D1591252

Democracy Imposed

RICHARD L. MERRITT

Democracy Imposed

U.S. Occupation Policy and the
German Public, 1945–1949

Yale University Press
New Haven and London

Copyright © 1995 by Yale University.
All rights reserved.
This book may not be reproduced,
in whole or in part, including
illustrations, in any form (beyond that
copying permitted by Sections 107 and
108 of the U.S. Copyright Law and
except by reviewers for the public
press), without written permission
from the publishers.

Designed by James J. Johnson and
set in Aster Roman type by The
Composing Room of Michigan, Inc.
Printed in the United States of
America.

A catalogue record for this book is
available from the British Library.

The paper in this book meets the
guidelines for permanence and
durability of the Committee on
Production Guidelines for Book
Longevity of the Council on Library
Resources.

Library of Congress Cataloging-in-Publication Data

Merritt, Richard L.
   Democracy imposed : U.S.
occupation policy and the German
public, 1945–1949 / Richard L.
Merritt.
      p.   cm.
   Includes bibliographical references
and index.
   ISBN 0-300-06037-8 (alk. paper)

   1. Germany—History—1945–
1955.   2. Germany—Foreign
relations—United States.   3. United
States—Foreign relations—Germany.
4. Military   government—
Germany—History—20th century.
5. Germany—Foreign public
opinion, American.   I. Title.
DD259.5.M47   1995
327.43073—dc20   95-4263
                                           CIP

10 9 8 7 6 5 4 3 2 1

To the airmen in my family,
defenders of our freedoms—
1st Lt. Paul J. Roberts, Jr., USAAF (DEC)
and
Col. Raymond J. Merritt, USAF (Ret.)

Contents

Figures

Tables

Preface

"Democratizing" Germany and taming its "aggressive spirit" posed an awesome challenge for U.S. policy planners at the end of World War II, a task that only hard-bitten Germanophobes or naive idealists could undertake cheerfully. Its accomplishment would require clarity of goals, complete cooperation among the occupying powers, and withal persistence in the face of inner doubts, resistance to external criticism, and acceptance of the glacial pace inherent to the process. None of these prerequisite conditions existed in 1945, yet within four years, the enemy of World War II had become America's partner in the new global struggle that people were calling the "cold war." Well might we ask, in light of this dramatic shift, how successful the U.S. effort to democratize and pacify Germany really was.

Several factors hinder a proper evaluation of the American role in postwar Germany. The United States controlled less than a third of the country's people and lands west of the Oder and Neisse rivers. U.S. influence in the rest of the country was only indirect, particularly in the Soviet zone of occupation, but in the British and French zones as well. Even in the U.S.-controlled areas the effects of American intervention in 1945–1949 cannot always be distinguished from the effects of other processes: a genuine desire on the part of many Germans, for example, to create a working democracy, lasting peace with their neighbors, humane resolution of the wartime and postwar migrations that threatened social solidity, and, more generally, progress toward modernizing German life.

Another obstacle to our understanding is the very sensitivity of the issue. Fueled by centuries of furor regarding Germany's proper place in the world—and intense ideological antagonisms during both the Nazi and cold-war eras—discussions of the U.S. occupation have frequently devolved into polemics. What did the Americans want in Germany? During the Nazi triumphs of the early war years, some vengeful Allies echoed Cato's *Delenda est Carthago:* Carthage must be destroyed. Did some still

harbor this grim disposition after victory? With the German threat de-
fused, a conciliatory element envisioned a democratic, peaceable Germany. Was this dream misguided from the outset? Would greater persistence in the postwar goals have produced another and presumably
better outcome? Did the American change of heart as the cold war deepened merely restore the quasi-feudal social structure of an earlier Germany? These are only a few of the questions that plague the conscientious
historian.

This volume approaches one dimension of U.S. occupation policy in
postwar Germany: the German people's response to it. It proceeds from
the view that historians too frequently have judged the U.S. occupiers
unfairly. The international change of heart occasioned by the cold war, a
change of heart that in Germany became apparent by mid-1947, led to
such profound policy shifts that even U.S. officials who later recounted
their stories of the occupation found it difficult to characterize accurately
the strategies of 1945–1947. Denazification policy, for instance, which in
1946 had seemed an important goal, was viewed a year or two later as a
nightmare—something that no policymakers in their right minds would
pursue. German replacements of U.S. officers, writing their memoirs a
decade or two later, were no more charitable in depicting this particular
policy.

Such changing perspectives in effect falsify history. Reconstructing a
personally experienced event, whether it be a public policy or a love affair,
requires intense effort to suspend the knowledge of hindsight. It is easy to
say retrospectively that this or that policy failed, and that people in the
know—that is, people like us!—understood or should have understood
that from the very outset.

When empirically valid data provide us with a check on the accuracy of
post hoc accounts, then it makes sense to explore their findings. Such data
are available for evaluating more scientifically the popular German reaction to the U.S. military occupation. Beginning in October 1945 the Occupation Military Government, United States (OMGUS) conducted state-of-
the-art public opinion surveys in the U.S. zone of occupation and, later,
elsewhere in western Germany. This study uses data from the OMGUS and
other surveys to ascertain not what the intellectual and policy elites
thought about American policy, nor what they assumed the German-on-
the-street was thinking, but rather to focus on German images from the
source: How did the German people themselves evaluate the U.S. military
occupation?

A second goal is more problematic. U.S. occupation policy and German
attitudes toward it give us insights into an intriguing intellectual problem. We know that a society's elite or rabble leaders can sometimes im-

pose changes on the entire population. But can such individuals have a similar impact on a foreign society? At a time when sociologists and others were not dealing systematically with the issue of exogenously induced change, the U.S. government was seeking in fact to implement such change. That is, American leadership took the stance that it could, through its occupation policy, change German society. The program was not over-reaching: it did not seek, as Hitler's regime had, to modify such deep-seated cultural elements of the German people as family, community, and religion. The U.S. target was to modify sociopolitical perspectives and behaviors in ways that might enhance Germany's prospects for democracy and peace.

This study, then, uses reports based on postwar surveys in U.S.-controlled Germany to evaluate the popular German response to a daring American project: imposed social change. The occupation experience of the British and French zones—not to speak of the Soviet zone—differed from that of the American zone. Yet, because the United States dominated the Western occupation arena while Britain and France had to face their own problems of postwar reconstruction, it was U.S. policy that set the tone for the new Germany. Analyzed over time, data from the U.S. occupation zone constitute a fair surrogate for samples from the whole of West Germany.

Several people helped me to realize this study. The first of these were the late Professors Karl W. Deutsch of Harvard University, Oron J. Hale of the University of Virginia, and Hajo Holborn of Yale University, each of whom taught me much about German history and politics. Professor Emeritus Gabriel A. Almond of Stanford University originally provided me with the OMGUS and HICOG survey reports, Frederick W. Williams shared his experiences in directing the OMGUS surveys, and Dr. Leo P. Crespi of the United States Information Agency helped me locate missing reports and imparted a wealth of firsthand knowledge about U.S. public opinion surveying in Germany.

A number of colleagues were kind enough to devote their time to reading and commenting on some of the book's chapters. The volume is much the better because of the thoughtful contributions of Ronald A. Francisco, University of Kansas; Arthur B. Gunlicks, University of Richmond; Arnold J. Heidenheimer, Washington University in St. Louis; Donald P. Kommers, University of Notre Dame; Andrei Markovits, University of California, Santa Cruz; Helmut Norpoth, State University of New York at Stony Brook; George K. Romoser, University of New Hampshire; Steven Thomas Seitz, University of Illinois at Urbana-Champaign; and Wade A. Jacoby, Massachusetts Institute of Technology.

Others have helped in various ways. Programs at the University of

Illinois at Urbana-Champaign provided important support: the Graduate Research Board; Institute for Communications Research, directed by Professor Clifford Christians; and Merriam Laboratory for Analytic Political Research, directed by Professor Dina A. Zinnes. Robert G. Muncaster, associate professor of mathematics at the Merriam Lab, offered computational assistance and helped me master the CricketGraphs used in this volume. Anthony King, University of Essex, England, suggested the book's main title. Thomas Schwartz, Vanderbilt University, did a fine job of evaluating the manuscript for Yale University Press. The final chapters were written while I was Fulbright Research Professor at the Humboldt Universität zu Berlin. And Dan Heaton of Yale University Press did his best to turn my academic prose into something that is readable.

Portions of the book have appeared in different form in other publications. Excerpts come from: Anna J. Merritt and Richard L. Merritt, eds., *Public Opinion in Occupied Germany: The OMGUS Surveys, 1945–1949* (Urbana: University of Illinois Press, 1970); Anna J. Merritt and Richard L. Merritt, eds., *Public Opinion in Semisovereign Germany: The HICOG Surveys, 1949–1955* (Urbana: University of Illinois Press, 1980); Richard L. Merritt, "Digesting the Past: National Socialism in Semisovereign Germany," *Societas: A Review of Social History* 7 (1977):93–119; and Richard L. Merritt, "American Influences in the Occupation of Germany," *Annals of the American Academy of Political and Social Science* 428 (November 1976):91–103. Chapter 7 is a modification of Anna J. Merritt, "Germans and American Denazification," in *Communication in International Politics*, ed. Richard L. Merritt, 361–383 (Urbana: University of Illinois Press, 1972); and Chapter 10 of Richard L. Merritt, "Öffentliche Perspektiven zur amerikanischen Erziehungspolitik," *Bildung und Erziehung* 34 (1981): 161–180.

The volume is dedicated to my cousin, Lieut. Paul J. Roberts, Jr., USAAF (DEC), and to my older brother, Col. Raymond J. Merritt, USAF (Ret.). It was the murder of Lieutenant Roberts—a pilot shot down on 27 October 1944 near Marburg, Germany, and, after landing safely in the rural county of Biedenkopf, killed by a local constabulary—that initially piqued my interest in the German people and their politics. He was ever present in my mind as I researched German attitudes in the years immediately after his murder. The much-decorated Colonel Merritt, who among other things spent almost seven and a half years at the "Hanoi Hilton" as a guest of the North Vietnamese government, has inspired me in ways too numerous to mention.

My primary debt is to my wife, Anna. She did an alligator's share of the work that led to our companion volumes—*Public Opinion in Occupied Germany* and *Public Opinion in Semisovereign Germany*—and also graciously permitted me to include as Chapter 7 of this volume a modified version of her article on denazification. She followed closely every stage of this project and is clearly my sine qua non.

To all these friends and colleagues I want to express my thanks—without, however, burdening them with responsibility for my mistakes of fact or interpretation. Complaints about such mistakes may be addressed to our Abyssinian cats, Leilt Nefertiti and Leul Akhenaton (a.k.a. Titi and Toni), who, in exchange for a large can of tuna, have agreed to accept full responsibility.

Abbreviations

ACC	Allied Control Council
AFM	American Forces Network
AMG	American Military Government (also OMGUS)
AMZON	American zone of occupation
APO	*Ausserparlamentarische Opposition*, extraparliamentary opposition
AUD	Action Community of Independent Germans
BHE	Union of Expellees and Victims of Injustice
BMG	British Military Government
CAD	Civilian Affairs Division, Joint Chiefs of Staff
CCS	Combined Chiefs of Staff
CDU	Christian Democratic Union
CSU	Christian Social Union
DA	German Alternative
DFP	German Freedom Party
DG	German Community
DIVO	*Deutsches Institut für Volksumfragen* (public opinion institute)
DKP	German Communist Party
DKP	German Conservative Party
DL	German League for People and Homeland
DP	German Party
DRP	German Reich Party
DRP (KV)	German Rightist Party (Conservative Association)
DVU	German People's Union
EAC	European Advisory Commission
ECSC	European Coal and Steel Community
EDC	European Defense Community
EMNID	EMNID K.G. (public opinion institute)
ERP	European Recovery Program (Marshall Plan)

FDP	Free Democratic Party
FMG	French Military Government
FRG	Federal Republic of Germany (West Germany)
GDP	All German Party
GDR	German Democratic Republic (East Germany)
GYA	American Youth Activities
HIC	Short identification of HICOG as source of data
HICOG	U.S. High Commission for Germany
ICD	Information Control Division, OMGUS (replaced by ISD in July 1948)
IfD	*Institut für Demoskopie* (public opinion institute)
IM	Informal collaborator with GDR Ministry of State Security (MfS)
IMT	International Military Tribunal (Nuremberg war crimes trials)
IPCOG	Informal Policy Committee on Germany
ISD	Information Services Division, OMGUS (replaced ICD in July 1948)
JCS	Joint Chiefs of Staff
KPD	Communist Party of Germany
MfS	GDR Ministry of State Security (also known as *Stasi*)
MG	Military Government or Military Governor
NATO	North Atlantic Treaty Organization
NLP	Lower Saxon Provincial Party
NORC	National Opinion Research Center (public opinion institute)
NPD	National Democratic Party of Germany
NS	See NSDAP
NSDAP	National Socialist German Workers Party (Nazi party)
NZ	*Neue Zeitung* (newspaper sponsored by OMGUS/HICOG)
OEEC	Organization for European Economic Cooperation
OMG	Short identification of OMGUS as source of data
OMGUS	Occupation Military Government, United States (also AMG)
OSS	Office of Strategic Services
OSS	Opinion Survey Section of ICD/ISD, OMGUS (replaced by RAB in September 1949)
PDS	Party of Democratic Socialism (replaced SED)
PG	*Parteigenosse*, or NSDAP member
RAB	Reactions Analysis Branch (replaced OSS in September 1949)
REPs	The Republicans (political party)
RIAS	Radio in the American Sector (U.S. radio/television station in Berlin)

RRG	German Broadcasting Corporation (until 1945)
SA	*Sturmabteilung,* NSDAP storm troopers
SHAEF	Supreme Headquarters, Allied Expeditionary Forces
SED	Socialist Unity Party (mainly in GDR)
SFB	*Sender Freies Berlin,* radio/television station in western Berlin
SMG	Soviet Military Government
SPD	Social Democratic Party of Germany (mainly in FRG)
SRP	Socialist Reich Party (FRG)
SS	*Schutzstaffel,* the NSDAP praetorian guard
Stasi	GDR Ministry of State Security (MfS)
SWNCC	State-War-Navy Coordinating Committee
TVA	Tennessee Valley Authority
UNWCC	United Nations War Crimes Commission
USFET	U.S. Forces, European Theater
VOA	Voice of America (U.S. overseas radio)
WAV	Economic Reconstruction Association (FRG party)
WSR	Frederick W. Williams survey research collection of OMGUS marginals

Introduction:
Changing German Society

The American occupation of Germany after 1945 was the most daring effort in modern times to transform a well-established Western society. Ancient warriors had often subjugated or slaughtered the losers, and European states after the fifteenth century had imposed their own institutions and values on non-Western colonies. But the religious and early Napoleonic wars, though conceived as engines of social change, effected no systematic programs. And as for changing a modern, Western society, the idea never received serious consideration.

World War II provided an unprecedented challenge. The United States and its wartime allies, anticipating military victory, knew that maintaining the peace meant taming Germany and the other Axis powers—not just immediately but for all time. Not to do so, they felt, would lead to disaster: given the inertial tendencies of all societies, Germany would resume its path toward European and perhaps even world domination as soon as the Allied troops returned home, fostering new and ever more terrible wars. Decisive, even daring, Allied action was imperative.

Yet one person's daring is another's folly. Foolhardiness, critics were quick to point out, flawed the *grand dessein*, perhaps fatally. In their view American policy planners were dreamers who underestimated the practical realities of the swamp called German society; their high-flown policies rested too much on ad hoc, seat-of-the-pants interpretations of exceedingly complex issues.

Alternative perspectives on U.S. occupation policy in postwar Germany are the stuff of this book. At its heart are several elements that shaped the images Americans used to pilot their policies. One was the understanding Americans had of Germany's role in World War II: who was responsible for causing the war, and who for its brutal excesses? How Americans answered such questions set the tone for their postwar response. A second element was concern about Germany's political, economic, and social system. It meant punishing miscreants, whether or not

1

they were members of Adolf Hitler's National Socialist German Workers Party (NSDAP, or the Nazi party). It also meant helping postwar Germans lift their political system, phoenixlike, from the ashes of World War II.

Influencing German Minds

None of these concerns was new, of course. Previous wars had brought similar policy challenges. What was new in the 1940s was a third element, a strategy: the United States and its wartime allies had both to convince Germans that the policies of Nazism were unacceptable in the comity of nation-states and to guide a revitalized Germany, one that was ready to eschew Nazi ideology in favor of democracy and global cooperation. This strategy looks beyond a national society's governmental and other epiphenomenal structures and focuses on the society itself. It presents occupiers as wise albeit firm teachers rather than vindictive persecutors. Not all victors are willing to adopt such a strategy. Indeed, during World War II it found acceptance in only two quarters. Soviet leaders and other Marxist-Leninists understood that extending the communist revolution required drastic policies and even the use of force to realize them.[1] And American writers and political leaders viewed directed social change as the path toward a safer, more liberal world. The focus of this book is not only the American dream of a democratic, peaceable Germany but also the extent to which the implementation of U.S. occupation policies persuaded the German people to change their ways.

By 1945 the rest of the Western world had long been baffled by Germans and German ways. Leaders and common citizens alike begged for insights—clues that might help them understand the oft-mentioned, ineffable, mystical, and sometimes deliciously dangerous "German problem." Why had Germans, within a span of three generations, initiated three major wars, the most recent of which had unleashed mass murders and destruction of astonishing proportions? Was it merely coincidental, or was a flawed "national character" at the root of these wars? If social interaction results from stochastic processes, then Germany's war involvements might be seen as a random roll of the global dice. Perhaps

---

1. The attempt to pacify and, in its own fashion, democratize the portion of Germany under Soviet control is itself an interesting case study of directed social change. The Red Army's protective role in the eastern German Democratic Republic proved to be the GDR's necessary and sufficient condition of stability. When Mikhail Gorbachev could no longer guarantee the regime's ability to control its own borders and population, eastern Germans quickly recognized means for ending the GDR in November 1989 and, less than a year later, incorporating its territory into the Federal Republic of Germany (FRG).

Germans were born harboring a "bad seed" that impelled them to lash out against their neighbors. Or were such traits not genetic but learned? If so, who taught them, to whom, and why? Alternatively, did Germany's aggressiveness derive from the country's political institutions, the failure of its people to embrace liberal democracy, or simply its corrupt or even mad leaders? Or, as Hitler claimed, were German actions not offensive but defensive, aimed at protecting the German nation from the hostile, envious, greedy predators hovering overhead?

The responses to such queries reveal a conception of German society and the German state that underlies many of the policies implemented in the postwar years. Overarching all these questions, however, was a central issue that haunted everyone: How could the wartime Allies prevent for a very long time any resurgence of German aggressiveness? The need to do so was clear to virtually all Americans. Few doubted the importance of punishing Hitler and his henchmen—not merely to consummate the Allies' right of retribution but more pointedly to demonstrate to Germans, future generations included, that modern civilization would not condone aggressors and genocidal murderers. Many victims of Nazi outrages applauded the Allied demand for unconditional surrender and the plan to destroy Germany's military prowess. Such policies were necessary, they said, to repudiate German myths about the fundamental invincibility of the country's arms and military leaders and to facilitate controls that Allied occupation forces would exert for years or even decades.

But punishment and tight controls were not enough. Such steps had been tried in the past, to little avail. A quarter-century earlier the World War I Allies imposed all sorts of limitations on defeated Germany, even conducting war crimes trials. Such measures found little acceptance among Germans, and willful German governments dismissed them quickly and contemptuously. Some critics blame the Allies for having settled on half-measures rather than insisting on strict controls. Others see the problem in the Allies' inability to address the German people directly. It is not surprising that common citizens, led by men who had spun an elaborate theory to explain away Germany's wartime defeat and who rejected the principles of Versailles, cherished intense hostility toward the Weimar Republic and were willing to follow their half-hearted democratic leaders on yet another military gamble. Whether the cause was Allied timidity or German resistance, this earlier stab at Allied control failed. Worse, it embittered the defeated Germans and created new resentments that spawned yet another worldwide conflagration.

How could the post–World War II Allies break the vicious circle of wrathful indignation and international conflict? The trick, some observers said, was to discard existing policies and German leaders—even those untainted by the Nazi past—for they remained linked to the social conditions that had led to the emergence of Nazism. From this perspective, what was needed was a new society capable of producing the leaders who could create a democratic, peaceable Germany.

How were Germans and Germany to be made more "democratic" and more "peaceable"? Wartime U.S. planners found the latter problem more manageable. The opinion of the nonfascist world cried out for a demilitarized Germany, one that had neither armed troops nor armament industries. The international coalition dedicated to the defeat of Nazism and Fascism even planned a worldwide organization that would provide the "united nations" with collective security. Although this idea smacked of protecting the rest of the world from Germany and other killer sharks, the Allies expected from the outset that a peaceable Germany would eventually join the United Nations Organization. The mechanism for Germany's permanent pacification thus existed. The task for U.S. and other policymakers was to persuade the German people to accept and adhere to the new international order.

Democratizing Germany was more problematic. *Democracy* was the mantra of the times. Hitler had scorned the very notion, but the Western democracies he had called degenerate—and the Soviet "people's democracy," as well—were tearing Germany apart through superior weapons, soldiering, and popular support on their home fronts. Democracy, orators never ceased telling us, and not National Socialism was the wave of the future. "Democracy is the worst form of government," Winston Churchill once quipped, "except all those other forms that have been tried from time to time." Well, then, after destroying its fascist dictatorship, why not "democratize" Germany?

The idea was deceptively simple: wise guidance provided to the mass of Germans—who would surely welcome opportunities to control their own fate—and firm external controls over recalcitrants could generate political institutions and practices at once stable and democratic. This was an idea that the wartime Allies could easily endorse, at least in principle. After all, didn't Great Britain, the Soviet Union, the United States, and, eventually, France enjoy some form of democratic governance? Never mind a growing sense that differences were greater than similarities; and never mind the growing reality that Allied leaders, meeting to plan strategy, ignored the specifics of democracy and focused on other issues they thought more pressing. Democratization as a desirable goal and the Allies' capacity, individually if not jointly, to implement social change in Germany became leitmotifs of thought about postwar Germany.

Democratizing Germany was a particularly bewitching notion in the United States. Americans had long viewed their constitutional system as a model for other countries to emulate. The visionary rhetoric of the founding fathers, nineteenth-century notions of manifest destiny, a test of fire during the Civil War, the peculiarly American version of imperialism as the twentieth century dawned, crusades for democracy in the two world wars—all sustained a dominant theme: the universal relevance of the American version of democracy. Policymakers in Franklin Delano Roosevelt's era extolled the American genius to solve social problems, citing evidence that ranged from the melting pot's proclaimed efficacy in freeing the New World from Old World ethnic strife to the New Deal's public-administration talents for social engineering. Such self-confidence made it relatively simple to spin out audacious plans to export American constitutional principles and practices to German soil.

Transforming Societies

The idea of transforming German society was both altruistic and pragmatic. As we shall see in Chapter 1, Americans were not fundamentally hostile toward Germans or Germany. Almost one in five Americans can trace some German ancestry (Cronin 1992), and large numbers, even if they had no direct ties, knew people of German heritage or recognized that, from frankfurters to Beethoven, German culture had significantly influenced the American way of life. Germans at home, they reasoned, had had a bad break in falling sway to authoritarian leadership and forms of governance. It followed that the German people deserved help in straightening out their politics so that they, too, could enjoy the blessings of liberty and justice for all.

But Germans would not be the sole beneficiaries of policies democratizing their country. A popular belief of the time was that democratic states do not start wars. Alexis de Tocqueville saw Americans in the 1830s as "lovers of peace."[2] During World War I President Woodrow Wilson spoke of his own democracy's "historical mission" to create "a peaceful international order based on world law" (Levin 1968:4).[3] And, indeed, the best social scientific research of the day (Wright 1942:847–848) found

2. People in democratic societies, Tocqueville wrote, are not inclined to seek military glory: "The ever increasing numbers of men of property who are lovers of peace, the growth of personal wealth which war so rapidly consumes, the mildness of manners, the gentleness of heart, those tendencies to pity which are produced by the equality of conditions, that coolness of understanding which renders men comparatively insensible to the violent and poetical excitement of arms, all these causes concur to quench the military spirit" (1835/1954:279).

3. As Wilson told Detroit businessmen in 1916, "You are Americans and are meant to carry liberty and justice and the principles of humanity wherever you go" (Levin 1968:18).

strong support for the proposition that democracies do not fight other democracies. It thus made sense to assume that democratizing Germany would dampen and eventually obliterate its aggressive urge. Democracy would reinforce inherently peaceable attitudes among the German people and instill peaceable policies in the German government. The whole world would be the winner. The question was how to accomplish this goal, how to change German society so that it would embrace democracy.

Social philosophers have taught us for two and a half millennia and more that societies change.[4] Not until the eighteenth century, however, during the Age of Enlightenment's exaltation of the power of human reason, was social change considered an issue meriting serious attention. Why does it occur? What causes it?[5] Why is the rate of change different from one society to the next? Why do societies rise and then fall, and new ones emerge in their place? The intellectuals sought universal truths to enrich their understanding of human existence. What they got were theories—fascinating, sometimes brilliant, but often deeply flawed theories; "classical" theories, as modern writers (Etzioni and Etzioni 1964) call them—that cut across time and space to explain the phenomenon of social change.

A central issue was the source of social change. Early perspectives stressed mainly exogenous factors. They crafted cosmic dramas that pitted frail human beings against overweeningly powerful, self-serving gods. Thus Athens' tragic poet Aeschylus (525–456 b.c.) saw vengeful gods making capricious demands that mortals ignored only at their peril. Ancient Jews scripted a similar world. The god of Moses was "a jealous god" who severely punished those who crossed him (Exod. 20:5) while, the psalmists (Pss. 46:1) added, succoring those who dwelled in the house of the Lord. Later social thought ranged from the rationalistic and iconoclastic view of the gods posited by Euripides (c. 485–406 b.c.) to the stance of early Christian theologians who saw social change as part of God's design for the Adamites, the children of Adam and Eve. In all these perspectives, gods dominated the cosmic drama and motivated the changes that occurred.

The Renaissance shifted the focus from gods to humankind. The Age of

4. "All is flux; nothing stays still," wrote Heraclitus (c. 535–c. 475 b.c.).

5. Moore (1968:366) defines social change as "the significant alteration of social structures (that is, of patterns of social action and interaction), including consequences and manifestations of such structures embodied in norms (rules of conduct), values, and cultural products and symbols." He distinguishes between "*social* change, which refers mainly to actual human behavior, and *cultural* change, which refers mainly to culturally meaningful symbols produced by human beings." In summarizing this complex field of study I have relied especially on MacIver and Page (1949), Etzioni and Etzioni (1964), LaPiere (1965), Moore (1968), Swanson (1971), Nisbet (1972), Vago (1980), and Sztompka (1993).

Faith gave way to a new secularism, one that, on its way toward reformation, relaxed the ties between God and his people. Social philosophers had long since posited that individuals could influence their own fate. Sophocles (495–405 B.C.) had abandoned Aeschylean gods to explore the fatal flaws that kept people from comprehending or carrying out the legitimate rules that the gods imposed on them. Various religions had given believers the option of violating the creed's commandments—albeit at the cost of certain damnation should they not repent in time. What was new in the Renaissance view of the cosmic drama was the sense of personal responsibility. As Shakespeare's Cassius (*Julius Caesar* 1,ii,140) put it,

> The fault, dear Brutus, is not in our stars,
> But in ourselves.

The eighteenth-century Westerner did not generally repudiate the bonds of faith. But widespread acceptance of religion's claim to be the factor primarily accountable for social change was a thing of the past.[6]

Social thinking of the Enlightenment went off in three other directions. One emphasized human beings as the agents of social change. Religion retained a role in the cosmic drama in spite of sweeping perspectival changes wrought by learning and discovery. But more important was the growing view that the force who had set the drama's stage and written its script was a benign god presiding over a just domain. The central dimensions of that domain were in principle discoverable—if only people would take the time to find the key to understanding. Those who did could enjoy previously unknown degrees of freedom in selecting among their social options. On the intellectual side, scientific advances added pieces to a jigsaw puzzle that scholars felt would eventually reveal a universally accepted vision of human existence, a vision consistent with prevailing ideas about the nature of humankind. On the practical side, we might use this knowledge to improve our lot in life—that is, to initiate the social change that is within our purview.

Not gods but individuals and societies and social movements, the philosophers said, stage the cosmic drama. Just as scientists had learned how the motions of planets influence our physical world, so social philosophers

6. Other exogenous linkages, some of them developed much later, have sought to replace religion's waning potency as the agency of social change: such environmental circumstances as climatic changes, race and other biological considerations, the invisible hand not of God but of the free-market economy, and such stochastic processes as cycles of wars among nation-states. Human beings, such theories claim, can neither fully apprehend nor control the elements that shape individual and social existence. The lot of mortals is thus to react to such factors as best they can. Precisely for this reason exogenous interpretations, while sometimes capturing attention, have failed to satisfy scholars seeking explanations for social change.

seeking to uncover the nature of the social universe focused on human desires, behaviors, and other endogenous factors. They saw such knowledge as the fountainhead for self-determination: once people understand how social processes affect their lives, they can cope better with them. To this Machiavelli would have added that improved understanding helps the Prince manipulate his competitors and the people at large. Other observers saw improved knowledge as a means for wise leaders to improve the human condition.

The search for a single, comprehensive model of the social universe eluded the philosophers. Instead of a commonly accepted path leading to social knowledge they found many alternative paths with mutually contradictory claims. Moreover, they stumbled upon ideological traps that blocked the search for truth. New theories were developed to respond to these perplexities. Karl Marx and other social philosophers found specific evils such as capitalism that prevented humankind from realizing its potential. Nihilists, Friedrich Nietzsche, and others proclaimed that the cosmic drama had no stage set and no script, that we are alone in the wilderness bereft of the ancient guidelines that could help us face an unknowable and changing future.

Enlightenment thought also expanded interest in the process of social change. How can we tell whether or not it is taking place? Is social change the story of relentless, upward progress? Some teleologists thought life was governed by natural processes leading toward an ultimate purpose. So did sociologists from Auguste Comte to Herbert Spencer and beyond, offering hope to a society whose members were weary of the vicissitudes of their miserable daily existence. Subsequent social philosophers, however, have viewed social change as cyclical: individual civilizations move up and down the scales of maturity, organizational sophistication, development, and talent. Oswald Spengler's cycles were never ending, but he held that a society's characteristics fluctuate between fixed zeniths and nadirs. Arnold Toynbee, less pessimistic, saw each new upward change reaching a higher zenith than had the previous one.

A third and ultimately more provocative set of questions that surfaced in the eighteenth century was practical: can political leaders or other elites change the society they govern, and if so, how? The concern here is not the moral issue of whether such people have a right to impose social change but rather the pragmatic issue of whether it is a feasible and worthwhile project for leaders to undertake.

Social philosophers of the Enlightenment quickly turned to designing thought systems and experiments aimed at testing the implications of such questions. Previous thinking had dwelt on the essence of human nature and on imagined utopian societies in which people would work peaceably together. The eighteenth century saw the emergence of a more practical bent. Perhaps the first major experiment in large-scale social planning came with the United States Constitution (1787). The men who drafted it and who used *The Federalist* papers to pen eloquent defenses of their positions designed institutions with checks and balances that would maximize the probability of desired, democratic outcomes. Of particular importance were the Constitution's first ten amendments, the Bill of Rights, which guaranteed civil liberties. The French Declaration of the Rights of Man followed suit two years later, as did the constitutions of other states that adopted the American idea of binding commitments to governmental procedures.

New ways of thinking about political phenomena continued to develop in the nineteenth century. Social philosophers began calling for institutional devices that they expected to change, if not human nature, then at least prevailing patterns of human interaction. Matthew Arnold advocated a "new culture" that, based on the world's best learning, could lead people to perfection. Auguste Comte called for a new moral science, the sociology he fathered, that would guide states toward realizing a better world. John Dewey saw nonauthoritarian, experimental education as a pathway to democracy. What did not emerge from all this thought, however, was a continuing dialogue between social philosophers and political practitioners—even though both increasingly recognized the need for controlled social change. Academics seemed content to continue expounding and disputing alternative, sometimes abstruse theories, while politicians seemed just as content to let them do so.

Government and civic-minded individuals, meanwhile, pursued a more immediately productive mode of thinking. Ignoring grand theorizing, legislators and executives in the United States took bold steps toward what Friedrich List had earlier termed social planning. The Homestead Act of 1862, for example, gave settlers unoccupied public lands in exchange for nominal fees and five years of residence, thereby both opening the new prairie cornlands and setting enduring land-tenure patterns. The Morrill Act of 1862 gave states public lands to establish colleges emphasizing agriculture, engineering, and home economics, and the Hatch Act of 1887 provided federal monies to support research and experiment stations. Such measures notwithstanding, social planning did not emerge as a routine procedure for addressing social problems.

The growing complexity of mass society in the United States and elsewhere created a drag on the push toward a merger of theory and practice. Urban centers, once small, homogeneous communities that were relatively easily managed, had become metropolises with unforeseen burdens; industries expanded and swallowed up their competitors; governments moved toward bureaucracies of gigantic proportions. Old solutions to social problems no longer sufficed. But how to replace them?

Joint problem-solving procedures, such as those initiated by the National Municipal League (Stewart 1950), were one good idea. Established in 1894 by representatives of various municipal reform groups that had convened in Philadelphia to discuss good city government, the League (now the National League of Cities) uses its educational program to develop and propagate model city charters, taxing systems, electoral balloting procedures, and plans for state administrative reorganization. Other such "good government" associations also emerged. Even the American Political Science Association, created in 1903, had as one of its main purposes providing a forum for discourse between political scientific knowledge and improved governmental procedures.

In part because of the growing importance of public policy, social philosophy moved to examine those issues as well. The expansion of learning provided an impetus. Institutions of higher education increased in size and scope, graduate programs burgeoned, and, in the United States, state governments broadened the curricula of their land-grant universities to include social scientific components. In both the United States and Europe thinkers at the interstices of theoretic and practical issues began to capture our intellectual attention: William James and his dynamic psychology, the Viennese psychoanalyst Sigmund Freud, and the behaviorist J. B. Watson; sociologists including the Germans Max Weber, Ferdinand Tönnies, and Karl Mannheim—not to speak of Woodrow Wilson, Charles Merriam, Harold Lasswell, and others who cast their lot with the emergent discipline of political science.

Yet by the early 1930s the concept of social change had lost momentum. The deterministic nature of many traditional theories encountered increasing resistance, and on a more practical level the ideas of the Marquis de Condorcet, Marx, Weber, and others seemed to have limited value in the real world. These theories viewed societies in the abstract or in relative isolation. Physical and cultural distances separating societies made it convenient to think of them as independent and to concentrate attention on idiosyncratic, internal problems and solutions. As integrated theories explaining and predicting complex social realities, they fell short.

Nor did they provide a systematic plan for changing societies. Although the U.S. Constitution and the Homestead Act represented steps in this direction, governments shied away from an enduring policy of social planning. Presidents Theodore Roosevelt and Woodrow Wilson tinkered with the idea, and President Herbert Hoover created an inchoate policy-planning staff in the form of his Research Committee on Recent Social

Trends. But piecemeal legislation and planning committees without economic or political bite would not accomplish meaningful social change.

After assuming the presidency in March 1933, Franklin Delano Roosevelt bridged the gap between theory and practice in policy planning. While still governor of New York he had set up a "Brain Trust," a top-level team of advisers recruited directly from academia and charged with the task of investing government policy with scientific knowledge. The original team did not survive long in the White House, but its fundamental message lingered on: government should seek the best information and brightest thinkers, whatever their governmental experience or political party affiliation. This concept of governance established a pattern of interaction between theoreticians and practitioners that has become routine in policy-making.

Roosevelt and his administration were convinced that science and technology could overcome the untoward forces of nature. For decades engineers had designed steel frames and elevators that made tall buildings soar into the skies; new fields of science such as geotectonics made it possible to construct skyscrapers even in high-risk seismic zones. Hoover Dam on the Colorado River, begun in 1931 and completed five years later, was considered one of the engineering wonders of the modern world. Airplanes transcended national and continental boundaries, radio brought news and entertainment into the homes of millions, and medical research was producing "miracle drugs" and operating procedures that promised to ease human suffering.[7]

Activists thought that social problems, too, begged for intervention by science and technology. Again, such ideas were not original with Roosevelt and his social planners. For years eugenicists had proposed to step directly into human lives to create a better, "purer" race.[8] Psychoanalysts had tried to heal wounded or ailing souls. Lasswell (1927), a political scientist, showed governments how to use modern techniques of propaganda to manipulate mass behavior. Educators had restructured public schools to turn them into agents of social change.

Roosevelt's New Deal had a larger framework in mind. To realize the American dream of equality and justice for all, the New Deal proposed to create a social safety net that could alleviate the damages caused by the

7. Scientists later persuaded Roosevelt that an atomic bomb was feasible and its use could shorten the war. The Manhattan Project that developed and tested the weapon, thereby changing the very parameters of society, was a model merger of science and government.
8. See Kühl (1994) and Chapter 8. The modern field of genetic engineering has been bedeviled by its link to the eugenics movement.

Great Depression and other sources of distress. Introducing Keynesian thinking into the economy would have this effect, social planners said. So would the Tennessee Valley Authority, perhaps the most complex bureaucratic structure created since the days of the Egyptian pharaohs.[9] Americans in the 1930s also saw legislation ranging from a social security system of old-age and unemployment benefits to jobs for the unemployed and tax policies to pay for the needed changes.

By 1940, though Americans still suffered from hard times, they enjoyed a certain ebullience about their nation's accomplishments and its future: pride about the peculiarly American form of democracy, satisfaction about their forebears' protection of the Union and the critical role Americans had played in Europe's Great War, and celebration of the management of important social change. Such successes in designing and maintaining a sociopolitical institution were not accidental, most Americans thought, but evidence that they were on the right track.

A New World

Americans around 1940 were particularly pleased with the way they had managed the need for social change. But the policies that effected that change were pragmatic, largely divorced from social theory. Observers have frequently remarked on the antitheoretic bias of political practitioners. The theoretic literature on social change was not relevant to political decision makers. Their lives focus on day-to-day concerns rather than the grand sweep of history; neither Aristotle nor Max Weber had much to say about resolving a conflict among the TVA's subsidiary agencies.

The absence of solid, empirically tested theory notwithstanding, the idea of public policy that would improve American society or any other society was in vogue.[10] Although theory never led directly to New Deal policy, politicians, administrators, and publicists used theory-based assertions, insofar as they could, to justify their policies. The idea itself remained potent: policy changes can transform whole societies.[11]

9. The TVA built for the impoverished people of the Tennessee River valley dams and reservoirs that provided cheap electric power, flood control, irrigation, recreation, industrial opportunities, and still more. See Lilienthal (1944).

10. The expected interaction between idea, theory, and practice did not reach fruition. The soundest link in "classic" writing was between idea and theory on the one hand and, on the other, between idea and policy. Scholarly attempts to give ideas a theoretic underpinning were far from convincing, and, as we shall see in Chapter 2, the idea-to-policy circuit was muddled.

11. The "three grand visions of human history which have left the strongest impress on both societal and sociological imagination"—namely, "evolutionism, cyclical theories and historical materialism"—have encountered "numerous critiques," according to

The context in which U.S. policymakers formed their occupation policies evolved substantially after 1940. Ares had captured the physical world, and the perceptual world also changed. With conflicts in Europe, North Africa, Southeast Asia, the Far East, and the Pacific threatening American security, planning a winning strategy of worldwide dimensions preoccupied policymakers. And as the shadows of Auschwitz-Birkenau, Stalingrad, Dresden, and Hiroshima loomed, the concepts that people had long used to frame their perspectives on reality were clearly inadequate. This phenomenon was manifest in three crucial ways.

First, new conceptualizations emerged. The new breed of political sociologists asked different questions about social change than had their predecessors. Emphasis on supernatural and social-class "causes" of change gave way to empirical questions. What agencies of change, policymakers wanted to know, had what impacts in which social systems? New research made it clear that the process of change—the specific phenomena affected and the level, duration, direction, magnitude, and rate of the changes (Vago 1980:10)—varies from one time to another, from one group of people to another. To the new scholars of social change this research quashed the notion of universal truth, yet their recognition of the value in much of the earlier thinking led to some ingenious efforts to merge the classic and modern traditions.[12]

Second, American policymakers did not keep up with new social scientific theorizing. The Roosevelt administration devoted its attention and energy to the country's long-standing domestic problems. It was content to dredge out of the distant past old paradigms that fit intuitive notions of social change but lacked real life.

Third, new issues of practical import addressed the theory of social change. Pre-1940 concerns with internal efforts to change societies increasingly seemed to be both parochial and passé. Political sociologists had a new focus: how do societies become "modern, civilized countries"?

Sztompka (1993:xv–xvi). Nevertheless, "such visions retain a strong influence on contemporary thinking, provide archetypes for common sense and are revived in ever new formulations in sociological discourse."

12. We see this in the ways textbook writers merge the various approaches. Steven Vago (1980:33–62), for instance, proposes as many as five broad categories: *evolutionary* theories seeing social progress as inevitable as societies move from less- to more-elaborated levels of development, organization, and civilization; *conflict* theories stressing system-transforming rivalry among social groups that compete for control over scarce resources; *structural-functional* or equilibrium theories emphasizing what aspects a society changes to maintain its overall steady state; *systems* or cybernetic theories concentrating particularly on information and communication; and *social-psychological* theories pointing to individual adjustments the collective effect of which is systemic change.

Other, presumably friendly, governments might offer "developing countries" models or technical assistance or economic aid. They might even
invade a country and force it to modify outmoded structures and processes. In this context, arguments that responsibility for social change lay
with the society itself, not with external actors in the global or regional
system, seemed quaint.

For at least some Americans in 1943–1944, imposition of "civilization"
was not what they envisioned for their country's occupation of Germany.
Most American thinking had a traditional focus: what must the Allies do to
defeat the Nazis and then ensure that Germany would not again aggress
against its neighbors? But prominent Americans eventually sought to
raise the ante. They wanted the Allies not only to clean up the status quo
but also to change German society. The reasons behind this goal were
mixed; beyond the defensive impulse to maintain direct controls over the
German state and discourage Germany from resuming its militaristic
ways, some hoped by democratizing Germans to enrich the human quality
of their life and to enhance democracy's global reach. But the implications
of the practical stance and the ostensibly altruistic one were the same.
Even ignoring claims of a genetic weakness in the German "soul," something in their social system made Germans respond aggressively to their
domestic and external environments. Only by changing key dimensions of
this social system could German aggressiveness be reversed. The United
States, because of its historical ties to democracy and its removal from
long-standing European quarrels, was among the Allies best suited to
direct Germany's social change.

In a way, attention by wartime planners to social change was misleading. The classical theorists focused on events in a single country or society,
or compared similar experiences in several societies. They emphasized the
processes of nation building and state building. How, for example, did
Italians or Germans or Americans learn to think of themselves as part of a
distinct nation, and how did each group learn to function effectively as a
nation-state? Those interested in the postwar German case, in contrast,
wanted to know how one socially advanced state might change the perspectives and behaviors of another.

A model of social change closer to the German case than nation building or state building was colonization. Western countries had for centuries
been expanding their areas of control into Africa, the Middle East, Asia,
and the Americas. Sometimes colonists eradicated the indigenous population, either deliberately, or because natives had no natural immunity to
imported diseases, or because indigenes chose to defend their property
and culture in the face of the colonists' overwhelmingly superior fire-
power. Survivors encountered relentless colonial administrators who, be-

sides seizing the natives' wealth and occasionally enslaving them, were intent on stamping out their culture. The words used by the occupiers differed—white man's burden, *la mission civilisatrice*, Christian duty, manifest destiny—but their meaning was the same: the imposition of the occupiers' politics, values, and culture on the indigenous population.

Americans did not like to think of themselves as colonizers. True, they had thrown the Spanish out of the Philippines and Puerto Rico, annexed Hawaii, purchased the Virgin Islands, and obtained other territories. Management of these lands, however, aimed at tutelage, not exploitation, and most U.S.-held territories were eventually to become free. U.S. leaders, meanwhile, criticized the European colonial powers and hectored for more sensitive treatment of colonies. Thus the fifth of President Wilson's Fourteen Points, proposed in 1918 as peace terms, called for an adjustment of colonial demands. At Versailles in the following year he even persuaded his wartime allies to treat their dependent territories as mandates to be given their independence in time. The collective self-image of the United States as an anticolonial state made it difficult for Americans to think of their occupation policy in such terms.

In the early 1940s neither U.S. policymakers nor common citizens had any explicit intent to colonize anyone. The organizational, financial, psychological, and other costs of such an undertaking were unthinkable. Furthermore, although full-scale colonization might work in such "primitive" societies as nineteenth-century Gambia or Indonesia, the mid-twentieth-century world was quite different. Earlier colonies had rarely had well-developed political structures or communication systems that included written languages, historical records, and information networks to integrate the entire region. Fragmentation was the norm—and, as the Romans observed, divided societies are easily conquered and easily ruled.

Germany in 1945 enjoyed a highly elaborated social structure and an integrated political system. Would-be colonizers could expect serious passive and perhaps even active resistance. Had Americans been asked in the early 1940s—they were not—whether they wished to colonize Germans as the Dutch and British had colonized Hottentots or the Spaniards Incas, they would surely have found the idea abhorrent.

Yet what Americans wanted might be called modified colonization. At the extremes, maximalists wanted German society fundamentally restructured, while minimalists were content to punish obvious war criminals but otherwise let Germans get on with their own lives. Between these extremists stood the bulk of Americans, seeking to reform German society modestly or transform only a few of its main dimensions. Just as nineteenth-century church groups sent missionaries into the colonies to convert the heathen masses, some twentieth-century Americans advocated a mission to democratize Germans. Just as the ideal colonial administrators exercised benevolent despotism, so military governors were expected to treat their German charges firmly but fairly. The notion of social change as policy was aimed at rectifying a society's faults, whether paganism or Nazism, while bathing the benighted in a brighter light of civilization.

The occupation of Germany was not the only U.S. effort to impose social change on other countries. The Marshall Plan was similar in one regard. The European Recovery Program (ERP), Secretary of State George C. Marshall said, was prepared to provide European countries with $16 billion to refurbish their war-torn economies, but it would not deal piecemeal with potential recipients. The ERP's insistence on unity spurred European countries to create the Organization for European Economic Cooperation (OEEC), under the aegis of which they would share economic information and develop consensus on how much aid was needed and how it would be distributed. Such forced cooperation was an important first step toward European economic and eventually political community. The United States' imposition of change on European states, however, was not the same as direct intervention.[13]

Meanwhile another international issue was reinvigorating the intellectual concern with social change. Decolonization beginning in the 1950s led policymakers and theoreticians to ask how an undeveloped or underdeveloped country could become "modern" not only economically and politically but also socially. The practical emphasis of modernization studies on the political and economic dimensions skewed the approach away from the traditional concerns that motivated U.S. policymakers as they contemplated what they should do about an authoritarian, aggressive Germany.

Social Change and U.S. Policy

Americans took a risk when, their minds firmly set, they marched inexorably toward the occupation of Germany. The idea of social change had caught their attention, and current thinking seemed to validate its

13. In another context (R. Merritt 1980b), I suggested that both strategic bombing in wartime Germany and U.S. occupation policy in postwar Germany were early examples of a form of international political communication that might be called "structural communication." Both sought to change perspectives (that is, the values and beliefs that produce attitudes) and behaviors. The difference lies in the magnitude, direction, and persistence of the changes they seek. Carpet bombing of cities aimed at changing beliefs about reality (namely, the inevitability of Germany's defeat) in ways that would change a specific kind of short-term behavior (in particular, the willingness to support Germany's war effort). The social-change dimension of U.S. occupation policy targeted values in ways designed to permanently change diffuse kinds of behavior.

authenticity as a plan for action. But what, exactly, was it? The idea itself had produced two centuries of inchoate albeit elaborate theorizing. Social philosophers used it to describe a reality—namely, that societies change over time—but their efforts to explain the process, why it occurs (and why not), was not convincing; and none paid close attention to the circumstances in which one country can direct another country's social change. Such shortcomings eventually led most political sociologists to abandon the search for universal explanations and to focus instead on more specific dimensions.

The idea of social change nevertheless thrived among wartime thinkers and planners. It confirmed the intuition of some that U.S. occupation would tame the Germans. Through education and public relations, and supported by a modicum of force, Americans could accomplish two goals: first, to convince Germans that their recent past was a disaster in not only a military but also a moral sense; and, second, to teach them how to create a more democratic, peaceable Germany. Whether or not the prospect of systemic transformation was scientifically sound, the United States adopted it as a basis for planning. Given that genesis, we may then ask, Did policy correspond with the idea? Did the policy produce concrete progress toward social change? What impact did the program, however conceived, actually have on German society?

This book assays yet another question: how did Germans respond to the American program of directed social change? The perspectives and behaviors of the country's politicians, bureaucrats, intellectuals, and other elites are well known. An analysis of public opinion data, however, provides a focus on the "forgotten German," the German-on-the-street who is affected by public policy, but who also helps to shape the behavior of the nation and its leaders.

Part I sets the stage. Chapters 1 and 2 characterize what the Americans and their leaders had in mind in 1945 when they embarked on the occupation of Germany. Chapter 3 also examines the use of public opinion surveying to measure German reactions to U.S. policies aimed at social change.

Part II focuses on Germans' postwar images of their country's recent past: what they thought about Hitler and Nazism, their national and personal sense of responsibility for criminal acts carried out in the Nazi era, and their attitudes toward war crimes trials and denazification procedures aimed at removing from important positions those who had supported the Nazi regime. The final chapter of this part traces the development of such attitudes in the years after 1949, when the formal U.S. occupation of Germany ended.

Part III explores popular moods toward U.S. policies that helped build a new Germany. Individual chapters assess the efficacy of the U.S. military as an agency of social change, public education and U.S. information programs, revitalization of the media, and the new German government established after the constitution was promulgated in 1949. The final chapter of the part traces the long-lasting effects among the German people of policy changes imposed by the American occupiers.

Part IV summarizes the overall impact on German society of U.S. occupation policy, particularly what U.S. experience tells us about the general process of directed social change. Is the palpable Germany that exists today, the Federal Republic of Germany, the ideal Germany that American planners wanted when in 1945 they went headlong into military occupation of the country?

I

America's Dream of a
Democratic Germany

The outbreak of World War II in September 1939 raised several dilemmas among Americans. The most immediate one was the role the United States was to play in the conflict. Doubtless most Americans hoped that they could avoid this war. After all, they said, their country had once before launched a crusade to rescue Europe only to be rebuffed afterward by those whom it had helped. That winds of war again buffeted Europe confirmed the wisdom of isolationism. Other Americans, however—in increasing numbers as the war went on—favored some form of U.S. intervention. They saw democracy and indeed Western civilization at stake. This policy dispute raged until the United States entered the battle in December 1941, whereupon isolationists and interventionists joined in the war effort.

More perplexing were other dilemmas, at once less clear-cut and more enduring. On the assumption that, with or without U.S. assistance, victory would eventually be theirs, what were the victors to do with Germany? Americans did not respond in unison to this question, either. Sympathy for Adolf Hitler's Germany was hard though not impossible to find in the United States, and few Americans approved of Germany's invasion of its European neighbors. Most Americans agreed that Hitler and his government deserved a thorough thrashing. However odious Germany's aggression was, though, it seemed consistent with European behavior over the past three or more centuries.

So what was the United States to do? The American preference before December 1941 was clear: to help one's friends if that could be done without getting directly involved in the conflict itself, and to hope for a victory that could restore the prewar status quo. After the Japanese attack on Pearl Harbor and the subsequent declarations of war against the United States by Germany and Italy, such a stance was not enough. The U.S. government had to forge a strategy that would win both the war and the peace. Hitler's regime had to go and the aggressors to be punished. Other Germans, followers rather than leaders, would surely suffer from wartime damages and postwar deprivation. Isn't this the fate of all people who lose wars? As the Roman historian Livy wrote: Woe to the vanquished!

It took some time for Americans to heed a rather different doctrine that for several decades had been percolating in political and intellectual circles: that the people themselves and the society that nourishes them are responsible for the actions of their leaders. Chapter 1 of this book traces the way in which such thinking evolved in the United States after the summer of 1939. It arose from the observations of publicists, cultural anthropologists, and others imbued with the concept of "national character"—the uniform, immutable ways in which members of a nation-state think and act. Thus "the Englishman" had these characteristics while "the Spaniard" or "the German" had those. It is but a short distance from this mode of thinking to believing that social engineering can modify a nation-state's character.

As World War II continued, the notion caught hold among some Americans that Germany's postwar occupiers, particularly the United States, could mold and "improve" German society. The idea was trendy: it offered a quick fix to a complex issue. The idea had an intellectual cachet: it offered a pseudoscientific explanation for such otherwise inexplicable German behaviors as Gestapo brutality, military persistence in a lost cause, and newly discovered horrors of the death camps. Popular American publicists and thinkers endorsed the idea in a growing number of books, newspaper columns, articles, and public speeches. Substantial numbers of the American people, as indicated by public opinion surveys, toyed with the dream of democratizing Germany.

But changing German society, however attractive a notion to contemplate in the wee hours of the night, made less sense as a policy. Chapter 2 characterizes the emergence of U.S. policy on occupied Germany. A president who was interested more in domestic issues and in designing a worldwide collective security arrangement did not provide consistent leadership in creating his government's occupation policy, and administration departments engaged in serious ideological disputes and bureaucratic infighting regarding who was to do what. Some policy elements aimed at transforming Germany's social system crept into U.S. planning. As a result, at war's end the United States did not have a tightly integrated occupation policy capable of withstanding the tests that it would face.

How did Germans react to the patchwork policy that emerged from Washington in mid-1945? This is the book's central question. It focuses on adult responses in the American zone of occupation to public opinion surveys conducted initially by U.S. occupation authorities and later by independent, German-owned polling agencies. Chapter 3 describes the background of German public opinion polling, procedures used after the war, and the overall reliability and validity of the data that emerged from such surveys. It thus serves as a technical introduction to Part II, which centers on changing images of Germany's past, and to Part III, which looks into changing images of Germany's future.

ONE

America's Wartime Images of Germany

Americans abruptly abandoned Europe after their dramatic and decisive sweep onto the continent during World War I. Their hasty departure was not foreseen when the combatants signed an armistice on 11 November 1918. Indeed, the next few months promised the United States a prominent role in both reconstructing war-torn Europe and creating a framework for lasting peace. Jubilant throngs cheered President Woodrow Wilson when he visited major European cities at the end of the year, and the other political leaders of the alliance that had defeated the Central Powers seemed amenable to accepting his Fourteen Points.

A combination of factors caused the United States to rethink its international role. The realization that the negotiators at Versailles were wheeling and dealing to promote their own national interests rather than the commonweal soured many Americans on participation in the peace-making process, as did a growing sense that the European powers would neither accept the preeminence of the United States nor repay their war debts. Partisan disputes at home led the U.S. Senate to reject the Versailles Treaty that Wilson so fiercely defended but which his opponents saw as a sell-out to European chauvinism. George Washington's injunction of a century and a quarter earlier again became the cry of the day: The new American republic should eschew permanent alliances.

Americans spent the next two decades trying to balance their conflicting interests. On the one hand, isolation from the strife of others was the norm. Not only did the United States refuse to join Wilson's League of Nations, it also abstained from active participation in the League and enacted legislation ensuring the country's neutrality should international war once again break out. Of particular importance were the neutrality acts, culminating in the legislation of May 1937 that sharply limited U.S. trade with belligerents. On the other hand, the realities of the modern world made strict isolation a self-defeating fantasy. U.S. political leaders could not ignore the fact that political and economic decisions made in

Europe impinged on Americans as well. Thus they felt constrained to play a role in promoting peace (Washington Naval Conference of 1922, Kellogg-Briand Pact of 1928, London Naval Conference of 1930), restructuring Germany's reparations payments (Dawes Plan of 1924, Young Plan of 1929), and protesting aggressive acts (Stimson Doctrine of 1932). Moreover, Americans were too tied to their European forebears to sustain any cultural isolation. Their partisan sensitivities showed through even when their formal utterances stressed neutrality.

German expansion in the late 1930s, especially the invasion of Poland on 1 September 1939, challenged American neutralism. The predominant cultural persuasion in the United States—notwithstanding the large number of German-Americans and Irish-Americans, and discounting popular animosities regarding unpaid war debts—favored Germany's foes, Great Britain and France. Americans could see in their daily newspapers that Germany was the cause and not the victim of a string of European confrontations. But, hamstrung by its neutrality acts, what was the U.S. government to do? So serious did the pending outbreak of war seem in April 1939 that President Franklin Delano Roosevelt wrote to both Adolf Hitler and Benito Mussolini, urging them to refrain from aggression and to join talks aimed at reducing armaments and enhancing world trade.

Four and a half months later, after the Wehrmacht's march into Poland, Britain and France declared war against Germany, but even then the U.S. government clung to neutrality. On 5 September, Roosevelt formally declared such a stance and admonished his fellow Americans to conform to the neutrality acts. His behavior, however, increasingly cultivated engagement, especially after the Wehrmacht invaded Denmark and Norway in April 1940, overran the Benelux countries a month later, and occupied France a month after that. On 22 June, the day of France's capitulation, Congress passed the first of several measures to strengthen U.S. defense capabilities. The Luftwaffe's attack on London and other urban centers—the Battle of Britain—was already under way. On 16 September, Congress authorized a military draft, and three months later the president moved both to organize America's defense and to help besieged England. "We must be the great arsenal of democracy," Roosevelt said.

Throughout 1941 pressures for U.S. involvement turned to action: enactment of the Lend-Lease Act (11 March), Roosevelt's proclamation of an unlimited state of national emergency (27 May), closure of German consulates in the United States (16 June), assistance to the Soviet Union after Germany's invasion (22 June), the North Atlantic meeting between Roosevelt and Britain's Prime Minister Winston Churchill to develop common war aims (14 August), and orders that U.S. ships menaced by German attackers should "shoot on sight" (4 September). Even before Germany declared war on the United States (11 December, four days after the Japanese bombed Pearl Harbor), the policy of neutrality had become a hollow shell.

America's debate about neutrality would eventually be replaced by a bipartisan legislative consensus on the country's need not only to defeat the Axis powers but also to play an active international role in the future—to shape events rather than merely to react to them. What is more, the wartime surge of the U.S. economy and Europe's severe deprivation put the United States in a unique position from which it could dominate the postwar climate. The publisher Henry Luce described it as the "American century," one that could realize the opportunities for world peace and harmony inherent in a sudden but justly deserved *pax americana*.

What did Americans want to accomplish, and how were they to build peace from the shards of Europe and its centuries of internecine struggle? At the core of this challenge was the modern variant of an ancient obstacle: the German problem. How were the United States and its wartime allies to deal with Germany, which thrice within seventy-five years had plunged Europe into disaster? Organizing a strategy merely to defeat Nazi Germany was insufficient; the Allies, under American leadership, needed to devise a strategy that would end German aggression forever.[1]

Public Perspectives Among Publicists

Deciding what to do about Germany required an understanding of both the cause of the events in which Americans found themselves enmeshed and their own country's capabilities and will to act. Those who saw World War II as merely the latest in a never-ending series of clashes among quarrelsome Europeans were inclined to avoid American involvement. So, too, were those traumatized by the Great Depression's impact on American lives. Others, seeing Nazism and Fascism as phenomena threatening Western civilization, were ready to leap to its defense—even if that meant abandoning their precious idea of neutrality—both to vanquish the aggressors and to share in postwar planning for a new and more peaceful world order.

President Roosevelt was among the latter. But he also understood that any U.S. policy toward Germany had to be informed by the mood of the

1. This book's focus on U.S. policy does not mean that the other Allied countries had no role to play in postwar Germany. The United States nevertheless dominated Western decision making. Its conception of what needed to be done in postwar Germany became the most influential, and, ultimately, its continued commitment to Europe and its financial support provided the ability to carry through any and all occupation programs (see Foschepoth and Steininger 1985).

American people. As Wilson's experience after World War I had shown, democratic leaders cannot lead where their citizenry will not go. And although creative leaders might easily shape public opinion when the issues are remote or the images inchoate, it is difficult to force an aroused, knowledgeable public to do something against its will.

But how can we ascertain what popular perspectives are? Before the mid-1930s, when George Gallup introduced to sometimes skeptical observers his new, "scientific" polling procedure, the concept of *public opinion* referred mainly to the views expressed by educated elites and skilled orators in public forums. Books and magazine articles on public affairs by scholars, intellectuals, and others outside government service were particularly powerful components of this "public opinion": they appealed to a wide range of readers, including policymakers, and they attracted more public attention than did other sources. The images that this literature projected both shaped and reflected what Americans were thinking about the German problem.[2]

The amount of attention such publications paid to the German problem was enormous. Perhaps at no previous time had publicists had the opportunity to spill more words on a current foreign-policy issue. Throughout the six war years they filled publishing houses and news bureaus with outpourings of opinions, ideas, and policy recommendations. The stakes at issue and the length of conflict no doubt accounted in part for the volume of commentary. But so did the growing number of publication outlets and above all a relatively new concept of governance that gave literate citizens the sense that their views could directly influence policy decisions.

The activist stance adopted by writers in these publications was a radical departure from the past. Generations earlier such authors as Baronne de Staël Holstein and Alexis de Tocqueville had written about the "national character" of their own population or foreign peoples whose lands they visited. But the books they wrote were typically in the tradition of belles lettres: historical, cultural, anecdotal, and descriptive, interested more in explaining than in changing the "character" of nations they studied, and withal sometimes remarkable in their political acumen.[3]

2. Because many relevant books published in England and Canada had U.S. editions and elicited commentary in U.S. newspapers and elsewhere, we shall view them as part of American intellectual perspectives on Germany. Newspaper editorials are another useful source of information on public attitudes. For a systematic content analysis of the world's "prestige" newspapers, see Pool (1970).

3. Examples of writing on German "national character" include Tacitus (c. 98/ 1970), Fichte (1808/1922), Jahn (1810), Staël Holstein (1810/1813), Whitman (1897), Shuster (1932), Müller-Freienfels (1922/1936), and Demiashkevich (1938). A plethora of vitriolic screeds also appeared during World War I.

Making the jump from description to policy recommendation was in principle possible, but most of these earlier writers, having no role to play in the policy-making process, saw no utility in trying to do so. The circumstances at the end of the 1930s gave writers free rein not only to recount the past and present but also to speculate about alternative futures that the Allies could pursue. Popular anger about the failed peace of 1918, advances in such scholarly fields as cultural anthropology and social psychology, and particularly a faith in the Allies' ability eventually to overrun the whole of Germany made speculation about the German problem and its solution a competitive sport among intellectuals and gadflies alike.

Anglo-American publicists shared common views about neither the nature of German society nor what postwar policy should be. The literature nonetheless contains some common threads.[4]

Who caused the war? Writers of this period did not dispute Germany's responsibility for World War II.[5] The question was, *Which* Germans? One group of writers emphasized particular elements of the country's politics. The German people, according to this camp, may have been naive in their understanding of politics. They may have gullibly accepted Hitler's promises until it was too late to prevent him from acting out his insane dreams of a Greater Germany. Some of them may even have been criminal in carrying out the Nazi regime's dictates. But—and this was a stance assumed not only by Germanophiles but also by those who held no brief for German society—the Germans as a people were victims, not perpetrators, of Nazism and its excesses. This conclusion raises another question: If not the German people, then who?

Scapegoats lay readily at hand. The obvious demon was Adolf Hitler himself, or the Führer together with his Nazi toadies. Liberal Germans who had fled the Nazi regime and had a personal stake in the country's postwar development were vehement in stressing this argument (see Hagen 1944). So were non-Germans who for various reasons abhorred Nazism. Thus the prominent New York trial lawyer Louis Nizer visualized postwar Allied occupiers trying and executing as many as a sixth of a million criminal conspirators.[6] Such internationalists as former Undersecretary of State Sumner Welles (1944:338) pointed to the German gen-

---

4. A good though brief account of about six dozen such publications is Lach (1945).

5. Not until many years after the war ended (e.g., A. Taylor 1961) did revisionist historians begin taking a different tack on Germany's responsibility. See Chapters 5 and 8.

6. "Death penalties," Nizer wrote (1944:96–97), "should be sought against each" arch-criminal and "the whole-hearted fanatical Nazis upon whom the ruling group relied"—roughly seventy-five thousand "leaders of German mass organizations" such as the Gestapo and Labor Front, and as many "subordinates who organized and taught the S.S., the Peasant Front and other such organizations."

eral staff, which "was using Hitlerism as its tool." The political left— again, especially refugees from Nazi Germany (see J. Braunthal 1943) —saw capitalists as the main instigators. And practically every writer could in one way or another castigate the "Prussian spirit"—whether the aggressive impulse was sui generis, brought to Germany by the Huns (Braybrook 1945), engendered by the military (Welles 1944), supported by capitalists (J. Braunthal 1943), or infused into the whole of the German people (Ludwig 1943, 1945).[7]

Was German culture to blame? An alternative approach centered on German society. Was German aggressiveness bred in the bone, part of a "national character"?[8] A notorious book by Theodore Kaufman (1941:94), which cited the German nation's "centuries-old inbred lust . . . for conquest and mass murder," drew but one conclusion: *Germany must perish!* Kaufman would have systematically sterilized all Germans—men, women, and children—who had the "power to procreate."[9] More moderate writers blamed centuries of wrong-headed enculturation rather than the political version of original sin. Lord Robert Vansittart (1941, 1943), who had gained international stature by early criticism of Hitler's Germany, and the German-born popular historian Emil Ludwig (1941:484) found Hitler and his men immediately responsible for the war but added that the German people stood wholeheartedly "behind Hitler."[10] The neurologist

7. Braybrook traced Germans directly to the warrior Huns of northern China, c. 3,000 B.C. Although he did not advocate such policies as sterilization, Braybrook (p. 41) urged the occupiers to impose the strictest possible controls on the "Hun-German ruling caste," which, he said, "is preternaturally clever," able to "stultify any Allied repressive plans, if these plans are announced in detail beforehand."

8. "Certain attitudes and character traits" of national populations, Erich Fromm (1942:79) wrote, "are not accidentally but necessarily connected, because they result from a basic form of relatedness to the world and oneself."

9. Behind this book lies an appallingly fascinating story. Kaufman, a theater ticket salesman in Newark, New Jersey, evidently wrote the book, set up a publishing company to produce it, and sought to market it by himself. After seeing his book, Nazi propagandists set out in July 1941 to "prove," via distorted information, that Kaufman was an intimate of President Roosevelt's and that Roosevelt himself had ostensibly dictated the book's main arguments; the book thus represented official U.S. intentions. These phony claims were used to rationalize the Wannsee Conference's decision of January 1942 to push toward a "final solution" of the "Jewish problem." By the 1960s Nazi apologists and extreme right-wingers were using the allegedly official "Kaufman Plan" to justify the Holocaust as an act of self-defense. See Benz (1989).

10. "So vast a majority of Germans . . . has been made bad by centuries of misteaching," Lord Vansittart (1941:vii) said, "that it will follow any Fuehrer, cheerfully and ferociously, into any aggression." According to Ludwig (1941:ix), "Hitler is not an adventurer cast up in Germany by the merest chance, but a truly German phenomenon," and, hence, "all well-intentioned efforts to make a distinction between him and the German character miss the point."

Richard M. Brickner (1943) put "five decades of German history" on a hypothetical couch to analyze the roots of German "aggression." What he found was that German society suffered from "group paranoia."

Other writers sidestepped the thorny debate on German national character. Germans, they said, were pretty much like everyone else— although perhaps, as the politically influential American journalist Dorothy Thompson (1942) pointed out, a bit more confused about their national identity. Thus differences neither caused nor explained German political behavior. Consider the norms of European politics after the Treaty of Westphalia in 1648 (see A. Taylor 1961). Did Hitler's war aims and foreign policies differ morally from those of Napoleon, Bismarck, or Pilsudski? Weren't they all skilled in "power politics," in the European game of Realpolitik? Moreover, many Western commentators asked, wasn't the raw deal accorded Germany at Versailles in 1919 enough to account for the German quest to reestablish the country's rightful place in the sun and control over its own security?

The war's closing phases muddied such views. The closer the Allies moved toward victory the less relevant deep-rooted psychological dimensions seemed. In June 1943 Britain's prestigious Royal Institute of International Affairs published a report on *The Problem of Germany* (RIIA 1943) that listed a dozen such psychologically based assumptions about why Germany had gone to war.[11] The committee promptly abandoned them. "Political action is not likely to be based on the clear and general acceptance of any set of assumptions as valid," it concluded (p. 12), and then went on to its main concern: postwar policy toward Germany.

The world was revolving on its axis. Beginning in mid-1944 (but see Gilbert 1981; Bird 1992) concrete information about the full scale of Hitler's genocidal policies—policies carried out for the most part, though not initiated, by common German citizens—shocked the world. Wars of aggression were a European tradition; craven, systematic barbarism was not. Even Germanophiles had to ask, Who are these Germans? Serious thinkers as well as political dilettantes (see Morgenthau, Jr. 1945) began again to censure the German nation. The report issued on 26 April 1945 by a group of U.S. medical scholars and practitioners as well as social scientists relied heavily on the arguments of one of its members, Richard Brickner: that "German aggressiveness" had "sprung out of German character"

---

11. These ranged from "The Germans are a congenitally aggressive people; and it is owing to their inherent aggressiveness that they remained . . . less civilized than other European peoples" to "Germany resorted to war in order to save Europe from Jewish and Bolshevik influence, and from the secular British policy of division; and to fulfill the task, which the present moment of history commands, of creating European unity" (RIIA 1943:86–88).

Figure 1.1
Attitudes Toward Occupation Policy

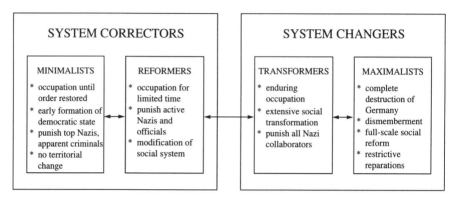

and that "deep-seated dualism in the German character" accounted for Germany's "group paranoia" (Lowrey et al. 1945:432–433).[12]

Musings about the German "soul" colored the kinds of policy recommendations writers made (see Figure 1.1). At one extreme maximalists called for either Germany's destruction through dismemberment and "pastoralization" or its virtually permanent subjugation under Allied controls. At the opposite extreme minimalists endorsed only those measures necessary to ensure an immediate and, they hoped, enduring end to German belligerency. Between the poles were reformers, who wanted limited changes, and transformers, who expected far-reaching changes in German society short of wholehearted transformation.[13] These contrasting views and the array of perspectives in between fueled sometimes vitriolic polemics among those seeking to influence U.S. public opinion and government policy.

Cleaning up the debris. One short-run focus of the debate found widespread agreement among publicists. Dismantling the Nazi war machine, both the Wehrmacht and the armaments industry, was a theme rooted in experiences after World War I. The Allies had accepted then a negotiated peace that preserved Germany's military establishment, albeit in reduced form, and permitted unrestricted industrial growth. This "leniency" had been repaid by Germany's fierce remilitarization in the Nazi years. No Anglo-American publicist wanted a repeat of this sorry story.

12. Participating social scientists were anthropologist Margaret Mead, educationist Lyman Bryson, psychologists Richard S. Crutchfield and Gardner Murphy, and sociologists Theodore Abel and Talcott Parsons. A professor of philosophy, Harry A. Overstreet, also participated.
13. The classification of system correctors and system changers ignores a fifth cate-

For the same reason many but not all writers agreed that the World War II Allies should demand Germany's unconditional surrender. Those preferring less rigidity felt that negotiating with Hitler's domestic enemies could save lives by bringing about an earlier end to the war. Some who distrusted the Soviet Union believed that coming to terms with Germany early would ease any Soviet temptation to pursue communism's allegedly inevitable westward march. Vera Micheles Dean (1943:295), editor of the influential *Foreign Policy Reports,* pointed out another potentially negative impact of insistence on such a decisive victory: it might bolster the German population's will to resist. The Allies, she said, should repeat as often as possible their intent to destroy the Nazi regime rather than the German people or German society. Making this point clear would encourage Germans to assist the Allied effort.[14]

An even more contentious issue, partition, addressed the heart of German unity. As far as most writers were concerned, returning territories taken by Germany after 1937 was essential.[15] But what about the pre-1938 Reich? If territoriality was at the root of German aggressiveness, then it made sense to partition the country. Thus Kaufman (1941:96) wanted to obliterate Germany by turning over its territorial units to neighboring countries. Welles (1944:342) proposed consigning East Prussia to Poland and dividing the rest of the country permanently into three parts.

The counterargument was that partitioning Germany would only make matters worse. Thompson (1942:21), who uncovered the confusion of Germans about their true national identity, found "wasteful and dangerous" any "attempt further to confuse the German mind" by creating territorial division.[16] The Chatham House report (RIIA 1943:34–37) pointed out that partitioning Germany would require detailed Allied agreement and even, because of the greater probability of unrest under partitioning, Allied arms.[17] Allied leaders, it continued, were keen about neither. The

---

gory of punitive Germanophobes, but their views were generally not taken seriously in the postwar policy-planning process.

14. The first of Dean's (1943:295) eight policy recommendations stated: "The Germans should be given an opportunity to participate in the liberation of their own nation, as well as conquered Europe."

15. A few felt that some territories unreasonably taken from Germany by the Treaty of Versailles and recaptured after 1937 should be ceded to Germany permanently.

16. "The history of Germany, unlike the history of the Austro-Hungarian Empire, has been a history of coalescence, not of disintegration," Thompson (1942:24) wrote. "Our one hope in stopping pan-Germanism is to insist on *national* Germanism, and the integration of the German nation as a strictly limited nation in a Europe of strictly limited nations" (p. 28).

17. "The only safe basis for policy is the expectation that the Germans will be determined to preserve their unity, except in so far as they are prevented by force," the

potential convulsions were simply not worth it. A conference of American medical experts and social scientists (Lowrey et al. 1945), with its emphasis on controlled social and institutional change, did not seriously entertain partition as a solution to the German problem.[18] Even Prussia was not to be broken apart or given away to other states—though, nodding to frequently voiced concerns about the aggressiveness of Germany's traditional elite, the team recommended that "landed estates in East Prussia be expropriated and divided, and the Junker class dispersed" (p. 419).

Other ideas found general albeit not unanimous concurrence among publicists. Writers had little doubt about the need for Allied military occupation, and they expected to see German war criminals severely punished.[19] The comprehensiveness of the trials nevertheless raised questions: Should they be show trials of only the top Nazis, or more far-reaching judicial proceedings? If the latter, who should stand trial—even lower-ranking party members (Nizer's sixth of a million), military officers down to the rank of corporal, or simply all Germans who could not demonstrate their innocence?

The publicists also expected Germany to pay reparations. Although most recognized the problem that this issue had caused after World War I, they were unwilling to absolve Germany of the damages it had inflicted in World War II. Some writers wanted to assess billions of dollars' worth of more or less punitive claims. Such a demand raised the question of how Germans might pay if willing or be forced to pay if not. Ingenious alternative plans, their authors claimed, would extract indemnity without crippling and hence unnecessarily embittering the German people. Dean (1943:295) proposed that the United Nations establish an "international raw materials commission," on which Germans would be represented, to "distribute the new materials needed for modern industry in such a way that no nation can accumulate stocks for use in war, and permit free

---

Chatham House study group concluded (p. 35). "The possibility would become a certainty should the victors themselves assert a vigorous nationalism."

18. Destroying the "central forms of social control . . . could be resented as an attempt to rob Germany of her nationality," the New York team said (p. 420). "A more subtle way of breaking up the monolithic state . . . would be to involve German industry and social control in various international organizations that would transcend national boundaries."

19. Dean and Ringwood (1943) warned against the "danger . . . that discussion about punishment of Nazi 'war criminals' may create the impression that Germany alone was responsible for World War II. . . . While Hitler and his associates can and should be held responsible for acts of commission that led to the outbreak of war, other nations now fighting Germany cannot be relieved of responsibility for their many acts of omission, due in some cases to failure—or refusal—to understand the international situation, and in others to sympathy on the part of many groups for the ideas of Nazism."

access by all nations to new inventions for the manufacture of synthetic products."[20]

The therapeutic value of all such procedures attracted writers' attention. Having Germans themselves clear the rubble of their destroyed cities, tend war victims, send their young men to rehabilitate war-torn Europe, sit on international reparations commissions, participate in criminal court proceedings from preliminary hearings to imprisonment and even execution—all were means to teach Germans most immediately how their country had gone wrong during the Nazi years and what the consequences of that were. Such steps, many writers argued earnestly, would have a salutary effect on German thinking.

Education for democracy? Making postwar Germans work not only for their own keep but to atone for leaders who had betrayed them and to restore the societies Nazism had sought to destroy implied a long-term, educational mission. Some wartime publicists frankly doubted that Germans were teachable (Kaufman 1941). The bulk, however, agreed enthusiastically on the value of education in democratizing Germany: the German people and especially German youth needed to learn how to be democratic, how to enjoy a "cooperative mentality" (RIIA 1943:69).

Their assessments nevertheless differed according to their diagnosis of the problem. The Chatham House study group (RIIA 1943), which saw the problem mainly in the perversity of the Nazi education system, the "immediate didactic purpose" of which was "to foster racial pride and aggressiveness in the service of the *Volk* and its Fuehrer" (p. 70), offered a political solution.[21] The Allies needed to create the proper political environment— for example, lifting "the yoke of Goebbels . . . from radio, press, and cinema" (p. 71), removing hard-core Nazis from positions of power at all levels of the education system, and preparing democratically acceptable materials for the classroom. "To make use of a moment which may be fleeting," the group added, "it might be a service to prepare in advance translations of representative new books banned from Germany, up-to-date textbooks free of the Nazi *Weltanschauung*, short objective histories of recent events, and the like" (p. 72). A new international education authority could also introduce German teachers to current ideas and practices in the rest of the world. However effective a political solution might turn out to be, compulsion clearly would not work; given the nature of the education process, it would doubtless be counterproductive. "A perma-

20. Dean (p. 195) also recommended that Germans "be required to supply labor and technical skill to the reconstruction of regions devastated by German armies."

21. "The key to the practical problem of re-education in Germany, even in the current sense of the teaching of the individual, is seen to be political organization in the broadest sense" (RIIA 1943:75).

nent new direction can be given to German education only if in Germany herself leaders arise under whom the German masses can learn, in terms which mean something to them, the lessons of democratic freedom, political responsibility, and international co-operation" (p. 75).

Others found the German education system's problem in centuries of hypernationalistic enculturation—enculturation that would require the Allies to penetrate deeply not only into public institutions but into German culture as a whole. The New York conference of medical experts and social scientists focused outspokenly on changing German attitudes and behaviors. Even in the best of circumstances, conference participants said in their final report, the education system could not do that.[22] Teachers and textbooks alone simply do not change attitudes. The conference thus provided a long list of possible changes not only in the education field (structures, content, teaching personnel, and extracurricular education) but also in the home, civil service, police systems, and other social settings. The conferees, who had in mind a "long-term program for the successful reintegration of a chastened, but especially a changed German people in relation with the other peoples of the world," produced twenty concrete suggestions, several dealing directly with public education, among them (p. 436):

5. The entire German educational system must be revamped in such a way as to effect a considerable degree of decentralization and the abolition of the state-dictated hierarchy.
6. All teaching should be aimed at developing independent thinking, respect for social contributions, and contempt for status as such. The importance of world unity and cooperation must be stressed.
7. Centers for adult education should be established, with programs approved by the Allied educational authority.
8. A program for the more adequate preparation of teacher personnel should be inaugurated at once, with a provision for teachers' colleges whose programs are subject to Allied approval.

The conference's overall program "*will not* mean that we shall be imposing our own particular way of life upon the Germans," its report concluded. "It *will* mean that we shall be helping to build attitudes that are essential to the continuance of a peaceful world" (p. 439; emphasis in original).

22. In line with Chatham House thinking, the New York conference agreed that, whatever role that system had to play, "new educational myths and concepts" could not "be imported from the outside" but would have to "come from the Germans themselves" (Lowrey et al. 1945:414).

Public Perspectives in Sample Surveys

Publicists set the tone for the public discussion and influenced common citizens as well as elected officials and their staff, but policymakers were anxious to know those citizens' unfiltered thoughts about the German problem. Courageous leaders will support unpopular policies they think right. They usually prefer, however, to have solid public support before stepping out on political limbs. Traditionally a politician kept an ear to the ground to ascertain how the grass roots were growing and where their intellectual sprouts were heading. George Gallup's polling techniques developed in the mid-1930s provided political leaders an opportunity to evaluate more precisely what the public was thinking.

This tool gave the Roosevelt administration insights into the American public's view of the German problem and its policy implications. The president clearly understood the importance of public opinion. After all, he led a country whose people had in 1919 backed out of their government's commitment to world and especially European politics. A strong segment of his own party and even more leaders in the opposition continued two decades later to lobby for isolation. When Germany's invasion of Poland on 1 September 1939 sparked World War II, American voices calling for their government's restraint were loud and clear. Yet Roosevelt believed that America's best defense, indeed, the future of the world, lay in defeating the Axis powers. Knowing how individual citizens—citizens who would cast ballots in the presidential election of 1940—responded to the rhetorical fusillades of isolationists and interventionists was of great practical importance.

According to public opinion polls, the people of the United States decidedly opposed involvement in a new European war. They took this extreme position before hostilities began and in the war's first two years moved only gradually from it. In July 1939 (Roper 1939a:84) only 3 percent of respondents reported a willingness to enter the fray should England and France go to war with the "dictator nations"—although 25 percent more said they would do so should it be clear that England and France were losing the war.[23] Figure 1.2 shows how this way of thinking evolved from the war's earliest days until shortly before the attack on Pearl Harbor that triggered active U.S. involvement. For the twenty-six

23. Elmo Roper, Inc., conducted *Fortune*'s surveys for several years. During the war years, however, the monthly magazine neither assigned authorship nor reported when the sampling took place. Here we shall use two conventions regarding the *Fortune* surveys: listing Roper as the author; and assuming that the interviews were conducted two months before the magazine reported the data. Support for the latter assumption comes from the fact that data in the *Fortune* issue of March 1944 were reported a year later (Roper 1945:454) to have been based on samples interviewed in January 1944.

Figure 1.2

U.S. Preparedness to Enter the European War, 1939-1941

Question: Should we send our army and navy abroad to fight Germany?

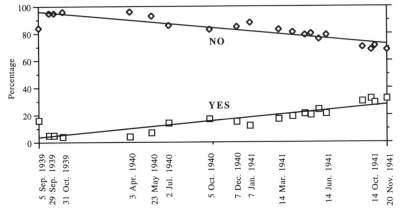

YES: y = 3.7730 + 2.9699e-2x R^2 = 0.781 F-Ratio = 64.5 Prob < 0.001
NO: y = 96.227 - 2.9699e-2x R^2 = 0.781 F-Ratio = 64.5 Prob < 0.001

Source: Gallup (1972).
Note: Questions vary across time but are consistent.

months as a whole, an average of four in five Americans opposed U.S. entry into the war. In the first war months 95 percent took that stance. And even in late fall 1941, after the fall of France, after the German invasion of the USSR, and after the U.S. Navy began its shooting war with German U-boats, more than two-thirds continued to resist their country's involvement.

Does that mean that Americans were indifferent to the war, its combatants, and its consequences? To the contrary, from the very outset they blamed Germany for starting it. A week after the German march into Poland and the Anglo-French declarations of war, five in six poll respondents saw Germany as the aggressor (Gallup 1972:178).[24] Moreover, Americans promptly chose sides. Asked specifically in August and September 1939 which countries they would "like to see win," five in six respondents named "England, France, and their friends" while only 1 percent claimed to favor "Germany and its friends" (Roper 1939b, c). Germany, though, was not the sole pariah as far as American imagery was concerned. Although more than half of the interviewees cited Germany

---

24. About 6 percent attributed the war to England and France or the Versailles Treaty, another 6 percent cited Poland and other actors on Europe's political stage, and 6 percent expressed no opinion.

when asked which "nation" was "the worst influence in Europe," a full third pointed to the Soviet Union (and 2 percent to England, 1 percent to Italy) (Roper 1940b:102).

Why had Germans started the war? "Hitler's greed for land and lust for power," answered more than half of a U.S. sample in October 1939 (Roper 1939d:120). Almost a third attributed the war to the injustices of Versailles. Only 6 percent, however, blamed it on England or France—the same percentage that cited the German people, who "always want to have things their own way, even if that brings a war."[25] This image of German guilt persisted, providing a bedrock for later U.S. efforts to aid Britain and even the Soviet Union, whom one in three considered Europe's worst influence.

And if Americans thought Germany culpable, they were equally of the opinion that the aggressors should pay for their crimes. In November 1939 punishment was at the top of their list of postwar priorities: half wanted to crush Hitler and his government while leaving the German nation intact, a fifth to exterminate the German nation and dismember the country, and one in seven simply to disarm the Germans and supervise any steps taken by a new German nation (Roper 1940a:90). But what did "crushing Hitler and his government" mean? Regarding Hitler personally, in January 1942 39 percent wanted him hanged or shot and 23 percent wanted him imprisoned (Gallup 1972:339). Only 6 percent proposed exiling him. Hermann Göring? Immediately after the war's end two in three wanted him killed and 15 percent wanted him otherwise punished (Gallup 1972:507). Nazi leaders? The survey of June 1942 found 35 percent favoring execution and 31 percent imprisonment (Gallup 1972:339).[26] Gestapo agents and storm troopers? In May 1945 nearly half called for immediate executions, a tenth for torture, starvation, or other forms of slow and painful death, and a fifth for various other kinds of punishment (Gallup 1972:507).[27] The Nazi party itself should be abolished, said 88 percent in January 1944 and 93 percent a year later (Roper 1945:254). The main direction of thinking,

25. The open-ended question permitted multiple responses. Another 15 percent gave other answers, such as traditional European hostilities, and 5 percent offered no views.

26. Small numbers of Americans wanted to inflict on Hitler (3 percent) and Nazi leaders (2 percent) slow torture or some other form of mental and physical suffering. Five percent proposed treating Hitler and the Nazi leaders "as Nazis have treated others." Taken together, about 77 percent of the sample sought vengeance: to end the lives of Hitler and his cohorts or otherwise make their lives exceedingly unpleasant.

27. Asked in April 1945 about "members of the Nazi party who defend themselves by claiming that they committed crimes under orders of higher-ups in the party," one in five spoke of execution, and three in five wanted to imprison them all (42 percent) or those who were tried and found guilty (19 percent). Three percent called for reeducation, 2 percent saw no need for action, and 15 percent gave no response (Gallup 1972:501).

then, was clear: Americans had blood on their minds when they looked at Nazi Germany's leaders.

Hatred of German leaders did not, however, extend to all things German. German culture merited serious attention, Americans said. In December 1939 only 8 percent accepted the argument that their "orchestras and bands . . . should stop playing German music" (Gallup 1972:196). Only 11 percent agreed that "American colleges and high schools should stop teaching the German language."

The German people, Americans said, merited sympathy or at least understanding. Most survey respondents seemed to find it difficult to differentiate between the lovable Mr. Schulz who ran the grocery store down the street and the masses of Germans in the homeland who, for whatever reason, had been swayed by brownshirted Nazis. Americans were simply not willing wholeheartedly to accept propaganda that treated the German people as archfiends. Less than one-third of the respondents to a survey conducted in September 1942 by the National Opinion Research Center thought it "necessary to hate our enemies in order to win the war" (NORC 1945:11). Two months later only 6 percent considered "Germans" to be their enemy, whereas 74 percent assigned that status to the German government (Gallup 1972:356).

The progress of the war nevertheless found Americans increasingly exasperated by the German people. Figure 1.3 shows how American attitudes toward this question changed from early 1942 until the end of 1944.[28] The perception of Germans as incurably warlike, which attracted an overall average of 26 percent, increased. The view of them as potentially good citizens (averaging 31 percent) declined. Two in five thought Germans, though not warlike, were weak and too easily led by ruthless rulers. This image—basically peaceful but gullible—persisted and, as we shall see, even became stronger as time went on. In February 1944 almost two-thirds of an American sample believed that Germans "would like to get rid of their Nazi leaders now" (a claim denied by 19 percent), but only 31 percent felt that it was within Germans' power to do so if they wanted to (53 percent denied that) (NORC 1945:9).

Irrespective of what motivated German behavior, Americans understood that their own country would have to confront the issue after the war. As we have seen, they differentiated among actors in the German

28. Responding to a similar question in October 1939, 67 percent saw Germans as peace loving and kindly but misled, 20 percent as possessing "an irrepressible fondness for brute force and conquest," and 4 percent as conquerors compelled by "the needs of Germany's expanding population" (Roper 1939d:120).

Figure 1.3

American Views of Germans, 1942-1944

Question: Which of the following statements comes closest to describing how you feel, on the whole,
about the people who live in Germany?

The German people will always want to go to war to make themselves as powerful as
possible.

The German people may not like war, but they have shown that they are too easily led
into war by powerful leaders.

The German people do not like war. If they could have the same chance as people in other
countries they would become good citizens of the world.

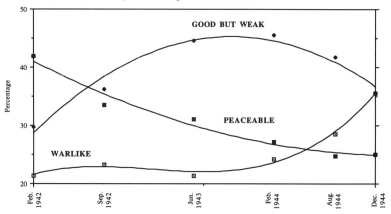

Warlike: y = 21.508 + 0.47461x - 5.0535e-2x^2 + 1.4301e-3x^3   R^2 = 0.992   F-Ratio = 78.1   Prob< 0.013
Good but weak: y = 28.605 + 1.6778x - 4.2322e-2x^2   R^2 = 0.953   F-Ratio = 30.1   Prob< 0.010
Peaceable: y = 40.996 - 0.88684x + 1.2139e-2x^2   R^2 = 0.971   F-Ratio = 50.0   Prob< 0.005

Source: NORC, 1945:6.
Note: The question for February 1942 differs somewhat from the others.

drama. Most culpable were Hitler, Nazi party and military officers, and lesser leaders who adhered loyally to policies set at the top. A strong American sentiment called for the removal, incarceration, or summary execution of these false prophets. Substantial numbers of interviewees believed that the German people, had they been able to do so, would themselves have toppled them. The Nazi leadership was Germany's evil genius, thwarting rather than realizing the will of the people.

At the bottom of the hierarchy of power were precisely these people: Germans, women and men, who served as nurses and Wehrmacht draftees and shopkeepers, who enjoyed their beer and frankfurters, who made Christmas tree ornaments and had given the world so many poets and thinkers. Most Americans accepted this image—even though many worried about the apparent naïveté of Germans and their proclivity to follow strong men who led them astray. Asked in 1943 and 1944 what kind of postwar policy their government should pursue toward the German people, half of an American sample called for a severe (9 percent) or strict

(41 percent) treatment (NORC 1945:15; multiple responses permitted). Two-thirds, however, recommended leniency.[29]

American public opinion saw yet another "actor" in the German drama beyond the leaders and followers: Germany itself. This putative entity—the political equivalent of the equally problematic notion of "national character"—consisted of a concatenation of government offices, industry, educational institutions, and other organized structures that together acted as a single unit.[30] It was at once the victim of Nazism's perversion of democratic principles and the faithful executor of those Nazi excesses. But to execute decisions made on high ultimately requires mass consent. The entity called Germany was thus instrumental in seducing the people, getting them at once to implement the leaders' demands and to provide the popular exultation needed to legitimate such acts.

How was the United States to handle this third actor? Figure 1.4 reflects the American public response when asked what to do about policy aimed at Germany as a country rather than the German people. In this case (without multiple responses) an average of almost three in four called for a severe (30 percent) or strict (41 percent) treatment, whereas about 12 percent recommended leniency.[31] These attitudes shifted over time, with a growing inclination to punish Germany severely (rising from 21 to 34 percent) and a diminishing inclination for leniency (falling from 17 to 8 percent). It was, then, Americans were saying, Germany and not the non-Nazi people that should be the target of U.S. occupation policy. This moral sleight of hand would later cause occupation decision makers severe problems in determining exactly what to do.

Rectifying the Old

What did the American people say they wanted their government to do in occupied Germany? First of all they expected to see Nazi miscreants

29. Because multiple responses were permitted and because some respondents gave ostensibly contradictory responses, suggesting both "strict supervision" and "lenient treatment," e.g., the sum of the responses exceeds 100 percent.

30. Referring to the nation-state as an actor in the international system is a rhetorical device with ancient roots. Monarchs were sometimes given the name of their country to symbolize their position as head of state: Shakespeare's Henry V spoke of the French king Charles VI as "our brother France." The device is also used as a mental shortcut: We say that "Germany invaded Poland" with no intent of suggesting that either Germany or Poland is a unitary actor with human characteristics. The idea of "Germany as an entity," however, as used by World War II pollsters, ran directly into an intellectual trap akin to that in which "national-character" analysts wallowed.

31. Some variation in responses to the two sets of questions may stem from slight differences in their wording or ways of coding the responses.

Figure 1.4

Dealing with Postwar Germany, 1943-1945

Question: What do you think we should do with Germany, as a country, after the war?
Supervise and control, disarm, eliminate Nazis, control industries
Treat very severely, destroy as political entity, cripple her
Be lenient, rehabilitate, reeducate, encourage trade, start fresh

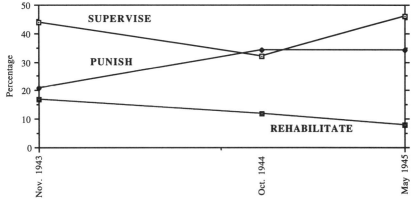

Source: Gallup, 1972:426, 470, 506.

punished and Germany made safe for a peaceable, civilized world. The key issues were:

Unconditional surrender. While the United States was still sitting on the war's sidelines, in November 1939, a majority of poll respondents wanted to see the Allies—at that time, Britain and France—prosecute the war until they achieved total victory (Roper 1940a:90). Only a third thought that they "should stop if Germany asks for peace," while well over half felt that the Allies "should continue until Germany is so badly beaten that she will never again rise as a nation." Five years later, however, American attitudes appeared to have mellowed. A NORC (1945:40) survey asked in December 1944: "If the people in Germany had their say, do you think they might surrender sooner if they thought we would help them get their peacetime industries going again after the war?" Seven in ten thought they would, two in ten thought not. It seems reasonable to assume that those who envisioned war-weary Germans keen to end the bloodshed might also conclude that the demand for unconditional surrender merely delayed the peace.[32]

32. In fact, as we have seen, publicists and others sometimes valued the peace process's form more than the fact that it was taking place. My assumption here is that the mass public simply wanted the war to end and cared little for strategic thinking.

Dismemberment. Americans were not of one mind regarding the advisability of partitioning Germany. Early in the war, in October 1942, almost two in three respondents opposed the proposition that Germany "be broken up completely" (Gallup survey reported in NORC 1945:27). As the war went on, however, the idea seemed less outrageous. This shift does not mean that Americans wanted Germany "divided up and given to other countries": a survey in fall 1944 that raised that issue found even fewer favoring it (26 percent) than had earlier accepted partition alone (NORC 1945:26). But when a Gallup (1972:501) survey in April 1945 returned to the issue of partition alone, support rose to 40 percent, and the share of undecided respondents, only 6 percent in the October 1942 poll, rose to 28 percent. Only half as many disapproved outright of the notion as before.[33]

Disarmament. Surveys found strong pressure for policies that would "completely demobilize the German Army and keep [Germany] from having any army again" (Roper 1945:254). Three in four took this stance in January 1944 and five in six did so a year later. An independent survey in January 1945 found 92 percent of a sample agreeing and only 6 percent disagreeing that "after the war, . . . Germany and Japan [should] be kept permanently disarmed" (Gallup 1972:485).

German forced labor. Americans were not averse to compelling German men to reconstruct war-torn Europe. In December 1943 a Gallup (1972:430) survey asked: "After the war should three to four million German men be sent to Russia to help rebuild destroyed cities there?" Half responded positively and 30 percent negatively. The same question, asked again in April 1945, found much more support for sending Germans to Russia: Almost five in six agreed and only 11 percent disagreed (Gallup 1972:502).

Roper and NORC surveys asked similar questions that referred not to "Russians" as recipients but to "devastated areas" or "some of the countries [the Wehrmacht] had fought against." These questions, too, elicited strong support. In the Roper (1945:254) survey 46 percent agreed in January 1944 and 62 percent a year later. The number opposing the idea dropped from 32 to 22 percent. In the NORC (1945:47) survey of December 1944, 51 percent responded positively but 41 percent negatively.[34]

---

33. Supportive evidence came from Roper (1945:254) surveys in January 1944 and January 1945: the percentage wanting to "break Germany up into smaller states" rose from 30 to 41 percent, while opposition declined from 41 to 34 percent.

34. Those who supported the idea were then asked whether or not the need for workers in Germany made any difference. More than half of the subsample (28 percent of all respondents) said that German workers should be sent overseas anyway. Fewer than a third of the subsample (16 percent of all respondents) wanted to give priority to German needs.

Reparations. A sharply worded question posed in 1942 by NORC (1945: 43) found many Americans eager to extract reparations from defeated Germany: 43 percent wanted "as much as is possible to get out of the Axis countries, even if it breaks them," 9 percent "none of the costs of the war," and 38 percent "something in between" the two polar positions. A more moderate question in fall 1944 elicited over twice as many agreeing (62 percent) as disagreeing (29 percent) with Allied plans to secure payments "either in money or goods" (NORC 1945:41). But, should wartime Germany give up its captured territories and punish Hitler and other Nazi leaders, then the ratio changed to 48 percent agreeing and 43 percent disagreeing. Americans were not sanguine, however, about prospects for actually getting any reparations bonanza. For every respondent expecting Germans to be able to pay (29 percent of the entire sample), two (57 percent) did not.[35] Asked an even milder question in January 1945, 87 percent of the respondents thought that "Germans should . . . be forced to make up in some way or another for the destruction they have caused in other countries," and only 8 percent disagreed (Roper 1945:259). Taken together the surveys found popular American support for the principle of reparations but little expectation of tangible results.

Creating the New

A second part of the American public's vision of U.S. occupation policy focused on the future of Germany. The occupation, to be successful, had to go beyond merely punitive measures such as rounding up and incarcerating Nazi leaders. It had to develop ways that would lead Germans toward international cooperation and even democracy. Some key issues were:

Military occupation. How long were U.S. troops to remain in Germany? Roper (1945:254) surveys found 73 percent agreeing in January 1944 and 86 percent a year later that the Allies should "govern Germany with an occupation force for several years." In August 1944 an open-ended question about the length of time occupation would last elicited a median estimate of two to three years (Gallup 1972:460). A third said that one year

35. Those agreeing with the idea of reparations (62 percent) or not responding to the question (9 percent) were then asked what the Allies should do if Germany did not pay. More than three-fourths of the subsample (55 percent of the entire sample)—were doubtful, saying either that nothing could be done (31 percent), time should be extended (18 percent), or the Allies should forget the whole thing (6 percent). The others, 23 percent of the subsample (16 percent of the entire sample), responded that Germany should be made to pay (11 percent) or that the Allies should use physical force (5 percent).

or less would be enough and slightly more thought four years or more were needed (Gallup 1972:460).[36]

Emergency assistance. What was the United States to do if occupied Germans were starving in the streets? Four in five were willing either to sell Germans what food they could pay for (39 percent) or to give them food as a gift if they could not pay (41 percent). One in six thought that the United States should "not send them any food at all" (NORC, 1945:23).

Education. Two-thirds of American poll respondents in August 1944 accepted and one in five rejected the idea that after the war "the Allies should supervise the education and training of German youth" (Gallup 1972:460). A principal concern was simple enough: whether or not there would "be enough of the right kind of Germans within Germany to re-educate the people along democratic lines" (Roper 1945:259). This question, asked in January 1945, found that 57 percent of respondents doubted that enough educators of such quality existed, but 22 percent thought otherwise.

Industrial reconstruction. Americans supported the timely reconstruction of Germany's nonmilitary industry.[37] Wartime destruction, they felt, had severely limited the German ability to maintain even a modicum of self-sufficiency. But how could the occupied country rebuild what it needed? Should "our government," Americans were asked in fall 1944 (NORC 1945:34–36), "help Germany get her peacetime industries going again after the war?" Three-fifths of the interviewees agreed and one-third disagreed. Of the former, well over half (33 percent of the total sample) were willing to help Germany rebuild even if that meant continued rationing at home. Why? The reason given by three-fourths of those favoring industrial assistance (44 percent of the total sample) was that the United States would benefit from a reconstructed Germany.

Restoring democracy. Should Germans be permitted to hold political elections? In February 1942 well over two-thirds of those expressing opin-

36. A Gallup (1972:503) survey in Britain at roughly the same time found the median response to be "up to 10 years." Almost a fifth expected the occupation to last up to five years, and 27 percent said up to ten years. Others thought it would last up to fifteen years (10 percent), twenty (16 percent), twenty-five (8 percent), or even more (10 percent). More than a tenth gave no response.

37. The distinction between military and nonmilitary industry may not have been clear to all respondents. Asked in January 1944 whether the Allies should "prevent the Germans from rebuilding their steel, chemical, and automotive industries"—that is, what Roper (1945:254–256) considered to be the country's "big war industries"—31 percent agreed and 53 percent disagreed. The next year evidently brought some clarification of what the stakes were. In January 1945 the ratio was 43 percent agreeing to 41 percent disagreeing. The latter survey also found that 51 percent were willing to permit the Allies to "try to find some way to let Germany remain an industrial nation without being a menace to the rest of the world," while only 33 percent opposed such an idea.

ions (62 to 28 percent) thought they should (NORC 1945:28–29). Two and a half years later, however, the ratio of support for elections dropped, with 56 percent willing to see Germans voting and 37 percent opposed. Respondents who thought Germans incurably warlike were less inclined to accept the idea of balloting (an average of 43 percent in the two surveys) than were those who saw Germans as good but too easily led (61 percent) or fundamentally peaceable (71 percent).

United Nations membership. Plans that emerged during the war to create an international security arrangement, the United Nations, raised considerable interest among Americans. In fall 1944 seven of ten believed that the United States should join that organization (NORC 1945:58). Of these, more than half (40 percent of the entire sample) also thought that Germany should be permitted to join.[38] More than a third (26 percent of the total), though, said that Germany should be excluded from membership.

The public opinion data reported here suggest a shifting American image of the war itself and of who had been responsible for starting it. In the early months of U.S. involvement, poll respondents were inclined to take a balanced view of what they understood to be a traditional war. That is, for large numbers of Americans, German leaders rather than the German people had "caused" it, and once the Allies had defeated the Wehrmacht and gotten rid of the Nazis, international life could begin anew. By mid-1944, however, attitudes were hardening. Americans were less likely to differentiate German leaders from German masses or to give either any benefit of doubt. They were more likely to take vengeance on postwar Germans and the German nation.

What accounts for this shifting perception? One factor was surely the growing psychological proximity of the European war. Before U.S. troops invaded French Morocco and Algeria in November 1942, few Americans other than seamen fought battles in the European Theater that cost American lives. The beginning of the Italian campaign in July 1943 and the Allied invasion of occupied France in June 1944 changed things substantially. It put ever more GIs on the front lines and ever more gold stars—symbolizing family members killed in action—on the front windows of American homes. Intellectual balance toward an abstract conflict dissipated. The German state and people were no longer abstractions. They were deadly realities.

38. Roper (1945:262) found in January 1945 that almost three-quarters of adult Americans were willing to accept Germany as a member "right away" (8 percent) or "after she has proved that she can behave decently" (65 percent). A fifth said that they would "never" tolerate German membership in the United Nations.

A second factor was the apparent irrationality of Germany's willingness to fight the war to its bitter end. A Hitlerian boast said that Nazis would see Europe go up in flames before letting Germany go down—and dutiful minions did their best to carry out this perverted fantasy. But Americans saw no reason for such behavior. The sentimental heroism of isolated handfuls of men at the Battle of the Alamo and Custer's Last Stand had no bearing on the millions of lives at stake in a protracted European war. By late 1943 it seemed clear that the Allies would eventually defeat Germany. By late 1944 the end was nigh. Why, then, did the Germans continue to fight, to shed an enormous amount of blood in a hopeless quest?

Finally, Americans were horrified when they learned the full dimensions of Nazi death camps, and their responses to survey questions manifest their loathing (Gallup 1972:504–505). Most accepted the reports as true (84 percent) or true but exaggerated (9 percent).[39] They also had a clear notion of the nature if not the scale of human carnage these camps wreaked across Europe.[40] Asked in May 1945 the extent to which they thought that "the German people . . . approved of the killing and starving of prisoners in Germany," almost five in six American poll respondents saw civilian complicity to be either entire (31 percent) or partial (51 percent); only one in eight denied it (Gallup 1972:508).[41] Three in five thought it would be a good idea (with 35 percent of the opposite opinion) to distribute throughout the land documentary films about the atrocities (Gallup 1972:505). Five in six reported an interest in seeing such movies, 87 percent thought that German prisoners of war in U.S. camps should be made to view them, and 89 percent said that "such pictures should be shown to all German people in Germany."

39. One percent termed the reports doubtful and 3 percent not at all credible. A key juncture for Anglo-American images of the concentration camps came in April 1945 when the British army opened Bergen-Belsen and published photographs depicting the camp's deplorable conditions, including inmates dying of typhus, typhoid, and starvation (Captives 1945).

40. The median response estimated that the camps had exterminated a million people (Gallup 1972:504).

41. In contrast, responses to a similar question showed that the Japanese were more widely viewed as bloodthirsty. More than three in five American respondents asserted that the Japanese people had entirely approved atrocities and another 25 percent saw them as having partly approved such acts. Only 6 percent denied that the Japanese people supported or knew anything about the atrocities (Gallup 1972:509).

A NORC (1945:11) survey in September 1942, before the major crimes of the Holocaust had begun, reported that 31 percent agreed and 61 percent disagreed that "the German people should be blamed for the cruelties to religious groups, the mass killings in occupied countries, and the tortures in concentration camps." Asked in fall 1944 who should be blamed "for the cruelties in this war," 2 percent cited the German people, 58 percent Nazi leaders, and 38 percent both.

Increasing personal involvement, incredulity regarding Germany's apparent *Götterdämmerung* mentality, and repugnance toward Nazism's wanton massacre of Jews, Slavs, Gypsies, and others—all contributed to a growing sense among Americans that the German people were willful perpetrators rather than hapless victims of Nazism. This perception, however, remained a minority view. The data reviewed here suggest that during the first part of the war the number of Americans fundamentally hostile to Germany and the German people rose from about a sixth to about a fifth.[42] Whatever the question, every fifth American respondent could be counted on to give a Germanophobic response. Events of the latter part of the war alienated another eighth of the American people. By war's end, then, as many as one in three respondents expressed deep hostility against Germans and Germany. But the majority still did not. Some doubtless were philogermanic, but most seemed simply to take a long view of the situation. They recognized that the war would end and that the U.S. government would eventually face a new Germany, one that might be more amenable to peace and democracy.

An Occupation Policy for Americans

In many ways American public opinion was consistent with the images of Germany that Anglo-Atlantic publicists were simultaneously projecting. Unanimity was rare. Consensus was most striking when writers and interviewees described how they thought Hitler and his cohorts should be treated. Otherwise, perspectives ranged from minimalist to maximalist. Just as the occasional writer, such as Kaufman (1941), took an extreme position, so, too, a few poll respondents expressed unusual harshness. The nature of public opinion surveying seldom permits nuances and refined lines of argumentation. Interviewers are trained to focus responses into limited numbers of categories. Subtle differences at the center are sometimes sacrificed and sharpness at the margins intensified. But at the same time that poll respondents appear bellicose and punitive, we find thoughtful publicists blithely proposing systematic sterilization or death sentences for a sixth of a million.

Diversity of opinion defies any notion of a single, integrated American image.[43] Using the minimalist-maximalist continuum characterized in Figure 1.1, however, we find most writers and interviewees somewhere in

42. Hostility toward Hitler and the Nazi regime was much higher. The estimates described here ignore the small percentage of Americans who consistently expressed no opinion on German matters.

43. A wide range of daily newspapers and weekly news magazines (see NORC 1945) produced roughly the same complex of variation.

the middle.[44] This is particularly true when we explore popular views of the past, including the war. So much horror had occurred that no one could claim that the European portion of World War II was "business as usual" in the international arena. But the justice and security that Americans wanted did not, for the majority, mandate Germany's brutalization. Germany—whether seen in its political or its cultural dimension—had to pay for its Nazi adventure and be prevented from repeating it or anything similar. More specifically, the Allies had to bring to justice the country's Nazi leaders. For tolerating such leadership, each German citizen also had to pay, in the form of reparations, some years of deprivation, and strict Allied surveillance until Germans could again be permitted to govern themselves. The actual extent of any one of these steps was less important than the principle they would establish. To accomplish this purpose Americans wanted a strict, no-nonsense, but relatively short-termed occupation, one that would not cripple the German people's ability to thrive and prosper.

More problematic was the future of German society. Where pollsters could offer specific questions, the distribution of perceptions among interviewees and publicists alike was similar. Many, for instance, saw the need to revamp Germany's education system, to make it more consistent with the principles of democratic society. But what in the education system needed revamping? Similarly, should the occupation forces restructure the media of mass communication, and if so, how? Such concerns raised a key, broader question: How should the Allies—or, better, the Americans—"democratize" and "pacify" German society? Early public opinion polling did not lend itself well to this question, but the diffusion of ideas emanating from publicists provided much food for thought.

Those responsible for setting U.S. occupation policy in Germany could thus draw on assessments of diffuse American perceptions. Where popular views coalesced around important issues, elected leaders and their administrative staffs tended to pay heed. But even in those circumstances, and certainly where attitudes were widely split, America's wartime perspectives on Germany provided one contribution to the policy-making process.

44. I am suggesting what amounts to a bell-shaped curve of perspectives, with perhaps 10 percent of Americans at either extreme and 40 percent in each of the two middle ranges.

TWO

● ●

U.S. Occupation Policy

U.S. policy planners faced a serious impediment to establishing the country's wartime goals toward Germany and crafting a plan to realize those goals: the planners were far from certain about what they were supposed to do. President Roosevelt was himself indecisive. Despite his oft-repeated intention to deal with the German issue, addressing such nitty-gritty matters as providing drinking water to a bomb-gutted city in Germany was not his métier. His forays into this policy arena as often as not only complicated the situation.[1]

Thinking About Occupying Germany

Roosevelt's forte was large-scale planning. Four months before the United States formally entered the war he met with Churchill in the North Atlantic to draft a document that would enhearten democrats throughout the world. The Atlantic Charter, later endorsed by fifteen other countries, spoke of "the final destruction of the Nazi tyranny" and the need for collective security in the postwar world. But it contained not a word about Germany's fate. On the first day of 1942 the two men, together with Soviet and Chinese representatives, signed the United Nations Declaration, which was eventually endorsed by forty-three other states. Each country pledged "to employ its full resources, military or economic," in the battle against the Axis powers, to cooperate with the other united nation-states, and "not to make a separate armistice or peace with the enemies." This declaration, too, bolstered spirits, and it provided the basis

1. This chapter relies heavily on Hammond (1963) and, among others, Ratchford and Ross (1947), Zink (1947), Arne (1948), Mosely (1950a, 1950b), USDS (1955, 1960, 1961, 1968, 1972, 1985), Feis (1957), Armstrong (1961), Snell (1963), J. Blum (1967), Gimbel (1968), Backer (1971, 1978), Kuklick (1972), Peterson (1977), De Zayas (1989), and J. Smith (1990).

for the United Nations organization set up in 1946. But what would happen to a defeated Germany went unmentioned.

Such grand designs were hardly cornerstones for concerted action toward Germany, and the president's inattentiveness magnified the policy vacuum. One key question was jurisdictional: Was the War Department or State Department to take the lead in drafting and implementing U.S. occupation policy? U.S. military men had governed defeated enemies since the Mexican War, so the War Department assumed that it would take on the main responsibility after World War II as well. In one of its early sallies into the field of postwar governance, the department established in mid-1942 a School of Military Government in Charlottesville, Virginia. The program barely survived a political maelstrom in October when President Roosevelt saw it encroaching on territory that he had staked out for himself. A month later the president assigned Secretary of State Cordell Hull "full authority for economic, political, and fiscal questions in liberated territories" (cited by Peterson 1977:31). Hull's new Office of Foreign Territories, however, was soon abandoned.

The contest between the War and State departments was more than simple bureaucratic infighting. The two departments approached the German problem in fundamentally different ways. The War Department envisioned a postwar world of relentless struggle for power among competing nation-states. Accordingly, the philosophically minimalist members of the Joint Chiefs of Staff (JCS) argued, it made sense for the United States to do as quickly as possible what had to be done in defeated Germany and then get out of the country to concentrate on other areas of potential conflict. Thinking in the State Department, initially moderate, leaned more toward creating a world cushioned by a global collective security arrangement. This strategy might include lengthy occupation of such aggressor countries as Germany. Champions of both perspectives, which were in many ways similar to the lines that publicists were peddling in the public arena, lobbied the president as best they could.

Casablanca Conference (January 1943). Roosevelt and Churchill moved toward fundamental policy decisions in January 1943 when they met in the French-Moroccan city of Casablanca. They voiced concern that foreign and domestic pressures might force the Allies to accept a German suit for a negotiated peace, one that could leave Germany unconquered and the Wehrmacht virtually intact. The disaster after the negotiated peace of 1918 was fresh in their memories. At the conference's closing session with the press, Roosevelt made what he later described as a spur-of-the-moment declaration: the United States and England had agreed, he said, that nothing short of Germany's unconditional surrender was acceptable.

The announcement from Casablanca had a double impact. In Germany, it gave Hitler's propaganda minister, Josef Goebbels, a needed opportunity to mobilize renewed popular support for the war effort, which was sagging seriously after major Wehrmacht defeats at Stalingrad and El Alamein. On 18 February, in a well-publicized address at Berlin's Palace of Sports, Goebbels proclaimed that only "total war" could save the German nation. "Do you want this total war?" he bellowed out. "Jawohl," his audience roared back (Massenkundgebung 1943). Any later reference to unconditional surrender triggered new claims that the Allies aimed to demolish German civilization. What impact such propaganda had on German behavior is by no means clear. But many who were in Germany at the time believe that it had a powerful influence on the popular will to continue fighting.[2] In the Allied countries, by contrast, the abruptness of Roosevelt's call for unconditional surrender led to some confusion. It took until October 1943 before their foreign ministers, meeting in Moscow, could accept the idea in principle. By then, in the U.S. political context, military leaders were acting in accordance with the new policy direction.

The Joint Chiefs of Staff responded on 1 March 1943 with its Civilian Affairs Division. CAD assumed responsibility for training military personnel and civilians to serve as occupation officials, prepared handbooks of technical procedures, and generally set the tone for the occupation that the JCS wanted. Military strategists as well as officers in war zones made it clear that any actions by bureaucrats not linked to the Pentagon—including those from the State Department—would be carried out only at the sufferance of the military.[3] For this and other reasons the State Department's Office of Foreign Territories was shut down. So was the White House's last thrust in this area, the Foreign Economic Administration, set up as late as September 1943. Two months later the president accepted the War Department's leadership role in coordinating and implementing if not setting policy on postwar Germany.

Conferences in Moscow (October 1943) and Teheran (November–December 1943). In October 1943 Secretary Hull met in Moscow with foreign ministers Anthony Eden of the United Kingdom and Vyacheslav Molotov of the

2. Armstrong, describing the emerging German stance, notes that "from that time on no consideration was given to any argument except that of victory. Defeat meant total destruction. Victory required total effort, Total War was no holds barred. The Total End justified Total Means" (1961:218).

3. Hammond (1963) cites four reasons why the War Department in 1942–1943 did not share information or otherwise cooperate with the State Department: It was seeking to protect its own information and hence control over its own affairs, legitimate its own responsibility for military governance, minimize the impact of the State Department's excessive attentiveness to British interests, and respond to conflicting images within the War Department about the State Department's role in policy-making. War-State conflicts were "less matters of substance than of procedure" (p. 325).

Soviet Union. Central to the agenda was the intergovernmental struggle against Nazi Germany. The conferees found agreement on several issues, such as returning Germany to its boundary of 1937 and punishing those who had committed atrocities.[4] Other matters, however, proved more problematic. Hull proposed removing from public life Nazi party members and any vestiges of Nazism, creating a reparations commission to compensate victims of physical damages caused by Germany, demilitarizing the country entirely, and removing its capacity to produce military hardware.[5] Finding no agreement on the specifics of these and other issues, the foreign ministers referred them to their heads of state and created a European Advisory Commission (EAC) to deal with them in greater detail. At the very least, then, the Moscow Conference established the parameters of tripartite consensus on the German problem.

The Teheran Conference took place a month later. The first time Churchill and Roosevelt were together with Josef Stalin, the leaders addressed several questions carried over from the foreign ministers' conference. What, for instance, did the president and prime minister mean by unconditional surrender as a policy, not a principle? Stalin opened the dialogue with a harsh, anti-German statement. Churchill and Roosevelt reasserted their acceptance in principle of unconditional surrender but skirted details. Eventually the Big Three consigned the issue to the EAC. Some weeks later, though, both Churchill and Roosevelt clarified their stances somewhat: they would adopt any wartime goals, including unconditional surrender, that would help them destroy Nazism and Germany's subsequent military threat—but they did not intend to enslave the German people. Roosevelt clung adamantly to the principle of unconditional surrender, budging only slightly despite pressure from the State Department and his military chieftains, who leaned toward a flexibility that could end the war more quickly.[6]

Another question touched on in Teheran was Germany's division. Early

4. The foreign ministers' "Declaration on German atrocities" was accepted a month later by the Big Three.

5. Hull proposed that "arms manufacturing facilities be dismantled" and that "importation and manufacture of arms, ammunition, implements of war, and materials essential to their manufacture, including all types of aircraft, be prohibited" (cited by Hammond 1963:316).

6. General Dwight D. Eisenhower, commander in chief of SHAEF (Supreme Headquarters, Allied Expeditionary Forces), and his chief of staff, General Walter Bedell Smith, argued that relaxing the demand for unconditional surrender would induce German generals to give up their useless fight—an idea that gained some credence from the plot of 20 July 1944 on Hitler's life. A State Department policy issued on 12 May 1944 gave Germany's satellites (Hungary, Romania, Bulgaria, and Finland) a strong incentive to withdraw from the war.

wartime thinking among the Allied policy planners had envisioned Germany's dismemberment into any number of political units. In December 1941 Stalin formally pushed for three independent countries: the Rhineland (including the Ruhr and Saar basins), Bavaria, and a third northern state that would be diminished in size by giving part of Prussia to Poland. During the next two years both the British Foreign Office and the State Department drafted, considered, and reconsidered similar plans: The Moscow Conference of foreign ministers dampened such thinking. There the ministers seemed to prefer some form of decentralization to partition. Meeting in Teheran a month later, however, the Big Three presented competing schemes to split up Germany into smaller units that could be more easily controlled. Finding no commonly acceptable position beyond their agreement in principle on dismemberment, though, they postponed the decision, turning the matter over to the EAC.

Of the other issues dealt with at the Moscow and Teheran conferences, one of the more potentially contentious was reparations. What should Germany be made to pay for its infamous behavior? This question, too, aroused unsettling, and unsettled, ghosts of the past. Demands for reparations had embittered the French after the Franco-Prussian war and the Germans after World War I. Did the victors of World War II need to reinvent such a disastrous wheel? Those calling for reparations responded, quite simply, that the European countries Nazi Germany had raped needed money and particularly equipment, and that good planning could avoid the errors committed in the past. Hull called for a reparations commission that could assess fair compensation for physical damages caused by Germany. Molotov, speaking of a Soviet Union laid to waste and millions of noncombatants killed by the Germans, had something more in mind. Again the issue moved on to the Teheran conferees, who again reached no resolution other than passing the buck to the EAC.

The issues that the Allied foreign ministers and heads of state addressed in fall 1943 were broad in scope—and sufficiently contested or complicated that the Allies generally chose to postpone considering them. This meant going home from Teheran to reconsider options and reassess priorities.

Dissent over such issues as partition had been brewing in the State Department long before Roosevelt boarded the *USS Iowa* on his way to Teheran. It had begun as early as January 1942 when the president appointed an Advisory Committee on Postwar Foreign Problems to aid State Department planning. Besides prominent individuals from the private sector, the committee included intradepartmental staffers. One of the latter, Under Secretary Sumner Welles, soon proved to be the committee's spark plug, outshining the chairman, the tiring, overburdened Secretary Hull. This unofficial hierarchy was particularly evident after Hull assigned to the committee the task of assessing the pros and cons of Germany's partition, a topic on which Welles felt personally competent. Welles could not persuade the members to adopt his position, but the committee's final policy statement of July 1943 was decidedly slanted to support partition. Secretary Hull signed the document but soon relegated it to his dustbin, suspended the committee's charges, and never called either the document or the committee back to life. Two months later, asked by the president what he thought of the policy statement, Hull was forthright. "Imposed partition," he said, "would be little short of a disaster both for Germany and for us" (cited by Backer 1978:22). Roosevelt nevertheless went to Teheran strongly committed to partition.

The policy conflict broke into the open soon after the president returned home. Welles, irked by Hull's brusque treatment of his policy statement, had resigned his position to present his views to the public. His enormously popular book, *The Time for Decision*, which appeared in July 1944, provided ample ammunition for those who wanted Germany dismembered. But not everyone accepted its premise, and opposition to partition rose in influential governmental circles as well. Military officers were particularly worried that dismembering Germany would leave western Europe no reliable buffer against an onslaught from the east. In July 1944 Hull signed a formal memorandum that, after considering the positive and negative merits of partition, recommended against it.

The conferences of fall 1943 and the mission that Roosevelt assigned to JCS gave it the impetus to beef up its postwar planning. The newly created, tripartite EAC, linked to each ally's foreign policy ministry, found it tough either to get from the military the information it needed or to coordinate planning activities. Even so an Anglo-American Combined Chiefs of Staff (CCS), responsible directly to Prime Minister Churchill and President Roosevelt, proceeded apace. By April 1944 it completed CCS 551, the first major, coordinated planning document spelling out the military's occupation strategy. Turning over to EAC questions of postwar policy, CCS 551 began stoutly:

> The administration shall be firm. It will at the same time be just and humane with respect to the civilian population so far as consistent with strict military requirements. . . . It should be made clear to the local population that military occupation is intended (1) to aid military operations; (2) to destroy Nazism-Fascism and the Nazi Hierarchy; and (3) to maintain and preserve law and order; and (4) to restore normal conditions among the civilian population as soon as possible,

insofar as such conditions will not interfere with military operations. (Cited by Hammond 1963:328)

The rest of ccs 551 outlined technical procedures to govern such concerns as the production, storage, and' distribution of food. What it virtually ignored were "high political" issues—the issues that animated those who saw a need to transform German society. As Hammond (1963:329) points out,

> The Supreme Commander was to "permit freedom of speech and press, and of religious worship, subject to military exigencies and the prohibition of Nazi propaganda; and establish local government, making use of Germans or of Allied officers. Military Government will be effected as a general principle through indirect rules." Fraternization was to be discouraged; and sweeping measures undertaken to destroy Nazism and Fascism, and the German General Staff and Supreme Command. Discriminatory Nazi legislation was to be revoked, but there was no absolute ban on the employment of Nazis. Political activity was to be forbidden or discouraged, but the Supreme Commander was to "permit the formation of a democratic trade union movement and other forms of free economic association."

Ccs 551, although by no means narrow or mild, was not the Carthaginian peace Germans feared. But neither was it the program of massive social restructuring that system-changing Americans wanted. Five months later, in September 1944, the U.S. Joint Chiefs of Staff incorporated a slightly modified version of the Anglo-American document into its own directive, JCS 1067.[7] But by this time the mood of other top U.S. decision makers was changing.

Morgenthau Plan

By August 1944 Americans who had hoped for a decisive policy that would end the German problem once and for all were alarmed. President Roosevelt seemed to be falling prey to the principles promulgated by such men as Secretary of State Hull and Secretary of War Henry Stimson.

7. Ccs 551, prepared under the auspices of the American-British SHAEF, was submitted to Eisenhower in his capacity as Supreme Allied Commander. The modified document, reworked under the auspices of the Joint Chiefs of Staff and retitled JCS 1067, was given to Eisenhower in his capacity as commander of American forces in Europe. "Ccs 551 was never rescinded," Hammond (1963:328) notes. "Its semi-successor, JCS 1067, was never endorsed by the British military chiefs, and applied only to the American zone in Germany and only in the post-surrender period."

In July Hull had endorsed his agency's Postwar Programs Committee's report, which rejected any partition. Stimson supported the JCS's evolving plan for a moderate occupation. The concern of the system-changers manifested itself among some outside the government whose views influenced the informed public (see Nizer 1944), and it led some government officials to quit their jobs and even make a direct appeal to the people (see Welles 1944). Some who remained in government service did what they could to prevent the United States from committing what they considered to be a grave error.

One of these insiders was in the position to influence top-level policymaking: Secretary of the Treasury Henry Morgenthau, Jr., a longtime friend of the president. A trip in August 1944 to London gave him and his staff associates the occasion to express their dismay about Allied policy toward Germany.[8] They devised an alternative policy that they thought at once workable and, given Germany's record of aggression, just. Morgenthau seized the occasion to present the plan to Allied Supreme Commander Eisenhower, U.S. Ambassador to the EAC John Winant, U.K. Foreign Minister Eden, and others. He heard support from all quarters— although later comments from those with whom he spoke questioned whether he had been listening carefully. Returning to Washington he spoke with Hull, Stimson, and, eventually, President Roosevelt. Morgenthau also gave the president a draft *Handbook of Military Government for Germany*, prepared by SHAEF and based on CCS 551.

Roosevelt found Morgenthau's argument persuasive and the SHAEF handbook, as he wrote on 26 August to Stimson, "pretty bad" (cited by Hammond 1963:355). It implied, Roosevelt said, "that Germany is to be restored just as much as the Netherlands or Belgium, and the people of Germany brought back as quickly as possible to their pre-war estate." Far from it, the president went on:

> It is of the utmost importance that every person in Germany should realize that this time Germany is a defeated nation. I do not want them to starve to death, but, as an example, if they need food to keep body and soul together beyond what they have, they should be fed three times a day with soup from Army soup kitchens. . . .
> Too many people here and in England hold to the view that the

---

8. Morgenthau's motivation has aroused considerable interest among observers and scholars. For a critical account, see U.S. Senate (1967). The family history of his son, Henry Morgenthau III (1991), confirms the general view that the secretary was deeply affected by news reaching the U.S. government in 1943 about atrocities the Nazis were committing against Europe's Jewry (see J. Blum 1967, Kimball 1976). Most players in U.S. policy-making, such as John J. McCloy (Bird 1992), found ways to ignore any need for action.

German people as a whole are not responsible for what has taken place—that only a few Nazi leaders are responsible. That unfortunately is not based on fact. The German people as a whole must have it driven home to them that the whole nation has been engaged in a lawless conspiracy against the decencies of modern civilization.

In the same letter Roosevelt accepted Stimson's interpretation of the military's mission in governing defeated Germany: "to see that the machine works and works efficiently." But what the "machine" was to be and what it was to do were once again open questions.

A furious round of meetings and negotiations over the next two weeks was designed to catch the president's eye on the German question before he met Churchill in Quebec on 11–16 September. Morgenthau emerged the clear winner in this bid for attention, partly because he had produced a timely memorandum, partly because Roosevelt leaned fundamentally toward his line of thinking about Germany's future, and partly because Morgenthau accompanied the president for a time on his motor-car drive to Quebec. The memorandum spelling out Morgenthau's plan was crucial because it quickly became a key talking point of British and especially American leaders. It contained fourteen points:

1. Demilitarization of Germany: disarm army, people, direct or indirect armament industry;
2. New boundaries of Germany: transfer parts of East Prussia, Upper Silesia, Saar, adjacent areas;
3. Partitioning of new Germany: create two autonomous, independent states, north and south;
4. The Ruhr area: dismantle industries, transfer as restitution, place basin under international control;
5. Restitution and reparation, including forced labor outside Germany;
6. Education and propaganda: close down until reorganized under complete Allied controls;
7. Political decentralization: dismiss policy-making officials, restructure to strengthen provincial governments;
8. Responsibility of military for local German economy: German people responsible for dealing with price controls, rationing, unemployment, etc., and for sustaining the German economy;
9. Controls over development of German economy: United Nations control over foreign trade, restrictions on capital imports, etc.; prevent new industrialization with military potential;
10. Agrarian program: break up large estates, divide among peasants; end primogeniture and entail;

11. Punishment of war crimes and treatment of special groups (e.g., Nazi organizations);
12. Uniforms and parades: not to be permitted;
13. Aircraft: current equipment confiscated; no Germans to operate or help operate;
14. United States responsibility: full military and civilian representation in international governance program; policing and civil administration by Germany's continental neighbors. (Reprinted in Morgenthau, Jr. 1945)

"Under this program," Morgenthau's report concluded, "United States troops could be withdrawn within a relatively short time."

What happened in Quebec and afterward is more the stuff of soap opera than of international decision making. But like a modern Lazarus the Morgenthau Plan kept rising from the dead to muddle discussions at home and abroad about U.S. policy toward occupied Germany.

Did Roosevelt accept the Morgenthau Plan? At the president's request Morgenthau presented it at dinner on 13 September to both Churchill and Eden. Churchill rejected it out of hand, but the next day he was persuaded, possibly by the British need for more U.S. lend-lease assistance, to modify his position. He helped draft an aide-mémoire that, ignoring most of Morgenthau's fourteen points, focused on German industry's complicity in Nazi aggression and hence the need to leave firms in the Ruhr and Saar basins "out of action and closed down." The aide-mémoire concluded: "This programme for eliminating the war-making industries in the Ruhr and in the Saar is looking forward to converting Germany into a country primarily agricultural and pastoral in its character. The Prime Minister and the President were in agreement upon this programme" (cited by Feis 1957:370).

The very idea—*pastoralizing Germany!*—was electric. Back in the United States, Roosevelt, engaged in a modest electoral campaign, encountered a storm of criticism. Morgenthau's report about his Quebec successes alarmed Hull, Stimson, and others who thought they understood what the president's German policy was (Feis 1957:370). A press leak of the plan on 21 September introduced the public to what most thought to be a bizarre notion and revealed the administration's policy-making disarray. The most immediate and obvious impact was felt in Roosevelt's reelection campaign, which suffered from the perception of blatant Executive confusion. The War Department, meanwhile, linking the apparent policy switch to Roosevelt's earlier criticism of the SHAEF handbook, began backtracking from its newly issued planning document, JCS 1067, and edging toward a more strict revision, one that, although not fundamentally maximalist, would be tougher against the Germans. Finally, Goebbels used talk of pastoralization to warn the German people what they had to expect should they lose the war—thereby stiffening, if only slightly, the German will to fight.

In reality, only a small part of the Morgenthau Plan gained acceptance at Quebec, and within a matter of weeks both Roosevelt and Churchill repudiated even that part. On 3 October, Roosevelt admitted that his decision had been hasty.[9] Later that month Churchill proposed a new and far more moderate policy directive. But the president repeatedly referred back to elements of Morgenthau's thinking, and the program permeated policy planning until long after the war ended. The thought that the Allies would pastoralize Germany also became part of a persistent folklore whose ghost lives today. In fall 1944, however, Roosevelt retreated, stunned by the effects of the blunder in Quebec and by the sharp attacks by his electoral opponent, Thomas E. Dewey. Acting Secretary of State Edward R. Stettinius, Jr., and others sought to press him.[10] Roosevelt the political fox simply became testy, preferring, he said, to defeat Germany before devising grand schemes to occupy it.

Moving Toward a U.S. Occupation Policy

Roosevelt's administration nevertheless had to try to make sense of the confusion. In the absence of clear, consistent guidelines from the White House, the relevant agencies—the State Department with its ties to EAC; the War Department, along with JCS and SHAEF (as well as CAD, the policy dimension of which had been on ice since early 1944); and the Treasury Department with its myriad financial responsibilities—were playing bureaucratic games to improve their own positions in setting agendas and policy outcomes. Meanwhile the British continued to cling to CCS 551 and ignore the American JCS 1067.[11]

9. Secretary Stimson, having lunch with the president, wrote in his diary: "He grinned and looked naughty and said 'Henry Morgenthau pulled a boner' or an equivalent expression, and said that we really were not apart on that; that he had no intention of turning Germany into an agrarian state and that all he wanted was to save a portion of the proceeds of the Ruhr for use by Great Britain." Stimson then read to him the Quebec report's key sentences. The president, Stimson recalls, "was frankly staggered by this and said he had no idea how he could have initialed this; that he had evidently done it without much thought" (cited by Feis 1957:372).

10. Stettinius substituted for the ailing Hull in November 1944 and replaced him as Secretary on 1 December.

11. Eisenhower's SHAEF focused mainly on presurrender directives derived from bipartite negotiations. In December 1944 it issued a new *Handbook for Military Government in Germany Prior to Defeat or Surrender;* and on 15 April 1945, three weeks before

Immediate revision of JCS 1067 was needed, both to accommodate conflicting demands from the various agencies and to make the document more useful for Winant's negotiations in the tripartite EAC. Initiatives in mid-November 1944 by both the State and War departments, the latter moving toward a draft revision, brought about in December a coordinating committee comprising the assistant secretaries of the State, War, and Navy departments (SWNCC). The draft envisioned a longer occupation, enhanced the occupation government's control machinery, and, at the insistence of the Treasury Department, added a provision that broadened the categories of Nazis and others to be arrested and brought to justice by the occupation forces—a measure that provided a basis for later denazification proceedings. SWNCC accepted the document in principle on 6 January and, after securing approvals from U.S. and tripartite agencies, on 12 February 1945 issued the revised version of JCS 1067.

By then Churchill, Roosevelt, and Stalin had been meeting for almost a week at Yalta. The conference had its contentious moments, mainly because Germany's pending defeat was now a stark reality. American and British troops were already in German territory, and the Red Army was poised on the eastern banks of the Oder River in preparation for its final assault on Berlin. Decisions long postponed required action. And decisions in principle failed to provide a solid basis for moving forward. Yet the war was not over, and delay remained just as tempting in the Crimea as before.

The Allies nonetheless made some important decisions at Yalta. They reaffirmed formally their demand that Germany surrender unconditionally.[12] Surrender would give the occupiers complete sovereignty—the "supreme authority" they needed, in the words of the final document signed at Yalta by the foreign ministers, "to take such steps, including the complete disarmament, demilitarization and the dismemberment of Germany as they deem requisite for future peace and security" (cited by Snell 1963:190). At the same time the Allies made full-scale partition less probable. Stalin's position and the implied threat of the foreign ministers' declaration notwithstanding, they effectively reversed their earlier agree-

Germany's surrender, it issued to army group commanders directives based on CCS 551. On shortcomings in the consistency of U.K. policy, see Foschepoth and Steininger (1985).

12. On 9 March 1945 Allen Dulles of the U.S. Office of Strategic Services (OSS) began meeting in Switzerland with the commander of the SS and German police forces in Italy, General Karl Wolff, to discuss the surrender of his command. Stalin termed the meetings a violation of the Allied prohibition of any separate peace arrangement and claimed that they demonstrated Anglo-American complicity with the Nazis to restructure postwar Europe (see Dulles 1947; Armstrong 1961).

ment in principle to partition Germany. German territories east of the Oder and Neisse rivers would be turned over to Poland and the Soviet Union; lands Hitler had absorbed—Austria, Czechoslovakia, parts of Poland—would be returned; and, according to an EAC protocol approved at Yalta, the rest of Germany would not be dismembered permanently but simply divided temporarily into occupation zones.[13] The principle of German territorial unity remained intact, with the whole of occupied Germany to be governed by an integrated Allied Control Council (ACC).[14]

Other key issues remained in limbo, including reparations. Roosevelt said that his government demanded only to retain German assets in the United States and perhaps to obtain some raw materials; Churchill spoke of Britain's potential need for German equipment and products; and Stalin sought to secure for the USSR both reparations in kind (factories, machinery, ships, railway equipment, power plants) and German labor for reconstruction. The Soviet leader suggested reparations of $20 billion, half of that sum going to the USSR. When Churchill urged that all three reduce their claims to a minimal level or risk condemning Germany to a grinding poverty sure to produce later problems, Stalin accused the Western countries of reneging on their promises. Roosevelt ended the dispute by calling for the creation of a reparations commission. Another issue postponed at Yalta was the disposition of eastern Europe's ethnic Germans, eight million of whom would eventually flow into Germany's western zones of occupation.

The public relations communiqué issued at the end of the Yalta Conference accentuated its achievements and obfuscated serious points of tripartite disagreement. It is particularly instructive, however, in indicating what the Allies had in mind about changing German society. The communiqué promised severity: the Allies would destroy the Nazi war machine, ban armaments industries, punish war criminals, exact reparations in kind to compensate for Nazi destruction, and wipe out the Nazi party and the last vestiges of Nazism. But the goal was not the German people's destruction. Extirpating Nazism and militarism would simply help peaceable Germans do what was necessary to rejoin the comity of nations.

The State Department, driven by policy changes from Yalta and the recurrence of conflict with the War and Treasury departments, began

13. Some contemporary commentators saw this arrangement as a de facto dismemberment of Germany along east-west lines, a view that became more common after Allied cooperation had broken down into a cold war. In 1990 Germans in fact restored their territorial unity—except for the lands east of the Oder and Neisse rivers.

14. The EAC had accepted a French decision-making role in its deliberations. At Yalta the Big Three extended this principle by granting France both an occupation zone and ACC membership.

immediately to draft a revised JCS 1067. Its proposed directive, initialed on 10 March by Secretary Stettinius, aimed at ending the feud among the three departments.[15] Very quickly, however, the directive encountered opposition from all sides, including the president. On 22 March in a meeting with department representatives, Roosevelt clarified his attitude on U.S. policy toward Germany—but without saying much that was new—and urged the departments to produce a coordinated proposal that reflected his views.

The newly created Informal Policy Committee on Germany (IPCOG), with its political, economic, and financial subcommittees, essayed to broker the compromise. Hitler's last-ditch effort to hold back the harbingers of infamy was coming rapidly to an end, and the intended U.S. occupiers needed clear directives. A proposal submitted to the political subcommittee by the War Department's CAD gave IPCOG a means to break through the deadlock—for instance, by accepting the State Department's long-standing insistence that the occupation's goals should include carrots as well as sticks. Meetings, alternative drafts, and a summary session produced a clause that emphasized the U.S. intention to prepare Germans for "political life on a democratic basis." IPCOG approved an integrated proposal on 26 April, two weeks after President Roosevelt's death and only days before Hitler's suicide and Berlin's collapse under the onslaught of the Red Army. On 11 May 1945, three days after Germany's formal capitulation, President Harry S Truman approved the newly revised JCS 1067.[16]

A few details of JCS 1067, issued as *Directive to Commander-in-Chief of U.S. Forces of Occupation Regarding the Military Government of Germany*, are particularly germane to U.S. efforts at social change (USDS 1985:15–32). Article 4, "Basic objectives of military government in Germany," specified that:

1. "It should be brought home to the Germans" that Germany's war and fanatical resistance had caused their economic and other problems and that the Germans could not "escape responsibility for what they [had] brought upon themselves."
2. The Allied occupation aimed neither at liberation nor oppression but rather at realizing "important Allied goals."

15. The interdepartmental problem arose from the deeply entrenched positions of each. The War Department, for instance, wanted to give the military governor as much latitude as possible to carry out his mission. This made sense based on the department's previous experience in military occupations. The Treasury Department, fearing that the conservative orientation of military men might make them treat Germans too leniently, wanted the military commander's procedures tightly controlled in Washington.

16. The new version was, technically, JCS 1067/8. Following common practice, however, I shall continue to call it JCS 1067.

3. "The principal Allied objective [was] to prevent Germany from ever again becoming a threat to the peace of the world." Essential steps included eliminating Nazism and militarism, apprehending and punishing war criminals, industrial disarmament and demilitarization, and "the preparation for an eventual reconstruction of German political life on a democratic basis."
4. Other objectives included reparations, restitution, and relief for victims of Nazism.

Among the provisions of Article 6, entitled "Denazification," were the removal of any legal or public-institutional stains imposed by Nazism and the exclusion of active Nazi party members or supporters from public and important quasi-public or private positions. Article 8, "Suspected war criminals and security arrests," targeted for arrest and prosecution eleven categories of people, ranging from Nazi party officials to "Any other person whose name or designation appears on lists to be submitted . . . by the J.C.S. or whose name may be notified . . . separately." Article 14, "Education," called for closing all educational institutions until the Allies had purged Nazi personnel, textbooks, and curricula, and then reopening at least the elementary, middle, and vocational schools. These directives indicate that JCS 1067 had moved substantially in the course of a year, from an almost exclusively minimalist concern with short-term management of a particular task—ending the dilatory effects of Nazism—to a far-reaching design for social transformation.

An Integrated Allied Occupation?

Jcs 1067, of course, governed only the American zone of occupation. Working out Allied consultation to develop joint policy presented a different set of challenges. Aside from domestic concerns and the continuing war in East Asia, each of the major powers was preoccupied with immediate problems in the German areas it controlled. A disagreement between Stalin and Truman over the transfer of troops to the occupation zones threatened to jeopardize any meeting at all.[17] But beginning on 17 July the conference took place in Potsdam, a city on the outskirts of Berlin that was rich in German and especially Prussian history.

The world had changed dramatically by mid-July, when Churchill (and later, after a general election in the United Kingdom, Prime Minister

17. After 2 May, when Berlin fell to the Red Army, the Soviets were reluctant to turn over to the Western powers their sectoral rights in the city. Truman's eventual threat to scuttle other agreements, including the planned conference at Potsdam, led to a resolution of the dispute on 1 July.

Clement Attlee), Stalin, and Truman met in Potsdam. The *Wehrmacht* had capitulated, and the Allies had declared Germany's unconditional surrender.[18] Truman was bringing onto the scene new American actors.[19] Two months of occupying Germany had tested in the field the early plans and theories, and tensions were mounting among the sometime Allies of east and west. And, although only Truman knew the details at the time, the face of modern warfare was about to change in Hiroshima and Nagasaki. The war against fascism was not over, of course: battles still raged in the Orient. In the U.S. decision-making system, interdepartmental jockeying continued unabated, supplemented, in fact, by the inclusion of a fourth agency, the Foreign Economic Administration (FEA). The Potsdam Conference offered the wartime Allies the best opportunity they would have to bring the European war to its conclusion.

The Potsdam Conference turned out, however, to be more the beginning of a new conflict than the end of an old one. Historians have rightfully emphasized the plethora of clashes that erupted there—clashes dealing not only with Germany's future but also with the expected Soviet contribution to the war against Japan, postwar structure of the East Asian Theater, planning for the United Nations, and a host of other issues.

This emphasis on East-West conflict muddies a fundamental accomplishment of the Potsdam Conference: it clarified the parameters that would govern postwar Germany's occupation. In no case was this clearer than with respect to the U.S. occupation of Germany. The meeting in Potsdam tacitly legitimized the American Military Government (AMG) that was already functioning reasonably well. General Eisenhower, commander of the U.S. Forces, European Theater (USFET), which had in May replaced the bipartite SHAEF, was nominally the military governor (MG). In fact, though, his deputy for military government, Lieutenant General Lucius D. Clay, was doing the work.

Clay found by mid-July that he could operate well in the existing occupation environment, though it was sometimes exasperating. Already complicated by a concatenation of directives, back-channel maneuvers, and

18. In fact EAC had developed a surrender document for German representatives to sign but, at the last minute, Eisenhower replaced it with a far simpler "act of surrender." By jettisoning months of tripartite labor, the Supreme Allied Commander deepened Stalin's growing suspicion about Western intentions and forced the by now quadripartite Allies to draft and, on 5 June, sign an awkward "Declaration regarding the defeat of Germany and the assumption of supreme authority by the Allied powers" that imposed on Germany the equivalent of an unconditional surrender.

19. Truman succeeded Roosevelt on 12 April and soon replaced Secretary of State Stettinius with James F. Byrnes. After Secretary of the Treasury Morgenthau resigned, piqued that he had not been invited to Potsdam, Truman appointed Fred M. Vinson, who saw his future more in the U.S. political arena than in reshaping postwar Germany.

criticism by reporters, congressmen, and other visiting firemen, that environment was further confused by deskbound planners without field experience, whose well-meant but untested decisions were woefully obsolete and difficult for administrators to carry out in sometimes gutted war zones. Clay kept a cool demeanor and a sophisticated understanding of what the occupation drama was about and what his own role in it was. He resolutely sought instructions from Washington—but demonstrated that he could carry on if they did not arrive, and make reasonable decisions anyway. The effect was to make jcs 1067 flexible as an instrument of control.

Preparing for the Potsdam Conference had forced both the State Department and the new president, meanwhile, to come to grips with occupation strategy. The former "improved" its interpretation of jcs 1067, and the latter, in the process of doing his homework, agreed to a brief, modified summary of that improvement. On arriving in Potsdam he presented the summary as an agenda proposal. Churchill and Stalin quickly accepted it. But putting Truman's summary on the agenda did not mean that it became tripartite (or quadripartite) policy. The British, for instance, continued to adhere to ccs 551. What Truman's action did was to spell out what U.S. decision makers had in mind—and, should the other conferees not concur, what policies the U.S. government intended to implement.

The new modifications broadened the military governor's prerogatives, something against which Morgenthau had fought ferociously for almost a year. Should interallied cooperation break down, for example, should the acc not function effectively, then each MG, in his own zone of occupation, could act in the acc's capacity. Another modification gave the MG more discretion in determining when Germans in his zone could begin holding public meetings and setting up democratic political parties that could work toward their country's reconstruction.

The expansion of the military governors' discretionary power gave the MGs greater de facto policy input. Consider, for example, the dilemma of reparations. How were foodstuffs, machines, tools, and other reparations in kind to be assembled, evaluated, and distributed to their intended recipients? At Yalta, Stalin had proposed that Germany be made to pay $20 billion, half of it to the USSR. At Potsdam he proposed that reparations payable to the USSR be extracted proportionally from each of the four occupation zones. Truman rejected this notion out of hand. The Anglo-American idea was that each occupying country could extract reparations in kind from its own zone, but this was unreasonable from the Soviet perspective: it would either have impoverished the more agricultural Soviet zone or forced the USSR to wait for years and even decades before it could secure its due.

Sharp exchanges led to a compromise: each occupying power would give to the designated recipients specified amounts of reparations goods—contingent on what the MG thought he needed to carry out his mission.[20] The compromise also encountered Soviet opposition, for it provided no joint control over an MG's potentially capricious decisions. But Stalin really had no choice: rejecting the Anglo-American compromise would have denied his country access to shipments from the more industrialized zones in the west. Not surprisingly, this policy soon broke down and greatly exacerbated East-West discord.

Other decisions reached at Potsdam also affected the way in which the quadripartite occupation of Germany would take place. Giving France veto power in the Allied Control Council enabled the French MG to obstruct its operations for two and a half years. Giving the Soviet Union (and its satellites) carte blanche to expel ethnic Germans from eastern Europe strained the ability of the Western MGs to cope with food, housing, social welfare, and other difficulties. The compromise giving to Poland and the USSR German territories east of the Oder and Neisse rivers—for a temporary administration that soon proved permanent—would deepen the building cold war. These and similar decisions significantly increased the prospective cost in time, money, and nerves to disarm and reconstruct Germany. By the time the Potsdam Conference convened, all parties recognized that the United States alone had the capacity to bear not only that added burden but also the cost of rebuilding the rest of war-torn Europe. "This generosity," Peterson (1977:63) pointed out dryly, "ran counter to the public and congressional mood."

The Potsdam Conference thus drew clear lines where the Allies previously had countenanced a blur. One obvious point was that the Soviet Union and Western powers were moving on a collision course. In their independent but presumably coordinated occupation policies, each chose the hedgehog's strategy of hunkering in: protecting its resources and procedural advantages, forming alliances with those of like mind, and warding off changes that might endanger the tenuous status quo. In the U.S. zone the strategy that emerged from Potsdam favored a military governor who had the freedom to operate at once efficiently and effectively and the wisdom to know what his limits were. The strategy favored policies to make possible a self-sufficient German economy sooner rather than later. And it set the stage for seeing Germans as allies in the new struggle against

20. A related and equally problematic U.S. decision restricted the dismantling of any industry below the level at which the MG judged it to have sufficient capacity for effective functioning. Except for the "merchants of death," industries in the American zone of occupation were not to be destroyed.

Soviet communism. The clear lines drawn in Potsdam undercut the war-time dream of an integrated occupation.

Occupation Policy Solidified—But Not for Long

The Potsdam Conference also marked the beginning of the end of the American dream to democratize Germany. The prominent themes that evolved from popular attitudes among Americans ultimately played a role in setting policy. Americans initially leaned toward traditional notions of correcting the German system and its international aggressiveness. This task-oriented approach focused on winning the war, abolishing Nazism as an international scourge, and preventing a recurrence of German aggression. Government policies seeking to accomplish such tasks, particularly the first two, found common support. As the war dragged on, however, many (but still a minority) of these Americans began to contemplate something more far-reaching. Germany needed to be taught a lesson, they said. The U.S. had to change the German system, not merely correct it, if democracy was to thrive. The American policy-making apparatus, influenced by Secretary Morgenthau with his special tie to President Roosevelt, followed suit and to some measure changed U.S. policy. Jcs 1067 in its form of May 1945 was the result.

But the policy shift from moderate reform to extensive transformation satisfied extreme ideologues of neither stripe. Neither minimalists wanting a "quick in, quick out" occupation nor maximalists wanting to cripple Germany forever made their way through a sometimes turgid policy-making process, which relied so much on negotiation and coordination. The case of jcs 1067 demonstrates that bureaucratic entities, especially when forged in the blood of conflicting agencies, gain a life of their own. Once Morgenthau's concept was on board, the ship of state was unable to toss it into the sea. By May 1945 U.S. military authorities were seeking to implement their mandate as best they could, however much they might personally have preferred a more traditional, even minimalist program. In the White House the new president felt honor bound to implement his predecessor's German policy even though he was far from enthusiastic about it. His trip to Potsdam was designed to strengthen the established U.S. occupation policy with its overtones of social change.

But resiliency in bureaucratic entities also depends on persistence. A change in the helm can quickly swing the ship's rudder. Thus Roosevelt's death and Morgenthau's resignation, which left the Treasury Department's hard-line staff members bereft of high-level support, gave heart to State and War department personnel discomfited by jcs 1067's harshness. At Potsdam the basic lines of U.S. occupation policy remained intact, but military authorities had more prerogatives than the system transformers had hoped. Truman was also beginning to sense that the wartime coalition could disintegrate on German soil and to ponder the implications of this possibility.

The ensuing months saw an evolution of this new line of thought. Systemic change began increasingly to be both impracticable and counterproductive. U.S. occupation officials were finding German realities more complex than wartime planners had imagined, and some did not deal well with the ambiguities of their situation. General George S. Patton, Jr., had to be relieved of his Bavarian command in September 1945 after publicly trivializing U.S. policy on denazification. Moreover, East-West cooperation was deteriorating; in December 1945 the State Department declined to carry out further dismantling of U.S.-zone industry, and in the following spring Clay ceased reparations shipments to the Soviet zone.

Back in the United States, restlessness was mounting on many fronts. The occupation was beginning to seem interminable. The GIs were not coming home as rapidly as Americans had hoped, and costs for supporting occupation and European recovery were skyrocketing. Internal fights about both the theory and the practice of U.S. policy in Germany continued to vex the administration. The press was sniping at occupation-related glitches in Germany and Washington. And, above all, the growing East-West conflict increasingly made the occupation appear to be an expensive, meaningless charade. Truman, facing a bitter congressional campaign in November 1946 and seeing ever more heat emanating from his German policy, contemplated ways to get out of the kitchen.

By mid-1946 the United States was moving resolutely toward Germany's economic and political reconstruction. In June at the foreign ministers' conference in Paris, Secretary Byrnes called for an economic merger of the four zones of occupation. Only the British responded, but before year's end the two countries had signed such an agreement. Byrnes's speech of 6 September in Stuttgart emphasized bilateral and trilateral cooperation from the days of ccs 551 to the Potsdam Agreement. He defined U.S. occupation policy in terms of demilitarizing and denazifying Germany, restoring local self-government, and introducing as rapidly as possible "elective and representative principles into the regional, provincial, and state administrations" (usds 1985:95).

Secretary Byrnes's message was stunning. U.S. occupation policy, he told the world, had never been more than moderately corrective. The maximalist provisions that had made their way into parts of jcs 1067 were ignored as if they had never existed.[21] From there it was a small step to

___

21. Byrnes, melding U.S. and quadripartite policy, said: "The Nazi war criminals

revising U.S. occupation policy still more. On 11 July 1947 JCS 1067, with all its system-changing overtones, was replaced by JCS 1779, with its emphasis on Europe's need for "a stable and productive Germany" (USDS 1985:124–135). "The necessary restraints" would "ensure that Germany is not allowed to revive its destructive militarism," JCS 1779 declared. And American troops would remain "as long as foreign occupation of Germany continues." The overall thrust was clear: The United States intended to proclaim its past policies a success and end its occupation of Germany.[22]

---

were to be punished for the suffering they brought to the world. The policy of reparations and industrial disarmament prescribed in the Potsdam Agreement was to be carried out. But the purpose of the occupation did not contemplate a prolonged foreign dictatorship of Germany's peaceful economy or a prolonged foreign dictatorship of Germany's internal political life" (USDS 1985:95).

22. Jcs 1779's Article 3, "United States policy toward Germany," stated: "As a positive program requiring urgent action the United States Government seeks the creation of those political, economic and moral conditions in Germany which will contribute most effectively to a stable and prosperous Europe" (USDS 1985:124).

THREE
· ·

Assessing German Perspectives

In early 1945 German villages and cities experienced what literally thousands of others across Europe had gone through in the previous three decades. Distant thunder began to roll, with jagged flashes reddening the skies. As the rumbling came ever closer, people knew that their community, too, would suffer the foreign army's onslaught. They also knew that, should their own military "defend" them, or if local zealots tried to stave off the inevitable, communal destruction and loss of life would be the consequences. Most people took cover until the storm passed on to the next village. In the interminable hours of terror, they prayed for survival and anxiously contemplated the future.

The morning after the storm was much the same for these shattered communities as it had been for those overrun so recently by the Wehrmacht. First individuals, then huddled groups emerged from bunkers and other hiding places. Surveying the carnage, they found that their would-be defenders who were neither killed nor captured had left the field for another battleground. In their place were swarms of foreign military authorities carrying out myriad assignments. Some officers were support staff for the front-line troops, others tallied the dead and tracked down stragglers, and still others addressed such immediate issues as public safety, health, and sanitation. Helplessly uncertain of the ultimate outcome, dazed Germans, like dazed Poles and French before them, knew only that their community had succumbed—for many, succumbed again—to foreign occupation.

Some Germans crawling from their refuges, however, encountered something unique in the history of warfare: batteries of foreign soldiers asking them—in German—to respond to questionnaires. Even before fighting had died down in some instances, social psychologists and sociologists in the Psychological Warfare Division of the U.S. Army entered captured towns. Their immediate task was to inform military authorities about the moods and concerns of the defeated Germans, and they hoped to accomplish this by applying the newest analytic techniques of the modern social sciences. One new technique relied on psychologically rooted depth interviews: sophisticated questioning over time that was calculated to reveal how people were thinking and what motivated them (Janowitz 1946; Janis 1963). Another survey used short questionnaires to assess wartime demoralization caused by strategic bombing (U.S. Strategic Bombing Survey 1945).

Systematic polling of randomly chosen samples of the public was well known in the Anglo-American world, particularly in the United States. In Germany, however, after a dozen years under Nazi dictatorship, the assessment of public opinion was virtually unknown and certainly untested. Would polling be worth its time and cost, given the other obligations facing U.S. occupation authorities? Supporters argued that reliable data about mass perspectives could tell them about the potential for resistance, support for Nazi leaders and objectives, expectations about the pending military occupation, and more. Such information, they said, had the tactical value of assessing German reactions to specific U.S. measures and the strategic value of predicting how Germans would respond over the long run to the transforming policies implicit in JCS 1067. The deputy military governor, General Lucius D. Clay, authorized the creation of a public opinion survey unit, which began its field operations in October 1945.

This book focuses on what pollsters found out about German perspectives on the American occupation. Before turning to specific attitudes, however, we must explore the growth of public opinion polling in postwar Germany, especially in the American zone of occupation (AMZON). The history and characteristics of opinion sampling are well known, but the particularly German developments merit examination: the use of surveying by American military authorities, the policy value and significance of its results, and the emergence of commercial polling agencies in West Germany.

From Idea to Systematic Measurement

The idea of public opinion was hardly new when GIs marched into defeated Germany in 1945. For millennia effective leaders had grasped intuitively the need to recognize the perspectives of politically relevant strata both at home and abroad. These elites traditionally included top political figures and sometimes leaders of military, clerical, financial, intellectual, and other "publics." Such actors played a role in the leader's success or failure, so it made sense for the leader to know what the others wanted, what they were willing to accept, and the likely consequences of compliance or noncompliance.

Before the advent of scientific surveying, leaders gleaned "public opinion" information however they could. Shakespeare's Henry V donned a cloak to disguise himself and moved among his troops to assess morale the night before the battle of Agincourt, and the poetic license in this depiction is not extreme. Governments spent considerable sums to learn what their rivals—and their constituents—were up to. They employed consuls, ambassadors, and spies to provide information about perspectives abroad. Eventually, powerful states, including the United States after its disaster at Pearl Harbor in December 1941, found intelligence agencies imperative for maintaining security at home. The popular image of intelligence emphasizes glamour and danger: cloak-and-dagger espionage, femmes fatales, dirty tricks. More typical if less notorious is the hard work of worker bees who evaluate newspapers, statistical documents, and other publicly available sources. Whatever its specific form, though, traditional intelligence has aimed at shrewd assessment of the attitudes and likely actions of a politically relevant stratum. Would entrepreneurs pay the taxes needed to refurbish the fleet? Could church leaders be counted on to provide moral support for the king's new wars? Would soldiers continue to fight if salaries fell into arrears? Did the enemy intend to launch an attack? Effective spies were the unacknowledged agents of policy.

The rise of mass participation in the political arena eventually created a new era of world communication. The traditional elites found themselves sharing political influence with larger segments of the population. Catalyzed by the modern press, common citizens discovered that with emerging electoral strength came the ability to mobilize for political purposes; the masses—and their demagogues—could for the first time play a significant role in politics. Leaders discovered that they could not function without responding to the demands of this new public. Some began to consider the international implications of these social changes. Influencing a mass population abroad, for instance, might usefully limit the maneuverability of its government. But how could this be done?

World War I was a watershed. Having come to realize that popular morale was as important a military factor as was the morale of men at the front, governments began searching for means to bolster mass support. Governments in the West recruited journalists considered to be experts on "public opinion" and adept in writing what the masses wanted to read. Their "propaganda" proved to be quite successful at home. Abroad, however, the effectiveness of propaganda was limited by poor understanding of social variation. Toward the end of the war, some propagandists began to investigate new ways for getting better estimates of popular moods, perspectives, and behaviors (Lasswell 1927).

In World War II, when "psychological warfare" took on "the character of a struggle for the attention, beliefs, and loyalties of whole populations" (Lerner 1949:8), propaganda specialists on both sides pursued information policies both at home and abroad. Heinrich Himmler's Gestapo (Geheime Staatspolizei, or Secret State Police) employed a network of informants who filed weekly reports on the popular moods, rumors, and morale of Germans (Boberach 1965). The Gestapo also relied on *V-Männer* or confidential informants (Weyrauch 1986, 1989). The United States, too, monitored popular German attitudes. Such "strategic" information came from reports by informants, wartime studies of "culture at a distance" (McGranahan and Wayne 1948; W. Langer 1972), interrogations of prisoners-of-war (Gurfein and Janowitz 1946; Shils and Janowitz 1948), and inferential studies of news the Nazis passed on to the home front (George 1959).

Systematic public opinion analysis was a logical successor of these techniques.[1] The use of structured questionnaires (or schedules) to secure politically relevant information dates to John Sinclair's late-eighteenth-century demographic study of Scotland (1791–1799). A century later Charles Booth (1892–1897) and B. Seebohm Rowntree (1901) in England and Frédéric Le Play (Pitts 1968) in France used such systematic procedures in their social surveys. And from 1907 to 1911 in Germany, Adolf Levenstein (1912) sent questionnaires to eight thousand workers in the world's first large-scale social survey. Newspapers, too, had experimented as early as 1824 with primitive straw polls of voting intentions (Gallup and Rae 1940:35; see also Robinson 1932).

Social scientists, using formal questionnaires and the systematic interviewing techniques developed by anthropologists, census takers, and others, began a revolution that soon reached beyond academia into practical politics. Major projects included an "actual house to house canvass" of precincts in eight Ohio cities (Donaldson 1914), questionnaires soliciting the views of two hundred "leaders of social progress" (Hart 1923), a representative sample of six thousand Chicagoans (Merriam and Gosnell 1924), and an experiment using matched samples (Gosnell 1927). By the late 1920s attitude surveys as research tools were well known and reasonably well developed. New techniques in the 1930s opened new paths for political analysis, while the inauguration of large-scale sample surveys of national populations (such as the Gallup Poll in 1934) both popularized the notion and began to provide a data basis for secondary analysis.

Despite Levenstein's early contribution and the growth of systematic public opinion analysis elsewhere, particularly in the United States, the

---

1. This is not to suggest that public opinion surveying is a form of intelligence in the traditional sense—spying—for its information-gathering procedures are applied overtly (see Crespi [1985:6]; and, for an alternative view, Rückmann [1972]).

procedure did not gain currency in Germany. Some social scientists experimented with it, but Nazism's racial policies and control of the universities forced most of them to flee the country. During the war, a young
German who, while studying journalism at the University of Missouri, had
become familiar with George Gallup's initial polling efforts, suggested in
his doctoral dissertation that sample surveys in Germany could assist the
Nazi regime to maintain effective control over the German population
(Noelle 1940). For whatever reasons, however, officials alerted to this suggestion did not follow it through.

U.S. Opinion Surveys in Postwar Germany

Not surprisingly, then, Germans did not know what to make of
the GI with his battery of questionnaires. A decade of strict police controls
led some to view the enterprise skeptically. But others so welcomed the
opportunity to express their views to unknown interviewers that the difficulty turned out to be fitting their lengthy comments into short questionnaires. The polls were substantially successful, particularly those gauging
the effects on morale of strategic bombing. With the support of Deputy
Military Governor Clay, the Office of Military Government, United States
(OMGUS) eventually formalized surveying operations. In October 1945, the
Intelligence Branch of the OMGUS Office of the Director of Information
Control set up the Opinion Survey Section, under the direction of Frederick W. Williams (1970). Other military governments also created survey
research units that met with varying degrees of success. Britain's Public
Opinion Research also proved to be useful, but the Soviet attempt quickly
died (Halpern 1949).

OMGUS Surveys

From October 1945 until September 1949, the Opinion Survey Section
carried out seventy-two major surveys, an average of one every third
week, and summarized their findings in 194 separate reports. The reports
themselves went to the highest levels of the American occupation authorities (Clay 1950a:283). Unfortunately, the completed questionnaires,
punch cards, and various documentary materials disappeared in the early
1950s—lost, some say, when the Rhine River overflowed its banks, or
destroyed when American archivists made an administrative decision
that punch cards were not worth preserving once the appropriate government agencies had analyzed them, or perhaps still packed in boxes in a

corner of some forgotten warehouse.[2] The reports, nonetheless, comprise a veritable wealth of readily available information on public perspectives in Germany during the occupation years (A. Merritt and R. Merritt 1970).

Questionnaires. The Opinion Survey Section was responsible for determining which questions would be asked of the respondents. Its task proved to be difficult, not only because various OMGUS agencies made competing demands for priority in the selection of questions, but also because few practitioners outside the Opinion Survey Section seemed alert to the methodological complexity of polling. Questions that are clear to an expert in a particular field, for instance, may be confusing when addressed to the lay citizen, an Opinion Survey Section procedural review observed, so questionnaires were pretested on small groups to ensure that the questions were "meaningful and understandable to the wide variety of types of Germans to be studied." And "improving" a single question's phrasing in succeeding surveys may invalidate any comparison of data over time. Although the Opinion Survey Section was prepared to abandon or modify ineffective items, its staff aimed at maintaining comparability.

Sampling. The Opinion Survey Section's initial intent was to concentrate solely on the American zone of occupation in southern Germany: Bavaria, Hesse, and what was then called Württemberg-Baden.[3] In March 1946, however, the section had begun surveying the opinions of West Berliners; somewhat later it expanded operations to Bremen (with its harbor city of Bremerhaven), a city-state in northern Germany under American military control. The first eight surveys, conducted between 26 October

2. The reports—for the OMGUS surveys (1945–1949), 2,081 pages in length, and, for the subsequent High Commission or HICOG surveys (1949–1955), 7,817 pages—are obtainable as microfilm or photocopies from the Archives Branch, Washington National Records Center, Washington, D.C., 20409; for the OMGUS series a set of questionnaires is also available (Box 233-3/5 and 233-5/5 [#1243]). Institutions providing access to the OMGUS and HICOG reports include the library of the United States Information Agency (1750 Pennsylvania Avenue, NW, Washington, D.C., 20547), the library of the University of Illinois at Urbana-Champaign, the Yale University library, the Center for West European Studies at Harvard University, and, in Cologne, Germany, the Zentralarchiv für empirische Sozialforschung. Questionnaires and IBM cards for some of the later HICOG surveys are available at the Roper Public Opinion Research Center, University of Connecticut, Storrs, Conn., 06268.

3. In 1945, when the Big Three accepted France as an occupying power, the American and British governments agreed to carve out a French zone from their own occupation territories. The United States split two provinces, Baden and Württemberg, and assigned the southern half of each to France. The French then established separate provinces: Baden (or South Baden) and Württemberg-Hohenzollern. AMG merged its two into a single province, Württemberg-Baden. In 1951 the FRG united all three as the single province of Baden-Württemberg (see Leibholz 1952).

and 13 December 1945, used area samples of 39 to 45 communities, with a sample size that ranged between 331 and 466 respondents. Beginning on 27 December 1945 the Opinion Survey Section interviewed approximately 1,000 persons in 80 communities. In April 1946 it increased this number to about 1,500 respondents in 141 communities, and a year later it was surveying roughly 3,000 persons in 241 communities.

The earliest surveys made little attempt to stratify the sample even by province (or *Land*).[4] By April 1947, when the section formalized its sampling procedure, it could note that "communities under 10,000 in size are systematically selected at random from lists which order all communities in [the American zone of] Germany according to size within the eight administrative areas. Towns over 10,000 in size are weighted out in the sample as separate items." The determination of individual respondents rested on the selection of every *n*th name from the list of ration card holders—which, in the earlier years at least, doubtless constituted a complete enumeration of residents in American-occupied Germany. A visiting consultant, Elmo C. Wilson (1948:9), commented in August 1948 that the use of such lists offered a "samplers' paradise" unparalleled in the United States. He characterized the Opinion Survey Section's entire sampling procedure as being "of the highest order."

Field work. The field staff carried out each interview in the respondent's home or workplace. For surveys in October and November 1945, American service personnel who could speak German "like natives" conducted the interviews; thereafter, Germans trained by the Opinion Survey Section carried out the field work. In all cases the interviewers informed respondents of OMGUS sponsorship of the surveys and assured them that their anonymity would be preserved. Interviewers were instructed to ask all scheduled questions and record all responses, including those by people who did not respond ("Didn't say," or *DS*) or who reported not knowing how to answer ("Don't know," or *DK*).[5]

---

4. The Federal Republic of Germany consists of the federal government and sixteen subnational units of government called *Länder* (singular *Land*). Although some English-language writers use the German term *Land* or, using the U.S. model, translate it as *state*, this volume avoids the definitional problem of the latter term and refers instead to the FRG's sixteen *provinces*.

5. Interpreting such *DS/DK* responses can be a problem. Consider a question to which 40 percent responded *Yes*, 40 percent *No*, and 20 percent *DS/DK*. Should we say that 40 percent responded positively but 60 percent did not? Or should we say that half of those answering the question gave positive responses and the other half negative? My general procedure is to report complete data—that is, 40 percent positive, 40 percent negative, and 20 percent nonresponsive—but it sometimes helps understanding to say something like "Half of the *informed respondents* (40 percent of the *entire sample*) agreed with the proposition."

Analysis. The staff of the Opinion Survey Section transferred the information from the questionnaires to punch cards, produced sometimes elaborate cross-tabulations of the data as well as longitudinal comparisons, and wrote reports for distribution to other OMGUS units. (These reports are summarized in A. Merritt and R. Merritt 1970.)

HICOG Surveys

With the formal end of the military occupation in September 1949, the U.S. High Commission for Germany (HICOG) replaced the Office of Military Government, and the Opinion Survey Section became the Reactions Analysis Branch within the HICOG Office of Public Affairs (Crespi 1980). Surveying operations continued unabated under the direction of Leo P. Crespi after 1948. By the end of 1950 the Reactions Analysis Branch had both expanded its sample to include the whole of the Federal Republic of Germany (FRG) and engaged the newly formed Deutsches Institut für Volksumfragen (DIVO) to conduct the field work. The data, whether stemming from surveys conducted directly under the auspices of the HICOG staff or those developed by DIVO, were analyzed and presented in periodic reports issued by the Reactions Analysis Branch. Later, in May 1955, when the FRG attained virtually complete sovereignty and a United States Embassy replaced HICOG, the Reactions Analysis Branch (which had been renamed the Evaluation Staff in July 1953) became part of the Research Branch of the Embassy's Office of Public Affairs.

The HICOG Reactions Analysis Staff carried out more than one hundred surveys of West German public opinion during its five and a half years of existence, analyzing the data and distributing them in 237 reports ranging in length from 4 to 369 pages. (These reports are summarized in A. Merritt and R. Merritt 1980.) Most of the surveys were of two types. Regular monthly surveys took about three weeks of field interviews with approximately 3,000 adults in the territory that had been the American zone of occupation, 500 in West Berlin, and 300 in the American-held province of Bremen and Bremerhaven. The monthly surveys generally used a "split-sample" approach, giving slightly different questionnaires to each half of a sample. In contrast to these elaborate, regularly scheduled polls, "flash" surveys, introduced in October 1950, sought to ascertain quickly the views of a relatively small number of people (about 640) living in major cities throughout the Federal Republic, not just in the American zone. The flash survey was replaced in March 1951 by an intermediate sample of 800 West Germans, selected nationwide on the basis of stratified probability procedures (see Table 3.1). At the same time, the regular surveys were broadened to include a representative sample from the whole of West Germany

Table 3.1   Interview Areas for Intermediate Sample Size, March 1951

Community Size Strata	Percent in Stratum in West Germany	Cases in Size Stratum	Cases by Zones		
			British	U.S.	French
250,000 and over	17.5	140	105	35	0
100,000–249,999	9.0	72	48	20	4
25,000–99,999	12.0	96	54	29	13
10,000–24,999	9.3	74	46	19	9
5,000–9,999	9.1	73	37	28	8
2,000–4,999	13.6	109	47	46	16
Under 2,000	29.5	236	78	114	44
Total		800	415	291	94

Source: HIC-69:a.

and West Berlin. Occasional special surveys targeted such samples as West Berliners or youth.

During the HICOG years the Reactions Analysis Branch and Evaluation Staff assumed another mission: assessing the perspectives of East Germans. Berlin's division in 1948 did not close the borders between its eastern and western sections. Until the German Democratic Republic (GDR) built the Berlin Wall in August 1961, access between the city's two halves was fairly free for many people. American authorities were able not only to observe life in the eastern part of the city but also to interview East Berliners and others from eastern Germany who visited West Berlin to see friends and relatives, shop, attend the theater and other public events, and even find employment. From 1950 to 1958, the Reaction Analysis Branch, Evaluation Staff, and the latter's successor, the U.S. Embassy's Research Staff, conducted at least 24 samplings of East German views on such diverse topics as life in the GDR, expectations of German unification, the relationship between the United States and the Soviet Union, and favorite radio programs (see R. Merritt 1975).

How useful were the surveys of postwar Germans conducted or sponsored by the United States? We shall ignore the fundamental, theoretic question about survey research: Do surveys tell us anything worth knowing? In the late 1940s critics in both the United States and Germany had their doubts. They saw polling as the result of the social scientists' misguided "empiricism"—an elaborate and withal expensive effort to discover the "truth" by posing meaningless questions to the wrong people. Critical German intellectuals, publicists, and politicians decried polling as a heavy-footed transfer of inherently American concerns to German circumstances, an emblem of the Americans' basic misunderstanding of German society. The issue of theoretic significance was irrelevant, however, once the U.S. military authorized a surveying program.

Two more practical questions remain about the usefulness of the U.S.-supported surveys. One concerns validity: Did respondents tell the truth, or did they answer questions in ways they thought the interviewers or someone else wanted? Another concern is reliability, or the reproducibility of survey results: Do independently conducted surveys produce similar results? Issues of validity and reliability were particularly acute during the earliest years of the occupation. When an agent of the armed occupier was conducting the surveys, after all, should we not assume that this fact influenced the responses given by those interviewed? Even in later years, however, American military and political authorities had to ask how accurate the survey findings were for their decision-making needs.

The American military pollsters paid close attention to these issues. On the one hand, they invited visiting experts to evaluate their program and recommend improvements (see Wilson 1948). On the other, they ran their own tests to monitor the validity and reliability of their work. The latter tests are particularly useful for retrospective analysis.

A test of validity: OMGUS surveys. In November 1948 the Opinion Survey Section designed a survey to test the validity of its other surveys. Specifically, it sought to ascertain how much bias OMGUS sponsorship introduced into the findings: Were respondents cowed by a belief that interviewers were doing the bidding of American military authorities and that saying the "wrong" thing could lead to some form of punishment? Two sets of interviewers, one saying that they represented the "Military Government," the other a "German public opinion institute," asked separate samples in West Berlin a variety of identical questions regarding political attitudes, particularly issues of occupation policy. In summarizing the results of this survey Crespi (1950:167–168), at that time chief of the Opinion Survey Section, wrote:

> Without in any way denying the importance of the sponsorship problems that were uncovered in some areas of questioning, it would not be unreasonable to hold that the major import of the present experiment is not so much the presence of sponsorship differences on MG questions but their relative absence. With only a third of the questions exhibiting differences at the 95 per cent level [of significance] and only 14 per cent at the 99 per cent level; with a maximum difference of 17.1 per cent and a non-significant average difference of 6.6 per cent on questions in large part selected to show up sponsorship differences if they exist, the

conclusion seems fair that on the score of sponsorship MG polling is an entirely workable method of inquiry in occupied Germany.

The areas of greatest difference seemed to be questions bearing on American prestige and, to a lesser extent, questions about militarism and National Socialism. Of these discrepancies, Crespi wrote: "It is on the side of caution not to take the obtained percentages entirely at face value. Perhaps a feasible suggestion is to apply in such instances a 10 per cent safety factor—the nearest round figure to the 11.1 per cent average sponsorship difference found on questions passing the 95 per cent level" (1950:168–169). But sponsorship differences do not necessarily mean that the OMGUS-sponsored surveys were less valid than those conducted by the "independent" German agency. Respondents may simply have given different versions of the "truth" to interviewers from different agencies, with neither version necessarily a more accurate reflection than the other of the respondents' "real" perspectives (see Bindman 1965). Those who would use the OMGUS surveys, however, must bear in mind the possibility of this 10 percent bias on some kinds of responses.

A test of reliability: HICOG surveys. Electoral studies in 1953 carried out across West Germany provide insight into the reliability of U.S.-sponsored surveys. From August to November of that year the Evaluation Staff of the Office of Public Affairs commissioned a set of three surveys to predict and explain the Bundestag election of 6 September (R. Merritt 1980a). Sample sizes, based on a stratified random sampling procedure, ranged from 664 to 1,270 respondents. All technical aspects of the survey were conducted by DIVO of Frankfurt-am-Main. Working closely with the Evaluation Staff, DIVO technicians used procedures similar to those developed when they had worked for the Opinion Survey Section during the OMGUS and early HICOG years. The final report was prepared by the HICOG Evaluation Staff (HIC-191).[6]

The research project used various sets of independent data to check the reliability of the HICOG surveys: (1) comparison of overall results between HICOG surveys with those conducted at the same time by other polling agencies (Noelle et al. 1956; Reigrotzki 1956; Hirsch-Weber and Schütz et al. 1957); (2) comparison of HICOG questions, asked in two dozen separate pollings from March 1951 to September 1953, with similar questions asked during the same period by a competing firm; (3) usefulness of the HICOG survey in predicting before election day what the electoral outcome would be; and (4) comparison of results from subgroups in the national

6. Numbers in parentheses refer to the OMGUS reports (e.g., "OMG-22" is series I, report 22) or to HICOG reports (e.g., "HIC-19" is series II, report 19).

population (divided by sex, age, level of education, religion, and occupation), contrasting reported voting in the HICOG postelection survey with actual voting as indicated by West German Federal Statistical Office representative statistics (Horstmann 1954) and with intended voting as gauged by an independent polling institute's preelection survey.

Allowing for the absence of any precise test of reliability and for the variability in the sets of data used to evaluate the HICOG surveys, the evidence consistently indicates that the HICOG data accurately mirrored West German public opinion. The HICOG preelection survey, for instance, closely approximated the actual outcome of the election, particularly when we control for differences due primarily to the timing of HICOG's postelection survey. An average unanticipated variance of only +1.5 percentage points, broken down according to the respondents' sex and age, distinguishes the HICOG survey from the FRG's official statistics, which were based on actual ballots of a representative sample of almost 320,000 West Germans. The HICOG surveys were clearly the state of the art of public opinion surveying at the time.

Surveys of East Germans. Interviews with East Germans visiting West Berlin posed other technical problems for the HICOG and Embassy surveys. Interviewers had not only to locate respondents from the East but also to protect these respondents from subsequent retaliation by East German authorities, who characterized the pollsters as espionage agents (Halpern 1949). To shield the respondents, interviews were conducted in private rooms at the popular industrial and agriculture fairs held every year in West Berlin. But how representative were these interviewees from the East? HICOG analysts could address this question only by comparing the East German responses to one another and to responses from West Berliners. The consistency of these comparisons over time, if it did not solve the issue of nationwide representativeness, permitted useful analysis of an important segment of that population.

Broadening West German Public Opinion Analysis

When the OMGUS surveys began in 1945, Germans had no experience with and little knowledge about scientific public opinion polling. The U.S. Army's venture into this field demonstrated to a wide variety of Germans—not just those who were tapped as respondents but prospective business leaders, politicians, and government servants as well—some of the uses and limitations of survey and market research. As had been true in the United States, this new and potentially productive technique piqued their interest. In a February 1946 poll 94 percent of American-zone Germans who answered the question (81 percent of the entire sample) said that the U.S. polling was a good idea (WSR-14).[7] It was "good to inform the Americans how we are thinking" and "we can make suggestions" or "speak our minds," most respondents agreed. A few, however, were resistant. Some intellectuals and politicians were reluctant to give credence to a politically laden device that they neither understood nor could control. Some voiced various ideological objections (Rückmann 1972), and others, consistent with the frequently noted "anti-empirical bias" of German society (Dahrendorf 1965/1967), expressed antipathy toward social scientific concepts and research.

Nevertheless, systematic public opinion analysis was in Germany to stay. Before the end of 1945, Karl-Georg Freiherr von Stackelberg (1975) had established in Bielefeld, British zone of occupation, the EMNID-Institut, which later conducted polling as the German affiliate of the Gallup International.[8] In 1946, in the French zone, Elisabeth Noelle and her husband, Erich Peter Neumann, set up the Institut für Demoskopie (IfD) in Allensbach-am-Bodensee, on the shore of Lake Constance.[9] The main target of both EMNID and IfD then and now is the business community. As in the United States, German entrepreneurs were quick to recognize the practical value of surveying. Knowing what the masses are thinking and desiring—what types of automobiles they are likely to buy, whether they prefer soap in blue or red packages, which kind of advertising is most persuasive—has an immediate impact on sales and profits. But from the outset the IfD also focused on political issues.

But beyond simply introducing Germany to the idea of the opinion poll, Opinion Survey Section and, beginning in 1949, HICOG's Reactions Analysis Branch trained a number of Germans in the practical art of poll taking. Some employees of these units were sent to the United States for

7. *WSR* citations refer to the collated volumes in Williams (c. 1947) rather than the survey numbers themselves.

8. The polling operations of EMNID, a recent brochure (c. 1990) states, provide Ermittlungen (ascertainment), Meinungen (opinions), Nachrichten (communication), Information, and Dienste (services).

9. From the outset the IfD was linked to the conservative Christian Democratic Union and its Bavarian affiliate, the Christian Social Union; Neumann, an early adviser to the FRG's first chancellor, Konrad Adenauer, was elected in 1961 as a CDU member of the Bundestag (Schmidtchen and Noelle-Neumann 1963). Almost a half-century after World War II, Leo Bogart (1991) launched a vitriolic attack against Elisabeth Noelle-Neumann, less for any specific acts during the Nazi era than for the ease with which she moved into the post-Nazi world—to gain positions of influence in West Germany, honors in the United States, and national and international prestige in the field of public opinion research—and for what Bogart and others saw as her shameless refusal to apologize sufficiently for her alleged Nazi past (see Bogart 1991; Chicago 1991; Noelle 1992).

academic or professional training. By 1950, when the Reactions Analysis Branch began to wind down the operations side of its surveys, Germans who had worked with these units were ready to set up their own polling agencies. At least one of these agencies, DIVO, would eventually contract with the Reactions Analysis Branch and its successors to carry out surveys for the Americans. The U.S. government also initiated scholarship programs that took a significant number of German graduate students and young instructors to American universities for study that included public opinion analysis. Many subsequently returned home to enter commercial polling agencies or conduct scientific research in that field.

Public opinion surveying, including market research, flourished in West Germany beginning in the 1950s. The press gave increasing attention to poll results, especially during electoral campaigns, and several firms began publishing regular yearbooks and newsletters to report results of general interest. Among the most important publications were the IfD's thrice-monthly *Allensbacher Berichte* (Institut für Demoskopie 1949 et seq.) and occasional reports covering one or more years, the first of which was *Jahrbuch der öffentlichen Meinung, 1947–1955* (Noelle et al. 1956). Others included, in Frankfurt-am-Main, DIVO's three volumes of data, *Umfragen* (DIVO-Institut 1958–1962), and, in Bielefeld, EMNID's monthly newsletter, *EMNID-Informationen* (EMNID-Institut 1949 et seq.). Then, too, academics began paying serious attention to politically relevant surveys (for early trends, see Diederich 1965; R. Merritt 1980a). By the 1960s West Germany was one of the world's most extensive users of public opinion procedures—a "surveyed nation," in the words of a public opinion analyst (Schmidtchen 1959).

This volume, focusing on the postwar German response to the American occupation policy, concentrates on the OMGUS surveys conducted from 1945 to 1949. For the bulk of this period these surveys continued to be the American military government's only sustained source of accurate data on public perspectives. As other agencies began to emerge, they sometimes produced relevant data that merit our attention. Similarly, post-1949 surveys by HICOG, the U.S. Embassy, and various commercial agencies can provide useful information about both subsequent shifts in public opinion and retrospective views of issues that had roused considerable interest during the occupation years. The goal is to integrate these various sources of public opinion data into an overall image of Germans' responses to American policies aimed at changing German society.

II

Changing Images of the Past

The World War II Allies were determined not only to wipe out Nazism but also to make Germans understand its evil nature and eventually accept democracy. What gave them the right to impose their collective will? Though concepts of natural law were invoked, in fact the Allies' military control sanctioned the ancient "law of the club." This principle alone gave occupation authorities the unquestionable right to implement policies that ranged from demilitarizing Germany to "denazifying" and reeducating the country.

In a sense, there was no limit to what the conquering Allies could do. Many Germans, cowed for years by Hitler's domination and unnerved by wild rumors emanating from various quarters, feared that once again the victors intended to impose a Carthaginian peace upon the vanquished. In other modern societies, however, concepts of justice, morality, and practicality constrain unwarranted actions. All of the Allied governments professed adherence to the latter orientation—without relinquishing their right to punish severely those who tried to thwart them. The question they faced was how to carry out their system-changing mission without running afoul of international social norms.

One answer lay in understanding what Germans thought about Allied policies. Some elements of the victor-vanquished link remained clear and unchangeable: the Allies initially rejected any suggestion that Germany needed a revitalized Wehrmacht. Other elements of the relation, though, presented options. In such cases, pushing through schemes that Germans did not understand or found intolerable was counterproductive: resistance could damage the entire occupation program. Besides, persuading Germans to change their attitudes and behavior required more than command. It demanded an understanding of popular moods and reactions.

The German response to Allied occupation policies was thus critical. Knowing what different segments of the German public had in their minds gave the Allies a tool for evaluating the effectiveness of their policies and for fine tuning the strategic mix of carrots and sticks. The new analytic instrument of public opinion surveys offered one key to this kind of understanding.

The American Military Government in particular understood the role that public opinion analysis would play in occupation policy: by assessing public thinking and responses to individual policy shifts, polling could enhance the MG's overall effectiveness.

This section of the book focuses on public responses to four important dimensions of Allied occupation policy. The first two chapters of Part 2 deal with Germany's immediate past and collective responsibility. Chapter 4 addresses popular German attitudes toward Nazism and particularly toward Adolf Hitler: Was Nazism a fundamentally bad idea or a good idea badly carried out? Had Hitler not led Germany into World War II, would he be ranked today as one of the country's most constructive leaders? Chapter 5 looks at German evaluations of Nazi "crimes": To what extent was Germany responsible for the war's outbreak? How can we understand the death camps and the Holocaust? Was German society as a collectivity guilty of committing or at least condoning these crimes?

Two subsequent chapters raise the issue of individual responsibility. Chapter 6 explores German responses to both the individuals brought before the International Military Tribunal and the judicial process itself: Were Hermann Göring, Rudolf Hess, and General Alfred Jodl personally responsible for Nazism's crimes? Were the Nuremberg war crimes procedures that tried them fairly carried out? When should such trials end? Chapter 7 addresses the responsibility of Germans who, occupying important positions, had joined the party and to some measure supported its criminal policies: Should these collaborators be brought to trial or otherwise punished? What legally and morally justifiable processes could assess their guilt? How reasonable were the denazification procedures carried out by U.S. military authorities?

A final chapter of this section goes beyond the immediate occupation years—and also beyond public opinion data alone—to look at the long-range impact on Germans of the Nazi regime: Were the years from 1933 to 1945 only an episode in German history, never to be repeated, or do unreconstructed Nazis and neo-Nazis await the day when they can return to power? How have Germans, individually and collectively, come to terms with their Nazi past? Do they say one thing in public but something else in private? Do young Germans express the same views as their elders, for whom Nazism had had a more immediate, personal impact? Chapter 8 helps us understand the social structure and process that were to emerge in Germany after the occupation.

· ·

FOUR

National Socialism in Retrospect

Until Germans themselves comprehended the fundamentally evil nature of National Socialism, Allied leaders felt, they might be tempted to resurrect it. The Allies resolved to convince the German people that Nazi Germany had been barbarism's greatest assault on Western civilization since Europe emerged from the Dark Ages. To this end they rewrote textbooks and undertook extensive information programs about Nazi crimes, they published photographic records of the infamous death camps and forced Germans to clean them up, and they staged a spectacular, yearlong trial of major war criminals.

Germans had only to look around them to know that National Socialism had failed. Adolf Hitler's government had collapsed ignominiously. Aerial bombardment and street fighting had laid waste to their cities, their factories, and their communication and transportation networks. Three and a half million Germans had died in Hitler's war. The much-vaunted Wehrmacht had been smashed in battlefields both east and west. Foreign troops again occupied the land. And every day more packs of war-weary refugees streamed into the West from eastern Europe.

The cost of the short-lived Nazi episode would have been manifest to Germans even had the victors not beaten their anti-Nazi drums. But how were these Germans to understand and come to terms with their recent history? What accounted for Hitler's accession to power in 1933? Why had Germans thronged so enthusiastically to carry out his demands? Was Hitler's war, which verged on national suicide, the consequence of National Socialism, of a flaw in German national character, of vindictiveness in Germany's jealous but stronger adversaries, or merely of bad judgment on the part of the country's political activists?

This chapter, in evaluating postwar German perspectives on Hitler and National Socialism, addresses three main issues. First, Hitler the man: How did the passage of time—a time used by the Allies to promote their own accounts of what Hitler had done and the implications of his actions—change his image in the popular mind? Second, did Hitler's ideology, the dream of National Socialism, make sense, had it ever made sense, to postwar Germans? Had the political program of his National Socialist German Workers Party (*Nationalsozialistische Deutsche Arbeiter-Partei*, or NSDAP) proved intolerable, or did Germans credit it with elements that deserved serious attention and that might yet gain high marks in the academy of history? Third, how enduring were these occupation-time perceptions? Some analysts feared that Germans might revert to old Nazi ways and new Nazi leaders once occupying armies went home. This concern has persisted: the emergence of a unified Germany in 1990 prompted international debate, and vicious attacks against foreigners by German "skinheads" more recently have occasioned concern about residual fascist impulses. What do public opinion data tell us about neo-Nazism's potential in modern Germany?

Hitler as a Leader

Postwar Germans were ambivalent toward Adolf Hitler. On the one hand, they psychologically distanced themselves from him and claimed to have resisted the intellectual dimension of his political philosophy. Most residents of the American zone of occupation (AMZON) said that they had not read the ideological underpinning of Nazism, Hitler's *Mein Kampf* (1925–1927/1939). In February 1946, 7 percent reported having read the book in its entirety, and another 16 percent remembered reading part of it (OMG-2).[1] Two years later these figures dwindled to 5 and 14 percent, respectively (OMG-92). Most AMZON Germans reported having viewed Hitler's leadership with skepticism. Only one in eight recalled trusting him as a leader up to the end of the war (OMG-22). Half claimed either never to have trusted him (35 percent) or to have lost their faith by the time war erupted in 1939 (15 percent).

AMZON Germans saw themselves as powerless victims of Hitler's deceptions. In April 1946 more than nine in ten agreed and only one in twenty disagreed with the proposition that "Hitler and his government were criminals and misled the German people" (OMG-19). Three-fifths of those

---

1. This chapter follows the notational conventions described in chapter 3. OMG citations refer to numbered reports written by the Opinion Survey Section of the Office of Military Government, United States (OMGUS); HIC to reports written for the U.S. High Commission for Germany (HICOG) by its Office of Public Affairs' Reactions Analysis Staff, renamed Evaluation Staff; WSR to early OMGUS surveys reported in the datacards of Frederick W. Williams (n.d.); IfD to the Institut für Demoskopie's *Jahrbücher*, edited by Elisabeth Noelle et al. (1956 et seq.), as well as IfD's thrice-monthly *Allensbacher Berichte* (IfD/AR); and EMNID to the monthly *Informationen* of EMNID K.G.

offering an opinion thought that Hitler and his government had never even intended to improve the German people's situation (54 percent of the entire sample, compared with 37 percent who credited Nazi leaders with good intentions). When asked in October 1946 whether they would like to have seen Hitler brought before the International Military Tribunal at Nuremberg, 72 percent of AMZON Germans responded positively and only 12 percent felt it better that he had been spared this ignominy (WSR-31). Rejection of Hitler grew stronger yet in later years. The share of West Germans reporting their willingness to vote again for a man like Hitler dropped from 14 percent in 1953 to 10 percent five years later and 5 percent in 1963 (EMNID-20:8/9, 35:10).[2]

Postwar Germans did not, on the other hand, wholeheartedly condemn all aspects of Hitler's political leadership. Was the Führer himself to blame for the consequences of the Third Reich? Among those who in July 1947 considered National Socialism to be either "a bad idea" or "a good idea badly carried out," a quarter blamed Hitler unreservedly (OMG-68). Almost three times as many attributed responsibility either solely to Hitler's advisers (25 percent) or jointly to Hitler and his advisers (45 percent).[3] Viewed somewhat differently, approximately the same number assigned some blame to Hitler (71 percent) as to his advisers (70 percent). Many even agreed that responsibility for Hitler's accession to power (43 percent) and maintenance in power (24 percent) rested with the German people themselves (OMG-94). Most postwar Germans, then, did not treat Hitler as a scapegoat for whatever went wrong from 1933 to 1945.

Indeed, these postwar Germans reported, much good came from Hitler's leadership. Perhaps recalling the earlier and sunnier days of Hitler's dozen years in power, they refused to repudiate him because of the darker years. Very few West Germans—10 percent in 1950 and July 1952, dropping to 2 percent in 1966–1976 (IfD-1:132, 6:58)—continued to see Hitler as Germany's greatest statesman, one whose true greatness would be recognized only later. In response to a closed-ended question asked in July 1952, the same share, one tenth, recalled Hitler's outstanding leadership (see Figure 4.1). More than three-fifths of the nationwide sample

2. In 1965 and 1967 this percentage was still lower, 4 percent. In 1968 a third of those supporting the new right-wing extremist National Democratic Party (NPD) said that, if the opportunity arose, they would in fact vote for a man like Hitler. Interpretation of such data must take into account changes in the population's age structure—specifically, the declining number of Germans having had direct experience with Nazism.

3. Almost the same percentage of those responding to the original question as either "bad idea" or "good idea badly carried out" put the blame on Hitler personally (26 and 25 percent, respectively), but the former responded far less frequently that the advisers alone were responsible (20 and 32 percent, respectively).

Figure 4.1

Retrospective Views of Hitler's Leadership, July 1952

Question: One hears widely differing views about Hitler. Which of the ones on this list
do you find the most fitting?

Hitler was the greatest statesman of the century: his true greatness will not emerge
until later. [Great]

Hitler made some mistakes, but he was an excellent leader. [Solid]

Hitler did much good, but it was greatly outweighed by his disastrous actions and
characteristics. [Flawed]

Hitler was an unscrupulous politician who bears the blame for many horrible deeds.
[Evil]

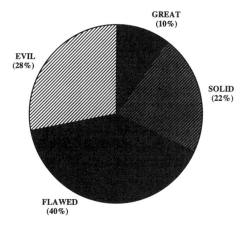

Source: IfD-1:136.

expressed more temperate views, 22 percent feeling that a few mistakes
did not damage his overall record of excellence and 40 percent recalling
positive aspects that were outweighed by his misdeeds. Twenty-eight percent saw Hitler as a depraved politician.

Surveys conducted during the next four decades continued to reflect
this ambivalence toward Hitler. Figure 4.2 shows a solid, albeit diminishing, acceptance in the Federal Republic of the proposition that, had it not
been for World War II, Hitler would be ranked as one of German history's
leading statesmen.[4] The number of West Germans who reject this premise, almost always greater, increased steadily between 1955 and 1978,
from less than 40 percent to more than half.[5] A national survey in spring

4. See also Geissler (1981:65).

5. A survey in May 1983 (EMNID-35:5/6) asked respondents to name the "three greatest Germans in our history." Hitler ranked fourth (14 percent), behind Konrad Adenauer

Figure 4.2

Hitler's Greatness Had World War II Not Intervened, 1955-1978

Question: Everything that was built up between 1933 and 1939 and much else besides was destroyed during the war. Would you say that, without the war, Hitler would have been one of the greatest German statesmen?

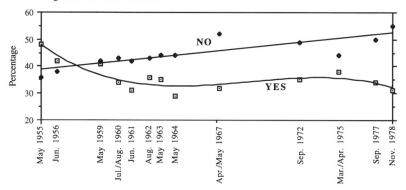

YES: y = 47.831 - 0.32924x + 2.2229e-3x^2 - 4.4392e-6x^3   R^2 = 0.797   F-Ratio = 11.8   Prob < 0.002
NO: y = 38.796 + 4.7713e-2x   R^2 = 0.709   F-Ratio = 26.8   Prob < 0.001

Source: Herdegen (1979:96).

1992 that included both eastern and western Germans found 27 percent agreeing and 69 percent disagreeing that, except for the war and his treatment of Jews, Hitler would today be ranked as one of Germany's greatest statesmen (Wild 1992:64).[6]

Irrespective of Hitler's strengths and weaknesses, a sizable number of postwar Germans said, his very role as chief of state gave him the right to rule. This concept of legitimated authority, rooted deep in Germany's cultural history, bedeviled Germans during the Nazi era—and Allied authorities afterward. It linked authority inextricably to obedience. In March 1946, for instance, two-fifths of AMZON respondents agreed that "the individual should always obey the orders of the state without question" (OMG-22). The same principle undercut efforts to remove Hitler forcibly from power. The number of survey respondents who censured the participants of the 20 July 1944 plot against Hitler's life increased from 11 per-

---

(42 percent), Otto von Bismarck (30 percent), and Johann Wolfgang von Goethe (25 percent). Among those giving Hitler high scores were teenagers (24 percent), Bavarians (23 percent), retirees (22 percent), and Catholics (20 percent).

6. Eastern Germans were more critical of the Führer. Among eastern Germans, the ratio of detractors to supporters was about four to one. That of western Germans was somewhat higher than two to one.

cent in February 1946 (wsr-15) to 24 percent in October 1951 (hic-114) and 30 percent a year later (IfD-1:138).[7] Some respondents thought the plot aimed to destroy Germany. Asked in 1949 (hic-17) whether Germany's wartime defeat was due to the military superiority of its enemies or "the treachery of a certain group of people within Germany," almost as many amzon Germans chose the latter explanation (38 percent) as the former (45 percent).

Further questioning in 1951 revealed that more than half of the West Germans who disapproved of the plot (13 percent of the entire sample) viewed it as treasonable rather than merely unethical or ill timed. When asked whether the families of plotters subsequently executed by the Nazis should receive help from the Federal Republic of Germany, 89 percent of those who supported the plot favored such restitution, but only 69 percent of the plot's critics agreed.[8]

By late 1952 (hic-167) three-fourths of those giving an opinion (58 percent of the total sample) said the plotters were not traitors. More than three-fifths of that group argued that the plotters wanted to save Germany from ruin (23 percent of all respondents) or end a futile war, thereby preventing further bloodshed (13 percent). But general sympathy for the plotters notwithstanding, a core of hard-line condemnation remained. Sentiment against the plot and its participants did not address its actual or potential impact on Germany's war effort or on other policies but, rather, the belief that nothing justifies lèse-majesté. It is the citizen's duty to obey government orders.

Nazism's Potential and Performance

Regardless of attitudes toward Hitler as a person or political leader, large numbers of postwar Germans in areas under U.S. control continued to express perspectives characteristic of National Socialist ideology (see Table 4.1).[9] Two caveats should be applied to these findings.

7. The variation of attitudes toward plot participants is in part an artifact of the polling process: figures in 1946 and 1952 reflected views of all respondents answering the question, while those in 1951 responded to a question that first spelled out what the plot was.

8. Of the 13 percent who opposed assistance, almost half thought that the relatives did not need it and somewhat more thought that they did not deserve support because the plot was traitorous or criminal. In April 1956, 49 percent of a national sample supported parents who, in a hypothetical situation, did not want the local school board to name a new school after one of the plotters; 18 percent supported the school board (IfD-2:145).

9. Table 4.1 shows that the ratio of those supporting such ideological propositions (an average of 22 percent of all amzon interviewees) to those rejecting them (67 percent)

Table 4.1   Public Attitudes Toward Nazi Ideology, April 1946

Percentage Giving "Agree" or "Disagree" Responses

	Yes	No
A civilian is an unworthy (lower) person compared to a member of the army.	9	89
In all probability foreign nations and races are enemies; therefore, one should be prepared at all times to attack them first.	10	82
If a pure German marries a non-Aryan wife he should be condemned.	10	85
The horrors committed by the Germans are an invention of the propaganda of our enemies.	12	70
An education encouraging people to have their own opinion is dangerous to the security of the state.	13	81
The communists and the social democrats should be suppressed.	15	75
Only a government with a dictator is able to create a strong nation.	18	75
This war was caused by a conspiracy between the international bankers and the communists.	18	62
The German people were victims of a conspiracy by other nations.	19	77
It would have been much better for the Allies to have had a war with Russia instead of with Germany.	20	48
The publication of no book that criticizes a government or recommends any change in government should be permitted.	29	62
Negroes are members of an unworthy (lower) race.	30	59
The Versailles Treaty was the source of the Second World War because it was too hard on Germany.	32	52
Jews should not have the same rights as those belonging to the Aryan race.	33	62
Extermination of the Jews and Poles and other non-Aryans was . . . necessary for the security of Germans.	37	59
Territories such as Danzig, Sudetenland, and Austria should be part of Germany proper.	52	36

Source: OMG-19.

was roughly one to three. Younger Germans were substantially more prone to accept Nazi ideology, the ratio of acceptance to rejection exceeding one to two: 32 to 62 percent for Württemberg-Badeners aged 17–27, and 33 to 61 percent for Marburg University students. Political prisoners were close to the AMZON average. The 16 questions of Table 4.1 were part of a battery of 110 in a "German attitude scale" provided for the OMGUS Surveys Branch by Morris Krugman (1949) of Columbia University. The survey was

First, we must wonder whether these patterns of response were "typically" German or whether Americans, French, and citizens of other industrialized countries might not have agreed to similar propositions. Systematic research, beginning with Stouffer's (1955) study of *Communism, Conformity, and Civil Liberties* in the United States, has in fact uncovered pockets of illiberality in many societies. Consider, for example, Father Charles E. Coughlin's religious anti-Semitism in the United States during the 1930s and 1940s (Athans 1991). Second, the data say nothing about the extent to which such perspectives antedated the existence of Nazism in Germany. Social scientists do not have any adequate means to compare German perspectives in 1945 to those in 1900 or 1925.

In March 1946, using questions similar to those in Table 4.1, OMGUS pollsters attempted to determine whether popular attitudes were affected by the perception that they reflected Nazi ideology (OMG-22; WSR-20). They used a split-sample technique, in which slightly but significantly different questions were asked of each half of a sample chosen randomly from a single population. This survey explored how political views varied according to whether or not the wording of the question attributed the ideas to Hitler himself. Thus half of a sample got the question, "Before the war it was often said that parts of Europe with considerable German minorities (e.g., Sudetenland) should be legally reincorporated in Germany; did you agree with that or not?" The other half got the same question, except that it began, "Before the war Hitler often said." The result of the split-sample test showed a modest difference: the first wording elicited positive responses from 36 percent of the interviewees, the second from 39 percent. A similar pair of questions posited the prewar sentiment that "international Jewry alone would profit from the war"; 14 percent agreed with the generalized proposition and 11 percent were willing to identify themselves with Hitler in accepting it. A third pair of questions, asking about the putative superiority of the "Nordic race," generated the same result. Overall, we see slight differences that are neither consistent nor statistically significant. Perhaps respondents recognized the National Socialist linkage of the questions irrespective of any mention of Hitler but the results suggest that Hitler merely tapped the underlying perspectives of Germans, then reinforced these perspectives through his propaganda.

This measure of popular postwar acceptance of Nazi-related ideas is

administered in April 1946 in six individual pollings. Table 4.1 reports data from 1,470 AMZON respondents. Smaller samples of young people (295 youths aged 17–27 in Württemberg-Baden and 214 students at Marburg University) found an average of 10 percent of them accepting more Nazi-oriented expressions than did AMZON respondents. Others sampled were political prisoners (84 detained, 95 released) and 182 West Berliners.

Figure 4.3
Nazism as Bad Idea or Good Idea Badly Carried Out, 1945-1949

Question: Was National Socialism a bad idea, or a good idea badly carried out?

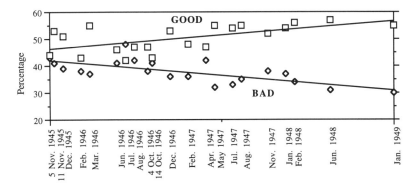

GOOD: y = 46.278 + 0.27165x   R^2 = 0.354   F-Ratio = 10.4   Prob < 0.004
BAD: y = 41.992 - 0.28653x   R^2 = 0.484   F-Ratio = 17.8   Prob < 0.001

Sources: OMG-22, 66, 68, 175.

reflected in attitudes toward Nazism in general. OMGUS surveys repeatedly asked AMZON Germans whether they considered National Socialism to have been "a bad idea" or "a good idea badly carried out." In thirteen surveys between November 1945 and April 1947, as Figure 4.3 shows, an average of 48 percent took the latter viewpoint. A month later this figure rose to 55 percent, where it remained fairly constant during the next two years. For the period as a whole, the percentage of respondents recalling Nazism as a good idea badly carried out rose by an average of more than 3 percentage points per year. Meanwhile, the average share of respondents describing Nazism outright as a bad idea dropped even faster.[10] A breakdown of the survey conducted in August 1947 reveals that respondents most likely to describe National Socialism as a good idea badly carried out were under the age of 30 (68 percent), former Nazi party members (67 percent), people with nine to twelve years of schooling (64 percent), Protestants (64 percent), West Berliners (62 percent), and Hessians (61 percent). These interviewees were more critical than others toward the postwar news media, democracy, and a government offering its citizens liberty rather than security (OMG-68).

10. An average of 12 percent did not know or could not say what they felt. In July 1966 a nationwide sample of university students found that 44 percent could report something positive about Hitler and the Third Reich (with three-fifths of these mentioning the resolution of Germany's economic crisis of the early 1930s), 38 percent could find nothing good to say, and 18 percent did not know (IfD-4:368).

Figure 4.4

Good vs. Evil in National Socialism, 1951-1952

Question: When you take everything into account, was there more good in the ideas of National Socialism or more evil?

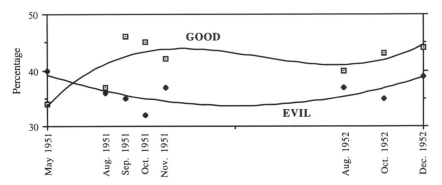

GOOD: y = 33.499 + 3.5652x - 0.38252x^2 + 1.1850e-2x^3   R^2 = 0.681   F-Ratio = 2.9   Prob < 0.167
EVIL: y = 39.181 - 1.1515x + 5.9315e-2x^2   R^2 = 0.490   F-Ratio = 2.4   Prob < 0.185

Sources: HIC-87, 118, 167.

Somewhat different questions asked after the occupation formally ended produced consistent results: sharp division in evaluating National Socialism. "When you take everything into account," West Germans were asked in eight surveys plotted in Figure 4.4, "was there more good in the ideas of National Socialism or more evil?"[11] An overall average of 41 percent saw more good and 36 percent more evil. Similar population groups emerged as temporizers in this period as in that covered by the question in Figure 4.3: Respondents aged 25 to 34 (the same age group as those under the age of 30 in 1947) were 10 percentage points higher than average in seeing National Socialism as good, the more educated 7 points higher, and Protestants 4 points higher.[12]

Nor did the passage of time fundamentally change popular attitudes toward Nazism. On the one hand, Germans acknowledged increasingly the negative side of the Third Reich. Four nationwide surveys from May 1964 to February 1979 (IfD-8:191) found a strong majority agreeing that the National Socialist state was not only wrong but criminal. In fact, the share of people accepting this argument rose from 54 to 71 percent while

11. See also Forschungsgruppe Wahlen e.V. Mannheim (1977), as cited in Geissler (1981:37).

12. The surveys of 1951–1952 asked no question about Nazi party membership. Bavarians ranked higher than Hessians (47 to 40 percent, respectively, for the last four surveys shown in Figure 4.4).

that denying it dropped from 38 to 25 percent. But, on the other hand, many Germans refused to ignore the Third Reich's positive side. Four nationwide surveys from April 1975 to February 1979 (IfD-8:191) asked respondents first to put aside the war and persecution of Jews and then to evaluate the Third Reich. An average of 36 percent agreed that, except for those policies, the Nazi regime had not been bad at all, while 42 percent gave it a negative evaluation in any event. More than half of the respondents to a national survey in spring 1992 said that National Socialism had only bad qualities (17 percent) or more bad than good qualities (36 percent); two in five saw both good and bad (42 percent) and 2 percent more good than bad (Wild 1992:64).

Other surveys that posed different questions to different samples came up with similar results. Consider Nazi labor policy, which among other things denied collective bargaining and the right to strike (OMG-11). In April 1946, the policy found support among about a third of both an entire sample of AMZON residents (slightly more of whom opposed it) and a subsample of those who had been trade union members before 1933 (48 percent of whom opposed it).[13] Or, what about the relative merits of National Socialism and communism? Asked to choose between them, the number opting for National Socialism increased from 19 percent in November 1945 to well over twice that many in February 1949, with the number preferring communism declining from 35 to 3 percent (OMG-60, 175). Among Bavarian university students, 55 percent of whom a year later would describe Nazism as a good idea badly carried out, 30 percent claimed that National Socialism would not necessarily have led to war. Two-thirds did see war as inevitable under Nazism (HIC-17).[14] National Socialism may have had its negative aspects, a substantial number of postwar Germans seemed to be saying, but compared to the available alternatives it had much to commend it.

When they turned to the NSDAP's concrete policies and performance, West Germans agreed strikingly in their evaluations (Table 4.2). To be

13. Support for Nazi wage control policy came from 42 percent of pre-1933 unionists who were not active in 1946, and 28 percent of both pre-1933 unionists active in 1946 ("old generation") and activists who had not been trade union members before 1933 ("new generation"). OMGUS analysts said: "Nazism made some inroads among the pre-1933 trade unionists, but the compromised unionists tend to remain outside the new free trade unions now being organized."

14. Those who thought National Socialism was not an inherently bad idea were considerably more inclined to think that Germany could have had a National Socialist government without going to war (45 percent) than were those who thought it basically a bad idea (10 percent). Asked for their reasons, students who saw National Socialism as having led inevitably to war responded primarily in terms of Hitler's delusion of grandeur (32 percent) or the hunger for power that drove NSDAP officials (21 percent).

Table 4.2 Good and Bad Aspects of National Socialism, 1951

	Entire Sample		Respondents Seeing in National Socialism: Nov. 1951	
	May 1951	Nov. 1951	More Good	More Evil
Good aspects of National Socialism (percentage giving response)				
Good job opportunities, living standards	41	46	60	42
Good social welfare	30	38	48	33
Good organization, discipline; security	8	10	14	10
Youth education, labor service, Hitler Youth, physical training of youth	5	9	12	7
Controlled and sound economic policy	4	9	13	7
Realizing the national ideas	2	2	5	1
Extensive construction (e.g., highways)	—	6	6	5
Other responses	6	7	8	6
Nothing was good	7	6	—	14
No response, no opinion	25	19	6	13
Bad aspects of National Socialism (percentage giving response)				
Preparation for war, rearmament, war	28	26	26	29
No freedom, dictatorship	20	29	25	38
Racial policy, persecution of Jews	19	30	37	32
Violence, cruelty, concentration camps	15	17	20	18
No religious freedom; church persecution	9	16	15	20
Poor foreign policy; imperialism	6	11	11	15
Dominant position of Nazi party	3	6	9	5
Other responses	11	8	10	8
Everything was bad	2	2	—	5
No response, no opinion	25	18	9	7

Sources: HIC-87, 118.
Note: Multiple responses permitted.

sure, those who found Nazism generally objectionable cited more negative than positive features, and the reverse was true for those finding more
good than evil in National Socialism. The population as an aggregate also
disagreed about such specific issues as compulsory labor service, and
what some saw as support for law and order, others termed an abridgment
of freedom. But the overall pattern of evaluations is consistent. Not a
single respondent said that the persecution of Jews was good or that Nazi
social welfare policies were bad.

After the occupation's formal end, survey teams that interviewed special samples on topics particularly important to them found similar results. In early 1950 AMZON Germans considered unemployment by far the
most serious problem facing the new West German government in Bonn.
More than a third of the sample wanted to reinstitute policies similar
to those implemented by the NSDAP in the 1930s to boost employment
(HIC-22)—especially the improvement and extension of transportation
and traffic facilities (14 percent), reconstruction (10 percent), and compulsory labor service (14 percent). A special survey of 544 unemployed
Bavarians (HIC-23) found that they were not only more concerned with
unemployment than was the overall population but also more knowledgeable about what the NSDAP had done to ease unemployment in the 1930s.
More than half of the unemployed interviewees favored reintroducing
public works programs and other policies used by the Third Reich to put
people to work, though they were no more inclined than the national
sample as a whole to institute compulsory labor. A survey in mid-1950
found young people reacting similarly (HIC-38). Almost a third could name
measures or institutions of the Third Reich that they would be willing to
see reinstituted, including labor service (12 percent), organizations like
the Hitler Youth (7 percent), and youth homes and camps (6 percent).
Three-fifths of the youth indicated that they would favor the establishment of a single youth organization for the whole of West Germany, and a
third of these even wanted its members to wear uniforms.

The overall tenor of these survey data suggests substantial popular
antipathy toward Nazi leaders but tolerance of some elements of their
political system. Postwar Germans said that they had been concerned well
before the war's end about the direction of the Third Reich but could do
nothing about it.[15] They were glad to see Hitler and his cronies gone, but

15. For some this inability to act against Nazism no doubt stemmed from concepts of
national loyalty (like those notions of legitimate authority that led to criticism of the 20
July 1944 plotters). Others saw themselves as powerless. A national survey in September
1977 (IfD-8:192) asked whether the German people had had any opportunity to change
Nazi policy regarding, say, the concentration camps or slaughter of Jews. For every

they did not reject everything Nazism had done. AMZON Germans, especially younger citizens who had come of age during the Nazi years, differentiated clearly between what they saw as National Socialism's good and bad aspects, and a fair number of them were willing to reinstitute elements that they thought had been positive.

Neo-Nazism as a Social Protest Movement

Acceptance of some Nazi policies, however, does not mean that Germans were waiting for the reemergence of Nazism itself.[16] Few wanted a new party like the NSDAP to take power in postwar Germany. An eighth of a nationwide sample in late 1951 said that they would welcome such an event, but only a quarter of those (3 percent of the total) added that they would do whatever they could to support it (HIC-118). A fifth said they were active opponents, who would do everything possible to prevent a new Nazi takeover. More than half stated either that they would not like such an event but would do nothing to oppose it (30 percent) or else that they would not care (23 percent).[17] Even among those who saw more good than evil in National Socialism (HIC-118), 43 percent indicated that they would resist a new Nazi takeover actively (13 percent) or passively (30 percent), and far fewer would support it either actively (7 percent) or passively (20 percent). Twenty-one years later, as Figure 4.5 shows, active opponents doubled from 20 to 40 percent and passive opponents increased from 30 to 39 percent; active supporters remained constant at 3 percent, while passive supporters declined from 10 to 3 percent; and the number of indifferent and uninformed respondents declined from 23 to 9 percent.

A concurrent trend was increased acceptance of a multiparty political system. The percentage favoring "a single, strong national party which really represents the interests of all classes of our people"—that is, a party implicitly similar to the NSDAP—dropped from 44 percent in December

---

respondent who responded positively (11 percent of the entire sample), more than six (68 percent) denied that such opportunities existed.

16. The term "neo-Nazism" is frequently attached both to parties espousing the leadership principle and ideology of National Socialism and to extreme right-wing parties that do not. In the latter case, "neo-Nazism" is a misnomer.

17. An independent sample in late 1953 provided similar results (IfD-1:276). In contrast, when asked in December 1952 (HIC-167) how they would react to an attempted seizure of power by communists, more than five-sixths of a national sample reported that they would oppose it actively (53 percent) or passively (32 percent), 1 percent that they would welcome but do nothing to facilitate it, and less than half of 1 percent that they would do everything in their power to bring it about. Postwar Germans may have had their doubts about National Socialism, but they wholeheartedly despised communism.

Figure 4.5

Personal Response to a New Nazi Party Seeking Power, 1951-1972

Question: Suppose a new National Socialist Party tried to assume power. How would you
react? Here are various alternatives. I would:

    (*a*) do all I could to prevent this happening. [Prevent]
    (*b*) be against it but would do nothing in particular. [Oppose]
    (*c*) not care. [Indifference]
    (*d*) welcome it but do nothing in particular to support it. [Favor]
    (*e*) welcome it and support. [Support]

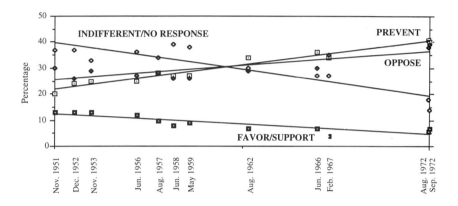

PREVENT: $y = 21.827 + 7.5284e\text{-}2x$ $R^2 = 0.956$ F-Ratio = 216.7 Prob < 0.001
OPPOSE: $y = 25.482 + 4.3481e\text{-}2x$ $R^2 = 0.682$ F-Ratio = 21.5 Prob < 0.001
FAVOR + SUPPORT: $y = 12.455 - 3.0745e\text{-}2x$ $R^2 = 0.0755$ F-Ratio = 30.8 Prob < 0.001
INDIFFERENT + NO RESPONSE: $y = 39.939 - 8.3032e\text{-}2x$ $R^2 = 0.810$ F-Ratio = 42.5 Prob < 0.001

Sources: HIC-118, 167; IfD-1:276, 2:277, 4:293, 5:231.

1952 to 25 percent in March 1956, while opposition climbed from 37 to 47
percent (HIC-230). Similarly, the percentage wanting "to see a party established which only had the good sides of National Socialism" declined by
almost half, from 40 to 23 percent, with the number opposing such an idea
remaining virtually constant (43 and 44 percent, respectively). The Nazi
leadership principle had still less support. Only one in six saw any need in
1956 to have, as before, "a national leader who rules Germany with a
strong hand for the welfare of all"; 55 percent felt no such need.

    This postwar lack of popular enthusiasm for a revitalized National
Socialism notwithstanding, neo-Nazism has emerged from time to time
since 1945. As we have seen, ideas associated with Nazism survived the
Nazi experience, the lost war, and occupation; a minority of Germans
remained unabashed admirers of Hitler's personality and goals. Not sur-

prisingly, then, neo-Nazi parties arose in the western zones almost as soon as occupiers permitted political parties to function.[18] Competing with a variety of nineteenth-century liberal, monarchic, and ultraconservative parties, the explicitly neo-Nazi parties had distinctive cachets. They carefully avoided open ties to the NSDAP—in part because their leaders recognized the popular animosity toward Hitler and his party, but more significantly because they realized that such a step would subject them to inquiries and restrictions by occupation and, later, FRG authorities.[19] Neo-Nazi parties nevertheless praised Hitler for his wisdom and perspicacious leadership, blamed Social Democrats and "international Jewry" for sabotaging the Third Reich, encouraged chauvinistic nationalism and xenophobia, criticized the Allied occupiers for what they called their wartime atrocities and postwar blunders, and pandered to those who felt that their neighbors were unfairly abusing Germans (Tauber 1967; Klingemann and Pappi 1972; Backes and Jesse 1985, 1989; Stöss 1989/1991). In some cases they even adopted slightly modified uniforms and other trappings of the National Socialist movement.

The first extreme right-wing parties to capture international attention were the Economic Reconstruction Association (*Wirtschaftliche Aufbauvereinigung*, or WAV) in the U.S. zone of occupation, mainly Bavaria, and the German Rightist Party (Conservative Association) or *Deutsche Rechts-Partei* (*Konservative Vereinigung*) in the British zone. The WAV was created as early as December 1945. Although it quickly ran afoul of U.S. occupation authorities by turning openly antidemocratic, it maintained—barely— its legal status. The WAV won more than 15 percent of the seats in Bavaria's parliamentary election of December 1946 and took twelve Bundestag seats in the first federal election of August 1949. Beginning in June 1946, the British zone's DRP (KV) sought to merge all organizations that opposed liberalism—without, however, directly attacking the liberal forms of government being established in western Germany. It achieved only modest successes, however, in provincial and local elections. After its leaders merged in 1947 with North Rhine-Westphalia's German Conserva-

18. Eastern Germany, under first the Soviet Military Government and then the German Democratic Republic, systematically suppressed both neo-Nazi movements and evidence that such tendencies existed among its "new German citizens." As became clear immediately after the GDR collapsed in fall 1989, the suppression was far from complete. Surveys conducted in 1990 (Fuchs and Schöbel 1992) "showed an extremely high percentage of authoritarian and alienated citizens in East Germany." See Chapters 8 and 13.

19. Article 9(2) of the FRG's Basic Law (*Grundgesetz*), or constitution, states: "Associations, the purposes or activities of which conflict with criminal laws or which are directed against the constitutional order or the concept of international understanding, are prohibited."

tive Party (*Deutsch-Konservative Partei*, or DKP) the DRP/DKP commanded 429,000 votes and won five Bundestag seats in 1949.

The national election of 1949 taught West German rightists the value of unity. A plethora of such parties spent too much time quarreling with each other and not enough emphasizing their common ties—and were punished by an electoral law that favored larger parties.[20] It made sense for the WAV, DRP/DKP, and other extreme right-wing parties to coalesce. Then, too, voters and activists who favored outright National Socialism increasingly abandoned conservative parties in the search for something new.

Socialist Reich Party (SRP). That quest was answered by the Socialist Reich Party (*Sozialistische Reichspartei*), set up in October 1949 only days after the occupation formally ended and Konrad Adenauer took office as the FRG's first chancellor. The SRP's leaders, most of them former Nazis, immediately seized the offensive. No longer hampered by the threat of intervention by the occupiers and enjoying the freedoms of a democratic climate, the SRP became postwar Germany's most serious effort to regroup Nazi activists. Its leaders spoke openly in support of Hitler and the Third Reich, propagated a new stab-in-the-back myth, and disparaged the notion of the Holocaust. They staged torchlight parades and assigned men wearing white shirts and red arm bands to keep order at rallies. In their speeches and publications they spewed out the grudges and propaganda of bygone days, and above all they attacked the FRG's liberalism and democratic principles. In 1951 the party even adopted Hitler's strictly hierarchical organizational principle, *Führerprinzip*.

When the SRP took 11 percent of the valid votes in Lower Saxony's parliamentary election in May 1951, winning 10 percent of the provincial parliamentary seats, the media in Germany and abroad suddenly became full of the party's outrages. Politically informed Americans wondered whether they were not witnessing the emergence of a new Nazi party—right under the eyes of the U.S. High Commission in Germany (see Middleton 1951; American Jewish Committee 1952). American politicians facing their own election in 1952 pressured HICOG officials, who asked their Reactions Analysis Staff to find out what was going on. Were West Germans succumbing so quickly and so submissively to a party committed to dismantling their democracy?

20. The 1949 electoral law distributed 400 seats, 240 of them in single-member constituencies and 160 according to a list (proportional representation) system, but required that, to gain any representation at all, a party had either to win a single-member constituency or gain 5 percent of the vote in any one province. Subsequent electoral laws raised the number of seats, gave constituencies and lists each half of the seats, and toughened the 5 percent hurdle by requiring that minimum percentage at the national rather than provincial level or, alternatively, winning elections in three constituencies.

HICOG pollsters learned that the SRP elicited little interest from the German-in-the-street. In May 1951 (HIC-87), two to three weeks after the SRP's stunning success in Lower Saxony, nearly two-thirds of West Germans and more than a third of Lower Saxons had not even heard of the party. The largest number of knowledgeable respondents described it not as a party offering something new but as an effort by former Nazis to restore the past. Five-sixths of a special sample of one hundred SRP adherents in Lower Saxony said the party aimed at both bettering economic and social conditions in Germany and expressing widespread discontent with the FRG's achievements, but barely half of other Lower Saxons and 42 percent of the rest of West Germans agreed. The reasons most frequently cited for SRP support were the FRG's "bad economic policy" (16 percent) and the feeling that "the government doesn't care for the little people" (15 percent). Almost nine in ten SRP sympathizers felt that the Western powers exerted too much influence on the FRG's decisions, and almost half of these went so far as to say that the Bonn government was merely a "puppet" of the "so-called" Allies.

A survey conducted a half-year later found little change. In November 1951 (HIC-118), only 4 percent more West Germans (from 37 to 41 percent) reported having heard of the SRP, and again the more knowledgeable respondents tagged the party as a neo-Nazi vehicle. When those aware of the SRP were asked why it had done so well in recent elections, the most common response, given by 8 percent of the entire sample, was that SRP voters were dissatisfied with the FRG's economic and social situation and attracted by National Socialism's social welfare ideas. Just as many said either that SRP voters hoped for personal advantages (4 percent) or that they simply liked the idea of National Socialism (4 percent).

Most West Germans did not take the SRP seriously. Except in Lower Saxony and in Bremen, where the party got 7.7 percent of the vote in October 1951, the SRP won little support in provincial parliamentary elections: 0.2 percent in North Rhine-Westphalia in June 1950, 1.6 percent in Schleswig-Holstein in July 1950, and 2.4 percent in Baden-Württemberg in March 1952. Nor did West Germans wish the SRP well. Of the 41 percent who by November 1951 had heard about the SRP (HIC-118) only one in twenty (2 percent of the entire sample) wanted to see the party flourish in West German politics and one in fourteen (3 percent of the total) hoped it would gain moderate influence. More than half wanted the SRP to have little influence (6 percent) or none at all (17 percent). Nine months later awareness of the SRP had grown, but so had opposition: 56 percent of a national sample had heard of the party, but almost four-fifths of those offering an opinion (44 percent of the total sample) expressed primarily negative views of the SRP, while only 6 percent had positive views (IfD-

1:274). Public opinion surveys also found virtually no electoral support: HICOG's election barometers carried out monthly from January to December 1952 (HIC-168; see IfD-1:255) found between 1 percent and less than a half of 1 percent saying they would cast their ballots for the SRP if the election were held "now."

West Germans' lack of interest in the SRP did not, however, mean that they felt comfortable with its presence. In May 1951 (HIC-87) more than a quarter considered it politically dangerous and 22 percent wanted to see it banned as an undemocratic party under the terms of Article 9(2) of the Basic Law. Why, West Germans were asked, did officials in Bonn want to prosecute and forbid the SRP—because it had the courage to speak truths to the West German government and occupying powers or because the party aimed at setting up a despotism? As many respondents in June 1952 suspected the latter as the former rationale (19 percent each) and another 11 percent agreed with both (IfD-1:274).[21] In January 1952 still less than a quarter favored proscribing the SRP and nearly a third did not (IfD-1:274), but after the Federal Constitutional Court banned the party in October 1952, 37 percent of respondents approved the decision, with 22 percent disapproving.

National Democratic Party (NPD). The Constitutional Court outlawed the Socialist Reich Party but could not quell the political yearnings of some former Nazis and their followers. SRP leaders simply joined other extreme right-wing parties to carry out business as usual. But the world in which that business took place was undergoing fundamental changes. The SRP's fate made it clear that neo-Nazism had its legal limits, and, besides, not many citizens thought it prudent or productive to oppose democracy outright. Most damaging to neo-Nazi ambitions, though, was the success of Chancellor Adenauer's conservative government. It was rebuilding the economy and providing other services, gaining Allied confidence, and winning public acceptance. Adenauer's Christian Democratic Union (CDU) and its Bavarian cohort, the Christian Social Union (CSU), won 49.9 percent of the Bundestag seats by 1953 and gained an absolute majority of 54.3 percent in 1957. This popular triumph made it difficult for the disputative neo- or would-be-Nazis to gain support.

---

21. This question followed one that, after cuing respondents about the SRP's leader and recent electoral success in Lower Saxony, nevertheless found 36 percent who had never heard of the party; the 51 percent no-response rate in the follow-up question addressed here includes these 36 percent plus 15 percent who claimed to know about the party but did not know or could not say why the West German government was trying to ban it. In a survey more than two years later 38 percent recalled that the proscription was due to the SRP's Nazi-like and antidemocratic character, and 6 percent said that the party had displeased the occupation powers (IfD-1:275).

These changing circumstances forced neo-Nazi movements and other ultraconservative parties to regroup. The German Community (*Deutsche Gemeinschaft*, or DG) split in 1950, with most members joining the broader Union of Expellees and Victims of Injustice (*Bund der Heimatvertriebenen und Entrechteten*, or BHE). Together with the German Party (*Deutsche Partei*, or DP), which before 1947 had been the Lower Saxon Provincial Party (*Niedersächsiche Landespartei*, or NLP), the BHE served in coalition governments with Adenauer; and for the 1961 federal election the BHE and DP merged into the All German Party (*Gesamtdeutsche Partei*, or GDP). Meanwhile, the spiritual successor of the SRP, the German Reich Party (*Deutsche Reichspartei*, or DRP), which in 1950 sprang from the earlier DRP (KV) and DRP/DKP, sought to make Nazism more acceptable to German voters.

Before the 1961 Bundestag election each of these parties had been running candidates in provincial and federal elections; some, notably the DG, BHE, and DP, though retaining elements of Nazi ideology, tried to distance themselves from the tainted past. Neither these parties nor the DRP, however, could overcome popular indifference. Public opinion surveys found them stagnant at low levels of support.[22] In the 1961 election the conservative GDP dropped to 2.8 percent of the vote from 8.0 percent in 1957, the DG remained constant at 0.1 percent, and the neo-Nazi DRP declined from 1.0 to 0.8 percent—none of them satisfying the 5 percent requirement for representation. At the same time they were losing membership and leaders to the more successful parties in Bonn. Those who remained pushed the ultraconservative groups increasingly toward the extreme right. Regrouping was needed again.

In November 1964 the DRP's leader, Adolph von Thadden, invited rump members of the BHE and DP to help found the National Democratic Party (*Nationaldemokratische Partei Deutschlands*).[23] The NPD soon established its preeminence among West Germany's extreme rightists. Balancing the requisites of partisan acceptability and constitutional legality, the NPD made its mark in several local and provincial elections. In November 1966 it won 7.9 percent of the provincial vote in Hesse and 7.4 percent in Bavaria, and five months later it claimed 6.9 percent in the Rhineland-Palatinate. Public opinion surveys showed a rise in support from 2 percent

22. Monthly polls (IfD-4:198–199) showed that the DP hovered around 4–6 percent beginning in January 1950 but declined to 1–2 percent around April 1961; the BHE, which enjoyed support of 7–11 percent beginning in July 1952, dropped to 2–3 percent by April 1961; and the GDP (which fused the DP and BHE) fell from 4 percent in May 1961 to 1 percent in August 1965.

23. Thadden explicitly excluded DG leaders, some of whom eventually merged with the German Freedom Party (*Deutsche Freiheitspartei*, or DFP) to form the neutralist Action Community of Independent Germans (*Aktionsgemeinschaft unabhängigen Deutschen*, or AUD).

in the first months of 1966 to 7 percent in summer 1968 (IfD-5:304–305). Many political observers in West Germany and abroad began to fear a resurgence of fascism and expected the NPD to clear the 5 percent hurdle in the federal parliamentary election of September 1969 (see Cameron 1966; Long 1968; Niethammer 1969).[24]

But this worst-case scenario was not played out. The NPD got 4.3 percent of the votes in the 1969 federal election and soon dropped out of provincial parliaments as well. What accounts for this meteoric rise and equally rapid fall of the NPD? Thadden and other party leaders attributed their early success to organizational talents and the persuasiveness of their message. These factors no doubt played a role, but other circumstances over which the NPD had no control gave the party an unexpected boost (see Nagle 1970; Klingemann and Pappi 1972; Stöss 1989/1991). One was an economic recession. Not having experienced unemployment or other economic difficulties since the early 1950s, West Germans were unnerved by an apparent economic crisis in 1966. A political crisis that fall exacerbated the people's anxiety. Chancellor Ludwig Erhard was forced to resign, and a "grand coalition" gave power to the CDU/CSU and Social Democratic Party (Sozialdemokratische Partei Deutschlands, or SPD), which between them controlled over 90 percent of Bundestag seats. In part as a result of what some termed an emerging "cartel of fear," unrest broke out in the universities and on the streets.

In short, the FRG's stability and its political viability came under threat in the late 1960s. What better time for a party such as the NPD to make mischief? Its leaders, who persistently inveighed against the manifest economic decline and political collapse of the FRG's vaunted democracy, solicited the support of anyone with a grievance, including even leftists who saw the grand coalition as a danger to democracy. The party offered a nostrum of solutions that would have delighted Josef Goebbels. For a short time the NPD gained some support from the disaffected—the high point was a 9.8 percent showing in Baden-Württemberg's provincial election of April 1968—but economic recovery, the grand coalition's ability to address important issues, the promise of return to political normalcy, and above all the NPD's failure to come up with new and interesting ideas made it decreasingly attractive to common citizens.[25] After the fed-

24. FRG judicial leaders overruled those who called for the NPD to be outlawed via Article 9(2) of the Basic Law; the experience of 1952 had demonstrated that such a step would give the party more attention than it deserved and would not prevent NPD members from replacing it with another, equally neo-Nazi party.

25. Before the 1969 election 2 percent or fewer thought that the NPD could best deal with such key issues as foreign policy, the economy, inflation, and education. Surveys in

eral election in September 1969 few West Germans (6 percent) expressed any regret that the party had gained no Bundestag seats. The NPD had already begun its slide into oblivion.

The Republicans (REPS). By the end of the 1970s neo-Nazism and perhaps even right-wing extremism seemed almost dead in the FRG. Observers agreed that some West Germans continued to be nationalistic, racist, and aggressive, and to harbor other attitudes reminiscent of Hitler and National Socialism. But this contingent could not translate these sentiments into effective political action. A survey in March 1980 found that 78 percent of West Germans did not think that radical right-wing groups posed a danger to the FRG. One in five did see a threat—largely because they feared a repetition of the country's history (20 percent), with its brutal terror (18 percent), weakened democracy (14 percent), and domestic unrest and fanaticism (13 percent). And 44 percent thought that those openly espousing National Socialism and its ideology should be ignored rather than turned into political martyrs (EMNID-32:6).

This complacency ended abruptly in September 1980 when a right-wing extremist planted a bomb that killed 13 and wounded 219 visitors to Munich's Oktoberfest.[26] In the following months neo-Nazi arsenals uncovered by police raids, shoot-outs between extremists and the police, and vandalism on Jewish gravestones suggested that the extreme right was shifting its strategy from partisan discourse to terrorism. The percentage seeing the radical right as a danger to German democracy grew from 20 percent in March 1980 to 56 percent the following fall and 78 percent in November 1981 (EMNID-33:12); the percentage in favor of prosecution for those who publicly praised National Socialism rose from 54 to 69 to 80 percent, respectively.[27] With the subsequent abatement of right-wing terrorism, concern diminished somewhat: the percentage describing the radical right as a danger to democracy dropped to 58 percent in March 1983 before rising to 71 percent in December 1983 and declining again to 62

January 1971 and November 1972 reported less than half of 1 percent crediting the NPD as the leader in these various areas (IfD-5:300–301).

26. The perpetrator, a member of a neo-Nazi paramilitary group (the Defense Sport Group, or *Wehrsportgruppe Hoffmann*) who evidently acted on his own behalf, was killed in the blast. The group was banned in 1980.

27. The right also threatened the left's predominant position as West Germany's leading terrorist danger. In March 1980, we have seen, only 20 percent saw any danger to democracy posed by the right. A year later, however, asked whether the radical right wing or the radical left wing was more dangerous, 9 percent expressed more concern with the right, 18 percent the left, and 66 percent both (EMNID-33:2/3). The same question asked in December 1981 elicited 15 percent for the right, 19 percent the left, and 60 percent both (EMNID-34:1/2). In each survey 5 percent attributed no danger to either.

percent in December 1985, but the willingness to prosecute rightists stayed at or above 70 percent (EMNID-37:9/10).

By this time various extreme right-wing groups were regrouping yet again. The most successful of these was the Republicans (*Die Republikaner*, or REPs). This party emerged in Bavaria in November 1983 under the leadership of two CSU defectors and a former television reporter who had gained notoriety with a provocative war memoir. Coalitions with other provincial groups eventually gave the REPs a national, if not wholly integrated, political base. The party had little immediate success: 3.0 percent in the Bavarian provincial election of October 1986, 1.2 percent in Bremen in September 1987, 1.0 percent in Baden-Württemberg in March 1988, and 0.6 percent in Schleswig-Holstein in May 1988. Disputes along regional lines further clouded the REPs' future.

But the party made a breakthrough in January 1989. Conducting an aggressively antiforeign campaign in West Berlin's provincial election, the REPs hit a raw nerve among voters. The city housed almost three hundred thousand foreign workers and their families—more than one in eight residents—and floods of ethnic Germans from Poland and other east European states, as well as asylum seekers from Sri Lanka and elsewhere, were coming in every day. Many West Berliners feared that this influx of foreigners was changing the city's character. The major parties skirted the issue and were indignant when the REPs chose chauvinistic confrontation as an election tactic. Some West Berliners saw this truculence as reason enough to vote for the REPs. The party also benefited from its own notoriety. Public attacks on the party's ideology and a bloody demonstration aimed at preventing a REPs rally not only captured voters' attention but also gave the party a public relations windfall: it could both lampoon fearful democrats who would abridge a tiny party's freedom of speech and underscore its own pledge once in office to ensure law and order. The REPs gained a reputation as a party of political protest and action.

When the REPs got 7.5 percent of the vote and 11 parliamentary seats in West Berlin, the alarming news quickly went around the world.[28] The party won 6.6 percent of the vote in Hesse's communal elections six weeks later. In June 1989 it entered the international arena. Winning 7.1 percent of the West German vote, the REPs placed six representatives in the European Parliament. Meanwhile, support for the party in public opinion surveys rose from 4 percent in February 1989 to 7 percent in May and June

28. West Berlin's peculiar legal status at the time, under Allied control, ensured that the REPs members would then be sent to the Bundestag—like other West Berlin representatives, without a formal vote.

of that year (Vor 1990). The REPs appeared to be a radical right-wing party on the rise.

But support soon began to wane. The REPs' poll rating slipped to 6 percent in fall 1989 and 2 percent a year later. In the first all-German federal election, in December 1990, the party garnered only 2.1 percent, still almost a million votes.[29] Subsequent surveys found the REPs hovering between one and two points, and party support fell to 1.9 percent in the federal election of October 1994.

These shifts raise two questions about the REPs' future. First, what counts for the decline before 1992? One cause was doubtless the euphoria that swept through Germany after the Berlin Wall opened in November 1989. The move toward merging East and West Germany simultaneously strengthened support for Chancellor Helmut Kohl—who quickly assumed the role of his country's unifier—and weakened any activity or political party that might endanger unity. All other issues, including those that had attracted voters to the REPs, became secondary to unification. But the party was the victim less of unforeseen circumstances than of its own internecine struggles, which spawned divisions and withdrawals (Gewaltige 1990). The party's representatives in West Berlin's parliament split into two factions that eventually became separate parties. Such conflict in turn succored rival parties that claimed best to represent the German right.

And the gains of other right-wing groups at the expense of the REPs raises the second question: Is the party's decline permanent? Surveys conducted in spring 1992 (FDP-Wähler 1992), when the REPs rebounded to 5 percent, suggest not. That this new support materialized just as anti-foreign protests broke out in Germany is not coincidental. Germans increasingly complained that the growing influx of refugees from developing countries and ethnic Germans from eastern Europe was destroying German society. Processing the asylants' papers and caring for them while their applications were under review was expensive. Those who found work were taking jobs from German citizens at a time of national economic stringency. And the government's open migration policy undermined its own efforts to use scarce resources to integrate the two Germanies. The government, however, seemed helpless: immigrants were coming into Germany at the rate of more than a thousand per day.

Such a situation was ideal for the REPs and other right-wing extremists—and they quickly exploited it. While the major parties sought to determine what was both fair to the immigrants and acceptable to

29. The REPs got 2.0 percent of the list votes in the former West German territory, 0.1 percent in former East Germany, and 4.1 percent in united Berlin. It thus got parliamentary seats at neither the federal nor provincial level.

Germans, rightists, demanding to "keep Germany German," staged public protests and violent attacks on foreigners. The government could control demonstrations, arrest criminals, and issue endless public statements, but neither the government nor the major parties could deal with the root of the problem: what could be done about the number of foreigners pouring into the land?

By the end of 1991, as the problem became acute, public opinion began to shift perceptibly. Surveys conducted from September 1991 to June 1992, after first noting that the issue of immigration had encouraged the rise of right-wing radical tendencies, asked respondents whether they sympathized with these tendencies (FDP-Wähler 1992:47). The number of respondents expressing such sympathies declined from 34 percent in September 1991 to 24 percent in December. From there, though, it rose to 25 percent in February, 33 percent in April, and 38 percent in June 1992.[30] Was German democracy endangered by radical and extremist movements? In spring 1992 (Wild 1992:69), 52 percent of Germans thought it was.

Right-Wing Extremism After the Occupation

A half-century of right-wing extremism in postwar Germany defies instant summaries. Some themes, nevertheless, are consistent. First, the radical right never possessed a unified perspective that could rally the masses. Each individual group had its own core principles, some of which hewed closely to the gospel according to Adolf Hitler, others of which diverged strikingly, in ways that left the various perspectives incompatible. What linked the parties was faith—faith that somehow, and notwithstanding his egregious blunders, Hitler had been on the right track. It was the responsibility of postwar Germans to realize the Führer's quest for an ideal Germany. What this shared dream meant in practice, however, was the source of bitter dispute.

Second, unable to agree on a unified perspective, the radical right's individual parties and other groupings fought resolutely to protect their own, independent views of what that perspective should be. Leaders of different groups found it difficult to function effectively in unison, and enduring coalitions proved illusory. This inability to coalesce was due only in part to ideological conflict among right-wing extremists. To a greater extent it represented a strategic decision diversely executed but frequently repeated—a penchant to pursue the chimera of ideological

30. Contrary to the conventional wisdom that right-wing extremism is erupting primarily in the former GDR, 41 percent of western Germans and only 27 percent of eastern Germans expressed sympathy for the movement's views in June 1992.

purity rather than the election victories that would produce political power. The extreme right could not find an integrator of Adenauer's caliber to bring it political success.

More germane to this chapter is yet a third point: most West German citizens wanted nothing to do with these navel-gazing ideologues, these quaint vestiges of a dead past who were futilely trying to resurrect it. Hitler and Nazism had failed disastrously. Though both had their good points, though neither was as unmitigatingly evil as the victorious Allies painted them, hitching the new Germany's star to them seemed, however romantic, politically foolhardy and even self-destructive. Public opinion polls and voting patterns persistently showed that few postwar Germans would support the SRP, NPD, REPS, or any other party that smacked of neo-Nazism. One after another, each radical right-wing party withered and died.

But this persistent failure does not mean that the FRG housed (or houses) no chauvinists, anti-Semites, racists, warmongers, dreamers of a restored feudal aristocracy, and other ultraconservatives eager to revoke the political developments of the past century. Such extremists exist in every country, and postwar Germany is no exception. The FRG is unique only in isolating them. It established new legal norms—Article 9(2) of the Basic Law, for instance, which curtails antidemocratic activities, and legislation enforced by judicial sanctions that prohibit baiting any group, including but not restricted to foreigners and Jews. At the very least such steps make those harboring antidemocratic sentiments hesitate to act them out or even express them in public. The FRG's successive governments, moreover, extended these legal norms to international affairs. Adenauer's support of Israel, Brandt's policy toward eastern Europe, Kohl's push toward a united Germany and a European Union, and similar measures have demonstrated to Germans that international cooperation works. Such gains, and five decades of economic growth and stability at home, make it difficult for neo-Nazi ideologues to gainsay their country's postwar accomplishments and unlikely that common citizens will jeopardize a democratic future for another radical right will-o'-the-wisp.

Concern with right-wing extremism in Germany is not misplaced, however. Although no evidence other than our memories of events that took place a half-century ago suggests that anti-Semitic outbursts are more likely to occur in the FRG than, say, in France or Poland, drastic changes in the world's political climate can change the behavior of any state.[31] A more persuasive reason for vigilance, though, is that right-wing

31. Germans have sometimes seemed fascinated by what the ancient Roman historian Tacitus (c.98/1970) termed a *furor teutonicus*, or German savagery, a tendency,

extremism has served a recurrent if not decisive function in postwar West German politics. The fear it engenders in the hearts of some compatriots, not to speak of many foreign observers, makes it a useful political tool.

Voting for such parties, or telling a survey interviewer of one's intention to vote for them, may reflect less acceptance of the parties themselves than a desire to express dissatisfaction with the ruling parties. If the influx of foreigners is your key concern, and if the main parties are unwilling or unable to address the issue, then how better to express your dissatisfaction than by supporting the right-wing extremist party that promises to deal appropriately with this problem? You may make this gesture even though you know that the party is unlikely either to gain parliamentary representation or, if it does, to carry out its announced policies. The goal is primarily to shake up the political establishment, to force the established parties to deal seriously with your concerns as a citizen. Similarly, disaffected youths such as the skinheads of the 1980s and 1990s can bring public attention to their perceived plight by smearing swastikas on Jewish gravestones, donning black shirts and other trappings of Nazism, and shouting "Sieg Heil!" at public meetings (Jugend 1990).

Politics as a theater for protest and self-expression poses a dilemma for democratic societies. Some citizens can claim that their civil rights have been violated irrespective of whether the theatrical gestures are countenanced or suppressed. One does not have to be Jewish to feel outraged by the latest act of anti-Semitic vandalism. And antiforeign demonstrations menace the myriad of Turkish workers and asylum seekers residing in Germany. But governments have found more effective means than police truncheons to address the legitimate concerns of their protesters.[32] It is this challenge—and not the phony threat of resurgent Nazism—that the Federal Republic continues to face.

Opposition from the Left

This chapter's focus on Nazism and later extreme right-wing parties slights another important aspect of postwar Germany's politics:

---

when thwarted, to respond both irrationally and violently. For some, the threat of resurgent Nazism has been a useful instrument, for example, to badger the Allies into concessions. In 1965 Franz Josef Strauss, the longtime leader of Bavaria's csu, Adenauer's former defense minister, and fifteen years later the cdu/csu candidate for chancellor, asserted that if Germany was subjected to "military discrimination" as it had been under the Treaty of Versailles, then a "new Führer-type . . . would promise and probably also acquire nuclear weapons" (T. Hamilton 1965). In general, however, the political effectiveness of the furor teutonicus is more persuasive in mythology than reality.

32. Chapters 8 and 13 return to the question of whether the antiforeign attacks of the 1990s might be expected to have a more lasting impact.

communism and the political left in general. The German left has a
rich but fragmented history. It developed before the German émigré Karl
Marx wrote his political tracts in London and before the formation of
social democracy in the 1860s. Equally long is the history of sectarianism
in the German left. The Social Democratic Party (SPD) set aside this tendency until World War I and the rocky months that followed, when splin-
tering produced several new socialist parties, including the Communist Party of Germany (*Kommunistische Partei Deutschlands*, or KPD). The
dream of socialist unity survived, but the multiplicity of parties raised a
practical question: Who would structure and who lead the unified movement to broaden the political force of the working class?

The events of the 1920s and 1930s scuttled any potential alliance between the traditional SPD and the burgeoning KPD. German communists,
expecting Soviet leadership in the inevitable worldwide revolution, saw
no reason to tolerate old-guard socialists. In the last years of the Weimar
Republic the two parties' thugs—as well as various right-wingers—even
engaged in street battles. But KPD strategists soon concluded that informal
alliance with National Socialists would serve multiple purposes: destroy
the Weimar system, force social democrats to accept KPD leadership, and
outmaneuver the Nazis for ultimate power over Germany. When the strategy failed, SPD and KPD stalwarts suffered severely under Nazism. An effort
in the 1930s to bring the parties together showed promise while communists were fighting fascists in the Spanish civil war but collapsed after the
Molotov-Ribbentrop pact of August 1939 led to German and Soviet inva-
sions of Poland and, within Germany, strained efforts at Nazi-communist
collaboration.

Post–World War II social democrats were therefore highly skeptical
about the KPD's future role in Germany. SPD leaders had learned to trust
neither the treacherous German communists nor their fickle comrades in
Moscow, who had other, non-German fish to fry. Relations worsened in
the first occupation year. To the surprise and dismay of German and
Soviet communists, the expected flight of the German people to the "truly"
antifascist KPD did not take place. The KPD's fawning obeisance to Moscow
undercut its appeal, as did memories of the party's past duplicity, Nazism's intense antibolshevik propaganda, and the Red Army's behavior in
defeated Germany. Few took seriously the KPD's new olive branch of
working-class solidarity.

If the communists could not win over the social democrats, their strategists decided, then they needed to outmaneuver the SPD by merging all the
socialist parties into the KPD. By the end of 1945 the Soviet Military Government (SMG) began forcing the SPD to merge with the KPD, and by April of
the following year it had put loyal Stalinists in command of a new Social-

ist Unity Party (*Sozialistische Einheitspartei Deutschlands*, or SED). SPD leaders in the western zones of Germany and sectors of Berlin, most notably Kurt Schumacher (see Edinger 1965), staunchly resisted. The SED became eastern Germany's dominant party, but in the West the SPD and KPD remained separate.[33] Among most German leftists, the communists' naked power play rankled—as did the SED's subservience to Soviet dictates.

Conservatives in western Germany would have preferred to see the KPD banned outright, but Four-Power occupation made this impracticable. Still, the party was not doing well. Only 2–3 percent of AMZON Germans said in 1945–1946 that they would vote for the KPD (OMG-3, 26, 60). In the first national parliamentary election of August 1949 (OMG-191; IfD-1) 5.7 percent of the voters supported the KPD, but four years later the number dwindled to 2.2 percent (R. Merritt 1980a). FRG lawyers, meanwhile, updating a penal code from the 1870s, made more specific the circumstances in which anticonstitutional political parties could be banned. Various rules applied to the KPD: subverting the state (the party had called for an overthrow of the "Bonn regime"), acting as an agent of a foreign power (that is, the Soviet Union), and more generally pursuing an "overall goal and activities" consistent with "Marxism-Leninism." Eventually the Federal Constitutional Court agreed to deal with the charges filed in 1951 by the FRG's prosecuting attorney. In August 1956 the court outlawed the KPD (Kluth 1959; Brünneck 1978).[34]

For the next two decades German leftists found it difficult to maintain a voice in the FRG's public forum. Soviet and East German totalitarianism had discredited communism's serviceability as a barrier to rightist encroachments into the citizen's daily life. In 1959 the SPD itself abandoned Marxism as one of the party's fundamental tenets, undercutting left-of-center social democrats. Moreover, general acceptance of cold-war rhetoric disheartened leftists who sought political change but not revolution. The replacement in 1966 of Chancellor Ludwig Erhard's conservative-liberal coalition with Kurt-Georg Kiesinger's "grand coalition" of center-right (CDU/CSU) and center-left (SPD) posed another kind of threat, especially given the SPD's abandonment of Marxism. The grand coalition parties, which together controlled 90 percent of the Bundestag seats, had the power to alter the FRG's political system dramatically.

In such a conservative environment, unreceptive to experiment, how could those to the left of center sustain and enhance the gains they had

33. Because of the city's Four-Power status, the SED continued to exist in the western sectors. Similarly, the SPD remained in East Berlin until it dissolved itself in August 1961.

34. The party would, in slightly modified form, be resurrected in September 1968 as the German Communist Party (*Deutsche Kommunistische Partei*, or DKP).

made in democratizing Germany? Their own party, the century-old SPD, seemed to be flirting with the right; and the Free Democratic Party (FDP), the only other party evidently capable of surmounting the 5 percent barrier, was as economically conservative as it was tiny. Some leftist theoreticians concluded that their only hope was to initiate an "extraparliamentary" opposition (*Ausserparlamentarische Opposition*, or APO)—a loose consortium of groupings distressed by the FRG's direction, groupings prepared to protest, resist passively, and even disrupt the staid sociopolitical canons of German life.

What later came to be called APO began with unrest in West Berlin. Students at the city's Free University took first to the lecture halls and then to the streets to protest the "cartel of fear" said to characterize West German politics under the grand coalition, as well as conditions at the Free University, U.S. involvement in Vietnam, and a visit by the Persian shah. Bewildered police officers, who did not know how to deal with public demonstrations, only fanned these small flames of dissent. Dissent eventually spread to every major urban center and university town, giving voice to a potpourri of groups that opposed nuclear power plants, environmental pollution, airport expansion, sexual discrimination, and a host of other social ills.

Dissent turned increasingly violent. Most German protesters followed the model pioneered at the University of California: provocation, designed to shake the complaisant into an awareness of sociopolitical wrongs and to inspire appropriate action. Protests organized loosely around the inchoate APO baited the police; scribbled slogans on public walls shocked those who value, above all, law and order in their public lives. Protestors increasingly turned to force and violence to accomplish their ends, in part because state authorities had set a brutal precedent. Bloody confrontations assumed an almost ritualistic character.

The very intellectual and geographical diffuseness of the era of unrest makes it difficult to say who its prime movers were and what they wanted. Activists represented a broad political spectrum. Their motivations ranged from idealism to an urgency to be where "the action" was—perhaps to bash a few heads and rob a few banks. The most visible leaders came from the left, though, and because their demands for sociopolitical change were so far-reaching, many Germans found it easy to identify them as the radical left and to equate them with the long-hated, treacherous Bolsheviks. Adding credence to this image, protests and violence continued long after September 1969, when the social democratic–liberal coalition assumed power in Bonn; ongoing protests fueled a growing fear that radicals sought if not to overthrow the government then at least to reduce its capacity to govern.

The protest movement shifted dramatically in the 1970s. One wing moved toward new forms of political activism. Some joined the SPD— although many social democrats were outraged by Chancellor Willy Brandt's "radicals decree" (*Radikalenerlass*) of 1972, which denied to unspecified "radicals" access to public-sector jobs (G. Braunthal 1990). Others created their own special interest groups or formed political parties, such as the Greens, to compete in the democratic process. Another much smaller wing turned to terrorism, justifying its acts in terms of the need for sociopolitical change and the inability of the current political system to accomplish it. As such terrorists as Ulrike Meinhof and Andreas Baader and such organizations as the Red Army Faction gained notoriety, growing numbers of Germans became alarmed with the terrorist threat.[35]

In spite of the sound and fury, in spite of the kidnappings and murders, the protest movement that began in the late 1960s did not radicalize German political society. Left-wing terrorism abated—in part, as we have seen in this chapter, only to be replaced in the late 1980s by right-wing terrorism.[36] West Germany's "danger" from the left diminished even more at the decade's end when East Germany began to fall apart. New GDR authorities and, eventually, those working under a united Germany not only offered information about the GDR's network of contacts with West German terrorists but also turned over to western offices suspected terrorists still under their jurisdiction. The SED also disintegrated. In the absence of overpowering governmental pressure, and given the opportunity denied since 1946, many SED members turned or returned to the SPD. Others regrouped under a new Party of Democratic Socialism (*Partei des demokratischen Sozialismus*, or PDS). The PDS gained some eastern German support in the parliamentary election of December 1990 but did not clear the 5 percent hurdle among western German voters.[37] In the October 1994 federal election, however, four PDS members won single-member constituency seats.

Only in part has the German left been restored to the status it enjoyed before the 1930s, but it continues to be a potent factor in political decision

35. In the polls of the mid- and late 1970s, terrorism was ranked as the second-most-significant problem facing the FRG, behind only immediate social crises (IfD-5:463–464, 5:101–103).

36. According to the Federal Office for the Protection of the Constitution ("Bestie . . ." 1992:25) acts of violence by left-wing extremists, which numbered 1,904 in 1986, diminished to fewer than 600 in 1990 before rising to 703 in 1992. Acts of violence by right-wing extremists, 189 in 1986, rose to more than 300 in 1990 and 2,003 in 1992. Leftists charge that police and judicial officers pursue the left more forcefully than the right.

37. In the dual system of the 1990 election, the PDS obtained 11.1 percent of the vote in the ex-GDR, which gave it 17 Bundestag seats, and, in the old Federal Republic, 0.3 percent and no seats. The SPD got 36.7 percent in the West and 24.3 percent in the East.

making. Years of national, provincial, and local leadership in the FRG have removed both the SPD's earlier stains of disloyalty to the German nation and its image as a home for mindless ideologues who can disrupt but not govern. Those who see the left not as a party but as a philosophy of governance weathered the isolation of the Adenauer era and, afterward, accusations of serving if not engendering the agents of terror.

• •

FIVE

Nazi Crimes Against the World

In summer 1939 most of the world seemed willing to treat Hitler and Nazism as a peculiarly German problem. Deplorable, yes, and meriting vigilance, but not something requiring intervention. Besides, what right had other countries to intervene? Germany had violated the Versailles Treaty, but even political leaders and citizens beyond Germany's boundaries felt that the victors of World War I had dealt unfairly with Germany and that almost two decades later the terms of the treaty were no longer valid. Moreover, Hitler insisted after the rape of Czechoslovakia that Germany had no further territorial demands on its European neighbors. Many observers assumed that time and the vicissitudes of domestic politics would tame Hitler's fury.

The invasion of Poland on 1 September forced Europeans to take seriously the German threat. The Blitzkrieg soon gave way to the "phony war," however, when Britain and France, no longer able to defend their Polish ally, began planning their own defenses. By spring 1940 it was clear that Hitler's Germany aimed at imposing its "new order" on the whole of western Europe, and by spring 1941 this dream of conquest had expanded to include the Soviet Union. The rest of the world had no option left but to condemn—and try to block—this naked aggression by Germany and its fascist cohorts, Italy and Japan.

Even so, for many observers Hitler's war represented international politics as usual (see A. Taylor 1961). Germany, they said, was doing little more than what other nation-states had always done and by which, when successful, they profited enormously. This is not to say that those holding this view liked what they saw. Most agreed that Germany was a menace that had somehow to be stopped, but the war itself was akin to an industrial accident—something that occurs from time to time even if we take preventive measures.

This opinion changed as World War II dragged on. The rest of the world began to see that Hitler's war was in fact different from those of years gone by. Its aims were not merely territorial aggrandizement, or loot, or increasing population size. It was a kind of war not fought in civilized Europe since the early Middle Ages—although some states had carried out such wars elsewhere against non-European populations. The goals of this war included extirpating or enslaving peoples who did not fit into German notions of the "Aryan" race. The consequence was a network of death camps where millions of Jews, Gypsies, homosexuals, Seventh Day Adventists, Russians, Poles, and other "inferior races" were slaughtered. No objective person, having learned what Germans had done ostensibly in the names of Christianity, the German nation, and a half-baked ideology, could claim that Hitler's war simply reflected the norms of international politics.[1]

But how did the German people view the war that they had fought and the crimes against humanity it had wrought? How did they account for what had taken place—not only the initiation of modern history's most destructive conflict but also the systematic extermination of masses in the Holocaust, as it has come to be called? Who or what was responsible for this horrendous event? This chapter examines how postwar West Germans responded to such questions that were posed formally in public opinion surveys. It also goes beyond these public responses to explore more deeply the ways in which Germans sought to come to terms with Nazi crimes against the world.

The Unprecedented War

Perhaps the most significant consequence of Nazism for most Germans was World War II. They had suffered terrible losses during the fighting, and afterward they were left with a country in ruins, occupied by foreign troops. American occupation authorities readily granted that Germans understood the consequences of the war. The question was whether or not the same Germans understood the causes of the conflict. Little doubt troubled the Americans themselves: Germans had unleashed the dogs of war in a mad effort to rule Europe and even the world. But which Germans? The brown-shirted, swastika-bedecked leaders who strutted about claiming the glory of world conquerors, or everyone who had grown up in German society?

The question of responsibility was important for an American occupation policy whose goal was to transform Germany into a peaceable democracy. If Nazi leaders were the culprits and common citizens the hapless

---

1. Of course, as we shall see in Chapter 8, some in Germany and elsewhere have made such claims.

tools of their machinations, then policy might simply remove these leaders from positions of power and influence, punish them as a cautionary lesson for would-be aggressors of the future, and identify the unencumbered democrats who could rule a future Germany. If, however, Nazi leaders only carried out acts sprung from the deepest roots of German society, then a mere change of governmental personnel would serve no purpose in the long run. Americans could reach no consensus on which of these extreme positions more accurately explained World War II.

To assess responsibility American occupation authorities first examined records to ascertain what had taken place during the Nazi era: who had done what to whom and in what circumstances. But they also felt obliged to plumb the labyrinthine dimensions of the "German soul": Were Germans inherently militaristic? Were they fated, unless controlled firmly by the Allies, to spawn yet another war? Answering this question was the special task of the OMGUS surveying unit.

What caused the war? From its inception the OMGUS surveying unit assessed German attitudes about war in general and about responsibility for the war just past. Surveys in April 1946 and August 1947 were inconclusive (see Table 5.1). Few respondents associated themselves publicly with overt warmongering: war for self-glorification, war to increase wealth, war as heroism and courage that ennoble the society, war as justification of the soldier's privileged status, war as the mother of inventions, war as legitimating such strategies as preemptive strikes against putative enemies. American-zone Germans had experienced war recently enough to eschew its romantic aura. But between a quarter and half of the respondents accepted propositions describing war as a natural, socially determined phenomenon. Sometimes, they said, war is even the most bearable of existing alternatives. A military presence is for this reason the nation-state's best defense.

Whether German responses to these questions were unique is impossible to determine. Perhaps random samples of Americans or French or Britons would respond similarly to similar questions.[2] OMGUS officers were divided on the question, and many Germans resented bitterly the easy assumption that their people were distinctly warlike. But the data

---

2. An expectation of violence dominated thinking in many countries. Surveys in late 1948 found that 32 percent of British-zone Germans believed both that "it will be possible for all countries to live together at peace with each other" and that this was "likely to happen" (Buchanan and Cantril 1953). The figures for the British zone of Berlin were 20 percent in August 1948 and 14 percent in October 1949. Surveys in other countries found less confidence in the possibility and probability of peaceful interaction: 11 percent in France, 10 percent in the United Kingdom, 8 percent in the United States, 7 percent in Italy, 5 percent in Norway, and 3 percent in the Netherlands.

Table 5.1 Public Attitudes Toward Militarism, 1946–1947

Percentage Giving "Agree" or "Disagree" Responses

	Agree	Disagree
Only by war can the human spirit be glorified.	2	95
There is some advantage in war (in contrast to "it doesn't pay to conduct a war").*	2	94
Fear is [not] natural, and those people showing their fear when faced with a dangerous situation should [not] be treated with understanding.	4	94
A man who shows no heroism or courage is unworthy.	7	91
The strength of a nation is weakened by democracy.	8	83
A civilian is an unworthy (lower) person compared to a member of the army.	9	89
In all probability foreign nations and races are enemies; therefore, one should be prepared at all times to attack them first.	10	82
The weakness of most West European schools is based on their lack of military discipline.	13	66
In general it's better to be on the winning side in a war than on the right side.*	18	74
The experience of enduring bombing and shellfire strengthens a man's character.	26	67
The Allies are absolutely [un]justified in not allowing Germany to have an army.	26	47
It is [not] a sign of weakness in a people's character to instigate a war.	27	59
The greatest strength of the American democracy is . . . based on its military power.	28	55
Our nation can . . . assume that other nations will attack her if we are on good terms with these nations.	29	64
A nation's rights are determined by that nation's power.	30	58
A man . . . improve[s] his character through bombing or shelling an unfortified village.	36	59
The education of children should . . . be based on military principles.	38	60
Democracy is a good form of government because it can develop a superior armed force.	38	44
A soldier has [a] claim to . . . special respect.	43	49

continued

Table 5.1   Continued

Percentage Giving "Agree" or "Disagree" Responses		
	Agree	Disagree
Germany should be allowed to have an army in order to be able to defend herself against aggression from other European nations.	44	47

Sources: OMG-19 (April 1946); and, indicated by asterisks (*), OMG-82 (August 1947).
Note: Wording sometimes emended—usually by adding or subtracting the word "not"—to make questions consistent in the response categories.

raise a second, ancillary question that is worth exploring: To what extent did individual respondents give internally consistent responses? That is, did those who gave "nondemocratic" answers to one question give similar responses to another one? The OMGUS research team used eleven Guttmann scales to evaluate such an issue (OMG-19; for notations see Chapter 4, note 1). The relevant scale here, "war and militarism," tabulated each person's "democratic" responses to five items.[3] More than four of five interviewees gave "democratic" responses to all five questions (43 percent) or to four of them (38 percent). Another 13 percent gave three such responses.[4] Barely one in twenty showed reluctance to endorse democracy, responding "democratically" to two questions (4-plus percent), one (1-plus percent), or none (less than 0.5 percent). In short, in spring 1946 very few American-zone Germans expressed hard-core militarism—and perhaps the climate of anti-democratic thinking was in fact no greater in postwar Germany than elsewhere.

Turning from philosophic perspectives to interpretations of recent history, responses to questions posed in April 1946 reveal a modest degree of consensus about responsibility for the war's outbreak (OMG-19). An average of more than two-thirds assigned blame to Germany: 80 percent said that Germany's own urge to dominate had led to its misfortune, 67 percent said that the country's neighbors had been nonaggressive, and 56 percent said that not only was Germany responsible, but its "leaders should . . . be

3. Whereas Table 5.1 reports the number of respondents reporting only "yes" or "no," the "war and militarism" scale also includes "no response."
4. Interviewees giving responses they evidently thought would please the American occupiers—that is, scoring high on OMGUS's "Flattery(?) Scale" by agreeing, for example, that "Germany has no musical genius to compare with the American Deems Taylor"—were somewhat less apt to take "democratic" positions on the "war and militarism" scale than were respondents not seeking to ingratiate themselves (OMG-19; Krugman 1949).

held as war criminals." Almost a quarter of the respondents, though, shifted blame to others, citing most often a conspiracy by other nation-states (19 percent), international bankers and the communists (18 percent), and the Versailles Treaty's injustice (32 percent).[5]

Later surveys dealt more directly with the central question—Who caused the war?—and asked respondents to name as perpetrators either Germany, other countries, or particular circumstances. In three surveys from November 1947 to September 1949 a growing number, averaging about a third of the respondents (26, 34, and 37 percent, respectively), cited Germany's responsibility. About a fifth that many (4, 7, and 9 percent, respectively) blamed foreign countries. A much larger but declining percentage (55, 41, and 36 percent, respectively) refused to fix direct blame exclusively on either Germany or the Allies.[6]

The results show moderate consensus among American-zone Germans, but an examination of the "particular circumstances" cited provides useful insights. In the September 1949 survey (HIC-1), more than a third of the respondents said that Germany caused World War II, and 9 percent blamed other countries. But 36 percent found less direct or one-sided causes of war: 4 percent indirectly blamed Germany by focusing on Hitler and the Nazi government, 13 percent said that Germany and other countries were jointly responsible, 12 percent blamed other countries indirectly, and the remaining 7 percent spoke of world conditions such as the capitalist system or the inevitability of war.[7] Figure 5.1 regroups the responses accordingly, showing that three of four respondents assigned responsibility to one or more countries or governments. Of that group 72 percent thought Germany or the Nazis responsible in part or in full for World War II and 45 percent thought other countries were.

By the mid-1950s, increasing numbers of Germans viewed their country as responsible for the war. Forty-three percent of a national sample put the blame on Germany in May 1955, 50 percent in May 1959, and 62 percent in spring 1967. Meanwhile, far smaller numbers named other countries as the aggressors (14, 11, and 8 percent, respectively), or said that both Germany and other countries were to blame (15, 10, and 8 percent, respectively). The percentage attributing the war to international

5. In response to another question, about half (53 percent) assigned blame to miscommunication: "Because other nations do not understand Germany, diplomatic relations are often strained."

6. The second survey was conducted in January 1949. The share not responding was 15 percent in 1947 and 18 percent in both 1949 surveys.

7. Most respondents who faulted other countries indirectly said that these neighbors envied Germany (5 percent), denied its territorial right to *Lebensraum* (4 percent), or imposed on it the unfair dictates of Versailles. A few blamed other countries for recognizing or protecting Hitler.

Figure 5.1

Responsibility for World War II, September 1949

Question: In your opinion, who was mainly responsible for the last war—Germany, other countries, or particular circumstances? If the last: What were they?

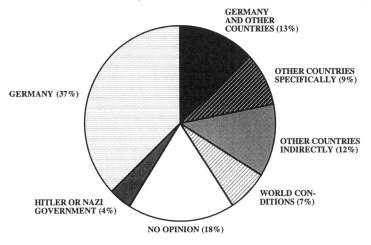

GERMANY
AND OTHER
COUNTRIES (13%)

OTHER COUNTRIES
SPECIFICALLY (9%)

GERMANY (37%)

OTHER COUNTRIES
INDIRECTLY (12%)

WORLD CON-
DITIONS (7%)

HITLER OR NAZI
GOVERNMENT (4%)

NO OPINION (18%)

Source: HIC-1.

capitalism or simply to fate remained small (9, 11, and 6 percent, respectively). In seven surveys conducted from October 1951 to May 1967 an average of 48 percent of respondents cited Germany as the cause for the war, 12 percent blamed other countries, 11 percent Germany and other countries, and 9 percent other causes, with 20 percent not knowing or not saying. Figure 5.2 shows, as percentages of those citing any country (an average of 72 percent for the entire sample), the changing share of both those mentioning Germany and those mentioning other countries. These data verify a building consensus—but by no means unanimity—on German responsibility for World War II.

Who lost the war? OMGUS pollsters, for whatever reason, never asked Germans why the Third Reich lost World War II. Not until the creation of the Federal Republic in 1949 renewed prospects of German rearmament did popular images of the country's past military effectiveness become a focus of surveys. We saw in Table 5.1 that substantial numbers of American-zone citizens thought that Germany needed an army. But what did lessons of the past tell us about the kind of military establishment it should have? Should the Wehrmacht be recreated, or was it forever discredited not only by its battlefield losses but by its National Socialist politicization? Would

Figure 5.2

What Country Started World War II? 1951-1967

Question: It is of course hard to say, but what would you think—Who actually is guilty
that in 1939 the war broke out?

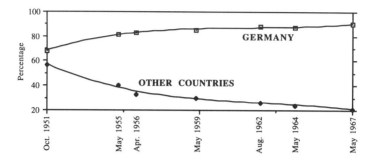

GERMANY: y = 68.094 + 0.41952x - 3.2436e-3x^2 + 8.7154e-6x^3   R^2 = 0.992   F-Ratio = 132.1   Prob < 0.001

OTHERS: y = 57.039 - 0.58716x + 3.9814e-3x^2 - 1.0060e-5x^3   R^2 = 0.989   F-Ratio = 93.6   Prob < 0.002

Source: IfD-4:146.

a refurbished military create a new stab-in-the-back legend, this time
blaming Germany's defeat on Hitler's amateurish meddling, on domestic
sabotage, or on foreign conspiracies?

The first HICOG survey in September 1949 (HIC-1) explored the perceived impact of conflict between the government and the military. It
posed questions in the form of two independent, mutually incompatible
propositions: first, Germany would have won had Hitler left fighting the
war up to the generals; and, second, Germany would have won had the
officers always carried out Hitler's wartime decisions and orders. One in
six American-zone residents accepted the first proposition and two-thirds
rejected it. One in nine, predominantly younger men, accepted the second
proposition and nearly three-fourths rejected it. As many as 28 percent,
then, blamed faulty leadership—either political or military—for the lost
war.[8]

A series of national samples from March 1950 to spring 1967 used a
more open-ended question but produced similar findings in assigning
responsibility for Germany's defeat (Table 5.2). If we collapse six individual responses—Hitler, generally bad leadership and policies, wrong conduct of war, German disunity, National Socialism and Hitler, and Germany's Jewish policy—into a single category of improper, confused, or
just plain bad leadership, then we find that over the 27 years this category

8. The maximum figure of 28 percent assumes that the 17 percent decrying Hitler's
bungling were distinct from the 11 percent complaining about the generals.

Table 5.2 The Lost War, 1950–1967

Responses to the Question:
What in your view is the cause for Germany losing the war? (percentages)

	Mar. 1950	Dec. 1952	May 1959	Apr./May 1967	Average
Faulty leadership	44	44	35	46	42
Hitler	11	13	11	17	13
Generally bad leadership, bad policies	15	14	9	12	13
Wrong conduct of war	6	6	6	9	7
German disunity (between party, Wehrmacht, SS)	7	6	6	3	6
National Socialism, Hitler	4	4	1	2	3
Germany's persecution of Jews	1	1	2	3	2
Own weaknesses, enemy's strength	33	32	40	34	35
Internal strife: Treason, sabotage	25	23	15	10	18
Miscellaneous	19	20	22	25	22
Germany attacked from all sides, worldwide hatred against Germany	2	—	—	—	1
Espionage	1	—	0	0	0
Other	6	10	8	5	7
Didn't say, didn't know	10	10	14	20	14

Sources: IfD-1:137, 4:146. Multiple responses allowed.

averaged roughly 42 percent (multiple responses permitted). The second most prominent class of response, stressing the material superiority of the Third Reich's enemies, averaged 35 percent.[9] Internal strife, including treason and sabotage, was mentioned by 18 percent of respondents overall, but its share diminished from 25 percent in 1950 to 10 percent in 1967.

Overall, postwar Germans never decided whether their country had lost the war (because of its own mistakes) or the Allies had won it (because

9. More Germans rated the United States Air Force as superior to the Luftwaffe than vice versa, for instance, but gave as their reason the superior technical and material advantages enjoyed by American airmen while crediting German fliers with superior training, skill, and courage (HIC-154).

of their superior resources), but the theory of an internal stab in the back lost ground steadily. Those responsible for their country's wartime destruction, postwar Germans seemed to say, were not members of some furtive underground but rather leaders who could not govern effectively and who seriously underestimated the strength of their foreign adversaries.

Germans and Jews

A second aspect of National Socialism that troubled postwar Germans was its treatment of Jews, other minorities, and even mainstream Germans who ran afoul of the regime. But what and when did they know about concentration camps and especially the mass murders?[10] It seemed inconceivable to many non-Germans that postwar Germans, even if they had not actively condoned these policies, were unaware of them. Germans who denied specific knowledge of the Holocaust or expressed abhorrence of the atrocities committed ostensibly in their name encountered skepticism from the world's press and Allied occupation authorities. An officer in the U.S. Army's Psychological Warfare Branch, who in June 1945 systematically interrogated a sample of roughly one hundred Germans, put it bluntly: "The mass of the German people," he said, had "no interest in admitting more than a minimum knowledge" (Janowitz 1946: 141). Hostile critics spoke of a "conspiracy of silence" among all Germans, irrespective of their degree of complicity in the heinous crimes (Bier, 1986).

Polling offered American military government (AMG) officials an opportunity to assess the evolution of popular sentiments about this complex of issues. How knowledgeable about the death camps were postwar Germans? Whom did they hold responsible? Did they have anything good to say about Nazi racial policy? With the Holocaust behind them, what did they think about Jews? And, ultimately, what should a revitalized Germany do about the crimes of the past?

Survey data suggest that most postwar Germans had only sketchy knowledge about Hitler's "final solution of the Jewish problem," but not because the Nazi government had secreted public information during the war or because the most horrendous death camps were outside Germany. Neither factor, even before 1945, prevented those who wanted to know from finding out what was taking place. After the fall of the Reich, they

---

10. Public opinion surveys focus on Jewry's fate because Jews were the largest single group victimized by Nazism; as such, Jews also function as representative of all persecuted groups.

could learn simply by talking with other Germans or availing themselves of the abundance of information provided by the Allies: brochures, movies, even forced visits to death camps. For whatever reason, the public's attention to this information was limited.

Early OMGUS surveys revealed an information gap. In mid-November 1945 (WSR-4), almost half of an American-zone sample either said they did not really know what had gone on in the concentration camps (40 percent) or gave no response to the question (9 percent). The rest claimed to know exactly what had happened, but responses to a follow-up question suggest that the "informed" respondents simply had the minimal information they needed or wanted. Asked why people were sent to the camps, and permitted to give as many reasons as they wished, almost two in three interviewees accurately cited political grounds and 14 percent the political indiscretions of the detainees. But only 6 percent mentioned religious reasons or a policy deliberately aimed at exterminating Jews. At the same time, asked what they had learned in recent weeks, only 29 percent mentioned the concentration camps; 12 percent said that they had learned of German aggression or the country's early war preparation (OMG-16).

The International Military Tribunal, which during the same week began its trial of major war criminals, provided the world with a wealth of information about monstrous Nazi crimes. The effect of this information, however, was mixed. On the one hand, some postwar Germans began to realize—or at least to admit to realizing—that they did not know the whole story.[11] What they had heard about the concentration camps turned out to be woefully incomplete. By late January 1946 (WSR-12) the number saying they knew exactly what had gone on there dropped to 38 percent, in contrast to those either reporting that they had incomplete information (57 percent) or giving no response (5 percent). On the other hand, even informed Germans learned more details. In April 1946 (OMG-19) seven in ten either agreed that investigations verified the mass murders or denied that claims about them were the invention of the enemies' propaganda.[12]

11. Critics point here to psychological repression (Janowitz 1946:142–143): people said they had no real knowledge as a means to distance themselves—at least in their own minds—from moral culpability. Germans clearly did not dwell on the issue. In November 1957 (IfD-3:70), for instance, given a list of eleven items that parents and their children might discuss together, such possibilities as family finances, jobs, and various aspects of the war ranked at the top, while "persecution of Jews during the Hitler era" ranked last among both respondents under the age of 25 (18 percent) and older ones (21 percent).

12. If we consider only those giving responses to these two questions—about one in five did not—then the average level of acceptance rises from 69 to 85 percent, in contrast to 15 percent who explicitly denied the reported evidence. In December 1946 (OMG-51), two months after the Nuremberg trial ended, the percentage accepting the former

The Nuremberg verdicts were handed out on 1 October 1946. Three days later OMGUS pollsters asked an American-zone sample what the trial had taught them (WSR-25; OMG-33). About seven in ten spoke of the concentration camps and 12 percent of the extermination of Jews and others (WSR-25). But new details did not necessarily produce coherent, deep-seated understanding. Asked in August 1949 how many of Germany's half-million Jews in 1933 still lived in Germany, fewer than a quarter could give an approximately correct answer; asked what had become of most of the others, only 30 percent responded correctly (IfD-1:129).[13]

However knowledgeable they were about Hitler's anti-Semitic excesses, scattered data show that most postwar Germans thought their former government's behavior appalling. The first OMGUS survey in October 1945 gave American-zone respondents a list of three statements and asked them to choose the one with which they most agreed: "0 percent said 'the Jews got under Hitler what they deserved'; 19 percent said 'Hitler went too far in his treatment of the Jews, but something had to be done to keep them in check'; and 77 percent said 'the measures taken against the Jews were·in no way justified'" (WSR-1). A query six months later, more complicated because it mixed Jews with other victims of Nazism, found 59 percent agreeing that the "extermination of Jews and Poles and other non-Aryans was not necessary for the security of Germans" (OMG-19). More generally, national surveys in 1951 found National Socialism's racial policy and persecution of Jews cited among the movement's worst aspects (see Table 4.2).

A deeper OMGUS concern than images of the past was the potential for anti-Semitism in postwar Germany. The survey unit made three separate attempts to approach this issue. Its major survey on basic attitudes, carried out in April 1946 (OMG-19), included four pairs of questions designed to tap this sentiment. Each pair had both a positively and a negatively worded question:

> 8 percent agreed that "the music of Jewish composers is no good,"* and 5 percent denied that "it is possible that musical composition can be beautiful in spite of the composer's race";
> 10 percent agreed that "if a pure German marries a non-Aryan wife he should be judged and despised," and 29 percent denied that "men

---

proposition about reliable research dropped to 59 percent, while those disagreeing rose to 20 percent and the number giving no response to 21 percent. Viewing only those giving responses, acceptance stood at 75 percent.

13. Of approximately 590,000 Jews who lived in Germany in 1931, perhaps 380,000 fled after 1933, 170,000 ended in Nazi death camps, and 30,000–40,000 survived; in 1949 about 25,000 Jews lived in Germany's four occupation zones and Berlin.

and women should be allowed to marry without making any distinctions between the races"*;

33 percent agreed that "Jews should not have the same rights as those belonging to the Aryan race," and 10 percent denied that "Jews should have the same rights as members of the Aryan race"; and

54 percent agreed that "in general, Germans are acknowledged as being the best workers in the world,"* and 50 percent denied that "Jews have always demonstrated that they are cleverer than Germans."

The data provide two different but compatible interpretations. First, in the initial (and most germane) three pairs, an average of one in six respondents gave what the OMGUS survey unit considered to be an anti-Semitic response. Their concerns focused more on racial "purity" and civil rights than on artistic competence. Second, a Guttmann scale of responses to the three questions indicated above with asterisks (*) showed that 17 percent were more and 83 percent less "nationalist and racist," a code phrase for attitudes OMGUS investigators considered to be the roots of anti-Semitism.[14]

Another survey conducted eight months later found public acceptance of nationalism and racism on the rise (OMG-49). A Guttmann scale demonstrated that the percentage who took this stance had more than doubled from the last survey, to 36 percent.[15] More-focused questions yielded another Guttmann scale aimed at assessing racism in general and anti-Semitism in particular. Respondents were asked to agree or disagree with eleven statements, eight of which, producing highly correlated responses, sorted respondents into five categories (see Table 5.3):

20 percent showed *little bias*, saying that "Germans are generally recognized to be the most skilled and diligent workers";

19 percent, leaning toward *nationalism*, said "some races are more fit to rule than others";

22 percent displayed *racism*, saying "some races are less worthy than others";

14. Three percent gave nationalist or racist responses to all three questions, 14 percent to two, 48 percent to one, and 35 percent to none. In fact, the Guttmann scale presented in this OMGUS report (OMG-19) added a fourth question about the civil rights of Jews. Two percent of the respondents gave nationalist or racist answers to all four questions, 7 percent to three, 15 percent to two, 43 percent to one, and 33 percent to none. Because subsequent surveys in December 1946 and April 1948 did not include this fourth question, and for the sake of continuity, this analysis focuses on the shorter scale.

15. Five percent gave nationalist or racist answers to all three questions, 31 percent to two, 59 percent to one, and 5 percent to none.

Table 5.3 Nationalism, Racism, and Anti-Semitism, December 1946

	Guttmann Scale				
	Little Bias	Nationalism	Racism	Anti-Semitism	Intense Anti-Semitism
Percentage in category	20	19	22	21	18
Jews should be permitted to (percentage within category answering positively):					
Eat in any restaurant	82	78	80	52	20
Marry non-Jews	98	98	95	90	72
Return to Germany	22	19	18	10	7

Sources: OMG-49; WSR-28.

21 percent, manifesting *anti-Semitism,* did not want to "work *under* a Jew" and were "against having a Jew live in the same apartment house"; and

18 percent, showing *intense anti-Semitism,* were "against having a Jew live on the same street"; would not "work *with* a Jew"; and agreed that "the racial origin of the composer affects the beauty of a composition."

These categories correlated in turn with the other three propositions respondents were asked to accept or reject (WSR-36): 91 percent of the total sample said "a German who marries a non-Aryan wife" should not "be judged and condemned"; 64 percent said "Jews should be allowed to go to the same restaurants as non-Jews"; and 15 percent said Jews should be helped "to rebuild their life in Germany" rather than "to emigrate to Palestine." Table 5.3 breaks down responses to these three propositions according to the categories established by the other questions.

A survey in April 1948 (OMG-122) produced apparently contradictory results. On the one hand, it uncovered even higher levels of nationalism and racism. Once again analysts applied a Guttmann scale to responses to the questions on eating, marrying, and returning to Germany. What they found was that the percentage of intensely biased respondents, who gave nationalist responses to two or three of the three questions, more than doubled again: from 36 percent in December 1946 to 74 percent in April 1948.[16] On the other hand, Guttmann scaling of responses to questions more overtly aimed at measuring anti-Semitism showed a decline. From December 1946 to April 1948 those categorized as having "little bias" rose from 20 to 21 percent, "nationalism" from 19 to 20 percent, and "racism" from 22 to 26 percent. Meanwhile the share of "anti-Semites" dropped from 21 to 19 percent and of "intense anti-Semites" from 18 to 14 percent.

The findings in April 1948 raise two fundamental questions. First, how do we reconcile growing racism with decreasing anti-Semitism? OMGUS analysts suggested that the consequences of the war and Allied policies had diverted "the pressure of prejudiced feeling" away from a focus especially on Jews (OMG-122).[17] That explanation suggests that nationalism and racism, though perhaps of intrinsic interest, were losing their social function as the root of anti-Semitism. Second, on the assumption that

16. In April 1948 (OMG-122), 43 percent gave nationalist or racist answers to all three questions, 31 percent to two, 23 percent to one, and 3 percent to none.

17. "Comments made by respondents indicate that Germans in 1948 are beginning to talk of Negroes, Russians, Balkans or Gypsies—in that order—as representatives of the 'inferior races'" (OMG-122:4).

anti-Semitism was the key issue pollsters wanted to address, was there a better and more direct way to measure it? The analysts' solution was to ask respondents whether they felt "very strongly" or only "fairly strongly" about their expressed views on the seven questions. Assessments might then be fine-tuned through gradient scores of intensity that varied from one sample group to the next—relative levels of intensity, for example, between Berliners and residents of Munich.[18] The practical effect of this procedure is that 18 percent of the population of the American zone could be categorized as anti-Semites, 55 percent not anti-Semitic, and the remaining 27 percent somewhere in between.[19]

Data from the occupation years show one fairly consistent pattern. About one AMZON German in six could be identified as a hard-core anti-Semite. Somewhat more, between a fifth and a fourth, cared little one way or another about Jewish questions. This group seemed likely to follow whatever the public policy trends were—to the advantage or disadvantage of Jews in postwar Germany.

What caused anti-Semitism? A survey conducted in August 1949 (IfD-1:129) asked West Germans this question directly. Almost two-thirds of the responses cited characteristics of the Jewish people (53 percent) or Jewish religion (12 percent), while only 30 percent attributed it to anti-Semitic propaganda. But the question used in this survey was flawed. Did interviewees respond according to what they themselves thought or according to their assumptions about what "other people" or "society as a whole" believed? If we accept the oft-cited assertion that public opinion respondents attribute their own views to others, then this flaw is not problematic. Without more sophisticated questions, however, we cannot be sure.

In October 1951 HICOG pollsters queried not the respondents' own attitudes toward Jews but rather historic circumstances (HIC-113). More than a fifth of the respondents held "the Jews themselves partly responsible for what happened to them during the Third Reich": Jews had pursued unfair business practices (10 percent), pushed themselves into positions of

18. A gradient score (or zero point) was derived "by giving weights to the percentages according to the number of anti-Semitic replies represented in Groups II ['nationalists'] to V ['intense anti-Semites']. According to this score, if there were absolutely no prejudice among a population group, the score would be zero. If everyone in the group [was] completely anti-Semitic, the score would be 300" (OMG-122:7). The gradient score of the American zone stood at 72.

19. In spring 1992 (Wild 1992:68) about a fourth of the respondents in a nationwide survey said that most (5 percent) or a large number (18 percent) of Germans are anti-Semitic. The remainder said there were only a few (52 percent) or practically no (25 percent) anti-Semites. One respondent in five claimed that anti-Semitism in Germany is dying out, 60 percent that it remains steady, and 18 percent that it is increasing.

power and influence (4 percent), or agitated against the Third Reich (4 percent). More than half of those surveyed denied that Jews had brought their suffering upon themselves, but 27 percent said that it would be best for West Germany's remaining Jews to emigrate (HIC-113), and again the reasons given for this point of view stressed negative characteristics attributed to Jewry.[20] However ambiguous they were, such surveys demonstrated repeatedly that ties between Germans and Jews remained problematic.

The formal passage of the occupation did not substantially alter German images of Jews and Jewry.[21] In January 1946 only 38 percent of AMZON Germans claimed to know exactly what had happened in the concentration camps. Later national samples responded similarly to related questions:

- In June 1961 a third of those who had been twelve or more years old at the war's end recalled having learned before then about the mass extermination of Jews. Fifty-eight percent reported getting such information only after the war, and 10 percent were not certain when they found out (IfD-3:229).
- In December 1988 West Germans over 60 years of age (that is, 17 years or older in 1945) were asked when they had first learned in a general sense about the mass murder of Jews (IfD-9:383). A third claimed to have had such knowledge either before 1939 (7 percent) or between then and 1944 (27 percent). More than half responded that they had learned this either in 1945 (34 percent)—the year when Allied troops penetrated Germany, opened death camps in the homeland, and initiated public information programs—or even later (17 percent).
- In early 1992, asked, "How many Germans in the Nazi era knew about the mass extermination of Jews?" (Wild 1992:64), a fifth said either "the majority" (16 percent) or "almost everyone" (5 percent). About three in five said "very few" (16 percent) or "a minority" (42

20. Almost as many preferred that Jews remain (26 percent), but far more (42 percent) seemed not to care one way or another. An independent, oft-posed question (IfD-4:96) asked whether or not it would be better for Germany to have no Jews. The number responding positively dropped from 37 percent in December 1952 to 19 percent in March 1965. In this case, however, we cannot assess whether such respondents were themselves anti-Semites seeking to protect Germany from the Jews, or humanitarians seeking to protect Jews from an unreliable Germany. For other examples of attitudes toward Jews, see IfD, passim, especially IfD-3:214–219.

21. Important accounts (and relevant literature) of changing German attitudes toward Jews not directly based on survey research are A. Markovits (1984), A. Markovits and Hayden (1986), and A. Markovits and Noveck (forthcoming).

percent), and a fifth said "less than half." The older the respondents, the less they attributed knowledge to Germans.

Such findings report a consistency across time. Between a half and two-thirds of the German people, talking either retrospectively about their own behavior or historically about the actions of others, reported having had no general information about the crime of the century. A sizable segment of the population, though, between a quarter and a third, said it knew about the atrocities.

Revising the history of the Holocaust, either to deny what had taken place or to minimize Germany's responsibility, found little support among post-occupation Germans. We saw earlier that in April 1946 only 12 percent of an AMZON sample openly claimed that the atrocities were invented by the enemy's propaganda, and 13 percent denied that investigations had verified the mass murders (OMG-19).[22] Four decades later 77 percent of a national sample thought the reports on the Holocaust were accurate, and 12 percent found them exaggerated (IfD-9:383). A survey in September 1987 (Bergmann and Erb 1991:306) produced almost identical results (79 and 13 percent, respectively). And a half-decade later, after historians had waged some major revisionist battles, 73 percent accepted and 15 percent questioned mainstream accounts of the Holocaust (Wild 1992:64).

Surveys conducted after the occupation ended suggest more complex dimensions of German attitudes toward Jews. A third to two-fifths of AMZON Germans, OMGUS pollsters found, were either overtly anti-Semitic or inclined toward anti-Semitism. An independent survey conducted in the last month of formal occupation, August 1949 (IfD-1:128), asked West Germans how they viewed Jews. Well over a third gave openly anti-Semitic (23 percent) or reserved (15 percent) responses, and fewer than half expressed tolerance (41 percent) or philo-Semitism (6 percent). In December 1952 the same question elicited a reversal of distribution: more than half (52 percent) gave negative responses (34 percent outright anti-Semitic) and less than a third (30 percent) positive ones. These shifts may have been attributable to then-current public debate on such issues related to Germany's anti-Semitic past as banning the Socialist Reich Party and paying "reparations" to Israel.[23] An EMNID survey in 1989 (cited in

22. In February 1986 a national sample was asked how many Germans in the Nazi era were anti-Semitic (Ifd-9:383). More than a third attributed anti-Semitism to most Germans, almost half to a minority.

23. How strong was anti-Semitism? In 1949 (IfD-9:409) a third thought it increasing (19 percent) or remaining constantly strong (13 percent), and somewhat more said that it was remaining constantly weak (4 percent) or decreasing (32 percent). Three years

Bergmann and Erb 1991:60) found that more than half of West Germans could be categorized as very (4 percent), somewhat (10 percent), or a bit anti-Semitic (40 percent); 46 percent were not anti-Semitic.

Opinions have split on whether the government should protect Jews by punishing those who commit anti-Semitic acts. In August 1949 (IfD-9:409) almost as many favored such a policy as a matter of principle (17 percent) or if the acts were serious (24 percent) as opposed it on principle (15 percent) or because it would be undemocratic (28 percent). An almost identical question in September 1987 (Bergmann and Erb 1991:306)—the earlier one spoke of "anti-Semitic" acts, the latter of acts "hostile to Jews"—produced rather different results. More than four in five supported legal actions in serious cases (43 percent) or in principle (39 percent), and only a tenth rejected such action on principle (5 percent) or because it would be undemocratic (5 percent).

What about the other side of the coin: Do Jews see Germans as anti-Semites? In a survey in 1990 of 377 West German Jews, 7 percent characterized Germans as strongly anti-Semitic, 62 percent as moderately so, and 30 percent as not anti-Semitic at all (Silbermann and Sallen 1992: 101). A quarter, however, saw anti-Semitism rising (p. 115), and a fifth termed anti-Semitic vandalism as something more than a political bagatelle (p. 109).[24] Would a concentrated information campaign by the Jewish community reduce anti-Semitism? "Yes, certainly," said one in five, and half thought it possible, but almost a third of the respondents were doubtful (p. 102).

Most non-Jewish Germans responding to public opinion polls are untouched by the anti-Semitism of Hitler and his latter-day disciples, or else they have learned how to avoid giving interviewers any "politically incorrect" responses. A questionnaire distributed in September 1987 to a West German sample uncovered the diversity of popular opinions (Bergmann and Erb 1991:309). Respondents were asked to read a list of statements and select the ones with which they agreed.

83 percent agreed: "I personally don't know of any guilt I have toward Jews";

75 percent agreed: "I make no distinction between Jews and other people";

---

later these figures were three-tenths (14 and 15 percent, respectively) and more than a third (13 and 24 percent, respectively).

24. Two-thirds described anti-Semitism as stable and 9 percent as dying out. More than two-fifths interpreted Jew-baiting as a threat to Jews in general, but only 13 percent saw a personal danger. Half viewed it as a general problem facing the FRG.

61 percent agreed: "I am ashamed that Germans have committed so many crimes against the Jews";

49 percent agreed: "I simply don't understand why some people basically have something against Jews";

40 percent agreed: "I believe that many are unwilling to express their real opinion about Jews";

34 percent agreed: "To form my own images, I would like to know Jews better";

23 percent agreed: "The entire topic 'Jews' is somehow unpleasant to me";

22 percent agreed: "I believe that the Jews are also responsible when they are hated and persecuted";

20 percent agreed: "When I talk about Jews, I'm always very careful, because you can only burn your fingers";

19 percent agreed: "I believe you always have to be careful with Jews";

19 percent agreed: "Before the war my family had Jewish friends and acquaintances";

15 percent agreed: "What I think about Jews I don't tell anyone"; and

10 percent agreed: "Earlier, my family was very much inclined against Jews."

A substantial majority thus reported having clear hearts about the past, and many expressed positive attitudes toward Jews. But significant minorities made it clear that the nexus of Germans and Jews is a taboo topic that only the foolhardy will address willingly. This sense of danger periodically creeps into the German body politic.

Collective Guilt

Postwar West Germans by and large denied personal responsibility for military aggression, genocide, or any other transgressions attributed to National Socialism. The idea of collective guilt was hardly foreign to them. Since the early occupation months foreigners and Germans alike have tried to drum into the national psyche a sense of shame for complicity in the crimes of Nazism. Moreover, as we have seen, Germans were both aware of and appalled by these crimes committed in their name. Ninety-four percent of an American-zone sample in April 1946 agreed that those guilty of war crimes should be made to stand trial (OMG-19). But only 30 percent saw the German people as a guilty party meriting punishment.[25] About one in five respondents answered a similar

---

25. In June 1945 Janowitz (1946:143) found "an almost universal tendency to lay responsibility upon the Nazi party or the S.S." among those he interviewed intensively.

Figure 5.3

German People's Responsibility for the War, 1945-1948

Question: Do you think that the entire German people are responsible for the war because they let a government come to power which plunged the whole world into war?

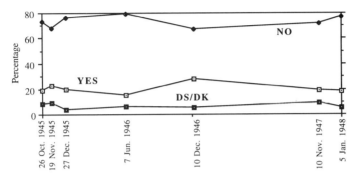

YES: Curvilinear fit not statistically significant
NO: Fit not statistically significant
DS/DK: Fit not statistically significant
Sources: WSR-1, 4, 9, 25, 36; OMG-100.

question positively in seven surveys between October 1945 and January 1948 (Figure 5.3). The relatively low level of interviewees not responding (averaging 7 percent) suggests that interviewees found the issue salient and that their views were well formed.

In December 1946, twenty months after the end of the war but only weeks since the Nuremberg trials ended, OMGUS pollsters sought to explore the concept of collective guilt more deeply (OMG-51). They asked American-zone respondents explicitly to accept or reject seven propositions relating popular behavior and Nazi crimes. Some drew on themes stressed by the Nazis: "Did Germany attack Poland in order to protect Germans living there from mistreatment by Poland?" and "Did the harshness of the Ver-

---

Other early questions muddled different aspects of the idea of collective guilt: 56 percent of respondents to an April 1946 survey rejected the proposition that "Germany was not responsible for the war and German leaders should not be held as war criminals," and 41 percent denied that "the German people should not be made responsible for the mistakes of their leaders and should not have to pay the price of war" (OMG-19). A similar survey conducted at roughly the same time, however, found that only 22 percent of AMZON respondents agreed that the German people were responsible for the war for having let "a government come to power which wanted to plunge the world into war"; most of those who disagreed with the proposition felt that because the government had begun the war, the government had to bear responsibility for it (OMG-22).

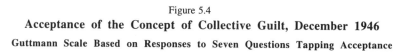

Figure 5.4

Acceptance of the Concept of Collective Guilt, December 1946

Guttmann Scale Based on Responses to Seven Questions Tapping Acceptance

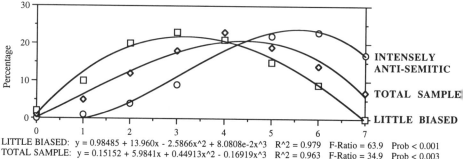

LITTLE BIASED: $y = 0.98485 + 13.960x - 2.5866x^2 + 8.0808e\text{-}2x^3$ $R^2 = 0.979$ F-Ratio = 63.9   Prob < 0.001
TOTAL SAMPLE: $y = 0.15152 + 5.9841x + 0.44913x^2 - 0.16919x^3$ $R^2 = 0.963$ F-Ratio = 34.9   Prob < 0.003
ANTI-SEMITIC: $y = 0.34848 - 3.5714x + 3.5509x^2 - 0.38636x^3$ $R^2 = 0.977$ F-Ratio = 57.0   Prob < 0.001

Sources: OMG-49, 51.

sailles Treaty give the German people a right to start a second world war?"
Others tapped themes stressed by U.S. occupation authorities: "Do you
believe that the German people are at least partly to blame for the acts of
the Hitler regime because they supported it?" and "Do you agree or disagree that research has shown that the Germans tortured and murdered
millions of helpless Europeans?" Rejecting the Nazi-oriented and accepting the OMGUS-oriented propositions represented sympathy for the collective-
guilt theme. The opposite pattern was a firm denial of collective guilt.[26]

A Guttmann scale applied to responses to all seven questions produced
a bell-shaped curve skewed to the rejecting side: almost one in five respondents took a strongly supportive position on collective guilt by giving two
or fewer theme-denying answers (see Figure 5.4). Twice as many took a
strongly negative position by giving five or more answers that denied the
collective-guilt theme. The mean score was 3.8; that is, the average respondent responded to almost four of seven questions with answers that
denied the concept of collective guilt. Figure 5.4 also indicates that respondents showing little racial bias were more supportive of collective guilt,
while intense anti-Semites were more negative.[27]

26. To the question about Poland's invasion, 46 percent gave the OMGUS-oriented
response, 21 percent the Nazi-oriented response, and 33 percent no response; distribution of answers to the the Versailles Treaty question was 68, 7, and 25, respectively; on
responsibility for supporting Hitler, 63, 31, and 5; and on torture and murder, 59, 20, and
21. The averages for these four questions alone, then, were 59 percent supporting the
collective-guilt theme, 20 percent denying it, and 21 percent not expressing a clear-cut
view.

27. Another set of questions asked at the same time explored the respondents' proclivity toward nationalism and anti-Semitism (OMG-49; see also Table 5.3). The average

Nor did the concept of collective guilt gain favor after the occupation ended. A nationwide survey conducted in October 1951 gave respondents a card showing three positions one could take "about the war and everything Germany did during the Third Reich" (HIC-113). Only 4 percent of the interviewees endorsed the proposition that "every individual German bears a certain guilt for Germany's actions during the Third Reich and everybody should acknowledge this guilt." Five times as many denied any sense of guilt but did report feeling some responsibility to rectify the Third Reich's wrongs.[28] Nearly two-thirds, however, flatly denied both collective guilt and collective responsibility. "Germans in general need feel neither guilty nor responsible for righting any wrongs," these respondents said. "Only those who really committed something are guilty as well as responsible."[29]

OMGUS pollsters treated collective guilt for Nazism's genocidal policies as part of a more general question regarding Nazism as a whole. The pattern of responses changed after summer 1949, when the Western Allies ended their full-scale occupation of West Germany and helped create the semisovereign Federal Republic. With a legitimate government in power, abstract issues of all sorts turned into political demands and claims. The debate about collective guilt and collective responsibility came to encompass such matters as restitution, protection of West Germany's remaining Jews, and "reparations" to Israel.

The attitudes of postoccupation West Germans toward such issues were generally consistent with what American-zone samples had said about anti-Semitism. They eventually accepted the idea of paying restitution to individual Jews who had lost their property, for example. As we have seen, a modest albeit growing number saw the need for restitution even if they denied a legal obligation to redress past wrongs (HIC-113, 167). Given a list of five categories of Nazi victims, however, West Germans were least responsive to the needs of "Jews who had suffered because of the Third Reich

---

collective-guilt scores for the five nationalism–anti-Semitism categories were: little biased, 2.9; nationalist, 3.5; racist, 3.8; anti-Semitic, 4.0; and intensely anti-Semitic, 4.8.

28. Four decades later (Wild 1992:61), when asked who was responsible for persecuting the Jews, one in five respondents said "all Germans, including those born after the war" (4 percent) or "all Germans who were adults then" (17 percent). A third tagged "Germans who at the time knew" about the Holocaust. Almost half cited only "those Germans who had taken part in the persecution." Were the German people as an entity guilty? A third thought they were, but 42 percent thought not and one in four expressed no opinion.

29. Somewhat more than a year later, in December 1952, these figures were, respectively, 5, 29, and 59 percent (HIC-167). The significant change was the added 8 percent who, while eschewing guilt, were willing to provide victims of Nazism with some form of restitution.

and the war" (HIC-113).[30] Even so, over three times as many (68 percent) favored such assistance as opposed it (21 percent). Principal reasons given for opposing aid to Jews were that they had enough to look after themselves (4 percent), had been adequately helped by various authorities (3 percent), or had exploited Germans in the past (3 percent).

West Germans further voiced support for legislation aimed at protecting Jews still living in the country. Again, initial surveys uncovered opposition: in October 1951 almost as many opposed (33 percent) as supported (38 percent) a bill under consideration by the FRG's Bundestag that would punish those who acted or expressed themselves in an anti-Semitic manner (HIC-113).[31] Later, after such legislation had been enacted, only a diminishing number of West Germans continued to oppose it.[32]

A more complicated issue centered on reparations to Israel (HIC-167). An agreement in August 1952 called for the FRG to pay the equivalent of $715 million to Israel as restitution for what had happened to Jews during the Third Reich. The agreement did not attract popular support among West Germans. Two of every three expressing a view (49 percent of the entire sample) urged the Bundestag to reject the proposal. Only about half that many (26 percent) supported it. The main reason for opposing it, given by 24 percent of the entire sample, was that the claims were excessive or burdensome or would hinder restitution programs in West Germany. About half as many (11 percent) argued that only those Jews who had actually suffered losses were entitled to claim compensation, not the state of Israel. Those favoring the FRG-Israeli agreement stressed primar-

30. The other four categories were war widows and orphans (to whom 96 percent were prepared to give support), those who had suffered bombing damage (93 percent), refugees and those expelled from the eastern territories (90 percent), and relatives of people executed because of participation in the 20 July 1944 attempt on Hitler's life (73 percent).

31. Opponents most commonly cited as reasons their belief that such a law would violate the democratic freedom of expression (9 percent) or principle of equality (6 percent), or else the fact that Jews already had the legal protection accorded to all FRG citizens (4 percent). Chapter 8 addresses a new dimension of conflict between the free-speech rights of publicists who denied that the Holocaust had occurred and the demands of Jews and other victims of Nazism who see such public statements as a violation of their human rights. On 13 January 1993, for instance, the British historian David Irving was fined $20,000 in Munich for publicly saying that gas chambers had not existed. Already thrown out of Canada because of his "lie of Auschwitz" thesis, in November 1993 Irving was expelled from the FRG.

32. In a May 1958 survey, 46 percent said that it was right that acts of anti-Semitism be punished by the courts; 20 percent said it was wrong and 4 percent that it depended on the circumstances (IfD-3:219). In a January 1960 survey, 78 percent argued that those displaying hostile behavior toward Jews should be punished; 7 percent disagreed and 5 percent said that it depended on the circumstances.

ily Germany's moral responsibility.[33] Eventually the government paid large sums to Israel and the public forgot the moral question (see Balabkins 1971; Feldman 1984).[34]

The fundamental principle of postwar Germany's obligations to individuals and governments victimized by Nazism nevertheless continued to capture attention, reflected in such issues as the trial of Adolf Eichmann and the right of NATO airmen to carry out low-altitude training over German soil. But unlike the question of compensation, the idea of collective guilt was abstract. The bulk of postwar Germans saw the issue as a meaningless irritant, a tool for German-baiting. This attitude reflected in part the lack of a programmatic upshot of collective guilt. The notion seemed geared more to making Germans ashamed than to providing them with clear instructions about how to redeem their country's standing in the world's good graces. It had little impact on those directly responsible for Nazism's sins: during the occupation years party supporters had to deal with military-government bureaucracies, not legislation appealing to some moral concept of collective guilt, and those accused of heinous crimes faced the London Charter of August 1945. Even these threats diminished as the U.S. government increasingly lost its taste for punishing postwar Germans.

Nor did collective guilt make much sense to postwar Germans. It was the right of conquest, they said, not a moral imperative that justified the Allies' military occupation. Why should Germans be held responsible for Nazi excesses simply because they are Germans? Some leaders and many Germans-on-the-street argued increasingly that the time had come to cease harping on the past.[35] But the West German government felt constrained—and to a significant degree forced by its new allies—to deal as best it could with practical implications embodied in the notion of collective responsibility.

33. Apprised that the Arab League had protested the agreement and threatened to break off trade with the FRG, the positive responses dropped sharply from 26 to 12 percent, and the number of those opposing the agreement rose slightly from 49 to 52 percent.

34. A survey in March 1989 (Mit Gestrigen 1989:151) found that 47 percent of a national sample thought the amount of reparations paid by the FRG was appropriate, 5 percent too little, and 46 percent too much.

35. In March 1989 (Mit Gestrigen 1989:154) a national sample was asked to comment on the following proposition: "We should stop dwelling on our past, because the others did things that were just as terrible." A six-point scale ran from strong disagreement (scored as one point) to strong agreement (six). The respondents ranked on average at 4.3 percent. Three years later three in five Germans (62 percent) agreed that "46 years after the war's end, we shouldn't talk so much about the persecution of Jews but finally draw a line with the past" (Wild 1992:68). A fifth (20 percent) disagreed and a sixth (16 percent) expressed no opinion.

SIX

· ·

Punishing the Guilty:
Nuremberg and After

Formal criminal proceedings against individuals transgressing international legal norms, especially the laws of war, were not a new idea in May 1945 when the Nazi regime collapsed. Precedents came from Greek mythology, religious texts, and recent history. After the Civil War, for example, the United States had tried and executed Captain Henry Wirtz, commandant of the infamous prison camp in Andersonville, Georgia; imprisoned, without trial, Confederate President Jefferson Davis for two years and Vice President Alexander H. Stephens for a short time; and disenfranchised Confederate loyalists (Foner 1990:190 et passim). After World War I the victorious Allies had sought to force defeated Germany to try and punish those responsible for the war itself or for specific war crimes. Germany's acceptance in principle, however, quickly turned into an apathetic reality that mocked Allied intentions (J. Willis 1982). The outbreak of World War II brought demands throughout the world for a new form of justice, one that had teeth in it.[1] Some favored simply lining Nazis up against a wall and shooting them. Others called for summary courts under military jurisdiction. Still others saw more formal trials as an opportunity not only to punish Nazi war criminals but also to strengthen international legal principles that could mitigate the scourge of war in the future.

The idea of war crimes trials in post–World War II Germany quickly generated dissent. Some Germans, continuing to rail about the Allied affront in demanding such trials a quarter-century earlier, saw no constructive purpose to be served by them. Others considered such trials a welcome means of punishing those who had led Germany into the abyss of 1945. The Allied leaders, meanwhile, disagreed among themselves and

1. Until the tide of war turned against Germany in late 1942, the Wehrmacht's War Crimes Bureau (*Wehrmacht-Untersuchungsstelle für Verletzungen des Völkerrechts*) developed plans to carry out war crimes trials against Soviet, British, French, and other enemies (de Zayas 1979/1989).

heard divided opinions at home. Key questions were, first, the relative merits of summary executions and judicial proceedings and, second, if trials were held, what form they should take (B. Smith 1977, 1981, 1982). Meeting in Moscow in November 1943, the Allied foreign ministers did little more than promise punishment to Nazi criminals. The Big Three accepted this proposal a month later in Teheran. During the next year a United Nations War Crimes Commission (UNWCC) was created while the issue was debated in Germany and across the North Atlantic. But not until August 1945, three months after the war with Germany ended, could the Allies—by now including France—agree in London on the charter that convened the International Military Tribunal (IMT) in Nuremberg.

War Crimes Trials in Postwar Germany

The trial envisioned by the London Charter was perhaps the most spectacular element of the quadripartite occupation of defeated Germany. In a sense, those who drafted the charter knew that they had little alternative. The angry mood of Nazism's victims would not have stood for permitting the men who had wreaked such havoc on the world—men such as Reich Marshal Hermann Göring and Foreign Minister Joachim von Ribbentrop—to retire to their mountain retreats to write memoirs glorifying Hitler's reign and justifying their own roles in it. Neither was it feasible simply to declare any wartime German leader an enemy of peace and shoot him on the spot. Far better, those who drafted the charter reasoned, would be trials in which the norms of justice might temper cries for vengeance, and which might expose to the world the enormity of Nazi crimes. Trials might even set precedents that would dampen the eagerness of future dictators and their underlings to embark upon such mad adventures.

The fundamental assumption of the Nuremberg trials was that individuals are responsible for their actions. They cannot hide behind the cloak of "state sovereignty" or anonymous governmental agencies. Constantin von Neurath and Franz von Papen, both leaders of the Third Reich's diplomatic corps, could not excuse themselves by claiming that, because they had acted on Hitler's behalf, they were not personally responsible for what they had done. By the same token, top policymakers of an organization or agency itself accused of war crimes could be charged with participation in an illegal conspiracy. Besides the Nazi party leadership, several agencies were indicted as groups: the Reich Cabinet, General Staff and High Command, Gestapo and State Security Service, the SS (or *Schutzstaffel*, Hitler's praetorian guard), and the SA (*Sturmabteilung*, or Storm Troopers, the party's bully-boys during its earlier days). The tribunal rejected the defense of Julius Streicher, the Nazi party's professional ideologue, anti-Semite, and publicist, that he was merely carrying out party dictates and hence inculpable.

Of what could individuals and organizations be accused? Signatories of the London Charter knew that they were creating international law when they specified four categories of war crimes: (1) planning and waging aggressive war, that is, crimes against peace, (2) conspiracy to carry out crimes against peace, (3) war crimes, such as murder or ill-treatment of prisoners of war or deporting civilians to slave labor, and (4) crimes against humanity, "namely, murder, extermination, enslavement, deportation, or other inhumane acts committed against any civilian population, before or during the war; or persecutions on political, racial or religious grounds in execution of or in connection with any crime within the jurisdiction of the Tribunal, whether or not in violation of the domestic law of the country where perpetrated."[2] The London Charter explicitly stated that individuals responsible for formulating or executing any of these crimes were "responsible for all acts performed by any persons in execution of such plan" (B. Smith 1982:215).

From 14 November 1945 until 1 October of the following year the International Military Tribunal sat in judgment on Nazis and state officials.[3] The justices, one from each of the Big Four, clearly represented the victors—a fact that the Soviet justice, Major General I. T. Nikitchenko, emphasized by wearing his military uniform. The Allies also selected rep-

2. What some characterize as the creative development of natural international law, others, favoring positive (codified) international law, may call perversion of the legal process. Many such complaints were lodged against the IMT: the London Charter established ex post facto law; IMT proceedings violated the time-honored twin principles of *nullum crimen sine lege* (there can be no crime in the absence of a law) and *nulla poena sine lege* (there can be no punishment in the absence of a law); principles applied to Germans were invalid because they were not also applied to people from other countries who had committed similar acts (the so-called *tu quoque* defense); individuals cannot be held personally responsible for acts of state; and, because the alleged crimes took place in territories under German control—in Germany's *imperium*—German courts applying German law were the only appropriate judicial agencies for trying the accused. Critics also raised procedural objections: the judges represented only the victors; by the nature of the tribunal the prosecution and defense enjoyed no true equality of power; complete documentation was not made available to the defense; defense attorneys were sometimes treated as though they themselves were on trial alongside their clients; evidence was evaluated differently according to the purpose it served; and the defense was inhibited from introducing certain kinds of evidence or witnesses. See Knieriem (1953/1959); Appleman (1954); Benton and Grimm (1955); and Woetzel (1962).

3. Originally, the IMT brought indictments against twenty-four men. Party leader Martin Bormann, however, was never found; Robert Ley, leader of the Reich's Labor Front, hanged himself before the trials began; and industrialist Gustav Krupp von Bohlen und Halbach was deemed too ill to stand trial.

resentatives from their own countries to serve as prosecutors while permitting German nationals and émigrés to defend the accused. Almost eleven months were spent reviewing evidence, listening to impassioned pleas and cool descriptions of horrifying events, and weighing the conflicting claims of legal principles; the outcome: eleven death sentences (plus another for Martin Bormann, tried in absentia), seven prison sentences ranging from ten years to life, and three acquittals. The tribunal also declared the leadership corps of the Nazi party, Gestapo and State Security Service, and SS to be "criminal organizations."

The Allies originally saw the IMT as the first of several tribunals, but British, French, and Soviet occupation authorities soon found different ways to deal with alleged war criminals in their own zones of occupation. U.S. authorities, by contrast, continued to stage major, highly publicized, albeit not strictly international, tribunals in Nuremberg. Between October 1946 and April 1949 a dozen such series of trials targeted 177 doctors, judges, lawyers, government ministers, SS and army officers, industrialists, and financiers.[4] At this time, when it was clear that the western zones of Germany would gain semisovereign status, the U.S. turned over to the emerging government responsibility for initiating further criminal indictments. U.S. military units also set up their own courts to try concentration camp guards, medical personnel who had injected poison into Polish and Russian human guinea pigs, and Germans accused of murdering American servicemen (such as the massacre of 142 U.S. prisoners of war near Malmédy in Belgium, and the killing of downed U.S. airmen) (Ziemke 1975:392–393).[5] And, although U.S. authorities neither initiated nor conducted any trials after 1949, they continued to maintain prisons, review earlier verdicts, and even carry out death sentences under the aegis of the U.S. High Commission for Germany (HICOG).

The new Federal Republic of Germany (FRG) soon began honoring its commitment to track down and prosecute other Nazi war criminals. War crimes trials continue today, a half-century after World War II ended.[6]

4. The twelve tribunals issued twenty-four death sentences, twenty life imprisonments, and ninety-eight shorter prison terms; thirty-five defendants were acquitted; eight indicted defendants committed suicide or were dismissed from the trials because of illness (T. Taylor 1949:91, 241).

5. These U.S. military tribunals, more than five hundred in number, indicted 1,941 individuals and convicted 1,517 of them, 324 to death sentences and 247 to life imprisonment (Rückerl 1980:28–29). In 1951 the U.S. High Commissioner, John J. McCloy, granted amnesty or sharply reduced sentences for those still held in U.S. prisons (see Bird 1992). The last U.S. prisoners were released in 1958 (but not those tried by the IMT in Nuremberg, who remained in the Spandau Prison in Berlin).

6. By 1978 the FRG had prosecuted almost 83,000 people for war crimes, convicting over 6,400 of them (with 12 condemned to death before the abolition of that penalty, and

They also continue to be controversial. Critics have accused FRG judicial officers and judges of dragging their feet, prosecutors have grown increasingly exasperated in being handed cases supported by insubstantial evidence, and international "Nazi-hunters" and highly publicized trials overseas have continued to excoriate both Nazi Germany and, by implication, all Germans. Bowing to heavy national and international pressure, the FRG even felt constrained to nullify its twenty-year statute of limitations on war crimes. Politicians, writers, educators, intellectuals, and others both in Germany and abroad have found Nazi war crimes trials an ongoing forum for their political and moral views.

Public Views of the International Military Tribunal

What did the German people think about these various war crimes trials? U.S. military government officials had a particular interest in assessing the popular impact of the IMT of 1945–1946 in Nuremberg. A crucial issue was the acceptance of its fundamental legitimacy. Would the trials create new resentment that might later erupt into new conflicts? Did Germans see the tribunal merely as a particularly vicious Allied propaganda campaign? What did they learn from the trials? OMGUS officials also examined the public perception of the trials' fairness. Did Germans see the IMT simply as a kangaroo court? Did the outcome satisfy common citizens, those who had lived through the Nazi era's moments of glory and its final ignominy? For OMGUS officials the success of the entire occupation program depended on what happened in Nuremberg and how Germans and others interpreted the trials.

Although most Germans in the American zone of occupation said that the Nuremberg tribunal was a good idea, closer inspection of the survey data challenges this response. The first question OMGUS pollsters asked in April 1946 determined that 94 percent of all respondents agreed and only 2 percent disagreed that "those German leaders who ordered the execution of civilians or prisoners-of-war should be put before courts as criminals" (WSR-23; OMG-19; for notations see Chapter 4, note 1). A subsequent question, though, asked, "Since Germany was not responsible for the war, should German leaders be brought to justice as war criminals?" Juxtaposing the ideas of war guilt and war crimes trials made the latter less palatable: about a third accepted the proposition that their leaders should not be tried, whereas 56 percent thought that, notwithstanding Germany's relative innocence, its leaders should be brought to justice.

---

another 151 given life sentences), and 4,700 cases were still on the docket (see Rückerl 1980). As Chapter 8 points out, such trials continue.

A half-year later, immediately after the Nuremberg verdicts were read, six out of seven people who expressed an opinion—72 percent to 12 percent—agreed that the Allies were legally justified in putting Nazis in the dock (WSR-31). When those who denied the Allies' right to judge were asked why, 37 percent (about 4.5 percent of the entire sample) said that such trials were the German people's task—which, of course, said nothing about whether or not the German people should or would pursue the task. Even more said either that the IMT had no legal precedent (21 percent) or that the Allies had also committed war crimes but were not being punished (18 percent). And when interviewers asked all respondents whether lesser Nazi leaders should be brought to trial, as many (43 percent) wanted to let things be as to prosecute further.

Public attention. Irrespective of their attitudes about IMT's legitimacy, AMZON residents had ample opportunities to learn about its proceedings. All four occupation governments made concentrated efforts to inform the masses about both the crimes with which the Allies charged defendants and the course of the tribunal itself. They distributed pamphlets, broadcast information first on Radio Luxembourg and then on German radio stations, and flooded the licensed press with news releases. They conducted exhibits and seminars, showed documentary movies, and forced some Germans to clean up the infamous death camps and bury the dead. Taking into account the wartime destruction and postwar dismantling of the country's communication network, Allied information campaigns aimed at instructing Germans about their country's crimes were extraordinary.

But did anyone pay attention? Contrary to what at least some American journalists wrote at the time, AMZON Germans responding to public opinion polls expressed deep interest in the Nuremberg trials.[7] Figure 6.1 reveals that, in seven surveys from December 1945 until October 1946, an average of 73 percent of the respondents said they read newspaper reports on the trials. Attention was particularly strong at the outset, when as many as five in six made this claim. But as the trials went on and on, growing mounds of evidence piled up by the prosecutors, though fascinating to experts and subsequent historians, deadened the minds of common citizens trying to comprehend what Nazism had done in their name. Today's news recounted more grisly stories than did yesterday's—and tomorrow's news promised to be even more horrendous.

Not surprisingly, then, the initial interest began to flag. By March

---

7. Daniell (1945:54), after pointing out the emphasis given to the trials in the newspapers, noted sardonically, "It was interesting to watch the Germans skip that part of their papers."

Figure 6.1

Newspaper Readership of the Nuremberg Trials, 1945-1946

Question: Do you read newspaper reports about the Nuremberg Trials?

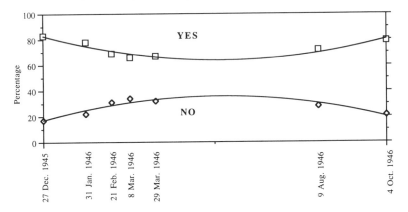

YES: y = 82.891 - 0.26188x + 9.0058e-4x^2   R^2 = 0.883   F-Ratio = 15.1   Prob < 0.014
NO: y = 17.227 + 0.25419x - 8.7331e-4x^2   R^2 = 0.870   F-Ratio = 13.4   Prob < 0.017

Sources: WSR-12, 20, 29, 31; OMG-60.

1946, for every two AMZON Germans who read the press reports, one did not (WSR-20). The percentage of readers rose to 72 percent in August, as the trials neared a conclusion, and to 80 percent in October, after the verdicts were announced (WSR-31; OMG-33). But those who followed IMT news in the press paid less attention to its details. In late March (WSR-20), only half of those who said that they read the reports did so completely. In August (WSR-29) the ratio of serious attentiveness dropped to three careful readers for every four less attentive ones. Further, substantial numbers did not care much about what the IMT news was saying. "Among readers," the OMGUS Opinion Survey Section reported about surveys in December 1945 and August 1946 (OMG-16), "the number of people who read articles all the way through . . . dropped from 64 percent to 51 percent and 'partial readers' . . . increased from 33 percent to 48 percent."[8]

Growing impatience with the IMT manifested itself in other ways. The bulk of AMZON Germans, for instance, thought newspaper reporting to be accurate. Figure 6.2 shows that from October 1945 to October 1946 an

8. Other OMGUS reports indicate that in March 1946, when 67 percent of the respondents said they were readers, more than half that number (36 percent) expressed great interest in the trial, but the remainder had only a passing interest (18 percent) or none whatever (12 percent); and that in August, when 72 percent were readers, 45 percent expressed very much interest in the news reports and 25 percent only a little (WSR-20, 29).

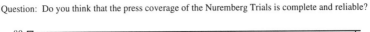

Figure 6.2

Reliability of Press Reporting on the Nuremberg Trials, 1945-1946

Question: Do you think that the press coverage of the Nuremberg Trials is complete and reliable?

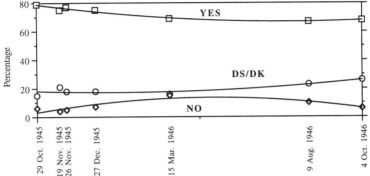

YES: $y = 78.785 - 8.9965e\text{-}2x + 1.7025e\text{-}4x^2$ $R^2 = 0.961$ F-Ratio = 49.6 Prob < 0.001
NO: $y = 3.0987 + 0.11124x - 2.9938e\text{-}4x^2$ $R^2 = 0.756$ F-Ratio = 6.2 Prob < 0.060
DS/DK: $y = 18.117 - 2.1274e\text{-}2x + 1.2913e\text{-}4x^2$ $R^2 = 0.741$ F-Ratio = 5.7 Prob < 0.067
Sources: WSR-1, 4, 5, 9, 18, 29, 31.

average of 73 percent of the respondents considered the reports complete and reliable, and only 7 percent disagreed. But over the course of these twelve months, the number either denying the newspapers' reliability—especially during the middle months when, to some Germans, the trials seemed interminable—or withholding an opinion increased from 21 to 32 percent.[9]

OMGUS pollsters used two other means to see how respondents evaluated the newspapers' performance in reporting the Nuremberg trials. First, they asked respondents to assess news coverage via a direct but more open-ended question. Table 6.1 groups the responses recorded by OMGUS analysts in three surveys conducted between December 1945 and October 1946. Again the data reveal high levels of support, but with some dissatisfaction during the trials' middle period. This phenomenon appears more clearly in Figure 6.3, which ignores "other" and the high percentage of irrelevant responses.

Second, in August and October 1946 OMGUS researchers differentiated

9. The data in Figure 6.2 suggest but are insufficient to verify the proposition that perception of inaccuracies in IMT reporting contributed to declining interest in the news accounts.

Table 6.1   Newspaper Treatment of the Nuremberg Trials, 1945–1946

Responses to the Question: What do you think of the way in which the
newspapers report the Nuremberg trials? (percentages)

	Dec. 1945	Feb. 1946	Oct. 1946
Good			
Good; satisfactory; tells the truth; objective; informative; just	51	46	44
Pretty good	12	13	9
Good in general, but: insufficient or dubious details; bad pictures	6	5	6
Incomplete; inadequate	3	4	3
Slow and tedious; dull; too much irrelevant material	3	4	*
Poor	5	8	6
Biased; much propaganda	3	4	3
Unjust; untrue; don't like it; can't believe it; humiliating	2	4	3
Other	1	2	*
Irrelevant response	30	31	41
No answer	1	—	1
No opinion; can't say	14	12	24
Don't (or rarely) read newspapers; don't or can't get newspaper	14	12	16
No interest in politics	1	—	—
Hope so; hope it is true	—	7	*

Sources: WSR-9, 14, 31.
*Less than one-half of one percent.

their general question, asking respondents to rate their newspaper's completeness and its reliability. Table 6.2 groups these data into a fourfold matrix. About a quarter of the respondents (averaging 25 percent of the two surveys) did not respond. Of the remainder more than three in five (averaging 48 percent of the total sample) considered the news reporting complete, and more than five in six (64 percent of the total) considered it reliable. An average of 8 percent thought their newspaper neither complete nor reliable.[10]

10. Viewing the average scores somewhat differently, 44 percent thought the newspapers both complete and reliable, 20 percent complete but not reliable, 4 percent

Figure 6.3

Quality of Newspaper Coverage of Nuremberg Trials, 1945-1946

Question: What do you think of newspaper coverage?

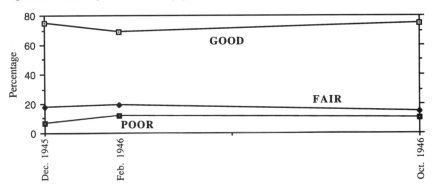

Sources: WSR-9, 14, 31.
Note: Didn't say/didn't know and "other" responses are omitted.

Tables 6.1 and 6.2 indicate that AMZON Germans generally approved of press coverage of the Nuremberg trials, and two factors magnify the force of that approval. As Table 6.2 suggests, readers were less satisfied with the newspapers' completeness than with their reliability. But this observation may reflect Germany's political and economic situation at the time: Allied occupiers, including the United States, had issued relatively few licenses to people who wanted to start newspapers, had restricted publications to one to three issues per week, and, because of the high cost of imported newsprint, had sharply curtailed the number of pages per issue. Newspapers were thus few in number and small in their news content, partly explaining complaints about inadequate coverage of important events. The public's professed satisfaction with Nuremberg reporting, moreover, was consistent with—perhaps even higher than—overall attitudes toward the quality of the media, as measured in surveys conducted long after the occupation ended. Given restrictions on how much the press could print, and given long-standing public views on the German press, its IMT reporting must be viewed as a media success.

Learning about history. The trials in Nuremberg substantially increased AMZON Germans' knowledge of the Nazi era. The learning curve was particularly steep during the IMT's earliest weeks. In late December 1945, six

reliable but not complete, and 8 percent neither complete nor reliable; 25 percent did not respond.

Table 6.2   Quality of Nuremberg Press Coverage, 1946

Responses to the Questions: Is newspaper coverage of the Nuremberg trials complete? Is it truthful? (percentages)

	Completeness					
	Yes		No		Total	
	Aug. 1946	Oct. 1946	Aug. 1946	Oct. 1946	Aug. 1946	Oct. 1946
Reliability						
Yes	43	45	20	20	63	65
No	4	3	10	6	14	9
Total	47	48	30	26	77	74

Source: WSR-29, 31.

weeks after the trials had begun, 84 percent of respondents to an OMGUS survey indicated that they had learned something new from them (WSR-9).[11] Almost two-thirds of the sample (64 percent of all respondents) said that they had learned of the concentration camps and 23 percent of the extermination of Jews and other groups; 13 percent said that they had known nothing about the evils of National Socialism before the trials.[12]

Similar questions posed to AMZON Germans in October 1946, immediately after the trials ended, reinforced the notion that more than ten and a half months of trials had taken a toll in ennui.[13] The number of those saying that the trials were instructive dropped from 84 percent in late December 1945 to 71 percent in early October 1946 (WSR-31). What the respondents found instructive also shifted somewhat: 71 percent referred

11. In August 1946 the OMGUS Opinion Survey Section reported: "The results of a study shortly after the Tribunal convened [on 14] November 1945 revealed that in the intervening few weeks 65 percent of the German people had learned something from the proceedings. In later polls the percentage of people having gained some information rose to 87 percent" (OMG-16). Precise data and dates for these surveys were not provided.

12. These data, juxtaposed with those from surveys reported to have taken place "in the intervening few weeks" after the IMT began, again show initially rapid growth of learning. In the earlier surveys, 65 percent reported learning something, 29 percent mentioned the concentration camps, and 0 percent the annihilation of the Jews; the later survey showed 87, 57, and 30 percent, respectively (OMG-16).

13. This interpretation suggests that some respondents simply did not recall when they had learned about issues raised in Nuremberg. An alternative interpretation is that the respondents were at the outset shocked by what they heard about the enormity of Nazi crimes, but in retrospect they realized that they had been aware of the reality of these crimes well before fall 1945.

to the concentration camps (up from 64 percent in December 1945), and the number who learned about characteristics of Germany's top leaders rose from 13 to 15 percent, but the share citing the extermination of Jews and mass murders dropped from 23 to 12 percent. Overall, however, what was learned remained fairly constant—and, even taking into account declining interest over time, the Nuremberg trials performed their educational function successfully.

Although large numbers of postwar Germans accepted the legitimacy of the Nuremberg war crimes trials intellectually—although they followed the proceedings with interest and used the occasion to learn something about their own country's history—the question remains how well they accepted it psychologically. Resigning themselves to the dictates of the occupation powers was one thing: the trials would take place irrespective of what Germans felt about them. It was quite another matter, however, to believe that the Allies were conducting the trials not only in their own immediate interest but also in the endurable interest of the German people. Germans, after all, had also suffered deeply from the corrupt and criminal men who had led the Nazi regime, and they had a manifest stake in ensuring that their future leaders would be free from any taint of Nazism. Popular German resistance to the trials would make little sense—provided that the IMT carried out its responsibilities fairly.

How, then, did Germans view the twenty-one men standing in Nuremberg's dock? Asked which of them were not guilty, AMZON Germans changed their answers over time (Figure 6.4). In the early months more than seven in ten thought that all the defendants were guilty, and a declining percentage thought that any should be let free.[14] By spring 1946, however, as defendants began presenting their cases, the mood shifted. A survey conducted toward the end of March (WSR-20) asked whether the accused had adequately defended themselves against the charges they had faced. Only 5 percent thought they had done so and 59 percent thought not, but more than a third did not know: firm views were giving way to vacillation. By August 1946 only 52 percent said that all the defendants were guilty. Three in ten found mitigating circumstances for one or more defendants and the same percentage did not know or could not say who was not guilty.

But were the German leaders standing trial in Nuremberg the only criminals? Many AMZON Germans disagreed. In a March 1946 survey 71 percent named others who they thought had committed war crimes (WSR-16). They listed, among others, Nazi leaders and politicians (23 per-

14. A somewhat different question asked earlier in March 1946 produced slightly different results: 71 percent said that all of the accused shared guilt for the preparation of the war, with 10 percent excepting some from blame and 1 percent absolving all of them (WSR-17).

Figure 6.4

Perceived Guilt of the Nuremberg Defendants, 1945-1946

Question: Which defendants do you think are not guilty? (Dec. 1945 and Mar. 1946)
Which defendants do you think are only lightly implicated or not at all guilty?
(Aug. 1946)

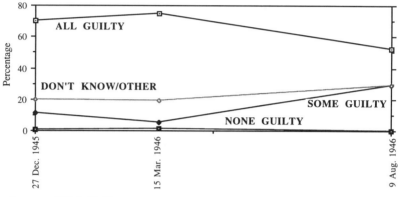

Sources: WSR-9, 18, 29.

cent) industrialists (9 percent), generals and other Wehrmacht officers (6 percent), Nazi activists and fanatics (5 percent), and SS officers (5 percent). (Six percent mentioned "foreign warmongers.") Of those who listed guilty parties, 77 percent thought they should be tried and 8 percent thought not. What about Hitler himself: would they like to have seen him stand trial? In October 1946 (WSR-31) a substantial majority (72 percent) said they would have liked that, while 12 percent thought it better that Hitler had escaped this disgrace.

One of the most creative and controversial prescriptions of the London Charter was the call for the "trial" of organizations. Collective responsibility was the fundamental principle. If the IMT judged an organization to have been criminally responsible for war crimes or crimes against peace or humanity, then any person proved to have occupied a leadership role in the organization was by definition guilty of having participated in an illegal conspiracy. The potential effects of the principle were far-reaching because it identified as criminals not only people who had actively carried out Hitler's aggressive and racial policies but also those who, for example, rose in the military ranks through leadership talents rather than ideological purity.

Three surveys conducted from before the Nuremberg trials began until after they ended found substantial support for the Allied indictment of organizations. Figure 6.5 shows that an average of almost three in five

Figure 6.5

Indictment of Nazi Organizations, 1945-1946

Question: The four Allies have indicted German organizations . . . in their entirety. In your opinion is this procedure justified?

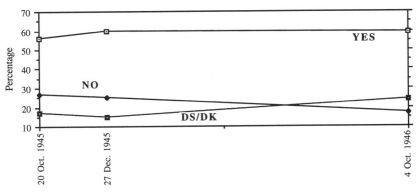

Sources: WSR-1, 9, 31.

AMZON Germans approved it. Those who objected declined from 27 percent in October 1945 to 17 percent in October 1946.[15] Deeper questioning found that the objection was not general but specific. Table 6.3 suggests that respondents were most hostile toward the Nazi leadership and the Gestapo and least hostile toward the SA and the General Staff. Still, 72 percent of an AMZON sample in February 1946 could give reasons why the General Staff was put before the court (WSR-15). Of those citing the military's responsibility for the war (47 percent of the entire sample), four-fifths thought that the indictment was justified. Only one in twelve (4 percent of the entire sample) denied any justification for trying the General Staff.

The trials' fairness. In ten surveys from October 1945 to October 1946, more than nineteen of twenty AMZON Germans who expressed an opinion said that the Nuremberg trials were conducted fairly (79 percent of the sample as a whole, compared with 4 percent who thought otherwise; see Figure 6.6). What perception of unfairness there was became evident during the tribunal's middle months. In October 1946, after its conclusion, 78 percent of the respondents said that it had been fair and 6 percent called it unfair. After hearing the verdicts, 55 percent of the respondents said that

15. In October 1946 the 17 percent objecting to the idea of collective responsibility were asked to state their reasons (WSR-31). Three-quarters of them responded either that such a proceeding could damage many innocent people (46 percent of the objectors) or that the organizations only did their duty (29 percent).

Table 6.3   Culpability of Nazi Organizations, 1945–1946

Responses to the Question: In your opinion, are the proceedings against organizations justified? (percentages)

	26 Oct 1945	4 Oct 1946
"No" respondents	27	17
Groups deserving punishments according to "no" respondents (see note):		
Nazi leadership	14	1
Gestapo	13	*
SS	10	3
Reich Cabinet	10	1
General Staff	8	4
SA	5	5
None of the above	1	5
Other or DS/DK	4	4

Sources: WSR-1, 31.
Note: In October 1945, those saying that collective responsibility was not justified were asked which if any organizations *should be indicted*; responses were reported as percentages of the entire sample. In October 1946, those saying that collective responsibility was not justified were asked which of a list of organizations *should not have been indicted*; responses were reported as percentages of those rejecting collective responsibility, but have been transformed here as percentages of the entire sample.
*Less than one-half of one percent.

the sentences had been just; a fifth called them too mild and only a tenth too harsh.

Immediately after the tribunal's end, OMGUS pollsters asked respondents what they thought were its "lessons" for the German people (WSR-31). The largest class of response (30 percent) to this open-ended question alluded to political leadership: never again to follow a dictator or parties that carried out one-sided economic and political policies. Almost as many AMZON Germans (26 percent) cited the imperative of peace, of never starting a war again. A handful mentioned justice (3 percent) or human rights (2 percent), and very few gave bitterly hostile responses: only 1 percent said the Nuremberg lesson was that there was no justice for Germans. The same percentages saw no lessons whatever or said that the German people would never learn.

German public and the Nuremberg trials. A strong majority of AMZON Germans responded positively to the Nuremberg war crimes trials of 1945–1946. Roughly three in four respondents lent the Allies their verbal support. Even taking into account the empirically based warning of OMGUS

Figure 6.6
Fairness of the Nuremberg Trials, 1945-1946

Question: Do you think that the [tribunal] was conducted fairly?

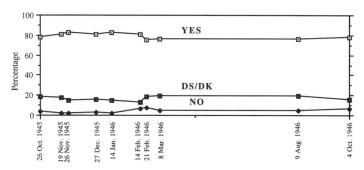

YES: Curvilinear fit not statistically significant
NO: Fit not statistically significant
DS/DK: Fit not statistically significant

Sources: WSR-1, 4, 5, 9, 14, 15, 29, 31; OMG-60.

analysts that responses to questions addressing attitudes toward National Socialism produced a 10 percent bias (Crespi 1950:167–169), we are left with about two-thirds of the population as supporters. Who were the others? Integration of figures from several surveys suggests that perhaps one in twelve respondents was a hard-core Nazi adherent who opposed the Nuremberg trials and any other element of the Allies' postwar strategy; another one in twelve was a more circumspect Nazi supporter—someone who often withheld opinions but, when the occasion arose, stressed weaknesses in Allied policies as reasons for rejecting them.[16] Even so, the massive, bitter opposition to the IMT that some of Germany's critics had predicted did not materialize.

The longer the trials went on, however, and the more redundant the evidence and lines of argumentation became, the more AMZON Germans lost interest in the trial and the more critics found reasons to complain. The Allied announcement in late summer 1946 that the trials would soon end renewed attention, as did the proclamation of the verdicts on 1 October. The slightly shifting trends of the previous year, together with a lack of enthusiasm about further war crimes trials, nevertheless made it clear to the Allies that the Nuremberg tribunal was taking its toll on German morale.

16. Roughly one in six respondents, matching the combined number of hard-core and circumspect Nazi supporters, might be identified as an uninformed or uncommitted person who would go whichever way the political wind was blowing.

The general consistency of public attitudes also raises the question of what Germans hoped to attain from the Nuremberg trials. One interpretation stresses self-justification, for themselves and for their nation. According to this view, the survey data expose a large body of politically disaffected and irresponsible Germans looking for scapegoats to exonerate themselves of blame for the crimes of the Nazi era.[17] A diametrically opposed interpretation emphasizes the norms of international community. Postwar Germans, according to this stance, wanted the International Military Tribunal to punish those responsible for the Nazi excesses. These leaders had not only failed to achieve their promised goal but in the process of failing had devastated Germany and turned Germans into a pariah nation. The defendants deserved to be punished—and, given the circumstances, the occupying Allies could best perform that task on behalf of the German people.

Still another interpretation, in the tradition of Realpolitik, views the idea of justice fairly executed as naive or at best disingenuous. The defeated Germans, it says, aimed to limit damage. They could not force the Allies to abandon their wartime pledge to carry out a war crimes tribunal, but, by supporting the IMT, they could accomplish other goals. They could, for example, soften Allied concerns about Germany's long-term intentions, jettison some of their own failed leaders of the past, avoid any stigma Germans might later have suffered by rendering judgments on their own, and demonstrate to the Allies that continued war crimes trials would be costly in terms of both money and German support for other Allied goals. The sooner the Allies could turn over to German authorities complete control of Nazi criminals, according to this interpretation, the better off all the countries would be.

Changing Public Views

Public opinion data derived from surveys carried out while the Nuremberg trials were taking place cannot answer definitively what postwar Germans hoped to attain. Surely each perspective—self-justification, international community norms, and Realpolitik—influenced some minds.

17. "Indeed," an American journalist wrote, "the attitude of most Germans toward the Nazi defendants at Nuremberg is very much like that of the legendary Russian family in a troika pursued by wolves who tossed their babies out behind them to appease the hungry animals" (Daniell 1945:53). Based on a "systematic interrogation" in early June 1945 of approximately one hundred civilians representing "a rough cross-section" of western Germans, Janowitz (1946) reported a similar phenomenon. Germans, he wrote, claimed "innocence" through "ignorance of the facts," which ostensibly only the Nazis possessed and mercilessly used to manipulate the innocents (p. 144).

A better test of which perspective prevailed is to assess the Germans' retrospective attitudes toward the IMT and other Allied trials and their attitudes toward proceedings initiated by German authorities. A chance to pursue such an assessment came in 1949, when the Western Allies granted a broad measure of sovereignty to the fledgling Federal Republic of Germany. Chancellor Konrad Adenauer honored his government's commitment to carry out new war crimes trials, but he also sought to end this responsibility and to reduce the sentences of Germans already convicted (Adenauer 1965/1966:300, 304, 409, 445, 447). Public opinion expressed in sample surveys followed suit. Three trends became evident in the early 1950s: disenchantment, impatience, and cynicism.

West Germans grew disillusioned about justice as dealt out by the occupying powers at Nuremberg and subsequent war crimes trials. Were the trials fair? As we saw earlier, an average of 79 percent in 1945–1946 called the original IMT fair and 4 percent disagreed. Referring to the broader range of trials four years later, however, only 38 percent evaluated them positively, and 30 percent said that they were unfair (HIC-57). In the survey in October 1946 only 9 percent said that the verdicts were too severe; more than three-quarters thought them just right (55 percent) or too mild (21 percent). Four years later, 40 percent of AMZON respondents said that verdicts had been too severe, 30 percent agreed with the tribunals, and 6 percent said that they had been too lenient. Asked in August 1952 about German generals still in prison, 63 percent of a national sample declared these men not guilty of the crimes for which they had been convicted; only 9 percent said that they were guilty (HIC-153).

The depth of this new sentiment came out later that year. Speaking before a meeting of former SS members, Major General Hermann Ramcke (Ret.) declared that the list of German war criminals was an honor roll, and that the Allies, who had bombed cities, women, and children, were the real war criminals. His remarks created a sensation in Germany and abroad. The West German public, however, did not find them remarkable: more than half of a national sample said that Ramcke's interpretation was essentially (31 percent) or partly (25 percent) correct (HIC-167). Only one in four rejected his comments.[18] Although support for his statement was greatest among those who said that they would welcome a new Nazi party's rise to power, it was also strong among opponents of such a party. Among those who said that they would do everything they could to prevent such a party from seizing power, a larger number agreed wholly (15

18. Another nationwide sample was asked merely for its reaction to a statement unidentified by source but essentially the same as Ramcke's: 46 percent reported that they liked it, 29 percent said they did not, and 25 percent offered no opinion (IfD-1:277).

percent) or partly (30 percent) with Ramcke's statement than disagreed with it (41 percent). Among passive opponents of a new Nazi party's efforts to seize power, 30 percent agreed without qualification and 28 percent agreed partly with Ramcke's statement, compared with only 30 percent who disagreed with it.

West Germans also grew impatient with the very idea of war crimes trials, particularly after the Landsberg decisions of January 1951 (Raymond 1951). A legal review of 101 previous sentences, forced on U.S. High Commissioner McCloy by American and German politicians (Bird 1992), reprieved 21 men from the gallows, commuted the sentences of 29 others (including the industrialist Alfried Krupp von Bohlen und Halbach, who was released), and released 3 sick men while confirming 7 death sentences (executed in June 1951). Of the German public who had heard of McCloy's decisions (64 percent of the total sample), 28 percent agreed with them while half disagreed (HIC-70). Further questions revealed that both those who agreed and those who disagreed felt that the original verdicts had been unjust. The former merely rejoiced at the reduced sentences, but the latter argued that all the men, including those sentenced to hang, should be set free. Only 7 percent of the respondents expressed any appreciation of the reasons for the trials in the first place, the importance of legal review of sentences, or the idea of clemency.

A year and a half later, in August 1952, only 10 percent approved and six times that many disapproved of the way the Western powers had handled the problem of war criminals in general (HIC-153). Most of those who disapproved said that the men then in prison had been unfairly convicted, the Allies had no right to try German officers, or people from other countries had committed war crimes but gone unpunished. One in five critics (12 percent of the total sample) simply said that the war had come to an end seven years before and that there was no longer any reason to keep such men in prison. Four percent even stated that the FRG should refuse to enter into any European defense arrangement until the prisoners were set free. Asked directly what should be done with those still in prison, about half of the critics called for their outright release, the others for legal review by Allied or West German courts.

Opposition to further war crimes trials continues to the present. In some instances the collective response to the issue was ambivalent. When the Israeli government brought Adolf Eichmann to trial in May 1961, many West Germans at both the beginning of the trial (68 percent) and its end eight months later (73 percent) agreed that it should be held in either Israel or the Federal Republic. Only one in seven argued that the passage of time had obviated the need for any such trial (Schmidt and Becker 1967:113). But as Table 6.4 shows, large majorities of those who gave an

Table 6.4 Views of the Eichmann Trial, May 1961

Response to the Question: You have surely heard of the Eichmann trial which has taken place in Israel. Opinions about it are quite varied. Here is a list of some things which many of our respondents to our surveys have said about the Eichmann trial. Would you please read them and tell me with respect to each point whether it is correct or not? (percentages)

	Correct	Incorrect	Impossible to say
People like Eichmann must be punished irrespective of whether or not they were soldiers.	72	10	18
What the communists are doing today is just as bad or even worse than that for which Eichmann is being tried.	61	17	22
I personally had nothing to do with that, and do not want to hear anything more about it now.	59	28	13
If Germany does not learn something from all this, it can easily happen again.	58	22	20
It would be best if one were to forget this affair and if we would focus our attention exclusively on the present and the future.	53	33	14
The worst of it is the damage it does to Germany's reputation in the world—Eichmann is a symbol.	51	29	20
In a practical sense the entire German people is on trial with Eichmann.	30	57	13

Source: Schmidt and Becker 1967:122.

opinion agreed both that it would be best to let bygones be bygones (53 percent) and that people like Eichmann should be punished regardless of whether or not they were soldiers (72 percent).[19] A similar degree of am-

19. In 1983 a former Gestapo officer, Klaus Barbie, was extradited to France to stand trial, convicted for crimes against humanity (Morgan 1990), and imprisoned until his death in September 1991. A West German sample, after being given clues about Barbie's identity, was asked whether or not "even today, almost 40 years after the end of the war, Nazi criminals should be prosecuted" (IfD-8:194). More than half said they should and fewer than a third responded negatively.

bivalence emerged in June 1964, six months after the opening of a trial of guards accused of crimes at the Auschwitz-Birkenau death camp. More than half of the respondents supported the trial either to remind their compatriots of the crimes committed under Nazism (17 percent) or to judge the accused and punish those guilty of such atrocities (36 percent). Thirty-nine percent, though, thought it best not to hold such a trial because the events lay too far back in history (DIVO-1964 [July I/II]).

A willingness to prosecute those responsible for spectacular crimes did not, however, spill over into a more general sphere. In January 1965, 60 percent favored and half as many opposed applying to war crimes the twenty-year statute of limitations written into federal law (IfD-4:166).[20] Asked why, 66 percent of those who wanted to end the trials argued that other countries had committed war crimes, 57 percent that "we as Germans should at long last stop fouling our own nest," 54 percent that so much time had passed that it was difficult to establish the guilt or innocence of the accused, and 40 percent that further trials would violate the statute of limitations (IfD-May 1965, cited in Schmidt and Becker 1967: 118). After the federal government declared the statute of limitations inapplicable to war crimes committed during the Third Reich, opposition to continued trials rose to 67 percent in January 1969 and support for them dropped to 23 percent (IfD-8:194).

Five years later a West German woman known for her public acts against government officials who had once been Nazis found little public support. In early 1974 Beate Klarsfeld tried unsuccessfully to kidnap a former SS officer to take him to France, where he had earlier been sentenced in absentia for crimes committed during the German occupation. Brought to trial herself for attempted kidnapping, Klarsfeld was convicted and sentenced to two months in jail. The case captured widespread attention in the FRG: 70 percent of one sample reported being aware of it, and exactly half of another sample expressed interest in Klarsfeld's trial (IfD-6:92; EMNID-1974 [26:8/9]; and Klarsfeld 1975). Asked generally whether criminals from the Nazi era should still be prosecuted, only a quarter responded positively and 60 percent disagreed. Of those who knew about the case, two-thirds argued that, however noble her intentions might have been, she had broken the law and had to be punished. A fifth of knowledgeable respondents (15 percent of the entire sample) countered that she should not be punished because she had only tried to take a convicted war criminal to the land where he had been sentenced to life

20. Among those who were not apprised beforehand of the statute of limitations, 54 percent expressed opposition to further trials and 34 percent said that if a crime should be uncovered, whoever had committed it should be punished.

imprisonment. Should German courts have the right to re-try individuals sentenced in a foreign court but who had not yet served their full time in prison? More than two in five respondents favored this idea, while one in four opposed it and almost a third offered no opinion. Generalized opposition to new war crimes trials did not necessarily absolve those whose war crimes were highly publicized.

Before the FRG permanently eliminated the statute of limitations for Nazi criminals in the 1980s, the issue stirred periodic controversy. A survey in 1974 (EMNID-1979 [31:2]) produced results similar to those of 1965: 60 percent wanted an end to war crimes trials, and 25 percent wanted to keep them alive. As the issue festered, however, West Germans became both more willing to articulate their sentiments and more supportive of continued trials. A survey conducted in 1978 found 64 percent wanting to call a halt and 34 percent favoring further prosecution. And a year later, after the spectacular television series "Holocaust" was beamed into German living rooms, opposition to continued trials dropped to 46 percent and support for them rose to 50 percent.[21]

Implicit in the growing disenchantment with past war crimes trials and opposition to new ones was a third trend, cynicism. Germans increasingly doubted that the original trials had been conducted solely to apply even-handed justice. At the time of the first Nuremberg trials, as we have seen, large majorities of AMZON Germans expressed satisfaction with the verdicts and accepted the indictment of whole organizations, such as the SS and the leadership corps of the Nazi party. As many favored the prosecution of less prominent criminals as did not (OMG-33). A half-decade later, however, West Germans were questioning the fairness of the trials themselves and the justice of the verdicts.

A dominant thread of the new mood was the sense that the earlier trials had been unjust. Survey after survey during the early 1950s documented the perception that the convicted military officers and others had only been doing their duty, that German courts rather than Allied military tribunals ought to have tried the cases, or that the punishments were too severe whatever the crimes had been. Asked in August 1952 why the generals who were still in prison had been tried at all (HIC-153), most of those who thought them not guilty of any crimes (63 percent of the sample,

21. A survey in February 1979 by the conservative Institut für Demoskopie (IfD-8:194) first reminded interviewees that the statute of limitations on Nazi crimes would presumably become effective at the end of the year (a fact of which 91 percent said they were aware). The survey then found that 47 percent of respondents personally favored drawing a line on the trials, and 40 percent thought that Nazi criminals should still be tracked down. See note 19, which linked a similar question to Barbie's prosecution.

compared with 9 percent who considered them guilty) responded that they had been imprisoned "to vent feelings of hatred and revenge against Germany" (11 percent), because the Allies feared the generals' influence and "keen military minds and qualities" (11 percent), because Germany had been defeated (10 percent), because the generals had carried out orders and performed their duty (8 percent), or to provide the Allies with scapegoats (6 percent).

What made this pill particularly bitter for Germans to swallow was their view that the military of other countries, too, had committed war crimes but gone unpunished. As we have seen, substantial numbers agreed at least in part with General Ramcke's assertion that the true war criminals were those who had bombed defenseless cities, women, and children (HIC-167). Survey respondents also cited commando raiders who killed prisoners, air strikes against civilian populations and virtually undefended cities such as Dresden and Hiroshima, the murder of German soldiers by partisans, the Katyn Forest massacre, and more general examples of Allied "war crimes." Continued focus on German war criminals seemed hypocritical. When opponents of new trials were asked their reasons, the answer they gave most frequently (66 percent) was that Germans should not be prosecuted so long as others were not also under indictment as war criminals. At the end of 1966, given a list of twenty-four political demands to evaluate, 58 percent agreed that there had been enough talk about German war crimes, that one should also take into account the crimes committed by others; only four propositions drew more support (IfD-4:204). At about the same time 52 percent of a sample of university students agreed (36 percent disagreed) that too little was said about war crimes committed by other peoples in World War II (IfD-4:368).

Fueling charges of injustice and hypocrisy was the perception that the Western Allies, and particularly the United States, were playing politics with the prisoners whom they had already convicted as war criminals. When Germans were asked in a 1951 survey why the Landsberg decisions had commuted some sentences and modified others, the largest single group (23 percent) said that the Americans had finally realized the injustice of the trials (HIC-63). But an even larger number, totaling 35 percent, cited various political motives clustered around the theme that the United States now needed German support in the cold war.[22] ("Not one respondent," lamented U.S. High Commission analysts, suggested "that the mod-

---

22. High Commissioner McCloy rejected as untrue a similar viewpoint, expressed in a BBC television program and widely reported in West Germany (Roth 1978): "Political or 'cold-war' considerations did not play the slightest role," McCloy said, in his decisions on such matters as the sentences of war criminals in the Landsberg Prison (McCloy 1978; but see Bird 1992).

ifications may have resulted from a careful, legal review of the issues involved.") A sampling of 110 mayors of West German cities and towns (HIC-67) yielded much the same distribution of responses, and a more detailed survey of a nationwide sample (HIC-70) corroborated the finding that Germans viewed the U.S. decisions as opportunism. The United States, according to this view, wanted to placate Germans and draw them into the Western camp in the struggle against the Soviet Union.

How Have the Nuremberg Principles Fared?

The public opinion data suggest some critical questions. First, how can we account for the dramatic shift in opinion between 1945 and the early 1950s? Second, what implications did this shift have for the U.S. government, and how could U.S. authorities best respond to it? Third, if U.S. occupation of Germany was an experiment in directed social change, how can we evaluate the effectiveness of the trials—and, by implication, the potential for any program aimed at directed social change?

Several explanations have been offered for the changing popular attitudes toward war crimes trials. The simplest focuses on characteristics of the trials themselves. The International Military Tribunal gained attention with its novelty and creativity—and the same qualities aroused emotions ranging from excitement to dread. The tribunal was intrinsically interesting to Germans who had lived through the Nazi era. Many of them were keen to see former Nazi leaders censured publicly and then punished. Others saw the IMT as a public spectacle, a theater of politics that promised—but ultimately did not deliver—high-level intellectual disputation and dramatic confrontations between the Nazi luminaries and their accusers. Then, too, the Allies produced forceful information campaigns to inform and persuade the masses. Even though AMZON Germans wearied as the Nuremberg tribunal dragged on for months (and 211 days of session), the trials remained a continuing source of attention that profited from a reputation of legitimacy.

Subsequent trials lacked these advantages. The novelty of war crimes trials had worn off. Defendants, for the most part lower-level bureaucrats and military officers who had not been in the public limelight, could argue more persuasively that they had only carried out orders. (The same could even be said of Eichmann and Barbie, though other characteristics of their trials propelled them into a glow of worldwide publicity.) Even the media, in West Germany and elsewhere, gave less attention to these trials than to their predecessors. The trials came to be seen as ever less salient to the immediate concerns of the German people and the world. With declining salience came less discriminating attention to details, a more insistent sense of déjà vu regarding each new trial, and more inclination to put an end to the very idea of war crimes trials.

A second explanation of changing public attitudes is the respondents' growing sophistication about legal aspects of the trials. Few denied the London Charter's creativity and most seemed to accept the need for "legally" punishing Nazism's major war criminals. In 1945–1946, however, debates about the IMT's status in international law found little opportunity for public attention. Allied media control helped stifle dissent, and so did the shortages of newsprint, means of transportation, and other communication resources. These restrictions, however, no longer prevailed in the early 1950s. Even if people did not understand the niceties of the legal argumentation, they had time to digest—and accept or reject— its dimensions. And the newly legitimated government under Chancellor Adenauer gave West Germans strength to resist the norms embodied in the London Charter.[23]

Evident inequities further fueled resentment in the popular image. The more the trials moved toward the lower echelons of government, military, or Nazi party service, the closer they came to the wartime experience of the German-in-the-street, the common citizen interviewed in public opinion surveys.[24] These citizens could understand and even empathize with a defendant's situational logic. To hear prosecutors, men who themselves had not faced such circumstances and seemed to prefer rhetoric to empathy, argue that a defendant "could" or "should" have done something differently infuriated Germans. And if the special circumstances of the IMT's trial of major war criminals made it acceptable to AMZON Germans, each new trial reopened the question of why Germans alone were on the dock. What about Katyn Forest, commando raids, terror bombing? The persistent repetition of technical problems raised in 1945–1946, such as principles of evidence, also rankled. More and more Germans said that West Germany, with its status after 1949 as an emergent member of the international comity of nations, deserved equitable treatment.

West Germans never rejected the Nuremberg principles in the early 1950s. Later surveys would demonstrate that strong majorities continued to support war crimes trials of Eichmann and other notorious Nazis. But

23. For example, in 1950, when the FRG signed the European Convention for the Protection of Human Rights and Fundamental Freedoms, it deposited a special reservation that restricted the application of "general principles of law recognized by civilized nations," that is, natural as opposed to positive or codified international law (Lozier 1963:31n55).

24. Doubtless some West Germans, fearing that a wider net could catch them, wanted a general amnesty rather than continued trials. Given the nature of public opinion polling, however, it is unlikely that OMGUS and other surveys would have included many potential defendants.

they came to believe that they had paid their dues for the sins of Nazism. The IMT played an important role, they agreed, and, if an Eichmann or some other criminal had slipped through the seine, he should be netted and tried. But new trials of lower-ranking officials—trials that relied on such tenuous principles of international law—only demeaned Germans; they were counterproductive to the construction of a stable European society.

Meanwhile, U.S. authorities in Germany and at home began to reassess their position on war crimes trials. They had ended the military prosecutions in 1947, and in April 1949 they concluded their twelfth and final Nuremberg tribunal of minor war criminals. Their activities after 1949 were confined mostly to reviews of earlier convictions, executions, supervision of others imprisoned in Landsberg, and lobbying the FRG's government to continue prosecuting Nazi war criminals. But U.S. authorities were alert to shifting public opinion and aware of the stream of polemic from West German politicians, lawyers, journalists, and others. These Germans wanted a freer hand for their government, and they wanted the Americans to release their prisoners.

Pressure in the United States also mounted, particularly in the climate of the cold war. Legal experts increasingly questioned the legality of the trials, often using the same arguments heard in Nuremberg from defense attorneys. Championed by hard-core anticommunists, they challenged the incarceration of only Germans when the Soviets were also known to have committed mass murder.[25] After courageous West Berliners endured the Soviet-imposed blockade from June 1948 to May 1949, America's popular iconography increasingly painted Germans not as the butchers of Auschwitz but rather as protectors of freedom and Western civilization against a communist onslaught. The Korean conflict that began in June 1950 further proved Soviet villainy and the need for a united defense in Europe. At the same time, the Korean commitment strained the U.S. budget. Did it make sense, some Americans asked themselves, to use valued resources of money and skilled personnel to clean up the detritus of past conflicts?

Some U.S. policymakers, seeing a serious military threat emanating from the Soviet Union, thought in short-range, tactical terms. In their eagerness to ensure West German support in the cold war, they may have been glad to jettison long-standing principles regarding war crimes trials. But the logic of the situation suggests that such a bargain was unnecessary.

25. In spring 1949 Senator Joseph R. McCarthy, a Wisconsin Republican, used a Senate subcommittee to terrorize U.S. bureaucrats and occupation authorities with his vituperative tirades in support of Germans who had been tried and convicted for the Malmédy massacre.

172 • Changing Images of the Past

The change in West German public attitudes toward all war crimes trials, including the IMT of 1945–1946, rendered U.S. insistence on outmoded, unpopular policies counterproductive. The longer U.S. authorities dallied in turning over to Germans all aspects of such trials, the more likely were West Germans, leaders and masses alike, to bridle against perceived U.S. recalcitrance. That resistance would, in turn, deprive the FRG of the popular support it needed to track down, prosecute, and punish other Nazi war criminals. To enhance the prospect of long-run support for the Nuremberg principles the United States needed to abandon its insistence on niggling execution of previous decisions based on those principles. U.S. authorities adopted this strategic shift in fall 1951.

The shift in public opinion toward war crimes trials does not mean simply that West Germans were ready to break completely with the Nuremberg principles. The FRG incorporated into its Basic Law and legal codes a number of the principles associated with the London Charter, particularly governing the military sphere. But on the other hand, neither the London Charter nor the many Allied trials in Nuremberg and elsewhere nor the security built into the FRG's Bundeswehr were necessary or sufficient to ensure that individual soldiers in the field of battle would behave as if they were responsible for their own behavior. Allied leaders and journalists were not the only ones distressed by the extraordinary rapidity with which the Nazi regime had been able to turn aside Western notions of civic morality. Democrats in postwar Germany were equally keen to adopt institutions and processes that would prevent similar collapses in the future. Their general success in accomplishing this aim was due more to their own experiences and efforts than to any "lessons of Nuremberg." Indeed, some observers within and without Germany have argued, the irregularities of the Allied attempt to punish war criminals ultimately weakened the German thrust toward democracy.

The data on public attitudes nevertheless suggest a problematic dimension of the Allied attempt to induce social change in postwar Germany. West Germans were quite willing to accept the original IMT proceedings in Nuremberg. But as the intellectual problems inherent in the trials became increasingly manifest and as the net cast by the Allies and later FRG offices grew wider, catching more and more "the good soldier" who had "merely followed orders," West Germans increasingly saw the entire effort as a witch hunt or, perhaps worse, a gigantic fishing expedition with no end. Some people rethought their attitudes toward even the early trials, a revisionism that threatened accepted views of the legitimacy of the Allied occupation and the democratic FRG that sprang from that occupation.

Public opinion followed, with a considerable lag in time, the lead of legal experts and West German politicians. And mass opinion, once it had swung into line behind the leaders, became ever more intractable on the question of war crimes trials—even those of Nazis accused of notorious crimes.[26] It was less the callous exchange of principles for cold-war expediency than this attitude shift—together with dampened enthusiasm for the realities of the Nuremberg principles, in contrast with the ideals—that inspired the transfer to Germans of further responsibilities for prosecuting Nazi war criminals. This transfer in turn strengthened the FRG's hand in carrying out the Nuremberg principles in myriad ways.

Ex-GDR and the Ghosts of Nuremberg

Curiously, however, when West Germans had the opportunity to clarify national policy on the legality of actions taken under totalitarian regimes, they seemed unprepared to do so. In 1990 the disintegrating German Democratic Republic accepted incorporation into the Federal Republic. Four decades of FRG rhetoric had proclaimed the GDR as an unjust state and solemnly inveighed against its communist leaders and their henchmen who had, among other repressive acts, fired on men and women trying to cross state borders to seek freedom in the West.[27] With the breach of the Berlin Wall and German unification, West Germans suddenly had the opportunity to give their complaints legal force: to prosecute GDR "criminals."[28]

The ghosts of Nuremberg fluttered in the wings. Had East Germans acted illegally when they carried out GDR laws and official orders that FRG politicians and jurists considered unacceptable? Or should they be exonerated because they had been following orders—for example, the explicit "order to shoot" at "border violators" trying to flee the country?[29] Similarly, could ex-GDR citizens be punished for not having behaved in ways that GDR law did not require? Could western German judges fairly

26. This attitude creates a dilemma: without general support for further prosecution of accused war criminals, notorious crimes were unlikely to come to light and their perpetrators brought to justice; but such criminals as Eichmann or Barbie were the only kind that most West Germans had any enthusiasm to prosecute.

27. The GDR had been seen as an *Unrechtsstaat*, or state of injustice, in contrast to the *Rechtsstaat*, or state (such as, presumably, the FRG) adhering to the rule of law.

28. This task was made more difficult by the West German judiciary's simultaneous dismemberment of the ex-GDR's socialist jurisprudence and its socialist legal institutions.

29. The order to shoot was made more horrendous, at least from western perspectives, by the installation of automatic firing devices that electronically identified and shot at a fleeing person. In all, over four hundred refugees lost their lives trying to escape from the GDR.

try those who had lived and worked under an entirely different legal system?

The most spectacular effort to bring GDR leaders to justice focused on the country's former SED party boss and head of state, Erich Honecker. Although other potential charges had been mentioned, such as an indictment for embezzlement, Honecker was eventually tried on thirteen counts of manslaughter, based on his role in issuing the order to shoot. The trial took almost three years to mount. Honecker had left the country clandestinely to hole up in the Chilean embassy in Moscow and did not return until July 1992, after Chancellor Helmut Kohl put pressure on Russia's President Boris Yeltsin. The uncertain state of the eighty-year-old Honecker's health caused further delay. He had already had a kidney tumor removed in January 1990 and was known to be fighting cancer. After much judicial debate and public discussion FRG judges concluded that Honecker should stand trial beginning on 12 November 1992.[30]

Why the Honecker trial? From the legal perspective, the order to shoot was manifestly illegal and the men who had ordered it deserved to be brought to justice. From the political perspective, a trial made sense, not only to punish wrongdoing but also simultaneously to give the world a forum to verify the FRG charge that the GDR was an unjust state—similar to Allied goals in 1945 when they established the IMT. But opposition began to surface, politically and judicially. Many doubted that Kohl's pursuit of Honecker's extradition was wholehearted, and the image of the frail but feisty old man in the courtroom began to haunt others. Nonetheless, the public supported the trial.[31]

The trial was badly handled. For days the court permitted Honecker's attorneys to make his health the primary issue. They claimed that his cancerous liver put him on the verge of death, and that to force him to go through a grueling trial would violate the right to human dignity guaran-

---

30. Honecker's codefendants were five other members of the GDR's National Defense Council (NVR): regional SED leader Hans Albrecht; Defense Minister Heinz Kessler; State Security (Stasi) Minister Erich Mielke; NVR Secretary Fritz Streletz; and Prime Minister Willy Stoph. Mielke and Stoph were excused from the trial on health grounds and because of Mielke's pending trial on another charge of murder. In September 1993 Albrecht was sentenced to four and a half years in prison, Kessler to seven and a half years, and Streletz to five and a half years.

31. In October–November 1991 (Im Osten 1991:63) an EMNID survey found that 63 percent of a nationwide sample thought Honecker's extradition important and 36 percent thought it unimportant. The proportion of eastern Germans who favored extradition was 6–7 percentage points less than of western Germans. Similar percentages favored putting Honecker before a court of law: 67 percent of a national sample in favor, 9 percent against, and 23 percent not caring one way or the other.

teed to him by Article 1(1) of the FRG's Basic Law.[32] The court obtained verification from the surgeon at the Moabit prison, where Honecker had remained since returning to Berlin in the previous July, but the defense team provided no corroborating evidence. The criminal court's presiding judge and his designated replacement were dismissed from the proceedings on a technicality. Eventually, on 12 January 1993, the Constitutional Court of Berlin threw out the case: Honecker's imprisonment and the assault against his dignity, the judgment said, violated his constitutional rights. The next day, amid consternation across the land among jurists, politicians, and common citizens, Honecker joined his wife and daughter in Santiago, Chile, where he died on 29 May 1994.[33]

The Honecker trial left many Germans with a bad taste in their mouths. The evidence that Honecker was near death was not convincing. It became even less credible when, after a twenty-hour flight from Berlin via Frankfurt-am-Main and São Paulo to Santiago, he strode off the plane to offer a press conference; when his Santiago physician reported that the cancer was operable and by no means life threatening; and when months passed with no visible evidence of physical decline. Similarly, the plea for human dignity rang hollow in some ears. "Did Honecker," asked those speaking for the mothers of the fugitives, "worry about our son's dignity when they shot him down at the border?"[34] Attempts to reverse the court's decision, and to investigate those responsible for it, failed. About half of the Germans responding to a Forsa-Institut survey conducted on the day of Honecker's departure thought that the judgment was based on political, not medical, considerations (Fisher 1993). The best that anyone could say about the trial was that it had demonstrated the survival of the FRG's Rechtsstaat.

32. A curious international dimension added pressure on the court. A prominent U.S. intellectual magazine, *The New Yorker*, published in its issue of 11 January 1993 a three-and-a-half page unbylined article on Honecker's trial. Readers had no way of knowing that the author was the wife of Honecker's defense attorney. This omission of crucial information—which the magazine's editor said followed *The New Yorker*'s normal procedures for the "Talk of the Town" section in which the article had appeared— doubtless lent credibility to the article's content, which characterized Honecker as a beloved hero among eastern Germans and a very sick old man whom the courts (and the German political system) were viciously persecuting.

33. A survey by the Institut für Demoskopie (IfD/AB 1993:3) reported later in January that 60 percent of a national sample (65 percent of the westerners and 44 percent of the easterners) disapproved of the court's decision, and 30 percent (27 and 40 percent, respectively) approved of it.

34. Berlin's Constitutional Court explicitly added that systematic violation of such rights by the GDR and its leaders was not grounds for ignoring their rights in a Rechtsstaat.

What particularly angered many was that, while Honecker escaped punishment, those who had carried out his order to shoot were being tried, about half of them convicted and sentenced to prison terms under GDR laws applicable at the time of the incidents.[35] Because the GDR did not issue a "shoot to *kill*" order, for example, killing a border violator was to be judged as murder. Some courts took into account, however, the sticky question of personal responsibility vs. superior orders. In one case the presiding judge ruled that, although the defendant was unquestionably guilty of murder, the court could not disregard that he had "functioned as a border guard." GDR law mandated a minimum sentence of ten years for murder, but the judge, taking into account the mitigating circumstance and a traditional German principle of leniency in the case of conflicting laws or penalties, sentenced the man to six years in prison. In October 1993 the Federal Supreme Court in Berlin reversed the decision and raised the sentence to ten years.

A potentially instructive courtroom drama is the Waldheim case. In 1950, guided by Soviet justice, GDR authorities charged 3,442 East Germans with war crimes committed during the Nazi era. The "trials" were in fact kangaroo court procedures carried out by sometimes unqualified judges. They paraded defendants through the Saxon city of Waldheim's town hall, rejected defense witnesses, gave the accused no chance to represent themselves, and, without demonstrating individual guilt, assigned prearranged sentences (Eisert 1993). Two-fifths of the Waldheim defendants died in prison, 32 of them executed. Four and a half decades later, the FRG has initiated procedures to try the only Waldheim judge still living, an eighty-eight-year-old man who spent his later years as a GDR judge.[36]

The Waldheim case tests two new principles about crimes charged against ex-GDR citizens. One concerns application of a statute of limitations. Because much time was lost in handling the caseload during the process of reorganizing East Berlin and the five new eastern provinces, West German authorities feared that serious cases might fall between the cracks. But legislation adopted in early 1993 coordinates procedures for cases occurring after 3 October 1990, the day on which the Union Treaty merger of the FRG and GDR became effective. Before then, and going back to the GDR's founding in 1949, any statute of limitations is suspended. The

---

35. By February 1993, eight trials had been completed, with eight of sixteen defendants convicted. An EMNID survey in October–November 1991 (Im Osten 1991:63) found that 33 percent of a nationwide sample supported these trials and 50 percent opposed them. Differential ratios for easterners (11:81 percent) and westerners (39:42 percent) recall earlier opposition of AMZON Germans to war crimes trials of common soldiers.

36. A problem proved to be finding qualified judges willing to sit in judgment on the case.

effect is to legitimate continued investigations of politically sensitive crimes that occurred throughout the GDR's existence.

Related to the issue of a statute of limitations is the question of how far back in time and to what magnitude of offense is the FRG's judiciary prepared to go? The case of an East Berlin judge, who from 1978 to 1986 convicted seventeen people who she knew were not guilty of crimes, is clear-cut. But in October 1993 the eighty-five-year-old ex-Stasi head, Erich Mielke, was sentenced to six years in prison for having murdered two policemen in 1931. Hans Modrow, Honecker's successor as head of state and by all accounts instrumental in overthrowing the GDR, was found guilty (but not punished) for election fraud.[37] Modrow's defense was that everyone had always known GDR elections to be fraudulent. He was being prosecuted, he insisted, because he had been fairly elected to the Bundestag in 1990. In December 1993 the GDR's spymaster, Markus Wolf, was sentenced to six years in prison for having conducted espionage operations before October 1990—quite successfully, one might add—against West Germany.[38] A Berlin court arraigned Wolfgang Vogel and his wife in January 1993 and in fall 1994 brought them to trial for perjury, blackmail, and tax evasion related to their roles in securing the release of the GDR's political prisoners.[39]

Unknown numbers of "lesser offenders" also face trials for acts that occurred before unification but were for political reasons never brought to trial in the GDR or are now deemed to have been illegal. Narrow interpretations of the laws to be applied and the length of time it takes to process cases have caused some popular unrest, especially among eastern Germans. Accustomed to the GDR's rapid handling of tort cases, they expected that unification and the Rechtsstaat principle would mean virtually instant redress for inhumanities that they had suffered under the communist regime. Persuading them that the wheels of justice grind slowly but inexorably is not an easy task—especially when "explanations" based on political motives are readily accessible.

Such charges of patent political motivation sting the FRG's judiciary. Its judges, cabinet officers, and other appointed officials tend to react

37. Modrow was accused of reporting officially that 98.5 percent of eligible voters had cast ballots for the SED in a local election even though only 90 percent of those eligible had voted.
38. The federal government evidently hoped that the seventy-year-old Wolf would, in exchange for a reduced sentence, identify his informants in West Germany. In May 1995 the Federal Constitutional Court decided that Wolf could not be punished just for serving as a citizen of an internationally recognized country. The court reversed the decision and freed Wolf.
39. From 1964 to 1989 Wolfgang Vogel negotiated the release of 33,755 prisoners and 215,000 relatives (see Whitney 1993). The Vogels were accused of soliciting money and property from those wanting to flee the country and of failure to report such payments as income.

defensively, reasserting their basic position—usually a variant of the FRG as a Rechtsstaat. They point out further that such claims, coming from the devil's henchmen—GDR officials desperate to save their own necks after abusing the political freedoms of their own citizens for decades—are at best self-serving, at worst an affront to the very idea of law and justice.

The apparent confusion and narrowness attending the trials of Honecker and other ex-GDR policy leaders suggest a failure to come to terms with the legal norms Germans supported and condemned during the occupation era. Meanwhile, eastern Germans are becoming increasingly convinced—as had their AMZON counterparts a half-century earlier—that the time has come to end such procedures.[40] The sickly smell wafting through the halls of German justice comes not from corruption but from indecision, palpably political justice, questions about the effectiveness of the vaunted Rechtsstaat, and popular disgruntlement.

40. EMNID surveys in 1990–1992 (Erst vereint 1993:56) asked eastern Germans to choose between two options: "One should draw a line ending our concern with the GDR's 40 years," or "One must first clarify how it all came about and who was guilty." The percentage preferring to dismiss the past and move on to the future increased from a quarter to a half: 23:73 percent in fall 1990, 38:60 percent in mid-1991, and 49:50 percent at year's end 1992.

SEVEN

Denazification
with Anna J. Merritt

One way of overcoming the Nazi stigma was to indict and try its leaders and punish the guilty. But what about the other Germans? If the leaders were evil men driven solely by the desire for personal gain, then the task was simple: remove them and turn governance over to the fundamentally democratic, peaceable German people. If, however, the leaders were committed ideologues, then the disease of Nazism may have affected other Germans as well. Shouldn't the Allies try to establish who had supported the Nazi regime and "denazify" Germany by removing regime supporters from positions of influence?

The Denazification Program

U.S. policy toward National Socialist members and fellow travelers evolved in early 1944. The first official step was the establishment of the Anglo-American Country Unit of Supreme Headquarters.[1] Its primary function was planning nonmilitary aspects of the prospective occupation. Out of these efforts came the *Public Safety Manual*, drawn up by the Public Safety Section of the Country Unit, and the *Handbook for Military Government in Germany*. The former, the first edition of which appeared in September 1944, called for the removal from public life or responsible positions of all individuals who had joined the National Socialist Party before 1933, as well as high-level officials in civil service, economic organizations, and the military. The Country Unit also suggested that the Special Branch of Military Government distribute *Fra-*

This chapter, originally published as A. Merritt (1972), was modified and expanded to include data not available when it was first written, and to meet this book's theoretic base and stylistic format.

1. In fall 1944 this binational unit was broken up and the American section renamed U.S. Group, Control Council for Germany. When the occupation began, further changes were made, and in fall 1945 the Office of Military Government, United States (OMGUS) was established.

gebogen, or questionnaires, to all Germans, while the Country Intelligence Corps would be in charge of making arrests. At about the same time the Country Unit itself issued the more general *Handbook*, which was subsequently turned down by President Roosevelt but nonetheless used unofficially by American Military Government personnel for a number of years. The section of the *Handbook* that dealt with the National Socialist Party was brief, calling only for the liquidation of the party.

Serious turmoil about the scope of the U.S. occupation arose in September 1944. Secretary of the Treasury Morgenthau's intervention into the policy-making process framed the debate: his call for severe intrusions into German society against the moderate view that was dominant in the War and State departments. The Morgenthau Plan never became official policy, but it created a climate of confusion that pushed policy planners in a maximalist direction. Increasing maximalist sentiment some months later was the news that Wehrmacht troops had in cold blood killed 142 unarmed American prisoners during the Battle of the Bulge.[2] Policy planners could not ignore a growing American demand for a tough occupation policy that would root out and punish any Nazi supporters.

The report issued after the Yalta Conference in February 1945 seemed to confirm Roosevelt's intention to include some aspects of the Morgenthau proposal in the final occupation program. The announced Allied intent was "to destroy German militarism and Nazism and to ensure that Germany will never again be able to disturb the peace of the world. We are determined to . . . wipe out the Nazi Party, Nazi laws, organizations and institutions, remove all Nazi and militarist influences from public office and from the cultural and economic life of the German people. . . . It is not our purpose to destroy the people of Germany, but only when Nazism and militarism have been extirpated will there be hope for a decent life for Germans, and a place for them in the comity of nations" (cited in Holborn 1947:154–155). No one was certain precisely how the Allies meant to implement this policy, but the Joint Chiefs of Staff drafted and redrafted its basic document, JCS 1067. By balancing conflicting demands within the Administration, JCS 1067 became increasingly a policy statement with more negative than positive overtones, one more concerned with eliminating certain things—Nazism in particular—than with creating something new and presumably better: "All members of the Nazi party who have been more than nominal participants in its activities, all active supporters of Nazism or militarism and all other persons hostile to Allied purposes

---

2. Just as the Malmédy massacre galvanized American thinking, so a similar event at roughly the same time, the murder of fifty British airmen who had escaped from Stalag Luft III in Sagan, Silesia, had the same effect in the United Kingdom.

will be removed and excluded from public office and from positions of importance in quasi-public and private enterprises."[3] President Truman carried the document into the Potsdam Conference to sell it to the other Allies. His success was mixed. On the one hand, the Allies agreed in principle on the need to deal resolutely with the devil's disciples. The final agreement of the conference stated: "Nazi leaders, influential Nazi supporters, and high officials of Nazi organizations and institutions and any other persons dangerous to the occupation or its objectives shall be arrested and interned. All members of the Nazi Party who have been more than nominal participants in its activities and all other persons hostile to Allied purposes shall be removed from public and semi-public office, and from positions of responsibility in important private undertakings" (cited in Zink 1957:165–166; for full text, see Holborn 1947:195–205; see also Feis 1960). On the other hand, although the Potsdam agreement was binding in all four zones of occupation and Berlin, its passage on denazification was vague enough that its practical implementation varied widely.[4]

In the U.S. zone AMG issued a clarifying denazification directive on 7 July 1945. The document established that all high-level civil servants who had joined the party before 1 May 1937 were to be removed from office. In addition, harking back to the *Public Safety Manual* and the *Handbook for Military Government*, it contained a list of 136 "mandatory removal and exclusion categories."

During this period perhaps the single most powerful figure in the drama of denazification appeared on the scene: General Lucius D. Clay, deputy and later military governor (MG) of the American zone. Almost immediately Clay became aware of the complexities involved in the undertaking. In his account of his four years in Germany, Clay (1950a:67) quotes part of his first report to General Eisenhower, at that time MG, concerning the problems facing the AMG officer: "His mission is to find capable public officials . . . at the same time, he must seek out and remove the Nazis. All too often, it seems that the only men with the qualifications

3. Cited in Fainsod 1948:42; for a full text of this fairly long section of JCS 1067, see Holborn 1947:157–172; USDS 1985:15–32.
4. Because the Soviet Union envisioned a totally new society, its zone showed the most sweeping changes. Many high-level Nazis in the Soviet zone fled to the West, many were imprisoned or given low-level jobs, and quite a few simply became loyal communists. Many top positions in the early postwar period were therefore filled with inexperienced people. This is one of several reasons why it took the Soviet zone somewhat longer than other zones to get on its feet; by the same token it did not have West Germany's problem with ex-Nazis in high places. For further comments on denazification in the other zones see C. Friedrich (1948:254–255) and Zink (1957:165–167), as well as Ebsworth (1960), R. Willis (1962), and FitzGibbon (1969).

. . . are the career civil servants . . . a great proportion of whom were more than nominal participants (by our definition) in the activities of the Nazi Party." Finding trustworthy people to help identify active Nazis was no mean task, especially when one considers how many anti-Nazis had fled the country, died in concentration camps, or been left physically or psychologically incapable of helping. The military forces had interned the highest-ranking and most obvious Nazi leaders as they swept north and east through Germany in the spring of 1945. Following this preliminary action, AMG required all Germans who held or were applying for high-level positions to fill out a questionnaire containing some 150 questions. By the end of 1945 public safety officers had looked at more than 1,650,000 questionnaires and had decided that more than 300,000 of the respondents should be permitted to work only as common laborers (Clay 1950a:69).

In addition to the practical problems the denazification program encountered in its early months, Clay faced the larger ethical problem of balancing his charge against tremendous economic pressures, the alleviation of which required manpower (Clay 1950a:16–19). Because directives were vague, each AMG official could do more or less what he deemed appropriate, so denazification was not uniform even throughout the American zone. This inconsistency gained notoriety in August, when Lieutenant General George S. Patton, Jr., was reported to have said at a press conference that the members of the National Socialist Party were pretty much like the members of the Republican or Democratic parties back home (see Griffith 1950:73–93).

Clearly, existing agreements and directives were not providing sufficient guidelines to fulfill the spirit of either Yalta or Potsdam. Additional clarifications were necessary (Clay 1950a:67–68). Law No. 8, issued by AMG on 6 September 1945, and Allied Control Council Directive No. 24 of 12 January 1946, signed by all four Allied powers, expanded the categories of persons subject to the denazification program. The former barred businessmen from their positions if they had been members of the Nazi party. The latter, reaffirming the ideas worked out at Potsdam, automatically classified as offenders many high-ranking officials from the National Socialist era.

Opposition to the denazification strategy of the AMG program, together with a growing feeling among U.S. officers that they could not possibly complete it by themselves within any reasonable amount of time, led General Clay and his associates to press for a German denazification law and a German denazification program under U.S. supervision (1950a:69–70).[5] The provincial ministers of justice were given the task of drawing up

5. Feeding U.S. officers' despair of completing the task, AMG had received 920,073

such a law in late 1945. After much discussion within the newly elected Provincial Council (*Länderrat*) and between AMG officials and the Germans, the Law for Liberation from National Socialism and Militarism was finally passed on 5 March 1946.[6] The law established five categories of Germans: Class I, major offenders; Class II, offenders (activists, militarists, profiteers); Class III, lesser offenders; Class IV, followers; and Class V, those exonerated. All persons over eighteen years of age were required to fill out Fragebogen—or, as they were frequently called to distinguish them from the questionnaires used in the first phase of denazification, *Meldebogen*—to determine the classifications. The machinery for this immense task consisted of 545 tribunals (*Spruchkammer*) and appeals courts employing over 22,000 persons.

By early 1946, then, the denazification program in the U.S. zone of Germany was operative, if controversial and somewhat confused. As hardliners and liberals debated the issue, authorities shuffled myriad vaguely worded and seemingly conflicting directives, laws, pronouncements, and announcements from various official sources. In fall 1945 antidenazification rumblings also began to be heard among the German people.

Later that year three events put the program in the limelight. In August the U.S. military governor granted an amnesty from all denazification proceedings to persons born after 1 January 1919. Then General Clay, in a speech before the fourteenth meeting of the Provincial Council in Stuttgart on 5 November, expressed dissatisfaction with the progress being made by the German denazification tribunals (see Gimbel 1968:106–110). Finally, on Christmas Day a second amnesty was announced for those with incomes during the Nazi era of less than RM 3,600 and taxable property valued below RM 20,000. The amnesty, which also included the disabled, affected some 800,000 persons, who, it was argued, had manifestly not profited by their party memberships.

By this time the discord between the United States and the Soviet Union had become increasingly apparent, and cold war had become an international fact of life.[7] Churchill had delivered his "Iron Curtain"

Fragebogen by 10 November 1945, representing only slightly more than 6 percent of the total AMZON population; of these, 277,118—30 percent—were still to be processed (OMGUS 1945b).

6. For details on the controversy between OMGUS and German leaders surrounding the writing of this law, especially regarding very basic differences in the legal systems of the two countries and the problem of presumptive guilt that formed the basis of the U.S. denazification policy, see C. Friedrich (1948:263–275), Griffith (1950:347–355), Gimbel (1968:103–106), and Niethammer (1972).

7. A detailed account of the controversy over denazification between the two occupying powers is contained in Griffith (1950:446–454).

speech in Fulton, Missouri, on 5 March 1946; the Truman Doctrine speech came one year and one week later; the Marshall Plan was publicly announced on 5 June 1947; and just one year after that, following the Western currency reform, the Berlin blockade was imposed. The cold war forced western Germany to choose whether or not to place its fate in the hands of the Americans. At the same time it compelled the United States to reevaluate its relationship with its former enemy. U.S. public opinion increasingly abandoned a retributive attitude toward Germans. If Germany was to be an ally, should not the German people be treated as trustworthy and capable? Could the denazification policy, a source of controversy from the outset and increasingly bogged down administratively, be squared with this new attitude?

During the spring and summer of 1948, American involvement in the denazification program was brought to a rapid conclusion.[8] German agents completed what was left in the Meldebogen files, then went on to search out, bring to trial, and punish others charged with crimes, a process that has continued, though with decreasing vigor, in the decades since.[9] But denazification itself, aimed at all Germans who had supported Nazism in any way, ended in spring 1949.

Popular Views on Denazification

What did the German public think about the U.S. policy of denazification—a policy that used sticks rather than carrots to direct postwar Germany toward democracy? AMG officers needed to know the answer because, they reasoned, a seriously disgruntled citizenry could sabotage the U.S. program. One important source of information was the licensed press, not only in AMZON but throughout occupied Germany. The newspapers' editorial pages concentrated on the need for denazification and the benefits of Law No. 8. At the same time, however, newspapers, magazines, and other printed sources carried pleas by a wide variety of personalities for still greater differentiation among levels of complicity, as well as warnings about potential repercussions of the program as it was

8. Denazification had been officially ended in the Soviet zone of occupation in February 1948.

9. Thirteen million Meldebogen were submitted; of these 3,000,000 pointed to chargeable offenses, but amnesties reduced the figure to 930,000 (cited in Clay 1950a:260). The final tally was 1,549 major offenders; 21,000 offenders; 104,000 lesser offenders; 475,000 followers. Nine thousand offenders received prison terms; 30,000 were sentenced to special labor; 22,000 were declared ineligible for public office; 122,000 were restricted in employment; 25,000 had their property entirely or partly confiscated; and 500,000 were fined.

being carried out.[10] OMGUS also gained information simply by asking people what they thought: officials cultivated personal contacts, talked with opinion leaders, interrogated informants, and initiated efforts to sample public opinion scientifically.

Evaluating the popular image of the U.S.-sponsored denazification program addresses five central issues. (*1*) How knowledgeable were AMZON Germans about the program? Were they alert to the provisions of Law No. 8 and its subsequent modifications, such as the Law for Liberation? Did they understand the program's functional aspects, that is, how it implemented basic OMGUS policy? (*2*) How did AMZON Germans view the denazification program from a philosophic perspective? Was it fundamentally a good or bad idea? Such a question, of course, begs for explanation. Hence: (*3*) Why did some respondents see denazification as a good idea? and (*4*) Why did others see it as a bad idea? Was the program reasonable and just? Or was it only a waste of time that the Allies and Germans could better use to address other, more important issues? Finally, (*5*) How did AMZON Germans assess the denazification program's operations? Did the Spruchkammer function effectively? Did occasional breakdowns damage the denazification policy itself?

Knowledge. The denazification proceedings initiated by Law No. 8 did not capture the undivided attention of AMZON Germans. In October 1945 more than a quarter of respondents to the first OMGUS public opinion survey reported that they were not aware of the law (WSR-1; for notations see Chapter 4, note 1). The same question asked two months later found the level of awareness rising only from 73 to 74 percent (WSR-9). Knowledge of the modified Law for Liberation, promulgated in March 1946, was even lower. Shortly after the law was passed 59 percent reported having heard of it, but less than half of these (28 percent of the entire sample) could describe with any accuracy the changes it brought (OMG-7). And in June 1946 only three in five respondents were knowledgeable about new provisions in Law No. 8 (WSR-25).

More detailed questions revealed a certain vagueness even among those who claimed to follow the denazification proceedings. Respondents who said in October 1945 that they were aware of Law No. 8 (73 percent of the entire sample) were asked a follow-up question (WSR-1): Were former Nazis prohibited from earning any living whatever? A third answered either incorrectly (13 percent of the entire sample) or not at all (11 per-

10. A strong plea for thoroughness mixed with compassion and reason was made in late 1945 and early 1946 by a longtime opponent of National Socialism, Ernst Müller-Meiningen, Jr. (1946). A number of biographies and memoirs from this period also emphasize these points: e.g., Edinger (1965:90–91), Heuss (1966), and Schmid (1967). On the fate of Gestapo informants, see Weyrauch (1986, 1989).

cent).[11] Several months later interviewers gave respondents a list of four alternative ways to carry out denazification:

1. American officials without German help;
2. Primarily American authorities with German advice and assistance;
3. Primarily German officials with supervision by American authorities; or
4. German authorities alone without supervision by American officials.

Interviewees were asked which of these characterized the existing system. In March 1946 only 36 percent correctly identified the third mode—primarily German officials under U.S. supervision; 14 percent responded incorrectly and 50 percent not at all (WSR-18; OMG-7). In June l946 (WSR-25) more gave correct answers (44 percent), but more gave incorrect ones as well (22 percent). In September 1946 (WSR-32), only 8 percent of AMZON Germans could even begin to describe how the Spruchkammer operated.[12]

The passage of time, and possibly General Clay's well-publicized speech before the Provincial Council in Stuttgart, made some impact. In December 1946 and January and February 1947, three separate surveys conducted in AMZON and Berlin dealt with denazification in general and Clay's speech in particular (OMG-55). Fifty-six percent of the people polled were able to identify the existing situation from among the four statements, though 23 percent were misinformed. But the new survey hardly showed widespread public interest. Former Nazi party members were more knowledgeable (73 percent) than those with just a former party member in the family (57 percent) or no affiliation whatever (53 percent). Educated citizens (78 percent of those with twelve years of schooling or more) and in the upper and upper-middle classes (75 percent) were also more knowledgeable than the general population. Able-bodied men chose the correct statement more often (68 percent) than did those unable to

11. OMGUS Law No. 8 specified that those identified as former Nazis could neither own nor manage businesses. Of the 49 percent who correctly said that the law did not prevent such individuals from earning their living, about a quarter knew fairly accurately what Law No. 8 did permit, and not quite half thought such people could work only as common laborers (WSR-1).

12. A question asked in December 1946 was written in a way that seems designed to maximize positive responses (WSR-36; OMG-55): "Have you heard or read that the American military governor, General Clay, criticized before the *Länderrat* the way in which denazification is being carried out?" Only 47 percent said that they had heard the speech. Informed respondents were then asked whether or not Clay's criticism was justified: 72 percent answered positively, 9 percent negatively, and 19 percent reported no opinions.

work (54 percent), and both were more knowledgeable than women who were able to work (49 percent).

Answers to a second question focusing directly on Clay's speech showed a similar pattern. Less than half of the AMZON population was aware of the speech, but former NSDAP members (79 percent) and the better educated and financially well off were best informed. OMGUS analysts discovered that 32 percent of their respondents had answered both informational questions correctly (OMG-55).[13] This level of knowledge compares closely with data from late 1945 to summer 1946. Among this group were stunningly higher proportions of the well educated, those enjoying upper-middle or higher socioeconomic status, and former Nazi party members; those with lower-level socioeconomic status, able-bodied women, and respondents with no family connection to the party were underrepresented.

Such figures suggest that during the early occupation months a substantial number of AMZON Germans, perhaps as many as a third, paid no attention whatever to the denazification process, another third enjoyed vague notions about it, and only the remaining third followed its proceedings with interest. Furthermore, the upper social classes and those who felt potentially at risk from denazification paid closest attention to shifting policy.[14] The bulk of Germans, however, had their minds on such matters as revitalizing the postwar German economy.

Philosophy. An early OMGUS attempt to systematically explore German political perspectives elicited solid support for the principle of denazification (OMGUS 1945c; Kormann 1952:56–62). In fall 1945 the Information Control Division interviewed nine mayors and twenty-four political leaders in seventeen AMZON cities and towns. Without exception, these men endorsed the principle of denazification. In fact, although a number of the mayors complained that dismissals had caused inefficiency in the administration of their cities, none suggested that known and genuine Nazis be retained to ensure governmental efficiency. Several respondents mentioned injustices in the program, and quite a few expressed fear that undemocratic procedures would cause—or already had caused—disillusionment in democracy. Law No. 8 was uniformly hailed as a great step forward, both because it permitted differentiation between activists and

13. Of the others, 39 percent answered one question correctly and 29 percent none.

14. One in five AMZON Germans said in June 1946 (WSR-25) that the new denazification law might penalize them personally (19 percent) or that they did not know whether or not it would (2 percent). Of such respondents, however, none thought they would be classified as major offenders, 5 percent as offenders, 9 percent as lesser offenders, 43 percent as followers, 19 percent as Class V exonerated persons, and 24 percent didn't know or couldn't say (WSR-25).

those who had been forced to join the party and because it called for some German participation. Most of the mayors were concerned over the possible long-range political effects of denazification. Would those who had been dismissed become radicalized? Would they turn against their society by joining the communists, starting a new right-wing party, or retreating completely from political life?

Common citizens in AMZON took a similar stance. OMGUS pollsters occasionally asked how reasonable their respondents considered denazification procedures to be and whether such procedures should even take place. Figure 7.1 reveals that in three surveys from October 1945 to September 1946 almost three-quarters of knowledgeable respondents said that the procedures were justified. In October 1945, almost three-quarters of the respondents reported being aware of Law No. 8, and two-thirds of that group (51 percent of the entire sample) said they thought it justified (WSR-1); two months later, with 74 percent reporting awareness, 49 percent found the law justified (WSR-9); and in September 1946, when 54 percent evaluated the quality of the denazification system's verdicts, 40 percent labeled them just (WSR-32).[15]

This positive attitude toward the principle of denazification continued until early 1949, when the U.S.-sponsored program was nearing termination. In January of that year two of three respondents said that it was "a good idea that through the denazification system those people who had furthered National Socialism in any form were held responsible for their actions" (OMG-182). Fewer than one in four disagreed. Even large numbers of former Nazi party members (56 percent) and those with a former party member in the family (59 percent) felt this way. Breakdowns by education and socioeconomic status reveal one highly significant trend among the two groups from which the German elites were drawn: slightly more respondents with twelve or more years of education said denazification was bad than said it was good, and 55 percent of those of upper-middle and upper socioeconomic status were opposed to the program, compared with 42 percent who termed it good.

Figure 7.1 also shows a stunning attitudinal reversal after the end of the occupation. Almost three-quarters of those who expressed views during the thirty-nine months from October 1945 to January 1949 described denazification as a good idea (averaging 52 percent of the entire sample). In a national sample conducted in May 1950, however, the number of

15. In September 1946, 12 percent termed the verdicts unjust and 2 percent gave mixed responses. Another question in the same survey asked, "Up to now, has the manner in which the [Spruchkammer] sessions were carried out been favorable for the defendants?" Three in ten answered positively, one in ten negatively, and six in ten gave a mixed or no response.

Figure 7.1

Reasonableness of the Denazification Process, 1945-1951

Questions: 1945: Have you heard of MG Law No. 8? If yes: Do you think the law is justified?
1946: Do you think for the most part that the verdicts have been just or not?
1949-1951: Do you consider it a good idea that through the denazification system those people who had furthered National Socialism in any form were held responsible for their actions?

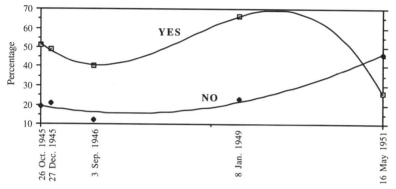

YES: $y = 51.871 - 7.3442e-2x + 1.3301e-4x^2 - 5.1242e-8x^3$ $R^2 = 0.997$ F-Ratio = 126.6   Prob < 0.065
NO: $y = 19.111 - 1.4726e-2x + 1.4139e-5x^2$ $R^2 = 0.961$ F-Ratio = 24.4   Prob < 0.039

Sources: WSR-1, 9, 16; OMG-181; HIC-87.

supporters dropped by half (26 percent) and the number of opponents more than doubled (from 19 to 46 percent).[16] Both before and after the occupation ended, more educated, better positioned respondents and especially Nazi supporters were most critical. It is not surprising that Nazi supporters were more inclined than others to reject the principle of denazification, but it is worth further consideration why postwar Germany's potential elites shared that negative attitude.

Attraction. Our discussion so far has skirted the fact that denazification aimed primarily at the Nazi PGs (*Parteigenossen*), the party faithful who had helped Hitler dominate German society and wreak havoc on the world. These included "big fish" who for years had savored their celebrity and grown rich from looted property, and they included leaders who in the name of the German people had orchestrated and carried out unspeakable atrocities. For individuals identifiable as potential criminals, military tribunals would seek justice, assess guilt, and execute the judgments. But

16. The HICOG report (HIC-87) provided no breakdown by province. Other data nevertheless suggest that, on such issues, the differences between AMZON and national samples were not significant.

less-visible party hacks, too, had at once benefited from Nazi corruption and abused those who did not toe the party line.

Many Germans who had suffered indignities from Nazism's rank and file hoped for retribution or at least justice. They understood Law No. 8's purpose. Asked in October 1945 (WSR-2) why the law restricted PGs to common labor as their means of livelihood, well over half responded in terms of political necessity, such as completely eradicating Nazi influence from all aspects of German life (42 percent) or preventing Nazism's rebirth (11 percent). A much smaller number saw it only in punitive terms: to punish the PGs (13 percent) or show them what work is (9 percent). AMZON Germans were also not averse (89 percent approved) to exchanging PGs for German prisoners of war held by the Allies at home and abroad (WSR-5). What should be done with their property? Almost two in three (WSR-8) thought it should be confiscated: distributed to the poor or needy (27 percent), used for social purposes (11 percent), given to victims of Nazism (9 percent), used for paying reparations (5 percent), or otherwise taken away (11 percent). Half that many said that PGs should be permitted to keep all of their property (5 percent), part of it (4 percent), or whatever they had not illegally acquired (23 percent).

Such intense animosity, coupled with a sinking feeling that hard-core Nazis would slip through the nets of justice, persisted in postwar German public opinion surveys. The first OMGUS survey in October 1945 (WSR-1), after questioning the respondents' views toward Law No. 8, asked directly, "Do you think the military government's measures toward former Nazis are, on the whole, too strict or not strict enough?" A quarter thought them too harsh, but more than a third called them too lenient.[17] Subsequent surveys inquired whether respondents approved of U.S. denazification policy and asked those who didn't to tell why. From November 1945 to October 1946 an average of 49 percent voiced approval, compared with 36 percent who said they disapproved (see Figure 7.2). During the same period, one in three of those who expressed dissatisfaction said that the proceedings were too soft (see Figure 7.3). Thus about three in five either supported U.S. policy or said that it should be strengthened.[18] Moreover—and this is consistent with the ever-broadening scope of former Nazis

17. Of the remaining 39 percent, almost half gave other responses (18 percent of the total) or none at all (17 percent), and one in ten (4 percent) said these measures were both too strict in some regards and not strict enough in others.

18. Respondents were asked in November 1945 (WSR-5) whether they personally knew any PGs who were being treated too harshly. Half of the 79 percent who gave responses said they knew no such people. The rest, permitted to give multiple responses, listed themselves (5 percent), relatives (13 percent), friends (4 percent), acquaintances (15 percent), and others (10 percent).

Figure 7.2

Satisfaction with Denazification Procedures, 1945-1949

Questions: 1945-1947: In general, are you satisfied or dissatisfied with the way in which
denazification is being carried out?

1949: What is your opinion about the way denazification procedures were
carried out—were they carried out the right way or not?

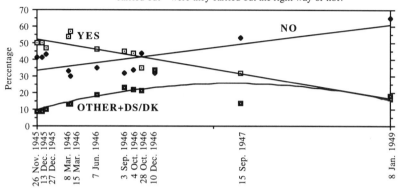

YES: $y = 51.992 - 3.1743e\text{-}2x$ $R^2 = 0.851$ F-Ratio = 57.1   Prob < 0.001
NO: $y = 33.237 + 2.3661e\text{-}2x$ $R^2 = 0.565$ F-Ratio = 13.0   Prob < 0.005
OTHER+DS/DK: $y = 9.5411 + 4.9983e\text{-}2x - 3.9248e\text{-}5x^2$ $R^2 = 0.529$ F-Ratio = 7.3   Prob < 0.011

Sources: WSR-5, 8, 17, 18, 25, 31, 32, 34, 36; OMG-7, 80.

Figure 7.3

Denazification's Treatment of Former Nazis, 1945-1947

Dissatisfaction Because "Too Soft," as a Percentage of "Too Hard" + "Too Soft"

Question: In general, are you satisfied or dissatisfied with the way in which denazification is
being carried out? If dissatisfied: Why?

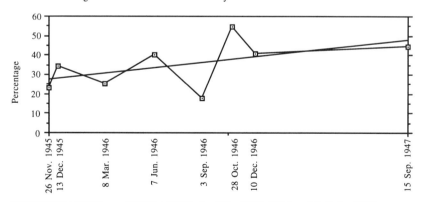

SOFT/(HARD + SOFT): $y = 0.27532 + 3.0268e\text{-}4x$ $R^2 = 0.287$ F-Ratio = 2.4   Prob < 0.160
Sources: WSR-5, 8, 17, 25, 32, 34, 36; OMG-7, 80.

granted amnesty—the concern with excessive leniency increased the longer denazification went on, by an average of 0.9 percentage points per month.[19]

The desire to punish PGs did not extend to all former Nazis. AMZON Germans regarded denazification procedures as different from war crimes trials. As we have seen, they supported the principle of bringing conspicuous Nazi criminals to justice. But public opinion findings reported increasing concern about what some Germans (and some Americans as well) considered fishing expeditions. Responses to questions asked in October 1946, immediately after the International Military Tribunal in Nuremberg sentenced the major war criminals, demonstrated this growing reluctance (WSR-31). Solid numbers of respondents continued to praise the IMT's conduct and verdicts, but as many respondents rejected the suggestion that lesser Nazi party members should be brought to trial as accepted it (43 percent each).

Further questioning shows diminishing bitterness toward lower-echelon PGs. Just as AMZON respondents were reluctant to accept war guilt for the entire German people, they were disinclined to attribute guilt to all PGs (WSR-31). One series of questions asked whether those who had joined the party before 1 May 1937—that is, during Nazism's formative period—were more or less guilty than those who joined later, when party membership was required for some categories of civil servants, such as public school teachers. A third said early members were more guilty, 18 percent cited late members, and 33 percent saw no difference between them. What about party functionaries—were they more to blame than nominal PGs? Seven in eight respondents said that the functionaries were more guilty (77 percent) or just as guilty (11 percent); most of the rest said that nominal PGs shared the blame (10 percent) or bore sole blame (1 percent). In short, AMZON Germans who thought that PGs deserved punishment made some small allowance to those nominal PGs who had joined late and taken no active role in the Nazi party.

What impact did denazification have on former Nazis? Two concurrent surveys conducted by OMGUS in September 1947 attempted to answer this question. One questionnaire was offered to a random sample of 300 known PGs, AMZON Germans whose Meldebogen had been kept on file

19. In September 1946, 40 percent of AMZON Germans reported that denazification was less severe than they had expected that it would be, while 27 percent thought it more so. The other respondents either offered no opinion (30 percent) or said alternatively that the reality was exactly what they had anticipated or that it was more severe in some respects, less in others (3 percent). The correlation coefficient on Figure 7.2—R squared equals 0.287—indicates that a linear model explains about 29 percent of the variance across time, but, at the 0.16 level of probability, this is not highly significant.

because of each individual's high level of activity in the party. The other survey questioned 3,000 randomly selected AMZON Germans. Among them were 359 admitted PGs, those who volunteered the information that they had been affected by denazification in some way or had been party members; the remaining 2,641 were unaffected respondents.[20]

The attitude toward denazification on the part of these three groups reinforces earlier findings. Greater differentiation of opinion comes with awareness. Far more of those who were not affected by denazification expressed satisfaction (34 percent) or no opinion (15 percent) than did those who admitted being PGs. Of the admitted PGs, 15 percent expressed satisfaction, 15 percent felt the proceedings too harsh, 2 percent thought them too mild, 61 percent had other reservations (in particular the contention that less important people were treated too harshly, important ones too mildly), and only 4 percent had no opinion. When the known PGs were asked whether or not they thought denazification was justified, 60 percent said it was.

The data suggest that Germans originally saw denazification as a means to punish those who had led their country to disaster and to prevent them from regaining political, economic, or social power. The German-on-the-street seemed pleased that U.S. occupation authorities were carrying out this task. But these attitudes shifted over time. One reason for the shift was a growing perception of inequity. Some PGs had joined the party not because they wanted to but because they had been forced to, and some PGs had not played an active role in the party. Accordingly, AMZON Germans increasingly questioned a denazification policy that continued to grind such nominal PGs through the wheels of justice, and they increasingly worried that soft procedures would let the "big fish" slip away.

Rejection. Some Germans doubted the efficacy of denazification. The interview in fall 1945 of thirty-three mayors and other local political leaders is a case in point (OMGUS 1945c). All of them supported the idea of denazification, and none wanted to keep former Nazis in municipal offices even if their loss reduced governmental efficiency. Some nevertheless feared that the questionable premises underlying denazification, along with its uneven implementation, could damage the prospects for German democracy.

More generally, from October 1945 to January 1949, as Figure 7.1

---

20. Five percent of the known PGs had been classified as major offenders (the highest category), while no admitted PG had been given this ranking. Fifteen percent of the admitted PGs and no known PG had been exonerated. These two groups resembled each other remarkably closely in background but differed markedly from the unaffected group. For example, 40 percent of the known PGs and 41 percent of the admitted PGs had nine years of education or more, compared with 16 percent of the unaffected (OMG-80).

shows, an average of one in five AMZON Germans directly opposed denazification. At the end of the period the figure was 24 percent, almost half of whom justified their claim by saying that Nazi party members had been idealists, that only criminals ought to be punished. A second argument centered on political freedom as the basis for democracy: "Many people today are members of parties—they also wouldn't like it if they were later punished for that; after all, we have freedom of thought and conviction" (OMG-182). This critical attitude was itself not very prevalent among German public opinion respondents. The notion that participation in an unsuccessful party could by itself lead to retaliation nevertheless supported widespread apathy toward things political. Keep away from politics, it said—and, indeed, numerous studies in subsequent years showed that early postwar Germans went to the polls in large numbers, but less out of conviction than out of a sense of duty (see Almond and Verba 1963:428–429; Dahrendorf 1965/1967:67–82; and A. Merritt and R. Merritt 1970:43–50).

Two surveys neatly link denazification and basic democratic principles (OMG-93). One sampled men to whom OMGUS officials referred as the "cream of the crop"—German prisoners of war sent during the war to Fort Getty in the United States for schooling in democracy and American values (see Ehrmann 1947). They were returned home after the war, with certificates showing that they had completed the course but otherwise no special provisions (such as employment). The second, discussed earlier, interviewed in September 1947 known Nazi party members, self-identified PGs, and unaffected respondents.

Seventy-eight of the Fort Getty trainees responded to a lengthy questionnaire sent them in spring 1947. These men were not typical Germans. Their original selection was based on relatively democratic political outlook, intelligence, and education. By the time of the survey 73 percent filled white-collar jobs or had professional status. They were also more willing to participate in local affairs and to join political parties than was the general public. Their responses to all the questions—ranging from the purely political to the highly personal—reflected a great deal of differentiation and critical judgment.

What to do with former Nazis and how to prevent their resurgence were not high-priority issues for the Fort Getty graduates. What impressed them most on their return to Germany? With multiple responses permitted, the largest number cited "corruption [and] red tape" (44 percent) and the "remains of Nazism and militarism, [evidence that] people did not learn from the past" (42 percent). Both responses suggest a call for action, the latter even hinting at punishing PGs. But, asked what they considered to be the most urgent problems facing the German people, less than a fourth of the sample mentioned denazification. Respondents attached far greater importance to such matters of everyday living as increasing production (73 percent) and stabilizing the food supply (60 percent), as well as the "reeducation of the German people" (49 percent). Moreover, 36 percent of the respondents cited the denazification program as an outright hindrance to the democratization of Germany. As one respondent put it, "The fact that denazification is frequently carried out in an unjust way makes it impossible to educate Germans in a democratic sense." Other arguments were that the whole program rested on legally inadmissible ex post facto law and that the truly guilty Nazis were not being tried.

Surveys in September 1947 of known Nazi party members, admitted PGs, and unaffected respondents (OMG-80) permitted contrasts between individuals who had committed themselves to Nazism and those who had not. For the committed, concern about denazification was more focused than the vague anxiety that all nominal PGs might be punished while leaders escaped.[21] Asked "In which realm do you think denazification has had the more important impact—in the economic or the political?" a majority of both known PGs (56 percent) and admitted PGs (54 percent) indicated the economic. In contrast, the unaffected split fairly evenly, with 31 percent saying economic, 30 percent saying political, and 39 percent expressing no opinion. When questioned about which of seven points they thought were the result of denazification, respondents from all three sample groups mentioned most frequently the lack of expert officials, followed by the lack of business experts and the feeling that former party members found themselves in economic need.[22]

Precisely what impact denazification had on the economic domain will never be known. A survey conducted in October 1946 (OMG-38) concerning job status revealed two dimensions of this issue. First, former PGs enjoyed higher socioeconomic status than others. A former party member was more than twice as likely as someone who had not joined the party to

21. An OMGUS report in September 1947 stated that 82 percent of the denazification cases dealt with "heavily incriminated" persons (cited in OMG-80:6). But those who felt that denazification was less important than getting the wheels of production rolling again may have found occasion to let an important person or former Nazi leader through relatively easily. As Zink (1957:164) points out, "The very fact that the net was so widely spread made it possible for certain shrewd and wily Nazi 'big boys' to get through the mesh." Even Clay (1950a:261) expressed doubts about whether it was possible to accomplish what the United States had set out to do.

22. The unaffected mentioned the third proposition less than half as often (23 percent) as did the other two groups (50 percent and 49 percent). In fact, the unaffected put in third place the assertion, "Active National Socialists are removed from responsible positions and replaced by people who are truly democratic."

have received at least some university training. Given Germany's traditional social and educational structure (see Dahrendorf 1965/1967), we
might expect a preponderance of these well-educated PGs to fill high-level
business and government positions, and indeed, 28 percent of the PGs held
such positions, compared with 12 percent of those who had not been party
members. Some former PGs, however, suffered demotions and other immediate burdens. Second, only 53 percent of those classified as professionals during the war were still in such jobs. For public employees the
figure was 40 percent. In contrast, 77 percent of the independent businessmen were still in their chosen fields, and for farmers the figure was 86
percent. The changes in job status were undoubtedly as much due to the
inevitable upheaval caused by war, especially a lost war, as to other
causes, including denazification (Gimbel 1968:171–178). Yet it seems reasonable to assume that, with so many party members in the groups in
which the most significant switches were made, there was more than a
coincidental relationship.[23]

Postwar Germans thus faced a dilemma. Those who had benefited
personally from Nazism, most specifically the former Nazi party members, wanted as little denazification as possible. But what about the Germans who had suffered Nazism's consequences? On the one hand many
were so disgusted with the behavior of PGs in 1933–1945 that they wanted
these moral lepers removed from positions of influence. On the other
hand, however, many Germans, including some who applauded the principle of denazification, believed that rebuilding their war-torn country
was a demand of highest priority that required assistance from its most
qualified individuals. If this meant returning at least noncriminal PGs to
influential positions, then so be it. In the circumstances, professional competence was more important than moral purity.

Effectiveness. Another question frequently asked by OMGUS pollsters
addressed the effectiveness of denazification procedures. "In general," interviewers inquired, "are you satisfied or dissatisfied with the way in
which denazification is being carried out?" Figure 7.2 shows that, from
late November 1945 until the Nuremberg war crimes trials came to an end
forty-five weeks later, an average of 49 percent reported being satisfied

23. A survey conducted in 1953 by the Operations Research Office of Johns Hopkins
University under the direction of John D. Montgomery confirms this assumption: "A
total of 8 percent stated that they had personally 'been disadvantaged' because of denazification, and an additional 15 percent stated that members of their families had.
Many more of the university graduates had felt its effects (23 percent) than those with
grammar school (6 percent) or high school (10 percent) education" (from an unpublished
manuscript by Professor Montgomery, who kindly provided us with portions of it; see
also Montgomery 1957).

and 36 percent dissatisfied.[24] The highest levels of dissatisfaction during this early period came in late 1945, when a review of Law No. 8 was under way. The mood improved in the following March after the new Law for Liberation was promulgated. Almost two in three who expressed views in mid-March 1946 gave positive responses (WSR-18). But the less knowledgeable were even more positive than the informed; those who had heard about the new law may well have seen that it did not encompass everything they had hoped.[25]

The mood began to darken again in summer 1946, at the time that U.S. policymakers were preparing for Secretary Byrnes's speech in Stuttgart.[26] By December AMZON Germans divided almost evenly among those expressing satisfaction, dissatisfaction, and indecision about denazification procedures. By September 1947 only 32 percent said they were satisfied and 53 percent dissatisfied. And by January 1949 the ratio dropped to 17 to 65 percent; that is, almost four in five who gave an opinion disapproved of the way denazification procedures were carried out. The "don't knows" reflected this mood change as well. Through June 1946 those not responding to the question averaged 12 percent. This figure rose to 22 percent between September and December 1946 before dropping to 15 percent in the late occupation era. These data suggest that a mood change of perhaps one in ten AMZON Germans went through a two-step pattern from satisfaction through uncertainty to dissatisfaction.

What forms did this growing dissatisfaction take?[27] As we have seen, of the 30 percent in March 1946 who had suggestions to make about handling denazification, a third said that nominal Nazis should be treated less harshly than activists and that greater care should be taken in determin-

24. The surveys cited in Figure 7.2 solicited reasons why respondents were dissatisfied.

25. A cross-tabulation between knowledge and satisfaction revealed that, of those who had heard about the new law in March 1946 (59 percent), less than half (28 percent of the entire sample) could provide concrete information about the changes (OMG-7). Of the knowledgeable, 52 percent were generally satisfied with it, but almost two-thirds of those who had not even heard about it also expressed their satisfaction. This negative relationship between knowledge and attitude toward denazification is consistent with findings that linked education and socioeconomic status to both Nazi party membership and skepticism about denazification.

26. Between March and December 1946, with but one exception, the level of dissatisfaction remained below that of late 1945. The strongest rise in 1946 was in the number of respondents who offered no opinion. This ambivalence diminished by September 1947, when the new U.S. policy that would terminate denazification became evident.

27. For a detailed and illuminating discussion of the opposition to denazification procedures on the part of such groups as the clergy and university professors, as well as individuals like the liberal editor of *Frankfurter Hefte*, Eugen Kogon, and deputy minister of political liberation in Hesse, Karl Heinrich Knappstein, see Griffith (1950:390–407).

ing who was an activist (OMG-7). The Fort Getty graduates leveled similar criticisms (OMG-93). Adverse comments in the survey focusing on Clay's Stuttgart speech (OMG-55) were broken down in the report according to whether respondents thought denazification too harsh or too easy. Three-quarters of those who thought it too harsh felt it punished the little people too severely, and another 10 percent mentioned inconsistencies in the judgments. Among those who were neither satisfied nor dissatisfied, 45 percent felt denazification was too harsh on little people, and 42 percent complained about inconsistent judgments. The knowledgeable group discussed in the same report—those able to pick the one correct statement out of four describing the existing situation—was also more likely to express dissatisfaction with that situation: among the satisfied, only 57 percent correctly characterized the program, but among those who thought the program too harsh, two-thirds knew how the program worked. Of those who felt it was too easy, 62 percent were knowledgeable.

By early 1949, when the U.S. denazification program was almost finished, large numbers of AMZON Germans thought that, whatever its merits, it had not been well carried out. Each category of respondent emphasized negative rather than positive sentiments. This was true of men (71 percent of whom thought the program poorly carried out, compared with 18 percent who thought it well carried out), and it was true of those with twelve or more years of education (85 to 12 percent), earning DM 750 or more per month (83 to 11 percent), with higher socioeconomic status (90 to 7 percent), and former NSDAP membership (78 to 17 percent). Even at this late date, almost 60 percent of the critics (37 percent of the total) complained that minor party members were punished too severely compared with major ones. About one respondent in eight declared that the Spruchkammer "did not judge objectively; accusers, judges, and witnesses could be bribed" (OMG-182).[28]

Sour frosting on the cake came from the numerous scandals that beset the tribunals. These ranged from "lost" evidence to perjury, from verdicts that reflected cronyism and political partisanship to judges pocketing bribes.[29] Corruption was not the norm, but, given the German judicial

28. How widespread corruption actually was is not known; in so large an operation there was bound to be some and, as usually occurs, a number of particularly juicy stories made front page headlines. For a listing and discussion of some of these, see Herz (1948:581–589) and HIC-8.

29. Zink (1957:164) writes: "The scandals arising out of the German administration of the denazification program were numerous and frequently sensational. The Munich Denazification Tribunal had to be thrown out and a new organization set up. It was commonplace for judges, prosecutors, and investigators to be charged by responsible persons with accepting bribes. Minor Nazis sometimes drew heavier penalties than the

system's traditional attention to detail and legislation, critics could hardly avoid interpreting the scandals as more or less systematic acts of passive resistance. The media encouraged this interpretation by blowing the events out of proportion. It became chic for the mass of Germans to look askance at the entire denazification process.[30]

The HICOG Reactions Analysis Branch decided in early March 1950 to ascertain what impact such events were having on AMZON Germans (HIC-8). Six weeks earlier a chief prosecutor and a commercial agent had been arrested in Württemberg-Baden, accused of accepting bribes in connection with denazification cases. The U.S. commissioner in Württemberg-Baden and the province's minister president turned the criminal investigation into a cause célèbre with mutually contradictory public statements, and the U.S. high commissioner, John J. McCloy, felt obliged to clarify his government's position.

The affair caught the public's attention. Three-quarters of the respondents had heard about what the survey described as a "denazification scandal," and over nine-tenths of that group (68 percent of the entire sample) could name the persons involved in it. Four in five who gave an opinion said that the incident was not unique but reflected many other, undiscovered cases. Nine in ten who responded thought that such incidents took place not only in Württemberg-Baden but elsewhere—and 7 percent thought they occurred even more frequently elsewhere. "Many people say that this scandal proves that the whole denazification process has been nothing but a fraud and money-making scheme," the interviewers commented before asking, "Are you also of this opinion or do you believe that denazification has had a real value?" More than half labeled it a swindle and only 29 percent thought denazification to be of real value.[31]

The data suggest that, as far as the AMZON public was concerned, the downfall of denazification was not fundamental hostility but weaknesses in the program itself, often made worse by members of the established elites. A substantial number of Germans rejected denazification from the outset, to be sure, and some no doubt looked for reasons to rationalize their skepticism. But the uncommitted abandoned their willingness to support the program as its weaknesses became manifest:

most active Nazi leaders. Influential Nazis managed in some instances to get their cases disposed of with little fuss."

30. With reference to a popular German powdered soap, *Persil*, the PG exonerated by a Spruchkammer could proudly boast of having received a *Persilschein*—whitewash.

31. Other questions found that more than seven in ten who gave an opinion (57 to 23 percent) sided with the U.S. commissioner in his jurisdictional dispute with Württemberg-Baden's minister president; nearly a third thought the latter was personally implicated in the scandal; and more than a third thought he should have resigned.

- Early failure to differentiate between hard-core Nazis and nominal PGs;
- Initial concentration on the "easy" cases—often with minor Nazis as their targets—followed by amnesties for higher-ranking officials;
- Unevenness of the verdicts;
- Evidence of corruption; and, of course,
- The economic and other costs of denazification at a time when Germans had other priorities.

Ultimately the country had a minority of citizens—perhaps a third or even a fourth of the electorate—who strongly opposed any resurgence of Nazism—any return to power of former PGs—and who saw denazification policy, however flawed, as a means to achieve that end, to move toward a more democratic Germany.[32] For various reasons, however, opponents of this group became increasingly powerful, and the nature of German society in the late 1940s and 1950s made ever more attractive to the masses the "purified" old rather than the untested new. Denazification became an easy target for its enemies.

Denazification and Restoration

The OMGUS surveys present a clear picture of the rise and fall of denazification in the attitudes of the German public. During the occupation period of 1945–1949, a majority of the adult population in the U.S. zone always favored the principle underlying the program. The shakiness of its legal underpinnings notwithstanding, the program promised to purge former Nazis from their dominant role in German politics, economics, and society. But the principle of denazification soon encountered roadblocks. U.S. heavy-handedness failed to account fully for differences between U.S. and German legal norms and to consider the possibility that many Germans—including some who for whatever reason had joined the Nazi party—might truly desire a new, democratic Germany. Procedural irregularities, including regional variations, uneven treatment of PGs, and outright corruption stirred further resistance. These irregularities, harped on by critics of denazification, aroused popular suspicion and anxiety.[33]

32. An independent national survey in September 1951 asked respondents what they considered to be the greatest error committed by the occupation powers and permitted them to give multiple responses (IfD-1:140). Only 6 percent named denazification; six other "errors" got higher rankings.
33. Independent national surveys found continuing support for denazification (IfD-1:142). In August 1948, well over half of those offering opinions thought that denazification was constructive—4 percent as necessary and successful, 10 percent as

Another source of growing disenchantment with the denazification program is more complex. Just as a direct question in the United States on blacks or Jews frequently elicits "politically correct" responses suitable to the American ideal of equality, a question in Germany concerning anti-Semitism prompts lip service to the democratic ideal that may or may not correspond to the person's true feelings. And just as most white Americans were shocked in the 1960s at the suggestion that their attitudes might be termed racist, it was difficult for the bulk of the German population to accept the notion of collective guilt implicit in the denazification program. Germans were willing to accept punishment of "the Nazis"—as long as this term referred to high officials or remained nebulous. But as soon as it became evident that denazification was a wide net ready to catch all manner of fish, Germans became uneasy. The obvious and well-publicized shortcomings of the program provided a simple solution to this psychological dilemma: dissatisfaction with denazification rested on injustices and inconsistencies in the program, but certainly the idea behind the program was very good. Casting further doubt on the future of the program, the trend toward increasing disenchantment with denazification was most marked among potential leadership groups and ex-Nazis.[34] On the other hand, strong minorities not only favored the idea of denazification but were also satisfied with the program as it was conducted during its entire and varied existence. The American denazification program, despite its palpable drawbacks, was in the public view not an unmitigated disaster.

What implications did the public opinion surveys have for policymakers considering what to do with the denazification program? At no point was opposition to denazification sufficient to warrant canceling the program. With sensible modifications to accommodate legitimate complaints about its procedures, the denazification program could, other things being equal, have carried on for a long period of time. But the circumstances of fall and winter 1945–1946, when the program was created, did not remain constant, and denazification had not garnered from either the German public or U.S. and German leaders the unquestioned support needed to sustain it in times when new priorities captured attention.

important but flawed, and 39 percent as necessary but incorrectly carried out—whereas 31 percent thought it both unnecessary and bungled and 9 percent saw it as Allied chicanery. In November 1953 half termed it constructive (5, 12, and 23 percent, respectively) and half useless (26 and 14 percent, respectively). Note that the percentage of negative responses (40 percent) remained constant during these five years.

34. Although these two groups exhibit many similarities, the poll data do not provide any proof that they were identical.

Shifts in the U.S. stance toward occupied Germany created the circumstances that deprived denazification of its momentum. That the United States had moved from a punitive to a reconstructive mode became clear by September 1946, when Secretary of State James F. Byrnes delivered in Stuttgart a highly publicized speech calling for economic recovery. The emerging cold war then led U.S. occupation authorities to consider Germans as future allies rather than merely defeated adversaries. This is not to say—as has often enough been said—that cold war pressures forced the United States to abandon its occupation policies, including denazification. Rather, given the new circumstances, U.S. occupation authorities had to evaluate the policy's various elements: Which were of highest priority and should be fought for? Which were of only marginal importance? Which could be maintained in a somewhat modified form? How could Germans be persuaded to take a more active role in implementing high-priority policies?

U.S. policy on denazification shifted toward a middle ground. OMGUS reduced the burden of a heavy caseload by granting amnesties to more categories of PGs. By 1948 those who had avoided prosecution, or whose cases had been postponed because of the enormous number of Meldebogen on file, were able to regain their former positions. OMGUS also transferred more authority to German tribunals and limited opportunities for direct control by U.S. officials.[35] Irregularities proliferated, discrediting the entire denazification program and making it easier for German politicians to enact legislation that undid many of its actual accomplishments.

The retreat of denazification did not mean a reascension to power by hard-core Nazis. National Socialism as a movement was and is dead. Its leaders, who had lost the war and brought to Germany both disgrace and disaster, were discredited. The deterioration of the denazification policy did mean, however, that those who had accepted, facilitated, or profited from the Nazi regime suffered only a temporary setback. Those who rose to positions of political and economic power in the Bonn republic were by and large the traditional, national conservatives of the Wilhelmine Reich and the Weimar Republic. Denazification, then, rather than bringing about a thorough reevaluation and the construction of something new, merely contributed to the restoration of the pre-1933 condition.

35. It is questionable whether or not the United States had ever had enough legally trained German-speakers who were knowledgeable about German law and society and who could properly supervise the denazification hearings of what early officials had estimated to be three million or more Germans.

Enemies of the People

From another perspective—what some observers see as a fundamental German intolerance of dissent—it is not surprising that Germans supported a denazification that did not impinge on their social framework (see Dahrendorf 1965/1967). According to this perspective, the populace had been willing to support and even reward Nazis because they represented the society's dominant authority, an authority based on the sociopolitical system that they had created out of Weimar Germany's chaos in 1930–1933. Discrediting the Nazi system thus meant discarding its representatives—or at least those who could not adapt quickly and persuasively to the new sociopolitical system that the Allies and their German agents were establishing. Individuals openly craving the reestablishment of that authority deserved the scorn they got, for they were undermining post-1945 hopes for reform.

With time, new enemies of the people emerged, not to restore former Nazis to public favor but to supplement them with new sources of danger. The conservative alliance on which Chancellor Adenauer built the FRG's first government studiously ignored the idea of making PGs responsible for the sins of Nazism. For democracy to take root on German soil, Adenauer said, required reconciliation, not divisive legal procedures. Besides, reconstructing Germany demanded the most qualified individuals, irrespective of their links to Nazism. Those accused of crimes should be investigated and brought to trial, but the Adenauer government saw no reason to rouse sleeping dogs. For more than a decade someone's Nazi past was not a topic for conversation. Sociopolitical elites endorsed the silence. Denazification fell victim to a willful, collective lapse of memory.

The new enemies were the same old gang, the Bolsheviks, reconditioned by Soviet leaders (and their East German lackeys) and ambitious for global conquest. The danger that they posed to Western civilization in general and West German reconstruction in particular justified for West Germans suppression of the freedom of speech constitutionally guaranteed to communists as well as other citizens, as well as the prohibition in 1956 of the communist KPD as an anticonstitutional party. Hostility toward the Soviet Union (see R. Merritt 1967) and fear of Soviet power produced strong German support for a defense force, even if it had to be integrated into NATO. In the 1950s and 1960s, having anything good to say about the East German regime or its Socialist Unity Party (SED) was tantamount to treason.

As we have seen, a new dimension of dissent erupted across West German society in the late 1960s—along with efforts to stamp it out. The dissent included sometimes violent confrontations with the police, an inchoate "extraparliamentary opposition," and, eventually, terrorist kidnappings and bombings. Traditional police methods to control crowds seemed merely to exacerbate the unrest. What to do about these "radicals" who were endangering German society became a major dilemma facing the country's political leaders.

The new chancellor elected in September 1969, Willy Brandt, faced public pressure for action to stop the radicals and their terrorism. Pressure came from the right, of course, with its traditional emphasis on law and order, but it also came from the left, from Brandt's own Social Democratic cohorts and trade unionists who, in some cases having themselves been burned by the radicals, labeled them extremists. By January 1972 the exasperated Brandt and the provincial governors saw no option other than to issue a "radicals decree" (*Radikalenerlass*), which promised to dismiss and deny public service employment to anyone acting in ways that threatened the FRG's free democratic order. This meant, for example, that a public school teacher could be fired for participating in a demonstration that turned violent. Civil libertarians howled, and legalists soon realized that making the decree conform with constitutional procedures sharply diminished its force—but substantial numbers of conservative politicians and the German public agreed in principle with the decree's implementation.[36]

The issue of German responses to dissent reemerged in the 1990s after the GDR's collapse and incorporation into the FRG. The situation was in part similar to that of 1945: FRG authorities, the "victors" in the cold war, seeking to discredit thoroughly the former regime of the "occupied" eastern Germans, vetted the East German public servants and collaborators to assess their reliability and eligibility to serve in a new, democratic Germany. For years public-sector employees in the former GDR—including judges, school teachers, clerks, scientists, and police officers—had more or less actively supported what West Germans considered an illegitimate and corrupt political system. The younger among them had even gone through education and recruitment processes that constituted political indoctrination.

To dump undesirable employees western Germans produced a plan

---

36. In a survey in July 1974 nearly a third of a national sample supported and almost half opposed a decision to let a member of the German Communist Party (DKP) teach in the public schools (IfD-6:98). Surveys in September 1973 and December 1975 showed substantially fewer willing to give a judgeship to DKP members (18:58 and 16:65 percent, respectively) or a professorship to members of the right-wing National Democratic Party or NPD (21:46 and 22:50 percent, respectively).

that had two important components.[37] To ensure a high degree of social stability, the replacement of all public-sector employees with newly trained personnel was rejected out of hand. A second parameter was more problematic: the plan had to be constitutionally justifiable. AMG had made it clear from the outset that it considered Nazism anathema and would not tolerate its collaborators. To secure the right to make such decisions was after all one of the reasons why the Allies had insisted on Germany's unconditional surrender. Western Germans in the 1990s, however, could not make such a full sweep. The FRG had neither banned communism nor outlawed the SED.[38] To dismiss people on these grounds would thus have been unconstitutional. Yet it was clear to westerners that staunch supporters of the SED regime had no politically responsible place in the newly unified Germany.

The Union Treaty, which the FRG and GDR provisionally accepted in August 1990 and which became effective on 3 October of that year, provided the basis for such a plan. In each region and area of the public sector, FRG offices established a personnel selection committee to evaluate all eastern employees. The extent of screening ranged from cursory checks of postal workers to penetrating questionnaires and interviews demanded of professionals such as judges and professors. What the different committees sought, though, was the same: evidence of support for the old communist regime, its policies, and its actions, at any but the most perfunctory level.[39] Those who did not pass muster were dismissed or transferred to other positions. High-level functionaries were particularly vulnerable: 88 percent of East Berlin's judges and prosecuting attorneys were offered early retirement packages or recommendations to find work elsewhere. Middle-level employees also suffered high attrition rates. The province of Brandenburg, for example, lost 20 percent of its school teachers.

37. An implicit third parameter was that the plan not be reminiscent of the past's discredited denazification.

38. In 1957 the Federal Constitutional Court banned the Communist Party of Germany (KPD) because of its antidemocratic stance. Berlin's Four-Power status nevertheless meant that until the German merger in 1990, a wing of the SED continued to operate legally in West Berlin. Meanwhile, the German Communist Party (DKP), a slightly modified successor of the KPD, took part in all FRG elections. The SED subsequently became the nationwide Party of Democratic Socialism (PDS).

39. According to Inga Markovits (1992/1993:127), the questionnaire for East Berlin judges proceeded from "the usual biographical inquiries" to "the nasty questions": "Were you a member of the Party? An unnecessary question, since every judge was. Were you exposed to Party disciplinary proceedings? Was your work ever the object of citizens' complaints? Were you a member of an IA senate [which Ministry of State Security or Stasi officers used for handling political crimes]? Were you a collaborator of the Ministry for State Security? Were you ever asked to collaborate? With what results?"

Personnel evaluations were in many ways a more efficient descendant of the AMG denazification program. Linguistic and cultural barriers to communication had disappeared, and so had the long, diffuse, and withal clumsy questionnaire that was supposed to guide denazification's proceedings. The new committee members were mostly although not always western Germans chosen because of their recognized expertise in a particular public-sector area. They thus could home in fairly quickly on the central issue: Was the individual capable of functioning effectively—and politically correctly—in a broad-based democratic environment?

Selection committee members had access to a cache of information that would have been the envy of AMG officers. Soon after the East German government began to disintegrate, some civic minded easterners found employees of the Ministry of State Security (MfS, or Stasi) destroying records. The files saved contained secret reports about GDR citizens written by Stasi officers, formal agents, and perhaps one hundred thousand or more informants or informal collaborators (*Informelle Mitarbeiter*, or IMs). Once the files were made generally available, eastern Germans found evidence that coworkers, lifelong friends, and even family members had been informing on them.

Eastern Germans were outraged when they learned about the Stasi files. That the state had routinely monitored its citizens was of course known to all. But the fact that institutionalized snooping extended so deeply into the social fabric was stunning news. The FRG quickly set up the Gauck Authority, headed by ex-GDR Pastor Joachim Gauck, to review the files and make them publicly available. The immediate goal, however, was not simply to provide freedom of information. The files were used to ferret out the SED's collaborators. Individual selection committees were then relentless in punishing IMs, those East Germans who had systematically betrayed their friends and associates.[40]

The parallel between AMG denazification hearings and FRG selection committees is instructive if imperfect. Unlike denazification, the selection committees were purely German instruments, focusing on a small category of public-sector employees. The latter procedure had no intent to review all ex-GDR citizens. Yet both used morally tinged but unquestionably political criteria to decide, during eras of severe unemployment, who would continue to hold their old jobs and who would not. Both encoun-

40. The Stasi files extend beyond public-sector employees. Irrespective of the pressures put on IMs to make reports, and the time, frequency, and usefulness of the reports they submitted, public knowledge of their "Stasi connections" has ruined the reputations and professional careers of politicians, church leaders, artists, and others in the private sector.

tered sometimes quite legitimate charges of unfairness and bias (see I. Markovitz 1992/1993). The greatest test of the work by the FRG committees, however, is yet to come. Adenauer sought national reconciliation by playing down the idea of denazification and even placing some former PGs in high positions. The FRG's conciliatory mood toward the SED regime's public servants has yet to emerge.

EIGHT

Coming to Terms with the Past

Recent German history has not lain dormant in dusty archives but is a living phenomenon that shapes the way people today interpret their past, their present, and their future. But history, in modern Germany and elsewhere, is malleable. We can agree that a certain event took place on a specified day yet dispute the event's causes and consequences. Moreover, history's impact varies according to the observer's life experience, memories, sensibilities, and a host of other characteristics. Its impact on societies is equally diverse. Countries are nevertheless consistent in trumpeting the glories of their past and ignoring or recasting their darker days.

How can we characterize postwar German perspectives on the Nazi episode in their history? Our starting point in the framework of this book was the empirical evidence of public opinion. Chapters 4–7 focus on some key dimensions of these public images, party and governmental activities, and especially the issue of collective and individual responsibility for Germany's Nazi past. By the mid-1950s the bulk of German responses to public opinion surveys expressed a fairly fixed, integrated point of view.

National Socialism. Chapter 4 established that postwar Germans— from the beginning of occupation to the present time—have had little interest in either resuscitating the National Socialist Party or putting a new Hitler into power. Both had played out on the world's stage their tawdry ideology, their confused, disastrous racism, and their military ineptitude. Both were thoroughly discredited in most German eyes. A sense of national shame pervaded their lives.

But this general rejection of Nazism is colored by two contrary impulses. First, acceptance of the regime's demise means neither that Germans were happy about the defeat nor that they abandoned out of hand every aspect of National Socialism and its Führer. Some of what Hitler said and did touched vibrant chords in many German hearts, and some elements—such as his idea of national identity—found and continue to find strong echoes in other countries. Second, although Germans recognized that they or their compatriots had succumbed to Nazism, they did not interpret this lack of political wisdom as manifesting any original sin. Some saw Germans as a strayed flock that repented its profligacy. Others acknowledged that the past must be remembered but insisted that it need not be dwelled on at the cost of meeting current and future needs. If the wartime Allies wished to foster the country's democratic development, then they needed the support of all Germans, including born-again democrats who may have made political mistakes in the past.

Nazi crimes. Chapter 5 showed that postwar Germans increasingly saw their country's Nazi government as a criminal regime. The more occupation authorities were able to rebut earlier Nazi interpretations with their own barrage of information and argumentation about the cause of World War II, the more Germans agreed that their country was the principal culprit. Similarly, as ever more Germans were confronted with reliable information about the death camps and mobile killing squads (*Einsatzgruppen*), larger numbers understood that Nazi genocide was a reality, not a figment of the enemy's fervid propaganda. Few remained who were willing to state openly that Jews or Gypsies or other victims had deserved their fate.

Popular acceptance of these basic tenets—Germany's blame for the war and Germany's crimes against humanity—did not erase popular attitudes toward other aspects of the war. Yes, Germans admitted, Nazi Germany had committed heinous crimes, but so had the Allies: the Red Army's massacre of Polish officers at Katyn Forest, U.S. and British commando raids that violated accepted principles of war, and the bombing of Dresden, among others. This attitude "relativized" Nazi crimes and diminished any sense of German complicity. It produced two kinds of popular responses that minimized German guilt for Nazi crimes. First, Germans observed, wars cause terrible things, things inflicted by all the combatants. Nazism should be condemned for its excesses, but atrocities were in the nature of war rather than something peculiar to Germany. Second, even granting German culpability, many asked rhetorically, how much longer were Germans to be pilloried in the court of world opinion for crimes committed by Hitler and his misguided cohorts? Continued war crimes trials, moral critics pointing accusing fingers, and Germans who foul their own nest have as little public support now as they did forty years ago.

Nazi criminals. As Chapter 6 reported, the initial International Military Tribunal (IMT) that met in Nuremberg (1945–1946) was a popular success in Germany. Attention flagged as the hearings dragged on, but most Germans found them both informative—sometimes horrifyingly so—and fairly conducted. For some time after the trials, most Germans applauded the IMT's sentences: the men convicted in Nuremberg got their just deserts. Only a few believed that the convicted defendants were scape-goats abandoned by the people they had served, or that these men were merely an alibi, a means for the other Germans to exculpate themselves. Larger numbers, though, questioned the usefulness of subsequent trials for any but the most notorious defendants. As the lesser trials carried out by the American Military Government (AMG) implicated lower-level offi-cers and even pillars of German society, popular support yielded to ambiv-alence.

Many Germans saw themselves as victims of Nazism, unwilling partic-ipants in a terrible social drama over which they had no control. The early trials were welcome vindications of their own self-perception. But even some of these people came to believe that further trials would be counter-productive, and those who had reason to worry about the results of those new trials agreed. Punish the unquestionably guilty, they said—but quickly —and then let's stop beating the dead horse of Nazism and get on with our lives. Relativists meanwhile reminded Germans and the wartime Allies not to forget that other peoples had also committed culpable offenses.

Denazification. Much the same line of thought, Chapter 7 showed us, characterized postwar German attitudes toward denazification. Initially, large numbers of Germans accepted the idea of punishing all National Socialists and their German collaborators. These were, after all, the people who had made Nazism work on a day-to-day basis, profited person-ally from the regime's gains, and made life hell for everyone else. But that retributive mood soon diminished as planners encountered problems in implementing their schemes. U.S. military authorities, realizing the enor-mity of their task, modified the process: making summary judgments on low-ranking Nazis while postponing cases involving major figures; put-ting denazification hearings increasingly under the control of Germans, some of whom sought to undermine the system; and granting expanded amnesties that released many of the bigger fish whose cases had been postponed. Germans began to see denazification in terms of U.S. confu-sion at the policy level and rampant corruption at the operational level. Eventually AMG had little choice but to terminate the denazification exper-iment.

Dimensions of Dealing with the Past

The opinion data are consistent in suggesting that by the 1950s the West German public had come to terms with the country's checkered past.[1] Nazism, without question a serious mistake, belonged to that past—small currents of neo-Nazi activities notwithstanding. The popular view holds that German society had been a victim of Nazism and its crimes, not the source. Those responsible for the crimes were, moreover, dead, in prison, or living in safe havens abroad. Germans who were enjoying the economic miracle of the new Federal Republic viewed past events with regret but felt little responsibility. A leading West German conservative politician, the late Franz Josef Strauss, articulated the popular attitude: "A nation that has achieved as much as we Germans have achieved has a right not to be constantly reminded of Auschwitz" (cited in Schneider 1990/1991:185).

How complete is the image expressed in public opinion surveys? Was it true that the whole of German society had by the 1950s come to terms with its Nazi past, or was the complaisance shown in the polls misleading? We cannot say how the respondents' public expressions correspond with their innermost feelings. Reports by psychologists (see Beradt 1966/1968; A. Mitscherlich and M. Mitscherlich 1967/1975) suggest some disjuncture between their public and private views. More to the point, did mass expressions vary so much from those of political leaders, moralists, and intellectuals that German society was riven? Many commentators have addressed this question, and their diverse interpretations may be grouped into four categories.

Nazism as aberration. Some observers, foreign and German alike, argued that Nazism had been an aberration. This notion of a new Germany —one that had "digested" its past—saw the German people as fundamentally peaceable and as seeking democracy even before World War I. But such peculiar circumstances as the disruption caused by Versailles, worldwide depression, and particularly the imminent danger of Bolshevik aggression gave way to the allure of a snake-oil salesman from Braunau (see Nolte 1963/1966). Hitler, with his charismatic qualities and early successes, had temporarily beguiled Germans, but with Hitler defeated and a divided Germany secured militarily from east and west, fascism would never reemerge. This sentiment of a new Germany was part of the international image that Adenauer sought to project for the Federal Republic.

Germany as repenting prodigal son. Other writers expressed amazement at the ease with which chameleon-like Germans had adapted to a

1. The oft-used metaphor *Vergangenheitsbewältigung* is described by the Harvard historian Charles S. Maier (1988:7) as "mastering the past, coming to terms with the searing experiences of World War II and collaboration in Nazi crimes."

new, democratic environment and welcomed a more responsible role in the Western world. The new Germans, they said, did not dismiss the dozen years of Hitler's Third Reich from memory. Without getting so tied up with the past that they became immobile, modern Germans accepted significant behavioral changes that would erase their image as Europe's "bad boy." The new Federal Republic of Germany was prepared to incur heavy political costs to prevent any recurrence of its predecessor's despicable record (see Prittie 1971). The FRG was stabilizing German society and defending Western culture against a communist onslaught (see Clay 1950b; Wallich 1955).

Germany as impenitent troublemaker. Dubious observers were less sanguine (see Russell 1969). When they surveyed the European scene they saw truculent, obdurate Germans who had come to terms with the past by denying Nazism as a problem. What, they asked, had the country's ideologues learned from the the previous half-century? That Germany's implacably hostile enemies were single-minded in seeking to destroy the country as a political actor! Accordingly, these critics went on, Germans would agree with or say whatever would encourage the Allies to go home and permit them to restore their pre-1945 or pre-1933 country. Such critics scorned the gullibility of the Western Allies, which, increasingly preoccupied by the cold war, elected to pacify the German public rather than to carry out their original intent to democratize the country.

"It wasn't me—Adolf Hitler did it."[2] Germans dealt with their country's Nazi past, according to this interpretation, by scapegoating individuals or groups putatively responsible for what was bad about National Socialism. Adolf Hitler, or "the Nazis," or the SS were to blame, these Germans asserted (see Reitlinger 1956). Common citizens—the man on the street, the woman in the factory, corporals and lieutenants, the child in school— had had no choice but to obey superior orders. To do anything else would have been to sign one's own death warrant (but see Jäger 1967/1982; Kitterman 1988; Block and Drucker 1992; Stoltzfus 1992). Such civil courage, however admirable in some circumstances, rarely occurs. Most people did what they were told. To prosecute or persecute Germans who were not personally guilty of crimes was unjust.

From a psychological perspective, as we have known since Biblical times, attributing blame to scapegoats can serve a useful purpose for an individual's personality and ability to function in society. Those who believe that the scapegoat sinned can absolve themselves of any responsibility for what went wrong. Those who, irrespective of whether they believe the claim, point publicly to scapegoats may find that this act

2. *Ich bin's nicht, Adolf Hitler ist es gewesen*, a 1984 play by Hermann van Harten.

deflects criticism. Even those who feel responsible may, if they repeat the denial often enough and vociferously enough, come to accept the manufactured "truths." Historical accuracy is not the central issue of this personal-psychological dynamic. Finding a plausible story that enhances one's own self-image—a "life-lie," in the words of the Norwegian playwright Henrik Ibsen—may make the difference between adjustment and maladjustment to one's environment, between sanity and breakdown.

From the social perspective, scapegoating can affect the way people live together. Entire societies accept particular interpretations of a phenomenon even if those interpretations do not correspond to reality. Social scientists call such images myths. Thus Americans continued to speak of their cities as melting pots merging diverse ethnics long after sociologists had discovered that such a process was not taking place.[3] Hitler's *Mein Kampf* is rife with nonsensical images—blood ties, social Darwinism, Jewish greed, Aryan supremacy, racial hygiene, and much else—that later became part of formally proclaimed German policy. Up to a point, socially sanctified myths serve an integrative function for those within the dominant group. But they can hamper the society's ability to deal with outsiders, whether within or without the country, and with realities beyond its own sphere. If an entire society can be persuaded that all of its woes were caused by Jews and socialists who undermined the Reichswehr and signed the Versailles Treaty, then aggressive actions against these troublemakers are inevitable.

For this reason observers have worried that twin myths might emerge in postwar German society: first, that only a single, identifiable actor, whether individual or collective, was responsible for all the sins of 1933–1945; and second, that Allied policies that cast a broad net were at best misguided meddling, at worst malicious German-baiting.[4] If Germans questioned the fundamental legitimacy of the occupation process, they could refuse to take seriously outstanding issues regarding the past. They could deny the existence of a problematic past or drag their feet in carrying out orders to rectify problems. Resentments over Allied occupation policies could also reopen quarrels that had already caused generations of conflict.

Did postwar Germans accept a mythologized scapegoating of the Nazi

3. "The melting pot . . . did not happen," Glazer and Moynihan (1963:v–vi) concluded after extending their findings about New York to other U.S. cities. "Principal ethnic groups" maintained "a distinct identity, albeit a changing one, from one generation to the next."

4. Another potential and equally destructive myth decried the "stab in the back," the putative sabotage of the German government by domestic groups, which prevented Germans from resolving their own problems.

era? Our review of public opinion data suggests that scapegoating indeed served postwar Germany as a convenient, popular social myth. Saying that Hitler or the Wehrmacht General Staff was to blame for everything that happened was both simple and to some measure credible. It justified calls to end war crimes trials, denazification proceedings, and other Allied impositions. And scapegoating, however simplistic, permitted Germans to cope with the past both individually and socially in ways that promised a return to normalcy.

But if the scapegoating myth was popularly accepted, the question of belief remains: Did the German people believe that one man or a small group was responsible? Short of conducting large-scale psychiatric interviews, we can find no complete answer to this question at the individual level (but see Beradt 1966/1968, and A. Mitscherlich and M. Mitscherlich 1967/1975). We can, however, gain some insights by exploring the collective behavior of postwar Germans, particularly the extent of their willingness to initiate inquiries and possibly criminal proceedings against former Nazis.

The Nuremberg war crimes trials opened Germans' eyes to what had gone on during the previous dozen years. The trials inundated the world with documentation of exactly what the Nazis had planned and what they had done. The credibility of the information contributed substantially to popular support for the tribunal process. This support was particularly strong for the first trials, which brought top Nazi leaders before an International Military Tribunal. The subsequent twelve tribunals that AMG conducted in Nuremberg likewise received substantial support (but see Buscher 1989). How durable were these attitudes?

Among the manifold effects of the Nuremberg trials, one of the most important from the Allied perspective was their educational function. After the trials, few Germans could in good conscience deny that the Third Reich had been guilty of warmongering and beastly crimes, including genocide. Continuing denial required a peculiar personality—one obtuse to the factual flood streaming from diverse quarters, or perhaps one interested less in understanding the truth than in scoring rhetorical points or starting beer-hall arguments.

"Auschwitz lie." Nonetheless, from 1945 onward deniers arose. Available evidence suggests that only a very small number of Germans rejected the testimony of the tribunals outright—perhaps only 1 or 2 or even 5 percent—and that some may well be sociopathic. It is thus tempting to treat them as amusing exotics, like people who insist that the earth is flat or visited by extraterrestrials. But the knowledge that many deniers have serious intent, and the recollection that equally bizarre claims made in the

1920s and 1930s contributed to the popular acceptance of Nazism, command our attention to their arguments.

Some deniers simply quibble about details or piece together scraps of information and interpretations that might mitigate German guilt. How do we know that six million Jews were murdered? Could the death toll not have been three million or "only" a few hundred thousand? Was the American military perhaps vindictive in describing as crematoria the simple baking ovens that produced the daily bread at Dachau? Perhaps it wasn't true, as Nazi propaganda had maintained, that a Polish attack against the German radio station in Gleiwitz triggered the outbreak of World War II. But what about Stalin, the slaughterer of millions of Russian kulaks? Didn't his Red Army also invade Poland? Such minimization can provide damage control for individuals and whole societies.

Other deniers go more to the heart of the issue. An international industry has emerged in recent years to debunk commonly accepted interpretations of National Socialism and its murderous policies. A major thesis purports to "unmask" the "Holocaust hoax." It didn't happen, deniers claim. Since Germany's Federal Constitutional Court has outlawed public expressions of this "Auschwitz lie" thesis, most of the argumentation comes from foreigners—the Americans David Hoggan (1961), Fred Leuchter (1989/1991; but see Bastian [1992]), and Arthur Butz (1977), and the British David Irving (1991).[5] Since 1980 advocates in a Los Angeles suburb have published the bimonthly *Journal of Historical Review* and have undertaken campaigns to recruit American students and instructors and to approach a mass public by appearing on television talk shows.[6] (Enthusiasts in the United States also distribute to a worldwide market— including Germans—a wide range of neo-Nazi publications and paraphernalia.)[7]

5. The illegality of the "Auschwitz lie" stance was reaffirmed in April 1994 by the Court's decision saying that a statement denying the Holocaust is not protected as free speech. German courts have thus had to evaluate publications (e.g., Walendy 1970/1981, deemed in April 1994 to deserve protection under the principle of freedom of opinion but not academic freedom) and documented assertions in terms of their constitutionality, and have imprisoned and fined offending Germans. The FRG has expelled both Irving, whose book *Hitler's War* asserts that the extermination of Jews was carried out without the Führer's knowledge, and the engineer Leuchter, whose *Leuchter Report* demonstrated "scientifically" that the Auschwitz-Birkenau concentration camp could not have engaged in mass exterminations.

6. These campaigns include letters (I received two in 1990 from the Sarich family in Winnetka, Ill., e.g.; see McCormick [1990]), advertisements (e.g., in November 1991 in Duke University's *Duke Chronicle*; see Ad 1991), and broadsides (e.g., *"Holocaust" News*, published in 1982 by Revisionists' Reprints, Manhattan Beach, Calif.).

7. Gerhard Lauch of Lincoln, Neb., claimed in January 1994 that his newsletter

What we see in the "Auschwitz lie" is a systematic effort to make history plastic: hard evidence and historical truths cast aside in favor of discourses that treat as equally valid any number of versions of the truth. Most historians have rejected both the approach and the more extreme published accounts. For instance, the gravity of James Bacque's (1989) assertion that Military Governor Eisenhower had sanctioned the killing of perhaps a million German prisoners of war interned in U.S. camps led eventually to the formation of a historical commission (Bischof and Ambrose 1992) that demolished the book's claim to scientific value—but the book still sits on the shelves of an unknown number of public libraries while the evaluative report remains primarily in the hands of historians. Politically and historically sensitive Germans and others have expressed a concern that the literature of the "Auschwitz lie" will capture the attention of people who will use it to support the projects of Germany's extreme right wing.

Reconstructing history. In the first postwar years such nationalistic and self-serving arguments were common but were not taken seriously. The Allies considered them remnants of Nazi propaganda rather than revisionism, and they felt that their own control of information would eventually reform German thinking. Germans who held such politically unacceptable beliefs generally chose not to voice them in public. Meanwhile, a new German information elite emerged—an elite comprising newspaper publishers, public school teachers, university professors, writers, and others who believed in Germany's role in causing the war, Nazi criminality, and even the imperative of cold-war defense against Bolshevism. Together they accepted a new "standard historical account" that tended toward criticism without going into paroxysms of anxiety about "socially flawed" Germans.

This high degree of historical congruency continued until the late 1960s. To be sure, hard-core ideologues of the right and the left occasionally published screeds rehashing old arguments, and some bitterly opposed what they called the "occupiers' history." Occasionally, too, an academic offered an eccentric thesis, only to encounter dismissal or the severe criticism of colleagues.[8] Two revisionist controversies sprang up in the 1960s. The first rose out of a dispute among historians about the cause of

---

went to "40,000-plus neo-Nazis in Germany" (Canon 1994); Bonn's Office for the Protection of the Constitution lists him as "the primary producer and importer of Nazi propaganda," which is illegal in Germany.

8. From the socialist world, of course, and particularly from the German Democratic Republic (GDR), came a plethora of tendentious writings that Western scholars and politicians by and large ignored.

World War I. The argument, which began with Fritz Fischer's (1961/1967) view that Germany had grasped toward world power, polarized historians both in West Germany and abroad. But such issues aroused little interest among German citizens. Events occurring a half-century earlier paled in relevance to matters erupting in the nuclear age.

The second wave of revisionism in the 1960s had more immediate significance. Germany's "new left" scrutinized the previous two decades and did not like what it saw: a "cartel of fear" that ruled the FRG; a postwar West Germany shackled to the past's capitalist mechanisms; the ominous creation in Bonn of a "grand coalition" that enabled the CDU/CSU and SPD to control West German society; and especially the FRG's support for the U.S. involvement in Vietnam. The social unrest that ensued is often encapsulated in such catchwords as "student revolt" and "state-sponsored terrorism" (see R. Merritt 1969). But the new perspectives of the left spawned serious efforts to rethink what had happened during the Third Reich and how postwar Germans had failed to deal adequately with their undigested history.[9]

Quarrel among historians. By the 1970s, then, with the reassessment of Germany's past attracting the attention of historians and others, some turned to the events of 1933–1945. The announced goal was simple: to use new evidence and historiographies as a means to account for Hitler and Nazism. The conclusions that some writers reached, however, suggested a different agenda. In challenging the interpretations that had prevailed since the late 1940s, they found Germany under Nazism far more understandable and its policies far more justifiable (see Augstein et al. 1987; Jarausch 1988; Maier 1988; Evans 1989). Critics were quick to attack. Charges and countercharges soon moved from polite discourse among colleagues to what came to be called the historians' quarrel (*Historikerstreit*), which included accusations of professional incompetence, political motivation, and Nazi apologetics.

Revisionist historians in the 1980s, though varying in emphasis, offered a fairly consistent image. One branch of the approach found historical and modern parallels to the Holocaust: the Turks in 1915 had slaughtered a million and a half Armenians, for instance, Stalin had executed or starved to death perhaps twenty million Soviet citizens, and Pol Pot's Khmer Rouge had in 1975–1978 killed one in seven Kampucheans. Nazism's mass murders were far from unique. A tragedy, yes, and even deplorable, but by no means beyond the pale of modern civilization.

Another revisionist branch held that German aggression had been a response to the very real threat from the Soviet Union. Stalin, these historians said, had been intent on world conquest. The USSR would eventually —and sooner rather than later—have invaded Germany and, given Stalin's annihilation of his opposition at home, put masses of Germans on the executioner's block.[10] For this reason, Ernst Nolte (1985, 1987b) tells us, Hitler was to some measure justified in initiating policies that, though seemingly brutal, might help Germans preserve themselves and their own nationality. This meant building up a strong war machine; it meant seizing neighboring lands to improve Germany's strategic position; it meant integrating the German people to fight a common foe determined to annihilate them. And the necessity of building a German sense of community in turn meant that Hitler needed a nationalizing ideology to differentiate Germans from non-Germans, such as Jews.

The Historikerstreit became public with the publication of Jürgen Habermas's (1986) attack against Andreas Hillgruber and Nolte and a counterbarrage by Nolte (1986; 1987a:171–179). Some applauded the debate's public nature. The issues were pertinent not only to academics; they addressed images that political leaders and common citizens alike held about their not-too-distant past, the politics of West Germany, and the FRG's relations with the rest of the world.[11] The public dispute forced somnolent citizens, many of whom had long ago written off Germany's Nazi episode as irrelevant to their current concerns, to rethink their views of what had taken place and why.

The Historikerstreit did not substantially change German attitudes about Nazism and its crimes. Arguments from the right, like those blaming everything on Hitler and his henchmen, may well have provided psychological succor to those who sought to minimize German responsibility for the events of the Nazi era. But the claim that Germany's behavior was not unique seemed far-fetched in the face of contrary evidence. What the

10. Andreas Hillgruber (1986; cited by Maier [1988:21]) wrote that the Wehrmacht protected its eastern front so ferociously not to complete the death camps' mission but "to defend the population from the orgy of revenge of the Red Army, the mass rapine, the arbitrary killing, and the compulsory deportations."

11. Jarausch (1988:285; footnotes omitted) neatly summarizes the emerging furor: "While rightist apologists urged 'an end to the collectivist confrontation with National Socialism,' leftist critics deplored the 'systematic relativization' of German crimes. Some European 'amnesia about the Holocaust' alarmed American journalists, while scholars like Charles S. Maier warned that 'revising the Nazi past for the Kohl era' could only lead to 'immoral equivalence' of the NS genocide with other mass killings, diminishing its singularity. Soon the wire services picked up the story, spreading concern in the Jewish community and beyond about this apparent German effort of exculpation from Hitler's atrocities."

dispute did provide was further evidence that German society had not yet eradicated its Nazi stain.

More problematic than outright denial or minimization, because it was more pervasive, was the possibility that Germans might simply disregard their recent history and behave as if these past events had no reality for present times. Chapters 6 and 7 pointed out how this could happen. The later Nuremberg trials, for instance, raised tricky problems. For one thing, they abandoned the earlier focus on the highest echelons of policy-making to distribute responsibility among those who had implemented the policies. This, we saw, had a double effect: sharpening popular concerns about the trials' fairness, and making such trials more difficult. A defendant's claim that he only carried out "superior orders," a claim dismissed out of hand by the IMT, carried more weight in the defense offered by junior officers, doctors, and common bureaucrats.[12]

Continuing such trials meant constant disruptions of personnel planning. Virtually from the day they entered Germany the Allied military and then their occupation forces needed skilled Germans to serve in responsible positions. Limiting access by former Nazis or Nazi sympathizers curtailed the availability of trained workers, and training people whom Nazism had not tainted was time consuming. Even before concern about the cold war grew, AMG officers and Germans alike were increasingly inclined to ease their strictures. Eventually those evaluating candidates for responsible positions in the new Germany abandoned any strict litmus test, instead differentiating rather loosely among degrees of complicity.

Occupiers and occupied collaborated to obliterate many procedures and modes of questioning that might be uncomfortable personally or inconvenient socially. The Allies were overwhelmed by new realities, some reflecting deeper understanding of what occupying powers can achieve and others stemming from changing global circumstances. It is difficult, many decades after the occupation, to gainsay the wisdom of such decisions. Their impact on the way Germans later dealt with their Nazi past is nevertheless clear.

A case in point was the postwar development of the medical profession in western Germany. When AMG officials reviewed charges against former

---

12. The Allied stance on "superior orders" was clear. Appleman (1954:191) writes of the IMT: "In referring to the plea of *respondeat superior*, the court held that it could be considered only in mitigation of the offense and went on to assert that mitigation of punishment does not in any sense of the word reduce the degree of the crime. It is more a matter of grace than of defense. In other words, the punishment assessed is not a proper criterion to be considered in evaluating the findings of the court with reference to the degree of magnitude of the crime."

Nazis and party supporters, they found particularly horrifying evidence that doctors had violated their Hippocratic oath to carry out policies of "racial hygiene": sterilization and other forms of eugenics, euthanasia aimed at "lives not worth living," bizarre experiments using human subjects.[13] Accordingly, in December 1946, only weeks after the IMT sentenced the major war criminals, AMG opened its first secondary trial in Nuremberg (T. Taylor 1949:159–168; *Trial* 1950; Appleman 1954:139–148). The "doctors trial" indicted twenty-two men and one woman for conspiring to commit and actually committing war crimes and crimes against humanity.[14] "Judged by any standard of proof," the verdict against these professional healers stated:

> The record clearly shows the commission of war crimes and crimes against humanity. . . . Beginning with the outbreak of World War II criminal medical experiments on non-German nationals, both prisoners of war and civilians, including Jews and "asocial" persons, were carried out on a large scale in Germany and the occupied countries. These experiments were not the isolated and casual acts of individual doctors and researchists working solely on their own responsibility, but were the product of coordinated policy-making and planning at high governmental, military, and Nazi Party levels, conducted as an integral part of the total war effort. (Cited in T. Taylor 1949:165)

Judgments handed out in August 1947 sentenced seven defendants to death by hanging, five to life imprisonment, and four to imprisonment for ten to twenty years; seven were acquitted.[15]

The doctors trial is instructive less for its proceedings and outcomes than for the German response to it. Media coverage provided the populace with basic information about the trial, but the German Chamber of Physicians went further. It commissioned an unknown, nontenured university lecturer, Alexander Mitscherlich, and his assistant, Fred Mielke, to attend

13. The modern Hippocratic oath instructs the physician that, among other things, "into whatsoever house you shall enter, it shall be for the good of the sick to the utmost of your power" and "you will exercise your art solely for the cure of your patients." On the question of why doctors should undertake such "medicalized killing," see Lifton's psychological interviews (1984, 1986).

14. Case No. 1 ("Medical Case") under Allied Control Council Law No. 10 was filed on 25 October 1946, opened on 9 December 1946, closed on 19 July 1947, and judgment declared on 19 August 1947. The defendants, who were also indicted for membership in a criminal organization (the SS), included eighteen physicians, Heinrich Himmler's personal adjutant and two other nonmedical administrative officials, and two "civilian" physicians (T. Taylor 1949:162–163).

15. The U.S. military governor confirmed the sentences on 22 November 1947, and the U.S. Supreme Court, on a vote of five to three, declined to review the case. The executions were carried out in Landsberg.

the courtroom proceedings in Nuremberg and to publish a brief account of the findings.[16] The report they wrote (Mitscherlich and Mielke 1947/1949) created a sensation. Firsthand experience with the German medical profession, skilled writing that emphasized the tragedy's human dimension as well as its technical side, and withal accurate reporting made the story gripping—and also made it clear that many members of one of Germany's most respected professions had enthusiastically supported Nazism's criminal medicine.[17]

This was not at all what the physicians' chamber had wanted.[18] Those who appointed Mitscherlich and Mielke evidently expected that the young men would produce a whitewash that would, at least in the minds of Germans, exonerate the doctors. The chamber nevertheless published *The Cynical Dictatorship*—and used the fact of publication to gain German acceptance into the World Health Organization. But at home the German medical profession treated the episode as a scandal. It shunned the authors and systematically ignored both the pamphlet and its second publication (Mitscherlich and Mielke 1947/1949)—except for one high-ranking, establishmentarian doctor, who, after savaging the book in a review for a professional journal, concluded that only "perverts" would read it. The reviewer found the book's precise factual presentation "directly irresponsible," "lacking the character of a documentation," and detrimental to the reputation of German scientists whose "honor is inviolable" (Hanauske-Abel 1986:272; footnotes omitted).[19] Ten thousand copies of the second publication sent to the medical association for distribution among German physicians evidently were destroyed, and Mitscherlich reported that

16. Why were such inexperienced men chosen to carry out this assignment? Higher-level medical professionals rejected it as a kiss of death to their careers. Mitscherlich, whose formal rank was *Privatdozent*, and Mielke considered the project sufficiently important that they were willing to put aside their own career objectives. See Mitscherlich and Mielke (1960/1962:9–22) and, for his later recounting of the events, Mitscherlich (1984:144–163).

17. The main chapters in Mitscherlich and Mielke (1947/1949) covered (1) experiments involving high altitude (subjection to low pressure), low temperature, and the drinking of seawater; (2) experiments with typhus and infectious jaundice; (3) experiments with sulfonamide, bone-grafting, cellulitis, and mustard gas; (4) collection of skulls of Jews for Strassburg University; and (5) the euthanasia program—direct extermination of racial groups and undesirable patients, and experimental work in mass sterilization.

18. This account of the fate of Mitscherlich, his book, and his personal standing derives mainly from Hanauske-Abel (1986) and Proctor (1988). I am indebted to Dr. Byron Ruskin, who brought this story to my attention.

19. The reviewer, Prof. F. H. Rein, dean of the University of Göttingen's College of Medicine, described the physician's vow in the Hippocratic oath to "be loyal to the profession of medicine and just and generous to its members."

"no one he met over the next ten years had ever heard of the book" (Proctor 1988:309).

In fact, not until the 1960s, when a West German publisher brought out a new, paperback edition of Mitscherlich and Mielke's *The Dictates of Inhumanity*, did Germans begin to pay serious attention to the partnership between National Socialism and the German medical profession.[20] Several studies two decades later (Lifton 1984, 1986; Müller-Hill 1984/ 1988; Baader 1986; Hanauske-Abel 1986; Proctor 1988; Kater 1989; Daum and Deppe 1991) have

- uncovered the true dimension of medical collaboration before 1945;
- disputed (Siegel with Green 1988; Rosner et al. 1991) the morality of using Nazi-generated data (see Alexander 1945; Molnar 1946; U.S. Air Force 1946; Beecher 1966; Pozos 1989; Wilkerson 1989);
- awakened Germans, who in the late 1980s demanded that their country's leading medical universities provide a decent burial to the skeletons, cells, and other body parts taken from victims of Nazi experiments rather than continuing to use them for teaching and research;
- pointed to the dubious scientific value of the Nazi experiments (Berger 1990); and,
- revealed the extent to which doctors closed ranks after 1945 to protect both their persons and their profession.

It became increasingly clear that, soon after the war's end, doctors had in effect coalesced to avoid any further punitive action. Who, they asked, was to be accused of what, and on what basis? Large numbers of them, perhaps half of Germany's doctors, had served under the government in the Third Reich, and Nuremberg's Medical Case had indicted only the highly visible, those occupying leadership roles in the Nazi party or clearly identified with specific programs.[21] Did it make sense to open a witch hunt to assess the innocence and guilt of the others? Were postwar Germany's valuable scientists to be condemned simply because they had followed political orders in 1933–1945?

The doctors resisted any action whatever. "We are professionals," the

20. According to Hanauske-Abel (1986:271; footnotes omitted), the German lack of interest extended even further: "Of 422 articles on medicine under National Socialism published worldwide between 1955 and 1979, only 2 originated in the Federal Republic, and the first monograph on 'Physicians under National Socialism' was printed only last year, half a century after the *Machtergreifung*." Two weeks after Hanauske-Abel's article appeared in the British medical journal *The Lancet*, Germany's Chamber of Physicians *(Bundesärztekammer)* expelled him and banned him from practicing medicine in Germany (Sholiton 1988).

21. Still other visible doctors, technicians, and administrators fled Germany or committed suicide.

German medical association was saying, "and we shall police our own. We don't need outsiders who do not understand our institutional culture and norms to impose on us their own notions about what is right and wrong." Least of all did the doctors want someone such as Mitscherlich—ostensibly one of their own but revealed as a turncoat—to rock their very successful and lucrative boat. Such perspectives are not peculiar to Germany, of course. Doctors in other countries are just as professionally self-protective. But in postwar Germany doctors simply eschewed any public discussion of potentially embarrassing issues: which of Germany's current medical college deans had obtained funding from Heinrich Himmler's racial research institute, which in addition to Nobel laureate Konrad Lorenz had "enthusiastically preached the gospel of racial purity using the vicious, inflammatory language of 'weeding out' and 'annihilation' of undesirable elements in society" (Bloch 1986), which in addition to Nobel laureate Werner Forssmann (1972/1975) had medically supervised executions of "criminals," and which presidents of the German Physicians Chamber in addition to Hans-Joachim Sewering had signed orders to euthanize a fourteen-year-old epileptic girl?[22]

The doctors' conspiracy of silence found support from the West German public. Increasingly restless about new trials of any kind, common citizens were not attentive to such social issues as "racial hygiene."[23] They wanted competent doctors and medical institutions; the activities of individual doctors before 1945 was irrelevant to this practical demand. People needed a physician who could cure a child's whooping cough. AMG and local German officials found this a hard argument to counter.

Even U.S. authorities backed off quickly from additional medical cases. Further indictments, besides encountering stiff German resistance, would have been difficult to bring to trial. Moreover, as medical experts evaluated the judgment handed down in Case No. 1, they began to understand that American doctors and institutions could well be subject to similar charges (see Baader 1986; Proctor 1988; Angell 1990; Hirsch et al. 1990; Reilly 1991; Annas 1992; Kühl 1994). It was easier to let even indictable

22. Lorenz later disclaimed "any understanding of the practical application of these figures of speech." Sewering's case erupted in January 1993 when the Chamber's support led to his selection as president of the World Medical Association. Objections against the former SS officer by German, American, Canadian, and Israeli doctors and the World Jewish Congress created enough publicity that Sewering, complaining about the WJC's "defamation campaign," withdrew from the position.

23. The issue of criminality considered appropriate for public opinion surveying was generic rather than specific. To the best of my knowledge neither OMGUS nor later German surveys touched on the criminal behavior of doctors who implemented policies of "racial hygiene."

physicians and medical researchers do their work, rise in their professional ranks, and sometimes win prestigious awards and appointments.

The postwar attitude toward the social responsibility of doctors thus shifted quickly if not dramatically in tone. At the outset U.S. authorities and probably most Germans would have agreed with two propositions: Nazi criminals should be prosecuted, and doctors have social responsibilities like other citizens—indeed, given their privileged status in society and their Hippocratic oath, greater responsibilities. Nonetheless, at least some German doctors violated their social responsibilities, but only a few of them were prosecuted, and the German people and U.S. authorities soon joined the German medical professionals in torpedoing further investigations.

But this story is not peculiar to the medical profession. By 1947 Germans who feared prosecution or job loss because of their pre-1945 behavior or affiliations could breathe more freely. AMG increasingly granted amnesty to groups in both categories, abandoned denazification as well as new trials in early 1949 (Bower 1982; Weingartner 1979), and soon began commuting death sentences and releasing those still in prison.[24] Meanwhile, "rehabilitated" military officers and public servants began finding good positions in government and industry. By 1950 the United States supported calls for a new German army. Nazi judges (J. Friedrich 1983; Müller 1991), as well as academics (Weinreich 1946; Heiber 1991) and industrialists (Borkin 1978; Bellon 1990), knew that punishment was a thing of the past.

Images of the Past in a Restored Germany

A mean preoccupation with tracking down the guilty had given way to emphasis on restoration of an eventually independent Germany. But few Germans, we have seen, wanted to restore what had led them to disaster in 1945. The model for Germany's future called for reincorporating the country's acceptable past, as modified by such postwar emendations as close alliance with the United States. But what past was acceptable? Conflict between those who called for the economic strength of Wilhelmine Germany and others who preferred the social structure of Weimar Germany, though divisive, was manageable. But any idea from

24. U.S. authorities, who hanged 308 war criminals in Landsberg, had by 1958 released all the others except those convicted by the Four-Power IMT in Nuremberg (Buscher 1989). As Chapter 6 noted, however, West German courts continued to indict people for pre-1945 crimes—more than 85,000 cases filed by the end of 1978 (Rückerl 1979/1980; and for a critical view, J. Friedrich 1984). Various other countries also tried and in some cases executed Nazi war criminals.

the 1930s required delicate and sometimes elaborate justification to overcome linkage to the "unacceptable" past.

For Germans in the West growth meant establishing economic stability, solidifying the new government, establishing an honorable role in western Europe, and helping to defend Europe from the East's expected onslaught. The country's rapid progress in all these regards was astonishing. By 1955 the FRG had worked an "economic miracle," establishing the basis it needed to become an international economic giant. That year the Western Allies granted West Germany virtual sovereignty and its own military under NATO control. Political unrest seemed to have dissolved: the federal election of September 1957 gave Konrad Adenauer's CDU/CSU an absolute majority of Bundestag seats. Germany, as Karl Deutsch and Lewis Edinger (1959) remarked aptly, was rejoining the powers.

The FRG came up with some creative solutions to long-standing political problems. Old challenges nevertheless reemerged, including pre-1933 Germany's apparent inability to modernize and liberalize its society simultaneously—a failing that some thought had led directly to authoritarianism and worse (see Dahrendorf 1965/1967). Should the new Germany only paper over such social conflicts, the result might well be a rigid structure straitjacketing any chance for German democracy.

Still, the FRG had to confront the question of what to do about former Nazis and their collaborators. The response under Adenauer was ambiguous: restoring German capabilities required the efforts of all Germans —provided that they were free of any glaring Nazi taint. The goal of economic development and social integration was clear and virtually uncontested, but vetting individuals was problematic. Although German courts still pursued identifiable criminals, this legalistic approach bypassed what was predominantly a social problem. What emerged was an informal rule of assumed political rehabilitation. Critics were irate when men prominent during the Nazi years gained new positions of power in Adenauer's government.[25] But the imperative of cooperation for reconstruction led most Germans to countenance this blemish.

Ignoring the unacceptable past while building an agreeable future

---

25. The most celebrated cases involved Theodor Oberländer, former SS officer and Nazi official who served the chancellor as minister of expellees, and Hans Globke, a Third Reich bureaucrat who in the mid-1930s had helped draft the Nuremberg racial ordinances, and who was Adenauer's chief of staff. Another cause célèbre involved Adolf Heusinger (Allen 1963). Though not a member of the NSDAP, he rose to the rank of lieutenant general to become the Wehrmacht's chief of operations and planning and, later, deputy chief of the German General Staff. After 1956 Heusinger became the new Bundeswehr's inspector general and a top-ranking NATO officer. For bitter attacks on Adenauer's stance, see Drożdżyński and Zaborowski (1960) and Tetens (1961).

sometimes created a chilling social pressure for conformity. The prevailing mode of political correctness demanded that Germans avoid any implication of guilt in the Nazi episode. Germans had learned soon after the war's end that reminding others of one's own Nazi past, openly touting Nazi principles or symbols, or supporting neo-Nazi movements were not the paths to success. Mainstream Germans, at least those contending for positions of influence, had to dissociate themselves from Nazism. Some found this task simple: they had only to reiterate what they had "always" felt, that Nazism was a bad thing. Others, however, including very prominent and capable people, were more deeply linked to the events of 1933–1945. Should they be exposed to the harsh light of public opinion or, like doctors, be protected because the new Germany needed them?

Until the late 1960s, streetwise Germans, those assuming leadership in politics and other walks of life, used several lines of defense to distance themselves from the issue of complicity in the Nazi past. They scapegoated the demon Hitler, for example, while exonerating those who had "only followed orders." They relativized, playing down the magnitude or German singularity of past events, or attributing them to the sins of youth for which individual Germans and German society as a whole had atoned sufficiently. More important strategies were withdrawal, building a conspiracy of silence; and dissociation, shunting aside issues of complicity rather than directly confronting links between past and present. And what were new Germans to do? Were they to don sackcloth, seek the world's forgiveness, and denounce Nazism on every occasion—though without going into details? For, after all, casting stones would only reopen sensitive issues and perhaps even shatter the ability to cooperate in building Germany's future.

None of these stratagems worked; the Nazi past simply did not drift from humankind's consciousness. None could forget, not the victims of Nazism, not thoughtful Germans humiliated by Nazi crimes ostensibly committed in their name, not citizens questioning whether they had done their best to mitigate Nazi policies and crimes, not conservatives railing against worldwide German-baiting, not even later generations who suffered from the cover-up.[26] The ideology espoused by Hitler and its brutal implications still ring loudly wherever politics and human behavior are discussed. "Auschwitz," "final solution," "SS," even "Einsatzgruppe" are ingrained in world culture. Only those who are utterly isolated from soci-

26. As a woman born in 1946 and raised in Hamburg wrote over four decades later, "The curiosity for certain subjects was simply bred out of us, conveniently and without fingerprints: the perfect crime. But it was the beginning of a life laced with deep mistrust and feelings of shame" (Reichel 1989:6)

ety or who willfully obliterate any hint of the past can escape the concept and reality of Nazism.

Nazism trivialized. This inescapable past is manifest in various ways. Some trivialize Nazism. Except in Germany and Austria, where their public display is forbidden by law, such symbols as the swastika or the SS death's head have become instruments for expressing ideas that have nothing to do with Nazism per se. For many years motorcycle riders in America emblazoned swastikas on their regalia to symbolize their outcast role in society. Any fool capable of engaging a tailor and paying the bill can don a Nazi—or, in Germany and Austria, pseudo-Nazi—uniform to wear to a social event or public demonstration, thereby ensuring public attention and press coverage. The terms "Nazi" and "fascist" are themselves epithets easily applied to anyone or any group with whom one disagrees, and Hitler's influence is blamed for everything from right-wing neo-Nazism to left-wing terrorism (see Becker 1978). Both wags and boors no less than his own admirers find it simple to parrot the wisdom of Hitler's words (see Butterfield 1991). One enterprising West German almost accomplished the feat of faking, selling, and enlisting general acceptance of "diaries" ostensibly penned by the Führer himself (C. Hamilton 1991). And others have made small fortunes producing underground video games that glorify Hitler and the Nazi era (Austilat 1989; Rauhaus 1989). Even Americans have gotten into the business of shipping Nazi documents and paraphernalia to German buyers.

Search for history. A more serious manifestation of the Nazi episode's continuing impact focuses on Nazism itself. One of modern history's most spectacular phenomena, Nazism draws the attention of many, for a variety of reasons. Some people have a prurient interest in Nazism as a cult of death and destruction (see Friedländer 1984). Most, however, are simply interested in trying to understand what happened and why it took place. How could a country that was the cradle of Protestantism and the source of avant-garde culture have taken the path offered by mass murderers? How could Germans have set up such an efficient killing process (even if individual death camps were themselves not always models of bureaucratic efficiency)? How could Hitler have initiated what history should have told him was a futile military campaign against the Soviet Union, and how could he have helped grind the Wehrmacht into that country's killing fields? Historians and cultural philosophers doubtless will debate such questions for centuries.

Nazism as bogeyman. Since 1945, we have seen, few people, Germans or others, have defended Nazism intellectually or politically. Proponents of particular nationalist and ultraconservative policies emerge from time to time, but they have little link to Nazism's aggression and criminality. Neither do "neo-Nazi" skinheads and most Republicans in contemporary Germany, or even Louisiana's Republican gubernatorial candidate in 1991, David Duke (Applebome 1991). Most intellectuals and political commentators have nothing good and much that is bad to say about Nazism. Some even use Nazism's negative image in a politically useful ploy: identification of a policy or an individual with Nazism, however fair or farfetched the association might be, can be a kiss of death.[27] Using Nazism as a political bogeyman is a worldwide phenomenon.

Overseas pressure. What became of Nazi criminals not tried in Nuremberg? The general confusion that accompanied the Nazi system's breakup in 1945—abetted at times by deliberate policy on the part of the occupation powers—permitted some Nazi supporters and even certified war criminals to flee the Fatherland. Occasionally the governments to which they repaired sought them out and extradited them to places where they could stand trial. Other governments were lax, however. They insisted on protecting those who had sought asylum, or, for reasons of national interest, blocked efforts to prosecute them. Meanwhile, professional "Nazihunters," such as Simon Wiesenthal (Wechsberg 1967) and Serge and Beate Klarsfeld (B. Klarsfeld 1972/1975), tried to track the fugitives down. The world's press recorded every triumph of the Nazi-hunters—especially when they brought to trial such notorious criminals as Eichmann and Barbie—and every report about the elusive "Angel of Death" at Auschwitz-Birkenau, Dr. Josef Mengele (Posner and Ware 1986), or Hitler's close associate, Martin Bormann (Posner 1991a). Eventually some recalcitrant governments were persuaded to cooperate with the search.[28]

27. Dr. Jack Kevorkian, under fire in the United States for aiding suicides, defended his actions by saying that he would "not follow the example of those immoral Nazi doctors," as were his colleagues who carried out "immoral laws" that deny people the right to choose their own death (Doctor 1991; see Bellant 1991).

28. U.S. policy toward former Nazis was haphazard until 1977, when a small branch of the Immigration and Naturalization Service was created to pursue and prosecute the fugitives. Two years later the branch was elevated to the Office of Special Investigations, U.S. Department of Justice. During the next thirteen years the OSI investigated 1,600 accused Nazi war criminals, filed eight-five cases, stripped the citizenship of forty-two individuals, and expelled thirty (Lewin 1992). See also Watts (1989) for bibliography and, for examples, Lasby (1971), H. Blum (1979), Dabringhaus (1984), A. Ryan (1984), Saidel (1984), Allen (1985), and Simpson (1988).

Other countries have dealt with the issue variously. On Canada's actions—e.g., the late 1991 revocation of Jacob Luitjen's citizenship and his expulsion to the Netherlands, where in 1948 he had been convicted in absentia for collaboration—see Troper and Weinfeld (1988) and Farnsworth (1991). In 1990 Argentina extradited Josef Schwammberger to Stuttgart, where in May 1992 he was given a life sentence. On the Lithuanian decision to open inquiries on those charged with wartime crimes against Jews, see Howe (1991). A Parisian court aroused public protest with its decision in April 1992 that not

These high-profile cases, the public trials that ensue, and the titillating prospect that a photo in tomorrow's newspaper will show the capture of yet another fugitive from Germany's dark past are constant reminders to Germans and the world that Nazi war criminals remain at large.[29] Other signs of the past emerge from time to time: historical accounts such as the 1993 movie *Schindler's List* that detail particular incidents or processes, publication of precise architectural drawings used to build the gas chambers in Auschwitz-Birkenau (Pressac 1989), or evidence from newly opened Soviet archives that the regular Wehrmacht as well as the Nazi-sponsored SS carried out mass murders of Jews (Tagliabue 1991).[30] The search to identify new criminals becomes more difficult with time, but fascination—morbid and otherwise—with Germany's Nazi past seems to be never ending.

The ways the Nazi past continues to affect the daily lives of foreigners and especially Germans is particularly evident in the evolution of cultural expression. West German literature in the early postwar period tended to stress the German soldier's heroism in the face of overwhelming odds, the incompetence and venality of Nazi hacks pretending to be military experts, or the devastation war brought upon the German people.[31] By the early 1960s, however, such German writers as Günter Grass, Heinrich Böll, Peter Handke, and Siegfried Lenz, identifying themselves as guardians of their country's conscience, adopted a different stance.[32] Their best-

---

only threw out Paul Touvier's case but also sought to exonerate all wartime collaborators (Riding 1992); in spring 1994 a provincial criminal court sentenced the seventy-nine-year-old Touvier to life imprisonment (Morgan 1994). In 1992 Australia also opened a trial of a man charged with carrying out Nazi killings.

29. In October 1992 Simon Wiesenthal identified in Graz, Austria, a seventy-four-year-old doctor, Egon Sabukoschek, who he said had been the Gestapo's "Jewish commissar" in Belgrade. Another recent case that captured international attention involved John Demjanjuk, a Ukrainian naturalized in the United States, who in 1986 was extradited to stand trial in Jerusalem. An appeal of his death sentence uncovered an apparent mistaken identity. Demjanjuk was returned to the United States, where his case was quashed, and then again to Jerusalem, where, in July 1993, the Israeli Supreme Court reversed his earlier conviction and freed him. Demjanjuk returned to his family in the United States.

30. Evidence from the Soviet Union's Jewish Anti-Fascist Committee (exterminated after the war by Stalin) and other sources (e.g., Browning 1992) contests the longstanding myth that, compared with the SS troops, regulars and even reserves in the Wehrmacht behaved in a civilized fashion.

31. Examples of these genres are, respectively, Hans Hellmut Kirst's trilogy of 1955, *Null Acht Fünfzehn* (*Zero Eight Fifteen*), Carl Zuckmayer's play of 1946, *Des Teufels General* (*The Devil's General*), and Wolfgang Borchert's "expressionist dirge for young soldiers" (Demetz 1986:234) of 1947, *Draussen vor der Tür* (*The Man Outside*). More generally, see Demetz (1970, 1986); L. Langer (1975); and J. Ryan (1983).

32. See, for example, Grass (1990). Some spiritual leaders of the Catholic and espe-

230 • Changing Images of the Past

selling novels and nonfiction dwelled on the failure of their parents' generation to address the Nazi threat, and the fear that their own generation
was unlikely to fare better against a similar challenge. This later literature
contributed to the German attitudinal change of the late 1960s: openness
to serious public discussion about what Nazism had been and what it
meant for modern Germans.

The new interest in Germany's recent past unsettled those who had
really wanted to bury it. For all their efforts to discredit Grass and the
others and to direct attention to other events, particularly the cold war
crisis, fascination with Nazism would not die. By the mid-1970s observers
in Germany spoke of a "Hitler wave." New trade books, including Joachim
Fest's (1973/1974) biography of Hitler, and such television programs as
"Holocaust," broadcast in Germany in January 1979 (Paletz 1981; Herf
1986; A. Markovits and Hayden 1986; Zielinski 1986), fueled this intense
social interest.[33]

Eventually, however, those with direct, personal experience with the
Nazi era began giving way to younger writers and intellectuals who lacked
that firsthand sensitivity. The new generation had to construct its own
images of the past from information gleaned from parents, teachers, and
others—and it had to ascertain the current significance of all those
streams of diffuse and sometimes conflicting evidence. Three trends began
to emerge in the 1980s. The first, as we have seen, was an effort to revise the
macroscopic image of Germany's past: the Historikerstreit that raised a
furor among intellectuals and professors but scarcely touched the general
public. More pertinent to society as a whole were the demands for concrete
information about the recent past and the transformation of the Nazi
episode into an objet d'art.

Microscopic studies. Questions arose in the 1980s, both in Germany
and elsewhere, that would have been unthinkable in the 1950s—questions
that discredited earlier whitewashing and purposive lapses of memory.
We have already seen that a new generation of academics, reared in the
climate of student revolts and My Lai, scrutinized what doctors, lawyers,
professors, business leaders, and other "respectable" Germans did in
1933–1945. Other writers dug more deeply into the familiar, exploring
how the past affected less-prominent people:

---

cially the Evangelical Lutheran churches played a similar role, as did the Jewish
community.
    33. Fest's 1977 film based on his book, *Hitler—eine Karriere* (*Hitler—a Career*), was
attacked in Germany for its revisionist nature; see Berlin et al. (1978) and Geissler
(1981).

- How children of death-camp survivors cope with the psychological burden they inherited (Epstein 1979);
- How sons and daughters of top Nazis respond to their fathers' convictions as mass murderers or their status as fugitives (Posner 1991b);
- How children grasp the significance of the stereotypical query, "What did you do in the war, Daddy?" (Reichel 1989);
- How French, Dutch, Ukrainian, and nationals of other countries overrun by the Wehrmacht react to new evidence about Nazi collaborators in their own ranks (Miller 1990);
- How Germans view women who informed on their neighbors to the Gestapo (Schubert 1990);
- How some citizens of Passau ostracized a teenage girl, Anna Elisabeth Rosmus, who tried to learn too much about the town's role during the Nazi era (Rosmus 1990);[34]
- How Holocaust writers themselves deal with the evidence (Rosenberg 1989).

Whatever its goal, this spate of literature—along with such dramatizations as "Holocaust" and "Heimat" on television and especially Steven Spielberg's moving film *Schindler's List,* which drew some criticism but enjoyed popular success—has given human dimension to Germany's Nazi experience.[35] The dozen years of the Third Reich represented more than a contest of giants. Villains and heroes existed—and they often seemed beyond human proportions—but masses of individuals were also caught up in the maelstrom, playing their own roles. It was time, the new generation of thinkers said, to pay closer attention to Nazism's effect on German humanity.

Nazism as an objet d'art. If historians and publicists present a sometimes dreary chronicle of the peril to Germany and civilization, others find artistic inspiration in Germany's Nazi past. Nazism as an object of art? Perhaps only devotees of the schlock that Hitler's tastes spawned in 1933–1945 would have thought this possible (Adam 1992). For the rest of the art world, few who wished to be taken seriously entertained such a patently absurd proposition. Most seemed rather to concur with Theodor Adorno's

34. Rosmus's story became the basis of Michael Verhoeven's internationally successful film *The Nasty Girl.* Schmemann (1989) reports that discrimination like Rosmus encountered exists in other towns, especially in the south of Germany.

35. "Holocaust" was presented on Channel 3 (equivalent to the U.S. Public Broadcasting System), but it received the highest viewer ratings in the FRG's television history. Between 32 and 39 percent of the market watched the four days of the series, which reached over twenty million Germans ("Holocaust" 1979). Sixty-three percent of a national sample reported seeing at least part of the series (Ifd-8:552).

dictum that writing poetry after Auschwitz would be barbaric (J. Ryan 1983:20).

An international shift in art forms nevertheless took place. Beginning especially in the English-speaking countries, with novels such as Joseph Heller's *Catch-22* and movies such as Stanley Kubrick's *Dr. Strangelove or: How I Learned to Stop Worrying and Love the Bomb* and Ken Russell's extravaganza *Lisztomania*, the new artistic style emphasizes the outrageous. It searches for inner, artistic truth rather than the literal, and gives little weight to historical accuracy. Characteristic of this trend in Germany, carried to its extreme, is Heiner Müller's play *Germania Tod in Berlin* (*Germania Death in Berlin*). As a *New York Times* drama critic wrote:

> In the play's most famous scene—the birth of a new Germany spawned by a sexual union between Hitler and Goebbels—Hitler, a beetle-eyed cross between Charlie Chaplin and Dr. Caligari, staggered onto the stage chugging gasoline. As he coupled with Goebbels, portrayed as a transvestite Valkyrie, the strains of *"Deutschland über Alles"* pounded through the theater to a disco beat. A chorus of angels, dressed in black leather and heavy metal, entered carrying a sign: "Germany a United Fatherland." . . . While the characters of Uncle Sam, John Bull and Marianne (the symbol of France) looked on in helpless stupefaction, the new Germany was born—half wolf, half pig. A gold neon swastika descended from the heavens to bless the event. (Holmberg 1990)

Of the same genre, although less flamboyant and confrontational, are Art Spiegelman's (1986, 1991) "cartoon" books *Maus* and *Maus II*. Spiegelman, the U.S.-born son of concentration camp survivors, transforms Nazis into cats and Jews into mice to re-create artistically his father's own experience in "Mauschwitz." Translations of *Maus* and *Maus II* achieved instant success in Germany and other countries.

These works of art point clearly to a geological change in culture, to a new reality. Nazism has transmogrified from a chapter of German history to an international archetype. What actually happened in 1933–1945, what people have said about it, and what effect both the real and reconstructed elements of Nazism have had are now a part of world culture, like the Spanish Inquisition and the U.S. Civil War. Children in Osaka learn about Hitler and Auschwitz—and "Mauschwitz." Swingers in Seoul can enjoy an evening at the "Hitler" bar or "Gestapo" cafe, literati in Buenos Aires have read Günter Grass's newest novel, and theatergoers in New York discuss Lillian Garrett-Groag's latest play, *The White Rose*, about university students in Munich who were executed for their anti-Nazi activities, or Charlie Schulman's outrageous comedy, *Angel of Death*, in which Josef Mengele leaves defeated Germany to become an entertainer and Oscar-winning playwright. Some critics find abhorrent the treatment of Nazism as art; for them it smacks of what Hannah Arendt (1963) called the "banality of evil": a reduction of events into cliches and snappy slogans that render trivial, hence even more likely to recur, their terrible human suffering.[36]

This new reality has modified but not changed the political world. War crimes trials will not disappear even when remaining old Nazis fade away. But western Germans have moved to the opposite side of the judicial fence from 1945: today they must deal with moral and legal questions about former GDR leaders, teachers, and border guards who fired at fleeing citizens. They must deal with the political acceptability of communist lawyers, professors, ambassadors, and others in the ex-GDR who are seeking new employment.[37] "It is as if we still saw the present in the rear view mirror of those terrible twelve years," the western German politician Klaus von Dohnanyi noted. "Again and again we use our memory of Hitler and the Nazi period as the measuring rod for current questions, although these two things have little to do with each other" (cited by Zitelmann 1990:78).

Most modern Germans doubtless understand that they are in a time warp. They would like to draw a line, a *Schlußstrich*, to terminate the historical account—so 69 percent of a national sample said in early 1989 (Zitelmann 1990:70)—and treat the German past just as other peoples treat their heritage.[38] That they cannot do so causes individual frustration and creates a potential for social unrest. The point is not that individual Germans carry with them wherever they go an indelible Nazi stain. "The past," as the German writer Peter Schneider (1991) points out, simply "throws longer shadows in Germany than elsewhere."

36. In a novel by Emily Prager (1991), an American woman named Eve on her fortieth birthday tattoos on her forearm the camp identification number of a woman killed at Auschwitz. Eve considers it a symbolic gesture to honor Holocaust victims, similar to POW/MIA bracelets worn by some Americans to commemorate soldiers captured or missing in action in Vietnam. One reviewer thought rather that Eve's action, "however well intentioned, comes across as the self-dramatizing act of someone suffering from a martyr complex, someone unaware of the trivializing effects of such a gratuitous act" (Kakutani 1991).

37. In September 1991, at their first all-German conference since 1933, psychologists dealt seriously with the need for eastern Germans to develop their own Vergangenheitsbewältigung, or coming to terms with the GDR past (Berger 1990).

38. Many Germans, including top political leaders, seemed surprised at the vehemence of international and even domestic protests in fall 1992 that forced the government to cancel a planned celebration of the fiftieth anniversary of the V-2 rocket.

III

Building a New Germany

. . . .

Part II assessed occupation-era German views of the country's recent past. Having Germans come to terms with their own past—understanding what their country had done, and understanding their own role in that history—was integral to the social change Allied occupation authorities hoped to foster. But social therapy was not their sole goal. The Allied military governments also wanted to create a new Germany, one that could surmount the weaknesses of the past. This task demanded German cooperation. This section of the book asks how Germans and Americans worked out a basis for cooperation and how Germans viewed the U.S. contribution to planning for the new Germany.

American-German cooperation required at least a modicum of mutual confidence between occupier and occupied. Chapter 9 explores German attitudes toward the American military and the American Military Government. Did the U.S. Army, in German minds, have the right credentials to make its occupation legitimate? No one doubted that the United States and its allies had taken over their land. But prospects for the occupation would have been bleak had Germans seen the occupation as an insupportable stain on their national character, or had they remained convinced of the Wehrmacht's prowess—convinced that the German army had been defeated not by fair battle but by a new stab in the back from internal enemies—or had they found AMG overbearing and impossible to work with. Alternatively, had AMG followed doctrinaire policies emanating from Washington or refused to bend to the practical exigencies of a foreign military occupation, it could have doomed any hope of turning Germany into a democratic, peaceable country.

Cooperative interaction between Germans and their American occupiers was the first prerequisite, but AMG also had to solve immediate problems of administration, ranging from public safety to sanitary engineering to principles of self-governance. Of particular importance were the public schools and public information programs. As they stormed into Germany the Allied troops shut down the schools, in part because they saw them as hotbeds of Nazism, in part because they did not have the control and material facilities needed to keep them open. But if the Allies were to reorient German society, then the first battle for democracy would have to be won in the schools. Chapter 10 focuses on the German response to AMG attempts both to transform the public school system and to establish information centers, youth activities, and other programs that could socialize Germans to democracy.

A key part of AMG's public information program was the reconstruction of the German media. Unlike the public school system, which the occupiers found intractably deep-rooted and stodgy, newspapers and radio were amenable to change—if for no other reason than that occupation authorities controlled the distribution of newsprint, assigned licenses to antifascists, and dominated the airwaves. Chapter 11 explores the kinds of media changes imposed by AMG and the German reaction to them. Did AMZON Germans heed newspapers and radio programming? Were they eager for the days when the American soldiers would go home, leaving behind Germans who could restore the powerful press barons and politically dominated radio broadcasting from years gone by?

Moving Germany toward democratic self-governance was a stepwise process: it began at the local level and, only after successes there, broadened to counties, provinces, and eventually—or so the Allies hoped—the nation. In fact, growing disputes between the tripartite Western Allies and the Soviet Union eroded inter-Allied cooperation on almost all levels. This conflict resulted in forty-one years of division before eastern Germans could merge their lands into western Germany's. Chapter 12 looks at AMZON German perspectives on this process of integration and disintegration. Of particular concern to AMG was the extent to which Germans in its zone of Germany and its sector of Berlin would align with the Tripartite Allies once a West German state was created.

The final chapter of Part III investigates the durability of political principles established in western Germany during the occupation years. Predictions by observers of Germany at the end of the 1940s ranged from a wholehearted acceptance of democratic ideals to a reversion to authoritarian belligerence. From the perspective of the 1990s, the Federal Republic has succeeded in a variety of ways, including the establishment of democratic principles of government and an international reputation for cooperation. But some incidents—most recently the eruption of right-wing extremism and xenophobia—raise questions about the depth of these successes and the extent to which political, economic, and other leaders have internalized the principles they are fond of proclaiming. Chapter 13 sets a framework for evaluating the extent to which the Federal Republic that exists today corresponds with the image of Germany that Americans had in 1939–1945 when they were contemplating a major effort to transform German society.

NINE

. . . .

U.S. Military as Mentors

Effective governance relies on widespread voluntary compliance with its norms and injunctions, laced with just enough compulsion to keep recalcitrants in line. Military occupations, by contrast, often find the ratio of compliance to compulsion reversed. Such regimes, imposed by force of arms and led by foreigners or their agents, face daily challenges to their legitimacy, as conquerors throughout history have learned, to their dismay. Nor have contemporary military governments—guided by the principle of temporary rule, not annexation—been significantly more popular with defeated peoples. Such regimes find it hard to win the hearts and minds of the vanquished or to squelch resistance movements.

With such thoughts in mind—and recalling Germans' record of active hostility to previous occupiers—the Allies of World War II developed plans for the military occupation of postwar Germany. Few expected ready German compliance. Allied generals expected the Wehrmacht to fall back to redoubts in the Bavarian Alps, from which it would conduct last-ditch defenses of the Fatherland. Lurid stories circulated about bands of fanatic youths, the "werewolves," trained by the Nazis to carry on guerrilla warfare after the war's end. At the very least, many Allied planners thought, the German people would undertake the kind of passive resistance that had proved so devastating during the French occupation of the early 1920s—destructive even of German interests.

The wildest fears of the Allies proved groundless, but Germans were understandably cool to the idea of yet another occupation by foreign troops. The Allied terms of "unconditional surrender" after the defeat and ignoble collapse of Nazi forces left little doubt in German minds that the occupiers intended to humiliate their country. A generation earlier German nationalists had turned a far less serious defeat and imposed peace into a basis for resentments that abetted the rise of the Third Reich. Would a similar sense of lost "national honor" inspire in Germans new and more virulent animosity? Then, too, was it obvious to Germans that the new masters—American, British, Soviet, and later French military forces—were militarily superior to Germans and would have defeated the Wehrmacht even without the help of Hitler's strategic blunders and the army's shortage of materiel?

Potential sources of popular opposition to the Allied occupation were plentiful. What actually occurred is the focus of this chapter, which explores that issue through the lens of public reaction to military government in the American zone of occupation. It evaluates data bearing on three interrelated hypotheses that link popular hostility toward the military regime to (*1*) a sense of lost national honor that demands the rejection of any foreign government exercising sovereignty over Germany; (*2*) denial of any inherent "right" of the U.S. military to tell Germans what to do; and (*3*) objections to specific policies adopted by the American Military Government from 1945 to 1949.

Lost National Honor as a Cause for *Ressentiment?*

Historians of Germany have made much of the putative importance of "national honor." Nationalists of various stripes have used the notion to further their ideological ends. During the ill-fated Weimar Republic in particular, rightists sought to explain away Germany's military defeat in World War I as the result of a "stab in the back" orchestrated by socialists and others, who then "sold out the Fatherland" and signed the "shameful" Versailles treaty. Hitler claimed to have thrown himself on his cot and wept when he learned of the armistice of November 1918. In later speeches he inveighed against the victors for having imposed on Germany the *Diktat* of Versailles. Still later, as bombs were crashing about his bunker in Berlin, he is reported to have expressed the bitter sentiment that Germany did not deserve to survive the inevitable dishonor.

The defeat and occupation of Germany in 1945 might well have given rise to a new nationalism seeking to restore the country's lost honor. The mass public in the American zone did not respond that way, however. Responding to six surveys from November 1945 to December 1946, for each person who said that "the occupation by the foreign powers" was "a national humiliation for Germany," twice as many denied that interpretation (see Figure 9.1).[1] In April 1946 (OMG-22; for notations see Chapter 4, note 1) the sense of national humiliation was strongest among the young

---

1. This proportion remained fairly constant over the thirteen-month period: an average of 30 percent saw the occupation as a national humiliation, 61 percent did not, and 9 percent did not say or did not know. A linear correlation shows a slight—and not statistically significant—convergence from November 1945 to December 1946.

Figure 9.1
Occupation as a National Humiliation, 1945-1946

Question: In your opinion is the occupation by the foreign powers a national humiliation for Germany?

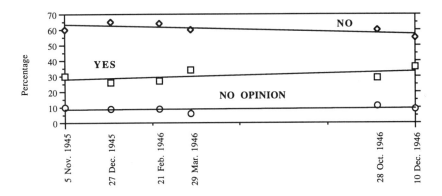

YES: $y = 28.062 + 1.2846e\text{-}2x$ $R^2 = 0.288$ F-Ratio = 1.617 Prob < 0.247
NO: $y = 63.308 - 1.4936e\text{-}2x$ $R^2 = 0.475$ F-Ratio = 3.623 Prob < 0.128
DS/DK: $y = 8.6304 + 2.0899e\text{-}3x$ $R^2 = 0.042$ F-Ratio = 2.282 Prob < 0.197

Sources: WSR-2, 9, 15, 20, 34, 36; OMG-22, 60.

(48 percent), the well educated (47 percent), government and white-collar workers (46 percent), and former Nazi party members (44 percent).

Perhaps a direct question is not the best way to get at the effects of such deeply traumatic events as a lost war, but other questions produce similar results. Much later, in November 1951, a national sample of adult women was asked what the most important points of the Potsdam agreement of July–August 1945 had been (IfD-1:140). Six in ten recalled nothing about the agreement. Of the remainder fewer than one in three (12 percent of the total sample) cited the "enslavement of Germany" or the "end of German independence." The loss of the eastern territories and the problem of expellees was mentioned more (20 percent), as was the division of Germany (19 percent). Demilitarization, denazification, and war crimes trials got nearly as much attention (11 percent), and 8 percent mentioned dismantling.

AMZON Germans recognized a kind of rough justice in the occupation. In April 1946 almost half said that the Allies were absolutely justified in not allowing their country to have an army; a quarter declared the opposite (OMG-19).[2] Substantial majorities of 60 percent in the American zone

2. Respondents split almost evenly, however, on the question of whether "Germany should be allowed to have an army in order to defend herself against aggression from other European nations": 45 percent agreed and 46 percent disagreed (OMG-19).

and 77 percent in the U.S. sector of Berlin called it just that "the Allies first help the Allied nations (e.g., France, Belgium, Holland) before helping Germany."[3] Seventy-four percent agreed (compared with 17 percent who disagreed) that "the countries who gave the Allies the most help, and who suffered most, should receive surplus food stuffs first." And as we have seen, majorities acknowledged the need for war crimes trials and denazification even if they disagreed with the way in which these policies were carried out.

Many AMZON Germans, having witnessed or learned from others how the fledgling democracy of the 1920s turned into a vicious war machine under the Nazis, doubted whether their country could quickly—if ever—develop truly democratic institutions and practices. By a ratio of almost three to one (63 percent agreeing and 22 percent disagreeing) AMZON residents said in June 1946 that "very few Germans have shown understanding or inclination toward democracy, as has been demonstrated during the last 50 years" (OMG-19). A somewhat larger number (69 percent agreeing and 23 percent disagreeing) argued that "Germany should be occupied for many years, until the German people are able to form a democratic government."[4]

This underlying skepticism about the German population's disposition toward democracy appears in a wide variety of other survey findings. A sample of 162 community leaders in February 1946, although virtually unanimous in approving the military government's incremental policy of giving more and more power to Germans, was almost as solid in insisting that these authorities retain final control (OMG-5). The reason most often given was that Germans might not be politically mature enough for sovereignty. A similar survey nine months later of 188 community leaders played down the concern about German political maturity (OMG-44), but three-quarters of the respondents thought that the American occupation would last at least ten years, and a quarter said more than twenty years. The median response was ten years.[5] Regardless of how long they thought

3. OMGUS analysts, in discussing this finding, added that "it takes unmitigated brashness for 25 percent and 20 percent of the people interviewed in the Zone and Berlin respectively *to indicate that they expect the Allies to aid Germany before extending help to the countries over-run by Germany during the war*" (OMG-22; emphasis in original).

4. The 3-to-1 ratio cited in the text is for the U.S. zone of Germany and the U.S. sector of Berlin; for Berlin alone it was 4.2 to 1, for youth in Württemberg-Baden 2.5 to 1, for Marburg University students 0.7 to 1, for released political prisoners 1 to 1, and for detained political prisoners 1.4 to 1 (OMG-19).

5. In contrast, 33 percent of a sample of AMZON Germans (WSR-28) thought that the U.S. occupation army would remain in Germany for as many as ten years, 19 percent between ten and twenty years, and 10 percent even longer; 17 percent said they would stay until circumstances had changed.

the occupation *would* continue, 76 percent added that it *should* last that long. Most of those offering reasons cited the need to "combat communism," "keep peace and order or watch political developments," or "prevent war and ensure peace"; a few mentioned the need to teach Germans democracy or reeducate German youth.[6]

Even the later occupation years saw a remarkable stability of opinion, though confidence in the ability of Germans to govern themselves democratically grew (OMG-74, 175). In four surveys from August 1947 to January 1949, an average of 47 percent responded that democracy could thrive in Germany, but 36 percent disagreed. (The high point of this indicator of self-confidence was June 1948, when the ratio of positive to negative responses was 53 to 29 percent.) Figure 9.2 shows another aspect of this underlying stability in attitudes. An average of almost one in seven was willing to see the occupation continue until Germany could form a good democratic government. More than half, however, maintained that the United States should reconstruct Germany as soon as possible. Figure 9.2 also shows both a modestly declining willingness to rely on the Allies to shape Germany's future and a growing desire to go it alone.

Latent fear of the antidemocratic tendencies of Germans nonetheless declined after 1947. Public opinion increasingly supported the idea of at least a semi-independent government. In mid-spring 1947, 55 percent were willing (30 percent were not) to accept a peace treaty immediately, even though its terms would be harsher on Germany (OMG-62). Seven in ten in August 1948 favored the creation of a provisional government for western Germany (OMG-136); of the 12 percent who opposed this notion, only a sixth cited the inability of Germans to govern themselves. Once the Parliamentary Council set up to create this government convened, large majorities (61 percent in both September 1948 and February 1949) aligned themselves with the move to form a West German government "now" (OMG-175). Opposition, due mainly to the realization that the development of such a government would seal Germany's division, declined from 17 to 11 percent.

One more question deserves attention: Did Germans want the "Ami," that is, the U.S. soldiers, to go home?[7] Presumably, if they saw the occupa-

6. Among seventy-eight former prisoners of war who had attended wartime courses in democracy at Fort Getty in Rhode Island, the largest share (42 percent) expressed the view that the Americans should stay "until Germany has become a truly democratic country" (OMG-93). Nearly a quarter urged the United States to remain until it had reached agreement with the Soviet Union, and one in three named a specific time period (14 percent saying less than twenty years, 12 percent longer or "forever"). Six percent pegged the end of occupation to the attainment of economic or social—but not political—normality in Germany.

7. Communists and others were writing graffiti on walls and singing songs that

Figure 9.2

Reconstruction of Germany, 1947-1949

Question: Which of these statements comes closest to your opinion?
- (A) Germany herself should bear the responsibility for her reconstruction under the supervision of the Allies.
- (B) Germany should be occupied by the Allies until she is able to form a good democratic government.
- (C) The Americans should reconstruct Germany as soon as possible in order to avoid her becoming a prey to communism.
- (D) The reconstruction of their country should be left to the Germans themselves without interference from the Allies.

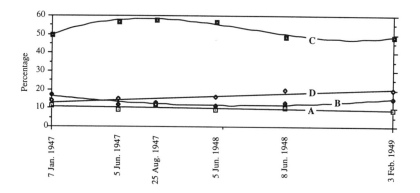

A: $y = 10.734 - 2.1831e\text{-}3x$ $R^2 = 0.221$ F-Ratio = 1.135 Prob < 0.283
B: $y = 16.342 - 2.4145e\text{-}2x + 3.0169e\text{-}5x^2$ $R^2 = 0.813$ F-Ratio = 6.508 Prob < 0.081
C: $y = 49.694 + 9.3573e\text{-}2x - 2.9699e\text{-}4x^2 + 2.2698e\text{-}7x^3$ $R^2 = 0.954$ F-Ratio = 13.814 Prob < 0.068
D: $y = 12.814 + 9.9684e\text{-}3x$ $R^2 = 0.698$ F-Ratio = 9.239 Prob < 0.038

Source: OMG-175.

tion as a national humiliation, Germans would have preferred all foreign troops to get out of the country, but few expressed such a wish. Only a quarter in May 1947 said that it would be better for Germany were the four occupying powers to leave at once, whereas 62 percent thought the opposite (OMG-72). Later responses to this question, shown in Figure 9.3, showed a bit more support for a Soviet proposal to remove Allied troops "within a year." More detailed questions asked of respondents from August 1948 to June 1949 (OMG-160, 187) and the third-order polynomial curves shown in Figure 9.3 suggest another dimension of this issue. On the one hand, AMZON Germans who did not want a quadrilateral withdrawal

---

demanded, "Ami go home." The term "Ami" persists today as a jocular—and sometimes pejorative—reference to an individual U.S. soldier (or all of them) in Germany.

Figure 9.3

Withdrawal of Occupation Forces, 1948-1949

Question: The Russians have proposed that all four occupying powers should leave Germany within the next year. Would you like to see this proposal carried out?

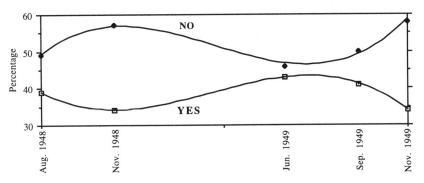

YES: $y = 38.975 - 3.5940x + 0.76048x^2 - 3.6223e\text{-}2x^3$ $R^2 = 0.999$ F-Ratio = 331.981   Prob < 0.040
NO: $y = 49.130 + 5.1243x - 1.0088x^2 + 4.7235e\text{-}2x^3$ $R^2 = 0.984$ F-Ratio = 20.529   Prob < 0.161

Sources: OMG-140, 160, 187; HIC-19.

thought it would leave them exposed to the threat of Soviet domination.[8] On the other hand, during the months before the formal promulgation of the Federal Republic of Germany (FRG), a somewhat increasing number—possibly as a bargaining ploy to put pressure on the Western Allies to move more rapidly toward the FRG's semisovereignty—was willing to risk any such danger.

The hypothesis that a people under alien military rule resists what it sees as a national humiliation seemed not to apply to AMZON Germans. (Later surveys found little difference on this score among residents of the British, French, and U.S. zones of occupation; see A. Merritt and R. Merritt 1980:40–43.) Only a minority saw the occupation in terms of national honor (Figure 9.1). Perhaps Germans were too stunned by the discovery that heinous crimes against humanity had been committed in their name to question whether foreign military rule disgraced them as a people.

AMZON masses and leaders were furthermore willing to accept tutelage in democratic governance from the Allies, especially during the early occupation years. Even toward the end of the occupation, in early 1949, large majorities called for the Allies to play a major role in Germany's recon-

---

8. Those who favored withdrawal minimized that danger. A handful of opponents to withdrawal also mentioned concern over the Germans' ability to govern themselves (3 percent) or the possibility of a Nazi renaissance (2 percent).

struction (Figure 9.2). Only one in five wanted no further interference from the Allies. Notably, however, during the later occupation years, the reasons given for accepting the continuing Allied role dwelled less on suspicion about the antidemocratic tendencies of Germans and more on what respondents saw as a growing external threat.

During this latter period, Germans expressed an understandably increasing willingness to take over the reins of government. The Allies, they said, should use their preeminence to develop German institutions as rapidly as possible, not to bolster their own dominance over the country.[9] Still, majorities did not want Allied military forces to withdraw from Germany. Indeed, their deeply felt need for protection, eventually institutionalized through the North Atlantic Treaty Organization, continues to the present day.

However reasonable may be the expectation that an occupied people resents profoundly and therefore resists the foreign regime, that response cannot be said to have characterized the U.S. zone of occupied Germany from 1945 to 1949. AMZON Germans understood and accepted the general principle of the occupation and did not channel any residual resentments into obstructive actions. They even encouraged the presence of foreign troops long after West Germany had achieved first semisovereignty in 1949 and then, six years later, almost full political independence.

The American Military's "Right" to Rule Germany

An occupied population can view its situation philosophically as not inherently unjust without accepting the legitimacy of the agents who carry it out—the agents' "right" to tell the population what to do. Such a right may be accorded ascriptively, that is, recognizing the moral superiority of the occupiers, or the occupiers may have "earned" the right through, for example, a convincing demonstration of their combat superiority (though ultimate victory may or may not be considered proof of such combat superiority). The behavior of the occupiers after they have taken charge may also lead the subject population to accept their right to rule, at least temporarily.

The right of the wartime Allies to occupy postwar Germany derived solely and simply from their military victory. That was enough. Agree-

---

9. In mid-September 1951, 41 percent of a nationwide sample expressed belief that the United States really wanted the semisovereign FRG to become an independent country as soon as possible, but 36 percent felt that the United States intended to keep the FRG in a dependent position as long as possible (HIC-103). Almost one in four expressed no opinion.

ments among the Allies spelled out, if not always in a completely clear manner, both the procedures for implementing the occupation and their concomitant rights and obligations. Their assumption of sovereignty over German territory was enunciated in the Berlin Declaration of 5 June 1945, issued almost a month after the Wehrmacht had laid down its arms. In declarations from the Atlantic Charter of August 1941 to the London Charter four years later, which set out the legal basis for the Nuremberg war crimes trials, the Allies repeatedly underscored the moral decay of Germany's Nazi leadership—by implication asserting their own moral authority.

Postwar Germans, though they admitted that Nazi crimes were legion, were less than convinced by the Allies' implied claim to moral authority. Few Germans, as we have seen, opposed the principle of punishing notorious Nazis and even "all those who ordered the murdering of civilians, or who participated in the murders" (OMG-19). But this national self-flagellation had another side. Germans could easily point to similar "war crimes" committed by the Allies. In December 1946, two months after the execution of those condemned by the International Military Tribunal in Nuremberg, five-sixths of a sample of AMZON adults argued that "both sides in this war committed many crimes against humanity and peace," and only six percent disagreed (OMG-51).

Among the most infamous Allied actions, from the Germans' viewpoint, was strategic bombing to demoralize urban populations. In April 1946, five-sixths of an AMZON sample correctly denied that "the air forces of the Allies only bombed military objectives in Germany" (OMG-19).[10] In a later survey in May 1952 (HIC-154) among the entire West German population, 62 percent said that American bombings of "French cities occupied by us Germans" was unjustified (16 percent disagreed). More than two-thirds thought that no circumstances whatever justified the wartime bombing of cities.[11] Criticism of American behavior in World War II was stronger among those who had personally experienced bombing attacks than among those who had not, and stronger still among those whose homes had been destroyed in such raids.

Respondents were more ambivalent about those responsible for the

10. In their "Flattery(?) Scale," described in Chapter 5, which sought to sort out respondents giving only answers which they thought the occupiers wanted to hear, OMGUS analysts gave points for insincerity to the 12 percent who agreed with this assertion.

11. Another 23 percent listed circumstances in which bombing of cities was justified: cities with war industries, e.g., armament factories (10 percent); those that are military targets, i.e., occupied by troops (8 percent); defended cities (5 percent); and cities from which civilians have been evacuated (2 percent).

bombing attacks. On the one hand, in May 1952 only 31 percent believed that U.S. airmen were "to be condemned . . . for what they did in Germany during the last war"; 54 percent said the pilots should not be condemned (HIC-154). Four of five who responded to the question said that, were they to meet an airman who had bombed Germany, they would treat him graciously. On the other hand, apprised of a remark by a speaker at a gathering of war veterans that "the real war criminals are those who made the unholy peace by themselves, who destroyed entire cities without military reasons, who dropped the bombs on Hiroshima, and who are producing the new atomic bombs," 46 percent of a national sample in November 1952 allowed that they liked the statement and only 29 percent did not (IfD-1:276).

The source of this ambivalence doubtless lies in Germany's history. Asked in May 1952 whether the United States Air Force had been a "chivalrous" opponent during World War II, the 16 percent who responded positively supported their view exclusively by reference to the combat behavior of American airmen, whereas the 50 percent who responded negatively focused equally exclusively on the bombing of cities (HIC-154). Those responsible for ordering the aerial attacks were to be condemned, not the American airmen—who had merely been doing their duty just as German soldiers had during those same evil days. To demand punishment for offending airmen would raise, at least in the respondents' minds, the specter of renewed investigations into German behavior during the war—something that few Germans wanted.[12]

Whatever positive feelings postwar Germans had about Americans—and their expressed feelings were mostly positive—they did not acknowledge that the U.S. military had acted in a morally superior fashion during World War II. Soldiers were soldiers, Germans said, and terrible things happen during wars. That American soldiers happened to be controlling postwar Germany had nothing whatever to do with a right based on higher morality.

Nor did Germans believe that American fighting men in World War II had been superior as soldiers. As Table 9.1 illustrates, Germans thought their own men better and considered Russian soldiers their toughest op-

12. As we have seen, AMZON survey respondents throughout the postwar years distinguished between legitimate wartime actions of soldiers and civilians on the one hand and the mass slaughters of Jews and other crimes ordered and carried out by fanatic Nazis on the other. They steadfastly rejected the notion of "collective guilt" of all Germans for these latter crimes, and by and large absolved soldiers who executed these commands, for whom disobedience to orders would have meant severe punishment or even death. Later opinion sharply opposed continuing trials of military men of whatever rank.

Table 9.1 Comparative Quality of Soldiers in World War II, 1951–1954

Questions: All in all, who in your opinion makes the best fighter as an individual? And who is in second place? And who is in last place?

	First Place			Second Place			Last Place		
	Dec. 1951	Jan. 1953	Jan. 1954	Dec. 1951	Jan. 1953	Jan. 1954	Dec. 1951	Jan. 1953	Jan. 1954
Americans	1	2	2	12	20	24	20	16	12
British	1	1	1	13	12	9	8	11	13
French	*	*	*	8	6	4	25	32	33
Germans	77	80	76	5	6	4	*	*	1
Russians	5	4	3	31	31	31	9	9	9
No opinion	16	13	18	31	25	28	38	32	32

Source: HIC-198
Notes: The various nationalities (percentages) were presented alphabetically on a card to respondents.
*Less than one-half of one percent.

ponents. Americans ranked a weak third (in 1951 ahead of only the French). These judgments are reinforced by comments made in 1954 by those who thought American soldiers inferior to former German soldiers. HICOG analysts categorized these as follows:

The German soldier had more courage, bravery, defiance of death and dare-devil spirit (or the Americans are deficient in these qualities)	20%
The German soldier had more endurance and stamina and was less demanding (or American soldiers lack stamina, demand too much)	18
The German soldier was more obedient and better disciplined (or Americans lack discipline, are too independent)	12
The German soldier had a more rigorous and better training (or the American lacks discipline and drill)	11
The German soldier was superior as an infantryman and as an individual fighter (or Americans are not good infantrymen or individual fighters)	9
The American soldier relies on the material and technical superiority of his weapons	8

The Germans have proved to be excellent soldiers through the ages	6
The German soldiers fought (unlike the Americans) for their homeland, their fatherland	4
The Germans are good soldiers (in general)	3
The American soldier lacks the combat experience of the German soldier	2
Other answers	2
No opinion, no answer	7
Total	102%

(HIC-198; multiple responses permitted)

Other surveys during the 1950s revealed that much of the negative opinion of American and other Allied soldiers derived from exposure not to men in combat but to personnel bivouacked in West Germany as part of the occupation forces.

Similar attitudes emerge toward American airmen. The data in Table 9.2 appear at first glance to be self-contradictory. Germans judged the USAF to have been the best air force during the war but rated American airmen second to Germans (and not far ahead of Royal Air Force pilots). More detailed questions elicited responses that praised Luftwaffe pilots for their skill, bravery, and daring. The USAF was ranked first, on the other hand, because respondents credited it with superior technical and material advantages: more and better planes, better equipment and armament, and more technical facilities.[13] Germans seemed to feel that, had their own airmen had these advantages, the Luftwaffe could have defeated any air force.

13. HICOG analysts in 1952 (HIC-154) seemed somewhat defensive in their interpretation: Germans who rated the Luftwaffe more highly, the analysts observed, stressed "the superior quality of the German airmen—in training, skill and courage who fought, they say, usually against heavy odds," whereas

those rating the U.S. Air Force best emphasize, almost entirely, superiority in resources, number of planes, equipment and technical facilities. While all of these factors did apply to the American Air Force especially from 1944 on, the fact that the planes coming over Germany were manned by men, not robots, appears to have escaped most West Germans.

Perhaps it is to be expected that a people who lived through mass bombing raids should emphasize number and material superiority of their one-time enemy. Also it is probably natural for a defeated country to assuage its national pride by emphasizing the bravery and skill of its defenders.

"But it also suggests," these HICOG analysts concluded, "that the bulk of the Germans are not yet able to face squarely all the facts in their defeat."

Table 9.2   Comparative Quality of Air Forces and Airmen
in World War II, May 1952

Responses to Two Sets of Questions: First, as far as you can judge,
which of these countries had on the whole the best air force in the
last war? And which holds second place? Second, by and large, who is,
in your opinion, better in combat as an individual airman?
And who holds second place? (percentages)

	Best Air Force		Best Airman	
	First Place	Second Place	First Place	Second Place
American	45	27	4	26
British	2	15	1	20
French	—	*	—	1
German	33	29	62	4
Russian	*	2	1	8
No opinion	20	27	32	41

Source: HIC-154.
*Less than one-half of one percent.

The implication of these findings is twofold. First, views of the quality
of U.S. fighting men and their equipment were critical in shaping the
Germans' willingness to undertake rearmament within a West European
or North Atlantic framework.[14] The improved image of U.S. soldiers from
1951 to 1954, shown in Table 9.1, is notable. This change can be attributed
in part to U.S. military successes in Korea, in part to a realization by
Germans that they had to rely on these American soldiers for their own
defense.

Second, for whatever reason—chauvinistic nostalgia, lack of information about the real qualities of the Allied forces in World War II, recent
experience with a more deskbound army of occupation—Germans cate-
gorically denied the combat superiority of the armies that now governed
their territories. In the eyes of Germans, it was not the fighting qualities of
the U.S. military that had earned it the "right" to occupy Germany.

In other circumstances such perceptions could easily have turned into
a dangerously scornful attitude contributing to revanchist nationalism.
The circumstances of postwar Germany's first decade, however, forced

14. Hɪc-119, 154, 174, 198 contain substantial information on perceptions comparing American and Soviet capabilities in terms of men and materiel.

Germans to rely increasingly on the American military and eventually to ally with it. Scorn and petulant rejection were not in Germans' interest. The question shifts, then, from judgments about past performance of the U.S. military, whether it had demonstrated moral or combat superiority, to estimates of whether or not Germans could get along with the occupation forces.

By its nature a military encampment gathers many mostly young men, separated from their families and other ties, frequently with time on their hands. Certain kinds of problems between soldiers and local civilians are likely to erupt. Place these young men in an alien and possibly hostile environment, give them authority over the civilian population and privileges (relatively high salaries, easy access to coveted commodities) that those civilians do not enjoy, and the probability of conflict rises sharply. The local population is also likely to see the soldiers as representative of the country from which they come. Arrogant, brutal, or insensitive behavior toward the occupied can worsen an already oppressive atmosphere, leading the occupied to resist the occupiers even when they might otherwise work together. By the same token, fair and sympathetic treatment of the occupied may make tolerable even the most unjust occupation.

German perceptions of the U.S. military as an occupation force incorporated two elements: the sensitivity of the military bureaucracy to the needs of an essentially civilian population and the characteristics and behaviors of individual soldiers. Unfortunately, OMGUS pollsters seldom directly assessed the first element. But this does not mean that OMGUS (or its Opinion Surveys Section) was insensitive to German concerns.

Consider, for instance, U.S. policy on fraternization (WSR-2). For various reasons military authorities had sought to prevent GIs from interacting personally with Germans. The policy proved to be difficult to implement, however, and caused resistance on both sides (Zink 1947:135; Murphy 1964:283–284). But, after abandoning the policy in summer 1945, military authorities considered reinstating it because of friction caused by uncontrolled German-American interaction. Survey findings in November 1945 (WSR-2) suggested that reinstitution of restrictions would only raise new popular resistance: only two in five of those expressing opinions (27 percent of the entire sample) agreed in principle with nonfraternization, and less than a quarter of that group wanted it reinstated.[15] The military government soon buried the idea.[16] Indeed, before long, the AMG

15. The OMGUS data card for the first question is incomplete: it reports that 27 percent disapproved of German women dating GIs, 42 percent were tolerant, and 17 percent gave a different response or none at all—leaving 14 percent unaccounted for.

16. I am not suggesting that OMGUS retreated from a new nonfraternization program only because of the survey results. The idea was doubtless stillborn, and even if it wasn't,

began initiating programs to enhance informal personal ties among GIs and Germans.

Regarding the behavior of American soldiers as a group, the German public took an understanding stance. In part this was because few of them knew much about the soldiers' insensitivities or peccadilloes. In late 1947 (OMG-34), at a time when Germans were still on very short rations, only about a third of the respondents felt that Americans were using German food supplies for themselves (29 percent, compared with 58 percent who denied it and 13 percent who did not know) or had heard that the Americans were wasting food (36 percent, with 64 percent denying it [OMG-91]). At a time when inflation was wrecking the economy, eventually forcing widespread bartering, only 5 percent blamed the occupation troops. At a time when the black market raged, seven in ten either denied (49 percent) or did not know about (21 percent) allegations that Americans in Germany were enriching themselves through barter activities (OMG-91).[17] At a time when property was more than normally prized because so much had been destroyed during the war, only 21 percent claimed to know of cases where American negligence had destroyed German property (OMG-94). Four years later, asked what the most significant error made by the occupation forces had been, only one in seven respondents in a national sample cited the troops' luxurious style of life and behavior (IfD-1:140).

Attitudes toward individual American soldiers were not much different —in part, again, because few AMZON Germans knew any. In September 1946 only 14 percent said that they knew an American well or fairly well, and another 20 percent had talked with an American, but almost two-thirds (66 percent) could claim neither connection (WSR-32; OMG-27).[18] A year later, in November 1947, about one in four respondents reported knowing an American personally, and about half of those knew more than four (OMG-94). By November 1949 almost one-third said that they had

---

by November 1945 OMGUS had a large number of competent advisers who could have quashed it. The survey data may nevertheless have strengthened the hand of those opposing the idea.

17. Commerce in contraband was so widespread, Zink (1957:138) wrote, that "it almost seemed like the classical story of Diogenes going about with a lantern to seek out an honest man. Not every American engaged in black-market activities of one kind and another during his stay in Germany, but this sort of activity was so general that there was very little criticism of it and indeed those who did not take advantage were often regarded as 'peculiar' or 'freaks.'" See Janis (1963) for data on intensive interviews with GIs regarding black marketing.

18. In October 1946, one in ten AMZON Germans reported having spoken with many Americans, twice that many to a few (WSR-31). It is remarkable, given German migrations to the United States, that in September 1946 (WSR-31) less than one in twelve AMZON Germans reported having received letters from there.

become acquainted with Americans since the end of the war, though more than half of those added that the acquaintanceship was casual (HIC-6). The Germans most likely to know Americans were not young women, as has often been supposed, but men in the upper and middle socioeconomic strata.

The scarcity of social interaction did not prevent AMZON Germans from expressing their views about the Amis. In November 1945 only one in six reported that their own attitudes toward the Americans had changed since the occupation began (WSR-2), and 37 percent felt that other Germans had become more friendly toward the occupiers in the previous few weeks.[19] Were the Amis friendly? In September 1946 three-quarters said that they were and 7 percent disagreed (WSR-32). Were the Amis typical Americans? In October 1946 half said that they were and 9 percent said they were not (WSR-31). What characterized the Amis? Almost two-thirds of the respondents could name positive traits, and more than a third could specify negative ones.[20]

Those who knew Americans personally had more differentiated views about them than did the others and were more tolerant of them (OMG-94). They were less upset about women they knew who dated Amis (19 percent opposed, compared with 22 percent of those knowing no Americans). But they were also more likely than others to think that American GIs were enriching themselves through the black market (42 percent), to have heard that Americans wasted or destroyed food (46 percent), to know of cases where Americans had destroyed German property through negligence (30 percent), and to have had unpleasant or irritating experiences with Americans (21 percent, compared with 10 percent among those who did not know Americans).[21]

American GIs got reasonably good marks for their behavior. In an April

19. Almost three in ten saw a change in Ami attitudes toward Germans; those reporting changes and those finding none (45 percent) were virtually unanimous in describing the Americans' good qualities (WSR-2).

20. Separate questions asked for positive and negative traits, with multiple responses permitted. On the positive side, 47 percent saw Americans as kind, helpful, good-natured, courteous, and neat, 10 percent said they were fond of children, 7 percent called them generous, and 8 percent identified other positive traits; one percent said Americans had no positive characteristics, and 36 percent gave no response. On the negative side, 14 percent complained that Americans were undisciplined, drank too much, and chased after German women, 5 percent said they were too self-concerned, 5 percent called them uncouth, and 14 percent cited other negative traits; 10 percent said Americans had no negative characteristics, and 55 percent gave no response.

21. Of the respondents who knew Americans, 38 percent said that the occupation had brought unnecessary and disagreeable restrictions (especially requisitioning, reported by 19 percent); 24 percent of those who did not know Americans made the same point (with 11 percent mentioning requisitioning).

1946 survey, 42 percent denied that Allied soldiers had "always acted correctly toward German civilians" (OMG-19).[22] Three and a half years later, however, just after the military government phase of the occupation ended, AMZON Germans described the behavior of the occupation troops in highly positive terms (HIC-6). Of those who saw American soldiers at least occasionally and had opinions on them (82 percent of the sample), almost three-quarters termed their behavior very good (6 percent of the total) or good (54 percent); more than one-fifth called it fair (13 percent) or partly good and partly bad (5 percent); and one in twenty-five said it was bad (3 percent) or very bad (1 percent). Criticism focused on the arrogance of the soldiers, who seemed to consider themselves "the victors and masters," as well as behavior attributed to a bad upbringing at home (HIC-119). Surveys in the early 1950s reproduced these results on essential points (HIC-119, 154, 174). In January 1954, for instance, 58 percent of an AMZON sample termed the behavior of American soldiers good, 23 percent fair, and 4 percent bad, with 15 percent undecided (HIC-198).[23]

Table 9.3 applies a relative perspective to attitudes toward American soldiers. The bulk of AMZON respondents thought that GIs behaved at least as well as or better than German troops would have in a similar situation.[24] But American soldiers did not fare so well in German eyes as the British did, and only slightly better than the French.[25] Table 9.4 shows the relative position of American soldiers even more clearly. They fared better in their own zone than elsewhere, but still not as well as the British overall.

A preponderance of Germans consistently felt that living with the American troops was getting increasingly easy. The share calling them more popular than before grew from 32 to 35 percent from November 1947 to September 1949, with the proportion seeing them less liked dropping from 22 to 12 percent (HIC-1). Asked about behavior of U.S. troops, 50 percent in November 1948 and 51 percent a year later termed it better

22. The 51 percent who agreed with the assertion were scored on the OMGUS "Flattery(?) Scale" (see note 10).
23. Comparable percentages for all of West Germany were 54 percent good, 20 percent fair, 3 percent bad, and 23 percent undecided; in Rhineland Palatinate, where U.S. bases were concentrated, and hence where Germans presumably had the best opportunity to observe American GIs, the distribution was 51 percent good, 28 percent fair, 6 percent bad, and 15 percent undecided.
24. HICOG analysts wrote: "On the assumption that the West German people would expect their soldiers to behave in an orderly, disciplined way (and this is the common view of the German people) in an occupation such as the present one in West Germany, the Allies appear to be predominantly favorably estimated" (OMG-119).
25. This hierarchy of regard is supported by zonal responses to a question about the behavior of the troops occupying the zone: subtracting the number responding "bad"

Table 9.3   Comparative Quality of Allied Occupation Troops, Fall 1951

Responses to the Question: Do you think that the (American) (British) (French) soldiers in West Germany in general behave the same as, better than, or worse than German soldiers would under similar circumstances? (percentages)

	Allied Troops		American		British		French	
	Sep. 1951	Nov. 1951	Sep. 1951	Nov. 1951	Sep. 1951	Nov. 1951	Sep. 1951	Nov. 1951
The same	59	65	57	63	61	66	52	61
Better	4	2	3	4	4	2	2	1
Worse	19	14	26	20	12	9	26	18
No opinion	18	19	14	13	23	23	20	20

Source: HIC-119.

than before; 5 and 10 percent, respectively, labeled it worse (HIC-6).[26] This same positive dynamic characterized the AMZON German image of relations between American soldiers and the German civilians: roughly half in January 1953 (44 percent) and January 1954 (58 percent) saw relations improving; only a minuscule proportion (2 and 1 percent, respectively) saw them worsening (HIC-198).[27] Conscious American efforts to improve public relations, participation by GIs in community projects and worthy causes, the ebb of World War II memories into the distant past, and, as suggested earlier, growing psychological identification with the victors-turned-defenders-and-allies—these factors all doubtless played a role in the German perception of increasingly positive bonds with American troops.

A discussion of German attitudes toward American soldiers would not be complete without a comment about black GIs in the immediate postwar period. During their occupation of the Rhineland in the early 1920s, the French used a large number of black Senegambian soldiers. Similar troops had fought in World War I side by side with French and other

from that saying "good" gave American troops a score of 47 (55 percent good minus 8 percent bad)—the same as French troops got in their zone of occupation (58 percent good minus 11 percent bad) but lower than the British score of 56 (61 percent good minus 5 percent bad) in their zone.

26. A barely noticeable positive rating and a doubling of the negative rating, HICOG analysts tell us, reflect reaction to a recent series of "incidents" in Franconia. Even so, the ratio of positive to negative ratings is more than five to one.

27. Comparable figures in 1954 for all of West Germany were 57 and 2 percent, for Rhineland Palatinate 61 and 2 percent.

Table 9.4 Comparative Behavior of Allied Occupation Troops, November–December 1951

Responses to the Questions: According to everything you have seen or heard, which soldiers behave themselves the best here in West Germany—the American, the British, or the French? And which soldiers behave themselves the worst here in West Germany, according to your opinion? (percentages)

	Best Behaved Soldiers in:				Worst Behaved Soldiers in:			
	West Germany	U.S. Zone	British Zone	French Zone	West Germany	U.S. Zone	British Zone	French Zone
American	19	24	17	13	9	7	8	14
British	27	22	31	19	2	3	2	1
French	2	4	1	8	23	28	23	12
All the same	11	6	12	15	8	6	8	12
No opinion	41	44	39	45	58	56	59	61

Source: HIC-119.

French colonial forces, and France officially viewed this force as the equivalent of any other military contingent. Germans, though, suspected that the assignment of people whom they viewed as half-savages to occupy one of the hearths of Western civilization was a calculated insult by the French.[28] Vehement protests appeared in the press and in public addresses against the "black outrage." Every alleged instance of misbehavior by a Senegambian soldier was exaggerated to enhance a scenario of rampant, politically motivated rapine and pillage. This frenzy soon fed Nazi racism.

It was against this background that Germans saw the arrival of black soldiers from the United States. Lack of information, anxiety, and a strain of racism characterized their response. Only 16 percent of Mannheim citizens, for instance, claimed in September 1946 (OMG-24) to have struck up any relationship with black soldiers, compared with 28 percent who reported such a relationship with whites. A survey five years later revealed little change. Although 55 percent of AMZON respondents expressed willingness to invite Allied soldiers into their homes, only two-fifths of that group (23 percent of the total) extended this willingness in principle to include blacks (HIC-119).

Contacts with blacks that Germans did have produced mixed results. Mannheim residents were inclined to see black soldiers as friendlier than whites (36 percent expressed this view; 16 percent the opposite). One in ten could describe having experienced or witnessed pleasant contacts, mostly involving blacks' friendliness to children (OMG-24). Fifteen percent, however, referred to unpleasant experiences, and slightly more said that blacks' behavior was not proper. The latter group, together with the 33 percent who said that their behavior was proper with some exceptions, complained most frequently about blacks' maltreatment of civilians (including murder, rape, and mishandling of women and girls) and drunken irresponsibility. Three in ten Mannheim citizens, half of them quite emphatically, reported that they feared blacks.

How many of the reported misdeeds and fears were grounded in actual fact is less important here than the magnitude of these negative perceptions, which are consistent with an overall pattern of racial bias observable in Germany during these years. About three in ten AMZON residents agreed in April 1946 (OMG-19) that "negroes, compared with the white race, are a lower race" and that blacks do not in general have the same

28. Hitler, in *Mein Kampf* (1925–1927/1939:448), had another explanation: "It was and is the Jews who bring the negro to the Rhine, always with the same concealed thought and the clear goal of destroying, by the bastardization which would necessarily set in, the white race which they hate, to throw it down from its cultural and political height and in turn to rise personally to the position of master."

abilities as whites.[29] (Not quite six in ten gave contrary responses to each question.) A special ability attributed to blacks, however, was their fighting skill. Forty-four percent of an AMZON sample in December 1951 reported believing that the black soldier, as an individual, would fight well; only 27 percent of the same sample responded similarly about American soldiers in general (HIC-119). Asked for their reasoning, the largest share gave responses with explicitly racial overtones. No evidence emerges from the surveys to suggest that stationing blacks in Germany affected German attitudes toward the occupation as a whole.

The German public's general tolerance for GIs may in part explain the refutation of a key hypothesis about the American military's "right" to rule Germany: that the success of an occupation rests solely on the quality of the occupiers, as measured either by the values that the occupied population ascribes to them or by their military achievements. Germans flatly denied the moral superiority of the Allies, and as we have seen, they felt that American soldiers and airmen were, as individual fighting men, inferior to their counterparts in the Wehrmacht and Luftwaffe. But the public attitude toward the U.S. occupation troops themselves, occasional misdeeds notwithstanding, was acceptance. The quality, character, and behavior of the American occupiers did not yield bitter and disruptive resentment—though the basis for such a reaction existed, had recalcitrant nationalists chosen to exploit it.

Germans acquiesced in part because few alternatives were available. A return to the Nazi dictatorship was out of the question, not only because the Allies would not have permitted it but also because Germans had little interest in restoring that discredited past. Nor did temporary regimes established under other occupying powers hold much promise. Few West Germans had any interest in coming under Soviet domination, and those Germans who already were soon began pouring out of the Soviet zone and the subsequent German Democratic Republic to fill the refugee camps of the West. Nowhere was the antipathy toward Soviet domination greater than in West Berlin. Its population had experienced life under the Red Army, and, during the Berlin blockade of 1948–1949, it took only a hint that the U.S. might withdraw to send most West Berliners into despair (OMG-132).

Even the other Western occupying powers seemed less attractive than the United States. AMZON respondents expressed their view in May 1946 that food rations were largest in their zone, smallest in the French and

29. "Racial prejudice was not closely related to fear of Negroes," OMGUS analysts concluded. "Such fear probably grows upon reports of mishandling of Germans by the troops rather than any ingrained stock of prejudice."

Figure 9.4

Treatment of Germany by the Individual Allies, September 1951

Question: Taking everything into consideration has what (America) (Britain) (France) has done in West
Germany since the end of the war been to the advantage or disadvantage of West Germany?

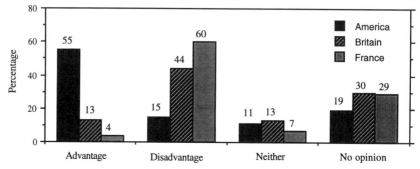

Source: HIC-103.

Russian zones (OMG-18). Somewhat over a year later, 84 percent of a similar sample (OMG-76) said that, if they had the information in 1945 that they
possessed at the time of the survey, they would have chosen to live under
the Americans (4 percent preferred the British), and 68 percent said that, if
they had a son, they would want him to live in the U.S. zone (5 percent
chose the British zone). Large majorities felt that economic conditions
were better in the American zone than under the British (67 percent),
French (76 percent), or Soviets (77 percent). And, as Figure 9.4 shows,
judgments made in September 1951 by a nationwide sample rated the
United States by far the most solicitous toward Germany's well-being:
The differences between positive and negative perceptions were for the
United States 40 (55 minus 15), for Britain negative 31 (13 minus 44), and
for France negative 56 (4 minus 60).

Such clues, together with other data showing an increasingly positive
image of the United States throughout the 1950s and early 1960s (see R.
Merritt and Puchala 1968:134, 249–260), suggest that, far from resenting
the U.S. influence, Germans retrospectively welcomed it.[30] But this over-

---

30. A study in depth conducted in summer 1947 in West Berlin found that large
majorities of respondents rejected anti-American statements regardless of how they
were presented (OMG-73). In gauging the American attitude toward Germany, respondents in November 1947 most commonly cited understanding (40 percent), followed by
indifference (35 percent) and sympathy (9 percent). In September 1949 half mentioned
understanding, indifference dropped to 20 percent, and sympathy remained fairly constant at 10 percent (HIC-1). (Four percent in each survey cited dislike and 2 percent
vengeance.)

all attitude of receptivity does not mean that they did not fault specific policies pursued by the American military government.

Specific Policies as Sources of Resistance

American military officials were called upon to perform many tasks in postwar Germany. Some were foreseen, and officials, trained mostly in academic or legal rather than military professions, spent months before the war ended attending special training schools to learn how to govern a foreign country. They were prepared to assume or delegate responsibilities at the local and regional level, and each no doubt realized that he would confront unanticipated problems not covered in the training manual.

Germans had to stand aside as these foreign military officers, many of whom spoke no German and had little understanding of local issues or traditions, took charge of institutions and processes that affected vitally every citizen's life. Egregiously wrong or stupid decisions, as we have seen, alienated some portions of that population. And critics have charged that major American policy decisions were sometimes counterproductive. The question here is how the mass of AMZON Germans evaluated the way in which AMG performed the tasks that it assumed or was assigned.

Many of these tasks were at the same time technical and delicate in nature. AMG had to restore community services: provide safe water, rebuild leaching fields, maintain fiscal controls, reconstruct bridges to revitalize traffic, disseminate information, and maintain such public records as birth and marriage documents, without which no modern society can function effectively. The military government had to determine how best to allocate the scarce resources available in the U.S.-controlled areas of postwar Germany, then revise its calculations to address such exigencies as the Soviet Union's June 1948 blockade of land and waterway traffic to and from the western sectors of Berlin.

In performing these tasks, which reflected mostly shared goals of Americans and Germans, AMG earned a reputation for competence and fairness. AMZON Germans did not blame the Allies for the inflation that reduced the economy to large-scale bartering. To the contrary, in early 1946 (OMG-25) large majorities felt that American and German authorities really wanted to prevent inflation (85 percent), were capable of doing so (79 percent), and would in fact do their best to hold prices at their then-present level (82 percent). Relatively few Germans, we have seen, seemed to feel that American soldiers were using the increasingly chaotic economic situation to enrich themselves (OMG-34, 91).

Other aspects of U.S. occupation policy drew similarly supportive responses. When AMZON Germans discussed taxation to equalize burdens caused by wartime losses (which 74 percent favored and 18 percent opposed), 40 percent wanted to put the program under U.S. administration, compared with 26 percent who favored German offices.[31] The reasons given by those favoring U.S. responsibility, OMGUS analysts pointed out, "were almost without exception variants of the theme that the Military Government would be more just and more objective than German officials" (OMG-169; underlined in original). AMZON Germans also supported U.S. youth programs and media policy. When West Berlin was blockaded, only a twelfth of AMZON Germans and a quarter of West Berliners thought that the Western powers could do more than they were to aid the beleaguered city (OMG-175).

Perhaps the most difficult issue was food rationing. Food was scarce in postwar Germany. Winters were harsh, and the war had disrupted planting and harvesting seasons, left large numbers of displaced persons who needed to be fed, and damaged the transportation network. The Allies, moreover, gave first priority to helping foreign peoples who had suffered under Nazism. As we have seen, that policy met with a mixed but largely understanding response, but AMZON Germans nonetheless reported that they were getting too little food to work effectively. Under all these pressures, however, AMG authorities were generally seen as fair in carrying out their rationing policy. The proportion of respondents who called the allocation and distribution procedures unjust was 3 percent in November 1945, reached a high point of less than a third in January 1948, then fell back within a year to a fifth (OMG-175).

Other AMG policies, which were based on values and goals that Germans did not share wholeheartedly, engendered unrest. Dismantling Germany's war industries was a case in point. The Allies intended to reduce the country's economic potential to a subsistence level. Asked in June 1946 about Allied plans, seven-eighths of those with opinions (49 to 7 percent of the total sample) thought the limits too severe (OMG-31). Dismantling industry to support reparation payments was particularly controversial. The median response to a question about how long the obligation for reparations might be expected to continue was nearly forty years, and about three-fifths of the informed respondents (44 to 29 percent of the total sample) thought the Allied imposition of industrial limits unjustified (OMG-59). Most of those who said it was justified referred to the victor's

---

31. Among the 32 percent who expected to have to pay something for this equalization (or *Lastenausgleich*), 51 percent favored the measures and 42 percent opposed them; among the 24 percent who expected to benefit, 95 percent favored and 2 percent opposed them (OMG-169).

Figure 9.5

Perceived U.S. Contribution to German Reconstruction, 1945-1950

Question: Do you think the Americans furthered or hindered the reconstruction of Germany?

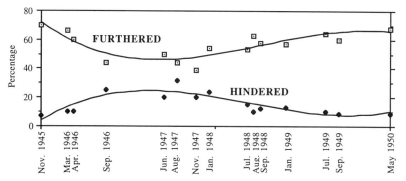

FURTHERED: y = 72.136 - 3.3156x + 0.12475x^2 - 1.2145e-3x^3   R^2 = 0.746   F-Ratio = 10.741   Prob < 0.001
HINDERED: y = 3.4120 + 2.8186x - 0.11313x^2 + 1.1699e-3x^3   R^2 = 0.733   F-Ratio = 10.079   Prob < 0.002

Sources: OMG-22, 60, 72, 85, 100, 175; HIC-30.

Note: The residual category includes "neither/nor," "both," and "no opinion"; in some cases figures are
estimated from charts; in April 1946 the question asked about Germany's "recovery and reconstruction."

right to impose restrictions, not the practical issues involved.[32] The others
objected to the lower standard of living that deindustrialization would
bring. Fatalism about the inevitability of such controls soon turned into
opposition.

Most AMZON Germans nevertheless accepted the bad with the good.
Figure 9.5 reflects a strong sentiment from 1945 through 1950 that the
United States had furthered rather than hindered German reconstruction.[33] What would have happened had AMG persisted in the original Allied
plan to keep the German economy at a subsistence level, bar active Nazis
from responsible positions in public or private life, and punish all those
guilty of broadly defined war crimes? The data suggest contradictory
answers. During the entire fifty-four months covered in Figure 9.5, positive responses outnumbered negative ones, implying a basic willingness
to tolerate U.S. policy. But the popular mood became increasingly hostile

32. Answers on industrial limitation came for the most part after interviewers explained to respondents what Allied plans were; before the survey, 64 percent had been
uninformed or misinformed about these plans (OMG-31).

33. Almost four times as many praised Americans as blamed them. In an April 1946
survey that focused not on AMG but on Americans in general, 52 percent agreed and 39
percent disagreed that "all the Americans are very much interested in the well-being of
the German people" (OMG-19).

until summer 1947, then improved sharply after a major shift in U.S. occupation policy set aside the wartime plans and procedures that Germans increasingly resisted.

With the strategic change in summer 1947 that resulted from the rethinking begun a year earlier, AMG stopped a downward trend in popular confidence about the U.S. intent to rebuild Germany. The trends suggest that, had OMGUS done nothing, hostile responses would have outstripped positive ones by the end of the year. Meanwhile, recalcitrance by the French and increasingly by the Soviets continued to stymie progress toward national reconstruction. The United States began after summer 1947 to demand inter-Allied cooperation to revitalize the German economy —a goal that Germans supported.

U.S. authorities encountered further resistance as a result of policies that favored some segments of German life to the detriment of others. Early decisions, each seemingly minor or routine—on personnel, the requisition of buildings for AMG offices, permission to rebuild a factory or export goods, issuance of publishing licenses and interzonal passes to attend meetings outside the U.S. zone—all these and other decisions had a cumulative impact that helped mold the later structure of Germany's new government. They also infuriated prominent Germans on whose feet the Americans had trod. In tones reminiscent of nationalist polemics of the 1920s, some challenged the legitimacy of the Bonn republic, which they termed the creature of Washington politicians. Others saw U.S. policies as an effort to restore the quasifeudal social structure that existed before the Nazis seized power. Even friendly critics thought intrusive the key role played by OMGUS officers in guiding the Parliamentary Council that drafted western Germany's constitution, the Basic Law.

A blatant example of U.S. interference was the mission to limit the spread of socialism in western Germany—which meant, for all practical purposes, strengthening the conservative Christian Democratic Union (CDU) and its Bavarian sister party, the Christian Social Union (CSU) (see Gimbel 1968:116–210). Kurt Schumacher, the outspoken leader of the Social Democratic Party (SPD), in particular bridled at what he saw as a naked abuse of power. A combat veteran who had lost an arm in World War I and what remained of his health in Hitler's concentration camps, the hard-bitten Schumacher was not about to brook ideological restrictions imposed by Americans. As his biographer wrote,

> A narrow, short-sighted view of American interests, he felt, guided American policy-makers in their efforts to block the endeavors of patriotic Germans to establish German democracy on firm anti-Communist foundations. Thus during the first years he characterized American

efforts to "democratize" as naive, and during the later years as just as undiscerningly anti-Communist. In effect, he said, the crude anti-Communist crusade of American policy-makers served merely to aid and comfort the sworn foes of democracy, the "reactionaries" behind [cDU leader and later Chancellor Konrad] Adenauer and the Communists. He claimed that American pressure for European integration and German rearmament was directed against the reunification of Germany and the democratization of the country through socialism. The United States, he asserted, was forcing upon West Germany policies that a German democrat and patriot was compelled to oppose. (Edinger 1965:185–186)

Schumacher saw in the U.S. military governor from March 1947 to May 1949, General Lucius D. Clay, "the man principally responsible for the failure of socialization measures in the British and American zones, and for the frustration of the Social Democratic drive for power in West Germany" (Edinger 1965:184).[34]

Because Schumacher was as vociferous in expressing his views as he was stubborn in defending them, and because he dominated the spD until a stroke incapacitated him in 1951, it seems reasonable to expect that his charge of AMG's structural bias filtered down to the party's rank and file. OMGUS data—analysts occasionally broke down responses according to the respondents' party affiliation—do not support this expectation. In fact, AMZON Germans identifying themselves as Social Democrats were by and large more supportive than others of AMG and its policies. A survey in April 1946 singled out spD members as especially "pro-democratic" in precisely this respect (omG-19). Later that spring they proved to be slightly more likely than cDU/csU supporters to express confidence in the desire of American and German authorities to prevent inflation (omG-25). Throughout the occupation period (Figure 9.5) spD supporters were more disposed than either the average AMZON respondent or cDU/csU adherents to praise U.S. efforts at reconstructing Germany.[35] In August 1950, a larger share of Social Democratic voters than cDU/csU supporters or the general population both feared that the withdrawal of the occupying powers from Germany would leave the country less secure politically and felt that the

34. As deputy military governor under first General Eisenhower and then General Joseph T. McNarney before March 1947, Clay was in fact principally responsible for conducting the U.S. occupation.

35. For those who credited the U.S. with furthering German reconstruction in four surveys from April 1946 to May 1950 (omG-22, 72; hiC-30), spD supporters ranked 8 percentage points higher (averaging 66 percent) than all AMZON respondents and 3 percentage points higher than cDU/csU supporters.

Western powers should do more to ensure the country's security (HIC-37).

Views on another issue provide an interesting sidelight to this image of a party with diverging leaders and followers. Social Democrats were far from unanimous on the key question of socializing industry. In November 1947, at a time when even CDU/CSU leaders, including Adenauer, were calling for public ownership of the means of production, almost equal percentages of SPD supporters favored socialization of all industry (17 percent) and no industries at all (18 percent); 47 percent wanted only heavy industry (coal, mines, iron and steel) socialized. Social Democrats were almost evenly divided between thinking that workers would be better off (41 percent) or worse off (40 percent) if industry were socialized (OMG-90).

These findings suggest that SPD supporters either did not hear or did not heed Schumacher's complaints.[36] Social Democrats viewed socialization measures more favorably than did other parties, to be sure. Almost two-thirds of them, compared with 37 percent of CDU/CSU supporters, endorsed at least some socialization of industry. Social Democrats continued to support U.S. policies and behavior despite mounting claims and evidence that the military government was blocking the party's pursuit of important social changes. Social Democrats considered factors besides the arguments of their party leaders in formulating opinions about the occupation.

German reactions to various U.S. policies undercut the hypothesis that an occupier's unpopular policies must necessarily spawn active resistance. Neither the imposition of controls on a subject population nor the hostility inspired among diverse but vocal groups had a significant impact in postwar Germany. Policies that sought to reestablish normal services or control an emergency situation met with general support for AMG's fairness. Potentially explosive policies designed to eradicate the remnants of Nazism—in part at the cost of the population at large—were abandoned before large-scale opposition to them emerged. Even policies that disadvantaged major segments of the population did not elicit antagonism among those—such as Social Democrats—presumably affected most by them.

36. If we assume that most trade union members also supported the SPD, then we might draw added evidence for the argument from a survey in late 1946 (OMG-35): trade union members expressed clearly their view that AMG had helped (66 percent) rather than hindered (4 percent) the growth of trade unions; almost two-thirds thought that the presence of AMG advisers at trade union meetings would be of "substantial" help.

The Tolerable Occupation

Unrealized expectations on both sides changed the character of the U.S. occupation of postwar Germany. In spring 1945, alert to what their own country had inflicted on other Europeans and agitated by the rhetoric surrounding the Morgenthau Plan, Germans feared the worst. Americans, expecting to find ersatz Hitlers behind every bush, prepared to encounter bitter, drawn-out resistance. But two years after the war's end, Germans and Americans were collaborating both to dismantle key occupation programs and to mold a new framework to protect Western civilization from renewed onslaught from the East. The Ami was not going home but becoming a constant in a changing German society. How do we account for this startling change of events?

First, most Germans grew to accept and even share the view of their occupiers that National Socialism and the Nazi regime were an abomination. The reasons for this varied from deep moral outrage to casuistic disdain of political leaders who had botched their opportunities. Enthusiasm for punishing former Nazis and their henchmen dwindled as the investigations and trials got closer to home, but the AMZON public never considered Nazi Germany's defeat and the subsequent occupation an unmitigated catastrophe, a national humiliation warranting a vengeful redemption. They accepted the need for at least temporary tutelage, viewed the Allied interregnum as a breathing space for anti-Nazi Germans to regroup, and ultimately looked to the United States not as their oppressor but as the defender of their freedoms. Such opportunities justified the minor injustices and even major discomforts that the occupation caused.

Then, too, AMZON Germans learned early that, if a country must be under the yoke of a foreign military power, it could do worse than have the United States as its occupier. When the troops first arrived, few Germans felt that the Americans—or the British or the French—had "earned" the wartime victory because of superior generalship or the fighting qualities of their men. Superiority, both quantitative and qualitative, in equipment and facilities had been decisive; had the Wehrmacht and Luftwaffe enjoyed such advantages, Germany might not have lost the war in the first place. This sense of inequity might have poisoned the German-American relationship, but it did not: U.S. military authorities behaved decently, GIs fraternized with the local population, and AMG soon abandoned its bureaucratic pettifoggery. AMZON (and other) Germans increasingly saw the Amis as more sympathetic to German concerns than were the other occupiers. Particularly in contrast to vindictive France and the unspeakable Soviet Union, the United States seemed most inclined to use justice to

Figure 9.6
German Confidence in U.S. Military Occupation, 1945-1950

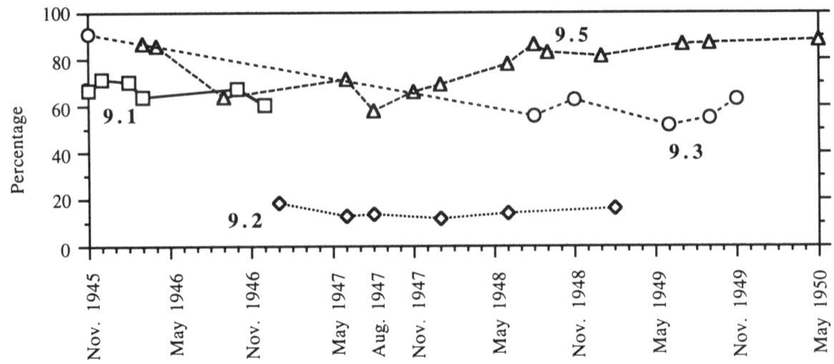

Figure 9.1: Acceptance of occupation (National humiliation? No/[Yes + No])
Figure 9.2: Opting for continuation of occupation (B/[A+B+C+D])
Figure 9.3: Desire to retain U.S. Army (Want withdrawal? No/[Yes + No])
Figure 9.5: Acceptance of U.S. reconstruction efforts (Furthered? Yes/[Yes + No])

temper the rigors of its occupation, least interested in profiting from the occupation, and most apt to further German reconstruction.

It was in the best interest of AMZON Germans to tolerate even unpopular AMG policies. The acceptance of Americans reflected in the survey data almost suggests that Germans chose to join those whom they had been unable to beat on the battlefield. A more plausible explanation is simply that Germans saw compliance rather than resistance as the most promising way to end the occupation.

A shift in U.S. occupation policy reinforced German cooperation. But improved German-American relations was not the only stake. Germans realized, too, that the United States would increasingly set the tone for both the occupation and the stance of the West toward the Soviet Union. Americans, meanwhile, were sensitive to any declining popular acceptance for the occupation. Figure 9.6 summarizes some dimensions of the disenchantment among AMZON Germans before mid-1947. Americans also understood the practical implications of the realignment in European politics that Bernard Baruch had characterized as cold war. This new strategic challenge, together with the diminishing efficacy of American policy in Germany, contributed to the U.S. decision in 1947 to modify its occupation policy.

The revised U.S. image of future relations with Germany eventually governed the Western approach. This new relationship spawned much hope and enjoyed moderate success in the American zone. AMZON Germans were more agreeable to key dimensions of the U.S. occupation—

including its continuation. Germans in other zones seemed to share these changing perspectives, partly because of the realization that, with lines between East and West in Germany hardening, British and French influence was bound to subside still more. Two years later, some hesitation from the other powers notwithstanding, the U.S. strategy finally brought forth a semisovereign Federal Republic of Germany that would later join the North Atlantic Treaty Organization. In one sense, then, post-1945 Germans were rewarded for their faith in alignment with the United States.

In another sense, however, the increasingly close tie to U.S. strategy produced an unplanned but long-lasting impact: common German citizens, those whom the pollsters interviewed, gradually abandoned national unity, if not as a dream then at least as a practical goal. Polls from the late 1940s to the 1980s revealed a deep German fear of falling under Soviet domination. Whether or not such a threat existed is disputable, but the perception is unarguable. As the cold war deepened and as German options grew more narrowly constrained, the German public was increasingly willing to substitute security for unity. The United States, meanwhile, at least after 1947, was increasingly willing to recruit German assistance for the apparently imminent global struggle. This conjunction of perception and need lessened tension between AMG officials and Germans—except for those who, like Kurt Schumacher, were unwilling to bend to the winds of change.[37] Until this environment of East-West hostility abated, national unity could remain nothing more than a dream.

The legitimacy of the occupation assumed new dimensions in this cold war climate. In the place of a victor-vanquished relationship emerged an inchoate German-American partnership. Expectations of a long, rigorous occupation gave way to the prospect of a future independent German government on a nearly equal footing. From the U.S. point of view, to restrain the German economy further was to risk hamstringing an emerging leadership, a strategy counterproductive to the goal of rebuilding solid institutions. Germans meanwhile grew increasingly impatient with anything that smacked of continued punishment for sins of a previous regime. The task after summer 1947 was to end, not extend, the occupation. Success depended on German-American cooperation, with acquiescence or, still better, active support from Britain and France. Acknowledging the legitimacy of the diminishing U.S. occupation provided the best route to a new independent Germany—and to the distant goal, unification.

37. German elites, especially intellectuals, have had, as A. Markovits (1989) points out, various and often contradictory reasons for their anti-Americanism. The German masses in contrast have been remarkably constant in their positive image of the United States and of Americans.

TEN

. . . .

Socialization to Democracy

U.S. occupation policy was meant to change people's minds as well as to understand their behavior. Whether Germans were merely politically inept, bewilderingly idealistic, or tainted with the original sin of authoritarianism was an interesting question, but AMG officers needed to know what to do on the day after their military victory. Such fanciful notions as Morgenthau's plan to turn Germans into happy, harmless shepherds were also of little practical use. What mattered was developing constructive ways to mold popular perspectives that could eventually support Germany's return to the comity of nation-states. The Allies understood from the outset that sending in the army would not be enough: until the goal was achieved, the Allies would have to deal on a day-to-day basis with the occupied Germans and help them become the people that a new Germany would need. But if force would not tame the Germans—and ultimately only the Soviet Union had to rely on the military to suppress its Germans—would persuasion be more successful? Could the Allies reeducate and reorient the Germans to accept democracy and to participate actively in the international peace process?

The United States, with a wealth of resources at its disposal, undertook by far the most extensive program among the Allies to socialize Germans to Western-style democracy. Wartime planning established some principles, and the Joint Chiefs of Staff charged the American Military Government with preventing "Germany from ever again becoming a threat to the peace of the world" and preparing for "an eventual reconstruction of German political life on a democratic basis" (U.S. Department of State 1985:18). Implementing such charges, however, frequently forced AMG to fly by the seat of its collective pants.

Through a wide array of programs in the U.S. zone, AMG sought in various ways to make the country safe for democracy. The capstone was its education policy. Regrouping the elementary and secondary schools was a major assignment, and staffing the schools with teachers and instructional material took years (see Zink 1947:147–164; Knappen 1947; Liddell 1949; Pilgert 1953; Bungenstab 1970; Lange-Quassowski 1979; Tent 1982; Hearnden 1985). AMG had other, quasieducational roles to play: establishing youth programs, libraries, exchange programs, and publications, for example.

This chapter evaluates the impact of such programs on postwar Germans living under U.S. control. How did they respond to AMG policy on education, reeducation, and reorientation? Were they susceptible to changes initiated or encouraged by the Americans? The wisdom of U.S. policy, its quality, or its effectiveness were secondary to the public perception—what common German citizens thought about this policy and its implementation.

Educating the Youth

The U.S. Army closed the public schools as it made its way into German territory in the last months of the war. Many public buildings had sustained damage, especially in the larger cities, and those that were more or less intact were needed for housing the GIs. Instructional materials and fuel to heat the buildings were unavailable, and withal the military wanted to ensure firm control over the movements and activities of individual Germans under their command. More important, however, closing the schools reflected the belief that they had been major contributors to Nazi power. The occupiers knew that the Nazis had sought to pervert the educational institutions, which had been among the glories of German culture, into tawdry propaganda centers. Accounts such as Erika Mann's (1938) *School for Barbarians* popularized a lurid image of what the Nazis had in mind and how they succeeded in indoctrinating Germany's impressionable children. The occupiers knew, too, that most if not all teachers had joined the National Socialist Teachers' League, that school officials were frequently Nazi party members who actively supported the war effort, and that some male instructors, during the closing phases of the war, carried their teenage charges into last-ditch battles that were as futile militarily as they were costly in young lives.[1] The Americans had ample justification to close the schools.

Virtually everyone who has gone to school has opinions about how schools should be run, and AMG encountered a variety of such views and demands. The far-reaching control Americans had over the politics and economics of thirteen million Germans gave them the opportunity to be-

1. Zink (1957:197–198) reports that the National Socialist Teachers' League enlisted 80 percent of the country's public teachers.

gin at the bottom to construct a new German society. They could hire and fire teachers and administrators, supervise administrative procedures, design curricula and write textbooks, introduce student councils and parents' associations, develop youth clubs, and issue licenses to publish new materials.

With the power to engineer social change through the education system came a heavy burden. The importance of public education and the potential impact of any changes U.S. educational planners might initiate put them in an often uncomfortable spotlight, targets of criticism from German educationists, school bureaucrats, politicians, and intellectuals, plus a plethora of Americans claiming expertise and the obligation to intervene. Critics on the political left argued that these educational planners were too soft on Nazism or that the policy was flawed by excessive capitalism, imperialism, or whatever. Critics on the right questioned whether it was necessary to reeducate Germans: would not simply removing Nazi leaders, they asked, better serve Germany's and America's broad policy goals? Pedagogues stressed the impracticability of trying to transfer educational institutions and practices from one culture to another—and even those who thought the experiment worth trying argued about how it would turn out.

With such criticism from without and policy disputes from within, it is no wonder that the turnover rate of AMG educational personnel was exceptionally high (Zink 1957:194) and that observers of recent German history disparage the U.S. attempt to restructure German education. What critics frequently ignore, however, is the program's actual impact on the German people, contrasted to its putative or planned impact. Many of the Germans who inflicted their advice and complaints on AMG officials had a vested interest in maintaining the educational status quo until they might once again control the schools. But what were U.S. policymakers hearing from their program's clientele—the parents, pupils, and others who were directly affected by it? Before turning to this question, let us review the main dimensions of AMG education policy.

U.S. education policy in Germany underwent major shifts between 1945 and 1949 (Tsuchimochi 1991). In the first phase the goal was to get the schools and other educational activities going again after the wartime destruction and postwar disruption—but in the process to remove former Nazis from teaching and other positions of responsibility, and eliminate racist and nationalist curricula. A second phase began with a report prepared in September 1946 by the U.S. Education Commission, led by George F. Zook. It called for a more aggressive, positive approach to "reeducation." The program it prescribed, which was embodied in AMG directives issued in early 1947, included a wide variety of reforms in the German education system, such as free tuition and textbooks, comprehensive schools, and plans for teaching civics.

By mid-1948, however, it was becoming increasingly evident that a West German state would be formed and that, even though some vestigial elements of the occupation might remain, the Allies would have little more to say about how Germans dealt with such domestic issues as education. A third phase of U.S. educational policy ensued, emphasizing German compliance with earlier directives on reeducation and reviewing the further options available to the U.S. government in structuring Germans' social environment. In October 1948, at a conference in Berchtesgaden, the new director of the OMGUS Education and Cultural Relations Division, Alonzo G. Grace, announced a new policy of "reorientation," which would encourage West German cooperation in defining and realizing programs to strengthen democratic sentiments among Germans.

Such major shifts in U.S. policy, together with the day-to-day exigencies faced by the occupation authorities, meant that different aspects of public education drew attention at different times. The initial focus was opening enough schools to get the children off the street. AMG officials increased the number of schools in operation from 5,821 in October 1945 to 9,756 seven months later.[2] The share of children aged 6 to 14 who were in school grew from 69 percent in October 1945 to 93 percent in May 1946. AMG then shifted emphasis to the problems of heating the classrooms, locating acceptable textbooks, and finding trained teachers.

Teacher training. Perhaps the most pressing problem, once adequate schoolrooms could be found, was a shortage of teachers. U.S. authorities had refused to recertify nearly two-thirds of the AMZON teachers because of their previous Nazi affiliations. Many of the teachers who had survived denazification hearings did so because they had retired before teachers were forced to join the National Socialist Teachers' League; some were too old or rusty to be effective in the classroom. When the schools opened on 1 October 1945, only 12,849 teachers met more than 1.1 million pupils—approximately 87 pupils per teacher (Knappen 1947:87). At least 16,000 additional teachers were needed.

Teacher-training institutes were geared to turn out only 2,000 teachers per year, but AMG authorities established crash programs at those institutes and created new ones. Candidates for admission were required to

2. Data from Knappen (1947:87), counting elementary schools only. An additional 402 secondary schools, beginning operation on 1 May 1946, accounted for 169,143 pupils and 5,349 teachers and had a shortage of 2,584 teachers (p. 90). A survey in August 1946 (WSR-29) found substantial approval of U.S. progress in opening the schools and universities: 70 percent expressed satisfaction, 8 percent had some reservations, and only 4 percent were not at all satisfied.

demonstrate academic ability and the "positive qualities of character and attitude" needed to be effective in democratization programs. No former member of the Nazi party was permitted to attend, and neither were former officers of the armed forces (OMGUS 1946a:4). Rather than the usual four years of university-level education followed by two years of supervised internship, candidates at such institutes received a short course and the injunction to return eventually to make up what they had missed. By early 1947 some forty teacher-training institutes operated in the U.S. zone.

Progress in providing sufficient trained, competent teachers was nevertheless slow. By May 1946 the number of teachers rose to almost 24,000, but because of the increased number of pupils—including many expellees from eastern Europe—a shortfall of more than 12,000 teachers continued to exist. Not until the end of the 1940s, after the United States had effectively given up on denazification, did the elementary and secondary schools of AMZON have an adequate number of teachers.

Textbooks. Even where teaching staffs were adequate, politically acceptable textbooks were in short supply. AMG authorities had rejected nearly half the textbooks submitted for their review (OMGUS 1946b:4). History books characterized the Third Reich as the culmination of the German nation's development; biology texts promoted racist theories; even algebra books evoked militaristic or racist sentiments. A typical arithmetic problem read: "The moneylender charged the farmer's widow 12 percent interest per year on a loan of six hundred marks for four years. Out of how much money did the Jewish swindler cheat the widow?" (cited in Knappen 1947:63–70).

At first Americans merely reprinted textbooks from the Weimar era (Knappen 1947:64)—when they could secure adequate supplies of paper and ink and access to printing presses—but eventually they were able to commission acceptable books by postwar writers. A directive issued in February 1947 created "textbook and curricula centers." These centers were stocked with samples of typical American texts and modern teaching aids and staffed by U.S. educators who could provide source materials and assist Germans to research, edit, and publish new textbooks. In the first two years of their operation the centers received more than eighty-four thousand visitors and lent more than thirty-nine thousand books. Grants from the U.S. Congress also helped resolve the textbook crisis; in 1948 alone Congress subsidized the printing of some 13.5 million textbooks in the American zone. Up-to-date history books, however, remained in short supply until well into the 1950s (Clay 1950a:300).

Education and AMG's role in setting education policy were not high priority items for AMZON Germans. Periodic questions asking interviewees about their "greatest cares and worries" elicited such responses as food, the fate of German prisoners of war, clothing, and unemployment, but never was education listed by more than one percent (WSR-1–36; OMG-29, 84, 93, 139; for notations see Chapter 4, note 1). Asked directly about the state of the schools, few respondents reported any problems. Three in five interviewed in November 1945 did not comment on problems in the schools and another fifth had no complaints (WSR-5). The attentive few (21 percent), however, saw problems galore. The chief difficulty was that teachers were too inexperienced (7 percent) or too few (4 percent). Four percent each deplored excessive "democratic indoctrination," too much use of ideas taken from U.S. schools, insufficient fuel, and short school hours. A survey a year and a half later in Württemberg-Baden produced similar findings. More than three out of four of those who expressed opinions (62 percent of the entire sample) considered the schools' teaching plans and type of instruction adequate, "under normal conditions, to meet the needs of German youth" (OMG-61).

Nor was the AMZON public particularly concerned about what the Allies were doing in the schools. In educational circles critics complained that U.S. policy was "made in Washington" and unresponsive to needs in the field, and that the administration and enforcement of policies were badly coordinated and often inconsistent (Liddell 1949:19). But the masses did not pay close attention to the reality of Allied policy or to the grumbling of their own education "experts." Asked in January 1948 about the schools' major faults apart from their poor physical condition and lack of instructional materials, only 3 percent of West Berlin respondents and none in Stuttgart indicated concern about "Allied interference" (OMG-95).[3]

The issue of teacher shortages was particularly problematic as long as AMG insisted on keeping former Nazis out of the schools. In a survey conducted in December 1945 (WSR-8) about two in five who gave an opinion (30 percent of the entire sample) thought that the denazification program for the teaching profession was too severe. The rest said that it was all right as it was (43 percent) or even too lenient (4 percent).[4] Two years later, however, in January 1948, few adults in either West Berlin (24 percent) or Stuttgart (14 percent) thought that excluding teachers who had once been

---

3. It is not clear whether or not West Berliners, in responding to the cue "Allied," were referring to interference by a single occupier (such as the United States or Soviet Union) or by all of them together.

4. A subsequent question (WSR-8) asked whether "too many or not enough Nazis" had "been removed from the cultural sphere," which in German terminology includes but is not limited to education. Sixteen percent answered "too many," but more than twice that number said "too few" (9 percent) or "all right as it is" (27 percent). Almost half gave ambiguous answers (1 percent) or none at all (48 percent). (The 101 percent total reflects rounding error.)

Nazis best served the education system (OMG-95). The majority in both cities would have preferred to retain the "good old capable and experienced teachers."

What about the content of public education?[5] An issue of recurrent interest addresses the ways in which Germans have sought to come to terms with their country's recent past: What and how should German youngsters be taught about the Nazi episode? OMGUS educationists found it difficult to rewrite textbooks and train new teachers who could present to their pupils a version of history not overwhelmed by nationalistic prides and prejudices. As a result, schools under U.S. control at first simply avoided teaching contemporary history. But AMZON Germans expressed little concern about the omission unless they were asked specifically about it. None, we saw earlier, raised this issue when asked in an open-ended fashion about school problems. A survey in January 1948 asked more directly what the failure to teach history meant (OMG-95). About half in West Berlin and Stuttgart said that it would have serious effects, but an equal number in West Berlin and 39 percent in Stuttgart said that it would not make much difference. Those West Berliners who thought that the chief aim of the schools was to instill in children a sense of order and conduct (47 percent of whom said the omission of recent history would have serious effects) or to provide vocational training (40 percent) were less concerned than were respondents who stressed the need to provide children with a general education (52 percent) or training in critical thinking (55 percent).

U.S. policymakers got mixed readings from their soundings of AMZON interest in other education matters. One policy, responding to the notion that fees kept children from poorer families out of the schools, especially the higher grades which would qualify them for admission to the university, mandated free schooling and textbooks for all pupils. German education officials generally resisted this idea and argued that free education would dilute the quality of the higher schools (see Gimbel 1968:241–243).

5. OMGUS surveys did not address the public philosophy of education. A schedule of 110 paired questions, the "German attitude scale" (OMG-19), came closest by touching on three broad themes: First, 60 percent agreed (38 percent disagreed) that "the education of children should not be based on military principles," and 66 percent disagreed (13 percent agreed) that "the weakness of most western European schools is based on the lack of military discipline." Second, 80 percent agreed (13 percent disagreed) that "the most important thing in educating a child is to develop his individual personality," that is, "they should be individuals and not educated only for the state," and 81 percent disagreed (13 percent agreed) that "an education encouraging people to have their own opinion is dangerous to the security of a state." Third, 94 percent agreed (4 percent disagreed) that "most people learn independent thinking through an appropriate education," and 83 percent agreed (13 percent disagreed) that "the best citizens of a country are those who, through their education, think first for themselves."

But when OMGUS pollsters turned to adults in Württemberg-Baden in May 1947, they found substantial support for the philosophy behind the U.S. position: 44 percent of the respondents said that the quantity and quality of education a child received depended on the financial and social position of its parents, while only 30 percent claimed that children received an education commensurate solely with their abilities (OMG-61).[6]

American officials were also eager to enlist more popular participation in the governance of the schools. They encouraged the formation of parent-teacher associations and teacher unions, as well as some form of student government. Almost three-quarters of a Württemberg-Baden sample in May 1947 indicated that they liked the idea that each county's schools should have a committee of inspection, to be elected by county residents; only 12 percent opposed the plan (OMG-61). Three years later large percentages of students at the universities of Munich (95 percent) and Erlangen (93 percent) reported that their student governments functioned effectively (HIC-17).[7]

More problematic was the issue of religious education in the schools. U.S. officials, coming from a social system that seeks to separate state and church matters, were inclined to favor a similar plan in Germany. Leading church officials, however, and many politicians as well had a contrary view, and so did the vast bulk of the mass public. Almost all respondents (97 percent) in December 1945 said they favored giving children religious instruction in the schools, most felt it should be compulsory (84 percent of the entire sample) rather than voluntary (11 percent), and most thought that members of the clergy (81 percent) as opposed to normal, lay teachers (10 percent) should provide this instruction (WSR-8). Twenty-eight months later the same 97 percent wanted religious instruction, though smaller majorities wanted it compulsory (71 percent, compared with 24 percent who preferred voluntary programs), and two-thirds wanted the clergy to provide the instruction (OMG-126).[8] Only 28 percent of AMZON Germans supported the idea of confessional schools; of these, 13 percent favored and an equal number opposed having common schools as well as confes-

6. An additional 12 percent said that the child's education depended on both factors.

7. In the same survey, 78 and 73 percent, respectively, said they opposed dueling associations, compared with 9 and 18 percent, respectively, who favored these *schlagende Verbindungen* so long associated with German nationalist traditions.

8. The Catholic South and Protestant North have different attitudes and policies concerning religion in the schools. Thus on options of compulsory or voluntary religious instruction, southern ratios varied from 74:21 in Bavaria to 68:27 in Württemberg-Baden and 67:28 in Hesse. Northern ratios in more urbanized climates were 51:41 in West Berlin and 39:54 in Bremen. For details on religion and politics in the FRG's early years, see Linz (1967) and Blankenburg (1967).

sional schools.[9] OMGUS officials ultimately decided to turn the matter over to German education and church officials. These data suggest that AMG had noticeable though not overwhelming success in persuading Germans to reduce the role of religion in the schools.

The data also suggest that AMG faced little resistance from the AMZON public in setting educational policy. For most Germans at the time, how the schools were conducted was secondary to more immediate issues. When Germans did focus on the schools, they tended to agree that their traditional structure worked to the disadvantage of some social groups, and they welcomed a participatory role for parents and students in decisions that affected them directly. AMZON Germans might have balked had U.S. authorities pushed education reforms that kept the church out of the school but probably would have supported a U.S. policy banning confessional schools. No doubt the freedom that German public opinion was prepared to give to U.S. authorities had its limits, but AMG never tested those limits.

Although educating the youth was important in shaping Germany's future, AMG had a more immediate cultural goal in mind, too: reeducating and reorienting those who had lived in or grown up during the Nazi era but were not among the roughly one in six Germans who were strongly committed to that regime's principles and actions. U.S. authorities used several means to achieve this goal. As we have seen, they abandoned nonfraternization and encouraged informal relations between Germans and GIs—"ambassadors in uniform," as they were sometimes called. AMG initiated recreational, educational, and career programs that were available to Germans in their leisure hours. These programs offered athletic activities, cultural events, movies, and access to the increasingly widespread information centers, the *Amerika-Häuser,* or America Houses. Officers used AMG money or raised foundation funds to bring American consultants to German organizations and send Germans on study tours to the United States. What impact did this outpouring of energy and goodwill have on Germans?

Youth Organizations

Getting teenagers into school was a simple matter compared with occupying their time usefully when the schools were not in session.

9. Almost two-thirds preferred common schools, and more than three-quarters of those (51 percent of the entire sample) wanted no confessional schools whatever. In the December 1945 survey 37 percent responded positively (and 47 percent negatively) to the question, "Should confessional schools, in which religious instruction is compulsory, be established in a community in which a sufficient number of parents request them?" (WSR-8).

Youth centers and related programs, AMG authorities decided, would provide a partial solution to this problem. In autumn 1945 directives authorized setting up province youth committees in each county under U.S. control. The committees, comprising Germans who were interested in working with young people and who had been cleared in denazification proceedings, were to encourage the establishment of sport clubs, religious organizations, and other special interest associations.[10] In addition, OMGUS urged GIs and their dependents to organize and direct groups within the framework of the German Youth Activities (GYA) program.

The aim of such projects was somewhat ambiguous. Some AMG officials candidly acknowledged that their primary goal was to keep the youngsters off the streets and out of trouble. GYA and youth committee activities, they said, would curb juvenile delinquency. Some of their colleagues, though, took the high moral ground. The programs, they argued, taught democracy both directly and indirectly. The U.S. military governor, General Clay (1950a:302), stressed the importance of "competitive sports and other recreational programs designed to keep alive in German children a sense of play." Still others expressed the hope that "democracy in action"—exposure to presumably democratic American soldiers—would foster democratic sentiments in young people. Not until 1947, though, did AMG develop guidelines that stressed civic education and training for democratic leadership (Liddell 1949:123).

American military personnel began to organize German Youth Activities as early as September 1945. Although their efforts focused primarily on sports, they also offered such activities as carpentry, metal working, handicrafts, and singing. Few German youths, however, seem to have been socialized into democracy through study or discussion groups (Liddell 1949:125). Even the athletic and other events did not always have the desired effect—mainly because those running the activities were neither inclined nor qualified to teach democracy. Young Germans may nonetheless have developed a greater interest in U.S. customs and life-styles. Eventually, too, AMG created five special schools for training in leadership, schools that by 1952 had taught to more than four thousand youth leaders the fundamentals of democratic youth work (Grace 1953:463).

Any evaluation of these programs must take into account at the outset that traditional German youth leaders were not enthusiastic about the U.S.-sponsored GYA. Members of the youth councils, established by OMGUS

10. AMG subsequently banned some sport organizations which were "by their nature apt to make people more military minded" (WSR-14). Only half of AMZON Germans said that they had heard of this decision, and only half of these knew what kinds of organizations were affected. Even so, 77 percent called the measure justified (11 percent said it was unjustified, and 12 percent did not know or could not say).

in counties and provinces to develop and coordinate youth activities, viewed GYAs as direct competition, and unfair competition at that. U.S. military installations and servicemen could offer children much better facilities—including food, heated rooms, and equipment—than could German groups. How, they asked, could German youngsters resist these blandishments? Such manifest abundance, critics said, "pauperized" the children. It made them feel all the more keenly the relative poverty of postwar exigencies. Such visits could seduce the children into desiring an American way of life or even accepting the role of *Schokoladenmädchen* who exchanged sexual favors for food (Liddell 1949:127). Such friction and misgivings were not eased by a tendency of some American officers, impatient with German ways, to "pull rank" on behalf of GYA programs.

The clientele of the GYA, on the other hand, the parents and children whom it was supposed to serve, enthusiastically supported the program. Not all AMZON Germans were aware of the individual programs, of course. Only 55 percent of a random sample of parents in November 1946 and 44 percent of youths aged 14 to 18 living in four major cities (Frankfurt-am-Main, Heidelberg, Kassel, and Munich) in March 1947 knew at least something about them (OMG-46, 56). And relatively few AMZON youngsters participated in them. Every ninth parent in the earlier survey who knew of GYA had a child who participated; 13 percent of the metropolitan youth in the later survey had participated. At the end of 1947, 15 percent of AMZON youth aged 10 to 25 claimed such membership (OMG-99).

Most of those who knew about GYA approved of the programs. Almost all informed parents (94 percent, or 84 percent of the entire sample) said in November 1946 that they would permit their children to participate (OMG-46). More than three-fourths of those whose children had participated (54 percent of the entire sample) said that the programs were good; 5 percent disagreed. Youngsters who expressed an opinion were even more positively inclined toward the programs (OMG-56): 97 percent of the knowledgeable group expressed favorable views (48 percent of the entire sample, compared with 1 percent who spoke unfavorably of GYA). Among youths who had participated (13 percent of the total sample in March 1947), almost three in four considered the programs well led; 12 percent said they were poorly led. The survey in December 1947 found that 36 percent of young people aged 10 to 25 who took part in some kind of youth activity were aware that the U.S. Army had donated goods or services to their club (OMG-99).

What prompted young Germans to take part in U.S.-sponsored activities? German parents and children were no more unified in what they expected from GYA programs than were the Americans who set them up. Asked in late 1946 about the most important aspects of the GYA, most parents responded that the programs kept the children off the streets (41 percent) or provided free-time activities (19 percent). Only a quarter thought that such programs would teach their children about the American way of life, and still fewer spoke of political goals (OMG-46). A few months later young respondents in four large cities were asked why they participated (OMG-56). The answers they gave were:[11]

Get candy and food	40
Chance for sports and games	26
Show our former enemies what Germans really are	23
Learn English	17
Get to know some Americans	10
Learn about America from soldiers	9
Learn about democracy	6
Have a change	6
Occupy leisure time	5
Learn how democratic organizations are run	3
Other reasons	2
Program has no value for me	11
Total (multiple responses permitted)	158%

More than half of the same sample, when asked for the single most important reason for their participation, responded, "to get supplementary food." Still, of those who knew enough about GYA to express an opinion, only 12 percent said that young people took part solely to occupy their time and keep warm whereas almost four times that many said that participants enjoyed the programs.[12]

U.S. policy involved a multiplicity of youth organizations besides GYA. The monolithic claims of the Hitler Youth and, more recently, the Free German Youth in the Soviet zone were widely thought to contribute to totalitarian modes of thought and behavior. AMG efforts to assess the attitudes of postwar Germans toward this issue were nonetheless not wholly successful. A survey in July 1950 (HIC-38) of AMZON Germans aged 15 to 25 and their elders found that 60 percent of the youths and 56 percent of the adults favored the establishment of a single youth organization in the FRG. About half as many in each group opposed it.[13] Six months later

11. The figures presented are means for the four cities.
12. The remaining 43 percent cited both motives.
13. Of those in favor of a single organization, 35 percent of the youths and 23 percent of the adults thought it should require uniforms. This was a mildly contentious point among U.S. officials. Some hated the thought of putting Germans into any uniforms. Others, with a deeper understanding of German society, or perhaps recollecting their

support for a single youth organization declined somewhat but still represented a majority of those who expressed an opinion (HIC-73).[14] To pinpoint respondents' attitudes, the questionnaire asked those who favored a single organization whether all other organizations should be forbidden. Only 21 percent of the youths and 17 percent of the adults favored banning alternative groups—that is, diametrically opposed U.S. policy.

Although not all people had heard of the GYA, then, and although a fairly small percentage of AMZON children actually participated in its activities, it received good marks from the German public. Most who were familiar with GYA thought it a good program. Those whose children participated in it as well as the participating children themselves strongly endorsed its underlying idea and its operation. Moreover, the advantages of a multiplicity of youth organizations rather than a single, overarching one—advantages which OMGUS stressed—were rejected explicitly by only one youth in five and one adult in six.

Cultural Exchange

When the U.S. concept of reeducation took shape, it included a component of German-American cultural exchange (Pilgert with Forstmeier 1951). Paragraph 27 of JCS 1779, issued in July 1947, called specifically for the reestablishment of international cultural relations. The objective was to strengthen German-American ties without denigrating the values of German culture. Indeed, those values were to be recognized and encouraged at all times insofar as they were consistent with democratic principles. The mode of action was manifold: cultural materials, especially literature, would be available to any interested Germans; Amerika-Häuser would proliferate; American experts would consult with German associations and institutions; and some Germans, selected for their promise as Germany's future elites as well as their clean political record, would be U.S. guests on overseas study groups. Such programs were designed to help Germans better understand democratic ideals by freeing them from nationalistic ideologies and restrictions, and to help German scholars, artists, and others to overcome the cultural isolation of the Nazi era. Through visits to the United States in particular, U.S. officials thought, Germans could acquaint themselves with democracy in both theory and

---

own days as Boy Scouts or members of other youth groups, recognized the constructive, socially integrative function of (nonfascist) uniforms.

14. Among those aged 15 to 24, 55 percent favored a single youth organization in the FRG and 32 percent thought there should be more than one; corresponding views of adults were 44 and 34 percent, respectively.

Table 10.1   Purposes of the German-American Exchange Program, July 1950

Responses to the Question: There are different opinions about the reason for the establishment of the exchange program by the Americans. Would you please name two of the following which, in your opinion, are closest to American intentions concerning the exchange program? (percentages)

	Youth (15–25)	Adults (over 25)
Further understanding between the two countries	66	66
Bring the Germans closer to democratic ideas	38	40
Make America's economic achievements available to Germans	34	35
Use German experience and knowledge for America's purposes*	19	14
Influence Germany's leading classes for the benefit of America*	7	5
Americanize Germany*	7	3
No opinion	15	19

Source: HIC-44.
Note: Multiple responses permitted.
*Negative responses.

practice and carry what they learned back to colleagues and broader groups in Germany.

The German-American exchange program initiated by U.S. authorities was favorably received in German public opinion, but it demonstrated again that the young were more skeptical about American motives than were their elders. Knowledge of the exchange program spread fairly rapidly. Although in January 1950 only 40 percent of AMZON residents had heard of it (HIC-12), six months later 57 percent of those aged 15 to 25 and 59 percent of those older than 25 knew about it (HIC-44). Table 10.1 shows that Germans viewed the program positively, but if we add the three categories of answers that impute to the United States self-serving motives (indicated on the table by asterisks), the young were half again as likely to suspect American motives (33 percent) as were those over the age of 25 (22 percent).

Most respondents felt that the German-American exchange program would redound to the benefit of their country. Surveys in January 1950 in the U.S. zone and January 1952 in the FRG as a whole asked for whom an overseas experience would be primarily beneficial (HIC-12, 151). A very small percentage (6 and 9 percent, respectively) named Germany. About three-quarters (78 and 74 percent, respectively) said that only the individual would benefit.

Nor were respondents concerned that sojourns in the United States would overly "Americanize" the participants. In January 1950 one in ten thought that this might be the case, but 55 percent thought not and 35 percent did not know (HIC-12). Six months later more confident views emerged: 70 percent of the adults and 67 percent of the youths feared no American contamination from exchangees; 6 and 8 percent, respectively, did (HIC-44). A somewhat different question, "Could a visit of several months in American have an unfavorable influence on a German?" asked in January 1952 of a nationwide sample, elicited agreement from 16 percent and rejection from almost four times that number.

In general, then, the German public considered the impact of the exchange program initiated during the U.S. occupation to be at worst benign, at best enriching. The bulk of respondents thought that the Americans had good intentions in pursuing the plan and that the individual exchangees—and perhaps Germany as well—would benefit from the overseas experience. Relatively few expressed a concern that excessive Americanism might contaminate the exchangees.

U.S. Information Centers

Yet another important component of the U.S. cultural program in occupied Germany and afterward was the network of information centers called Amerika-Häuser, where visitors could read magazines and books, use reference works and other library facilities, attend lectures, see films, view art exhibits, and participate in other activities. By 1955, when the FRG gained virtual sovereignty and most U.S. programs began to be phased out, twenty-two such centers existed in major West German cities and West Berlin.

The Amerika-Häuser and their offerings became fairly well known to West Germans (HIC-31, 76, 181, 210). Surveys conducted between May 1950 and April 1955 found that an average of 64 percent of AMZON respondents (up from 49 percent in October 1948) and 48 percent of all West Germans knew that such centers existed in the larger cities. Very large and increasing numbers (78 percent in the U.S. zone, 86 percent in the FRG) of those aware of the centers could also specify some of their offerings. Only a few respondents (averaging 10 percent in the U.S. zone in 1950, 9 percent in the FRG in 1955), however, had actually visited an Amerika-Haus.[15]

15. The American information program also included bookmobiles and German-American reading rooms in areas where no Amerika-Häuser existed. Only one in

HICOG analysts estimated that, in all, three and a quarter million Germans older than 15 years of age had made a total of 35.9 million visits in 1954 to U.S. Information Centers (HIC-210).

The typical visitor to an Amerika-Haus was not the average West German citizen. One in three was a high school or university graduate (compared with 4 percent of the general population). The information center visitor was far more likely than the general population to be a professional man, well off financially, active politically, and young. Only 18 percent had no knowledge of the English language (86 percent nationwide). Two in five (compared with 17 percent nationally) had contact with someone in the United States, and 7 percent (2 percent nationally) had been to America.

Predictably, visitors to U.S. Information Centers evaluated them positively. The overall impressions of most were excellent (23 percent), very good (45 percent), or good (29 percent), and many more thought the quality of Amerika-Haus facilities to be improving (41 percent) rather than deteriorating (8 percent). The focal point of visitor interest was each center's collection of books, mostly about the United States or activities of Americans. (When asked what benefits they had obtained from their visits, the largest number mentioned increased knowledge of the United States.) A majority in fall 1954 hoped for continued U.S. direction and financial support for the Amerika-Häuser once West Germany achieved sovereign status, 43 percent wanted joint U.S.-German control, and only 2 percent thought it best for German agencies to take over the centers (HIC-210).

Reorientation

U.S. policies aimed directly at democratizing or reorienting Germans encountered stiff resistance among the country's vocal elites. Some resented what they saw as an American obsession with democracy as a social panacea and took delight in pointing out failures of democracy in the United States itself. Others resented what seemed to be American claims of moral superiority based on military might and objected to patronizing, condescending, and sometimes even undemocratic attitudes and actions from AMG officials and their HICOG successors after 1949. Bitter comments about AMG efforts to "Americanize" Germany were widespread among these vocal elites. Some in the United States and elsewhere even feared that German overreaction to perceptions of American indoctrina-

---

eight West Germans was aware of HICOG's ancillary information services, one in nine of the bookmobiles or reading rooms; only about one in a hundred had actually used any of these facilities.

tion might touch off a new international crisis, if not immediately then certainly after Germans had regained their full sovereignty.

But, again, what about the German-on-the-street? Surveys during the early years of the occupation demonstrated that large majorities of AMZON Germans were eager both to learn more about democracy and to institutionalize it in German society. Interviewed in spring 1947 (OMG-93), prisoners of war at Fort Getty, Rhode Island (Ehrmann 1947), who had taken courses on democracy said that programs to reeducate the German people were the country's third-most-urgent need (mentioned by 50 percent)—behind increased production (73 percent) and stabilized food supplies (60 percent), but ahead of German unity (49 percent). In January 1950 survey respondents placed political matters such as democracy and cooperation second on the list of civic characteristics that Germans could learn from Americans. A survey six months later confirmed and filled in the details of a general willingness to learn from Americans (HIC-10, 40).

Although relatively few (34 percent) were aware in January 1950 that U.S. High Commission officials in West Germany were engaged in a program to bring Germans closer to democratic ideals, 59 percent nevertheless welcomed the idea (HIC-11). Only 30 percent argued that the Americans should leave that task to Germans. Asked what effect such a U.S. program might have, two-thirds of those who gave opinions (45 percent of the entire sample) said that the effect would be favorable. The remainder thought that it would have little or no effect (20 percent) or an unfavorable one (2 percent). The more socially mobilized among the respondents (the highly educated, those living in cities, men, those with higher incomes), it may be added, tended to be rather more skeptical than others about the program's probable success, but still more prepared than the rest to welcome it. Respondents in general were certain that the program was designed to familiarize Germans with democratic ideas (59 percent) rather than to "Americanize" them (10 percent).[16]

In July 1950 HICOG pollsters learned that young Germans reacted differently to such questions than did their elders (HIC-40). Whereas 56 percent of the adults welcomed U.S. efforts to familiarize Germans with democratic ideals, only 51 percent of the youth aged 20 to 25 and 42 percent of those aged 15 to 19 did so. The younger the respondents, the more likely

16. An additional 9 percent thought the U.S. aim was a bit of both. These figures are similar to the distribution of responses to a more direct question asked in August 1949 (HIC-11) about whether the United States was trying to Americanize Germans: 71 percent said there was no such U.S. intent, 10 percent said there was, and 6 percent called it a bit of both. Of the 16 percent who said that there was at least an element of Americanization in the U.S. plan, more than a third added that the American influence was a positive one.

they were to prefer leaving the task of democratic socialization to Germans: 36 percent among the teenagers, 34 percent among those in their early twenties, and 27 percent among those older than 25 years of age. Estimates of the U.S. program's success revealed the same pattern: youths were almost twice as apt as adults to predict little or no success as to anticipate much success.

Although the data indicate that young Germans were more resistant to the U.S. reorientation program than were those over the age of 25, all age groups agreed that a successful program would have its greatest impact among younger Germans. Older respondents voted roughly two to one in both January and July 1950 (HIC-11, 40) to welcome rather than condemn U.S. reorientation efforts; younger respondents voted approximately four to three in the same direction. But among the younger respondents who predicted that the program would enjoy much or some success, 38 percent expected that it would influence younger people, compared with 14 percent who said that it would influence their elders. It was, of course, precisely at the younger Germans that U.S. officials primarily aimed their reorientation efforts.

One program that U.S. authorities sought to implement was a series of "town hall meetings" in villages and even in medium-sized cities. After several such meetings in autumn 1948, interviewing teams queried both common citizens and mayors about the outcomes. In Reilinger (Württemberg-Baden) a solid majority of a random sample (OMG-155) said that the meetings were either very useful (30 percent) or somewhat useful (48 percent), while only a sixth rejected them either mildly (8 percent) or strongly (8 percent). Those who knew of or who had attended meetings termed them a good idea (95 percent, compared with 4 percent who thought not) and said that they would attend the next such meeting (63 percent, compared with 23 percent who said they would not).

After a series of town hall meetings, public forums, and other assemblies in Bavarian towns, scarcely a quarter of the Bavarians surveyed claimed any knowledge of them (OMG-159), but solid majorities of the knowledgeable (74 percent) and the participants (88 percent) endorsed them. The mayors of towns where such meetings had been held were far more positive toward them (78 percent favorable, 16 percent unfavorable) than were the mayors in towns where no such meetings took place (22 percent favorable, 41 percent unfavorable). OMGUS analysts observed, moreover, that "there seems to be a tendency for those mayors who have not used a town meeting to expect it to be of most value in informing *the people* about the rationale behind acts of the government. On the other hand, mayors who have held such meetings tend to think of them as having their greatest value in informing *the officials* about how the people are thinking" (OMG-159; emphasis in original). These data on public reactions to town meetings reinforce the other data presented in this section: AMZON Germans and, later, the West German public were receptive to the U.S. program of reorientation. Indeed, they seemed to be intrigued by the notion that democratization might improve the quality of life in Germany itself.

U.S. cultural policy in occupied Germany and in the FRG presented policymakers in Washington with a dilemma. The direct appeal of the policy was to a relatively small percentage of West Germans, but its impact on that segment—which comprised the more socially mobilized Germans—was considerable. Given the uniquely favorable conditions under which the information program operated—a measure of continuing U.S. control over semisovereign Germany, the high priority that top-level U.S. officials gave to the task of enlisting German support for a tight Western alliance, and substantial if declining sums to spend in the pursuit of this goal—and given both the German predisposition to go along with the West (particularly if the option were falling under Soviet influence) and a certain resistance to any overt U.S. propagandizing, it would seem that the program fulfilled its potential. The question faced by policymakers, then, was whether or not its successes justified the cost in money and time. That elements of the program continue to the present day, albeit reduced still further in scale, reflects to some measure the firm basis it attained during the OMGUS and HICOG years.[17]

Perceptions, Policies, and Opportunities

The occupation of Germany provided opportunities—for both U.S. and German policymakers—to reevaluate traditions and past social priorities in education and other cultural dimensions. To some extent Americans and Germans agreed on shortcomings inherent in these traditions and hence the need to make changes. Sometimes elements of both policy-making communities could even agree on specific measures. Thus Social Democrats and General Clay united on the need to restructure schools to end insidious distinctions based on socioeconomic status of families. But PTAS and up-to-date textbooks proved to be no match for the deeply encrusted, class-ridden school system of the past. The occupation also provided the opportunity for bullheaded persistence to encounter

17. The United States Information Agency continues to send VOA programs to West Germany, maintain Amerika-Häuser or other USIA posts (bilateral centers, reading rooms, information centers) in fifteen cities, organize exhibits, and otherwise conduct informational activities in the FRG, including until 1992 operating RIAS in West Berlin (with German direction and joint German-American financing).

passive resistance. As it turned out, however, the occupiers did not stick long to the letter or even the spirit of JCS 1067. The AMG did not ignore German concerns, and the occupied did not treat U.S. education and cultural policy as an oppressive and unwarranted intrusion into German life by ill-informed and ill-advised foreigners. The potential conflict did not take place.

Does this mean that occupiers and occupied satisfactorily restructured postwar German education and culture? U.S. programs provided for teacher training, textbook preparation, youth organizations, support for founding the Free University of Berlin, cultural exchange, and even the Amerika-Häuser, where hundreds of thousands of young Germans, yearning to find out more about the "American way of life," gained access to newspapers, magazines, English language courses, and opportunities to talk with Americans. We can in retrospect fault such programs for their naïveté in some regards and their excessive ambitiousness in others. Moreover, and for various reasons, not all of these programs had the support from OMGUS that would have helped them thrive. Yet as a whole, U.S. policy in the education and cultural spheres significantly helped to shape postwar German society. Public opinion surveys conducted in the American zone of occupation and then in all of West Germany show that this policy was also popular with the German people.

In one important sphere, however, public education, a kind of German-American compromise eventually resulted that benefited few in the long run (see Robinsohn and Kuhlmann 1967; R. Merritt et al. 1971a, 1971b). Scientific, artistic, interpersonal, and other kinds of international exchanges and interactions continue unabated to the present day. But German educationists by and large adopted a strategy of benign opposition. Tolerate U.S. efforts at reform, they seemed to be saying, for sooner or later the Amis will go home. What did it matter that some of the measures proposed by OMGUS held out the promise of an improved education system and enhanced equity for all Germans, and what did it matter that, insofar as their views could be ascertained, the clientele of the education system was warmly receptive to the ideas U.S. educational officers were trying to implement? The pervasive and ultimately indomitable tactic was to resist rash changes that might thwart German educationists once the occupation should end.

Faced with this recalcitrance, U.S. officials in Washington and Germany ultimately chose to cut their losses. The complicated policies they sought to apply became easy targets for U.S. congressmen trying to make a name for themselves as budget cutters, for journalists out to prove that OMGUS was either mollycoddling the Germans or arrogating to itself overweening power in matters rightfully German, and withal for German critics who were less interested in reform than in their own roles, present and future, in the education system.

In such circumstances the undisputably popular German support for key aspects of AMG education and cultural policy counted for nothing. The more important realities were budgetary constraints, the need for West German support in the worldwide struggle against communism, and the stubbornness and disruptive power of German education "experts." Accordingly, U.S. policymakers retreated from the field of education into policies of reeducation and reorientation, which in turn gave rise to an immensely popular and fruitful program for German-American cooperation in the fields of education and culture.[18]

The effect for the German education system was largely a restoration of what had existed before the Nazis carried out their *Gleichschaltung*, or forced coordination. Parts of this system had merit, such as three-track schooling, but even it was somewhat antiquated for the post-1945 era. German educationists in the American zone of occupation wasted an opportunity to explore seriously the possibilities of educational reform. Another quarter-century would pass before many of the ideas spawned during those four years of occupation would be institutionalized—experimentation with comprehensive schools, broadening meaningful participation in educational decision making, and extensive revision of textbooks to remove excessively nationalistic perspectives. Hildegard Hamm-Brucher (1970:154; see also Bungenstab [1970]), then the Free Democratic Party's nationally known expert on education, commented: "It is difficult to imagine how many detours, mistakes, ideologically-laden fights, and unsound investments we could have saved ourselves if the suggestions on schools and reforms made by the Allies in the first postwar years had been carried out." Instead, consolidation of power and postponement of change had won the day.

18. An aspect that merits greater attention than it has hitherto received is the extent to which U.S. policymakers in Germany were convinced that pushing through extensive educational reforms would only help the Social Democratic Party, which was objectionable to them on other grounds.

ELEVEN

Media as Democratizers

Poor communication—both between the occupiers and public and among Germans themselves—bedeviled the early months of the occupation. Restricted opportunities to travel, virtual collapse of the postal and telegraph system, and residue of wartime destruction combined with an Allied ban on local media to leave Germans dependent upon the ubiquitous rumor mills, such Allied military radio programming as the American Forces Network (AFN), and bulletin boards that posted official orders and personal messages, especially inquiries and information about missing family members.[1]

U.S. occupation officials understood the need to reestablish effective communication channels that could accurately inform the German people. Some projects to rebuild technical linkages, such as the postal and telegraph system, were fairly straightforward. Others, however, forced the occupiers to deal directly with outstanding political issues. The occupiers had more in mind than simply replacing personnel who had enthusiastically supported National Socialism, printing new postage stamps, and permitting military convoys to transport the mail from one part of Germany to another.

Germany's media system, for example, demanded full-scale re-creation. The print media had virtually collapsed in the face of Nazi pressure, and Josef Goebbels had co-opted radio for his aggressive propaganda campaigns. This chapter explores the German public response to U.S. occupation policy regarding newspapers and the radio.[2]

1. Commentators on the transition period from the arrival of U.S. troops until the formal establishment of OMGUS describe the debilitating effects of German rumor mills (see Peterson 1990). By February 1946 (WSR-14), however, two-thirds of an AMZON sample said that they had not heard any rumors lately. The rumors heard most frequently centered on war with the USSR (mentioned by 10 percent) and a pending devaluation of the German currency (8 percent).

2. Because of inadequate survey data, films, books, theater performances, concerts, exhibitions, and other dimensions of the U.S. information program are excluded from the discussion.

From Weimar to Bonn

For centuries Germans have been in the forefront of the media industry. Johannes Gutenberg's movable metal type revolutionized the world of communications in the 1450s, and in Germany as elsewhere mass newspapers appeared four centuries later. In the early years of the twentieth century Germans made both technical and artistic contributions to radio and cinema. By the time the Weimar Republic was established in 1919, Germans had become among the most media-conscious people in the world—only to have their triumphs perverted fourteen years later when Adolf Hitler gained absolute power. Allied occupation officers confronted the challenge of revitalizing the media in post–World War II Germany within the context of that rich but checkered history.

Historians and democratic theorists still debate the nature and role of the press during the Weimar years. On one hand, the quality newspapers were without question models of their type, but on the other, the sensational boulevard press and the flagrantly partisan political press scandalized responsible journalists. On one hand, newspaper editors prided themselves on their independence, but on the other, conservative publishers controlled the purse strings and the editors, perpetuating a system characterized by some as feudal aristocracy (Dahrendorf 1965/1967). On one hand, politicians praised their country's freedom of the press, but on the other, the government retained press controls that dated to the 1870s and readily banned opposition newspapers during years of crisis.[3] Even if Weimar Germany may be seen as a legitimate venture toward democracy —itself a subject of debate among historians (see Koszyk 1972:452–453)— the press failed to fulfill its vaunted role as democracy's defender.

Broadcasting in Weimar Germany was more severely restricted. Only in the 1920s did the radio become a useful medium for addressing the masses, and German political authorities moved quickly to put it under strict state control and regulation.[4] Except for information programming broadcast by the Postal Ministry on the Wireless Service (*Dratloser Dienst*), radio stations were regional and controlled by provincial governments. Funding came not from advertising but from users' fees, which radio owners paid monthly to the Postal Ministry, which generally super-

3. Freedom of the press was a statutory reality, at least: "Within the limits of the general laws," Art. 118 of the Weimar constitution proclaimed, "every German has the right to express his opinion freely in words, writing, print, pictures, and in other ways. . . . There is to be no censorship."

4. The Statistisches Reichsamt (1926:95) reported that in January 1924 Germany, with a population of 63 million, had only 1,500 privately owned radio sets. By January 1926 this figure had risen to 1 million and by March 1930 to 3.2 million (Statistisches Reichsamt 1933:157).

vised the stations' operations. Nationwide programming coordination came through the German Broadcasting Corporation (*Reichsrundfunkgesellschaft*, or RRG). Private societies of radio listeners conducted research on listening habits and preferences and sought to influence the RRG's quality of programming.

Hitler, who understood early the political need to control the media and use them to sway the masses, found in Goebbels an ideal collaborator.[5] Together they persuaded and coerced politicians, administrators, and businessmen into believing that Germany's ability to master the challenges it faced required firm hands controlling its communication. National Socialist changes were to be fundamental, not merely cosmetic. As Goebbels said, "instead of being a state-supervised medium of free intellectual expression of the individual, the press under a totalitarian system performs public duties and is responsible to the nation" as organized in and by the Nazi state (cited in Research and Analysis Branch 1944:48).

The Editorial Law of April 1933—not three months after Hitler's accession to power—codified Goebbels's theory. It made newspaper editors and journalists directly responsible to the state. They continued to be nominally responsible to and draw their salaries from the publishers, but the Propaganda Ministry was their de facto employer. It hired and fired the publishers' employees, told them what to print, and disciplined them for any deviations from the party line. Publishers remained only formally in charge of the newspapers. The government could and frequently did ban their newspapers and confiscate their equipment to meet other needs. The National Socialist Party, meanwhile, began both competing with the independent press by publishing its own newspapers and favoring some publishing concerns at the expense of others. In short, "the privately owned press was despoiled and replaced by a giant Nazi publishing monopoly" (Hale 1964:14).[6]

5. In *Mein Kampf* Hitler (1925–1927/1939:330) wrote that "the State . . . must not let itself be misled by the boast of a so-called 'freedom of the press,' and must not be persuaded to fail in its duty and to put before the nation the food that it needs and that is good for it." In inveighing against Germany's pre-1914 press, he asked (pp. 330–331): "But what food was it that [this press] put before [the German] people? Was it not the worst conceivable poison? Was not the worst kind of pacifism inoculated into the heart of our people, at a time that the rest of the world was about to throttle Germany slowly but surely? Did not this press, even in times of peace, instill into the brains of the people doubts about the rights of their own State, in order to restrict it from the beginning in the choice of the means for its defense? . . . The activity of the so-called liberal press was the work of gravediggers for the German people and the German Reich."

6. As evidence for this conclusion, Hale cites "the acquisition by the party of the Eher Verlag and the *Völkischer Beobachter;* the development of the local Nazi press by the Gauleiters; the confiscation of the Socialist and Communist publishing properties; the conversion of the newspapers publishers' association into an instrument of party

The Nazis quickly seized control of broadcasting as well. Even before 1933 they dominated the leading radio listeners' society. Within months after taking power they took charge of the RRG and the Postal Ministry and set up the Reich Chamber of Broadcasting, which among other things trained broadcasting personnel and engineered commercial standardization to produce the inexpensive, low-powered, but enormously popular three-tube radio set, the People's Receiver (*Volksempfänger*).[7] By 1935 the Propaganda Ministry's Broadcasting Division assumed the RRG's programming responsibilities. Such organizational coups and technical innovations gave Goebbels what he needed to create a gigantic propaganda machine. His message could saturate the entire German audience (see Kris and Speier 1944), and, although he could easily beam programs overseas, the low-powered Volksempfänger prevented most Germans from receiving news from the outside world.[8]

When on 7–8 May 1945 German representatives accepted the Allied demand for unconditional surrender, U.S. occupiers were not prepared to deal seriously with Germany's postwar communication system.[9] Wartime planning had produced three goals: destroying the Nazi propaganda machine, persuading Germans that Nazism was indeed dead, and documenting and interpreting the facts. This planning also inspired some procedural directives, such as Law No. 191 (12 May 1945), which among other things banned almost all media and most entertainment activities, and Regulation No. 1, which authorized the licensing of such controlled activities as publishing newspapers (Dunner 1948:276). But the U.S. media effort had already lost valuable time. From 7 February, when American GIs first entered Germany, to 7 March, when they crossed the Rhine River

---

control and exploitation; the enforcement of special ordinances to effect the transfer of hundreds of privately owned papers to the party publishing combine; and the further acquisition and trustification of newspaper properties under the guise of wartime necessity during World War II."

7. Radio ownership rose from 5.4 million in 1933, when Germany had 66 million citizens, to 9.6 million in 1938 when, excluding Austrians, it had 68 million (Statistisches Reichsamt 1934, 1938).

8. Whether Goebbels's propaganda was successful at home or abroad is another question. Despite the fears of Allied experts, the overseas propaganda seems not to have enjoyed popular acceptance (Welch 1983). Even the home broadcasts eventually encountered an overwhelming credibility gap, illustrated by the irreverent motto, "If Goebbels said it, it cannot be true." Once, for instance, Goebbels accurately announced on the radio that an expected British air raid on Kiel had turned back. So lacking in credibility were his remarks that his announcement prompted a mass exodus by Kiel citizens.

9. JCS 1067 listed in Paragraph 8b(8) under suspected war criminals and security arrests "Nazis and Nazi sympathizers holding important and key positions in . . . (f) the press, publishing houses and other agencies disseminating news and propaganda."

at Remagen, to 11 April, when they reached the Elbe River, to 7–8 May, when hostilities ended, the military's posture toward German society was simply to stop all activities linked to Nazism. Meanwhile, German media specialists who had been victimized by Nazism emerged from their hiding places to volunteer assistance to the Americans—only to be rebuffed. Not until September did the OMGUS Information Control Division (ICD) even begin to move from the punitive to the reconstructive mode.

What did the ICD do during that half-year and more? Relying primarily on its own resources it moved in several directions to accomplish its prescribed goals. It shut down German newspapers, seized movie films, took over radio stations, banned presentations of operas and plays, arrested communications personnel and artists who had furthered Nazi propaganda, and undertook what came to be viewed as counterpropaganda: efforts to persuade Germans that each of them shared responsibility for the crimes of Nazism and that democracy was both necessary and desirable. One product of ICD efforts was a large number of restless people with time on their hands, fearful of their fate and denied reliable information, eager consumers at the rumor mills. To fill the communications gap ICD set up U.S.-produced newspapers in ten cities under AMG's jurisdiction, created three magazines, and began showing movies.[10] ICD also reconstructed radio stations in Frankfurt, Munich, and Stuttgart, which broadcast proclamations and announcements for the general public and news and entertainment for GIs, all calculated to support AMG operations.

In fall 1945 ICD shifted its emphasis.[11] It continued its missionary work against Nazism but added communication programs that fostered democracy and, increasingly, the "American way of life." This overt proselytizing notwithstanding, ICD officials realized that their goal was not to transform the German media but rather to rectify some Nazi-era problems and turn the print media back to the Germans. They published a new German-language newspaper, *Die Neue Zeitung*—"the American newspaper in Ger-

10. Twice-weekly newspapers were published until October or November 1945 in Augsburg, Bamberg, Berlin, Bremen, Frankfurt-am-Main, Heidelberg, Kassel, Munich, Straubing, and Stuttgart; their circulation in August 1945 was 3.8 million (Pilgert with Dobbert 1953:15). Magazines included the monthly and later biweekly *Heute*, the bimonthly *Amerikanische Rundschau*, and, jointly with the British military government, *Neue Auslese*.

11. On the activities of the Information Control Division (after July 1948 the Information Services Division), see the monthly reports of the military governor (numbered from 1 [20 August 1945] to 50 [1 August–20 September 1949] and designated here as OMG/MG) and occasional "functional" reports of the Information Control Division or Information Services Division (designated respectively as OMG/IC or OMG/IS). For accounts by participants, see Dunner (1948), Pilgert with Dobbert (1953), Zink (1957), Hurwitz (1972), and Wolfe (1979); see also Pross (1965), Roloff (1976), Hartenian (1984), and, for a critical view, Nahr (1991).

many," its masthead proclaimed—as a model of quality newspapers in the United States.[12] ICD in addition published pamphlets and literary works, created American Information Centers, and organized exhibits, concerts, movie shows, and theater performances. Officials sought to make the U.S. presence in occupied Germany cultural rather than solely military.

When *Die Neue Zeitung* appeared, ICD began issuing licenses for setting up German newspapers. U.S. licensing policy explicitly rejected candidates with any taint of Nazism and those who could not demonstrate their democratic orientation.[13] It favored divided responsibility, giving preference not to single editors but to editorial teams whose members represented different political-party preferences; and, rather than party-driven reporting, it insisted on independence. Editors, once licensed, could hire any non-Nazi they wanted and print whatever they considered appropriate —subject to standard laws of journalism (such as libel) and provided that they neither advocated Nazi and racist activities nor criticized Allied operations. Unlike the French military government, the ICD did not screen publications, relying instead on postpublication reviews. Editors who violated the rules faced temporary suspension of publication, reduced newsprint allocation, canceled licenses, and even prosecution under military government courts.[14]

Efforts to foster a postwar German press moved slowly but conscientiously. ICD issued its first license on 31 July 1945 to seven politically diverse men who established the *Frankfurter Rundschau*.[15] The editors were allocated newsprint to circulate 415,000 copies. The number of licensed newspapers grew to eight in September 1945, thirty-one in March

12. *Die Neue Zeitung*, which began publication in Munich on 18 October 1945, was later published in Frankfurt and West Berlin as well. Its total edition in June 1948 was 1.9 million copies; but by July 1949, near the end of the occupation, circulation had dropped to 426,000 (cf. OMG/IC 1948, 36:7; and OMG/MG 1949, 49:44).

13. Until November 1947 ICD followed Information Control Regulation No. 1, which required registration of minor communications employees. Regulation No. 3, which replaced No. 1, abolished this procedure (OMG/IC 1948, 36:4). ICD/ISD refused to the end to grant licenses to political parties—although in 1948 it began permitting parties to publish "information sheets," which were also subject to postpublication evaluation (OMG/IS 1948, 39:9–10; and OMG/IS 1948, 42:11).

14. In June 1946 "the *Süddeutsche Zeitung*, in Munich, was ordered to reduce its size from six pages to four for a period of 30 days, after it had three times published articles critical of Allied policy" (OMG/MG 1946, 12:14). For other examples, see OMG/IS 1948, 39:12–13; OMG/MG 1948, 41:37; OMG/IS 1948, 42:11; and OMG/MG 1949, 44:39. The United States was not alone in this stance. In February 1948 French military authorities cited similar reasons for a three-month suspension of the sale in the French zone of the *Rhein-Neckar Zeitung*, published in Heidelberg, that is, in the U.S. zone (OMG/IC 1948, 36:5).

15. Three of the editors were social democrats, two communists, one conservative (Center Party), and one independent. Two social democrats and the independent resigned by the following winter (OMG/OSS-34; Roloff 1976:42).

1946, and sixty-one in June 1949, when the ISD granted its last license to the *Weissenberger Zeitung* in Bavaria. Allocated circulation rose to 4.2 million by March 1946, after which the figure remained stable until licensing ended. To mother its fledgling press, ICD/ISD provided technical advice on how to run a newspaper, imported consultants from the United States, staged a major International Press Exhibition in Munich in May–June 1948, provided editors with study visits to the United States, and established the Munich School of Journalism to train young would-be journalists.

Delays in implementing an independent German press stemmed in part from conflict between ICD and German politicians and bureaucrats— conflict in which U.S.-licensed editors usually joined ranks with the occupiers. ICD wanted to ensure that its version of a free press could survive the end of the occupation. Some Germans, though, wanted to centralize the media at the local, provincial, and eventually federal level, to make government offices the only legitimate source of "official" information. U.S. officers challenged the notion of information management. In June 1946 U.S. Military Governor General McNarney wrote: "Military Government directed its licensed press to oppose vigorously tentative attempts by German Government officials to force the press and radio to receive official news only through official press bureaus, and any other efforts to hinder the free operation of German information services. It is expected that the press in the U.S. Zone will assume strong leadership similar to that of the press in America in all questions affecting the community good, and it must be in a position to examine critically the acts of German governmental officials and should have direct access to official sources of information" (OMG/MG 1946, 11:21–22).

In late spring 1948 ICD reported that the power struggle between government and the press continued (OMG/IC 1948, 36:5). The newly licensed *Nordsee Zeitung* of Bremerhaven "took action to maintain a free democratic press when the Mayor of Bremerhaven ordered city officials not to grant interviews or to give statements directly to the press, and established a central press bureau to censor official news releases. The paper challenged the censorship decree and began carrying recipes for housewives instead of municipal releases. The *Weser Kurier* of Bremen supported the stand taken by the Bremerhaven paper, and the censorship order was later withdrawn." During the following year, while occupation authorities were trying to negotiate an end to licensing and U.S. control, they had to overcome resistance from provincial governments that were distrustful of "free" media.

Broadcasting again presented a more complicated issue. U.S. authorities, although their own country preferred private to public radio, realized that Germans, like other European peoples, were more comfortable with government-sponsored radio (see Pilgert with Dobbert 1953; Mettler 1975; Hartenian 1984). At the outset, ICD personnel themselves operated the stations whose openings they authorized in Frankfurt, Munich, Stuttgart, and, eventually, Bremen. By June 1946 they had found enough qualified, politically acceptable employees that ICD staff members could be limited to supervisory positions while Germans ran the stations (OMG/IC 1947/#24:20).

Broadcasting in Berlin presented challenges both diplomatic and technical. The Red Army captured the city in the last days of World War II, and the Soviet military government (SMG) maintained sole control over it for three months. During this period SMG took over Radio Berlin, located in what had been designated as the British sector of occupation. When the Western military governments occupied their sectors of Berlin, however, they found the SMG unwilling to accept any kind of shared control over Radio Berlin.[16] U.S. officials decided by fall 1945 that they needed their own station, and they created Radio in the American Sector (*Rundfunk im amerikanischen Sektor*, or RIAS) which began operations in February 1946 as a "wired wireless" (*Drahtfunk*)—wireless broadcasting sent through telephone lines. Because few Berliners in those trying months had telephones, however, the impact of RIAS was minor. In September 1946 RIAS began operating with a 1-kilowatt transmitter, upgraded in March 1947 to 2 kilowatts. Three months later, the installation of a former Wehrmacht mobile transmitter expanded daytime coverage to the entire city, and in spring 1949 RIAS had a new 100-kilowatt transmitter (OMG/MG 1947, 24:29; OMG/MG 1949, 35:38). RIAS had become a major source of radio broadcasting not only in the western sectors of Berlin but also in the whole of Germany under Soviet control.[17]

By mid-1947 AMG policymakers could see that the collapse of Four-Power control over Germany was inevitable, and the London conference of foreign ministers in November–December confirmed that judgment. But U.S. designs had by then shifted to an eventual union of at least the western zones into a single state, albeit one of semisovereign status. The occupiers could then go home, without relinquishing the accomplishments to

---

16. After the Berlin blockade began in June 1948, Western pressure on Radio Berlin's Soviet-supported staff and the Soviet desire to strengthen its broadcasting capabilities led to the station's relocation to East Berlin; the abandoned property in the British sector eventually became the home of Sender Free Berlin (*Sender Freies Berlin*, or SFB; see R. Merritt 1986). After Germany's unification in 1990, the dominant western German authorities totally dismantled Radio Berlin (R. Merritt 1994).

17. The reorganization of Germany's electronic media following the country's unification in 1990 all but wiped out RIAS (R. Merritt 1994).

which they had contributed or residual controls over German politics and society. Such designs produced a sharp shift in the interaction between AMG officials and their German interlocutors.

The shift in thinking meant that ICD (or its successor, ISD) would eventually entrust to Germans complete control of both the press and radio. But which Germans? ICD officials hoped to use the months before newspaper licensing ended to strengthen the licensed firms enough to stand on their own. The licensed newspapers had to have sufficient circulation and reputation to survive the onslaught of new newspapers likely to emerge after licensing ended, as well as the competition of newspapers from AMZON and elsewhere that might seek to play a national role and squeeze out local newspapers. The strategy required AMG lawyers no less than the licensed publishers themselves to negotiate with provincial governments (and with the Parliamentary Council that drafted the West German Federal Republic's constitution) to ensure that newspapers would continue to have maximum freedom from unwarranted governmental controls. It took almost a year of wrangling—from September 1948, when AMG authorized steps to end licensing, until July 1949, when it finally accepted Bavaria's much-revised proposal—to produce mutually acceptable press laws.

ICD strategy also focused on the ownership of newspaper property. During their first weeks in Germany, U.S. authorities had confiscated printing plants and their machinery. Later the owners, many of whom U.S. authorities thought had contributed significantly to Nazi propaganda, wanted their property back—and by implication the opportunity to reestablish their earlier, usually very conservative, press empires. In the meantime AMG had turned over much of the property to licensed editors of the new, democratically oriented press. To prevent the return of this property to the legal owners, AMG devised a dual strategy. It gave the new newspapers a legal right to retain the confiscated property for an additional five or even eight years, and it underwrote the modernization of machinery for the new newspapers, rendering the older property hopelessly out of date.[18]

18. A regulation of September 1947 that permitted licensed newspapers to retain such property, paying fair rental, "was made necessary by the unwillingness of ex-Nazi owners of printing plants to sell or lease their properties even though, because of their political histories, they could not qualify as licensed publishers. The owners' refusal to negotiate voluntary leases had placed the U.S.-licensed publishers in an insecure position and would have hindered the development of a free and democratic German press." In February 1948 AMG used RM 25 million it had received in license fees to form a press cooperative bank that could "make loans to newspaper publishers and news agencies licensed in the U.S.-occupied Area," and "distributed equitably among the newspaper

OMGUS encountered further resistance from some Germans over radio broadcasting. U.S. officers insisted on decentralized programming and rejected direct governmental controls. Provincial government representatives in AMZON preferred to re-create the German Broadcasting Corporation (RRG) of the 1920s, which the Nazis had centralized and subordinated to the Propaganda Ministry. It took two years of negotiation to develop broadcasting legislation in the four U.S.-controlled provinces that was at once acceptable to both parties and consistent if not uniform. Each law put its province's radio (and, later, television) under the jurisdiction of a provincial public broadcasting corporation which had "a representative council functioning as a board of directors. To ensure equitable representation of the public interest, these radio councils are composed of delegates proposed for appointment by various cultural, educational, and economic groups or agencies and include one representative of the *Land* government. However, delegates are pledged to serve the general public interest regardless of their personal or political connections. To carry out its policies, the radio council appoints a station manager (*Intendant*) and an administrative council" (Pilgert with Dobbert 1953:31).[19]

In July 1949, two months after the Federal Republic of Germany began operations in Bonn and two months before it formally gained semi-sovereignty, AMG and the provincial government of Württemberg-Baden agreed on the fourth and last AMZON broadcasting law.

Attention to the Media

What impact did U.S. communication policy have on post–World War II Germany? An important gauge was the reaction of the German-on-the-street. Given the weight of the messages they wanted to convey to all occupied Germans, OMGUS authorities had an interest in finding out what the popular response was. And given the financial and other costs of ICD's activities, politicians in the United States had an inter-

---

publishers" the remaining RM 23 million from these fees (OMG/IC 1948, 36:5). OMGUS also lent its counterpart funds from the European Cooperation Administration to remodel newspaper plants.

AMG officials recognized the need for at least the appearance of equity (OMG/MG 1948, 42:41; cf. OMG/IS 1948, 42:8–9): "Military Government recognizes that, if the licensed press is to maintain itself as a free press in a post-occupation Germany, it must experience competition and learn to combat the challenges it is now equipped to face." Nevertheless, such "competitive processes" must be "entered into while corrective action can still be taken by Military Government, if necessary, to prevent the development of serious dangers to the growth of a democratic press."

19. The federal government later set up broadcasting corporations, *Deutschlandfunk* and *Deutsche Welle*, that aimed at overseas listeners.

est in finding out the program's cost effectiveness. Did AMZON Germans read the licensed newspapers? Did those with radios listen to what their local station was broadcasting? If they paid attention to neither, was this because they were trying to make a political statement or simply because they were not much interested in what communication media—U.S.-sponsored or otherwise—had to offer? As time went on, were Germans more or less inclined to pay attention to the OMGUS-supported media?

The Opinion Survey Section of the Information Control Division (OSS/ICD) first tried to ascertain and report information about the newspapers' readership in an October 1945 survey. Ninety percent of the sample interviewed read newspapers, and 61 percent read them regularly (WSR-1; for notations, see Chapter 4, note 1). Surveys over the next three months (WSR-4, 7, 11) found that 85 percent got newspapers, that 79 percent bought them, and that radio listeners were more likely (81 percent) to be regular newspaper readers than were nonlisteners (71 percent). Beginning in January 1946 the standard question asked whether respondents read newspapers regularly, occasionally, seldom, or never. The mode of reporting, however, shifted two years later, from three categories (regular, occasional or seldom, and never) to two (regular or occasional and seldom or never).[20]

Figure 11.1 reveals a high degree of consistency over time in AMZON newspaper readership if we use the two-category reporting procedure. From January 1946 to November 1949 an average of three in four respondents reported that they were regular or occasional newspaper readers. The remainder said that they seldom or never read newspapers—that they had no time or inclination to do so or could not afford them. Variations occurred among regions under U.S. control. More linked than their country cousins to channels of social mobility, city dwellers were more avid newspaper readers. The city-states of Bremen and especially West Berlin enjoyed higher levels of newspaper readers than did the provinces of Bavaria, Hesse, and Württemberg-Baden.

Public opinion researchers found early that two structural difficulties

20. We might speculate why this reporting shift was made. The earlier procedure showed a drop in regular readers (from 75 percent in January 1946 to 56 percent in January 1948) and increases in both occasional or infrequent readers (from 21 to 33 percent) and nonreaders (from 4 to 11 percent). Averages for the only three surveys for which complete data are reported (April and May 1947 and January 1948) found 59 percent read newspapers regularly, 17 percent occasionally, 16 percent seldom, and 10 percent never. These data suggest that, contrary to the evidence of Figure 11.1, newspaper readership actually declined somewhat over time. Given AMG's policy goals, however, the distinction between regular and occasional readers may have been less illuminating than that between readers of any significant frequency and respondents who were essentially nonreaders.

Figure 11.1

Media Attention, 1946-1949

Regular and Occasional Newspaper Readers and Radio Listeners

Questions: Do you read a newspaper? How often?
Do you listen to the radio? How often?

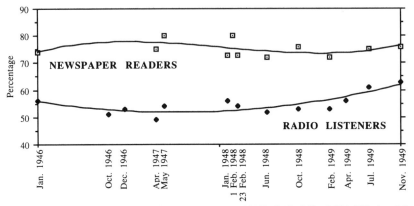

NEWSPAPER: $y = 73.986 + 0.72257x - 4.1824e-2x^2 + 5.9087e-4x^3$ $R^2 = 0.247$ F-Ratio = 0.8
Prob < 0.548
RADIO: $y = 55.804 - 0.46049x + 1.2813e-2x^2$ $R^2 = 0.683$ F-Ratio = 10.8   Prob < 0.003

Sources: WSR-1, 11, 33, 36; OMG-175; HIC-17S.

restricted the impact of OMGUS radio broadcasting (WSR-1). First, fewer than one in four AMZON Germans could understand English fairly well (3 percent) or a little (20 percent). This discovery fortified the presumption that U.S.-sponsored radio stations would have to rely heavily on German personnel and German programming if ICD wished to communicate effectively with the German people. Second, a third of the respondents did not own radio sets, and another 12 percent reported that their sets were broken and had not been repaired; barely half said they had functioning sets.[21] This limitation would not be resolved until the currency reform of June 1948 revitalized West Germany's economy, increasing employment and unleashing German purchasing power.

Not surprisingly, then, as Figure 11.1 shows, for three years beginning in January 1946 radio listening stayed at a fairly even plane, averaging 53 percent. With economic prosperity listenership began to soar. Independent surveys, which asked only whether or not people were radio listeners and not about the extent to which they listened, found that the proportion of West Germans who said that they were listeners rose steadily from 76

21. Two months later the researchers learned that 29 percent of AMZON homes relied on the low-powered Volksempfänger (OMG-1).

percent in December 1948 to 92 percent in February 1955 (IfD 1956:62). Radio-listening patterns would change after the advent of television, but access to radio broadcasting continues to be an important ingredient in modern German life.

Evaluating the Media

What did AMZON Germans think about the papers they read and the radio broadcasts they listened to? The question may seem banal: people pay attention to media that provide interesting information, we might assume, and if people are dissatisfied with the information content, they will simply switch to other media. From decades of research, however, we know that intellectual interest is but one of many reasons why people pick up a newspaper or turn on a radio. Social pressure, ennui, situational circumstances, and other conditions play a role. In postwar Germany, too, especially during the early period, media options were limited. The occupiers restricted newspapers from crossing provincial and even local boundaries, and low-powered receivers made it virtually impossible to listen to programs from any other than the local station.

Icd officials were in a seller's market: AMZON Germans would read whatever newspapers and listen to whatever radios they could find. What is remarkable is that, except possibly during the earliest occupation weeks, U.S. authorities did not respond more imperiously than they did. Instead, they persistently broadened the basis of German participation in shaping the media. And they employed market-research techniques to evaluate popular reactions and try to improve media quality—in short, to adapt the product of a seller's market to make it more acceptable to the buyer.

For three years oss/icd researchers asked whether respondents considered the press very good, good, fairly good, or poor. Table 11.1 indicates that, while the majority of respondents who answered the question gave newspapers high marks, the proportion of adverse comments grew from fall 1945 to fall 1948.[22] Figure 11.2 shows this shift in clearer focus by collapsing "Very good" and "Good" into a single category of "Positive" responses and omitting "Other" and "No answer." AMZON newspaper pub-

---

22. Two other early surveys produced comparable responses with higher negative scores. In November 1945 (wsr-4) respondents were asked for their thoughts about newspapers. Thirty-four percent responded "Excellent" or "Very good," 28 percent "Fair," and 11 percent "Poor," with 30 percent giving other or no responses (multiple responses recorded). A more complicated procedure used in June 1946 (omg-21) scaled responses to diverse questions into a single set of categories labeled "Very good" (18 percent), "Good," (34 percent), "Fairly good" (27 percent), and "Poor" (21 percent).

Table 11.1   Evaluation of the Newspapers, 1945–1948

Responses to the Questions: How do you like [your] newspaper? Do you think
[it] is very good, good, fairly good, or poor? (percentages)

	Oct. 1945	Oct. 1946	Nov. 1948
Very good	11	4	5
Good	51	35	43
Fairly good	24	32	37
Poor	4	5	6
Other	—	2	—
No answer	10	22	9

Sources: WSR-1, 31; OMG-37.

lishers encountered very little outright hostility (an average of 5 percent
across the three surveys) or diffidence (14 percent), but they noted growing
skepticism among readers.

The first major opportunity to evaluate the new media's effectiveness
came when Germany's major war criminals stood before the dock at
Nuremberg's International Military Tribunal. Allied authorities were eager to create the impression of fairness while at the same time informing
the mass of Germans about the crimes carried out under National Socialism. Failure to achieve these goals would have represented either an indictment of Allied media policy or evidence that Germans would resist

Figure 11.2

Evaluation of Newspaper Quality, 1945-1948

Question: How do you like [your] newspaper? Do you think [it] very good, good, fairly good, or
poor? (Note: "Very good" and "Good" are collapsed into "Positive.")

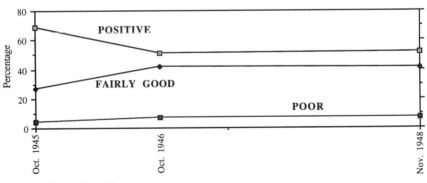

Sources: WSR-1, 34; OMG-37.

any foreign criticism of their wartime leaders and their actions—either of which would have undermined the Allied program of social change.

The data reported in Chapter 6 indicate that AMZON Germans were neither bored with press coverage of the IMT nor skeptical of it. An average of nearly three-fourths of them from 1 January to 4 October 1946 reported reading newspaper accounts of the trial, and a like number found the reporting complete and reliable. Although AMZON Germans seemed to weary as the trial—and press reports—dragged on, the Allied-controlled media met the test of German acceptance.

The increasing importance of radio broadcasting in the immediate postwar years did not make much impact on German assessments of U.S. communication policy. AMZON Germans did became somewhat more confident about the accuracy of the radio compared with that of the newspapers.[23] But radio listeners were increasingly less likely to see radio broadcasting as their main source of news (OMG-1, 45, 106), and they continued to see newspapers as the source of more comprehensive reportage (OMG-1, 58).[24]

After enduring a dozen years of complete state control of radio broadcasting, how did AMZON Germans evaluate the system that U.S. occupation officials were trying to create? OSS/ICD questions about the quality of radio news and the news in general, like similar questions about newspapers, went through word changes but produced rather similar results. The only reported questioning on radio news took place in December 1946, when the OSS/ICD field staff asked those who said they were radio listeners (53 percent of the entire sample) whether "the news service" had "become better and more complete since the end of the war" (WSR-36). More than half of the radio listeners (27 percent of the total sample) thought it better, compared with two-fifths (11 percent) who thought not. More than a quarter of the radio listeners (15 percent of the total sample) did not know or could not say whether or not the quality of the news had improved.

Subsequent questions, not addressed solely to radio listeners, drew fairly consistent responses. Figure 11.3 shows that from January 1947 to July 1949 an average of half the AMZON Germans considered postwar media news to be more reliable than what Germans had received during the

23. When respondents were asked "Which news is more trustworthy—that of the radio or that in the newspapers?" three in ten of those giving answers favored the radio (21 percent of the entire sample) rather than newspapers (50 percent) in January 1946. Radio's share improved to one-third (22 to 44 percent) a year later and to more than half (29 to 27 percent) in January 1948 (OMG-100).

24. In February 1947 (OMG-58) 43 percent of all respondents thought the newspapers more complete, 12 percent said radio broadcasting, and 35 percent reported no differences between the two.

Figure 11.3

Evaluation of Media News Quality, 1947-1949

Trustworthiness of Today's News Relative to Wartime News

Question: Does the news today (in Germany) appear to you more trustworthy, or less trustworthy, than that published (in Germany) during the War?

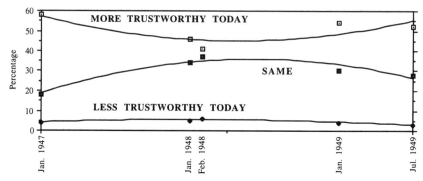

YES: $y = 57.050 - 1.5542x + 4.9490\text{e-}2x^2$ $R^2 = 0.665$ F-Ratio = 2.0   Prob < 0.335
NO: $y = 4.0344 + 0.21620x - 8.5254\text{e-}3x^2$ $R^2 = 0.877$ F-Ratio = 7.2   Prob < 0.123
SAME: $y = 18.525 + 2.0024x - 5.8030\text{e-}2x^2$ $R^2 = 0.915$ F-Ratio = 10.7   Prob < 0.085

Sources: OMG-58, 175; HIC-17S.

war. Only one in 25 respondents thought the wartime news more reliable, but 29 percent said that OMGUS-sponsored news was neither better nor worse than what Goebbels and his Propaganda Ministry had produced.

Closer inspection of the data analyzed in Figure 11.3 reveals some interesting patterns. The four surveys from January 1948 to July 1949 (OMG-175; HIC-17S) found an approximate average of 4 percent who considered the "news today" to be equally trustworthy to that published during the war, but another 27 percent who called it equally *untrustworthy*. The bland response of "Same" thus masks criticism of U.S. communication policy. On the other hand, critics of the U.S.-sponsored news tended also to be more supportive of Nazism than were respondents who liked that news.[25]

25. In January 1947 (OMG-58) OSS/ICD researchers cross-analyzed the question on media accuracy with another question on views of National Socialism. Among respondents who answered both questions, 89 percent of those who thought current news less accurate than wartime news also thought that Nazism was "a good idea badly carried out" rather than a "bad idea." Of those who found no difference in the quality of the news, 75 percent took a favorable stance on Nazism. Only half of respondents who said that current news was more accurate than wartime news had positive impressions of Nazism.

Free vs. Controlled Media

When American occupation authorities envisioned a free press in Germany, they thought in terms of a tradition ingrained in U.S. political thought: freedom of expression nurtured for more than two centuries by independent newspapers and more recently by private radio broadcasting corporations. They found the history of communications in Germany appalling—intensely partisan newspapers before 1933 and government controls of all the media during the Nazi era—and wanted to remedy the shortcomings of that system. They nevertheless faced a dilemma: Their fundamental commitment to an open media system emphasized education through the free flow of information and ideas among people who have something to say. Their assigned mission in occupied Germany, however, stressed training—or, perhaps more accurately, indoctrination—that would restrict politically unacceptable information, ideas, and personnel. Could AMG teach democracy, critics asked, by following an undemocratic media policy?

One practical manifestation of the Americans' dilemma was the relation of newspapers to local governments—which were, after all, agents of the military government, especially during the early occupation period. Germans were eager for an independent press. Seventy-one percent of the respondents to a December 1945 AMZON survey said that newspapers should have the right to criticize the civil government, and 8 percent thought not (WSR-6). But did the press in fact have the right to criticize the government? In October 1946 (WSR-34) more than three-fourths of those who expressed an opinion (48 percent of the total sample) denied that their local newspaper was too much under the influence of the local government. Only one respondent in seven disagreed—and only half of these (7 percent of the entire sample) thought the press insufficiently critical of local government.[26]

Subsequent questions angled more directly toward the principle of press freedom. Responses showed both solid support for it and a significant perception that the German press was being kept from that ideal. More than three in four respondents to a November 1946 survey (WSR-35) agreed that the German people should have complete freedom of speech (compared with 14 percent who disagreed).[27] Eight months later (OMG-77)

26. A survey a month later (OMG-37) found that the ratio of those who found local governments intrusive to those who did not varied in West Berlin (11 to 77 percent), Bavaria (14:60), Hesse (17:54), and Württemberg-Baden (21:48).
27. Freedom of speech was nevertheless not one of postwar Germans' highest values.

64 percent said that German editors should "be allowed to print every-thing they consider to be correct" (23 percent disagreed). But in July 1947 (OMG-77) less than half of AMZON respondents said that their zone of oc-cupation had a free press and that the newspaper they themselves read was free. More than a quarter responded negatively to each question.[28] And when the notion of press freedom was expanded to allow a newspaper to print everything its editors thought correct, only 23 percent of the sample thought that German newspapers had that right, whereas 60 per-cent disagreed. Respondents blamed this limitation on the occupation authorities.[29]

Another series of questions asked in July 1947 (OMG-77) addressed links between newspapers and political parties. Through their screening of li-censees U.S. occupation authorities had from the outset tried to sidestep a partisan press in favor of independent editors, but many Germans were not aware of this policy. Asked whether they believed that most papers were "edited by political parties or politically independent people," only 42 percent of AMZON respondents correctly answer the latter. The rest either thought that representatives of political parties edited the news-papers (20 percent) or did not know one way or the other (38 percent). Nevertheless, postwar Germans agreed that the press should be indepen-dent. Asked whether they preferred "to have newspapers published by political parties or by politically independent people," 75 percent of AMZON and 81 percent of West Berlin respondents chose an independent press (compared with 6 and 12 percent, respectively, who favored party-based newspapers).[30]

Distaste for a partisan press was not, however, absolute (OMG-77). Of

Asked in July 1947 (OMG-77) which of four political qualities was most important to them, 31 percent listed free trade, 22 percent freedom of religion, 19 percent free elec-tions, and only 14 percent freedom of speech. Fourteen percent declined to answer the question.

28. About half of those who answered these questions positively held their convic-tions strongly (averaging 24 percent of the entire sample), about a fifth less so (10 percent), and the rest (14 percent) said they only thought that what they were saying was in fact the case. In West Berlin, with its ready access to Soviet sector newspapers, figures were firmer: 66 and 63 percent, respectively, believed the publications were free; 23 and 31 percent, respectively, did not.

29. Those who said there were restrictions cited Allied censorship (27 percent), the Allies' reluctance to accept criticism or challenges to their authority (15 percent), or Allied control of the newspapers (2 percent). The remainder mentioned "today's condi-tions" (5 percent) or gave no response (11 percent).

30. The level of information made a difference. Among informed AMZON Germans—that is, those who knew that the U.S. policy did not permit a party press—92 percent favored an independent press and 4 percent a party press. Among uninformed respon-dents who thought that U.S. policy aimed at a party press, 81 percent favored an inde-pendent press and 13 percent a party press.

the 75 percent who preferred politically independent editors, more than a third (27 percent of the entire sample) said they would favor it "if each political party were also allowed to publish a newspaper in their state (or *Land*)." So in addition to the 6 percent of AMZON Germans who preferred a party press to an independent press, 27 percent were willing to live with either, whereas 37 percent wanted only an independent press, and 30 percent were undecided.[31] These figures suggest a permissive majority of 57 percent who were willing to tolerate either kind of newspaper.

We saw earlier that AMZON Germans enthusiastically favored complete freedom of speech. To what extent, then, did they think that U.S.-sponsored radio broadcasting furthered this goal? Asked in January 1946 (OMG-1) whether they believed that the radio was censored, the responses were about equally divided among those saying "Yes" (19 percent), they "Supposed so" (19 percent), and "No" (21 percent)—but the remaining two in five offered no response. A survey nine months later produced similar results.[32] The same survey, carried out in October 1946 (OMG-45), found two in three of the sample denying that radio programming contained too much propaganda. One in six respondents complained about excessive propaganda.

AMZON Germans wanted freedom of the airwaves, and some were sensitive to censorship and propaganda, but they proved willing to restrict freedom for at least one category of dissidents in occupied Germany. Asked in November and December 1946 (OMG-48, 100) "Who should speak on radio?" 77 percent were willing to grant the privilege to all Germans and 71 percent to trade union leaders, but they were more hesitant about permitting Communist Party members to do so. More than half accepted the idea, but a quarter did not. Figure 11.4 indicates that this latent hostility to communists grew sharply by the beginning of 1948. The decline over time in the percentage of interviewees who did not volunteer responses suggests that the issue was increasingly salient.

An Enduring Media System

Media policies established by OMGUS survived the formation in summer 1949 of the Federal Republic of Germany and the U.S. High Com-

31. For the U.S. and British sectors in Berlin these figures were 12, 42, 35, and 11 percent, respectively. Looking only at informed AMZON Germans, the figures were 4, 37, 48, and 11 percent, respectively.

32. In October 1946 more than half of AMZON Germans said that they were radio listeners, and two-thirds of these felt that radio was censored (OMG-45). By contrast, in the U.S. and U.K. sectors of Berlin, where the SMG-controlled Radio Berlin dominated the airwaves, 48 percent of the entire sample perceived such censorship. Three-fifths of the Berlin respondents reported too much propaganda in the radio, and only one in three did not.

Figure 11.4

Freedom of Media Access for Communists, 1946-1949

Question: Should members of the Communist Party be allowed to speak on the radio?

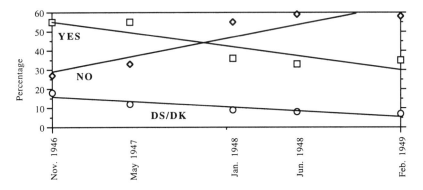

YES: y = 55.063 - 0.92902x   R^2 = 0.777   F-Ratio = 10.4   Prob< 0.048
NO: y = 29.048 + 1.3146x   R^2 = 0.844   F-Ratio = 16.2   Prob< 0.028
DS/DK: y = 15.889 - 0.38554x   R^2 = 0.850   F-Ratio = 17.0   Prob< 0.026

Sources: OMG-48, 100, 175.

mission for Germany. Whatever its real or imagined weaknesses, its overly ambitious programs and its naïveté regarding German society and the dynamics of social change, U.S. policy gained credence in the community's political life. Among other accomplishments, it is to the credit of U.S. media policy that:

- The print media were sufficiently established by 1949 that they would not fall back into the hands of publishers linked to Germany's feudal, aristocratic past;
- The main thrust of newspapers continues to be independent rather than explicitly partisan;
- The substantive and typographical format of the new German newspapers, put in place by editors and journalists who had learned much from U.S. (and British) tutelage, has continued;
- Radio stations, and eventually television stations as well, remain under the provinces rather than reverting to federal dominance;[33] and

33. In 1961 the FRG's Constitutional Court squelched an effort by Adenauer's government to create a federal radio and television station.

- Radio and television stations operate as public law corporations under the direction of councils whose members represent various walks of public life.[34]

These are not small accomplishments. Such U.S.-sponsored changes set the tone for Germany's current, democratic media system.

But again: How did AMZON Germans respond to the U.S. media policy? The most striking aspect of public perspectives is the consistency of responses over time. Unfortunately, in assessing communications OMGUS pollsters seldom posed the same question twice. Priorities on media issues were in perpetual flux, and experimentation to improve the quality of individual questions was common. Then, too, we are relying not on datasets but on summary reports supplemented by index cards. The time-series data that are available nevertheless make it clear that AMZON Germans voiced quite stable views about newspaper readership, radio listening, and quality of reporting.

That consistency suggests that postwar Germans thought the media important. An abundance of social-psychological testing reveals that people have stable views on issues that they regard as significant. Less salient issues give people response alternatives. They can search their minds to uncover their "true" thoughts, or parrot the most recently heard opinion that seems to satisfy the interviewer, or even respond capriciously. The data reviewed here, in contrast, indicate well-established opinions among reliable if changing samples of AMZON Germans.

From this assumption of salience it follows that Germans held views on media-related issues that neither U.S. occupiers nor anyone else could easily manipulate. Does this mean that the OMGUS dream of using the media to democratize German society was thus bound to fail? U.S.-sponsored public opinion surveys cannot answer this question. The surveys show that AMZON Germans preferred certain programming, wanted reliable news reporting, and bridled against obtrusive propaganda. They also reveal that many respondents, while preferring an independent press, were willing to live with at least some partisan newspapers. But AMZON Germans were never queried about the policy of providing the licensed press with funds and confiscated, low-rent property to enhance their viability in a competitive, postoccupation Germany, or about the hard negotiations that AMG carried out with provincial parliaments to ensure that public law

34. Broadcasting's main structural change since the occupation ended is the possibility created by court order in 1981 to set up commercial stations. Although OMGUS could not assume credit for this German innovation, U.S. occupation officials had extolled the virtues of private broadcasting.

corporations rather than provincial or federal offices would control radio broadcasting.

AMG sought to protect what it considered to be the public interest of the German people. Opinion polling was never conceived as a foolproof way of learning what this public interest was, and critics can easily inveigh against the occupiers for presuming to know the German public interest. But the survey data do clearly show that popular concerns centered on media programming and overall impact rather than legal (or even constitutional) technicalities. Historical experience in Germany shows that the public is likely to accept large chunks of whatever structure the appropriate authorities devise, and U.S. officials had reason to believe that any structural changes not achieved by the end of the occupation would never be realized. In this sense the public seemed to be permissive—as indeed it was when structural details were being hammered out. Moreover, in a half-century since, no popular sentiment about revamping Germany's media system has emerged. This resistance was particularly evident when western German decision makers integrated into their structures the media of the former German Democratic Republic. Western Germans disdained such changes as alternative media systems that could jeopardize a system that had worked successfully for decades (R. Merritt 1994).

The survey data also reveal that AMZON Germans by and large accepted the practical implications of U.S. media policy. Table 11.2 collapses into a single statistical base five different questions, all but one of which was asked several times between October 1945 and July 1949. We may group all five sets of responses into four categories: "Good," "Pretty good" (which we shall call "Ambivalent"), "Poor," and "No answer" (which includes both "Other" and "Irrelevant response").

Table 11.2 shows emphatic German support for U.S. media policy. One of every two respondents supported particular aspects of that policy while only 6 percent opposed them.[35] Could these figures be expected to hold up after OMGUS and HICOG had left the country? Typical of such later attitudes were responses in June 1955 and October 1982 by national samples asked about television programming (IfD-1:85, 8:553). More than half (51 percent in 1955, 55 percent in 1982) indicated that they were very happy or happy with it, compared with 6 and 5 percent, respectively, who were unhappy; two of five in each survey were either ambivalent (40 and 36 percent) or had nothing to say (3 and 4 percent). The similarity of these figures to OMGUS data evaluating newspapers (Table 11.1 and Figure 11.2)

---

35. Among those who gave an opinion, these figures are 65 and 8 percent, respectively.

Table 11.2   Overall Views of U.S. Media Policy, 1945–1949

| | Responses to Five Questions (percentages) | | | |
	Good	Ambivalent	Poor	No answer
Do you like your regular news-paper?[a]	50	31	5	14
Is the news more accurate than during the war?[b]	50	29	4	17
How did newspapers handle the IMT news?[c]	47	11	6	36
Was IMT reporting complete and/or reliable?[d]	44	24	8	24
Is the press free from local govern-ment influence?[e]	48	5	7	40
Average	48	20	6	26
Average excluding "No answer"	65	27	8	—

[a]"How do you like [your] newspaper? Do you think [it] is very good, good, fairly good, or poor?" (See Table 10.1 and Figure 10.2; three surveys from October 1945 to November 1948.)
[b]"Does the news today (in Germany) appear to you more trustworthy, or less trustworthy, than that published (in Germany) during the war?" (See Figure 10.3; five surveys from January 1947 to July 1949.)
[c]"What do you think of the way in which the newspapers report the Nuremberg trials?" (See Table 5.1; three surveys from December 1945 to October 1946.)
[d]"Do you think the newspaper reports of the Nuremberg trials are complete? Are they reliable?" (See Table 5.2; two surveys from August 1946 to October 1946.)
[e]"Do you think that the newspaper is too much under the influence of the local government or not?" (WSR-34; one survey in October 1946.)

strongly hints that the surveys were tapping into common social attitudes that have nothing to do with any occupying power.[36]

AMZON Germans had few illusions about U.S. media policy. They could see that AMG officials directly or indirectly shaped political dimensions of the news. They could see that some programming had propagandistic elements—condemning Nazism and then Soviet behavior while consistently touting democracy and the American way of life. But only a small percentage of AMZON Germans bitterly resented such facts of life under foreign occupation. A larger number simply expressed skepticism, and a majority was unconcerned about or unaware of the issues.

36. The similarities are even more striking if we discount respondents giving no answer. Average scores of newspaper figures in the three surveys from 1945 to 1948 (Table 11.1) are "Good," 58 percent; "Ambivalent," 36 percent; and "Poor," 6 percent. Analogous average figures for the two television surveys are 55, 39, and 6 percent.

Recalcitrants. Breakdowns of the data make it easy to characterize the relatively few hard-core critics. During the OMGUS era respondents who harbored negative views of U.S. occupation policy in general were most likely to lodge complaints about the quality of reporting, the value of *Die Neue Zeitung* and other AMG organs, and the occupiers' manifestly inconsistent policies as well as their encroachment on what such respondents saw as the inherent rights of Germans. Such recalcitrants also tended to be the people most likely to find something good to say about Germany's Nazi past. Their defiance of occupation authority made it unlikely that U.S. media policy could "reeducate" this recalcitrant minority for democracy.

Straddlers. More perplexing were the AMZON Germans whose perspectives seemed to straddle any number of fences. Table 11.2 placed about one in five respondents in that category, but many people who gave no responses should doubtless also be included. A more detailed breakdown of responses to a similar question (see note 25 above) suggests that, besides a few recalcitrants, occupied Germany had a sizable number of disaffected citizens. Irrespective of whether they could be called unreconstructed Nazis who still accepted major components of Hitler's ideology, roughly a fifth of AMZON Germans were thoroughly disgusted with both the Nazis who had led Germans to disaster and the U.S. authorities who had conquered and then occupied Germany—and for them to differentiate between the policies of the two was as meaningless as to distinguish Tweedledum from Tweedledee.[37] The practical implication was that they were not enthusiastic about U.S. media policy, but neither would they try to block it.

Reaching this heterogeneous group of straddlers for any persuasive communication proved difficult. Whether their stances in interviews stemmed from genuine ambivalence, an unwillingness to be pinned down on issues they did not think were salient, or ignorance masked with a veneer of neutrality is difficult to determine. What they had to say on any given issue varied, but their overall disaffection was consistent. Perhaps the best for OMGUS planners was that the straddlers' heterogeneity militated against any formal opposition among them.

Supporters. The largest set of respondents seemed ready to believe that Nazism had failed Germany and that foreign occupation was therefore inevitable. The best course of action in the circumstances, they said, was

37. Data about television viewing in 1955 and 1982 belie this interpretation. On an issue that had nothing whatever to do with Germany's checkered history, an average of 38 percent of all respondents expressed what we have called ambivalence or straddling. This response pattern has persistent social roots.

to accept the losses of the past, see what could be learned from the occupying powers, and then move on to reconstruct their country, to move Germany toward a better future. For most, a strategy of survival took precedence over grand schemes to build the new Germany; they would be content to reestablish their own jobs and carry on their own lives. Both the strategy of national reconstruction and that of personal survival implied the irrationality of quarreling with the occupiers over specific policies. Let the occupiers do what they will, the accommodationist argument continued, while trying to minimize any damage that their zealousness might cause. Eventually they would return home, leaving Germans to do more or less what they wished.

The supportive Germans, we might assume, were most open to efforts toward directed social change. Their strategies called for instrumental policy-making, accepting whatever was necessary to move toward the dominant goal of independence and security. It follows, then, that they should have been accessible to OMGUS programs that prescribed what they should reject and what they should adopt—and so OMGUS survey data show they were.

Such styles of decision making encourage flexibility rather than stability. The pressures that lead in one direction today may lead in a different one tomorrow. For this reason, even as OMGUS media officials sought to woo supporters, they initiated policies that would ensure the postoccupation continuity of U.S. media accomplishments. OMGUS's media-based, directed social change tried to convince its supporters that the imposed and negotiated media innovations would help them meet their more fundamental goals.

The OMGUS strategy of directed social change in the field of communications was complex but by and large successful. Popular German support for U.S. communication policy was considerably stronger than critics have been willing to recognize, and the policies themselves had an impact on the West German media that continues today. At the same time, the data show the limitations facing any government that uses strategies of control to achieve goals of social reform. Germany's political stage was filled with recalcitrants and straddlers, and many supporters had goals that only partly matched those of U.S. occupation authorities. Control—coupled with public relations rather than persuasive communication—ultimately played the dominant role in democratizing Germany's media system.

· ·

TWELVE

Federal Governance

However much Germans—buoyed by the feeling of relief following the demise of National Socialism and the cessation of hostilities, the support offered by at least some Allied officers, and the promise of new policies the Allies were implementing—may have accepted the postwar presence of the Allies, it was nevertheless a foreign military occupation. The Allies offered—or imposed—tutelage in "democracy." Many Germans listened and learned, but few wanted the occupation powers to play the role of older siblings permanently, however well-meaning and wise they might be. Eventually the occupiers had to let Germans govern themselves. But when, how, and what kind of governance?

The occupation began with several premises. At its core was the principle of Four-Power unity: the Allies agreed to collaborate in all important spheres affecting the occupation. By ensuring a regular flow from one occupation zone to another of vital commodities (including in-kind reparations), the Allies hoped to facilitate implementation of diverse policies. Close Allied collaboration would also prevent Germans of any political stripe from subverting policies or playing off one military government against another. Another key premise was that at least some Germans wanted to replace their authoritarian regime with a democracy. Some antifascists might hope only to restore Germany's pre-1933 mode of government, but others would surely be receptive to new ideas about political policy and practice, ideas that the occupiers were eager to offer. This chapter explores German reactions to the shifting hopes and dreams of the occupation's earliest days.

Occupiers and the Occupied

Occupation by foreign troops was a new experience for some Germans. They wondered how long this imposition would last, and they questioned the occupiers' intentions. Even if few believed the commonplace that the Allies intended to impose on hapless Germans a Carthaginian peace, they might well wonder what the victors had in mind and whether their wartime coalition had the resolve to carry out its intentions. For their part the Allies, already doubting their own ability to cooperate fully in the occupation, might ask how willing and able Germans were to speed toward democracy after more than a dozen years under the yoke of authoritarianism.

Germans heard different messages about long-term Allied goals both before foreign troops reached their soil and afterward. Some commentators on both sides, who claimed to have the ear of top echelons of power, spoke of an occupation that would last for decades if not generations. Others suggested—some with anticipation, some with regret, but even more with bitter irony—that the Allies would go home after punishing a few Nazis and destroying the most visible manifestations of the National Socialist regime. In the meantime, bombed out buildings, closed schools, food shortages, a dearth of material and equipment, and a breakdown of municipal services were elements of everyday life for Germans—as were military government officers, too frequently surly young men who did not speak German well and had little interest in German problems but who toted conspicuous weapons. Few AMZON Germans questioned the legitimacy of the occupation—in February 1946 seven in eight declared it necessary and only 7 percent disagreed (WSR-15:16; for notations, see Chapter 4, note 1)—but they wanted to know what was to become of them and their country.

How long would the Allied occupation last? OMGUS pollsters themselves, going into the field in fall 1945, doubtless had no clear answer. They nonetheless understood the role that expectations can play in a population's morale. Table 12.1 shows that at least half of the AMZON residents thought in terms of years in each of three surveys through July 1946. But images darkened early. The number of interviewees who expected an occupation of less than a decade first rose and then diminished between fall 1945 and the following summer, while the number who envisioned a longer stay rose from a third to half. Others thought in terms of contingencies. The occupation, about a tenth of them said, would endure until Germans learned how to govern themselves democratically. Only one in twenty argued that the world, not Germany, needed to change.

This does not mean, however, that a long-lasting occupation was what AMZON Germans wanted. Although an average of 41 percent expected the occupation to endure for a decade or more, only 15 percent desired this outcome.[1] A fifth said that the Americans should occupy Germany until a

1. Asked directly in April 1946, though, 69 percent of an AMZON sample agreed that

Table 12.1 Anticipated Length of the Occupation, 1945–1946

Responses to the Questions: How long do you expect the U.S. occupation
army to stay in Germany? How long should the Americans
occupy Germany? (percentages)

	Expectation				Desire
	Nov. 1945	Mar. 1946	Jul. 1946	Average	Dec. 1945
Less than a decade	18	23	12	18	16
Ten or more years	32	42	49	41	15
Until Germany is democratic	9	8	12	10	12
Until the world has changed	6	5	5	5	21
Other, didn't say/didn't know	34	24	24	27	42

Sources: WSR-2:2, 9:2, 20:4, 28:18. OMG-22 lists slightly different figures for March 1946.
Note: Questions and response categories differ slightly.

greater measure of peace and order could be secured. Whether respondents taking this stance feared world disorder threatening Germany or rather the probability of German mischief in such a dangerous environment is unclear.

Why should the occupation take so long? Early on, the Allies had pledged to move expeditiously toward a democratic, peaceable Germany, and Germans expected the Allies to honor this pledge. In three surveys from October 1945 to March 1946 an average of 70 percent of AMZON Germans told interviewers that they thought the Allies would "cooperate effectively in rebuilding Germany and Europe" (Curve A-1 in Figure 12.1), and only 16 percent anticipated no such cooperation.

Even by March 1946, however, German hopes for inter-Allied cooperation were sinking.[2] Furthermore, an assertion that the Allies would rebuild Germany itself found less credibility (Curve A-3). Acceptance of this proposition fell from 35 percent in March 1946 to 8 percent less than two

---

"Germany should be occupied for many years until the German people are able to form a democratic government" (WSR-23:28). A third that many rejected this view and 8 percent offered no opinion.

2. In October 1945 seven in ten responded positively about the prospects for Allied cooperation, 12 percent negatively, and 17 percent did not know or could not say (WSR-1:5). Ignoring nonrespondents, then, 85 percent of those offering their opinions were optimistic. The latter figure remained the same in January 1946 but dropped two months later to 74 percent.

Figure 12.1

Prospects for Allied Cooperation, 1945-1949

Questions: A-1. Do you think the Allies will cooperate effectively in rebuilding Germany and
Europe?

A-2. Do you think the Allies will cooperate successfully to leave behind at the end of
the occupation period a unified Germany?

A-3. Do you think that the Allies will cooperate successfully in the reconstruction of
Germany?

B. Combined responses to A-1 + A-2 + A-3.

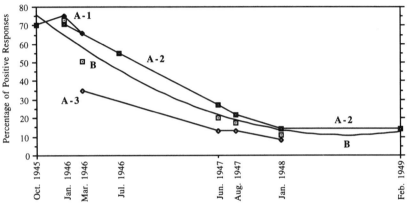

B: $y = 75.705 - 3.8081x + 5.5643e\text{-}2x^2$ $R^2 = 0.947$ F-Ratio = 44.3   Prob < 0.001.

Sources: WSR-1:5, 28:29; OMG-22, 63, 100, 175.

years later.[3] Another frequently asked question probed perspectives on
whether or not the Allies would abandon a still-divided Germany (Curve
A-2). Here optimism dropped fairly steadily from 71 percent in January
1946 to 14 percent in January 1948 and February 1949.

Collapsing these various trends into a single one (Curve B in Figure
12.1) shows a growing disillusionment about Allied concert to the benefit
of Germany. Those who cited Allied noncooperation, pressed for specifics,
confirmed in March 1946 what Western political observers had known for
months: the French balked at German reconstruction, but increasingly
the Soviet Military Government was downright obstructionist.[4] These

3. During this period AMZON Germans claimed to understand the reason underlying
Allied policy but nevertheless criticized the Allies (and especially the United States) for
giving priority to other European states in distributing food, industrial assistance, and
other forms of aid. Thus in March 1946 two-thirds expected the Allies to reconstruct
"Germany and Europe," but only a third expected them to do the same for Germany
alone (OMG-100).

4. Half of the AMZON respondents reported seeing noncooperation (OMG-22). Half of
these (24 percent of the entire sample) referred to the Soviet Union, 4 percent to France,
and 13 percent to both the USSR and France. Only 1 percent cited either U.S. or British
recalcitrance.

divergent Allied attitudes later evolved into full-blown hostility. By late 1947, while U.S. statesmen were leaning on their French colleagues to accept the Anglo-American lead toward a common German policy, they could not prevent an East-West schism.

Besides its long-run effect on German society and government, the ability of the Allies to cooperate had a more immediate and equally vital impact on the reconstruction of the German economy. During the war all the Allies had spilled resources and blood to destroy major parts of Germany's wartime economy. Afterward they gutted its industries to collect reparations and deindustrialized much of what remained, particularly armament industries. Doubtless few postwar observers expected much Allied enthusiasm for reconstructing that economy.

Probably just as few, however, had any reasonable notion of how long Germany's economic recovery would take, what it would cost, and who would foot the bill. Experts and publicists alike bandied about widely ranging estimates of the likely cost. And although military government authorities insisted that Germany would have to suffer for its Nazi episode, they recognized as well that the country needed substantial foreign assistance to regain economic self-sufficiency and even a modest standard of living for its people.

"How long do you think the reconstruction of Germany will take?" AMZON Germans were asked in March 1946 (WSR-20:5). Estimates ranged from a decade or less to a half-century or more, and the median response was between thirty and forty years.[5] Were these respondents optimistic "about the possibility that reconstruction" could "be accomplished with some degree of speed and energy"? About three in five AMZON Germans said they were, while a third (35 percent) were not (WSR-20:6).[6]

The slow pace of reconstruction troubled the Germans. In March 1946 about as many respondents said it was slower than expected (40 percent) as termed it faster (41 percent), and large numbers wanted even greater progress (WSR-20:7).[7] Eventually it did improve. In May 1947 as many as a sixth thought that it would not "take long to rebuild the German economy"

5. A fifth estimated up to nineteen years, the same number from twenty to thirty years, 15 percent said thirty to fifty years, and another fifth thought it would take fifty years or more. Seven percent said, simply, "A long time." In early 1946 no one could foresee the "economic miracle"—attributed by Wallich (1955) to cold war effects, Germany's geographic distribution of industry and population, and policy decisions made by occupation authorities and, later, Germans—which in eight years returned West Germany to the economic peak of 1936.

6. In urban environments, such as the American and British sectors of Berlin, the ratio of optimistic to pessimistic respondents was as high as 73 to 26 percent.

7. Almost three in four West Berliners thought that reconstruction was proceeding more quickly than expected, 16 percent more slowly.

Figure 12.2

U.S. Help vs. Hindrance in German Reconstruction, 1945-1949

Question: Do you think the Americans have furthered or hindered the recovery and reconstruction of Germany?

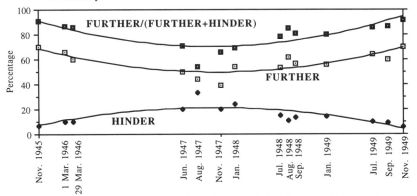

FURTHER: $y = 68.541 - 1.6104x + 3.3911e-2x^2$ $R^2 = 0.698$ F-Ratio = 12.7   Prob < 0.001

HINDER: $y = 7.1192 + 1.2069x - 2.6440e-2x^2$ $R^2 = 0.639$ F-Ratio = 9.8   Prob < 0.004

FUR/(FUR+HIN): $y = 90.885 - 1.8244x + 3.9612e-2x^2$ $R^2 = 0.675$ F-Ratio = 11.4   Prob < 0.002

Sources: WSR-2:17, 16:16; OMG-22, 63, 76, 100, 175; HIC-1, 17S.

Note: Some protocols seemed more willing to accept responses of "Neither."

(OMG-72). Among the 70 percent who thought it would take longer, six in ten (42 percent of the total sample) set as its probable time span ten or even fewer years. In the course of fourteen months, the expected length of reconstruction had dropped from more than a generation's time to less than a decade.

If the apparent prospects for economic recovery were improving, then why was it not taking place? Were the Allies dragging their feet? Our empirical findings underscore two points. First, compared with the other occupiers, the United States was gaining German respect for its constructive policies and actions. For those months when direct comparisons were possible, the Allied MGs in general were 15 percent less likely than OMGUS to be considered helpers and 15 percent more likely to be charged with obstruction.[8] Second, the image of the U.S. role changed dramatically, as is shown in Figure 12.2. From the high point of November 1945 AMG's image sank and German frustration rose steadily until August 1947.

At roughly that time U.S. policymakers began to reverse their overall

8. Assessment of the Allies' furtherance declined from 44 percent in September 1946 to 32 percent in January 1948, and that of hindrance doubled from 25 to 50 percent (WSR-32:10; OMG-72, 76, 100).

Table 12.2   How Reconstruction Can Be Achieved, 1945–1947

Responses to the Question: How can, in your opinion, the rebuilding of
Germany best be accomplished? (percentages)

	Oct. 1945	Feb. 1946	Mar. 1946	May 1947	Average
Religion	43	37	33	17	33
Hard work	62	59	71	57	62
New, strong leader	12	10	10	7	10
Return to traditional values	4	4	2	2	3
New political orientation	30	32	26	13	25
Other, didn't say, didn't know	7	7	5	9	7

Sources: WSR-1:9, 15:4, 20:9; OMG-72.
Note: Multiple responses permitted.

German strategy. The new policy directive, JCS 1779, issued in July 1947, was devised to end the Allied occupation and build a new German state. Further U.S. measures pushed to unify at least the western part of Germany, downplay denazification and war crimes trials, reform German currency, and encourage a constitutional assembly. Such steps restored German confidence, which flagged only slightly toward the end of 1948 when progress toward independence seemed to stall. But even during this period an average of four in seven respondents said that the Americans were furthering Germany's reconstruction. This view rebounded by the end of 1949 to 70 percent—where it had been four years earlier.

The partial breakdown of inter-Allied cooperation led to an obvious question: How could Germans contribute to their own country's resuscitation? For AMZON Germans the answer was simple: put Germans in charge of economic policy. Asked in July 1946 (WSR-28:25) what would happen "if economic policy were directed by a central German government," 79 percent said it would be better and 3 percent worse.

What should the German people do collectively to ease their country's economic distress? Four times during the first two occupation years OMGUS pollsters gave AMZON Germans a list of possible social behaviors (Table 12.2). Interviewees stressed their country's traditional social values—the work ethic and religion (although emphasis on the latter steadily diminished). Avoiding re-creation of Germany's recent past was important but far from central. An average of one in four referred to a need for new political direction, a democratic restructuring of German society. Only 3 percent on average suggested that a new Führer be empowered.

The survey conducted in May 1947 also asked how the individual German could help rebuild Germany (OMG-72). Again the most frequently selected response was "Hard work" (55 percent). Far behind were the individual's "Unity and cooperation" (10 percent), willingness to "Contribute all his abilities" (10 percent), "Honest work and personal integrity" (9 percent), and "Social participation" (7 percent).

Was the promise of hard work sufficient to convince the occupiers that Germans were ready to assume leadership of a new Germany? Skeptics argued that, as the experience under National Socialism demonstrated, Germans were inherently incapable of governing themselves either democratically or peaceably. Postwar Germans themselves, as we have seen, recognized that the mess created by their country had brought international disrepute. Germans knew that the price of past deeds was a more or less lengthy foreign military occupation, and they were willing to bear this price. Willingness to govern themselves, moreover, did not necessarily equal ability to do so. If Germans had to reform themselves, as the Allies insisted, then how were they to know when they would be ready to govern themselves?

From November 1945 to January 1949 OMGUS staffers posed slightly varying but functionally equivalent questions to tap popular views on this issue. Figure 12.3 shows only a middling degree of self-confidence. An average of 51 percent accepted the German people's competence to rule themselves, but 30 percent did not.[9] Even more revealing, acceptance diminished and skepticism rose during the occupation years. AMZON Germans seemingly became more wary about their own capabilities the closer they approached their semisovereignty. Although the statistical support for this conclusion is tenuous, it is nevertheless intriguing to consider that Germans found the transition to democracy more complicated than they had thought it would be.

Early empirical tests by the OMGUS Opinion Survey Section also gave analysts cause for concern about German commitments to the kind of democracy that U.S. authorities had in mind. For instance, in April 1946 interviewers administered a "German attitude scale" of 110 propositions designed to establish oppositional pairs: democratic vs. undemocratic, racist vs. nonracist, and so forth (see Chapter 4, note 9). Table 12.3 cites AMZON German responses to four propositions designed to assess attitudes toward Germany's future—or, more specifically, the extent to which Germans were ready to accept "supervised responsibility." A Guttmann scale

9. In August 1947, when 79 percent agreed that the German people were "capable of learning how to govern themselves in a democratic way," only 59 percent said that Germans had learned how to do so (WSR-29:12; 29:13). The negative responses were 6 and 17 percent, respectively.

Figure 12.3

German Capability of Self-Governance, 1945-1949

Questions: Nov. 1945: Do you think that the German people as a whole are today more capable
of self-government than they were three months ago?

Dec. 1945-Aug 1946: Did the Germans learn, in the past few months, how to govern
themselves?

Aug. 1947-Nov. 1949: Do you believe that the Germans today can actually govern
themselves democratically?

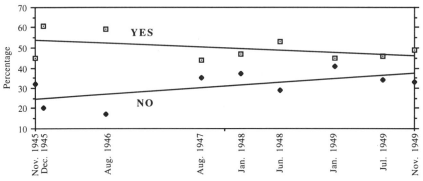

YES: y = 53.751 - 0.15946x   R^2 = 0.202   F-Ratio = 1.8   Prob < 0.193
NO: y = 24.528 + 0.26261x   R^2 = 0.363   F-Ratio = 4.0   Prob < 0.084
Sources: WSR-2:19, 9:6, 29:12; OMG-74, 197; HIC-17S.

cross-tabulating the responses showed that only 5 percent gave "democratic" answers to all four propositions. Twenty-seven percent responded democratically to three propositions, 33 percent to two, 24 percent to one, and 14 percent to none. If we combine the two most democratic groups and the two least democratic, we find that one in three AMZON Germans wanted their compatriots to accept supervised responsibility and slightly more did not.[10]

Other propositions posed in April 1946 (OMG-19) recalled National Socialist ideology. How many Nazi-supported responses would they elicit? The results showed that 15 percent of AMZON Germans were willing to suppress left-wing parties, 18 percent agreed on the importance of a dictator in creating a strong nation, 29 percent would censor publications critical of the government, and 38 percent accepted the proposition that "Democracy is a good form of government because it can develop a superior armed force."

10. The sum of the data reported in OMG-19 is 103 percent. The source of this discrepancy is not indicated but may be mainly rounding error.

The extent to which "supervised responsibility" equates democracy is of course problematic. Perhaps for this reason OSS/ICD analysts found that the "Future of Germany" scale was "the most negative set of responses recorded" among the eleven sets they explored.

Table 12.3 "Future of Germany" Scale: Supervised Responsibility, April 1946

	Responses to Four Propositions (percentages)		
	Democratic Responses	Undemocratic Responses	Didn't Know/ Didn't Say
Responsibility for the reconstruction of Germany should be placed in the hands of the German people under the supervision of the Allies.	(Yes) 75	(No) 19	6
Germany should be occupied for many years, until the German people are able to form a democratic government.	(Yes) 69	(No) 23	8
Germans should be allowed to take care of reconstruction without interference from the Allied occupation forces.	(No) 35	(Yes) 59	6
America should reconstruct Germany as fast as possible, before the German people fall prey to Communism.	(No) 10	(Yes) 82	8

Sources: WSR-23; OMG-19.

More encouraging to OSS/ICD analysts must have been AMZON German attitudes based on four other scales derived from the same survey. Each scale used four propositions, each spelling out a putative characteristic of democracies. Thus the "fallible leadership" scale included such assertions as "In a good government, discussions of proposed legislation should not be limited" and "Sometimes it is necessary to make suggestions or to criticize official policies even to a superior." Interviewees were asked to accept or reject each of them, and the numbers of "democratic" responses were then tallied. As Table 12.4 shows, an average of 75 percent strongly supported the OMGUS image of democratic values, and an average of only 8 percent strongly resisted it.

The entire range of data stemming from this survey (OMG-19), which took place almost precisely a year after the fall of Berlin and collapse of the Third Reich, thus provided a mixed reading of German attitudes. In some regards respondents accepted what OMGUS analysts considered to be the basic principles of democracy. In others, however, substantial numbers

Table 12.4 "Government, Democracy, Authority" Scales, 1946

Guttmann Scale Responses to Four Sets of Questions (percentages)

	Democratic Respondents	Undemocratic Respondents
Necessity of political information and interest	72	8
Independent thinking as a value	71	10
Fallible leadership	78	6
Independence and rights of individuals	77	7

Source: OMG-19.

Note: Each scale consisted of four questions. "Democratic respondents" gave "democratic" answers to three or four questions, while "undemocratic respondents" gave "democratic" answers to one or zero questions.

hearkened back to the attitudes of the previous, publicly discredited era. U.S. authorities were left with doubts about German preparedness for assuming the reins of democratic power.

A significant number of AMZON Germans, too, continued to have doubts. In May 1947 (OMG-72) three-fifths of a sample said that it would be "better for Germany if the four occupation powers were to get out at once," but a quarter disagreed. Respondents expressed confidence in the provincial governments (53 percent agreeing, 27 percent disagreeing) and the churches (65:26), but they registered concern about the political parties (35:46). Two months later, however, 70 percent agreed and only 10 percent disagreed that a central government should be established (WSR-28:27). A month after that, as we have seen, 6 percent thought that Germans were incapable of learning how to govern themselves democratically, and 17 percent claimed that they had not yet learned to do so.

Occupiers and occupied alike began with fixed albeit skewed images about their respective roles in postwar Germany. The Allies counted on inter-Allied cooperation to deal with their administrative tasks and their charges—a presumably naive German population consisting mainly of fanatic Nazis who would resist anything the Allies did, and a few enlightened but ineffective democrats who would accept Allied directions. Instead they found contentious Allies and fairly docile Germans who seemed more interested in getting on with life than in squabbling with the occupiers. Germans for their part realized that their political future rested on the Allied ability to work together, and they grew nervous as dissension seemed to break the ranks of the occupiers.

Secretary of State James F. Byrnes's address in September 1946 in

Stuttgart presaged a new era of the Allied occupation, predicated on reconstruction rather than punishment. In the ensuing months the East-West split deepened, and the Western powers strove to refocus their energies; in July 1947 a more liberal directive was handed down, modifying OMGUS policies (JCS 1779). But winding down the occupation would require cooperation among the Western occupation authorities to enact rapid strategic changes in their respective roles, as well as programs to convince themselves that at least semisovereign western Germans could act responsibly. Credible Soviet efforts to ameliorate relations with the Western cohorts might well have thwarted this Western initiative. But Soviet actions only exacerbated tensions, convincing the Western Allies that moving toward separate occupation authorities was the right path to take. What was effectively a Four-Power agreement to disagree led American, British, and French officers to pay close attention to the shape of democracy each envisioned for its occupation zone.

Germany's New Political Architecture

The role politics played in the patently political arena of immediate postwar Germany was curiously muted. Many postwar Germans, who had seen NSDAP members assailed in later denazification proceedings, shied away from creating and joining new parties. The occupiers were for their part ambivalent. At the outset they were not keen to broaden political activities, for they were unwilling to let any German group significantly constrain their own policies. This was less true in the Soviet zone, where occupation authorities treated communists at once as their lackeys and as Germany's future governors.[11]

Yet neither Western occupiers nor occupied Germans could avoid eternally the nexus of politics. MGs increasingly had to rely on Germans to carry out their orders, perform vital services, and in effect teach the foreigners German ways. After SMG began to permit parties in its occupation zone, Western MGs saw no alternative but to follow suit. The new parties, however, having no direct role to play in making Allied policies, remained at the periphery of OSS/ICD's attention. Analysts traced the development of parties, shifts in party preferences, and the importance of partisan orientation as variables explaining and predicting individual political attitudes but otherwise did not explore the parties' publicly expressed stances toward "political" issues.

11. SMG resurrected the Communist Party (KPD) and then, as it began losing popular support in Soviet-occupied Germany to the Social Democratic Party (SPD), forced the latter to merge with the KPD into a Socialist Unity Party (SED). Old-line communists, with Soviet support, dominated both the KPD and the SED.

The earliest OMGUS surveys revealed little popular enthusiasm for political activity. Surveys conducted in January and March 1946 (OMG-3) found that:

- Only half of the AMZON Germans felt themselves sufficiently informed about political events, and most of the remainder reported no effort to get more information;
- More than three-quarters were not yet and did not intend to become members of a political party;
- Whereas seven in ten knew that political meetings were allowed, fewer than a third of these informed citizens claimed to have attended one; and
- About two-thirds of those eligible to vote in elections held in January 1946 in fact did so.[12]

In April 1946, three-quarters of the respondents flatly said that, if they had a son leaving school, they would not like him to pursue a political profession (OMG-10). Typical of the comments were "Politics is a dirty business" and "One is a politician for ten years and then lands in a concentration camp." The percentage who thought politics a worthy profession (14 percent) was considerably lower than that in England (25 percent) or the United States (21 to 25 percent). In September 1946, just before referenda on provincial constitutions and elections to provincial parliaments, a series of questions demonstrated that only one in five potential voters was sufficiently interested to have even the barest information on the issues at stake (OMG-26).

Similar findings emerged from surveys in mid-1947, more than two years after the beginning of the occupation. About two in five felt sufficiently well informed about current political events, and only one in five of those who claimed insufficient information wanted to get more.[13] Almost four in five of the rest either had not bothered to seek further information or did not care to (OMG-72, 74). Levels of political information varied. Although 88 percent knew the name of their town's mayor, only 47 percent could name their province's premier and 60 percent could adequately define a secret ballot. Two-thirds preferred to leave politics to others rather than concern themselves personally with it (Figure 12.4).

Indeed, just as few expressed interest in politics, few reported being active politically. Nine in ten AMZON respondents indicated in May 1946 that

12. Turnout in German elections before 1933 and after 1949 was traditionally (although not recently) nearly 90 percent.

13. More properly, averaging figures for the two surveys shows that 41 percent reported having sufficient information and 57.5 percent not, 12.5 percent wanting more information and 45 percent not.

Figure 12.4
Interest in Politics, 1946-1949

Question: Are you yourself interested in political affairs or do you prefer to leave that to others?

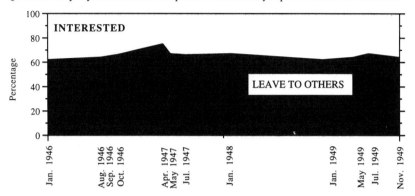

LEAVE TO OTHERS: $y = 66.203 - 2.0847e - 2x$ $R^2 = 0.009$ F-Ratio = .01 Prob < 0.769

Sources: OMG-175; HIC-17S.

they were personally doing everything possible to help rebuild Germany—
but only 7 percent agreed to help carry out the census of October 1946
voluntarily, 6 percent did volunteer work in their local community, and no
more than 4 percent were members of political parties. As many as 40
percent claimed no preference for any political party—a figure half again
greater than for the occupation period as a whole.[14] AMZON Germans were
inclined to ascribe responsibility for governance to officials rather than
to voters: asked about poor government, 38 percent held government officials responsible and 26 percent the voting public, with 12 percent assigning responsibility to both. Regarding good government, 48 percent
credited government officials, 21 percent the voters, and 13 percent both
equally.

Even two years later, on the eve of the FRG's promulgation, political
participation remained at relatively low levels (OMG-191). As before, few
felt well informed about politics: fewer than one in six could venture a
guess about whether or not their provincial constitutions contained provisions for initiatives and referenda (and, of those who answered, scarcely
more than half were correct), and 58 percent could name the province's
premier. Two in five knew in May 1949 that the Parliamentary Council,

14. Extrapolation from charts giving data from January 1946 to February 1949
(OMG-175) suggests that an average of about 25 percent of AMZON German interviewees
denied any party preference, compared with 30 percent who said they preferred the SPD,
25 percent the CDU/CSU, and 10 percent other parties; 10 percent gave no response.

which had been meeting in Bonn since the previous September, had drawn up a provisional constitution for West Germany, and fewer than half of these had any familiarity with this Basic Law. Nor was interest in politics much greater. Two-thirds continued to prefer leaving politics to others (Figure 12.4), only 38 percent thought that their fellow citizens had any significant interest in politics, and, when asked the cause of low participation in the affairs of state, 61 percent pointed to a general lack of interest, 20 percent to a lack of opportunity. Whereas three in four expressed a willingness to work an hour daily without pay for their country's economic reconstruction, only a third of that group was prepared to accept an invitation to take on a responsible position in the community's political life.

Yet political participation in U.S.-controlled areas, though low and fairly stagnant, was substantial compared with that in other countries. In the late 1950s, Gabriel Almond and Sidney Verba (1963) found West Germans more interested in and knowledgeable about politics than citizens of four other democracies. The German sample ranked below Americans and the English on the one hand but above Italians and Mexicans on the other in percentage of respondents who believed that individuals should participate actively in the life of their community, that their activity can influence the course of political events, and that they would receive serious consideration both in a government office and from the police. Almond and Verba concluded that "awareness of politics and political activity [in West Germany], though substantial, tends to be passive and formal. Voting is frequent, but more informal means of political involvement, particularly political discussion and the forming of political groups, are more limited. . . . And norms favoring active political participation are not well developed. Many Germans assume that the act of voting is all that is required of a citizen." West Germans, Almond and Verba found (1963:428–429), were satisfied enough with what their government was doing for them (see also Buchanan and Cantril 1953 and R. Merritt and Puchala 1968). Otherwise they felt no strong emotional attachment to the West German political system. OMGUS data a decade earlier pointed to a similar detachment from politics. But whether this detachment was a long-standing characteristic of German political behavior, or whether it stemmed from a postwar malaise, a feeling that Germany was paying now for too much political activity in the past, these data cannot tell us.

If few AMZON Germans professed a profound interest in politics or desire to join new political alignments, they nonetheless paid attention to political issues that directly affected them. Several such issues had complicated Allied-German relations during the early occupation period. One was food rationing. Not enough foodstuffs existed in the early postwar years to provide high-protein nourishment for all of shattered Europe's masses. Someone had to assume responsibility for feeding these people— to secure, store, and allocate dangerously limited supplies, and also to seek assistance from around the world. In western Europe the U.S. government, with only marginal help from its allies, took on this task. Germans, whose deposed regime was blamed for the crisis in the first place, were low on the priority list of recipients. However justified on practical and moral grounds this decision may have been, it deeply embittered some AMZON Germans. Germans took a similar interest in the treatment of refugees, expellees, and displaced persons who streamed into the Western occupation zones. How were they to be housed in heavily damaged Germany? How were they to be fed when indigenous Germans were suffering severe food shortages? How were they to find work in a country facing forced deindustrialization? In short, what was to be done with literally millions of new Germans?[15]

Such problems could be addressed as natural consequences of the sort of war that Europe had just fought. They nevertheless demanded immediate attention. The United States had little choice but to help substantial numbers of Germans. Despite a few vocal objections from some quarters, most AMZON Germans saw the U.S. effort to be effective and as fair as possible given the circumstances (A. Merritt and R. Merritt 1970:15–21). Yes, such issues raised political problems in the U.S. zone and elsewhere, but they did not spawn widespread divisiveness or rancor, or force the Allies to take sides. Problems that emerged after summer 1947, however, had more to do with unanticipated battles among former associates than with expectable outcomes of a lost war. Germans had good reasons to be concerned about how such contests affected their own future.

The Allies had pledged in 1945 someday to unite the four occupation zones and Berlin. The first major effort toward that end came in the second half of 1946, when the U.S. and British governments agreed formally to fuse economic control of their zones into what came to be called "Bizonia."[16] French reluctance and outright Soviet resistance stalled further

15. From 1945 through 1951 western Germany received 7.95 million ethnic Germans expelled from the Soviet Union, Poland (including former German territories east of the Oder and Neisse rivers), and other east European countries; as many as 1.65 million more fled from Soviet-controlled eastern Germany (Merkatz and Metzner 1954:118–119). This meant that expellees and refugees accounted for almost a fifth of West Germany's population in 1951.

16. In November 1946 (WSR-35:19), 84 percent of AMZON Germans approved and 2 percent disapproved of "the unification of the British and American zones." Later surveys revealed that 31 percent of respondents had heard of the Bizonal Economic Council by October 1947, 41 percent by January 1948, and 60 percent by March 1948 (OMG-107). The last of these surveys also discovered that 39 percent of the entire sample thought

Figure 12.5
Prospects for a United Germany, 1946-1949

Question: Do you believe the Allies will cooperate successfully to leave behind a united Germany at the end of the occupation?

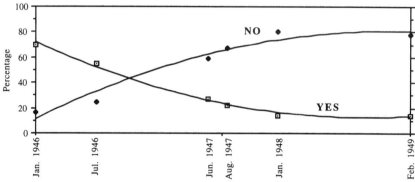

YES: $y = 71.990 - 3.6656x + 5.6107e\text{-}2x^2$ $R^2 = 0.992$ F-Ratio = 197.4   Prob < 0.001
NO: $y = 10.856 + 3.9685x - 5.6594e\text{-}2x^2$ $R^2 = 0.962$ F-Ratio = 37.9   Prob < 0.007

Sources: WSR-28:29; OMG-63, 100, 175.

movement, however. As we have seen, German assessments of inter-Allied cooperation were bleak by mid-1947, and respondents grew ever more pessimistic when asked directly whether or not the Allies could unify Germany before leaving the country (see Figure 12.5). Again the watershed of summer 1947 stands out. By then it was clear that both some Western Allies and the German people were eager for policy changes that would cut the Gordian knot.

Exacerbating the touchiness of the situation was the failure in 1947 of successive Quadripartite conferences of foreign ministers. East-West relations, already awkward at the practical level, broke down at the diplomatic level as well. Amzon Germans accused the Soviet foreign minister, Vyacheslav M. Molotov, of having torpedoed the Moscow conference of March–April. The collapse of the conference disheartened Germans: almost half doubted that the Allies could conclude a peace treaty by summer 1948 (omg-62, 63), and only one in seven expected the following November's conference in London to result in an agreement (omg-75). A spot survey after the breakdown of the London Conference in mid-December revealed an overwhelming sentiment among West Berliners that the Soviets were to blame (omg-86). One in three felt that it meant Germany's division, and 15 percent said that conditions would deteriorate or that war would ensue. One in four expected a continuation of the status quo.

---

that the bizonal unification had aided "the unification of all four zones"; 22 percent disagreed.

By early 1948 Germans were ready to accept a state that encompassed only the three western zones of occupation. American, British, and French representatives, together with colleagues from Belgium, the Netherlands, and Luxembourg, met in London in February 1948 to lay the groundwork for such a government. Of the relatively few survey respondents who later claimed to know anything about the London proposals, the bulk favored them (OMG-131). And, when apprised of the proposals' substance, 78 percent of all AMZON Germans (89 percent in West Berlin, 93 percent in Bremen) reacted positively. Support dropped to 72 percent when interviewers mentioned the possibility that only representatives from the western zones would be able to help set up the government, but events soon put an end to these hypothetical considerations anyway.

The key breakthrough in the East-West dilemma was the long-overdue western German currency reform in June 1948. Allies and Germans alike, as we have seen, had wrestled with economic problems from the onset of the occupation. The goal of reform was both to meet immediate needs and to create a rational economic policy that could help revitalize the country. OMGUS surveyors, even in their earliest questionnaires, explored a plethora of general and specific, sometimes time-bound issues: inflationary trends, the standing of the Reichsmark, rent and price controls, rationing, the black market, and other problems emanating only in part from the Allied inability to cooperate fully in redeveloping the German economy.

Economic pressures during the first two occupation years increasingly unsettled AMZON Germans, who saw economic chaos on the horizon. In January 1946, for instance, 67 percent of the respondents reported that their incomes were adequate; two years later this percentage had declined by ten points (OMG-100). Between January and June 1946 half the population believed that anti-inflationary measures would fail (OMG-60). Diminishing belief in the fairness of the ration card system fueled nagging worries about the adequacy of food supplies. Meanwhile, larger numbers of AMZON Germans recognized the growing importance of the black market in their lives. Although half denied the existence of a black market in their community in February 1946, two years later 71 percent knew of one. A more general mood of pessimism underscored all these trends: in December 1945 nearly eight in ten thought that economic conditions would improve, but by April 1947 only 45 percent thought so (OMG-100).

AMZON Germans were unclear about the sources and solutions of their economic woes. Asked why ten times as much currency was in circulation in July 1946 as before the war, most attributed it either to black market dealers (66 percent) or Nazis and war profiteers (33 percent), and 17 percent were unable to suggest any reason at all (multiple responses recorded). Yet a plurality of 40 percent in the U.S. zone and a majority of 52 percent in West Berlin opposed a currency reform at that time. Presented with alternative schedules for carrying out such a reform, however, 44 percent in the U.S. zone favored an immediate adjustment over delaying it until economic conditions should improve (12 percent) or until a new government should be formed (16 percent). In the meantime, most of those who expressed opinions preferred to keep their own reserves in goods rather than cash or bank accounts (OMG-32).

Once instituted in June 1948, the currency reform received enthusiastic support (OMG-133). Nine in ten termed it necessary, and more than half thought that it should have been implemented earlier.[17] Fifty-four percent expected the new Deutschmark to be strong enough to avoid any significant erosion of value, 58 percent believed that they would get along better during the coming year because of the currency reform, seven in ten intended to make additional purchases, and most expected the reform either to limit (71 percent) or to overcome (14 percent) the black market's profitability. Some dissatisfaction nonetheless existed, particularly with the ten-to-one conversion rate. This rate, more than one in three AMZON Germans said, treated small savers more harshly than the rich.[18] More than three-quarters expected—correctly, as it turned out—that the currency reform would lead to increased unemployment (OMG-32), but only 14 percent of western Germans actually expected to lose their jobs (IfD-1:148).

Currency reform ultimately produced both blessings and curses. On the one hand, after some temporary dislocations, it permitted the three western zones of Germany and the three western sectors of Berlin to begin moving toward a strong, unified economy. West Germany's development within a decade into Europe's economically most powerful state reflects the success of currency reform.[19] On the other hand, though, the currency reform was a symbolic step for Germans throughout the occupied territories toward what proved to be a forty-one-year division of Germany into East and West.

17. Independent surveys (IfD-1:148) found in June and July 1948 that the currency reform had pleased substantial majorities (71 and 74 percent, respectively) of western zone Germans (17 and 16 percent, respectively, were displeased). Should it have been delayed? In June 70 percent thought not and 21 percent were willing to wait.

18. An independent sample (IfD-1:151) found in July 1948 that 79 percent of western Germans felt that the currency reform had favored particular social groups—especially businessmen (62 percent), industrialists (38 percent), and capitalists (20 percent). Few thought reform benefited factory workers (9 percent), craft workers (6 percent), or retirees (2 percent).

19. Seven-eighths of national samples agreed in April and November 1952 that "since the currency reform West Germany had been given a great economic boost" (IfD-1:153).

When the Western Allies announced on 18 June 1948 that they were implementing a currency reform in their occupation zones (later expanded to include West Berlin), the USSR responded quickly. The Soviets initiated a currency reform for their own occupation zone and the whole of Berlin. The Western Allies rejected its applicability in their sectors of Berlin and extended their own currency reform to those sectors. The Soviets responded forcefully: they closed the roads and canals leading to Berlin's western sectors from the three occupation zones of western Germany. The West's reaction was just as quick. The Western Allies imposed a counterblockade on Soviet-controlled Germany, and U.S. and British authorities agreed to airlift sufficient supplies to sustain West Berlin's viability. But the Allies knew that undermining the blockade ultimately rested on the morale of the city's leadership and its 2.1 million citizens. Ernst Reuter, West Berlin's dynamic Social Democratic leader and later governing mayor, and other prominent Berliners gave their assurances immediately. But what about the mass of West Berliners?

Spot surveys, bolstered by more substantial investigations later, revealed that Berliners in the western sectors stood solidly behind the West and its airlift. Four weeks after the blockade was imposed 98 percent of a West Berlin sample agreed that the Allies were doing the right thing (OMG-130).[20] Throughout the blockade about nine in ten were confident that the Americans, British, and French would stay in Berlin as long as they remained in Germany. The West Berliners were apprehensive, naturally, as they fought for political survival. In July, a month after the blockade began, 52 percent doubted that the airlift could carry them through the harsh winter months that were expected. Seventy-seven percent nevertheless felt that the Western powers were doing their utmost to relieve distressed conditions in Berlin, and 84 percent thought that the airlift could provide them with sufficient food.

Confidence grew with the success of the airlift. By October 1948 almost nine in ten expected the airlift to bring them adequate provisions during the winter (OMG-141, 150). Meanwhile, 88 percent of the West Berliners said they preferred their present circumstances, however bad they might be, to unifying their city under the SMG and its communist footmen (4 percent). The percentage of those who said they would leave Berlin if given a chance dropped from 43 percent in July to 30 percent in October. AMZON respondents were only somewhat less sanguine. From July 1948 to Janu-

20. A remarkable consequence of the blockade was the way in which it linked Americans and Berliners—and, to a lesser extent, western Germans as well. America's public image of Germans shifted dramatically and almost overnight from "recalcitrant enemies" to "brave freedom fighters."

ary 1949 nine in ten said that the Western position was correct, and about two-thirds remained convinced that the Americans would stay in Berlin. Fifty-six percent thought that the airlift was providing sufficient food to maintain rations at their preblockade levels (OMG-144, 175).

Ultimately the airlift exceeded every expectation. The Soviet decision in May 1949 to lift the blockade was widely interpreted as a triumph for both U.S. hardness and West Berliners' tenacity. West Berliners continue to celebrate this teamwork in their loyalty to the West in general and the United States in particular. But the blockade also left a divided Berlin—a city that symbolized the division of Germany as a whole. The Federal Republic emerging in western Germany no longer had Berlin as its focus of attention. Three in five AMZON residents said in August 1947 that Berlin should be Germany's capital, but when the FRG's founding fathers in 1949 located their provisional capital in Bonn, two of every three AMZON Germans who expressed an opinion concurred with the choice (OMG-71, 180).[21] Berlin itself became a vibrant symbol of the united Germany that used to be, a brightly shining symbol of the united Germany that many hoped for in the future.[22]

Government for Western Germany

The Soviet-imposed blockade of Berlin made a western German state inevitable. Since February 1948 the Western Allies had been discussing plans for such a government with the Benelux countries, and by early June the French had agreed both to include its zone in the currency reform and to advance the idea of a trizonal fusion. The USSR bitterly protested what was becoming increasingly apparent: a formal division of Germany that removed the SMG from any control over a new western German state. In March 1948 Soviet representatives stormed out of an Allied Control Council meeting, and in June they left Berlin's Quadripartite governing body (known by its Russian name, Komandatura)—not to return until 1990. The SMG gave teeth to its protest in March by imposing a brief and limited blockade on the island city and in June by launching the full-scale Berlin blockade.

Such measures simplified Western policy-making. Critics of the Western intent to unify three if not four occupation zones (plus Berlin) found the cold war reality undermining their formal arguments. Citizens of ev-

21. In May 1949, the month when the Basic Law sealed both Germany's division and Berlin's separate status under Quadripartite rule, 77 percent of AMZON Germans continued to think that Berlin should be the country's future capital (OMG-180).

22. In spring 1992 the Bundestag of the newly united Federal Republic of Germany voted to restore Berlin's status as capital city.

ery Western nation, reeling from the Soviet takeover of Czechoslovakia in February 1948, quickly found it necessary to unify western Germany both to help the Germans resist Soviet predations and to add their resources to the defense of Western democracy. The Tripartite Allies became adamant about ending the impasse but had not resolved the specifics of what kind of government western Germans should have. That it should be "democratic" was without question. But such issues as the structure of governance yielded vigorous debate among Allies and Germans alike.

AMZON Germans agreed with the Western Allies that democracy would be the best form of government for Germany. Neither a monarchy nor independence for the provinces was appealing.[23] Nor did a communist form of government have much support. In August 1947, before the complete breakdown of inter-Allied cooperation, 71 percent of an AMZON sample could find nothing good to say about communism (OMG-74).[24] Both monarchy and communism ranked lower yet in a general preference poll than they had in March and July 1946. In contrast, as Table 12.5 reveals, more than seven in ten respondents who offered views expressed their preference for democracy over other governmental forms.

Instrumental orientation to democracy. But what did AMZON Germans mean when they praised democratic governance? A survey in mid-1946 found them accepting the commonplace: 25 percent spoke of freedom of speech or individual freedoms, 14 percent of equal justice for all or equal rights and duties, 12 percent of the people's influence on government or governmental honesty, another 12 percent of equality, unity, and the sovereign rights of people, and 7 percent of social welfare or reasonable living costs and wages (WSR-28:21, multiple responses permitted). Large numbers of respondents were silent: almost two in five had no definition of democracy to offer (WSR-28:21), one-third had neither good nor bad things to say about democracy (OMG-74), and 44 percent did not specify democracy as their preferred form of government (Table 12.5). Moreover, surveys in April 1948 and January 1949 (OMG-175), while finding that 58 percent of

23. Surveys in March and July 1946 found that only one in six accepted the idea of a monarchy and three in five rejected it (WSR-19:20); one in five entertained the notion of an independent Bavaria (WSR-28:24). Two years later 95 percent of all AMZON respondents expressed a preference for a democratic government in western Germany alone and only 1 percent for a communist central government for all of Germany (OMG-131). The strongest supporters of a monarchy were women unable to work (22 percent), respondents sixty years of age and older (22 percent), CDU/CSU adherents (19 percent), and those of upper-middle or higher socioeconomic status (OMG-74). See Boynton and Loewenberg (1974).
24. Only 16 percent could name some good points of communism. In contrast, 36 percent reported that democracy was entirely a good idea whereas 30 percent could name some faults (OMG-74).

Table 12.5   Views on Alternative Forms of Government, 1947–1950

Responses to Two Sets of Questions: First (in 1947), what kind of government
do you think Germany will have in about ten years—just your best guess?
Which would you personally like best? Forgetting about politics, which do you
think would be best for Germany from the economic viewpoint? Second (in
1950), what form of government do you regard as the most suitable
for a united Germany? (percentages)

| | August 1947 | | | Feb 1950 |
	Expected	Preferred	Best	Best
Monarchy	3	11	8	6
Dictatorship	2	2	5	3
Democratic republic	40	56	47	48
Socialist	9	10	9	3
Communist	11	*	1	*
Other	—	—	—	7
Didn't say/didn't know	35	21	30	33

Sources: OMG-74; HIC-15.
Notes: Recorded data in 1947 did not include an "Other" category. For 1950 the chart
collapses two categories—"Democracy" (45%) and "Republic" (3%)—into a single category of "Democratic republic."
*Less than one-half of one percent.

AMZON Germans were unwilling to give up any of a list of five democratic
rights "if the state would thereby promise you economic security," discovered that about 34 percent deemed those rights negotiable. What rights
would they relinquish to attain economic security? The dispensable rights
were to:

Vote for the political party you like	22%
Read all the books and magazines you wish to read	15
Work in the place you like	13
Express your opinion freely	7
Bring up your children according to your view	1–2

These findings suggest that at least a third of the AMZON population had
less than a firm commitment to democratic values.

Closer investigation suggests that AMZON Germans had an instrumental orientation to democracy: they expected their government to produce
certain "deliverables." As Figure 12.6 demonstrates, the commodity they
prized most was economic security. Such traditional democratic values as
free speech and press freedom—favored by an average of 30 percent from

Figure 12.6

Preferences for Economic Security vs. Political Freedoms, 1947-1949

Question: Which of these two types of government would you, personally, choose as better:
A government which offers the people economic security and the possibility of a good income [or]
A government which guarantees free elections, freedom of speech, a free press, and religious freedom?

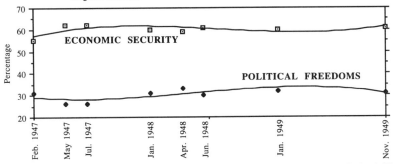

SECURITY: $y = 56.956 + 1.0995x - 7.9542e\text{-}2x^2 + 1.5220e\text{-}3x^3$ $R^2 = 0.458$ F-Ratio = 1.1   Prob < 0.438
FREEDOMS: $y = 28.965 - 0.43404x + 5.5716e\text{-}2x^2 - 1.2425e\text{-}3x^3$ $R^2 = 0.461$ F-Ratio = 1.1   Prob < 0.434

Sources: OMG-72, 74, 100, 175; HIC-17S.

Note: Early questions referred to economic security and "full employment" or "a good living."

February 1947 to January 1949—gave way in popular perspectives to ، ne desire for economic security (60 percent).[25]

Structure of government. What governmental structure should the future Germany have? The share declining to respond to this question dropped from 23 percent in July 1946 to 12 percent two years later, suggesting that the topic was capturing growing attention among AMZON Germans. Figure 12.7 shows that throughout this period a substantial number favored a decentralized form of government. An average of one in five respondents (21 percent) wanted some form of federalism: provinces would carry out major functions while the center, besides conducting foreign policy and ensuring national security, would perform a coordinative, administrative function. About as many favored either a looser confederation (13 percent) or independence for each of the provinces (9 percent).

The most startling finding in Figure 12.7 is the greater—and steadily increasing—preference for strong centralization. Under such a system power would reside in the center, and the traditional provinces would

25. Asked in November 1946, "Which should come first—the economic or political unity of the four zones in Germany?" 63 percent chose the former and 8 percent the latter (WSR-35:20).

Figure 12.7

Preferred Form of Democratic Governance, 1946-1948

Question: There are four kinds of government possible for future Germany. Which one would you prefer?

A strongly centralized government which would govern the four zones from Berlin.
A federal government in Berlin, but with most responsibility left to the provinces.
No central government; a confederation of provinces with each province self-governing.
Little cooperation of provinces; each province would be independent.

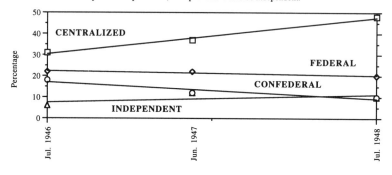

CENTRALIZED: y = 30.450 + 0.68471x R^2 = 0.990 F-Ratio = 101.3 Prob < 0.063
FEDERAL: y = 22.327 - 8.2803e-2x R^2 = 0.807 F-Ratio = 4.2 Prob < 0.289
CONFEDERAL: y = 17.079 - 0.31210x R^2 = 0.882 F-Ratio = 7.5 Prob < 0.223
INDEPENDENT: y = 7.5754 + 0.14650x R^2 = 0.361 F-Ratio = 0.6 Prob < 0.592

Source: WSR-28:26; OMG-74, 131.
Note: The question in July 1946 asked about preferences for "duration of the occupation."

either serve as the center's administrative agents or be replaced by more rationally organized regional offices.[26] By July 1948, when the Western Allies were rapidly moving toward setting up a constitutional convention for Trizonia, almost half of AMZON Germans called for this form of government.[27]

This highly centralized form of German government was precisely what the Western Allies did not want. They remembered the ease with which Hitler, having weakened and isolated regional power bases and governmental structures, had used his highly centralized government to pursue his goal of conquest. French authorities were particularly insistent about this equation of centralized government and aggressive German power, but the Americans and British, too, with their experience in feder-

26. The latter form of centralized power was adopted by the Soviet zone in fall 1949 for its German Democratic Republic.

27. Somewhat earlier, in February 1948, an independent survey (IfD-1:145) asked young people in southern Bavaria and southern Württemberg whether they preferred a central or confederal system. More than four in five chose the former, 15 percent the latter.

alism and local governance, favored limits on centralization in Germany. The Allies could also point to relatively peaceful eras when Germans had relied on loose confederations of government.

In early June 1948 the Allies made their intentions clear. The Tripartite Allies and the Benelux countries, after two and a half months of negotiations in London, produced procedures for unifying western Germany and spelled out what they expected from the Germans (U.S. Department of State 1985: 143–146). The concluding communique from London, dated 7 June, prescribed international control of the heavily industrialized Ruhr valley, continued presence in Germany of the Tripartite Allied military and management by the Allies of German foreign policy, reaffirmation of the prohibition of German armed forces, and creation of a provincially based constituent assembly instructed to draft the constitution of a federal government.[28] On the first day of the next month Allied authorities summoned a meeting of the provincial premiers, who were instructed to arrange for such a constituent assembly.

Moving toward a constitutional solution. The popular German response to the Six-Power London meeting was mixed, and apathy was a significant portion of that mix. In early July 1948 only two in five reported having heard of or read anything about the conference, and only half of these knew what its outcomes were.[29] The 20 percent who were knowledgeable responded positively though not enthusiastically to the London proposal. Although 18 percent of that group saw no advantages and 24 percent offered no opinion, the others referred to better living conditions (36 percent), a step toward independence (14 percent), or a bar to communism (8 percent). More than a third of the knowledgeable group did not know of any disadvantages to the proposal or could not say, and 8 percent expressly said there were none. Among those who mentioned disadvantages, the largest share (26 percent) spoke of Germany's division. About 8 percent each cited such issues as the probable loss of independence, loss of control of the Ruhr, and economic dependence on the Western powers. Asked to summarize their views, only 6 percent of AMZON Germans reported having

---

28. Article III(A) of the communique stated in part (U.S. Department of State 1985:145):

The constitution should be such as to enable the Germans to play their part in bringing to an end the present division of Germany not by the reconstitution of a centralized Reich but by means of a federal form of government that adequately protects the rights of the respective states [that is, provinces], and which at the same time provides for adequate central authority and which guarantees the rights and freedoms of the individual.

29. The city-states of Berlin (34 percent) and Bremen (41 percent) contained larger proportions of knowledgeable citizens.

a very favorable opinion, though 52 percent were favorable; 28 percent were unfavorable and 3 percent very unfavorable.[30]

Oss/ICD interviewers, after instructing the entire sample about specific issues emerging at the London conference, found more interest in the outcomes (OMG-131). One question focused on the role of the provinces in a constitutional assembly. Told about the planned assembly, respondents were asked: "Should the separate provinces of *all* of Germany elect representatives to attend this convention?" AMZON Germans supported this proposition by a ratio of 78 to 5 percent. Seven in eight respondents said that, if this structure was adopted, they would want their province to take part. Would it be acceptable if only the western occupation zones were to participate? Almost three-quarters found this arrangement tolerable, compared with 11 percent who did not. Seventy-two percent thought that linking the French zone to the Bizonal Economic Council would be a step toward unifying Germany, compared with 6 percent who disagreed. Two-thirds of those who knew about the proposed Ruhr statute opposed it.[31] But if AMZON Germans did not find the London protocols ideal, respondents nonetheless strongly endorsed the Allied decision to move ahead toward creating a new Germany.

Jockeying for position. Western Germany's political leaders were less enthusiastic. Their points of contention, many in number and degrees of magnitude, included a preference for centralized rather than federal authorities, outrage that the Allies sought to impose a government on Germans, and concern that a constitution for western Germany would eliminate options for national unification. The provincial premiers, instructed by the Allied military governors to meet with them on 1 July in Frankfurt-am-Main, met again separately a week later and decided unanimously to

30. We must recall that these figures refer only to the 20 percent of AMZON respondents who were knowledgeable. The 58 percent who gave positive responses thus represented only one in eight of the population.

A simple scale ranging from "Very favorable equals positive 2" through "No opinion equals 0" to "Very unfavorable equals negative 2" provides average scores of 0.30 for AMZON Germans, 0.56 for Berliners, and 0.39 for Bremers.

31. About three in four AMZON Germans interviewed in July 1948 knew that the London conference had addressed the issue (OMG-131). Fifty-five percent of that group knew that the proposed statute would put the Ruhr basin under international control. Thirteen percent thought (incorrectly) that the Ruhr basin would remain German under international control, 10 percent that it would be separated from Germany, and 8 percent that it would be under French control. One in seven either gave another answer (2 percent) or did not know (12 percent). But seven months later only 46 percent reported having heard about the Ruhr agreement, and seven months after that awareness dropped to 30 percent. Of the total sample, 7 percent in February 1949 and 9 percent in September 1949 thought it was a good agreement, whereas opposition dwindled from 23 to 7 percent (HIC-1).

reject the London protocols. It was the Allied MGs' turn to express outrage. MGs and Germans nonetheless agreed that the formal occupation should end, and multilateral talks and tête-à-têtes throughout summer 1948 produced an acceptable compromise. Of particular importance, at least symbolically, was agreement that a "parliamentary council" (not a "constitutional assembly") would draft a "basic law" (not a "constitution"). Key was the provisionality of any council decision, a contingency that left open the possibility that someday, after the whole of occupied Germany had been unified, its citizens might draft a truly German constitution. By 1 September 1948, then, the Parliamentary Council could begin its work.

A month earlier, in the first days of August 1948, OMGUS pollsters undertook again to assay German attitudes toward the plan to create a provisional government (OMG-136). Seventy percent of AMZON Germans endorsed the plan—mainly because "Germany needs a government of its own" (39 percent) or because of the need to improve the country's economic conditions. Of the skeptics, 12 percent of the sample, half expressed either the need for an all-German government (6 percent of the total sample), while others (2 percent each) said that a western German government would widen the East-West split or that Germans cannot govern themselves.

Few liked the strings that the Allies attached to the plan (OMG-136). Asked specifically who should control German foreign policy, half of the respondents, with a higher concentration among the more highly educated and those in higher socioeconomic strata, wanted the German government to have this responsibility; a quarter wanted to continue entrusting it to the Allies. Two-thirds of the sample were confident that the Allies, should they continue to control German foreign policy, "would keep in mind the best interests of Germany"—an assurance that only 15 percent repudiated. Would a Western initiative have any impact on Germany's East-West split? Almost half, again especially those in higher educational and socioeconomic groups, thought the split would widen, but a third said that it would not make any difference.[32]

Soviet prodding. If one cost of the Western plan was that Germans must accommodate Allied interests, a risk was that the Allies might be misinterpreting Soviet intentions. Soviet leaders insisted that they would endorse steps toward unifying the whole of Germany—if Germans would

32. Surveys conducted in September 1948 and February 1949 found similar responses to this question (OMG-175). Those who envisioned a widened split rose to 51 percent in September 1948 and then fell five months later to 44 percent. Those who expected no influence dropped to 26 and 28 percent. Of those offering opinions, the share expecting the gap to widen moved slightly from 58 to 66 and 61 percent.

repudiate the London protocols and persuade the Allies to cooperate with Moscow. Western officials rejected the Soviet proposal as nothing more than disruptive propaganda. Did Germans share that assessment, or did they fear that, by moving toward Western integration, they were forgoing their country's last real opportunity for unification?

Between early August 1948 and late June 1949 OMGUS interviewers posed two questions about Soviet proposals. One assessed response to the suggestion that "all four occupying Powers should leave Germany within the next year," the other to the notion that the World War II enemies should sign an "immediate peace treaty." It is impossible to gauge the extent to which the questions may simply have tapped deep-seated antag- onisms toward the USSR or the occupiers as a whole.[33] More promising is the proposition that Germans saw the Allies as rational decision makers seeking primarily to improve their positions in the global arena.

Even the assumption of rationality produces mixed interpretations. In summer 1948, before the Parliamentary Council had even met, two in five AMZON respondents said they liked the idea that a Four-Power agreement would ensure that the occupiers left Germany, while half rejected it (OMG-140). Support dropped that autumn to 34 percent, and rejection rose to 57 percent (OMG-160). In late June 1949—long after the Western Allies had accepted the Parliamentary Council's Basic Law, several weeks after the Berlin blockade ended, and only days after a Four-Power conference of foreign ministers in Paris had called for greater cooperation regarding Germany (U.S. Department of State 1985:269–270)—attitudes reversed again. Support rose to 43 percent and rejection dropped to 46 percent (OMG-187), and the Soviet idea of an immediate peace treaty found little enthusiasm (OMG-185): 22 percent advocated acceptance and 57 percent opposed it.

These findings suggest two patterns. One is that AMZON Germans, who were committed to a unified Germany, readily embraced any plan that seemed to offer the least hope, even if it meant jettisoning firm agree- ments.[34] A second pattern reaffirms the respondents' deep distrust of the

33. Postwar Germans harbored a strong antipathy toward the USSR and Soviet communism that took immediate form in their fear of Soviet aggression. For instance, throughout the period from January 1947 to February 1949 approximately half of AMZON Germans agreed that "the Americans should reconstruct Germany as soon as possible in order to avoid her becoming a prey to Communism" (OMG-175). For comparative data, see R. Merritt (1967).

34. Shortly after the FRG's promulgation and shortly before that of the GDR, in September 1949, 93 percent of an AMZON sample reported that they were "fundamentally for . . . a re-union of Germany" and only 3 percent said they were against it (HIC-1). During the next two decades reunification and economic issues vied to top the German list of the most important problems facing their country (IfD-3:482; IfD-4:387). As the

Soviet Union. Fifty-seven percent of the respondents felt that Germany would be politically less secure should the occupying powers withdraw.[35] They feared civil war and chaos most (25 percent of the entire sample), but 16 percent also reported fearing the Soviet Union and communists. More than half thought that the Soviet motivation in making the proposal was to get the Western powers out of Germany so that the USSR could exert its control. Only 2 percent believed that the Soviet proposal for an immediate peace treaty represented a sincere effort to establish peace for Germany, and 82 percent saw other political motives at work.

Drafting the Basic Law. Provincial representatives to the Parliamentary Council began meeting on 1 September 1948, Soviet attempts to scuttle their activities notwithstanding. The Council's proceedings enjoyed "an atmosphere of compromise and provisionality" (Merkl 1963:61) and sometimes initiated sharp conflict with the Allied authorities (see Clay 1950a; Golay 1958). On 22 November the Tripartite military governors felt constrained to instruct the Council that the basic law should provide:

> for a Bicameral legislative system in which one of the houses must represent the individual states and must have sufficient power to safeguard the interests of the states; . . .
>
> that the executive must only have those powers which are definitely prescribed by the constitution, and that emergency powers if any, of the executive must be so limited as to require prompt legislative or judicial review; . . .
>
> that the powers of the federal government shall be limited to those expressly enumerated in the constitution and in any case, shall not include education, cultural and religious affairs, local government and public health; . . .
>
> that the constitution should provide for an independent judiciary to

---

country found economic prosperity in the mid-1950s, reunification took first place with an unprecedented consensus (45 percent in January 1959), but the economic crisis that began in 1965 elevated prosperity to top ranking (62 percent in January 1967).

35. One in five AMZON respondents had no such fear. The ratio of fear to confidence dropped from 65:17 (or 79 percent of respondents who expressed opinions) in November 1948 to 57:21 (73 percent) in June 1949 and 53:23 (70 percent) in November 1949 (HIC-3).

A cross-tabulation of two questions asked in June 1949 shows that only 54 percent of the respondents expressed opinions about both (*a*) whether or not the occupiers should leave and (*b*) whether or not their departure would endanger German security. Two-thirds of this group reported consistent attitudes: 25 percent did not want the occupiers to leave and feared for German security should that event occur, whereas 11 percent welcomed and saw no danger from the departure. But 14 percent of those wanting the occupiers to leave also feared the consequences (OMG-185, 187).

review federal legislation, to review the exercise of federal executive power, and to adjudicate conflicts between federal and land authorities as well as between land authorities, and to protect the civil rights and freedom of the individual. (U.S. Department of State 1985:193–194)

The Allies' letter chastened German constitution drafters—but also intensified their work.

The Parliamentary Council's final draft of its Basic Law was submitted to the Allied authorities on 10 February 1949. The response on 2 March noted general acceptance but added several critical comments, "suggested" some new paragraph wordings for the Council to consider, and deleted any reference to Berlin as a province in the future federal government (U.S. Department of State 1985:204–206).[36] Almost ten weeks of partisan dispute among Germans ensued, most of it focusing on the Allied provision for federal powers in public finance. By May, however, the deadlock was broken. On 8 May the Parliamentary Council adopted its redrafted version, in mid-May the provincial parliaments accepted it, and on 23 May the Basic Law was proclaimed.

From this study's perspective what is most remarkable about the nine-month process leading up to the Basic Law's promulgation, given both the provisional constitution's importance for Germany's future and its media coverage, is the popular lassitude it seemed to inspire. In March 1949, while the Parliamentary Council was working out Allied demands, only one in five western German interviewees expressed "serious" interest and another third indicated "some" interest (IfD-1:157). Almost as many declined to answer due to indifference (40 percent) or lack of knowledge (6 percent). Surveys conducted later that spring, after the Basic Law's promulgation, found that only 42 percent of AMZON Germans knew that the Parliamentary Council had completed its work (OMG-183A). Of these fewer than half—18 percent of the entire sample—said that they were "acquainted with the Basic Law."[37] Twenty-eight percent of the sample indi-

36. The Western Allies did not want to jeopardize their right to protect at least the western sectors of Berlin. They felt that the Soviet Union might interpret West Berlin's inclusion in the Federal Republic as a violation of Four-Power rights, at once rendering these rights null and void and justifying a Soviet demand that the Western Allies remove their military forces from the city (see R. Merritt 1973). This Western interpretation of Berlin's political status pertained until Germany's unification in 1990.

37. An independent survey carried out in May in the whole of western Germany (IfD-1:157) found that two-thirds either did not know what the Basic Law was (51 percent) or were undecided whether it was good or bad for western Germany (14 percent); the rest rated it either positively (30 percent) or negatively (5 percent).

Figure 12.8
Formation of a West German State, 1948-1949

Question: Do you, in principle, approve or disapprove of the formation of a West German state now?

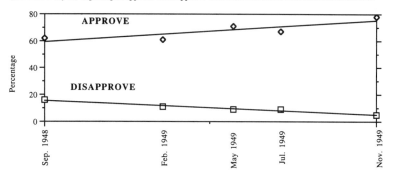

APPROVE: $y = 59.388 + 1.1367x$ $R^2 = 0.738$ F-Ratio = 8.4   Prob < 0.062
DISAPPROVE: $y = 15.523 - 0.74640x$ $R^2 = 0.968$ F-Ratio = 90.7   Prob < 0.002

Source: HIC-3.
Note: The survey of November 1949 omitted the word "now."

cated that, if given a chance, they would vote in favor of the new constitution; 6 percent said they would vote against it.[38]

Though the plan for a provisional government had its negative side, Germans seemed to be saying, it was manageable, and it was at any rate necessary to move in that direction. Figure 12.8 shows an emerging consensus among AMZON residents. In September 1948, when the Parliamentary Council first met, the ratio of those for to those against forming a German government was four to one. By November 1949, shortly after the Federal Republic of Germany began to function, this ratio was sixteen to one.[39]

Other early evaluations showed that the new Federal Republic of Germany enjoyed guarded popular support. Two-thirds of the respondents in November 1949 reported that they were satisfied "with the activities of the West German government up to now," compared with 7 percent who were dissatisfied (HIC-3). Having stabilized their country's status somewhat, West Germans were less worried about the consequences should the Quadripartite Allies leave Germany. A survey in February 1950 found

38. A breakdown found that 70 percent of informed AMZON Germans said that they would vote for the Basic Law (compared with 13 percent who would vote against it); 37 percent of the uninformed would favor and 7 percent oppose it (OMG-183A).

39. The number approving the FRG's formation increased from 62 to 78 percent, and those disapproving decreased from 16 to 5 percent (HIC-3).

that, after more than a half-year's experience with FRG-style democracy, AMZON Germans continued to express support for a democratic republic (Table 12.5).

Substantial numbers nevertheless had their qualms. Was West Germany truly independent? More than two in five felt that the Western powers exerted too much influence on the FRG's decision making, and more than a third of these (15 percent of the entire sample) termed the FRG "a puppet government."[40] Should the Western powers give more authority to the FRG? More than half said they should, and only 13 percent did not think it necessary. Was the FRG truly democratic? In February 1950 (HIC-15) almost as many said "no" (29 percent) as said "yes" (36 percent).[41] Did the FRG work "according to democratic principles"? Half said that it did, but a fifth thought otherwise.

Public opinion data from the late 1940s present a complex image of changing popular attitudes toward the future German government. Germans knew that the wartime Allies were there for good reason. Moreover, as suggested elsewhere, many of them were pleased that foreign occupiers could carry out the dirty job of reconstruction that Germans might find difficult to manage. They nevertheless wanted the Allies to move to the side as soon as possible, to let "democratic" Germans take over control of their country. The breakdown of the wartime alliance disrupted the dream of steady progress toward this goal. In those circumstances, what should Germans do?

The masses wanted democracy, to be sure, but they prized economic and military security even more, as well as, eventually, sovereignty. To achieve those ends they must work with the Tripartite Allies—pressuring them to resolve at least western Germany's economic chaos, reinforcing their preoccupation with the USSR's putatively aggressive intent, and persuading them that it was again "safe" to create a new German government. If they must make concessions in drafting a constitution and state apparatus, then so be it. A secure, independent Germany, they seemed to be saying, could eventually put things right again. As it turned out, however, the political and social patterns initiated during the occupation years set in motion dimensions of a Germany that would prove to be enduring.

40. Of the 42 percent who complained about Allied dominance—28 percent did not—three-fifths (25 percent of the entire sample) denied that the FRG was a puppet government (HIC-3).

41. Office of Public Affairs, Reactions Analysis Staff researchers added (HIC-15:5): "Among the informed group there is a marked hesitancy to call the West government truly democratic. Among the people who are able to define the term democracy, opinions are almost evenly divided pro and con, with 40 percent for 'truly democratic,' 38 percent 'not especially so,' and 24 percent unable to make up their minds."

THIRTEEN

• •

Creating the Future

How durable were the social changes fashioned by the American Military Government and the other Western Allies? Chapters 9–12 have focused on the ways Germans in the American zone of occupation viewed several U.S. policies. The questions that AMG-sponsored pollsters asked AMZON respondents did not cover all relevant issues, in particular key economic issues. But a consistent image of AMZON Germans emerged from the data.

Germans and U.S. Policies

Capitulation to the Allies in May 1945 in effect set Germans free. It gave them the opportunity to choose among political strategies that offered alternative futures. They could sullenly defy the occupiers to "reform" them. They could work toward social change, perhaps replacing the country's capitalist framework with a full-scale socialist state or even a "people's democracy." They could ape the social and institutional structures of one or more of the occupiers, or devise a German amalgam of various structures. To some degree the Allies could shape the choices available, and many—perhaps most—occupation policies aimed at precisely that goal. German response to that tutelage rested in part on the perceived legitimacy of AMG, in part on the policies it pursued.

American occupiers. Chapter 9 assayed German public acceptance of the American occupation. The world expected Germans to deny the occupation's legitimacy—because they wanted to preserve Hitler's Third Reich, because they resented violation of their national sovereignty, because they felt that the Allies had not earned Germany's defeat in battle, because the Allies, given their own behavior during the war, had no moral right to impose controls over Germany.

The German response, however, was more conciliatory than expected. Germans embraced a new concept of national honor: their national honor

349

had been besmirched not by the lost war but by the capitulation to Hitler, under whom their country had followed policies and committed crimes that no civilized population could tolerate. Germans themselves had besmirched their country's national honor. That the Allies would occupy defeated Germany, even if the defeat reflected more German material inferiority than fighting skills, was a natural consequence. In this moral sense, Germans accepted their country's occupation.

In a practical sense, furthermore, they could scarcely ignore the fact of occupation. Resistance was senseless; better to cooperate with the occupiers until they went home. Cooperation might give Germans a better opportunity to help shape occupation policies. Besides, the occupiers could accomplish tasks that Germans might have found difficult to undertake alone—punish war criminals, for instance, and restructure German society to minimize any recurrence of the Nazi menace.

For western Germans, particularly in the American zone, the occupation turned out to be less fierce than they had feared. After some initial bluster and strict policies (such as food rationing), AMG moved into a problem-solving mode: How could it restore transportation and other vital services? How could it maintain civil order? What about economic and even political reconstruction? AMG seemed to offer paths to a rosier future. Moreover, as the occupation continued, it grew increasingly clear that the United States and a revitalized, democratized Germany had much in common, not least their mutual concern about Soviet intentions in western Europe. Western Germany's foreign military occupation became increasingly tolerable.

Socialization. Among the programs undertaken by AMG to reorient German society, the most extensive, highlighted in Chapter 10, focused on youth and public education. AMG sought to change the schools not only by removing Nazi personnel and ideology but also by introducing new programs, classroom materials, instructors, and teaching methods, and by giving parents and even pupils a greater share in decision making. American youth programs offered opportunities to participate in organized athletic activities and learn various skills—as well as providing sweets and warm rooms on cold winter days. AMG and other U.S. agencies also initiated various ways to enhance American-German cultural exchange.

Such programs were popular with the German public but not always with traditional authorities to whom the military governments felt obligated to pay attention. To these authorities the goal was stabilizing German society, not introducing new ideas—however well these ideas worked elsewhere. Such recalcitrants wanted only to excise any deleterious remnants of Nazi indoctrination from the country's public schools, then restore the education system that, they felt, had worked so well before 1933.

Other AMG policies also encountered reluctance. Leaders of traditional programs for youngsters recognized the value of AMG's German Youth Activities program but itched for the day when they could take over full responsibility for Germany's youth. Similarly, although most German leaders and intellectuals endorsed cultural exchange programs, they expressed critical views, ranging from the sour grapes of the denied applicant to a fear of multifarious forms of U.S. cultural domination.

The full test of AMG cultural programs would come later, in some cases long after the occupation ended. But opposition among education authorities did not kill school reforms. Obvious popular acceptance persuaded some administrators of the need to implement such changes. Although AMG-sponsored youth programs did not survive the occupation, cultural exchange continues to thrive. Germans in fifteen cities continue to enjoy Amerika-Häuser and bilateral German-American Institutes. The Federal Republic of Germany has also invested substantial sums in such cultural-exchange programs as the Fulbright Commission (established in part to subsidize recipient countries' payment of counterpart funds for U.S. assistance), German Academic Exchange Service (*Deutscher Akademischer Austauschdienst*), and German Marshall Fund.

Toward democratic media. In contrast to such fields as public education, in which traditional albeit non-Nazi forms and personnel were initially restored, remnants of the past, Chapter 11 pointed out, were the losers in postwar print and electronic media. The Tripartite Allies were convinced that Hitler's control over the media had enhanced his ability to control the German people. Those media personnel who had cooperated with him and even those who did not actively resist him were in effect considered guilty of complicity. If they could not be brought before military tribunals, they should nonetheless be barred from playing any role in re-creating the German media.

Allied media policies endorsed such historical impressions. AMG's press licensing, for instance, largely eschewed institutions and personnel that had flourished in both the Weimar and National Socialist eras. It systematically discriminated in favor of applicants who could demonstrate both their innocence regarding the past's political sins and their willingness to publish democratic newspapers independent of political partisanship. The Tripartite Allies also sought to ensure political and cultural variation on the airwaves by placing radio under provincial rather than centralized control. The strategy in each case was to preclude formal or even informal amalgamations that a strong national leader could use to gain control over the masses.

The German public by and large supported AMG media policy. Those denied licenses complained bitterly, as did those content with the media and, perhaps, other aspects of the forbidden past. Most Germans, however, considered the AMG-promoted media to be fair, reliable, and, in comparison with past journalism, politically neutral. Technical and procedural changes wrought during the Nazi era and four years of occupation, moreover, had dulled the competitive edge of those who had not been active. By the end of the occupation representatives of the old media found themselves outdistanced in the new industry. As a result, media strategies established in 1945–1949 continue to shape the industry.

New government. In Chapter 12 we saw that, as the dust of war began to settle in 1945, Germans worried about the fate of their nation and the prospect of returning to normal governance. But many saw rainbows on the otherwise cloudy horizon. They rejoiced at having survived the war's ravages, and they rejoiced anew when they learned of the Potsdam Conference's relative mildness.[1] Allied plans to get rid of high-level Nazis, moreover, gave the new Germany a fighting chance. Many Germans even expressed the need for a slow but thorough occupation to prevent their compatriots from slipping back into the disastrous patterns of the past, but withal they hoped for speedy independence.

Emerging conflict between East and West shattered this hope. Increasingly it seemed that if Germany was to be granted a modicum of independence, it would be at the cost of national unity (and the loss of its eastern territories). The AMZON public expressed dissatisfaction with this turn of events. Self-interest inspired support for the U.S. stance in the cold war. This meant accepting Western decisions to initiate a currency reform, support West Berliners blockaded by the Soviets, and convene a Parliamentary Council that would create a government for their three zones of occupation.

Public opinion surveys did not go into detail about the forms of government the Parliamentary Council might offer, but occasional attempts to gauge feeling about federalism versus centralism nevertheless revealed an open-minded majority. Germans did not want a dictatorship, be it national socialist, communist, or whatever. Given a free choice, for a variety of reasons, they leaned toward a centralized form of government: they were most familiar with that mode of governance, which had existed under the twelve years of Nazism; Germany's past federal schemes had

1. The mood was perhaps best expressed by a prominent academic who was then approaching his teens. When he learned about the Potsdam decisions he reports having breathed a sigh of relief and exclaimed, "*Wir sind noch einmal davon gekommen*—We escaped again."

produced imperfect results; and many believed that central controls could most rapidly solve postwar Germany's most pressing problem, economic instability. Their preferences notwithstanding, though, Germans were willing to live with a federal structure. Accordingly, surveys in the years after the Basic Law's promulgation found few Germans who advocated a shift from a federal to centralized form of government.

The Western Allies convened their provincial governors in July 1948 and commissioned an ad hoc body to draft a constitution for their zones of occupation. The resulting Parliamentary Council, sixty-five delegates chosen on a proportional basis from party representatives in the individual provincial governments, began its deliberations on 1 September 1948 and continued until 12 May 1949, when it completed its draft of a Basic Law. Allied approval two months later called for the establishment of the Federal Republic of Germany and the election of its government. Subsequent surveys found the bulk of German citizens strongly supportive of their new Basic Law and Federal Republic.

In fact, public opinion surveys during the entire occupation period of 1945–1949 revealed considerable agreement among Germans about shaping the future, and especially about U.S. policies. Initial doubts on both sides notwithstanding, Germans and Americans soon came to a pragmatic understanding regarding goals, priorities, and even procedures. Although AMZON Germans resisted some policies, they saw increasingly that AMG officers were flexible on issues that did not touch on core U.S. policies and that most of these core policies had advantages for Germans as well as Americans. But how sincere was the popular call, raised presumably under the duress of foreign military occupation, for a democratized Germany? What would Germans do after the occupation ended?

Continued Political Growth

When the occupation formally ended in summer 1949, American and German leaders expressed hope and expectation for a new democratic era—even if it could not include eastern Europe and the newly minted German Democratic Republic in the Soviet zone of occupation. Others were less sanguine. Some critics thought that Germans, once they had the chance, would revert to their authoritarian ways. Some feared that inherent weaknesses doomed the American dream for a democratic Germany. Some simply believed that, as the memory of World War II's horrors receded, issues other than the need for Western solidarity and international cooperation would capture the attention of Germans and their wartime opponents. Germany's friends were as anxious as its critics to see whether the Nazi episode was an aberration in the country's history or something enduring, and as ready, if the latter, to take whatever steps necessary to prevent a recurrence of the Nazi menace.

The success of U.S. policies varied from one realm to another. In public education, for example, AMG authorities had some success in putting "democratic" teachers into the classroom. They fired Nazi party members and hangers-on, rehired those who had left the teaching profession under Nazi pressure, and recruited some with clean records even if they had no formal pedagogical or administrative training. But those whom the Americans hired, whatever their democratic predispositions, still taught in a traditional education system that did not adapt well to new ideas. This traditional system, its supporters said, could educate German children perfectly well once the Allies had removed Nazis from power.

Beginning around 1969, however, a variety of circumstances led to the revitalization of the German public education system. Traditionalists, especially those trained before 1933 who had regained control after the Allies backed away, were retiring, and younger administrators were more receptive to new ways of organization and pedagogy. At the same time, social democrats and liberals were increasingly keen—for different reasons —to revamp public education. The old guard's system—a minuscule educated elite dominating the broad masses whose educational opportunities were limited—was keeping pace with neither the changing social preferences of Germans nor the society's practical needs in a rapidly changing global economy.

Changes proposed, discussed, and partially implemented during the occupation years found greater acceptance in the 1970s. Civics teaching became the norm, as did parent-teacher associations, participation of parents and children in career choices, and modification of rigidly tracked programs. Universities were opened to students from broader socioeconomic backgrounds. In effect, most of the changes sought by the Americans in 1945 were effected—two to three dozen years later, under German impetus. Some reforms had unanticipated consequences that caused new problems. Wider access to university education, for instance, gave rise to an academic proletariat, as many graduates became overqualified for available jobs.

In contrast to teeth gnashing that accompanied efforts to change public education, U.S. occupation authorities found it relatively simple to create a new media system. They confiscated the press lords' printing presses and the state-owned radio stations' transmitters, and they barred from the postwar media virtually anyone associated with the old guard. AMG media officials knew that they had a limited time to get their reforms in place. The occupation would end sooner or later, and the disenfranchised would seek redress—specifically the return of their property so that they could go into business again.

But U.S. media officials depended upon several assumptions. First, they trusted, the occupation would continue long enough and their own policies would be sufficiently successful that controls could protect the infant media industry. Second, the reemerging press lords would be frustrated by obsolete equipment and inadequate personnel. Third, the population would become committed to the notion of an independent press, unwilling to tolerate even the pre-1933 system of a partisan press, still less an ideologically based media imposed by some latter-day Goebbels.

All three assumptions were fulfilled. Germans became enthusiastic about the AMZON print and electronic media, as well as similar ones in the British zone, and the press lords of earlier eras were neutralized. A decade and more later, though, print media in the FRG faced another kind of crisis—much like the crisis that their counterparts in the United States, Britain, and most other democracies confronted. Rising costs and the economic imperative for large-scale efficiency shut down many newspapers, especially those in small towns, and prompted fear of monopolization. In spite of federal legislation to curtail monopolistic trends, a few large firms came to control most of the country's newspapers and news magazines.[2]

Ghosts of the past haunted the Parliamentary Council's meetings in 1948–1949 when its members drafted a Basic Law for western Germany. However much they disagreed on other matters, the delegates were united in wanting a constitutional document that would prevent a new anti-constitutional party such as Hitler's NSDAP from seizing power. Members of various political parties had different interpretations of what had caused the Weimar Republic's demise and the rise of National Socialism, but compromises brought a solution that was acceptable to majorities in both the Parliamentary Council and the provincial legislatures that were to ratify the document.[3]

Some provisions of the Basic Law explicitly addressed the failure of past German democracy. The Weimar Republic, for instance, had interpreted democracy in terms of the citizen's absolute rights of free speech and free association and had thus tolerated political parties that funda-

2. With the unification of Germany in 1990 came enforced privatization of the ex-GDR's state-owned newspapers. Regional newspapers were at least initially able to retain their readership, but some form of consolidation seems inevitable (see R. Merritt 1994).

3. Only Bavaria rejected it. Support came from the middle (SPD, FDP, and most of Adenauer's CDU); the KPD, DP, and CSU provided the opposition. See Gunlicks 1989; Klatt 1989; Renzsch 1989.

mentally opposed democracy and the Republic itself. When two such parties—the National Socialists and the Communists—between them gained majority votes in the Reichstag, they could collaborate in destroying the Republic. And that, in the view of perhaps most postwar Germans, is precisely what happened. Article 9 of the FRG's Basic Law, while granting the citizen's right to "form associations and societies," establishes a clear constitutional limitation. According to Article 9(2), "Associations, the purposes or activities of which conflict with criminal laws or which are directed against the constitutional order or the concept of international understanding, are prohibited." Article 21(2) extends this principle to freely formed political parties: "Parties which, by reason of their aims or the behavior of their adherents, seek to impair or abolish the free democratic basic order or to endanger the existence of the Federal Republic of Germany, shall be unconstitutional. The Federal Constitutional Court shall decide on the question of unconstitutionality." Article 21(2) led to the banning of both the right-wing Socialist Reich Party (SRP) and the Communist Party (KPD), and it has since been used to ban new right-wing extremists.

Then, too, the Weimar German president's direct election gave him popular support in overriding the wishes of the parliamentary body, and the president's constitutional prerogatives gave him enormous power. Articles 54–61 of the Basic Law reduce the president's status and power. The president, who is selected by a special Federal Assembly of Bundestag members and elected representatives of the provincial parliaments, now has mostly ceremonial functions.

In late Weimar Germany an anticonstitutional majority of Nazis and Communists could block the Reichstag's ability to function by voting the existing chancellor "no confidence" and then refusing to agree on his successor. Article 67 of the Basic Law mandates that before the Bundestag can vote a chancellor's "no confidence," it must first agree on and vote for a successor. Such provisions have worked well. Replacing the Weimar Republic's dual executive with clear lines of authority has limited the potential for disruption and facilitated the FRG's political process.

But what was the government to do should an emergency crop up that threatened the political system? Article 48(2) of the Weimar Constitution gave the federal president the right first to declare the existence of such an emergency and second to exercise dictatorial powers in dealing with it.[4] In

4. Article 48(2) of the Weimar Constitution stated: "If the public safety and order in the federation are seriously disturbed or endangered, the federal president may take the measures necessary for the restoration of public service and order and may intervene if necessary with the assistance of the armed forces." The president had to report such measures to the Reichstag, which could revoke them.

the early 1930s Federal President Paul von Hindenburg's increasing re-
liance on Article 48 contributed to a political climate that persuaded him
to appoint Hitler as chancellor. Hitler soon secured Hindenburg's assent
to Article 48 and used it to sweep away Weimar's constitutional provisions. Abuse of the principle in the early 1930s led to so much contention
about new procedures among postwar constitution drafters, Germans and
Allied advisers alike, that it seemed wise to table the issue—and so it
languished unresolved for nineteen years. Constitutional amendments in
June 1968 did not resolve all of the conflicts but did give the FRG a working procedure.[5] As amended, the Basic Law sharply delineates the government's freedom of action should there be a breakdown of public security
and order at the provincial level or higher (Art. 35), a state of defense (Art.
115) or tension (Art. 80a), or a legislative emergency (Art. 81).

In these and other ways, such as creating a Federal Constitutional
Court (Articles 92–94), participants at the Parliamentary Council sought
to learn from the past, and especially to protect their fledgling democracy
from its domestic enemies. They were aware, of course, that no system is
perfect, that none guarantees protection against a willful demagogue with
strong popular support and a plentiful cache of weapons. They were nevertheless keen to do the best they could to avoid a Germany that could
again succumb so easily to dictatorial power.

A Democratic Germany?

Modifying existing institutions and procedures was an important part of the revitalization of Germany. But Germany also needed to
persuade the rest of the world that it had changed both genuinely and
profoundly. Establishing international or at least Western acceptance of
the FRG as a democratic state was a key element of any would-be West
German policy in the postoccupation period.

Konrad Adenauer's conservative government, elected in August 1949,
knew that even those who wished Germany well would not forget the
country's past status as global pariah. One condition of reversing this
image was the adoption of basic principles of human rights. To some
measure the Parliamentary Council, with guidance from the Tripartite
Allies, had accomplished this goal when it drafted the West German "bill

5. From fall 1966 until summer 1969 the cdu/csu and spd formed a "grand" coalition
government that controlled more than 90 percent of the Bundestag seats. This concentration of power enabled them to resolve a number of long-standing legislative disputes
and even to enact such constitutional changes as, in June 1968, provisions for emergency
legislation. Thus Article 35 provided for nonlegislative emergencies caused by a "natural disaster or an especially grave accident."

of rights." But the world wanted deeds, not words. The lofty goals proclaimed in the Basic Law had to be realized in the political marketplace of everyday life. A second condition was thus righting the wrongs, as much as possible, of the Nazi regime. Germans could not bring the dead back to life, but they could compensate for past injustices suffered by the living and the dead.

Civil liberties. The Germans who drafted the Basic Law focused sharply on means to protect citizens from governmental abuses of power. The first twenty articles were devoted specifically to basic rights in the FRG, among them:

- Article 1(1): The dignity of man shall be inviolable. To respect and protect it shall be the duty of all state authority.
- Article 3(1): All persons shall be equal before the law.
- Article 3(3): No one may be prejudiced or favored because of his sex, his parentage, his race, his language, his homeland and origin, his faith, or his religious or political opinions.
- Article 4(1): Freedom of faith, of conscience, and freedom of creed, religious or ideological, shall be inviolable.
- Article 20(1): The Federal Republic of Germany is a democratic and social federal state, [with] all state authority [emanating] from the people.[6]

Other basic rights addressed freedom of expression, marriage and family, education, assembly, and movement, as well as the right to choose one's trade, occupation, or profession.

The Federal Republic would later encounter difficulties in interpreting and implementing some of the basic rights granted to everyone in the land. The establishment in January 1956 of the Bundeswehr made it necessary, for example, to rewrite Article 4(3): "No one may be compelled against his conscience to render war service involving the use of arms." This right stemmed directly from the Nazi government's utter rejection of the concept of conscientious objection. Those who tried to avoid military service under the Nazis were likely to end up in concentration camps or worse, and postwar Germans were alert to guard against such fundamental violations of human rights. But whereas some wanted to strengthen citizens' rights to follow their own religious or moral convictions irrespective of state interests, others gave precedence to a stable military defense. After bitter dispute the Bundestag drafted legislation that regularized

6. Article 20(4), added in June 1968, provided that "all Germans shall have the right to resist any person or persons seeking to abolish that constitutional order, should no other remedy be possible."

such details as liability for service, conscientious objection, and alternative service. In June 1968 the grand coalition could transform a modified version of this legislation into a new Article 12a in the Basic Law.[7]

Population movements. Another issue with roots in the past dealt with citizenship and population movements. Under Nazism civilian and military officials had banished undesirable German citizens, transferred slave laborers from one camp to another, slaughtered "impure" ethnic and religious groups, and—less directly, through the Third Reich's energetic but eventually disastrous war—created a mass of displaced persons, refugees, and expellees. Postwar Germans were ambivalent about what was to be done. Some were still guided by years of poisonous propaganda about the superiority of the Aryan race. Others feared that an unreconstructed Germany would provide only misery to immigrants who might seek refuge there.

The data reviewed here suggest that most Germans felt the need to redress the balance, to demonstrate that the new, democratic Germany could act responsibly, and the Basic Law helped to make that case. Article 116(1) defines "Germans" as those possessing German citizenship, refugees or expellees of German ethnic origin who had been admitted to German territory within its pre-1938 boundaries, and "the spouse or descendant of such a person." Article 16(1) guarantees that "no one may be deprived of his German citizenship," and Article 116(2) adds that those deprived of German citizenship in 1933–1945 on political, racial, or religious grounds, and their descendants, were eligible to regain it. After vowing that "no German may be extradited to a foreign country," Article 16(2) promises that "persons persecuted on political grounds shall enjoy the right of asylum." Besides seeking to rectify the sins of the past and atone for Nazi violations of international norms, these provisions assured ethnic Germans expelled from east Europe and Germans in the Soviet zone of occupation that they had a home in western Germany.

In the circumstances of the late 1940s such provisions seemed reasonable. Even though they would have preferred to push the burden onto others (see A. Merritt and R. Merritt 1970:18–21), West Germans tolerated the influx of ethnic Germans expelled from east Europe (*Vertriebene* or *Umsiedler*) or fleeing from there (*Aussiedler*), as well as refugees from eastern Germany (*Flüchtlinge* or *Übersiedler*). By September 1950 the number of such immigrants had reached 9.6 million, almost one-fifth of the popu-

7. Article 12a(1) states that young men "may be required to serve" in the Bundeswehr, but Article 12a(2) adds: "A person who refuses, on the grounds of conscience, to render war service involving the use of arms may be required to render a substitute service."

lation of the FRG. Similarly, in 1948–1949 it was simple to offer refuge to those suffering persecution. Few west Europeans would find such an opportunity either useful or attractive, the Red Army prevented east Europeans from exploiting the offer, and few people from the rest of the world were likely to make their way to West Germany. As we shall see, however, the chickens hatched in 1948–1949 would come home to roost after the cold war ended four decades later.

Restitution and Reparations. The FRG has made serious—although, critics say, nevertheless inadequate—efforts to compensate the victims of Nazi crimes. Among the programs:[8]

- Germans who remained in western Germany after the war received compensation for wartime losses of property and personal injuries, loss of soldiers and other family members killed in the war (estimated at $830 million in 1950), war-related disabilities, public welfare, and restitution or compensation for confiscated property.
- Later provisions gave restitution and indemnification to foreigners and Germans who did not return to Germany after 1945.
- Refugees and expellees, nearly ten million of whom had entered the FRG by 1950, received immediate aid (*Soforthilfe*), "equalization of burdens" (*Lastenausgleich*) payments amounting to perhaps $380 million annually, and public welfare estimated at $120 million in 1948–1950 and $240 million in 1952 alone—with total direct costs for 1951 estimated at $880 million and indirect costs (for example, additional school building) at $740 million.
- Western countries, by the end of 1949, obtained reparations amounting to $517 million (in 1938 dollars), including $293 million in confiscated German assets abroad, $147 million in industrial equipment, and $43 million in German merchant vessels.
- From the Luxembourg Agreement of September 1952 Israel received $820 million in foreign aid in 1953–1965; other agreements accounted for $620 million in 1961–1979 (Feldman 1984:89–121).
- Germans who in 1933–1945 lost homes and commercial buildings in the area that later became the GDR could seek redress from the German government. An agreement with the United States in May 1992 extended this possibility to non-Germans.[9]

8. Data here are from Merkatz and Metzner (1954), Balabkins (1971), Feldman (1984), and elsewhere. For the first two decades after the currency reform I use the (rounded) exchange rate of DM 4.2 to the dollar.

9. The U.S.-German agreement signed in May 1992 gave the United States $190 million to distribute to Holocaust victims and their heirs. This program proved to be problematic. Although the U.S. government did not issue application forms until Sep-

The financial figures make it clear that the West German government paid dearly for World War II—and so does the FRG's acquiescence in the loss of its eastern territories. Some of the sums were doubtless comparable to those borne by combatants that had no responsibility for the war's outbreak. A state that repudiated its guilt might have refused to pay some of the other costs, and even one that acknowledged its responsibility might have tried to avoid paying. In short, it is possible to fault the FRG for not having given enough to Nazi victims or for having made excessively cumbersome the means to gain such assistance, but the government deserves credit for at least trying to recompense some of those who had suffered so grievously.

West Germans have sometimes had difficulty accommodating their principles and their practices of popular democracy. Adenauer, for instance, expressed strong support for civil liberties, yet in his own administration he brooked no opposition on important issues. Officials who flouted this principle were soon replaced. In 1958 Adenauer tested constitutional principles when he apparently decided to seek the presidency contrary to terms of the Basic Law.[10] Similarly, when the news magazine *Der Spiegel* uncovered confidential information about disarray in the new German military, Adenauer authorized heavy-handed retaliation that caused a worldwide scandal (Bunn 1968).

Some segments of the populace have also accepted only halfheartedly the practical dimensions of civil rights. We have seen that substantial numbers of AMZON Germans were willing to curtail the rights of communists to speak on the radio. Some Germans have since found it difficult to cope with those who seemed to threaten the peace, if not the political system itself, as occurred during the student demonstrations of the late 1960s. As in the United States, France, and elsewhere, the German police were baffled when confronting unruly protesters who were intelligent and came from comfortable if not wealthy homes. It took them years to learn new strategies of mob control. More recently, ugly attacks by right-wing extremists against foreign workers and asylum seekers have sometimes won popular support.

How do we interpret such incidents? Are civil liberties and the rights of

---

tember and neither government publicized the program widely, the deadline for submitting claims was 31 December 1992. Worse, lawyers for claimants complained that the ceiling for an individual compensation was a small percentage of the current value of the property claimed, and that the FRG government, which would be the recipient of settled property, was pressuring claimants to take minimal cash payments instead of suing for restitution (Holmes 1992).

10. Public opinion surveys his party commissioned (see Neumann and Noelle 1961/1962) contributed to his decision to abort his candidacy.

foreigners endangered in the Federal Republic of Germany? Earlier findings suggested that at war's end perhaps one in six Germans actively supported Nazism as a concept. This number dropped by the occupation's end to one in eight and is even smaller today—perhaps one in twenty or even forty, comparable to the percentage who support similar concepts in other Western democracies. But repudiating Nazism in favor of democratic principles does not mean that Germans accept uncritically everything the FRG does. On the one hand, substantial numbers oppose a particular administration and particular policies, and some blame the "Bonn system" for what they see as a popular malaise.[11] A recent general survey about satisfaction with Germany's political system found growing unrest (Deutsche 1992). In the western provinces the percentage who expressed satisfaction declined from 78 percent in 1991 to 65 percent a year later, and in the eastern provinces, formerly part of the GDR, the percentage dropped from 52 to 48 percent.[12]

On the other hand, surveys over the years have consistently shown that most Germans believe that democracy has taken root in German soil. In September 1953, 44 percent of a West German sample said that democracy in West Germany had become stronger in the course of the few years previous (5 percent thought it weaker and 18 percent about the same), and more than three-quarters of those who expressed opinions believed that Germans could govern themselves democratically (HIC-191; for notations see Chapter 4, note 1). Surveys in mid-1954 revealed that, by a ratio of more than five to one, West Germans were satisfied with the progress that the FRG was making on the road to freedom and independence (HIC-202). Four decades later neither party leaders nor political pollsters even address the prospects for substantial changes in the FRG's governmental structure. From the popular perspective it is not the structure of the system that is problematic but rather the ways in which human beings manipulate the system for their own ends.

11. Such Germans found a kindred spirit in H. Ross Perot, who in the U.S. presidential election of 1992 steadily attacked the "mess in Washington" rather than coming up with concrete proposals for change.

12. The reasons for east-west variation are too numerous for analysis here. One point nevertheless bears mention: support in the eastern provinces for the Party of Democratic Socialism (PDS), successor to the communist Socialist Unity Party (SED), has hovered between 9 and 14 percent. As new problems have bedeviled what had promised to be a quick and painless merger, eastern Germans have expressed doubt about the inherent efficacy of the German federal system—in the October 1994 national election the PDS garnered 0.9 percent of the vote in the western provinces, 17.6 percent in the eastern provinces, and 4.4 percent overall—but few want a return to the communist-ruled GDR.

A Peaceable Germany?

German leaders after 1949 were motivated not only to get their house in order but also to regain respectability in the international community. For centuries German governments had had rocky relations with their neighbors. The last two wars initiated by Germany also involved the world outside Europe. But World War II and the dawn of the nuclear age made it evident that the time had come to forge a less violent world, one in which the nations and nation-states of the world could coexist peaceably.

That goal demanded that Germany proceed in two directions simultaneously. One required that the country come to terms with its own neighbors. Some neighbors and even many eastern Germans had been lopped off the European map, but it still made sense for Germans to encourage and even take the lead in integrating western Europe. The other requirement was for German security. The world was still a dangerous place, one in which powerful states might find it worthwhile to gamble for global control. No German government could ignore such realities. The trick was to find ways to protect Germany from potential predators without alarming neighbors who had in the past suffered from German predations.

Linkage in Europe

The Adenauer government considered accommodating the European states, especially France, as a primary challenge. Whether Britain would play an active role in European affairs was unclear, and Adenauer reasoned that any progress must have Franco-German cooperation as its linchpin. His strategy was to endorse French initiatives and accept the French lead in matters that affected the continental powers. By the time Adenauer left the chancellorship in 1963, he and Charles de Gaulle had made great strides toward solidifying a Franco-German entente—an entente whose ultimate goal, bolstered by Italy and the Benelux countries, was the economic if not political unification of western Europe.

Throughout the early 1950s West Germans supported steps toward a united West Europe. Surveys in September 1952, March 1954, and June 1954 found an average of 74 percent supporting such an idea and only 7 percent opposing it (HIC-200). Presented with a proposal for a single common government to make decisions only on matters concerning West Europe as a whole, 74 percent in September 1952 and 72 percent in June 1954 favored it and 4 and 7 percent, respectively, opposed it. Those who accepted the proposal were then asked whether they would continue to support a common West European government if its decisions, made on behalf of the whole community, should affect West Germany adversely. An average of 82 percent of the supporters (60 percent of the entire samples) endorsed this "Europeanist" notion, and 8 percent opposed it. The more mobilized sectors of the population—men, the well educated, the wealthy—were most in favor of such a political union.

The most significant practical step toward West European unity during this period was the European Coal and Steel Community (ECSC). Proposed in May 1950 by the French foreign minister, Maurice Schuman, and signed in April 1951, the agreement creating ECSC went into effect in July 1952 after first the FRG and then France, Italy, and the Benelux countries ratified it. Two months later 79 percent of a national West German sample said that they had heard of the Schuman plan, and about two-thirds of these (53 percent of the entire sample) were aware that it dealt with coal and steel or with heavy industry in general (HIC-169S). Of this percentage, in turn, more than half (28 percent of the entire sample) favored West German participation in ECSC, and less than a third (15 percent) opposed it. When all respondents were informed of the nature of the plan, half were in favor of West German participation and one in five opposed it.

Other issues stirred more debate. The European Defense Community was twice the source of moderate West German resentment toward France—first, in the months before the contractual agreement of May 1952, when it appeared to some that the French were planning to use EDC to limit West Germany's autonomy; and second, from late 1953 to the summer of 1954, when the French were resisting ratification. More than half of German respondents who expressed opinions (41 percent of the whole sample) said that France, if it failed to ratify EDC, should be disregarded in future defense planning (HIC-200).[13] The Saar question was also divisive. Barely half of a West German sample knew about an agreement signed in October 1954, which called for "Europeanizing" the Saar before a plebiscite rather than returning it outright to Germany (HIC-206), but more than half of those who expressed opinions said that the Bundestag should reject the agreement. More than half of the total sample felt that France's claims in the Saar were not at all justified (compared with 3 percent who termed them predominantly or fully justified).

West German problems regarding EDC and the Saar would not stand in

13. Should the French turn down EDC (which they later did), then another 15 percent in the June 1954 survey (HIC-200) would have had West Germany give up all plans for Germany's rearmament and 18 percent would have had West Germany make renewed efforts to induce France to give its approval to EDC.

the way of further progress toward European unity. Nor, as opinion data obtained over the years by the Institut für Demoskopie show, did the West German public abandon the idea. Four general principles emerge from those data: First, most respondents had sketchy images rather than solid information about what the European movement involved. Second, they nevertheless advocated further institutionalizing the European community.[14] Third, they supported efforts specifically to promote political integration.[15] Fourth, they were increasingly pessimistic about the prospect of seeing in their lifetime a United States of Europe.[16] Today European linkage involves a wide range of contentious economic and political issues. The FRG is nevertheless in the forefront of those states pushing toward greater European integration.

Military Alliance with the West

Breaking up the German military, as we have seen, was the Allies' first goal upon occupying the country. They shared a general European sentiment that the Prussian Army and its successor, the Wehrmacht—especially as fine-tuned by the likes of a Frederick the Great or Bismarck or Hitler—were responsible for centuries of conflict and three generations of major conflagration.[17] They vowed to prevent any further scourge from threatening the world's security. And the Allies found support from the German people for the goal of a nonmilitarized Germany.[18]

Yet less than a half-decade later the four wartime Allies were planning the rearmament of two separate Germanies.[19] Virtually every pretense of

14. In four surveys conducted from September 1955 to May 1967 (IfD-2:342, 4:454), the number prepared to cast a referendum vote for a United States of Europe rose from 68 to 78 percent (averaging 75 percent); 6 percent said that they would vote against the idea.

15. Five surveys conducted between March 1970 and March 1979 (IfD-3:544, 5:561, 8:598) found a stable average of 71 percent favoring and 10 percent opposing the idea of transforming the Common Market into the political arm of a United States of Europe.

16. The share of optimistic views declined from 41 percent in February 1953 to 31 percent in March 1979 (averaging 34 percent); the share of pessimistic attitudes, averaging 39 percent, rose from 29 to 47 percent (IfD-2:342, 4:453, 6:286, 8:598).

17. The same sentiment also led the Allies in 1945 to break up the old Prussian provinces.

18. To this it must be added that many in occupied Germany expected eventually to see a new German army. Surveys in April and August 1946 found respondents about evenly split in addressing the statement, "Germany should be allowed to have an army in order to defend itself against aggression from other European nations" (45 and 44 percent, respectively, accepted the proposition, and 46 and 47 percent saw no such need).

19. In the strictest sense the term "rearmament" cannot be applied to a political

inter-Allied cooperation had been abandoned, and by late 1949 American military officers, perceiving a Soviet threat to west Europe, were agitating for a West German contribution to the Western defense structure (Martin 1963). In a December interview with an American journalist, Chancellor Adenauer let it be known that, although he opposed creation of a separate West German army, he would favor participation by German military units in some type of Western defense system (Steininger 1989). After the outbreak of the Korean war in 1950, German rearmament was a foregone conclusion; the only questions concerned timing and form.

Independent German military. Polled immediately after Adenauer's press statement in December 1949, three of five AMZON Germans said that they opposed the establishment of any army in West Germany, and only one in four favored such a plan (HIC-9). By spring, however, the ratio of those opposed to those favoring fell to 56:39, and shortly after the outbreak of hostilities in Korea, it dropped still further to 45:43—a slim plurality still opposed to an independent West German army (HIC-36). Those who favored an army cited security (16 percent) and, more specifically, protection from the Soviet Union (14 percent). Those opposed expressed an antipathy toward war (15 percent), fear based on the "loss of loved ones in the last war" (8 percent), and the observation that Allied controls would prevent the FRG from organizing an army (8 percent).[20]

The indecisiveness or contention implicit in these findings was more apparent than real. A clear-cut majority (63 percent) of AMZON respondents, for example, felt that West Germany could not be defended without German help (HIC-36). Almost half of those who opposed an army in August 1950 were willing to accept it as part of a more general West European army—yielding a total of almost two-thirds of the sample who were amenable to some form of rearmament. At issue in West German public opinion was the organizational framework for rearmament.

Atlantic pact. By this time the main line of discussion among the Tripartite Allies and in the FRG was the integration of German units into a broader, supranational military arrangement. Whether out of conviction or practical necessity, the West German public quickly endorsed this new

---

entity that did not exist before 1949 and had never been armed. The term is nevertheless generally used in discussing the creation of a West German military establishment after 1949.

20. A series of thirteen surveys conducted by the Institut für Demoskopie from November 1950 to February 1955 (IfD-1:372–373) yielded an average of 41 percent who favored an independent German army and 40 percent who opposed it. The periods of ascendancy for an independent army were the months before the adoption of a contractual agreement (see below) and the months between August 1953 and November 1954— that is, when EDC was undergoing severe criticism and eventual rejection in France.

Figure 13.1

Participation in Defense of Western Europe, 1950-1955

Questions: (Aug. 1950-Feb. 1952) Supposing West Germany would join the Atlantic Pact and be asked . . .
to participate in a general army for the defense of West Europe. Would you favor or oppose?

(Feb. 1952-Jan. 1955) Are you, in general, for or against West Germany's participation in the
defense of Europe?

(Feb.-Aug. 1954) In general, are you for or against West Germany's participation in the EDC,
that is, the West European Defense Community?

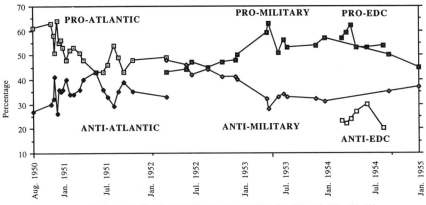

Source: HIC-58, 60, 64, 69, 80, 88, 94, 117, 130, 141, 144, 168, 177, 180, 193, 196, 199, 200, 203.

idea. Those who had approved in August 1950 (HIC-36) the creation of a West German army indicated by a ratio of almost two to one that they preferred that West German units be part of a broader Western defense arrangement rather than independent.[21]

A proposal under consideration in 1950–1951 would have brought the FRG into the North Atlantic Treaty Organization (NATO), thereby requiring contribution to a general army for the defense of Europe. Figure 13.1 shows that, in twenty-one surveys between August 1950 and late February 1952, an average of 52 percent of those interviewed favored NATO membership and 35 percent opposed it. High points in the curve occur after the initial phase of the Korean war and shortly after the Chinese army began to push United Nations troops southward, suggesting that fear of communist aggression underlay support for a strengthened NATO. The overall trend of declining support for a tie to NATO, on the other hand may be attributed to increasing Social Democratic opposition to any German rearmament whatever (although substantial numbers of poll respondents

21. In responding to several questions asked in this survey, only one in eight advocated a completely independent West German army. As note 20 suggests, however, the percentage open to this alternative was considerably higher.

who identified themselves as Social Democrats continued to support all such plans), or to growing interest in a West European rather than Atlantic defense structure.

West European army. During most of the early 1950s, solid majorities of West German respondents favored some form of participation by FRG troops in the defense of West Europe (Figure 13.1). But in what form? The plan that captured most attention proposed a European Defense Community (EDC), which would integrate twelve West German divisions into a European army. Proposed by René Pléven in late 1950 and subsequently endorsed by American leaders, EDC took shape in an agreement initialed in May 1952 and ratified by the Bundestag in March 1953.[22] The French parliament refused ratification in August 1954, however, and EDC died quickly.

West Germans had mixed emotions about EDC. On the one hand, it would have provided a framework within which to create a military—which West Germans increasingly thought was vital to the attainment of full sovereignty. On the other hand, many suspected that the original EDC proposals were really designed to keep West Germany perpetually under Allied—specifically, in this case, French—control, and that the FRG would be denied equality. Chancellor Adenauer fought hard for a contractual agreement with the Tripartite Powers that would ensure equality. The agreement was granted in May 1952, but throughout the period when EDC was under debate, most West Germans who expressed an opinion preferred a West German national army that would participate in the defense of West Europe (averaging 44 percent in eight surveys from November 1951 to August 1954) to the integration of German divisions in a general West European army (25 percent; HIC-117, 131, 196, 200, 202).

Before the contractual agreement was signed, West Germans voiced their suspicion in the form of generalized opposition to participation in West European defense (Figure 13.1). In the three months before May 1952, an average of 45 percent opposed such participation, compared with 44 percent who favored it (HIC-141, 180). During the negotiations, 55 percent said that they would favor some form of participation, provided that it guaranteed the FRG's equality of treatment; 14 percent expressed opposition even with such a guarantee (HIC-135). Support for defense participation edged up to a high point in April 1953, when 63 percent favored and 28 percent opposed it (HIC-177-S). Then support declined fairly steadily through January 1955, when 45 percent favored participation and 37 percent opposed (HIC-207).

22. The EDC treaty was tied up in West German constitutional litigation for more than a year.

The decline after mid-1953 coincided with the growing intensity of debate in France on the advisability of rearming West Germany in any circumstances. But even at the end of the decline, a majority of those who gave opinions favored some form of West German participation in West European defense. EDC itself, moreover, was popular after the Bundestag ratification—in part, no doubt, because West Germans looked favorably on any policy advocated by the government, and also in part because respondents saw it as a means to accomplish full sovereignty for the FRG.[23] Even this support declined in the months before the French parliament defeated EDC (Figure 13.1).[24]

Rearmament under NATO. The failure of EDC sent Western leaders in search of a new plan for West German rearmament. Conferring in Paris in October 1954, they agreed to end the occupation of West Germany, revitalize the Western European Union, and permit the creation of a virtually independent West German defense force under NATO command. The new plan corresponded closely to the German preference for a national army that would participate in the defense of West Europe rather than the integration of German divisions in a general West European army (see HIC-202).

Subsequent surveys found continued support among West Germans for some kind of military contribution. Was it necessary, they were asked in January 1955, for the FRG to have an army? Regardless of whether or not they personally liked the idea, 60 percent thought an army necessary and only 25 percent did not (HIC-207).[25] Moreover, although differences in

23. In June 1951, three in five favored the FRG's adherence to the Atlantic Pact and, with it, participation in a general army for the defense of Europe, and half as many opposed it. Four in five said that they would either welcome their government's decision to accept such a proposition (22 percent), accept it however unenthusiastically (45 percent), or oppose it without doing anything about it (13 percent). Only two percent said they would actively oppose such a decision (HIC-88). Several weeks later, 26 percent called themselves enthusiastic supporters, 45 percent passive supporters, 14 percent passive opponents, and again 2 percent termed themselves active opponents (HIC-94).

24. In five surveys from late February to June 1954, an average of 57 percent favored participation in EDC (28 percent very much so and 29 percent somewhat), and 25 percent opposed it (14 percent very much so and 11 percent somewhat). In late August, just before the French parliament turned down EDC, extreme opinion at both ends of the scale had declined: 23 percent favored participation very much and 31 percent somewhat (a total of 54 percent), and 10 percent opposed it very much and another 10 percent somewhat (a total of 20 percent). The number of those expressing no opinion increased from an average of 18 percent in the first half of 1954 to 26 percent in August (HIC-196, 199, 200, 202).

25. Sixteen percent said it was absolutely necessary, 16 percent very necessary, and 28 percent somewhat necessary; 11 percent termed it not so necessary and 14 percent not at all necessary.

age, party identification, religion, and other demographic elements colored the way people responded to this question, majorities in each of fifty-one categories of respondents listed in HICOG survey reports recognized the need for a German military, even Social Democrats, 54 percent of whom agreed. Similar although smaller majorities in all categories of partisanship (except those who expressed no party preference) thought the federal government should have the right to draft men, if necessary, for service in the new army.

With the promulgation of the Paris agreements in May 1955, the Federal Republic of Germany was well on its way toward rearming—with the explicit blessing of the Tripartite Allies and the support of its own population (HIC-213). What had been unthinkable ten years earlier was now accomplished fact. On 1 January 1956 the German Defense Forces, or Bundeswehr, formally took shape.

Taming the Military

What made this shift in policies acceptable was a concomitant shift in the focus of the new German military. The first obligation of the Bundeswehr was to ensure Germans and the world that it would contribute to both democracy and peace. Germans had already suffered enough from the "state within the state" that was the Prussian Army, from the Imperial Reichswehr, which preserved the privileges of the elite by muzzling the rights of the masses, and from the Weimar Republic's Reichswehr, which Hitler easily transformed into a political tool. Postwar Germans wanted a military that would be under tight external control, responsible to civilian authorities, and linked to the Western defense system—an integral part of the Allied architecture for European security.

The issue of linkage had been resolved by inclusion of the FRG in NATO. From the West German perspective, then, the central question was how to create a military establishment at the same time effective and non-threatening to Germany's new allies, one that would not raise the specter of Hitler's war-machine-run-wild. Effectiveness the Bundeswehr would have to develop itself—and attaining it proved to be more difficult than experts had anticipated. But what about the Bundeswehr's role (and not solely its image) as an agent for democracy and peace?

The FRG adopted two fundamental principles. First, the military would be under civilian control. The minister of defense is responsible to the indirectly elected chancellor and accountable to the directly elected Bundestag through its standing Defense Committee.[26] Second, military

---

26. Article 45a(2) of the Basic Law, adopted in March 1956, states: "The Committee

personnel, officers and common soldiers alike, are viewed as "citizens in uniform." That is, a uniform means neither that a man can lord it over civilians nor that he has given up his basic rights as a citizen of the FRG.[27] The principle of "citizens in uniform" had several implications from the beginning, when a Personnel Screening Committee (*Personalgutachterausschuss*) evaluated all applicants to military positions at the rank of colonel and above—most specifically in terms of their democratic attitudes and behaviors.[28] All commissioned and noncommissioned officers periodically participate in seminars at the Armed Forces Academy for Internal Leadership (*Schule der Bundeswehr für innere Führung*) that stress the practical meaning of the "citizens in uniform" concept. Another feature of the new Bundeswehr is the role of the Parliamentary Commissioner (*Wehrbeauftragter des Deutschen Bundestages*), who evaluates, reports on, and if appropriate rectifies any complaint that the basic rights of any military personnel have been violated.[29] The commissioner's annual reports to the Bundestag serve to monitor the state of democracy in West Germany's armed forces.

None of these procedures has worked perfectly. The Personnel Screening Committee clashed with the defense minister over some candidates, the idea of internal leadership was ignored by some junior officers seeking military advancement, noncommissioned officers occasionally maltreated their draftees, and, some years after the first Wehrbeauftragter had to resign in disgrace, his successor publicly criticized the Bundeswehr for failing to live up to democratic norms. To make matters worse, the federal government let the Bundeswehr lag as an effective military unit for a time, and when a news magazine exposed the military's weaknesses, the government's excessive intervention alarmed civil libertarians everywhere (Bunn 1968).

Over the course of four decades, though, the Bundeswehr has fulfilled its primary mission: to create a fighting force that is at once effective and firmly under civilian control. The federal government has eased the military's image problem by expanding service alternatives for conscientious

---

on Defense shall . . . have the rights of a committee of investigation. Upon the motion of one fourth of its members it shall have the duty to make a specific matter the subject of investigation."

27. Article 12a(1) of the Basic Law effectively prohibits women from serving in the Bundeswehr.

28. Sutton (1960) reports that, by the time the Personnel Screening Committee had completed its work in August 1957, it had turned down 100 of 600 cases and accepted 486 candidates unconditionally and 14 conditionally.

29. The role of Wehrbeauftragter, patterned after the Swedish Ombudsman, was codified in March 1956 as Article 45b of the Basic Law.

objectors, granting some latitude to the peace movement, and, until a united Berlin was integrated into the FRG in 1990, permitting young men to move to West Berlin, where they avoided otherwise obligatory military service. Each step helped lift from the FRG's armed forces any stigma from the Nazi past.

Some even say that the FRG has gone too far in asserting its nonaggression. Article 87a(1) of the Basic Law, adopted in March 1956, establishes that "the Federation shall build up Armed Forces for defense purposes," and Article 87a(2) adds that "apart from defense, the Armed Forces may only be used to the extent explicitly permitted by this Basic Law." In November 1982 the Kohl government, prodded by Foreign Minister Hans-Dieter Genscher of the FDP, interpreted these provisions to mean that the FRG could not provide military assistance to the United States, at that time concerned about imbalance in the Iran-Iraq war.[30] The SPD opposition was delighted with this narrow reading. In subsequent years Kohl and other prominent Germans drummed it into the German public consciousness. The Kohl coalition used the principle to justify its refusal to send troops to support the United Nations–sponsored expulsion of Iraq from Kuwait in 1991 and applied the same creed to sit out the U.N.-sanctioned humanitarian intervention into Somalia two years later. After criticism at home and abroad, however, the government reversed its decision in mid-1993 and, after a favorable ruling by the Federal Constitutional Court, sent 1,500 soldiers to Somalia.

The claim that the FRG is constitutionally prohibited from responding with force of arms ignores other dimensions of the issue (Kielinger 1991). Article 24(2) of the Basic Law, for example, states: "For the maintenance of peace, the Federation may enter a system of mutual collective security." Article 43 of the United Nations Charter, which the FRG eagerly accepted in 1973, clearly obligates members to join in U.N. peacekeeping missions.[31] These provisions justified a German role in both the Persian Gulf

30. The prominent German newspaper editor Josef Joffe (1992) wrote that the Kohl government's evasion in 1982 was "based on a constitutional myth" and nothing more than "a nice but cunning way of refusing the Americans' demands for assistance." Popular support for a German role in U.N. peacekeeping operations diminished from June to October 1992, the latter EMNID survey taking place when prospects were growing for intervention into Bosnia-Herzegovina and Somalia (Asylstreit 1992:61; FDP-Wähler 1992:44; Schöppner 1992). Asked what Germany should contribute to international peacekeeping activities, 38 and 46 percent, respectively, wanted to restrict it to the defense of Germany in the framework of NATO; others were willing to accept a noncombative (44 and 37 percent) or combative role (14 and 15 percent). In October 1992 western Germans were more restrictive than eastern Germans (63 to 38 percent); and SPD supporters were slightly more restrictive (51 percent) than the general population.

31. Article 43(1) of the U.N. Charter states: "All Members of the United Nations, in order to contribute to the maintenance of international peace and security, undertake to

war and Somalia, if not also the protection of Bosnia and Herzegovina from Serbia. Critics at home and abroad have bitterly complained of apparent German duplicity. The more cynical among them expected a coalition to develop between fiscally conservative Christian Democrats and pacifist Social Democrats that would significantly modify Germany's acceptance of Article 24(2) and force the FRG to renege on its U.N. obligation. A more recent Federal Constitutional Court ruling in July 1994 explicitly gave the government approval for overseas military operations after gaining the Bundestag's support.

The Continuing Challenge

The four goals of the Adenauer government—compensating for German crimes, guaranteeing civil liberties and other democratic processes, coming to terms with the FRG's western European neighbors, and ensuring West German security from external threat within an internationally constructive environment—were in place by 1955 when the Tripartite Allies granted the Federal Republic virtually complete sovereignty.[32] In normal circumstances observers might have concluded that West Germany had rejoined the powers (Deutsch and Edinger 1959).

But the circumstances, as we have seen, were not normal. Leaving aside complaints about the FRG lodged during cold war years by hardcore ideologues, the world pays close attention to what happens in Germany. Journalists, academics, political officers, and others are quick to remark on events that recall the dark past. The harshest critics say that modern West Germany should provide more restitution and compensation than it does, that an apparently democratic system is a thin veneer covering antidemocratic inclinations, and that the FRG's push for West European integration is merely a sophisticated version of Hitler's thrust for European domination. Writers have often seen a chimera in place of the real emergent Germany.

By the same token, West Germans have not always been their own best friends. Individuals have sometimes shown a remarkable lack of sensi-

---

make available to the Security Council, on its call and in accordance with a special agreement or agreements, armed forces, assistance, and facilities, including rights of passage, necessary for the purpose of maintaining international peace and security" (Arne 1948:145).

32. What remained were various emergency provisions, mostly assumed by the FRG through constitutional amendments in 1968, and Quadripartite functions such as control over Berlin, the Berlin air corridor, and convicted war criminals still in the Spandau prison (the last of whom, Rudolf Hess, died in 1987). Quadripartite agreements at the "Two-plus-Four" meetings in spring 1990 established the FRG's complete sovereignty.

tivity to the national image. In winter 1989–1990, for example, when Chancellor Kohl was trying to ram through German unification, Polish representatives repeatedly asked whether he intended to honor long-standing agreements with both the FRG and the GDR recognizing the German-Polish border on the Oder and Neisse rivers. Kohl, responding like a cagey used car salesman, seemed bent on obfuscation. Political analysts deemed his evasiveness a tactical ploy to weaken right-wing opposition—even within his own coalition—to a unification that did not return to Germany the territories east of the Oder and Neisse. The strategy left the Poles to wonder whether a unified Germany would be a revanchist Germany. National and international outrage mounted until Kohl acknowledged that the FRG would honor the previous territorial commitments. The stance was apparently what he had planned from the outset, but the circuitous route cost Germany in the international environment.

Another example of insensitivity occurred after the Gulf War, when U.S. intelligence services reported that German firms had sold Iraq poison gas and material for building nuclear weapons (Lewis 1992). The German government denied the allegation, apparently before carefully investigating it. By the time the FRG admitted that German industry had violated national laws in shipping such goods and announced that those responsible would be prosecuted, the damage to the country's international reputation had been done.

Or consider the international censure in late summer 1992, when high-level German business and government leaders planned a major celebration in Peenemünde to honor the fiftieth anniversary of the flight of Nazi Germany's first guided missile. Historically minded critics were quick to point out that the Peenemünde facility had used slave labor and had killed ten thousand Jews, Poles, and others (Neufeld 1995). The bitter English response also took organizers by surprise. Queen Elizabeth was scheduled to visit Germany in mid-October, and London and Bonn exchanged a flurry of official communications. Indicative of popular British sentiments was the press response. Almost the entire front page of London's *Daily Mirror* on 26 September was devoted to pictures of Hitler and a V2 rocket in flight, under the headline "*Donner und Blitzen!* Fury as Germans celebrate 50th anniversary of murderous V2 rocket." The international furor and protests against the event by Germans themselves persuaded the government to cancel it.[33]

33. Ironically, the centerpiece of the queen's visit was a trip to Dresden, where she sought to ameliorate bruised German feelings over a statue being erected on London's Parliament Square of Air Vice Marshall Sir Arthur Harris. "Bomber" Harris had organized the destructive aerial attack of 13–14 February 1945 on the virtually unarmed city.

Related and equally troublesome is the apparent slowness of the German government to formulate creative responses to national crises. Other governments share this shortcoming, of course. It took the United States more than a century to address the social demands deriving from the Civil War, and the former Great Powers have been slow to absorb the policy implications of their diminishing status. Such examples suggest that responsiveness is particularly slow among political authorities who are not in full accord with the mission assigned them either by legislation, court decision, or changes in international politics. The same pattern is visible in the difficulty the West German government encountered in the 1960s and 1970s in coping first with the student protest movement and then with the Baader-Meinhof gang, the Red Army Faction (RAF), and similar terrorist groups.

The most recent threat to German democracy emerged after the collapse of east European communism in the late 1980s and the rapid disintegration after summer 1989 of the German Democratic Republic. Newly opened borders inspired a mass migration of easterners into the FRG. In the best of circumstances such a population movement can tax any government's ability to meet public needs. The German case was more problematic, however. The country had suddenly to deal with sentiments and practicalities that the cold war conflict had masked. It had to confront virtually invisible but nevertheless overwhelming economic differences between eastern and western Germans. And it had to answer for a new time the timeless question: What is the German nation and what is it to become?[34] Is it to retain and strengthen its cultural and social distinctiveness? Or is it to accept the influx of immigrants who will inevitably challenge that heritage?

Ethnic Germans. Part of the migration problem of the 1990s had its roots in the attitudes and policies of the late 1940s. Among the tasks that the Parliamentary Council's constitution drafters took on in 1948–1949 were to ensure Germans living in the Soviet zone of occupation that the new West German state would not abandon them, to ease the assimilation of ethnic Germans whom the east European states had expelled, to nullify

---

Karl J. Dersch, director of the firm German Aerospace (DASA) and chairman of the organizing committee for the Peenemünde commemoration, was later found to be flying in his garden an imperial naval war flag, the black, white, and red banner illegally but commonly used by right-wing extremists and skinheads. His claim that he did not know the flag's meaning notwithstanding, he was dismissed from DASA.

34. The German nationalist Ernst Moritz Arndt phrased this question best in his patriotic song of 1813, *Was ist des deutschen Vaterland?* (What is the Germans' Fatherland?). The question—which Arndt answered in terms of language and culture: Germany is wherever Germans live—became a catchword for almost two centuries of German writers concerned with their national identity.

Nazi laws that had deprived Jews and others of their German citizenship, and to demonstrate to the world West Germany's intent to pursue liberal policies toward other peoples abused by their governments. These tasks were embodied particularly in Article 16 of the Basic Law.

While the formula written into the Basic Law served immediate purposes, it was a Pandora's box that would be opened along with eastern European borders. Article 16(1) stated: "No one may be deprived of his German citizenship." This was meant to restore citizenship to those from whom it had been taken away, East Germans, and ethnic Germans in east Europe who had streamed into West Germany after 1945. But who is an "ethnic German"? In principle it is anyone who can demonstrate the most tenuous German tie. And in principle, millions of ethnic Germans had the right, in perpetuity, to return "home to the fatherland." In 1948–1949 the practical side to such principles seemed more tiresome than germane.

By 1990 shifting tides in world politics put these principles in a different focus. Until then, Stalinism in east Europe made it risky for ethnic Germans who had not been expelled in the immediate postwar months to assert their ethnicity or to seek egress. The FRG's assertion of their right to do so may have scored propaganda points—especially in reinforcing the government's claim as the only legitimate successor of the Germany stripped of sovereignty by the Allies in 1945—but it accomplished little else. In the late 1980s borders were loosened both by political upheaval and by the willingness of economically strapped east European countries to ease emigration rules. The floodgates were opened for Poles whose grandfathers had served in the Prussian postal service or the Wehrmacht, for Volga Germans whose families had been in Russia for centuries, for Transylvanian Saxons, non-German spouses of ethnic Germans, and others with even more tenuous ties to the "fatherland." Their right to "regain" their citizenship in the FRG challenged the heart of Article 16(1).[35]

Asylum seekers. The second sentence of Article 16(2)—"Persons persecuted on political grounds shall enjoy the right of asylum"—was another time bomb. Who, political leaders might well have asked themselves in 1948–1949, was likely to seek political asylum in Germany? West Europeans? Some did, but most who sought work or new opportunities found the United States and Canada more attractive. East Europeans? Until 1989 few could cross East-West barriers. Third World citizens? It was difficult for them to get to Germany, and most could find refuge elsewhere. The right of asylum existed, but few used it.

35. Resettled ethnic Germans averaged 52,000 annually in 1979–1987 and then rose to 203,000 in 1988, 377,000 in 1989, 397,000 in 1990, and 222,000 in 1991. Of GDR citizens 344,000 fled or moved to the FRG in 1989, and 238,000 in the first half of 1990. (Data from the German Information Center, New York.)

Again changing circumstances turned what may have once seemed a harmless promise into a menace to the Federal Republic. The shift began in the late 1970s, when East German agents began to fly large numbers of Sri Lankans, Indians, Nigerians, and others into West Germany to seek political asylum. For the GDR this policy was doubly useful: it netted the government hard currencies from the airplane ticket sales, and it disrupted life in the FRG. The GDR's collapse in late 1989 ended this irritant, but at the same time open boundaries permitted people to use cheaper land routes to Germany—and the number doing so soared. From 1978 to 1988 an annual average of 61,000 foreigners applied for asylum in the FRG. But as the floodgates opened growing numbers of Romanian Gypsies, Russian Jews, Yugoslavs fleeing their troubled land, and Third World citizens made their way to German soil. In 1989 their number rose to 121,000, in 1990 to 194,000, in 1991 to 256,000, in 1992 to 438,000, and in 1993, when in mid-year tougher procedures were put in place, almost 323,000—more than a million in three years.

It was evident to German officials that many of those seeking asylum yearned not to breathe the invigorating air of freedom but rather to find work.[36] Legislation implementing Articles 16(2) and 19(4) nevertheless entitled each to a fair hearing. Applicants could expect to wait six months and sometimes longer for their hearings, but because they were denied employment during that time, they received FRG housing and subsistence allowances.[37] Should the claim for asylum status be denied—as happened in about nineteen of every twenty cases—then appeals might extend the case to as many as five years. Some whose asylum claims were denied were eventually deported. Many more simply disappeared into the FRG's porous environment—having cost the government tens and even hundreds of thousands of dollars in handling each claim.

Foreign contract laborers. West Germany's economic miracle added yet another dimension to the country's population dilemma. The FRG's economic growth in the 1950s was nourished by a constant influx of Germans fleeing the GDR. East German officials denounced the "headhunting" that was plundering the GDR economy, stopping it in 1961 with the Berlin Wall. But the West German economy still needed new workers. With the government's blessing, industries began to recruit foreign con-

36. The same could be said about the 3.1 million GDR citizens who had fled to West Germany in 1949–1961. Those who could demonstrate political exigencies got more federal funding and other perquisites, but those who could not make such claims were nevertheless permitted to remain as FRG citizens.

37. Art. 19(4) of the Basic Law states: "Should any person's rights [e.g., 'right of asylum,' as specified in Art 16(2)] be violated by public authority, recourse to the court shall be open to him."

tract laborers, euphemistically called guest workers. After completing
their contracts, most of the early arrivals—Italians, Yugoslavs, Greeks—
returned to homelands where new jobs were opening up. Another major
group of guest workers, however, Turks, found few such incentives. Though
encouraged in various ways by the German government to return home,
many chose to remain in Germany.[38] At the end of 1987, of 61.2 million
people living in the FRG, as many as 4.6 million were foreigners, a third of
them Turks.[39]

By 1990, the year of Germany's unification, its disruptive population
explosion—the influx of ethnic Germans and asylum seekers, the extended stays of guest workers—began to exacerbate other policy problems. The most significant of these was the unanticipatedly high cost of
unifying the country. West German planners for unification had counted
on a quick transfer of power, with conservative economic policies that
might cause modest dislocations. In fact, unified Germany soon faced
serious economic problems. Money was scarce: the government was committed to using all available resources—even increasing taxes—to refurbish industry and public services in the ex-GDR. Jobs were also scarce: in
the new federal provinces of eastern Germany the real rate of unemployment (that is, including those with make-work jobs or "training" positions) soared, reaching 40 percent in some locations. Many of the unemployed in both parts of Germany were young men with minimal education
and no marketable skills.

Presented such exciting if unsettling conditions, Germans responded
variously. Some envisioned a bright future for the unified Germany that
would eventually resolve its economic woes. Others worried about increased taxes and inflation. Still others were nationalistically offended.
They saw guest workers taking jobs from Germans, ethnic Germans on the
government dole but unable to speak German, economic opportunists
exploiting German largesse by claiming to be politically persecuted at
home, and withal "foreigners" on every street corner, in every department
store, at every park. Such images provoked those who had other grievances about life in the newly unified Germany. The volatility of the situation required the firm hand of government.

Instead of a firm hand the government provided handwringing, as
elected officials acknowledged solemnly that something had to be done.
Popular concern mounted, and so did that of publicists, ecclesiastics, and

38. Aliens who have lived in Germany for ten years may apply for naturalization;
when they have resided for fifteen years they are eligible for German citizenship.
39. United Germany at the end of 1992 had about 81 million inhabitants, 6.5 million
of them (8 percent) Turks. They are thus about three times more numerous in today's
FRG than were Jews in the Germany of 1931.

university professors, who expressed divergent assessments of the problem's nature and its most appropriate solution. The media, by nature dwelling on quotidian events, exacerbated the sense of danger. Change was needed, but few had a clue about what could be done that would not make the situation worse.

Meanwhile, some Germans began to demonstrate resolve if not political acumen. A few young people—aged fifteen to twenty-five, most of them men, though many were championed by women, unemployed or holding down dead-end jobs that left them with time on their hands, alienated from the world they "never made," sometimes organized as packs—adopted the population issue as a means to express their multifarious grievances.[40] They learned quickly that their protest, whatever its substance and whatever its goals, captured more attention if they could identify the "cause" with Nazism. Beating up a bank clerk or a shoemaker earned them little more than a citation from the local police. Beating up a foreigner and shouting "*Sieg Heil*," however, was almost certain to command front-page coverage in *Die Welt* or even *The New York Times*. Painting swastikas on Jewish gravestones had a similar effect.

The government thus faced a double threat. It had to deal forthrightly with the population transfer issue and neutralize the skinheads and other right-wing extremists. Because constitutional amendments require two-thirds majorities in both houses of parliament, any motion to revise Article 16 of the Basic Law needed support from majorities of both major parties, CDU/CSU and SPD. But the emotion-laden issue inspired bitter contestation both across the parties and within each, and among the general public as well.[41]

Three years of unusually acrimonious debate in public opinion and in the Bundestag led the major parties to agree in January 1993 on a revision of Article 16. The first paragraph of the revised article maintains in principle the right of the politically persecuted to asylum. Subsequent paragraphs, however, block access to citizens of European Union states or of any third country that guarantees the application of the Geneva Convention on Refugees and the European Convention on Human Rights.[42] The

40. "I, a stranger and afraid / In a world I never made"—A. E. Housman, *Last Poems*, 12.

41. An EMNID survey in November 1992 ("Bestie" 1992:65) reported that 10 percent of Germans wanted Article 16 eliminated, 46 percent wanted it limited, and 39 percent wanted it left alone. A similar question about Article 19, which guarantees asylum seekers the right of appeal, found 24 percent favoring elimination, 43 percent limitation, and 29 percent retention.

42. Bundestag legislation was to set up procedures for assessing whether a third state complies with the Geneva and European conventions. Article 16(5) sharply restricts applicants' right to appeal should their claims be denied.

new Article 16 may well reduce the number of asylum seekers and the cost of processing applications, and in the grand scope of governance the time required to forge an acceptable policy may seem reasonable.[43] In the immediate circumstance, however, the process of enacting yet another ad hoc constitutional change gave the FRG government a devastating appearance of dalliance.

The government moved just as slowly against the skinheads and other right-wing extremists, who were gaining worldwide attention by their unprovoked attacks—2,283 in 1992 and 1,322 the next year—against foreigners.[44] Domestic violence, particularly abuse of the defenseless, is an embarrassment for any democratic country. Germans, given their record under the Third Reich, are particularly sensitive about such behavior. At best, they fear, tolerance of such behavior creates the impression that xenophobia is a legitimate form of political expression in the FRG. At worst, it could unleash a chain of violence that can destroy a country's democratic processes—as indeed happened in the 1920s and 1930s.

Few Germans in the 1990s encourage violence against foreigners, homosexuals, Jews, and others. Perhaps 41,000 people are affiliated with right-wing extremist movements, but many more have attended their rallies and even chanted gleefully as skinheads tossed Molotov cocktails at foreigners' housing. In a survey conducted in September 1992, almost a third of young people aged sixteen to twenty-four endorsed right-wing extremist sentiments: 1 percent said they were ready to use force against foreigners, 13 percent accepted fascist ideas, and another 15 percent were clearly xenophobic (Fast 1992). Two months later almost one in three adult Germans moderately (27 percent) or decisively (5 percent) supported the rightists' call to expel foreigners ("Bestie" 1992:58). At roughly the same time a review of essays written by fourteen- to fifteen-year-olds in the eastern German city of Leipzig found that one in ten students was "uncompromisingly xenophobic" (Wüllenweber 1992).

Still, most Germans repudiate such stances. The same survey in which 32 percent supported the rightists' call to expel foreigners found more than twice as many moderately (24 percent) or decisively (43 percent)

43. The numbers seeking asylum dropped from 430,191 in 1992 to 322,599 in 1993 and 127,210 in 1994.
44. In late 1992 the Agency for Protection of the Constitution reported the existence of seventy-six extreme right-wing groups. In addition to about 5,000 skinheads and other "neo-Nazis," these included the National Front (24,000 members; banned in November 1992), the German Peoples Union (*Deutsche Volksunion*, or DVU; 25,000 members), the long-standing NPD (6,700 members), the German League for People and Homeland (*Deutsche Liga für Volk und Heimat*, or DL; 800 members), the German Alternative (*Deutsche Alternative*, or DA; 300 members; banned in December 1992), and the Viking Youth (*Wikinger Jugend*, banned in November 1994).

opposed to such a course ("Bestie" 1992). A follow-up survey days later, after a brutal murder of a Turkish woman and two children in the town of Mölln, showed support for expulsion dropping by more than a third.[45] And if 10 percent of Leipzig youths are outspokenly xenophobic, 90 percent are not. Beginning in autumn 1992 demonstrators in some of the largest rallies held in postwar Germany proclaimed the people's solidarity with foreigners and asylum seekers.

Many Germans remain unsettled by the government's apparent inability to deal decisively with the influx of foreigners. An EMNID survey in October 1992 (Asylstreit 1992:63) asked respondents to rank fifteen issues in terms of their relative importance. At the top of the ranking were "Fighting unemployment" (74 percent) and "Taking hold of the problem of foreigners" (73 percent). But widespread concern does not mean that Germans will act or even seek passively to pressure the government. Those who do, it can fairly be complained, initially encountered only lukewarm opposition from the German government. Too many local policemen, critics observed, stood idly by as gangs of skinheads firebombed foreign housing; criminal investigations proceeded too slowly, too many magistrates minimized the crimes, and the Federal Office for the Protection of the Constitution was slow in determining which groups were sufficiently anticonstitutional to be banned.

International crisis? As governmental indecisiveness fanned the flames of xenophobia in the Federal Republic, it also jeopardized the FRG's budding reputation for stability and tolerance of diversity. By the early 1990s the German press was reporting that:

- diplomatic personnel in Germany were expressing fear for their lives;
- violence in Berlin and its suburbs was spurring speculation on when—and whether—Germany's capital should be transferred to the city;
- Berlin's bid to host the Olympic Games in 2000 had encountered opposition, amid queries about the FRG's ability to guarantee the safety of the athletes (with sotto voce references to the bloody 1972 Olympiad in Munich);
- prominent Israeli and Jewish leaders around the world were again questioning whether it was safe for Jews to stay in Germany, and Turks in Germany and Ankara were asking a similar question about their own compatriots;

45. In the latter survey one in five moderately (15 percent) or decisively (4 percent) endorsed the demand, whereas four times that many moderately (8 percent) or decisively (69 percent) rejected it.

- world banking was reevaluating the wisdom of investing capital in Germany, especially in the five new federal provinces;
- business firms were becoming wary about long-term German production; and
- tourism was finding foreigners less interested in German sojourns.

The occurrence of such anomic outbreaks in other European countries, the United States, and elsewhere does not deflect global attention from those in Germany. Whether or not the facts justify the attention, whether or not the media blow isolated instances out of proportion, whether or not the FRG has made solid accomplishments in the pursuit of democracy and peaceability, foreign observers decry Germany's violent society and inability to govern. The foreign press has played a particularly devastating role. Previously, most media had treated the population issue as a peculiarity of German politics. But when gangs of youths using the symbols and rhetoric of Nazism began to beat asylum seekers and firebomb their residences, when they began to burn down Jewish memorials at concentration camps, and when governmental authorities seemed incapable of preserving law and order, then media anxiety turned a problem of national law enforcement into a putative Fourth Reich.

Does the new right wing endanger German democracy? Given the paucity of active extremists, their difficulty in coalescing nationally, and their preference for regurgitated Nazi slogans rather than thoughtful ideology, their prospects for success seem at least as slim as those of postwar Germany's previous right-wing parties. If the revised Article 16 helps to abate the influx of foreigners, if the government vigorously prosecutes illegal acts, and if economic growth provides more jobs, then the basis of the extremists' support will dissipate.

Can the right-wing extremists find new grievances that will feed popular discontent, on the other hand, as did the Nazis in 1933? The journalist Fritz René Allemann (1956) phrased an excellent response to this question with the title of his perspicacious book, *Bonn Is Not Weimar.* The recently manifested willingness of the masses to take public stances against xenophobic outbursts and the unwillingness of leaders to condone criminality suggest that what led to the demise of Weimar's democracy is not apt to repeat itself in the 1990s. Postwar Germany's problem is not the lack or even the weakness of democratic processes. More problematic is the execution of those processes by parties and political leaders who have not adequately thought through the broad implications of actions taken in narrow areas.

IV

Social Change in
Post-1945 Germany

Germans in the U.S. zone of occupation, Part III has shown, had a reasonably consistent image of their country's circumstances and its prospects. They would have preferred, of course, to have no foreign occupiers at all. Yet a substantial number of Germans doubted the democratic steadfastness of their compatriots should the occupiers depart too soon, and others did not want Western defenders to leave them at the mercy of the Red Army and the new dictatorship arising in the Soviet zone.

The survey data also indicate that the AMZON German public, in contrast at times to its emerging leaders, supported key changes that U.S. occupation authorities sought to implement. Citizens generally welcomed their country's tutelage in democratic values—even though some AMG officers and enlisted men abused their authority in their transforming zeal or quest for personal gain, and even though U.S. policy, after an initial flurry of activity, inclined more toward compromise than dramatic social change.

Germans' images of the present and future were colored by the past. Few postwar Germans relished a return to a new Hitler or to Nazism. Most endorsed policies aimed at removing from positions of political or social influence those who had created or sustained the evil that had befallen the land of philosophers and poets.

The description of the public opinion data nevertheless leaves open questions addressed at the outset of the study: the military success of the U.S. occupation, the success of the occupation as social engineering, and the abiding impact of the U.S.-German experiment in imposed democracy. Chapter 14 reviews the U.S. military occupation of Germany as a velvet revolution—one that began with a tinge of fire and brimstone but ended as a gentle basis for enduring international cooperation.

FOURTEEN

• •

German Society Changed?

The goals of U.S. occupation policy in post-1945 Germany were at once far-reaching and modest. Policymakers had embraced the doctrine of imposed social change, but at the rhetorical level only. U.S. policy sought neither to enslave Germans nor, comments by the disaffected notwithstanding, to "Americanize" them. The goal was not to transform such basic—some would say immutable—elements of culture as family, community, and religion. It was rather to modify the ways in which Germans dealt with sociopolitical issues: constraint and liberty, poverty and wealth, war and peace. Occupation policy insisted that Germans create a political system that would provide them with democracy and guarantee the world a greater measure of safety, and the policy was designed to help them do so.

The American approach had various sources. It reflected, for one, the pride of Americans in the accomplishments of the democracy their forebears had carved from the tyranny of George III. Then, too, Americans believed that they could apply to the social realm their "can-do" style of problem solving, so effective in approaching such physical puzzles as providing power and electricity to the impoverished Tennessee valley. Accompanying this buoyant spirit was a fundamental misreading of two centuries of scientific examination of the processes of social stability and social change. In the United States by the late 1930s, the very term "social change" had become a catchword for progressive thinking—or contentious theorizing—about various ways in which societies learn, adapt, and expand or contract. The compelling catchword offered a surface understanding of complex processes, an understanding that, once it was introduced in political discourse, was too compelling to ignore.

What this American enthusiasm for social engineering was to mean in practice changed as World War II went on. At first, policymakers and the American public considered traditional ways to punish such international miscreants as states who started wars or refused to pay their debts. Task-oriented Americans wanted to win the war, abolish Nazism and fascism as international scourges, and prevent the recurrence of German aggression.

With time, broader expectations and demands emerged and fed on each other. Thus the doctrine of unconditional surrender made the war longer and more costly in terms of human lives, social structures, and property. Strategic bombing, though it had a minimal effect on morale, raised the social costs of war. Calls resounding in the vigorous tones of Cato's *Delenda est Carthago* increasingly demanded Germany's destruction. Thinkers and policymakers who held various perspectives—minimalists, reformers, transformers, and maximalists—raged about the nature of the "German problem" and the best way to shape U.S. intervention. That military planners under the Joint Chiefs of Staff were eventually able to excise the excess and draft a modestly coherent document (JCS 1067) was a major accomplishment.

U.S. occupation policy emerged from a congeries of JCS drafts and revisions, edicts, ad hoc decisions, justifications, public debates, and assumptions—such as the presumed endurance of inter-Allied cooperation. The rich insights produced by this decision making process all pointed to the efficacy of foreign intervention as a means to impose change on a modern society. Taken together such elements constitute, at least through the retrospective spectacles of history, a single, overall "occupation policy," one that is judged less according to its individual parts than as a historical entity, like the Thirty Years' War or the Great Depression.

This concluding chapter evaluates the overall impact of U.S. occupation policy on Germany. Our starting point is not the wise or foolish leaders, nor the spinners of words that enthrall or confuse, but rather the common German citizen—or, rather, the mass of German citizens who offered their views to public opinion pollsters. How did these Germans respond to U.S. occupation policy? A second question addresses the efficacy of imposed social change. Would postwar Germans have moved in the same or similar sociopolitical directions had the United States not intervened? Implicit in the latter query is a third question: How can we assess the long-range impact of U.S. occupation policy? In 1949 when the German people gained semisovereignty, or in 1955 when they were almost completely responsible for their own fate, or in 1990 after unification, did they abandon what they had learned under Western and particularly American tutelage?

Winning Over the Enemy

Most Germans in the American zone of occupation accepted the military occupation imposed by the United States in 1945–1949, tried to learn from what the Americans had to say, and experimented with new programs that had the potential of improving their country's politics and society. The four occupation years became the basis for an enduring American-German entente that went beyond military alliance to the broader sociopolitical realm.

But American-German relations were scarcely that warm when the GIs stormed into Germany to smash the Third Reich. The substantial number of German immigrants in America notwithstanding, ties between the two peoples were not deeply rooted in history, and the two wars of the twentieth century estranged them still further. Although each side had become desensitized to wartime propaganda about the other's inhumanity, each also had suffered such severe wartime losses that neither thought of embracing the former foe. Even a half-century after the event American and other Allied organizers saw no reason to invite German participants to celebrations commemorating D-Day. One assumption was—and remains —clear: Americans entered war-ravaged Germany as foreign occupiers, not as liberators. Those Germans who had not been manifestly victimized by the Nazi regime but who thought that their hatred of Nazism would give them privileged status among the intruders were quickly disabused of this notion.

The American Military Government (AMG) began its work with a dual mission. One was to tear down the destructive elements of Germany's past that had caused the world such grief. This mission assigned traditional tasks to the occupiers. They were to stop the fighting, pacify the population, weed out obdurate leaders and petty bureaucrats of the past, and restore law and order—a task expanded in this case to include rebuilding municipal services, finding adequate food for the citizenry, and identifying reliable police officers and other public servants to replace those tainted by their ties to Nazism. Germans no less than Americans understood the reason for carrying out this mission—provided that it was carried out fairly rather than vindictively.

Although American officials feared widespread German opposition, they encountered neither Nazi-inspired guerrilla warfare nor sustained passive resistance among civilians. Instead occupation officers found that, while Germans did not welcome the renewed presence of foreign troops and muttered over their occupiers' ignorance of German ways, they were willing at least at the outset to acquiesce in what seemed to be an unintrusive way to rebuild their shattered homeland. How did this popular acceptance manifest itself?

The survey data demonstrate that the German public under AMG supported U.S. occupation policies, sometimes enthusiastically, even with respect to ostensibly sensitive issues: punishment of Nazi war criminals and removal of Nazi party members and collaborators from positions of influence. Later surveys found substantial nationwide support for those elements of AMG policy that continued to be broad concerns, such as trials of notorious criminals and support for victims of Nazi crimes. After German unification in 1990 the experience of the occupation era provided guidelines, albeit imperfect guidelines, for the FRG's treatment of eastern Germans.

But if German public opinion accepted U.S. occupation policy, the society's political and intellectual elites were less accommodating. AMG had cashiered top-level German policymakers, those linked too closely to Nazism. But lower-level civil servants retained in office proved to be resistant to change. They were inclined to believe that they knew better than did AMG officers what Germans needed and were willing to tolerate.[1] They seemed to care little about whether policy was good or bad—provided only that they had control over it. For them Allied plans were a threat.

AMG's second mission was to teach Germans to govern their affairs democratically while guaranteeing security to neighboring states—even if this meant imposing ideas and procedures that elicited German skepticism and even opposition. Reorienting German society was fraught with difficulties. Most Germans and Americans could agree on the need to punish Nazi leaders and compensate their victims, but not all shared a common image of what a democratic, peaceable Germany would be. AMG sought to restructure the media, rethink public education, and reorganize German governance and other aspects of the sociopolitical arena.

Again, AMZON Germans were supportive of most AMG programs. Even in areas where respondents disagreed with U.S. plans they seemed receptive to new ideas. Not only did large percentages of AMZON Germans accept the U.S. military's authority, they also held positive images of individual Americans and of the United States as a nation and sought to emulate U.S. popular culture and incorporate or copy its artifacts. At least until they came to understand that AMG was abandoning some of its programs, AMZON Germans bore with AMG's lead in education and other policy areas.

By early summer 1947 the relationship between occupier and occupied began to change. The expense, financial and otherwise, of maintaining a full-fledged occupation, the need to pay closer attention to an apparent Soviet bid for world hegemony, and domestic political pressures were among the factors that modified U.S. thinking about the urgency of some occupation goals. The maximalist perspective was already defunct in

---

1. Sociopolitical elites from the left were particularly recalcitrant. They "represented" the masses (at least in their own minds), and seemed to believe that they did not need to ask what people were actually thinking.

practice if not principle. With JCS 1779, issued in July 1947, the U.S. government abandoned the notion of deep-seated social change. It did not, however, desert the more modest campaign for selective reforms that could bring about systemic transformation. AMG pushed war crimes trials and denazification into ever more reluctant German hands, giving up, meanwhile, new planning for education and economic innovation. Americans nevertheless clung both to gains made in democratizing such areas as the media and to efforts at shaping the new German state.

Strains between Americans and Germans eased in ensuing months. Germany's emergent policy elites, including those whom AMG had hired to fill various positions, were gaining ground. As the Americans yielded on many of the issues they had pursued, they made it clear that the time had come to free Germany from occupation. AMG and German officials realized that they shared key goals, which required cooperation, not stiff-backed insistence and resistance. At the very least cooperation would push Germany toward a degree of independence that would allow occupation troops to withdraw and the new policy elite to take charge.

Sometimes cooperation was grudging. Doctors who joined ranks under the German Physicians Chamber to protect their profession against charges of medicalized killings showed an arrogance of power, as did the Chamber's nomination as president of the World Medical Association of an SS doctor who had sent at least one child to die at a euthanasia center. A different but equally awkward issue arose in January 1951 when Adenauer's government pressured U.S. High Commissioner McCloy to release 101 convicted war criminals still incarcerated in the Landsberg prison.

Such policy disputes also emerged in what both sides considered to be more central areas, such as the process of creating a government for the three western zones of occupation. As we have seen, the Parliamentary Council was from the outset engaged in a struggle for power between occupiers, particularly AMG, and occupied. Among the conditions on which the Tripartite Allies insisted was a federal system—notwithstanding popular preferences, particularly among Social Democrats, for centralized power (Renzsch 1989:28–29)—including an upper house of parliament to reflect provincial interests and concerns and a federal constitutional court. Such AMG advisers as James K. Pollock and Carl Joachim Friedrich, who provided Parliamentary Council members with technical advice, inspired the 5 percent clause that prevented fringe parties from clogging parliament as they had in Weimar days and for the positive vote of no confidence that prevented the lower house from dismissing a chancellor before electing a replacement.[2] It would be inaccurate to credit the Allies

2. The 5 percent clause appeared in the FRG's first electoral law and was later

with every innovation in German governance, but their significant role in shaping the Federal Republic of Germany is indisputable.

If, as we are told, the winners write the history books, U.S. occupation policy produced two sets of winners, in the short term, at least. American military officers and civilians wrote the first accounts of what they had accomplished. But in subsequent years German experts and policy players wrote *their* stories—often explaining what they could have done earlier had the occupation authorities accepted their advice, how they were able to circumvent Allied policies and proposals, and how efficiency improved once the foreign occupiers departed. Not until decades later did revisionist historians without a personal stake in the events of the occupation era begin searching for more balanced perspectives.

The evidence of this study, based on survey research embodying state-of-the-art techniques available in the late 1940s, suggests the need to reconsider the impact of the U.S. military occupation on German society. On the kinds of issues suited to public opinion polling, AMZON Germans consistently supported U.S. policy. Even on issues that elicited skepticism, the response tended toward compliance rather than rejection. With diminished presence of the occupiers, German elites assumed control, but survey-based evidence from subsequent years does not show widespread changes in attitudes toward the occupation era's accomplishments.

Externally Induced Social Change

U.S. officials planning for the occupation of Germany, far from paralyzed by the absence of any coherent theory of social change, were animated by the practical opportunity to modify a society. Germany in 1945 was ripe for reform, even transformation. The manifest failure of Nazism and the confusion of potential leaders made the German people receptive to discourse on governance. Their willingness to explore new ideas introduced by Western military governments, and particularly AMG, helped make the MGs more willing to take risks in their occupation policies—risks that would not have been possible before the Allies controlled German life. The result was an astonishing feat of imposed social change.

The U.S. program was not the first attempt to revolutionize German society. An even more far-reaching scheme, at least potentially, had come from within the country: the Nazi plan to change the entire German nation. It reached deeper into German roots than anything the Americans

---

legitimated by the Federal Constitutional Court. It remains a statute rather than a constitutional part of the Basic Law.

ever considered. At all levels of society Hitler, Goebbels, and the other Nazi brain benders used psychologically sophisticated procedures to control perspectives as well as behaviors. The procedures included both sticks, in the form of unmitigated terror, and carrots—appeals to what some commentators have called the popular German dream for national unity, racial integrity, and "wholeness."

The Nazis wanted a society in which each individual, group, and institution was wholeheartedly committed to the national cause as defined by the Nazi party. All their activities were subjected to forced synchronization (*Gleichschaltung*) to achieve this goal. The deep culture of community was targeted: the family, by persuading youths to honor the Führer rather than their parents; interpersonal ties, through a system of informants that undermined neighborhood trust; and religion, by co-opting the clergy to serve the party's ideological purposes. The more pliant culture of society was another focus: sociopolitical structures and behaviors ranging from social groups to information management to governmental policies. But as profound as the party's social changes were, the twelve years of Nazi rule ultimately were not enough to effect an enduring transformation.

Was the U.S. program, limited to four years, more successful? The bulk of the evidence reported in this study suggests that it was. Evaluating subsequent German behaviors in terms of U.S. policies is instructive:

- AMG preached personal responsibility for actions and pursued the principle in the Nuremberg war crimes trials; German authorities have conducted subsequent tribunals, including recent trials of ex-GDR leaders and border guards.
- AMG insisted that Germans accept collective responsibility (if not guilt) for atrocities committed against Jews; since the occupation the FRG has paid "reparations" to Israel, prosecuted those who harass Jews, and conducted public relations campaigns to sensitize Germans to the status of Jews and Jewry.
- Under the Americans, West Germany participated in the Marshall Plan and shared responsibilities under the OEEC; the FRG has since taken other concrete steps to enhance European unity.
- AMG restructured the West German media system; Germans have maintained and expanded this system.
- The occupiers placed restrictions on a German army; popular sentiment postponed the rearmament of the FRG and contributed to the concept of "citizens in uniform" and the nation's reluctance to enter into international disputes.
- AMG mandated governance stressing civil liberties, federalism, and a constitutional court; since occupation, Germans have retained the Basic Law's main dimensions without question.

Such examples suggest that postwar Germans took seriously U.S. insistence on Germany's democratic and peaceable future. But can we demonstrate a genuine causal link, or are we falling into a *post hoc ergo propter hoc* trap?

In confronting this question we must consider first the extent to which Germans were predisposed, even before war's end, to accept the programs that AMG and the other Tripartite Allies might propose. The data show that substantial numbers of German respondents were disgusted by what Nazism had done and increasingly realized that Nazi actions were not accidental but were consistent with and even prefigured by Nazi ideology. Other reports tell us that Nazi efforts to change German society, especially at its deeper levels, had backfired. Some Germans, having assimilated the Nazi line, found it difficult to recant and recover their core values. Others were sufficiently soured by the apparent inability of traditional community leaders to defend these values—the tolerance of Nazism by church leaders, for instance, or businessmen or academics—that they vowed never again to trust them or their successors. Still others learned from the Nazi episode that only by clinging steadfastly to the traditional values of family, the human ties of community, and religion could they guard their integrity against the sieges of Nazism or other *isms*.

To some measure, then, AMG enjoyed a ready market for its product. Attitudes toward the recent past, concepts of what it meant to be German, and hopes for Germany's future were far from homogeneous. Few Germans wanted to return to thoroughly discredited Nazism or anything like it. A modified version of Weimar Germany was attractive to those who had played formal roles in that regime, but it, too, had a dismal reputation. According to many Germans and foreign observers, the Weimar system, by engendering recurrent conflict and economic disasters, had paved the way to totalitarianism. Nor was a return to Imperial Germany realistic or desirable. So, what alternative was there to acceptance of what the Allies were proposing in 1945—what other than chaos or an indefinite foreign occupation? A predisposed population was doubtless a key ingredient to the occupation policy's success.

Another approach to the question of validity takes a different tack. How likely is it that, had the U.S. military occupation not taken place, Germans would nevertheless have taken the path toward democracy and peace? Consider two hypothetical, counterfactual examples:

• Suppose that German military officers and civilian leaders had overthrown the Nazi regime in late summer 1944 and sued for peace. Suppose further that the peace plan, calling for significant changes but retaining German sovereignty, won Big Three acceptance.

• Suppose that the Allies had offered Germans a minimalist plan based on formal acceptance by a newly elected German government, immediate destruction of Germany's military potential, and a pledge to restore Nazi-seized lands and pay reparations. Suppose also that the German opposition to Hitler had accepted the plan.

The central question of either scenario, each of them consistent with previous European peace plans, is: If the (hypothetical) new German leadership had wanted to make substantial social changes like those that U.S. military authorities initiated after 1945 and the German people agreed, could the government have done so? To take a simple example, could the new Germany have dethroned Weimar Germany's press lords and installed entirely new publishers and editorial teams? Probably not. To have done so would have violated a host of democratic principles, capitalist realities, and legal procedures.[3] Could the new Germany have created a military predominantly under civilian control and based on the concept of the citizen in uniform? Such a transformation would likewise have been unlikely. Shifting from a central to a federal form of government, or strengthening the provinces' political power, or establishing a constitutional court would have been equally problematic. Post–World War I Germany had ultimately refused to honor its Versailles pledges to punish the guilty, pay reparations, and reduce the country's military potential. Why should a new sovereign Germany have behaved any differently?

In this sense the AMG plan to transform German society was a convenient last resort. Many Germans, common citizens and sociopolitical elites alike, were searching for ways to create a more democratic and peaceable country. They might, over time, have been able to do so themselves. Allied policies nevertheless provided them with golden opportunities: first, to rid themselves of some of the more odious dimensions of the ancien régime while simultaneously assigning responsibility for change not to themselves but to the foreign occupiers; and, second, to experiment with new institutional procedures that, if they proved to be unworkable or burdensome, would be subject to revision or removal after the placated foreign troops returned to their homelands.

3. Our hypothetical examples raise a fundamental problem touched on in earlier chapters. If Germans, acting on their own, would not have carried out sweeping social changes, by what right could the Allies impose such changes on them? The answer lies in the realm of power politics: with restrictions according to common dictates of humanity, the "right of occupation" (*quod in armis est*) gave the Allies freedom to determine and, as much as possible, realize what they wished to accomplish. Whether or not it was morally correct or politically advisable to act anticonstitutionally and dictatorially to impose democracy and constitutionalism on anyone (Germans, but also children, animals, and the infirm) is an important issue that cannot be addressed here.

In sum, the relative weakness of individual supporters of alternative proposals for change and the absence of a consistent plan for change strengthen the empirically based perception that U.S. occupation policy positively influenced postwar West German reconstruction. Was this policy as effective as it might have been given the circumstances? The answer depends on an understanding of the dynamics of exogenously induced social change.

The tendency of societies is toward stability rather than change.[4] A population and its leaders endorse policies that maintain the social status quo. But a modern social system interacts with its environment. It cannot insulate itself against shocks from the outside (a destructive earthquake or the sudden collapse of a neighboring government) any more than against those from the inside (labor unrest, or a dynamic leader with a new vision, such as Martin Luther or Adolf Hitler). Even strict border controls cannot prevent the potentially disruptive exchanges of people and perspectives that force a social system to adopt new ways. Nor can social systems avoid the cumulative impact of its actions and the actions of its neighbors. Dumping toxic waste into the Baltic Sea may not have been problematic a hundred years ago, but the accumulated ecological damage of this practice now threatens the area's existence.[5]

Given the tendency toward social stability, those who would change the social system must legitimate their programs. Social change typically proceeds from the evolving dispositions of the sociopolitical elite: new leaders come to power and try to effect changes, rewarding perspectives and behaviors that support the new policies. Should the elites fail to meet the needs or expectations of other population strata, however, then revolution might ensue, with the masses acting as the agency of change.

Intervening foreigners seldom can establish the legitimacy enjoyed by a people's own leaders and followers, but neither the elites nor the masses of postwar Germany were in a position to prescribe the changes to be made, less still to impose them. Germans, as the survey data indicate, initially may have balked at accepting the U.S. military occupiers as a legitimate agency of change. But, first, no other such agency existed— discounting the Soviet Union's offer to play this role. Second, Germans

4. Ignored here is the potential disruptiveness of systemic ultrastability and the radicals who would overthrow it.

5. In another forum it would be instructive to expand on these various sources of change: endogenous shock (Nazi assault on German community), endogenous cumulation (the century of German anti-Semitism and the Nazi propaganda that made the Holocaust possible), exogenous shock (Anglo-American aerial bombardments of German cities), and exogenous cumulation (Western shift in the nineteenth century toward liberal democracy, largely ignored in Germany). Important variables are the timing, severity, and enduringness of the shock or event, and the groups most affected by it.

perceived the cost of resisting change to be significantly greater than the cost of accepting the occupiers' program. Third, Germans were primed to accept changes similar to what the Americans had in mind.[6] The Americans, after all, were only seeking social changes and not attacking the roots of German community. Fourth, U.S. military authorities eventually proved amenable to modified changes that most Germans could accept.

Was U.S. occupation policy the best that it could be? The data suggest that the occupiers could have done better. The confusion of ideas and policies, especially in the war's last year, suggested a lack of clarity in American goals and policies—a weakness that critics in Germany and the United States would exploit. The policy shift in mid-1947, while diminishing the occupation's overall impact, brought U.S. planning closer to what the newly emerging German allies considered appropriate and all but removed its punitive dimensions. The shift responded, the survey data tell us, to what Germans wanted from the future state: security, well-being in a broad sense, and—plainly third in their ranking—such social values as personal freedom, free elections, and a free press. In effect the U.S. government declared victory in the war against Nazi tyranny, criminality, and aggression. Together with its new German allies, it began to prepare for a widespread, albeit modified, restoration of the country's pre-1933 sociopolitical system.

A Half-Century Later

The ultimate test of the U.S. military occupation's effectiveness was its endurance over time. Various chapters in this book have addressed aspects of this topic: perspectives from 1945 to today on the spirit of Nazism, treatment of perpetrators of and collaborators in state-sponsored criminality, and constitutional as well as policy revisions. What do these scattered findings suggest about the U.S. occupation's endurance?

The End of Nazism?

Post-1949 West Germany and, since 1990, unified Germany have continued to combat National Socialism as a sociopolitical movement. They have been less successful, however, in treating it as a sociocultural phenomenon—in part because of the persistence of ideas associated with Nazi ideology, in part because of the phenomenon's functionality for social systems.

6. The German mood in 1945 was substantially different from the truculent noncooperation of 1919, partly because occupation policies of 1945 took greater account of German needs and were bolstered by an intense public relations campaign.

Sociopolitical movement. If any Germans did not yet know in spring 1945 that Nazism was a plague visiting on them unmitigated disaster, they were soon enlightened. The meaning of a foreign occupation pressed on them daily, and Allied information programs hammered them with detailed, indisputable evidence of Nazi criminality. Most Germans responding to public opinion polls could find some merits in Nazism, but they despised the system conceptually and they blamed Nazi leadership for bringing destruction and shame upon their country. Sustained support for neo-Nazism was minuscule.

What accounts for this antipathy? Few Germans who pay attention to history deny that Nazism was a ghastly mistake. Even the revisionism of the late 1980s barely touched popular German thinking. Debate over justifications and ultimate causes—of the rise of Nazism, Hitler's accession to power in 1933, the outbreak of war, the Wehrmacht's fierce and futile defense on the eastern front, the Holocaust and other atrocities—was an exercise bordering on irrelevance. The salient fact was that Hitler and the Nazis had created the machinery of destruction that eventually led to Germany's virtual extinction. What was important was preventing the recurrence of Nazism or any similar movement.

As is true of any people, however, not all Germans are sensitive to their own country's history. They ignore the evidence and hold fast to scraps of bizarre revisionist notions. Since 1945 small, noisy, and usually short-lived but authentic neo-Nazi movements have sprung up in Germany. Openly praising the Führer and his party, espousing Nazi ideologies, adopting trappings reminiscent of the NSDAP (uniforms and symbols as well as gestures and slogans), and proclaiming their intention to restore the National Socialist regime, these parties have not gained popular support. Yet few democrats feel comfortable about ignoring their presence and potential, for extremist movements of the right and the left have demonstrated their capacity for fomenting serious disruption. The danger always exists that, as happened in the last years of the Weimar Republic, one or another of these movements may catch hold among larger segments of the population.

The FRG has dealt seriously with such parties and associations. Adenauer's first government got the Federal Constitutional Court to ban the Socialist Reich Party (SRP). A later chancellor, Kurt-Georg Kiesinger, considered trying to ban the National Democratic Party (NPD) before the 1969 election but concluded that the party was too insignificant to warrant giving it the international publicity that a court case would provide. The interior minister in 1980 banned the Defense Sport Group, at the end of 1992 the Nationalist Front, the German Alternative, and the National Offensive, and in November 1994 the Viking Youth. Critics charge the government with acting too slowly to suppress the extreme right, but these tiny bands of the disaffected are like mushrooms that spring up after a rain: what is banned today will regroup tomorrow under a different name. What is under investigation today will tomorrow carefully tread the path of legality.

Sociocultural phenomena: intellectual shards. Historical sophistication and dissociation from the baggage of National Socialism do not necessarily mean that Germans reject all principles associated with Nazi ideology. Right-wing elements within more broadly based parties do not typically advocate the restoration of National Socialism or the elevation of a new Hitler. Such a hidden agenda is incidental to the plea they make for support—although instructive in understanding politicians and their behaviors. Right-wing politicians, even if they are authentic neo-Nazis, usually have enough political savvy to recognize the limits of legality and palatability, and to collect votes rather than unmarketable kudos applauding their ideological salvos.

Such parties are more common in local and provincial arenas than at the national level, where the 5 percent clause is more difficult to satisfy. A local party that criticizes a specific decision to increase the area's quota of asylum seekers can draw substantial support—especially if the dominant parties seem to waffle on the issue. So can a national party like the Republicans (REPs) that adapts its electoral strategy to sometimes conflicting local conditions. In addition, the right wings of such parties as Bavaria's Christian Social Union (CSU) can gain support by convincing the voter that they alone stand between the Scylla of neo-Nazis and the Charybdis of "liberals" who would sell out the German nation's traditional values. The successful right-wing faction, by increasing its influence over the party as a whole, can then parlay its gains into the national political arena.

Sociocultural phenomena: Nazism as drama. Germany's Nazi episode has spawned intense, worldwide interest. Scholars and artists, filmmakers and dramatists, politicians and preachers, novelists and satirists find in the Nazi episode a treasure-trove for the imagination, an infinite resource for study of the human condition, even a source of mass titillation. Others use the episode to rebuke contemporary Germans, and some use German sensitivity to past behaviors to blackmail the FRG even when it is pursuing perfectly legitimate policies.

Such abuses have led some Germans to wonder rhetorically why Germany, a half-century after war's end, should still be the world's whipping boy. German politicians, fearing backlash, usually—but not always—suppress complaints that smack of whining. Can't German naysayers display greater understanding of the needs of their own country? Can't foreign observers recognize the FRG's contributions to international peace and international development? It seems likely that popular fascination with Nazism will continue, and so will the willingness to use and sometimes misuse Germany's recent past as a means to score political points. But to say that because an incident happened a half-century ago it should be put aside does not persuade the person whose psychological scars keep the episode as fresh as if it had taken place yesterday. For all our efforts to exorcise it, the horror of Nazism stays with us.

Sustaining a Nonaggressive Democracy

Post-1949 Germany has been more successful in building the future than in disposing of the past. The development of the Basic Law is proof, as are federalism, a Federal Constitutional Court, the establishment of a military, and Germany's ties to its European neighbors—and Allied and particularly U.S. intervention was the genesis of each.

Basic Law. Observers from the United States and other countries where constitutional change is difficult to effect occasionally question the apparent ease with which Germans can and frequently do amend their Basic Law. This image of a fluid constitution is misleading.[7] First, amendments have made no change in core values. Second, the Basic Law is a much more comprehensive document than that of most other countries. The U.S. Constitution, for example, offers nothing comparable to the Basic Law's right of asylum (Article 16). The functional equivalent is the U.S. immigration code, which undergoes periodic changes. It is also true that proposed changes in the Basic Law need obtain only the vote of two-thirds of both houses of parliament and that party discipline generally ensures that parliamentary members follow party dictates.[8] But getting rival parties to agree on a change is difficult, and no single party has ever achieved the two-thirds majority needed to impose constitutional revision unilaterally.

In practical terms, those wanting constitutional changes must negotiate an acceptable package among the dominant parties. This consensus-building process can be very time consuming, and it is not always success-

7. The revision of Article 16 in June 1993 was the Basic Law's thirty-seventh amendment, the most extensive of which, adopted on 31 August 1990, accommodated changes made by the Union Treaty.

8. A modified proportional representation system forces practically all Bundestag members to follow party decisions, particularly if the party considers the issue under discussion to be important. Those who break party discipline on important issues may find it difficult to retain their positions on the next party ballot. Bundesrat members are agents of and hence get voting instructions from the party-bound provincial governments.

ful. Wholesale changes would be even more difficult to organize. In fact, until 1990 West Germans did not pursue a full-scale revision of the Basic Law drafted in 1948–1949.[9] They chipped away at parts that needed changes: provisions in 1955–1956 for the Bundeswehr, in 1968 for emergency legislation, and in 1993 for asylum rights.[10] But each amendment has worked to enhance the FRG's "free, democratic basic order."

The Basic Law gained additional credibility as a constitutional document after German union in 1990. More than forty years earlier the Parliamentary Council's drafters of the Basic Law had refused to call their document a constitution. They preferred the more tentative term to indicate the provisional nature of the document and the possibility that, after the signing of treaties formally ending World War II and uniting Germany, a constitutional convention could draft a full-scale constitution. This opportunity arose in 1990. The new Germany empowered a blue-ribbon commission to explore constitutional modifications or even to call a constitutional convention that would draft a new one. Until then, FRG and GDR representatives negotiating the Union Treaty agreed, the Basic Law would prevail throughout the country. As the constitutional commission slipped into inactivity, the provisional Basic Law took on a look of permanence.

Federalism. Provincial independence, so prized by U.S. military authorities and eventually accepted by the Parliamentary Council, has increased the provinces' political influence. The provinces have broadened the domains under their jurisdiction. Their defense of the Bundesrat's constitutional powers offers an example. Provincial complaints resulted in court decisions that multiplied significantly the kinds of Bundestag laws that require the Bundesrat's explicit concurrence (Pinney 1963). The provinces have also blocked federal incursions into their jurisdiction. Consider Chancellor Adenauer's effort, stifled in 1961 by the Federal Constitutional Court, to create a national radio and television station under control of the federal government. In 1990, while the FRG was in the process of incorporating the ex-GDR, the old provinces of western Germany maneuvered successfully to protect provincial rights both east and west. By insisting on individual partnerships between the old and new provinces

9. Most assuredly, opponents of various constitutional amendments saw them as fundamental changes in the nature of the Basic Law. The major parties and most citizens, however, have not expressed concern about any losses of constitutional privilege.

10. The idea of emergency legislation—for instance, what the FRG should do in the event of a nuclear attack—was hotly contested between the conservative CDU/CSU and the leftist SPD. Eventually it took a grand-coalition government to secure acceptable changes.

on all matters assigned to them by the Basic Law, they curtailed federal encroachments and ensured provincial diversity.

Federal Constitutional Court. Although a precedent existed in Weimar Germany's Constitutional Tribunal (Leibholz 1952:723), the Federal Constitutional Court established by the Parliamentary Council was a new institution in German legal history. The three Western military governors, in their aide-mémoire of 22 November 1948 (USDS 1955:194), called for "an independent judiciary" that would review federal legislation and executive power, adjudicate federal-provincial conflicts, and "protect the civil rights and freedom of the individual." Not all legal experts were enthusiastic. Social Democrats expressed concern that the inherently conservative nature of courts can countermand legislative decisions, whereas Christian Democrats considered the emphasis on civil rights excessively liberal. The parties nevertheless reached an early consensus on a Federal Constitutional Court (Articles 92–94) that would have an almost immediate impact on the FRG's judicial process (Kommers 1976, 1989, 1994).

Bundeswehr. The formal termination of the occupation in mid-1949 left West German security in the hands of the Tripartite Allies. Agreeing on the need to draw the FRG into West Europe's defense structure, the Allies explored several alternatives, ranging from an independent German military, which they found thoroughly unacceptable, to an integrated union such as the European Defense Community, later vetoed by the French parliament. The Allies finally agreed in 1954 to create a Bundeswehr within the framework of the North Atlantic Treaty Organization.

The price extracted from West Germans was an assurance that the military would support democratic processes instead of becoming, once again, a "state within the state." From the outset the FRG carefully carried out its military-political obligations. It took several years to get the Bundeswehr effectively operational, and as we have seen, lapses by both civilian and military leaders produced sometimes spectacular—albeit not crippling—domestic political crises. Internationally, careful attention by the Bundeswehr to its original charter eventually led other NATO members to accept the West German role in Europe's defense and even to place Germans in top military positions.

Current concerns about the FRG contribution to NATO derive from what some observers see as German overkill of its original intention to create a democratic and peaceable army. The Bundeswehr, critics complained, was not aggressive enough in the cause of peace. Few NATO members had initially quarreled with the Kohl government's interpretation of Article 87a(1) in the Basic Law. This interpretation, pressed by Foreign Minister Genscher, sought to restrict German military activities to the protection of NATO countries. As the cold war abated, however, and new kinds of international dangers arose, German inflexibility neither helped its allies nor served the cause of international security to which the FRG was committed as a United Nations member. In spring 1993 Bundeswehr units were nevertheless sent to Somalia as part of the United Nations' peace-keeping and humanitarian mission.

European Community. As they surveyed damage caused by the war and asked how both to repair the destruction and prevent its recurrence, some farsighted Europeans and Americans increasingly saw the need to enhance European cooperation and to move toward integration. Some even proposed a United States of Europe. Economic, political, and social problems complicated reconstruction, however, and the prospect of despairing masses in France, Italy, and elsewhere embracing communism was compelling. The need to rescue the European economy assumed ever greater urgency.

In 1947 the Truman administration proposed the Marshall Plan, which would provide European countries with at least $16 billion for economic reconstruction. To avoid the chaos likely to ensue should each country independently have to petition the European Recovery Program (ERP), President Truman insisted that aid recipients jointly develop a program for ascertaining needs, distributing funds, and evaluating the effectiveness of the program. The beneficiary states responded by forming the Organization for European Economic Cooperation (OEEC), which required for the first time ever that the European states exchange vital economic data and initiate extensive joint planning. West Germany, still an occupied country without a government, got its own package of funding and after gaining semisovereignty in 1949 became part of the ERP-OEEC nexus.

The U.S. decision to include West Germany (and West Berlin) in the European Recovery Program represented a significant shift in U.S. occupation policy. AMG policy before mid-1947 emphasized restraining Germans from lashing out against their neighbors, but the focus shifted increasingly toward encouraging German cooperation with those neighbors —or at least those in the noncommunist world. Through AMG, West Germans began receiving economic assistance, printed materials extolling European cooperation, and even feelers about the acceptability of a European army that would include German units.

AMG and Washington policymakers were marketing to western Germans a new product: the idea of Europe and the dream of European unity. This product found eager acceptance in West Germany. Liberals envisioned an end to Europe's internecine struggles, conservatives a common European market that could compete successfully with the U.S. economy. Implicitly, many realized that cooperative European unity was a desirable alternative to the domination that Hitler had sought: it would enhance German security, stability, and well-being and restore Germany, albeit within a European cooperative, to the status of a great state. And no doubt some Germans saw the budding plan for European cooperation as a means to end the Allied military occupation.

The next steps were up to Europeans rather than Americans. The "inner six" and later the "outer seven" established the European Coal and Steel Community, the European Common Market, and a host of other European institutions. West Germany consistently played a leading role in promoting and actually realizing western Europe's systemic transformation. AMG and the U.S. government had played a key role in Europeanizing Germans, but it was German leadership after 1949 that capitalized on the transformation.

German Civility and German Illiberality

The German record in the past half-century—sustained constitutionalism and civil liberties, power-sharing federalism, civilian-controlled military, peacemaking with neighbors—suggests significant shifts in exactly the directions in which the U.S. military government had pointed the country. Germans by and large have learned to behave democratically and peaceably. Sometimes, though, as such critics as Dahrendorf (1965/ 1967) have remarked, it seems that a basic illiberality underlies this learned civility and emerges from time to time to cause domestic consternation and international bewilderment.[11]

Past regime criminals. Germans will doubtless welcome the impending conclusion of criminal investigations into wartime events. Bringing top Nazis to justice was an essential AMG policy, one that the German public largely endorsed. Lengthy trials in Nuremberg, however, and changing ideas about American-German cooperation exhausted AMG's resolve. German jurists, many of whom had from the outset questioned the legal basis for such trials, took charge of them and moderated their bite. The masses began to weary of them, especially when investigations reached into the lower echelons of Germany's social hierarchy. Public pressure at home and abroad nevertheless forced the trials to continue.

Just when it seemed that the ravages of time—deaths, illnesses, lost evidence, fading memories—would bring an end to the trials, the FRG suddenly inherited all of the legal concerns pertaining to East Germany. Few western Germans doubted that their government had the legal right

---

11. The same criticism has been directed at the United States and other countries. The question here focuses on the long-range impact of a program specifically seeking to reform or transform Germany.

and moral obligation to prosecute the "criminals" who had brutalized the eastern German people for four decades in the name of a "people's democracy." What exactly was the FRG to do? Specific questions raised by jurists reflected those asked and answered and debated ad infinitum during the occupation years: Did one state have the right to judge the actions committed by citizens of another now-discredited state? Can an individual (such as a border guard along the Berlin Wall) be held responsible for carrying out a superior's order (to shoot at fugitives)?

The western German judiciary seemed daunted by this new version of old challenges. In a trial that captured international attention, prosecutors brought charges against Erich Honecker, the former East German head of state. But crossed signals and extreme sensitivity to the rights of the accused earned Honecker a release and a first-class airplane ticket to Santiago de Chile. Cases against such GDR leaders as Hans Modrow and Markus Wolf relied on questionable premises, suggesting that the FRG state's attorneys were grasping at straws. Critics claimed that the new trials were driven more by political vengeance than by justice. Meanwhile, continuing indictments and convictions of low-ranking officials made eastern Germans increasingly restless. Western German judicial officers, unlike their U.S. predecessors in occupied Germany, nevertheless continued to push relentlessly ahead, charging and trying major and minor offenders.

Past regime collaborators. Punishing those who had performed the devil's handiwork was another important dimension of the U.S. occupation. What became of the millions of Germans who before 1945 had committed themselves to Nazism by joining or otherwise supporting the party? We have seen them in the newsreels of the times: uniformed party stalwarts marching at the Nuremberg rallies, shining-faced youths transfixed by the sight of their Führer, masses cheering Hitler's speeches and shouting "Sieg Heil!" as he paraded down the streets of Germany. The mission of AMG was to search out and punish the most active of them. But the elaborate plan to "denazify" German society soon fell prey, as we have seen, to its own impracticability—a weakness that neither AMG enthusiasm nor popular German support could ameliorate. U.S. officers were pleased in 1949 to suspend denazification; West German politicians were just as pleased to help scuttle it forever.

Ironically, their successors returned to similar but more refined procedures after Germany achieved unity in 1990. The new targets were eastern Germans who had actively collaborated with and benefited from the GDR government. In a totalitarian country, where state-owned enterprises prevail and the dominant party insists on demonstrative loyalty, nominal party members inevitably abound. The Union Treaty of 1990 did not prescribe pursuit of SED members, but it specified that those who had collaborated with the GDR regime in carrying out its illegal activities be removed from important public-sector positions: judges, professors, leading municipal-service employees, and other public servants. The discovery of Stasi (Ministry of State Security, or MfS) surveillance files jeopardized the jobs of its informal collaborators (IMs), who had informed on their fellow citizens. Penalties for political links to the GDR's "unjust" state also extended to elected officials as well as to athletes, writers, and others in the private sector.

Low tolerance for dissension. The principle of denazification survived not only in its 1990 adaptation to eastern Germany's collaborators. Its philosophical underpinnings remained a model for German response to political dissent. The conceptual model functioned at two levels. One addressed pre-1945 circumstances: it punished those who, by supporting the past political system, had harmed their fellow citizens and German society as a whole. At a second level denazification had a post-1945 dimension: it prevented access to power and influence by those who had not adapted rapidly and completely to the newly emerging German democratic order. Although AMG procedures did not systematically focus on the second dimension, the principle was implicit. Quasi-legal procedures, this principle made clear, could be used to curtail dissidents, those who did not endorse the current political system.

The FRG would later use this second dimension of the denazification model to rid itself of several categories of people who dissented from the prevailing political order.[12] Most postwar Germans were quick to censure leftists, whom they accused of seeking Germany's overthrow and transformation into a communist "people's republic." The early 1950s saw criminal justice procedures used to restrain communists, and in 1956 the Federal Constitutional Court banned their political party, the KPD. In the 1970s the FRG adopted a "radicals decree" to control left-wing radicals. National and provincial authorities were to identify public-sector employees who did not enthusiastically support—that is, who complained too vehemently about—the FRG's "free, democratic basic order" and to evaluate them. Employees labeled left-wing radicals would be dismissed from their positions and denied further access to government jobs.

After union in 1990 the all-German government dominated by western German laws refined earlier procedures to restrict yet another category of citizens: "criminal" dissenters. The targets were eastern Germans who

12. Current German concerns about harassment of asylum seekers and other foreigners reflect a popular reluctance to accept those who think differently, that is, existential or social rather than political dissidents.

had cooperated too closely with the GDR regime (Stasi IMs, for example) or who had committed "illegal" acts against the FRG (conducting espionage for the MfS, for example).[13] International law had long permitted a state that captured a spy in its own territory to prosecute the agent according to its national law, and since 1945 states such as Israel and the United States had skirted international dictates, kidnapping suspected criminals and transporting them to their own countries for trial. The German version of this convention dates back to the Adenauer administration's interpretation of the Basic Law: because, it claimed, the FRG was the sole legitimate successor of the German state that in 1945 had turned over its sovereignty to the Allies, all Germans (including those who lived in the GDR) were citizens of the FRG, and any action by a German that threatened the FRG's "free, democratic basic order" constituted treason.[14] This principle permitted Germany's post-1990 judiciary to indict and convict the GDR's spymaster, Markus Wolf.

Few would deny a state's right to protect itself from its internal (and external) enemies. But postwar Germans have found it difficult to define the lines that divide defending the system from a clear and present danger, blocking legitimate albeit troublesome dissent, and punishing those who acted in good faith under a different political system.

Brittle policy-making. Another dilemma derives from the German governmental process. Like that of other highly bureaucratized states, the process is sometimes cumbersome. In normal circumstances this may not be problematic. In exceptional times it can hamper governmental effectiveness and even exacerbate its problems.

Political unrest in the late 1960s and throughout the 1970s exposed one practical shortcoming of German governance. Other democratic states that have experienced student protests, violent confrontations, and terrorism have wrestled with the challenge of responding firmly without violating the citizen's civil rights. But such unrest in Germany had more the character of a civil war. That university students, Germany's privileged children and future leaders, could be as disagreeable and as violent as old-line SA toughs shocked the police into entering a kind of class conflict

13. The procedure is moderate compared to the one initiated in 1945 at the IMT. Simple membership in an organization judged illegal, such as the NSDAP or the SS, made a person criminally liable in principle. In practice, however, not just membership but specific crimes had to be demonstrated to establish criminality.

14. This claim to sole representation found its most prominent manifestation in the "Hallstein doctrine." Drafted in 1955 by Adenauer's state secretary, Walter Hallstein, it denied diplomatic recognition, and hence economic assistance, to any state that granted such recognition to the GDR. The policy, which severely hurt such Third World countries as India, was abandoned in 1968 by the grand coalition.

that raged for years. Eventually German police learned the difference between handling unruly, even hostile crowds and warding off the vanguard of insurrection. Later, when terrorists robbed banks and killed hostages, German authorities again overreacted. Airports and civic centers took on the appearance of armed camps, and a few responsible leaders even demanded retributive execution of previously convicted or detained terrorists.

Unified Germany provided another example of ineffective crisis management in confronting the link between economic pressures and what was then a growing influx of foreigners seeking asylum. When skinheads and right-wing extremists interpreted popular concern about the economic and social consequences of immigration as support for their verbal and physical attacks against foreigners, authorities were slow to maintain public order and protect the rights of foreigners—and sometimes even winked at violence from the right and its claims of preserving national identity. Political officials were even slower in making appropriate constitutional and practical changes.[15] Both at home and particularly abroad the German government assumed a disastrous image of impotence or callousness, and by late 1992 concern about the specter of renewed right-wing violence was worldwide. By July 1993, when constitutional change was promulgated, the nexus of asylum applicants, economic stress, and right-wing extremism had become an enduring crisis.

Toward a Modern Germany

These characteristics—a willingness to strain legality in the search for a higher morality, low tolerance toward political and social dissent, and difficulty in responding quickly and appropriately to crises—have long troubled Germany watchers. Such manifestations of underlying philosophy suggest a German attitude that social conflict is intolerable violence, a threat to sociopolitical existence rather than a rudiment of human interaction with both positive and negative consequences.

From this broader perspective we may recast our understanding of the U.S. military occupation's long-range impact on postwar Germany. On the positive side, the Tripartite Allies and especially AMG helped sometimes reluctant Germans to move toward modernity, democratic at home

15. Because the Basic Law's original Article 16(1) unconditionally guaranteed foreigners the right of political asylum in Germany, any changes restricting this right required a constitutional amendment rather than a simple legislative enactment. It thus took four years for Kohl's right-center government to reach agreement with the SPD and to sign necessary treaties with neighboring countries, most notably Poland and the Czech Republic.

and pacific internationally. The Germans themselves deserve credit as well. They could have undermined the policies imposed on them. They could have carped against the Allies for weaknesses that became apparent only later. They could have refused to assert their own creativity in solving the Federal Republic's problems. They could have instituted sweeping constitutional and structural changes as soon as the occupation soldiers went home. But the Allies pushed West Germans to go in what has proved to be a mutually rewarding direction.

Allied and U.S. intervention did not cure all of Germany's ills, however—as few could have expected it would. Did the intervention aim at the right targets? Certainly the practical policies discussed in this book were appropriate individually and as key parts of an overall plan. They enhanced a particular orientation toward the Nazi past. In setting and implementing policy AMG seemed to proceed from the assumption that the events of World War II resulted from rational action: national leaders making reasoned choices to enhance their country's standing in the international arena.

Most Western analysts would quickly add that Nazi leaders made irrational policy choices that abundantly justified their dismissal, judicial punishment, and replacement by new, better-trained leaders. But the clarity of action that arose from Germany's political rationality under Nazism, as inappropriate as it may have been in its international context, pointed the way toward equally clear-cut responses. For many Germany watchers the manifest traits of the Nazi episode were the main event in a changing world drama. The data reviewed here suggest that Germans and Americans enjoyed compatible perspectives about the way to cleanse the country's false political model created by Nazi rationality.

The process of cleansing thus accomplished, did AMG still have a reason to remain in Germany? The Americans chose to remain, although with modified responsibilities. One reason was that the occupiers hesitated to leave Germany without evaluating its emerging political elite, providing the support needed to make and carry out tough decisions, and ensuring that the new Germans made the proper constitutional and institutional changes. Was the new political model working, or would Germans again slip into a skewed rationality that produced inappropriate decisions? Hindsight makes it difficult to deny the FRG's success in establishing sound political institutions, processes, and even outcomes. Available data also suggest strong popular support among the German people.

But concern about factors beyond transparent political characteristics continued to plague Germany watchers. Some observers had viewed the Nazi episode as a symptom of something deeper and more enduring: a "Prussian spirit," perhaps, or the manipulation of entrepreneurial jackals, or personal anxieties manifest as collective aggressiveness, or a German bent for authoritarian politics and governance. Occupation policy addressed all of these possibilities: it broke up Prussia and curtailed German industry, it proscribed an independent army devoid of civilian constraints, it strengthened a free press and constitutional guarantees of freedom.

Such steps unquestionably helped to change Germany's social fabric. In their comprehensiveness they augment our understanding about the post-1945 relationship between the Nazism of the past and the German society of the present. The explanation seems to lie less in the oft-claimed failure of Germans to achieve integrated nationhood than in their willingness to dwell on such an issue. The idea of nationhood has worried Germans since the age of nationalism began. They have decimated forests with writings that question whether or not Germans are a nation—if so, what its defining characteristics are or should be, and if not, who is to blame. As an intellectual concept German nationhood thrives today as it did two centuries ago. In the meantime no one has come up with a description of the phenomenon that is uniformly convincing to Germans, not to speak of the rest of the world.

This does not mean that the idea of German nationhood has remained abstract, appropriate for rhetorical excursions but not for the practical realm of politics. Indeed, Germans have acted too much to implement particular conceptualizations of nationhood. For Hitler and Nazi ideologues the tribal image was powerful. They spoke as though it would be possible to restore in unified form the Germanic tribes of yore that had baffled Tacitus; their policies of racial extermination, enslavement of inferior tribes, the imperative of tribal loyalty, and forced synchronization all aimed at realizing such a goal. It is this German record of acting out destructive fantasies that unsettles foreign observers when they see similar behaviors in today's ostensibly democratic, peaceable Germany— outrages committed against foreign workers and those seeking asylum, the Brandt government's radicals decree, open violence fomented by the left and the right, the search for means to punish "disloyal" supporters of the ex-GDR, financial policies benefiting Germany at the cost of European unity. Such apparently isolated events suggest a pattern that smacks too much of Germany's dismal past.

But the Federal Republic of Germany is not treading the path that almost two-thirds of a century ago led to National Socialism. Contemporary Germans seek the blessings of modernity and seem willing to accept its perils. Nor is the modern world a collection of isolated, mutually hostile tribes throwing rocks or even nuclear missiles at each other. It is a world of competitive but highly integrated economies with information-rich populations and a growing sense that mutual survival requires close, voluntary cooperation. In such a high-tech, high-powered world Germans cannot afford to play the nationalist games of the past. In a country that has often enough succumbed to such an ardent and treacherous lure, the most appropriate stance may be the catchphrase that the Amis introduced to the culture of occupied Germany: "Take it easy!"

References

Ad. 1991. Ad on Holocaust stirs debate. *The New York Times,* 10 November.

Adam, Peter. 1992. *Art of the Third Reich.* New York: Harry N. Abrams.

Adenauer, Konrad. 1965/1966. *Erinnerungen 1945–1953.* Stuttgart: Deutsche (1965). Trans. Beate Ruhm von Oppen. *Memoirs 1945–53.* Chicago: Henry Regnery (1966).

Alexander, Leo. 1945. *The treatment of shock from prolonged exposure to cold, especially in water.* Washington, D.C.: U.S. Department of Commerce, Office of Publications Board. Report 250 (CIOS Target, No. 24: Medical).

Allemann, Fritz René. 1956. *Bonn ist nicht Weimar.* Cologne: Kiepenheuer & Witsch.

Allen, Charles R., Jr. 1963. *Heusinger of the Fourth Reich.* New York: Marzani & Munsell.

―――. 1985. *Nazi war criminals in America: Facts—action: The basic handbook.* New York: Highgate.

Almond, Gabriel A., and Sidney Verba. 1963. *The civic culture: Political attitudes and democracy in five nations.* Princeton: Princeton University Press.

American Jewish Committee. 1952. *Neo-Nazi and nationalist movements in West Germany.* New York: American Jewish Committee.

Angell, Marcia. 1990. The Nazi hypothermia experiments and unethical research today. *The New England Journal of Medicine* 322:1462–1464.

Annas, George J. 1992. Changing the consent rules for Desert Storm. *The New England Journal of Medicine* 326:770–773.

Applebome, Peter. 1991. Duke: The ex-Nazi who would be governor. *The New York Times,* 10 November.

Appleman, John Alan. 1954. *Military tribunals and international crimes.* Indianapolis: Bobbs-Merrill.

Arendt, Hannah. 1963. *Eichmann in Jerusalem: A report on the banality of evil.* New York: Viking.

Armstrong, Anne. 1961. *Unconditional surrender: The impact of the Casablanca policy upon World War II.* New Brunswick, N.J.: Rutgers University Press.

Arndt, Hans-Joachim. 1978. *Die Besiegten von 1945: Versuch einer Politologie für Deutsche samt Würdigung der Politwissenschaft in der Bundesrepublik Deutschland.* Berlin: Duncker & Homblot.

Arne, Sigrid. 1948. *United Nations primer.* 2d ed. New York: Rinehart.

Asylstreit. 1992. Asylstreit entscheidet Wahl. *Der Spiegel* 46 (26 October):58–65.

Athans, Mary Christine. 1991. *The Coughlin-Fahey connection: Father Charles E. Coughlin, Father Denis Fahey, C.S.Sp., and religious anti-Semitism in the United States, 1938–1954.* New York: Peter Lang.

Augstein, Rudolf, et al. 1987. *"Historikerstreit": Die Dokumentation der Kontroverse um die Einzigartigkeit der nationalsozialistischen Judenvernichtung.* Munich: R. Piper.

Austilat, Andreas. 1989. "Wen greifen wir an?" Nazisoftware auf dem Schulhof: Jugendschützer setzen auf Gegenmassnahmen ohne Sanktionen. *Der Tagesspiegel,* 10 December.

Baader, Gerhard. 1986. Medizinische Menschenversuche im Nationalsozialismus. In *Versuche mit Menschen in Medizin, Humanwissenschaft und Politik,* ed. Hanfried Helmchen and Rolf Winau, 41–82. Berlin: Walter de Gruyter.

Backer, John H. 1971. *Priming the German economy: American occupational policies, 1945–1948.* Durham, N.C.: Duke University Press.

———. 1978. *The decision to divide Germany: American foreign policy in transition.* Durham, N.C.: Duke University Press.

Backes, Uwe, and Eckhard Jesse. 1985. *Totalitarismus—Extremismus—Totalitarianism: Ein Literaturführer und Wegweiser zur Extremismusforschung in der Bundesrepublik Deutschland.* 2d ed. Opladen: Leske und Budrich.

———. 1989. *Politischer Extremismus in der Bundesrepublik Deutschland.* Vol. 1, *Literatur.* Cologne: Wissenschaft und Politik.

Bacque, James. 1989. *Other losses: An investigation into the mass deaths of German prisoners in the hands of the French and Americans after World War II.* Toronto: Stoddart.

Badstübner, Rolf. 1990. *Friedenssicherung und deutsche Frage: Vom Untergang des "Reiches" bis zur deutschen Zweistaatlichkeit, 1943 bis 1949.* Berlin: Dietz.

Balabkins, Nicholas. 1971. *West German reparations to Israel.* New Brunswick, N.J.: Rutgers University Press.

Bastian, Till. 1992. Der "Leuchter-Report." *Die Zeit* 46 (25 September):90.

Becker, Jillian. 1978. *Hitler's children.* Rev. ed. London: Panther.

Beecher, Henry K. 1966. Ethics and clinical research. *The New England Journal of Medicine* 274:1354–1360.

Bellant, Russ. 1991. *Old Nazis, the New Right, and the Republican Party: Domestic fascist networks and their effect on U.S. cold war politics.* Boston: South End.

Bellon, Bernard P. 1990. *Mercedes in peace and war: German automobile workers, 1903–1945.* New York: Columbia University Press.

Benton, Wilbourn E., and Georg Grimm, eds. 1955. *Nuremberg: German views on the war trials.* Dallas: Southern Methodist University Press.

Benz, Wolfgang. 1989. Judenvernichtung als Notwehr? Vom langen Leben einer rechtsradikalen Legende. In *Rechtsextremismus in der Bundesrepublik: Voraussetzungen, Zusammenhänge, Wirkungen,* ed. Wolfgang Benz, 169–188. Frankfurt-am-Main: Fischer Taschenbuch.

Beradt, Charlotte. 1966/1968. *Das Dritte Reich des Traums*. Munich: Nymphen-burger (1966). Trans. Adriane Gottwald. *The Third Reich of dreams*. Chicago: Quadrangle (1968).

Berg, Lilo. 1991. Die innere Mauer überwinden: Psychologen diskutieren über die Chancen für ein neues Selbstverständnis der Deutschen. *Süddeutsche Zeitung*, 2/3 October. Trans. Psychologists discuss in Dresden how Germans can come to terms with past and present. *The German Tribune*, 20 October.

Berger, Robert L. 1990. Nazi-science: The Dachau hypothermia experiments. *The New England Journal of Medicine* 322:1435–1440.

Bergman, Werner, and Rainer Erb. 1991. *Antisemitismus in der Bundesrepublik Deutschland: Ergebnisse der empirischen Forschung von 1946–1980*. Opladen: Leske und Budrich.

Berlin, Jörg, Dierk Joachim, Bernhard Keller, and Volker Ullrich, eds. 1978. *Was verschweigt Fest? Analysen und Dokumente zum Hitler-Film von J. C. Fest*. Cologne: Paul-Rugenstein.

"Bestie." 1992. "Bestie aus deutschem Blut." *Der Spiegel* 46 (7 December):22–65.

Bier, Jean-Paul. 1986. The Holocaust, West Germany, and strategies of oblivion, 1947–1979. In *Germans and Jews since the Holocaust: The changing situation in West Germany*, ed. Anson Rabinbach and Jack Zipes, 185–206. New York: Holmes & Meier.

Bindman, Aaron M. 1965. Interviewing in the search for "truth." *Sociological Quarterly* 6:281–288.

Bird, Kai. 1992. *The Chairman, John J. McCloy: The making of the American establishment*. New York: Simon & Schuster.

Bischof, Günter, and Stephen E. Ambrose. 1992. *Eisenhower and the German POWs: Facts against falsehood*. Baton Rouge: Louisiana State University Press.

Blankenburg, Erhard. 1967. *Kirchliche Bindung und Wahlverhalten: Die sozialen Factoren bei der Wahlentscheidung Nordrhein-Westfalen, 1961 bis 1966*. Olten: Walter.

Bloch, Felicity. 1986. Medical scientists in the Nazi era. *The Lancet*, no. 8477 (15 February):375.

Block, Gay, and Malka Drucker. 1992. *Rescuers: Portraits of moral courage in the Holocaust*. New York: Holmes & Meier.

Blum, Howard. 1979. *Wanted! The search for Nazis in America*. New York: Quadrangle/The New York Times.

Blum, John Morton. 1967. *From the Morgenthau diaries*. Vol. 3, *Years of war, 1941–1945*. Boston: Houghton Mifflin.

Boberach, Heinz, ed. 1965. *Meldungen aus dem Reich: Auswahl aus den geheimen Lageberichten des Sicherheitsdienstes der SS, 1939–1944*. Neuwied: Hermann Luchterhand.

Bogart, Leo. 1991. The Pollster & the Nazis. *Commentary* 92 (August):47–49.

Booth, Charles, et al. 1892–1897. *Life and labour of the people in London*. 9 vols. London: Macmillan.

Borkin, Joseph. 1978. *The crime and punishment of I. G. Farben*. New York: Free Press.

Bower, Tom. 1982. *The pledge betrayed: America and Britain and the denazification of postwar Germany*. Garden City, N.Y.: Doubleday.

Boynton, G. Robert, and Gerhard Loewenberg. 1974. The decay of support for monarchy and the Hitler regime in the Federal Republic of Germany. *British Journal of Political Science* 4:453–488.

Braunthal, Gerard. 1990. *Political loyalty and public service in West Germany: The 1972 decree against radicals and its consequences*. Amherst: University of Massachusetts Press.

Braunthal, Julius. 1943. *Need Germany survive?* London: Victor Gollancz.

Braybrook, Charles. 1945. *Here is your Hun: A five thousand year saga of Hun wars, murder, rapine, and savagery*. London: W. H. Allen.

Brickner, Richard M. 1943. *Is Germany incurable?* Philadelphia: J. B. Lippincott.

Browning, Christopher R. 1992. *Ordinary men: Reserve police battalian 101 and the final solution in Poland*. New York: Aaron Asher.

Brünneck, Alexander von. 1978. *Politische Justiz gegen Kommunisten in der Bundesrepublik 1949–1968*. Frankfurt-am-Main: Suhrkamp.

Buchanan, William, Hadley Cantril, et al. 1953. *How nations see each other: A study in public opinion*. Urbana: University of Illinois Press.

Bungenstab, Karl-Ernst. 1970. *Umerziehung zur Demokratie? Re-education-Politik im Bildungswesen der US-Zone, 1945–1949*. Düsseldorf: Bertelsmann.

Bunn, Ronald F. 1968. *German politics and the Spiegel affairs: A case study of the Bonn system*. Baton Rouge: Louisiana State University Press.

Buscher, Frank M. 1989. *The U.S. war crimes trial program in Germany, 1946–1955*. New York: Greenwood.

Butterfield, Fox. 1991. Report says paper employee put Hitler quotes in *Dartmouth Review*. *The New York Times*, 10 January.

Butz, Arthur R. 1977. *The hoax of the twentieth century*. 2d ed. Brighton, Sussex: Historical Review Press.

Cameron, James. 1966. A shadow no longer than a crooked cross. *The New York Times Magazine*, 11 September, 94+.

Canon, Scott. 1994. Nebraska Nazi has following in Europe. *The Kansas City Star*, 21 January.

Captives. 1945. The captives of Belsen: Internment camp horrors, British officer's statement. *The Times* (London), 19 April.

Chicago. 1991. Chicago professor is linked to anti-Semitic past. *The New York Times*, 28 November.

Clay, Lucius D. 1950a. *Decision in Germany*. Garden City, N.Y.: Doubleday.

———. 1950b. *Germany and the fight for freedom*. Cambridge: Harvard University Press.

Crespi, Leo P. 1950. The influence of Military Government sponsorship in German opinion polling. *International Journal of Opinion and Attitude Research* 4:151–178.

———. 1980. Foreword. In A. Merritt and R. Merritt 1980:xxiii–xxvi.

———. 1985. Some reflections on U.S. public opinion surveys in post-war Germany. Paper prepared for the quarter-century celebration of the University of Cologne's Zentralarchiv für empirische Sozialforschung, 1 October. Mimeo.

Cronin, Anne. 1992. This is your life, generally speaking: A statistical portrait of the "typical" American. *The New York Times*, 26 July.

Dabringhaus, Erhard. 1984. *Klaus Barbie: The shocking story of how the U.S. used this Nazi war criminal as an intelligence agent.* Washington, D.C.: Acropolis.

Dahrendorf, Ralf. 1965/1967. *Gesellschaft und Demokratie in Deutschland.* Munich: R. Piper (1965). Trans. *Society and democracy in Germany.* Garden City, N.Y.: Doubleday (1967).

Daniell, Raymond. 1945. "So what?" say the Germans of Nuremberg. *The New York Times Magazine*, 2 December, 5+.

Daum, Monika, and Hans-Ulrich Deppe. 1981. *Zwangssterilisation in Frankfurt am Main 1933–1945.* Berlin: Campus.

Davidson, Eugene. 1959. *The death and life of Germany: An account of the American occupation.* New York: Alfred A. Knopf.

———. 1966. *The trial of the Germans: An account of the twenty-two defendants before the International Military Tribunal at Nuremberg.* New York: Macmillan.

Dean, Vera Micheles. 1943. What future for Germany? *Foreign Policy Reports* 18:282–295.

Dean, Vera Micheles, and Ona K. D. Ringwood. 1943. What should be done with "war criminals"? *Foreign Policy Reports* 18:296.

Demetz, Peter. 1970. *Postwar German literature: A critical introduction.* New York: Pegasus.

———. 1986. *After the fires: Recent writing in the Germanies, Austria, and Switzerland.* San Diego: Harcourt Brace Jovanovich.

Demiashkevich, Michael John. 1938. *The national mind: English, French, German.* New York: American.

Deutsch, Karl W., and Lewis J. Edinger. 1959. *Germany rejoins the powers: Mass opinion, interest groups, and elites in contemporary German foreign policy.* Stanford: Stanford University Press.

Deutsche. 1992. Deutsche mit der Demokratie unzufrieden. *Berliner Zeitung*, 27 October.

De Zayas, Alfred M. 1979/1989. *Die Wehrmacht-Untersuchungsstelle.* Munich: Universitas/Langen Müller (1979). Trans. *The Wehrmacht war crimes bureau, 1939–1945.* Lincoln: University of Nebraska Press (1989).

———. 1989. *Nemesis at Potsdam: The expulsion of the Germans from the East.* 3d rev. ed. Lincoln: University of Nebraska Press.

Diederich, Nils. 1965. *Empirische Wahlforschung: Konzeptionen und Methoden im internationalen Vergleich.* Cologne: Westdeutscher.

DIVO. 1958–1962. Deutsches Institut für Volksumfragen (DIVO Institut). *Umfragen: Ereignisse und Probleme der Zeit im Urteil der Bevölkerung.* 4 vols. Frankfurt-am-Main: Europäische.

Doctor. 1991. Doctor in suicides assails U.S. ethics: Kevorkian, in first talk since women died, likens other physicians to Nazis. *The New York Times*, 3 November.

Donaldson, W. T. 1914. *Compulsory voting and absent voting with bibliographies.* Columbus: Ohio Legislative Reference Department, Bulletin no. 1 (April).

Drożdżyński, Aleksander, and Jan Zaborowski. 1960. *Oberländer: A study in East German policies.* Poznan: Wydawnictwo Zachodnie.

Dulles, Allen Welsh. 1947. *Germany's underground.* New York: Macmillan.

Dunner, Joseph. 1948. Information control in the American zone of Germany, 1945–1946. In Carl J. Friedrich and Associates, *American experiences in military government in World War II*, 276–291. New York: Rinehart.

Ebsworth, Raymond. 1960. *Restoring democracy in Germany: The British contribution.* London: Stevens & Son.

Edinger, Lewis J. 1965. *Kurt Schumacher: A study in personality and political behavior.* Stanford: Stanford University Press.

Ehrmann, Henry W. 1947. Experiment in political education: The prisoner-of-war schools in the United States. *Social Research* 14:304–320.

Eisert, Wolfgang. 1993. *Die Waldheimer Prozesse: Der stalinistische Terror 1950: Ein dunkles Kapitel der DDR-Justiz.* Esslinger: Bechtle.

EMNID. 1949 et seq. *EMNID-Informationen.* Bielefeld: EMNID K.G.

Epstein, Helen. 1979. *Children of the Holocaust: Conversations with sons and daughters of survivors.* New York: G. P. Putnam's Sons.

Erst vereint. 1993. Erst vereint, nun entzweit. *Der Spiegel* 47 (18 January):52–62.

Etzioni, Amitai, and Eva Etzioni. 1964. *Social change: Sources, patterns, and consequences.* New York: Basic.

Evans, Richard J. 1989. *In Hitler's shadow: West German historians and the attempt to escape from the Nazi past.* New York: Pantheon.

Fainsod, Merle. 1948. The development of American Military Government policy during World War II. In Carl J. Friedrich and Associates, *American experiences in military government in World War II*, 23–51. New York: Rinehart.

Farnsworth, Clyde H. 1991. Canada revokes citizenship of Nazi. *The New York Times*, 12 November.

Fast. 1992. Fast jeder dritte Jugendliche "konsequent ausländerfeindlich." *Der Tagesspiegel*, 30 September.

FDP-Wähler. 1992. FDP-Wähler wollen Schäuble: Spiegel-Umfrage über die politische Situation im Monat Juni. *Der Spiegel* 46 (29 June):40–47.

Feis, Herbert. 1957. *Churchill, Roosevelt, Stalin: The war they waged and the peace they sought.* Princeton: Princeton University Press.

———. 1960. *Between war and peace: The Potsdam Conference.* Princeton: Princeton University Press.

Feldman, Lily Gardner. 1984. *The special relationship between West Germany and Israel.* Boston: Allen & Unwin.

Fest, Joachim C. 1973/1974. *Hitler: Eine Biographie.* Berlin: Ullstein, Propyläen (1973). Trans. Richard and Clara Winston. *Hitler.* New York: Harcourt Brace Jovanovich (1974).

Fichte, Johann Gottlieb. 1808/1922. *Addresses to the German nation.* Trans. R. F. Jones and G. H. Turnbull. Chicago: Open Court.

Fischer, Fritz. 1961/1967. *Griff nach der Weltmacht.* Düsseldorf: Droste (1961). Trans. *Germany's aims in the First World War.* New York: W. W. Norton (1967).

Fisher, Marc. 1993. Germany releases dying Honecker: He leaves for exile in Chile. *International Herald Tribune,* 14 January.

FitzGibbon, Constantine. 1969. *Denazification.* New York: W. W. Norton.

Foner, Eric. 1988. *Reconstruction: America's unfinished revolution, 1863–1877.* New York: Harper & Row.

Forschungsgruppe Wahlen e. V. Mannheim. 1977. Repräsentative Bevölkerungsumfrage November 1977 (ZDF-Politbarometer). Mimeo.

Forssmann, Werner. 1972/1975. *Selbstversuch: Erinnerung eines Chirurgen.* Düsseldorf: Droste (1972). Trans. Hilary Davies. *Experiments on myself: Memoirs of a surgeon in Germany.* New York: St. Martin's (1975).

Foschepoth, Josef, and Rolf Steininger, eds. 1985. *Die britische Deutschland- und Besatzungspolitik 1945–1949.* Paderborn: Ferdinand Schöningh.

Friedländer, Saul. 1984. *Reflections of Nazism: An essay on kitsch and death.* New York: Harper & Row.

Friedrich, Carl J. 1948. Denazification, 1944–1946. In Carl J. Friedrich and Associates, *American experiences in military government in World War II,* 253–275. New York: Rinehart.

Friedrich, Jörg. 1983. *Freispruch für die Nazijustiz.* Reinbek-bei-Hamburg: Rowohlt Taschenbuch.

———. 1984. *Die kalte Amnestie: NS-Täter in der Bundesrepublik.* Frankfurt-am-Main: Fischer Taschenbuch.

Fromm, Erich. 1942. On the problems of German characterology. *Transactions, The New York Academy of Sciences.* Ser. II, 5 (November):79–83.

Fuchs, Dieter, and Carolin Schöbel. 1992. Personality traits and political action in East and West Germany. Paper presented at the 15th Annual Scientific Meeting, International Society of Political Psychology, San Francisco, 4–8 July.

Gallup, George H. 1972. *The Gallup Poll: Public opinion 1935–1971.* Vol. 1, *1935–1948.* New York: Random House.

Gallup, George H., and Saul Forbes Rae. 1940. *The pulse of democracy: The public opinion poll and how it works.* New York: Simon and Schuster.

Geissler, Rainer. 1981. The effects of the film "Hitler—eine Karriere" on the knowledge of and attitudes towards National Socialism: An example of historical-political socialization through mass media. *International Journal of Political Education* 4:263–282.

Geissler, Rainer, with Jürgen Delitz. 1981. *Junge Deutsche und Hitler: Eine empirische Studie zur historisch-politischen Sozialisation.* Stuttgart: Ernst Klett.

George, Alexander L. 1959. *Propaganda analysis: A study of inferences made from Nazi propaganda in World War II.* Evanston, Ill.: Row, Peterson.

Gewaltige. 1990. Gewaltige Flut. *Der Spiegel* 44 (26 November):90.

Gilbert, Martin. 1981. *Auschwitz and the Allies.* New York: Holt, Rinehart and Winston.

Gimbel, John. 1968. *The American occupation of Germany: Politics and the military, 1945–1949.* Stanford: Stanford University Press.

Glazer, Nathan, and Daniel Patrick Moynihan. 1963. *Beyond the melting pot: The Negroes, Puerto Ricans, Jews, Italians, and Irish of New York City.* Cambridge: M.I.T. Press and Harvard University Press.

Golay, John Ford. 1958. *The founding of the Federal Republic of Germany.* Chicago: University of Chicago Press.

Goldschmidt, Dietrich. 1983. Transatlantic influences: History of mutual interactions between American and German education. In *Between elite and mass education: Education in the Federal Republic of Germany,* ed. Max Planck Institute for Human Development and Education (Berlin West), 1–65. Albany: State University of New York Press.

Gosnell, Harold Foote. 1927. *Getting out the vote: An experiment in the stimulation of voting.* Chicago: University of Chicago Press.

Grace, Alonzo G. 1953. Education. In Edward H. Litchfield et al., *Governing Postwar Germany,* 439–468. Ithaca, N.Y.: Cornell University Press.

Grass, Günter. 1990. *Deutscher Lastenausgleich: Wider das dumpfe Einheitsbegot.* Frankfurt-am-Main: Luchterhand. Trans. Krishna Winston and A. S. Wensinger. *Two states—one nation?* San Diego: Helen and Kurt Wolff.

Griffith, William E. 1950. The denazification program in the United States zone of Germany. Ph.D. diss., Harvard University.

Gunlicks, Arthur B., ed. 1989. Federalism and intergovernmental relations in West Germany: A fortieth year appraisal. Special issue of *Publius: The Journal of Federalism* 19 (Fall):1–238.

Gurfein, Murray I., and Morris Janowitz. 1946. Trends in Wehrmacht morale. *The Public Opinion Quarterly* 13:78–84.

Habermas, Jürgen. 1986. Vom öffentlichen Gebrauch der Historie. *Die Zeit,* Overseas ed. 41 (14 November):4.

Hagen, Paul. 1944. *Germany after Hitler.* New York: Farrar & Rinehart.

Hale, Oron J. 1964. *The captive press in the Third Reich.* Princeton: Princeton University Press.

Halpern, Henry. 1949. Soviet attitude toward public opinion research in Germany. *The Public Opinion Quarterly* 13:117–118.

Hamilton, Charles. 1991. *The Hitler diaries: Fakes that fooled the world.* Lexington: University Press of Kentucky.

Hamilton, Thomas J. 1965. Strauss warns of "new Führer." *The New York Times,* 27 August.

Hamm-Brücher, Hildegard. 1970. Versäumte Reformen. In *Nach 25 Jahren: Eine Deutschland-Bilanz,* ed. Karl Dietrich Bracher, 151–165. Munich: Kindler.

Hammond, Paul Y. 1963. Directives for the occupation of Germany: The Washington controversy. In *American civil-military decisions: A book of case studies,* ed. Harold Stein, 311–464. University: University of Alabama Press; a Twentieth Century Fund study published in cooperation with the Inter-University Case Program.

Hanauske-Abel, Hartmut M. 1986. From Nazi Holocaust to nuclear holocaust: A lesson to learn? *The Lancet*, no. 8501 (2 August):271–273.

Hart, Hornell Norris. 1923. *Progress report on a test of social attitudes and interests*. Iowa City: University of Iowa; Iowa Child Welfare Research Station, University of Iowa Studies in Child Welfare, 2:4.

Hartenian, Lawrence Raymond. 1984. Propaganda and the control of information in occupied Germany: The U.S. Information Control Division at Radio Frankfurt 1945–1949. Ph.D. diss., Rutgers University.

Hearnden, Arthur. 1985. The economic branch of the Military Government of Germany and the schools. In *The political re-education of Germany and her allies after World War II*, ed. Nicholas Pronay and Keith Wilson, 97–106. London: Croom Helm.

Heger, Heinz. 1972/1980. *Die Männer mit dem rosa Winkel: Der Bericht eines Homosexuellen über seine KZ-Haft von 1939–1945*. Hamburg: Merlin (1972). Trans. *The men with the pink triangle*. Boston: Alyson (1980).

Heiber, Helmut. 1991. *Universität unterm Hakenkreuz*. Part 1, *Der Professor im Dritten Reich; Bilder aus der akademischen Provinz*. Munich: K. G. Saur.

Herdegen, Gerhard. 1979. *Demokratie-Verankerung in der Bundesrepublik Deutschland: Eine empirische Untersuchung zum 30jährigen Bestehen der Bundesrepublik*. Allensbach-am-Bodensee: Institut für Demoskopie Allensbach.

Herf, Jeffrey. 1986. The "Holocaust" reception in West Germany: Right, center, and left. In *Germans and Jews since the Holocaust: The changing situation in West Germany*, ed. Anson Rabinbach and Jack Zipes, 208–233. New York: Holmes & Meier.

Herz, John H. 1948. The fiasco of denazification in Germany. *Political Science Quarterly* 63:569–595.

Heuss, Theodor. 1966. *Aufzeichnungen, 1945–1947*. Tübingen: Rainer Wunderlich, Hermann Leins.

HIC. See A. Merritt and R. Merritt 1980.

Hillgruber, Andreas. 1986. *Zweierlei Untergang: Die Zerschlagung des Deutschen Reiches und das Ende des europäischen Judentums*. Berlin: Wolf Jobst Siedler.

Hirsch, Jerry, Gordon Harrington, and Barry Mehler. 1990. Review article: An irresponsible farewell gloss. *Educational Theory* 40:501–508.

Hirsch-Weber, Wolfgang, Klaus Schütz, et al. 1957. *Wähler und Gewählte: Eine Untersuchung der Bundestagswahlen 1953*. Berlin: Franz Vahlen.

Hitler, Adolf. 1925–1927/1939. *Mein Kampf*. Munich: Frz. Eher Nachf. (1925–1927). Trans. Helmut Ripperger. Boston: Houghton Mifflin (1939).

Hogan, Michael J. 1987. *The Marshall Plan: America, Britain, and the reconstruction of western Europe, 1947–1952*. New York: Cambridge University Press.

Hoggan, David L. 1961. *Der Erzwungene Krieg: Die Ursachen und Urheber des Zweiten Weltkrieges*. Tübingen: Grabert.

Holborn, Hajo. 1947. *American Military Government, its organization and policies*. Washington, D.C.: Infantry Journal.

Holmberg, Arthur. 1990. In Germany, a warning from Heiner Müller. *The New York Times*, 8 July.

Holmes, Steven A. 1992. Nazi victims face deadline on claims. *The New York Times*, 31 December.

"Holocaust." 1979. "Holocaust": Die Vergangenheit kommt züruck. *Der Spiegel* 33 (29 January):17–28.

Horstmann, Kurt. 1954. Wahlbeteiligung und Stimmabgabe nach Geschlecht und Alter sowie die Art der Kombination der Erst- und Zweitstimmen. *Wirtschaft und Statistik* 6 (January):9–13.

Howe, Marvine. 1991. Lithuanian vows inquiry on Nazis. *The New York Times*, 17 November.

Hurwitz, Harold. 1972. *Die Stunde Null der deutschen Presse: Die amerikanische Pressepolitik in Deutschland 1945–1949*. Cologne: Wissenschaft und Politik, Berend von Nottbeck.

IfD. *See* Institut für Demoskopie 1949 et seq. and Noelle-Neumann et al. 1956–1993.

Im Osten. 1991. Im Osten liegt die SPD noch vorn. *Der Spiegel* 45 (25 November): 54–65.

Institut für Demoskopie. 1949 et seq. *Allensbacher Berichte*. Allensbach-am-Bodensee: Institut für Demoskopie.

Irving, David. 1991. *Hitler's war and the war path, 1933–1945*. London: Focal Point.

Jacobson, Edmund. 1944. *The peace we Americans need: A plea for clearer thinking about our allies, our foes, ourselves and our future*. Chicago: A. Kroch and Sons.

Jäger, Herbert. 1967/1982. *Verbrechen unter totalitärer Herrschaft; Studien zur nationalsozialistischen Gewaltkriminalität*. Olten: Walter (1967). 2d ed. Frankfurt-am-Main: Suhrkamp (1982).

Jahn, Friedrich Ludwig. 1810. *Deutsches Volkstum*. Lübeck: Niemann.

Janis, Irving L. 1963. Group identification under conditions of external danger. *The British Journal of Medical Psychology* 36:227–238.

Janowitz, Morris. 1946. German reactions to Nazi atrocities. *The American Journal of Sociology* 52:141–146.

Jarausch, Konrad H. 1988. Removing the Nazi stain? The quarrel of the German historians. *German Studies Review* 11:285–301.

Jews. 1941. Jews of Hanover forced from homes. *The New York Times*, 9 September.

Joffe, Josef. 1992. Was geht uns Somalia an? *Süddeutsche Zeitung*, 9 December.

Jugend. 1990. Jugend und Gewalt in Deutschland. *Der Spiegel* 44 (12 November): 36–65; 44 (19 November):157–174; and 44 (26 November):154–166.

Kakutani, Michiko. 1991. Wearing the Holocaust like an M.I.A. bracelet. *The New York Times*, 19 November.

Kater, Michael H. 1989. *Doctors under Hitler*. Chapel Hill: University of North Carolina Press.

Kaufman, Theodore N. 1941. *Germany must perish!* Newark, N.J.: Argyle.

Kielinger, Thomas. 1991. The Gulf War and the consequences from a German point of view. *Aussenpolitik*, English ed. 42:241–250.

Kimball, Warren F. 1976. *Swords or ploughshares? The Morgenthau Plan for defeated Nazi Germany, 1943–1946.* Philadelphia: J. P. Lippincott.

Kitterman, David H. 1988. Those who said "No!": Germans who refused to execute civilians during World War II. *German Studies Review* 11:241–254.

Klarsfeld, Beate. 1972/1975. *Partout ou ils seront.* Paris: J. C. Lattes (1972). Trans. Monroe Stearns and Natalie Gerardi. *Wherever they may be!* New York: Vanguard (1975).

Klatt, Hartmut. 1989. Forty years of German federalism: Past trends and new developments. *Publius: The Journal of Federalism* 19 (Fall):185–202.

Klingemann, Hans D., and Franz U. Pappi. 1972. *Politischer Radikalismus: Theoretische und methodische Probleme der Radikalismusforschung, dargestellt am Beispiel einer Studie anlässlich der Landtagswahl 1970 in Hessen.* Munich: R. Oldenbourg.

Kluth, Hans. 1959. *Die KPD in der Bundesrepublik: Ihre politische Tätigkeit und Organisation, 1945–1956.* Cologne: Westdeutscher.

Knappen, Marshall. 1947. *And call it peace.* Chicago: University of Chicago Press.

Knieriem, August von. 1953/1959. *Nürnberg: Rechtliche und menschliche Probleme.* Stuttgart: Ernst Klett (1953). Trans. *The Nuremberg trials.* Chicago: Henry Regnery (1959).

Kommers, Donald P. 1976. *Judicial politics in West Germany: A study of the federal constitutional system.* Beverly Hills, Calif.: Sage.

———. 1989. *The constitutional jurisprudence of the Federal Republic of Germany.* Durham, N.C.: Duke University Press.

———. 1994. The Federal Constitutional Court in the German political system. *Comparative Political Studies* 26:470–491.

Kormann, John G. 1952. *U.S. denazification policy in Germany, 1945–1950.* Bad Godesberg: Historical Division, Office of the Executive Secretary, Office of the United States High Commission for Germany.

Koszyk, Kurt. 1972. *Geschichte der deutschen Presse.* Vol. 3, *Deutsche Presse, 1914–1945.* Berlin: Colloquium Otto H. Hess.

Kris, Ernst, and Hans Speier et al. 1944. *German radio propaganda: Report on home broadcasts during the war.* London: Oxford University Press.

Krugman, Morris. 1949. A study of German prisoners of war. *American Journal of Orthopsychiatry* 19:525–536.

Kühl, Stefan. 1994. *The Nazi connection: Eugenics, American racism, and German National Socialism.* New York: Oxford University Press.

Kuklick, Bruce. 1972. *American policy and the division of Germany: The clash with Russia over reparations.* Ithaca, N.Y.: Cornell University Press.

Lach, Donald F. 1945. Bibliographical article: What *they* would do about Germany. *The Journal of Modern History* 17:227–243.

Lange-Quassowski, Jutta B. 1979. *Neuordnung oder Restauration? Das Demokratiekonzept der amerikanischen Besatzungsmacht und die politische Sozialisation der Westdeutschen: Wirtschaftsordnung—Schulstructur—Politische Bildung.* Opladen: Leske und Budrich.

Langer, Lawrence L. 1975. *The Holocaust and the literary imagination.* New Haven: Yale University Press.

Langer, Walter C. 1972. *The mind of Adolf Hitler: The secret wartime report*. New York: Basic.

LaPiere, Richard T. 1965. *Social Change*. New York: McGraw-Hill.

Lasby, Clarence G. 1971. *Project paperclip: German scientists and the cold war*. New York: Atheneum.

Lasswell, Harold Dwight. 1927. *Propaganda technique in the World War*. New York: Alfred A. Knopf. Republished 1971. Cambridge: M.I.T. Press.

Lautmann, Rüdiger, Winfried Grikschat, and Egbert Schmidt. 1977. Der rose Winkel in den nationalsozialistischen Konzentrationslagern. In *Seminar: Gesellschaft und Homosexualität*, ed. Rüdiger Lautmann, 325–365. Frankfurt-am-Main: Suhrkamp Taschenbuch.

Lautmann, Rüdiger, and Erhard Wisman. 1990. *The persecution of homosexuals in Nazi Germany: Sexual politics in a fascist state*, ed. Jack N. Porter. Lewiston, N.Y.: Edwin Mellen. Vol. 14 of Studies in German thought and history.

Leibholz, Gerhard. 1952. The Federal Constitutional Court in Germany and the "Southwest Case." *The American Political Science Review* 46:723–731.

Lerner, Daniel. 1949. *Sykewar: Psychological warfare against war, D-Day to VE-Day*. New York: George W. Stewart. Republished 1971. Cambridge: M.I.T. Press.

Leuchter, Fred A. 1989/1991. *The Leuchter report: The first forensic examination of Auschwitz*. London: Focal Point (1989). Trans. *Ein Ingenieursbericht über die angeblichen Gaskammern in Auschwitz, Birkenau und Makjdanek, Poland* (1990).

Levenstein, Adolf. 1912. *Die Arbeiterfrage, Mit besonderer Berücksichtigung der sozialpsychologischen Seite des modernen Grossbetriebes und der psychophysischen Einwirkungen auf die Arbeiter*. Munich: Ernst Reinhardt.

Levin, N. Gordon, Jr. 1968. *Woodrow Wilson and world politics: America's response to war and revolution*. New York: Oxford University Press.

Lewin, Tamar. 1992. For U.S. Nazi hunters, a mixed year. *The New York Times*, 6 July.

Lewis, Paul. 1992. Iraq admits buying German materials to make A-bombs. *The New York Times*, 15 January.

Liddell, Helen. 1949. Education in occupied Germany: A field survey. In Helen Liddell, Edmond Vermeil, and Bogdan Suchodolski, *Education in Occupied Germany/L'education de l'Allemagne occupée*, ed. Helen Liddell, 95–148. Paris: Marcel Rivière.

Lifton, Robert Jay. 1984. Medicalized killing in Auschwitz. In *Psychoanalytic reflections on the Holocaust: Selected essays*, ed. Steven A. Luel and Paul Marcus, 11–33. Denver: University of Denver, Center for Judaic Studies, Holocaust Awareness Institute; and New York: Ktav.

———. 1986. *The Nazi doctors: Medical killing and the psychology of genocide*. New York: Basic.

Lilienthal, David E. 1944. *TVA: Democracy on the march*. New York: Harper & Brothers.

Linz, Juan J. 1967. Cleavages and consensus in West German politics: The early fifties. In *Party systems and voter alignments: Cross-national perspec-*

tives, ed. Seymour Martin Lipset and Stein Rokkan, 283–321. New York: Free Press.

Long, Wellington. 1968. *The new Nazis of Germany*. Philadelphia: Chilton.

Lowrey, Lawson G., et al. 1945. Germany after the War: Round table, 1945. *American Journal of Orthopsychiatry* 15:381–441.

Lozier, Marion E. 1963. Nuremberg: A reappraisal. *Bulletin of the Columbia Society of International Law* (later *Columbia Journal of Transnational Law*) 2:22–33.

Ludwig, Emil. 1941. *The Germans: Double history of a nation*. Trans. Heinz and Ruth Norden. Boston: Little, Brown.

———. 1943. *How to treat the Germans*. New York: Willard.

———. 1945. *The moral conquest of Germany*. Garden City, N.Y.: Doubleday, Doran.

MacIver, R. M., and Charles H. Page. 1949. *Society: An introductory analysis*. New York: Rinehart.

Maier, Charles S. 1988. *The unmasterable past: History, Holocaust, and German national identity*. Cambridge: Harvard University Press.

Mann, Erika. 1938. *School for barbarians*. With int. by Thomas Mann. New York: Modern Age.

Markovits, Andrei S. 1984. Germans and Jews: The continuation of an uneasy relationship. *Jewish Frontier* 51 (April):14–20.

———. 1989. Anti-Americanism and the struggle for a West German identity. In *The Federal Republic at forty*, ed. Peter H. Merkl, 35–54. New York: New York University Press.

Markovits, Andrei S., and Philip S. Gorski. 1993. *The German left: Red, green and beyond*. New York: Oxford University Press.

Markovits, Andrei S., and Rebecca S. Hayden. 1986. "Holocaust" before and after the event: Reactions in West Germany and Austria. In *Germans and Jews since the Holocaust: The changing situation in West Germany*, ed. Anson Rabinbach and Jack Zipes, 234–257. New York: Holmes & Meier.

Markovits, Andrei S., and Beth Simone Noveck. Forthcoming. The world reacts: The case of West Germany. In *The world reacts to the Holocaust*, ed. David Wyman. Baltimore: Johns Hopkins University Press.

Markovits, Inga. 1992/1993. Last Days. *California Law Review* 80:55–129 (1992). Expanded and trans. *Die Abwicklung: Ein Tagebuch zum Ende der DDR-Justiz*. Munich: C. H. Beck'sche (Oscar Beck) (1993).

Martin, Laurence W. 1963. The American decision to rearm Germany. In *American civil-military decisions: A book of case studies*, ed. Harold Stein, 643–663. University: University of Alabama Press; a Twentieth Century Fund study published in cooperation with the Inter-University Case Program.

Massenkundgebung. 1943. Massenkundgebung im Berliner Sportplatz: Volksentscheid für den totalen Krieg. *Völkischer Beobachter*, 19 February.

McCloy, John J. 1978. Ein Brief von John McCloy. *Der Tagesspiegel*, 19 March.

McCormick, John. 1990. The Holocaust's new lessons: In Winnetka's 8th grade, a war of remembrance. *Newsweek* 116 (3 December):52.

McGranahan, Donald A., and Ivor Wayne. 1948. German and American traits reflected in popular drama. *Human Relations* 1:429–455.

Merkatz, Hans Joachim von, and Wolfgang Metzner, in cooperation with A. Hillen Ziegfeld, eds. 1954. *Germany today: Facts and figures.* Frankfurt-am-Main: Alfred Metzner.

Merkl, Peter H. 1963. *The origin of the West German republic.* New York: Oxford University Press.

Merriam, Charles Edward, and Harold Foote Gosnell. 1924. *Not-voting: Causes and methods of control.* Chicago: University of Chicago Press.

Merritt, Anna J. 1972. Germans and American denazification. In *Communication in international politics,* ed. Richard L. Merritt, 361–383. Urbana: University of Illinois Press.

Merritt, Anna J., and Richard L. Merritt, eds. 1970. *Public opinion in occupied Germany: The OMGUS surveys, 1945–1949.* Urbana: University of Illinois Press.

———. 1980. *Public opinion in semisovereign Germany: The HICOG surveys, 1949–1955.* Urbana: University of Illinois Press.

Merritt, Richard L. 1967. Visual representation of mutual friendliness. In *Mathematical applications in political science,* vol. 3, ed. Joseph L. Bernd, with the assistance of Archer Jones, 96–119. Charlottesville: University Press of Virginia. Rpt. in R. Merritt and Puchala 1968.

———. 1969. The student protest movement in West Berlin. *Comparative Politics* 1:516–533.

———. 1973. The tangled tie: West Germany and the Berlin problem. In *Politics in Europe: Structures and processes in some postindustrial democracies,* ed. Martin O. Heisler, 341–368. New York: David McKay.

———. 1975. Public perspectives in closed societies. In *Foreign Policy Analysis,* ed. Richard Merritt, 101–117. Lexington, Mass.: Lexington.

———. 1980a. The 1953 Bundestag election: Evidence from West German public opinion. *Historical Social Research/Historische Sozialforschung* no. 16 (October):3–38.

———. 1980b. Transforming international communications strategies. *Political Communication and Persuasion* 1:5–42.

———. 1986. Divided airwaves: The electronic media and political community in postwar Berlin. *International Political Science Review* 7:369–399.

———. 1994. Normalizing the East German media. *Political Communication* 11:49–66.

Merritt, Richard L., Ellen P. Flerlage, and Anna J. Merritt. 1971a. Political man in postwar West German education. *Comparative Education Review* 15:346–361.

———. 1971b. Democratizating West German education. *Comparative Education,* 7:121–136.

Merritt, Richard L., and Donald J. Puchala, eds. 1968. *Western European perspectives on international affairs: Public opinion studies and evaluations.* New York: Frederick A. Praeger.

Mettler, Barbara. 1975. *Demokratisierung und Kalter Krieg: Zur amerikanischen Informations-und Rundfunkpolitik in Westdeutschland, 1945–1949.* Berlin: Volker Spiess.

Middleton, Drew. 1951. Neo-nazism: "A cloud like a man's hand." *The New York Times Magazine*, 1 January, 9+.

Miller, Judith. 1990. *One, by one, by one: Facing the Holocaust.* New York: Simon & Schuster.

Mit Gestrigen. 1989. Mit Gestrigen in die Zukunft? Spiegel-Umfrage über Hitler, die NS-Zeit und die Folgen. *Der Spiegel* 43 (10 April):150–160.

Mitscherlich, Alexander. 1984. *Ein Leben für die Psychoanalyse: Anmerkungen zu meiner Zeit.* Frankfurt-am-Main: Suhrkamp.

Mitscherlich, Alexander, and Fred Mielke. 1947/1949. *Der Diktat der Menschenverachtung.* Heidelberg: Lambert Schneider (1947). Trans. Heinz Norden. *Doctors of infamy: The story of the Nazi medical crimes.* Exp. ed. New York: Henry Schuman (1949).

Mitscherlich, Alexander, and Margarete Mitscherlich. 1967/1975. *Die Unfähigkeit zu trauern: Grundlagen kollektiven Verhaltens.* Munich: R. Piper (1967). Trans. Beverly R. Placzek. *The inability to mourn: Principles of collective behavior.* New York: Grove (1975).

Molnar, G. W. 1946. Survival of hypothermia by men immersed in the ocean. *The Journal of the American Medical Association* 131:1046–1050.

Montgomery, John D. 1957. *Forced to be free: The artificial revolution in Germany and Japan.* Chicago: University of Chicago Press.

Moore, Wilbert E. 1968. Social Change. In *International Encyclopedia of the Social Sciences,* ed. David L. Sills, 14:365–375. New York: Macmillan and Free Press.

Morgan, Ted. 1990. *An uncertain hour: The French, the Germans, the Jews, the Barbie trial, and the city of Lyon, 1940–1945.* New York: William Morrow.

———. 1994. The hidden henchman. *The New York Times Magazine,* 22 May, 30+.

Morgenthau, Henry, Jr. 1945. *Germany is our problem.* New York: Harper & Brothers.

Morgenthau, Henry III. 1991. *Mostly Morgenthau: A family history.* New York: Ticknor & Fields.

Mosely, Philip E. 1950a. Dismemberment of Germany: The Allied negotiations from Yalta to Potsdam. *Foreign Affairs* 28:487–498.

———. 1950b. The occupation of Germany: New light on how the zones were drawn. *Foreign Affairs* 28:580–604.

Mosse, George L. 1966. *Nazi culture: Intellectual, cultural and social life in the Third Reich.* New York: Grosset & Dunlap.

Müller, Ingo. 1991. *Hitler's justice: The courts of the Third Reich.* Cambridge: Harvard University Press.

Müller-Freienfels, Richard. 1922/1936. *Psychologie des deutschen Menschen und seiner Kultur: Ein volkscharakterologischer Versuch.* Munich: C. H. Beck'sche (Oskar Beck) (1922). Trans. Rolf Hoffmann. *The German: His psychology and culture: An inquiry into folk character.* Los Angeles: New Symposium (1936).

Müller-Hill, Benno. 1984/1988. *Tödliche Wissenschaft: Die Aussonderung von Juden, Zigeunern und Geisteskranken 1933–1945.* Reinbek-bei-Hamburg:

Rowohlt Taschenbuch (1984). Trans. George R. Fraser. *Murderous science: Elimination by scientific selection of Jews, Gypsies, and others, Germany 1933–1945.* Oxford: Oxford University Press (1988).

Müller-Meiningen, Ernst, Jr. 1946. *Die Parteigenossen.* Munich: Kurt Desch.

Murphy, Robert. 1964. *Diplomat among warriors.* Garden City, N.Y.: Doubleday.

Nagle, John David. 1970. *The National Democratic Party: Right radicalism in the Federal Republic of Germany.* Berkeley: University of California Press.

Nahr, Wolf-Dietrich. 1991. *Die befohlene Pressefreiheit.* Berlin: Volker Spiess.

Neufeld, Michael J. 1995. *The rocket and the Reich: Peenemünde and the coming of the ballistic missile era.* New York: Free Press.

Neumann, Erich Peter, and Elisabeth Noelle, eds. 1961/1962. *Umfragen über Adenauer: Ein Porträt in Zahlen.* Allensbach: Institut für Demoskopie (1961). Trans. *Statistics on Adenauer: Portrait of a statesman.* Allensbach: Institut für Demoskopie (1962).

Niethammer, Lutz. 1969. *Angepasster Faschismus: Politische Praxis der NPD.* Frankfurt-am-Main: S. Fischer.

———. 1972. *Die Mitläuferfabrik: Die Entnazifierung am Beispiel Bayerns.* Berlin: J. H. W. Dietz Nachf. Rpt. 1982.

Nisbet, Robert, ed. 1972. *Social change.* New York: Harper & Row.

Nizer, Louis. 1944. *What to do with Germany.* Chicago: Ziff-Davis.

Noelle, Elisabeth. 1940. *Amerikanische Massenbefragungen über Politik und Presse.* Frankfurt-am-Main: M. Diesterweg.

———. 1992. Letter to the editor. *Commentary* 93 (January):9–15.

Noelle, Elisabeth, and Erich Peter Neumann, eds. 1967. *The Germans: Public opinion polls, 1947–1966.* Allensbach: Institut für Demoskopie.

Noelle-Neumann, Elisabeth, et al. 1956–1993. *Jahrbuch der öffentlichen Meinung.* 9 vols. to date. Allensbach: Institut für Demoskopie.

Nolte, Ernst. 1963/1966. *Der Faschismus in seiner Epoche.* Munich: R. Piper (1963). Trans. Leila Vennevitz: *Three faces of fascism.* New York: Holt, Rinehart and Winston (1966).

———. 1980. Die negative Lebendigkeit des Dritten Reiches: Eine Frage aus dem Blickwinkel des Jahres 1980. *Die Frankfurter Allgemeine Zeitung*, 24 July.

———. 1985. Between myth and revisionism? The Third Reich in the perspectives of the 1980s. In *Aspects of the Third Reich*, ed. Hansjoachim Wolfgang Koch, 17–38. London: Macmillan. Abridged German-language version in Nolte 1980; unabridged German-language version in Augstein et al. 1987:13–35.

———. 1986. Vergangenheit, die nicht vergehen will: Eine Rede, die geschrieben, aber nicht gehalten werden konnte. *Die Frankfurter Allgemeine Zeitung*, 6 June. Rpt. in Nolte 1987a:171–179.

———. 1987a. *Das Vergehen der Vergangenheit: Antwort an meine Kritiker im sogenannten Historikerstreit.* Berlin: Ullstein.

———. 1987b. *Der europäische Bürgerkrieg 1917–1945: Nationalsozialismus und Bolschewismus.* Frankfurt-am-Main: Ullstein, Propyläen.

NORC. 1945. *Germany and the post-war world.* Denver: National Opinion Research Center. Report no. 24 (January).

OMG. *See* A. Merritt and R. Merritt 1970.

OMG/IC. *See* United States, Office of Military Government for Germany, U.S. Zone, Information Control Division.

OMG/IS. *See* [United States,] Office of Military Government for Germany, U.S. Zone, Information Services Division.

OMG/MG. *See* [United States,] Office of Military Government for Germany, U.S. Zone.

OMGUS. *See* United States, Office of Military Government, Office of the Director.

Paletz, David L., ed. 1981. Special issue: Reactions to "Holocaust." *International Journal of Political Education* 4:1–180.

Peterson, Edward N. 1977. *The American occupation of Germany: Retreat to victory.* Detroit: Wayne State University Press.

———. 1990. *The many faces of defeat: The German people's experience in 1945.* New York: Peter Lang.

Pilgert, Henry P. 1953. *The West German education system, with special reference to the policies and programs of the Office of the U.S. High Commissioner for Germany.* Bad Godesberg: Office of the U.S. High Commissioner for Germany, Office of the Executive Secretary, Historical Division.

Pilgert, Henry P., with Helga Dobbert. 1953. *Press, radio and film in West Germany, 1945–1953.* Bad Godesberg: Office of the U.S. High Commissioner for Germany, Office of the Executive Secretary, Historical Division.

Pilgert, Henry P., with Friedrich Forstmeier. 1951. *The Exchange of Persons Program in Western Germany.* Bad Godesberg: Office of the U.S. High Commissioner for Germany, Office of the Executive Secretary, Historical Division.

Pinney, Edward L. 1963. *Federalism, bureaucracy, and party politics in western Germany: The role of the Bundesrat.* Chapel Hill: University of North Carolina Press.

Pitts, Jesse R. 1968. Le Play, Frédéric. In *International encyclopedia of the social sciences,* ed. David L. Sills, 9:84–91. New York: Macmillan and Free Press.

Plant, Richard. 1986. *The pink triangle: The Nazi war against homosexuals.* New York: New Republic.

Pool, Ithiel de Sola, et al. 1970. *The prestige press: A comparative study of political symbols.* Cambridge: M.I.T. Press.

Posner, Gerald L. 1991a. The Bormann file. *The New York Times,* 13 November.

———. 1991b. *Hitler's children: Sons and daughters of leaders of the Third Reich talk about their fathers and themselves.* New York: Random House.

Posner, Gerald L., and John Ware. 1986. *Mengele: The complete story.* New York: McGraw-Hill.

Pozos, Robert. 1989. Can scientists use information derived from concentration camps? Paper presented at the conference on the meaning of the Holocaust for bioethics, Minneapolis, 17–19 May. Transcript available on tape no. 7 of official recording. Minneapolis: University of Minnesota, Center for Biomedical Ethics.

Prager, Emily. 1991. *Eve's tattoo.* New York: Random House.

Pressac, Jean-Claude. 1989. *Auschwitz: Technique and operation of the gas chambers.* Trans. Peter Moss. New York: Beate Klarsfeld Foundation.

Prittie, Terence. 1971. *Konrad Adenauer, 1876–1967.* Chicago: Henry Regnery.

Proctor, Robert. 1988. *Racial hygiene: Medicine under the Nazis.* Cambridge: Harvard University Press.

Pross, Harry, ed. 1965. *Deutsche Presse seit 1945.* Bern: Scherz.

Ratchford, Benjamin Ulysses, and William D. Ross. 1947. *Berlin reparations assignment: Round one of the German peace settlement.* Chapel Hill: University of North Carolina Press.

Rauhaus, Gerd. 1989. Rassenhass als Komputerspiel. *Nürnberger Nachrichten,* 5 January.

Raymond, Jack. 1951. 21 Nazi criminals saved from death. *The New York Times,* 1 February.

Reichel, Sabine. 1989. *What did you do in the war, Daddy? Growing up German.* New York: Hill and Wang.

Reigrotzki, Erich. 1956. *Soziale Verflechtungen in der Bundesrepublik: Elemente der sozialen Teilnahme in Kirche, Politik, Organisationen und Freizeit.* Tübingen: J. C. B. Mohr (Paul Siebeck).

Reilly, Philip R. 1991. *The surgical solution: A history of involuntary sterilization in the United States.* Baltimore: Johns Hopkins University Press.

Reitlinger, Gerald. 1956. *The SS: Alibi of a nation, 1922–1945.* London: Simon and Schuster.

Renzsch, Wolfgang. 1989. German federalism in historical perspective: Federalism as a substitute for a nation state. *Publius: The Journal of Federalism* 19 (Fall):17–33.

Riding, Alan. 1992. Rulings jar France into reliving its anti-Jewish role in Nazi era. *The New York Times,* 10 March.

RIIA. 1943. *The problem of Germany: An interim report by a Chatham House study group.* London: Royal Institute of International Affairs and Oxford University Press.

Robinsohn, Saul B., and J. Caspar Kuhlmann. 1967. Two decades of nonreform in West German education. *Comparative Education Review* 11:311–330.

Robinson, Claude E. 1932. *Straw votes: A study of political prediction.* New York: Columbia University Press.

Roloff, Gerhard. 1976. *Exil und Exilliteratur in der deutschen Presse 1945–1949: Ein Beitrag zur Rezeptionsgeschichte.* Worms: Georg Heintz.

Roper, Elmo, Inc. 1939a. The Fortune Survey: XXIII. *Fortune* 20 (September):64–65+.

———. 1939b. The Fortune Survey: Supplement on War. *Fortune* 20 (October):unpaginated.

———. 1939c. The Fortune Survey: Supplement II on War. *Fortune* 20 (November):unpaginated.

———. 1939d. The Fortune Survey: XXV. *Fortune* 20 (December):78–79+.

———. 1940a. The Fortune Survey: XXVI. *Fortune* 21 (January):56–57+.

———. 1940b. The Fortune Survey: XXVIII. *Fortune* 21 (March):54–55+.

———. 1945. The Fortune Survey. *Fortune* 31 (March):254–262.

Rosenberg, David, ed. 1989. *Testimony: Contemporary writers make the Holocaust personal.* New York: Times.

Rosmus, Anna Elisabeth. 1990. Should German movies look back? *The New York Times,* 21 October.

Rosner, Fred, et al. 1991. The ethics of using scientific data obtained by immoral means. *New York State Journal of Medicine* 91:54–59.

Roth, Edwin. 1978. Brisanter Bericht im britischen Fernsehen. *Der Tagesspiegel,* 26 February.

Rowntree, B. Seebohm. 1901. *Poverty: A study of town life.* London: Macmillan.

Rückerl, Adalbert. 1979/1980. *Die Strafverfolgung von NS-Verbrechen 1945 bis 1978.* Heidelberg: C. F. Müller (1979). Trans. Derek Rutter. *The investigation of Nazi crimes 1945–1978: A documentation.* Hamden, Conn.: Archon (1980).

Rückmann, Kurt. 1972. *Demoskopie oder Demagogie? Zur Meinungsforschung in der BRD.* Frankfurt-am-Main: Marxistische Blätter.

Russell, Lord of Liverpool. 1969. *Return of the swastika?* New York: David McKay.

Ryan, Allan A., Jr. 1984. *Quiet neighbors: Prosecuting Nazi war criminals in America.* San Diego: Harcourt Brace Jovanovich.

Ryan, Judith. 1983. *The uncompleted past: Postwar German novels and the Third Reich.* Detroit: Wayne State University Press.

Saidel, Rochelle G. 1984. *The outraged conscience: Seekers of justice for Nazi war criminals in America.* Albany: State University of New York Press.

Schmemann, Serge. 1989. Landsberg journal: The prostitutes leave, but Nazi ghosts linger. *The New York Times,* 1 July.

Schmid, Carlo. 1967. *Der Weg des deutschen Volkes nach 1945.* Berlin: Haude & Spenersche.

Schmidt, Regine, and Egon Becker. 1967. *Reaktionen auf politische Vorgänge: Drei Meinungsstudien aus der Bundesrepublik.* Frankfurt-am-Main: Europäische.

Schmidtchen, Gerhard. 1959. *Die befragte Nation: über den Einfluss der Meinungsforschung auf die Politik.* Freiburg-im-Breisgau: Rombach.

Schmidtchen, Gerhard, and Elisabeth Noelle-Neumann. 1963. Die Bedeutung repräsentativer Bevölkerungsumfragen für die offene Gesellschaft. *Politische Vierteljahresschrift* 4:168–195.

Schneider, Peter. 1990/1991. *Extreme Mittellage: Eine Reise durch das Deutsche Nationalgefühl.* Reinbek-bei-Hamburg: Rowohlt Taschenbuch (1990). Trans. Philip Boehm and Leigh Hafney. *The German comedy: Scenes of life after the wall.* New York: Farrar, Straus & Giroux (1991).

———. 1991. Facing Germany's newer past. *The New York Times,* 30 September.

Schoenbaum, David. 1965. Nazi murders and German politics. *Commentary* 39 (June):72–77.

Schöppner, Klaus-Peter. 1992. Vertrauen der Wähler ist geschwunden: Ost und West befürchten immer höhere Belastungen durch die Vereinigung. *Berliner Zeitung,* 29 October.

Schubert, Helga. 1990. *Judasfrauen: Zehn Fallgeschichten weiblicher Denunziation im "Dritten Reich."* Frankfurt-am-Main: Luchterhand.

Shils, Edward A., and Morris Janowitz. 1948. Cohesion and disintegration in the Wehrmacht in World War II. *The Public Opinion Quarterly* 12:280–315.

Sholiton, Faye. 1988. One man's fight to keep memory alive. *Cleveland Jewish News*, 25 November.

Shuster, George N. 1932. *The Germans: An inquiry and an estimate.* New York: Dial.

Siegel, Barry, with Nina Green. 1988. Can evil beget good? Nazi data: A dilemma for science. *The Los Angeles Times*, 30 October.

Silberman, Alphons, and Herbert Sallen. 1992. *Juden in Westdeustchland: Selbstbild und Fremdbild einer Minorität.* Cologne: Wissenschaft und Politik.

Simpson, Christopher. 1988. *Blowback: America's recruitment of Nazis and its effects on the cold war.* New York: Weidenfeld & Nicolson.

Sinclair, Sir John. 1791–1799. *The statistical account of Scotland: Drawn up from the communications of the ministers of the different parisches.* 21 vols. Edinburgh: Creech.

Smith, Bradley F. 1977. *Reaching judgment at Nuremberg: The untold story of how the Nazi war criminals were judged.* New York: Basic.

———. 1981. *The road to Nuremberg.* New York: Basic.

———. 1982. *The American road to Nuremberg: The documentary record, 1944–1945.* Stanford: Stanford University, Hoover Institution Press.

Smith, Dorothy Snow, and Wilson M. Southam. 1945. *No Germany; therefore, no more German wars.* Ottawa: n.p.

Smith, Jean Edward. 1990. *Lucius D. Clay: An American life.* New York: Henry Holt.

Snell, John L. 1963. *Illusion and necessity: The diplomacy of global war, 1939–1945.* Boston: Houghton Mifflin.

SPD-Fraktion. 1978. SPD-Fraktion rügte Äusserungen des Abgeordneten Hansen. *Der Tagesspiegel*, 8 March.

Spiegelman, Art. 1986. *Maus: A survivor's tale: My father bleeds history.* New York: Pantheon.

———. 1991. *Maus: A survivor's tale II: And here my troubles began.* New York: Pantheon.

Stackelberg, Karl-Georg, Graf von. 1975. *Souffleur auf politischer Bühne: Von der Macht der Meinungen und den Meinungen der Mächtigen.* Munich: Moderne Industrie.

Staël Holstein, Anne Louise Germaine, Baronne de. 1810/1813. *Allemagne.* Paris: H. Nicolle (1810). Trans. *Germany.* London: John Murray (1813).

Stark, Holger. 1992. Berliner fühlen sich nicht wohl: Infas-Umfrage. *Berliner Zeitung*, 19 October.

Statistisches Reichsamt. Various years. *Statistisches Jahrbuch für das Deutsche Reich.* Berlin: Reimar Hobbing.

Steininger, Rolf. 1989. *Wiederbewaffnung: Die Entscheidung für einen westdeutschen Verteidigungsbeitrag: Adenauer und die Westmächte, 1950.* Erlangen: Dr. Dietmar Straube.

Stewart, Frank Mann. 1950. *A half century of municipal reform: The history of the National Municipal League.* Berkeley: University of California Press.

Stoltzfus, Nathan. 1992. Dissent in Nazi Germany. *The Atlantic Monthly* 270 (September):86–94.

Stöss, Richard. 1989/1991. *Die extreme Rechte in der Bundesrepublik: Entwicklung, Ursachen, Gegenmassnahmen.* Opladen: Westdeutscher (1989). Trans. Lindsay Batson. *Politics against democracy: Right-wing extremism in West Germany.* New York: Berg (1991).

Stouffer, Samuel A. 1955. *Communism, conformity, and civil liberties: A cross-section of the nation speaks its mind.* Garden City, N.Y.: Doubleday.

Sutton, John L. 1960. The Personnel Screening Committee and parliamentary control of the West German armed forces. *Journal of Central European Affairs* 19:389–401.

Swanson, Guy E. 1971. *Social change.* Glenview, Ill.: Scott, Foresman.

Sztompka, Piotr. 1993. *The sociology of social change.* Oxford: Blackwell.

Tacitus, Publius Cornelius. c. 98/1970. *The Germania.* In *Tacitus:* The Agricola *and* The Germania, trans. H. Mattingly and S. A. Handford. Harmondsworth, Middlesex: Penguin.

Tagliabue, John. 1991. Nazi archives in Moscow detail fate of Jews. *The New York Times,* 17 November.

Tauber, Kurt P. 1967. *Beyond eagle and swastika: German nationalism since 1945.* Middletown, Conn.: Wesleyan University Press.

Taylor, A. J. P. 1961. *The origins of the Second World War.* London: Hamish Hamilton.

Taylor, Telford. 1949. *Final report to the Secretary of the Army on the Nuernberg war crimes trials under Control Council Law No. 10.* Washington, D.C.: U.S. Government Printing Office.

———. 1992. *The anatomy of the Nuremberg trials: A personal memoir.* New York: Alfred A. Knopf.

Tent, James F. 1982. *Mission on the Rhine: Reeducation and denazification in American-occupied Germany.* Chicago: University of Chicago Press.

Testimony. 1991. Testimony uncovers tales of Nazi terror in wartime Poland. *The New York Times,* 14 November.

Tetens, T. H. 1961. *The new Germany and the old Nazis.* New York: Random House.

Thompson, Dorothy. 1942. *Listen, Hans.* Boston: Houghton Mifflin.

Tocqueville, Alexis de. 1835/1945/1954. *Democracy in America.* 2 vols. Ed. Phillips Bradley. New York: Alfred A. Knopf (1945); Vintage Books (1954).

Trial. 1950. *Trial of war criminals before the Nuernberg military tribunals under Control Council Law No. 10.* Vols. 1–2, *Medical Case.* Washington, D.C.: U.S. Government Printing Office.

Troper, Harold, and Morton Weinfeld. 1988. *Old wounds: Jews, Ukrainians and the hunt for Nazi war criminals in Canada.* Markham, Ontario: Penguin Canada.

Tsuchimochi, Gary H., ed. 1991. *The U.S. occupation of Germany: Educational reform, 1945–1949.* Bethesda, Md.: University Publications of America.

United States, Office of Military Government, Office of the Director. 1945a. The German press. *Weekly Information Report* 16 (10 November):22–23.

―――. 1945b. Denazification: Unfinished business. *Weekly Information Report* 18 (24 November):16–17.

―――. 1945c. German political leaders on denazification. *Weekly Information Report* 19 (1 December):30–35.

―――. 1946a. Status of German schools. *Monthly Report of the Military Governor: Education and Religion* no. 10 (20 May):1–19.

―――. 1946b. *Textbooks in Germany, American zone.* Bad Godesberg: Office of the Military Governor (U.S.).

[United States,] Office of Military Government for Germany, U.S. Zone (OMG/MG). 1945–1949. *Monthly report of the military governor.* Lithographed by the adjutant general, OMGUS; issued from July 1945 to August-September 1949.

United States, Office of Military Government for Germany, U.S. Zone, Information Control Division (OMG/IC). 1945–1948. *Monthly report of the military governor: Information control.* Lithographed by the adjutant general, OMGUS; issued from July 1945 to June 1948.

[United States,] Office of Military Government for Germany, U.S. Zone, Information Services Division (OMG/IS). 1948–1949. *Monthly report of the military governor: Information services.* Lithographed by the adjutant general, OMGUS; issued from July 1948 to 1 August–20 September 1949.

United States, Office of Strategic Services, Research and Analysis Branch. 1944. *Civil Affairs Handbook—Germany.* Sect. 12, *Communications and Control of Public Opinion.* Washington, D.C.: Headquarters, Army Service Forces, Manual M 356-12 (4 April).

United States, Strategic Bombing Survey, Morale Division. 1947. *The effects of strategic bombing on German morale.* 2 vols. Washington, D.C.: U.S. Government Printing Office.

United States Air Force, School of Aviation Medicine. 1946. *German aviation medicine, World War II.* Washington, D.C.: Department of Air Force, Surgeon General, U.S. Government Printing Office.

United States Department of State, Historical Office, Bureau of Public Affairs (USDS). 1955. *Foreign relations of the United States, diplomatic papers: The conferences at Malta and Yalta, 1945.* Department of State Publication 6199. Washington, D.C.: U.S. Government Printing Office.

―――. 1960. *Foreign relations of the United States, diplomatic papers: The conference of Berlin (the Potsdam Conference), 1945.* Department of State Publication 7163. 2 vols. Washington, D.C.: U.S. Government Printing Office.

―――. 1961. *Foreign relations of the United States, diplomatic papers: The conferences at Cairo and Tehran, 1943.* Department of State Publication 7187. Washington, D.C.: U.S. Government Printing Office.

―――. 1968. *Foreign relations of the United States, diplomatic papers: The conferences at Washington, 1941–1942, and Casablanca, 1943.* Department of State Publication 8414. Washington, D.C.: U.S. Government Printing Office.

―――. 1972. *Foreign relations of the United States, diplomatic papers: The conference at Quebec, 1944.* Department of State Publication 8627. Washington, D.C.: U.S. Government Printing Office.

United States Department of State, Office of the Historian, Bureau of Public Affairs (USDS). 1985. *Documents on Germany 1944–1985*. Department of State Publication 9446. Washington, D.C.: U.S. Government Printing Office.

United States Senate, Committee on the Judiciary, Subcommittee to Investigate the Administration of the Internal Security Act and Other Internal Security Laws. 1967. *Morgenthau diary (Germany)*. 2 vols. Washington, D.C.: U.S. Government Printing Office.

Vago, Steven. 1980. *Social change*. New York: Holt, Rinehart and Winston.

Vansittart, Lord Robert Gilbert. 1941. *Black record: Germans past and present*. London: Hamish Hamilton.

———. 1943. *Lessons of my life*. New York: Alfred A. Knopf.

Vor. 1990. Vor der Wahl noch eine Wende? *Der Spiegel* 44 (1 November):36–48.

Waldman, Eric. 1964. *The goose step is verboten: The German army today*. New York: Free Press.

Walendy, Udo. 1970/1981. *Wahrheit für Deutschland: Die Schuldfrage des zweiten Weltkrieges*. Vlotho-am-Weser: Volkstum und Zeitgeschichtsforschung (1970). Trans. Monika Fleck and William Albach. *Truth for Germany: The guilt question of the Second World War*. Vlotho-am-Weser: Volkstum und Zeitgeschichtsforschung; U.S. distribution, Torrance, Calif.: Institute for Historical Review (1981).

Wallich, Henry C. 1955. *Mainsprings of the German revival*. New Haven: Yale University Press.

Watts, Tim J. 1989. *Nazi war criminals in the United States: A bibliography*. Monticello, Ill.: Vance Bibliographies, Public Administration Series, P 2612 (March).

Wechsberg, Joseph, ed. 1967. *The murderers among us: The Simon Wiesenthal memoirs*. New York: McGraw-Hill.

Weingartner, James J. 1979. *Crossroads of death: The story of the Malmédy massacre and trial*. Berkeley: University of California Press.

Weinreich, Max. 1946. *Hitler's professors: The part of scholarship in Germany's crimes against the Jewish people*. New York: Yiddish Scientific Institute (YIVO).

Welch, David, ed. 1983. *Nazi propaganda: The power and the limitations*. London: Croom Helm; Totowa, N.J.: Barnes & Noble.

Welles, Sumner. 1944. *The time for decision*. New York: Harper & Brothers.

Weyrauch, Walter Otto. 1986. Gestapo informants: Facts and theory of undercover operations. *Columbia Journal of Transnational Law* 24:553–596.

———. 1989. *Gestapo V-Leute: Tatsachen und Theorie des Geheimdienstes Untersuchungen zur Geheimen Staatspolizei während der nationalsozialistische Herrschaft*. Frankfurt-am-Main: Vittorio Klostermann.

Whitman, Sidney. 1897. *Imperial Germany: A critical study of fact and character*. Meadville, Pa.: Chautauqua-Century.

Whitney, Craig R. 1993. *Spy trader: Germany's devil's advocate and the darkest secrets of the cold war*. New York: Times.

Wild, Dieter, ed. 1992. *Spiegel Spezial: Juden und Deutsche*. Hamburg: Spiegel, Rudolf Augstein.

Wilkerson, Isabel. 1989. Nazi scientists and ethics of today. *The New York Times*, 21 May.

Williams, Frederick W. 1970. Foreword. In A. Merritt and R. Merritt 1970:xvii–xxi.

Willis, F. Roy. 1962. *The French in Germany, 1945–1949*. Stanford: Stanford University Press.

Willis, James F. 1982. *Prologue to Nuremberg: The politics and diplomacy of punishing war criminals of the First World War*. Westport, Conn.: Greenwood.

Wilson, Elmo C. 1948. Report on ICD opinion surveys. Memorandum prepared for Colonel Gordon E. Textor, director, Information Control Division, Office of Military Government for Germany (U.S.), 4 August. Spirit duplication.

Woetzel, Robert K. 1962. *The Nuremberg trials in international law, with a postlude on the Eichmann case*. London: Stevens & Sons; New York: Frederick A. Praeger.

Wolfe, Robert. 1979. From information control to media freedom: The reverse course in United States occupation policy for Germany. Paper presented at the 93rd annual meeting of the American Historical Association, San Francisco, 28–30 December.

Wright, Quincy. 1942. *The study of war*. Chicago: University of Chicago Press.

WSR. N.d. Williams, Frederick W., Some results of public opinion polls of the German public. Ms., c. 1947, consisting of xeroxed 4-by-6 index cards reporting marginal responses to selected questions in OSS/ICD surveys, from no. 1 of 26 October 1945 to no. 36 of 10 December 1946. Accessible in the Library of the University of Illinois at Urbana-Champaign under call number Q.940.9342/G3125s.

Wüllenweber, Hans. 1992. 90% of eastern teenagers reject violence. *Mannheimer Morgen*, 10 December. English-language version in *The German Tribune*, 18 December.

Zielinski, Siegfried. 1986. History as entertainment and provocation: The TV series "Holocaust" in West Germany. In *Germans and Jews since the Holocaust: The changing situation in West Germany*, ed. Anson Rabinbach and Jack Zipes, 258–283. New York: Holmes & Meier.

Ziemke, Earl F. 1975. *The U.S. Army in the occupation of Germany, 1944–1946*. Washington, D.C.: United States Army, Center of Military History.

Zink, Harold. 1947. *American Military Government in Germany*. New York: Macmillan.

———. 1957. *The United States in Germany, 1945–1955*. Princeton, N.J.: D. Van Nostrand.

Zitelmann, Rainer. 1990. Vom Umgang mit der NS-Vergangenheit. In *Bewusstseins-Notstand: Thesen von 60 Zeitzeugen—Ein optimistisches Lesebuch*, ed. Rolf Italiaander, 69–79. Düsseldorf: Droste.

Index

77, 79–80, 83, 185. *See also* topics of surveys

Opinion polls. *See* American public opinion; German public opinion; Public opinion

Organization for European Economic Cooperation (OEEC), 16, 403

OSS. *See* U.S. Office of Strategic Services (OSS)

Overstreet, Harry A., 30n

Papen, Franz von, 147

Parsons, Talcott, 30n

Partitioning of Germany, 31–32, 31–32nn15–18, 42, 52–53, 57, 60–61, 61n13, 241

Party of Democratic Socialism (PDS), 119, 119n37, 205n38, 362n12

Past: approaches to dealing with, 145n35, 178n, 210–24, 211n, 233n37; and continuing interest in Nazism, 227, 227–30; disregard for, 219; and Germany as impenitent troublemaker, 212; and Germany as repenting prodigal son, 211–12; and Holocaust denial, 214–16, 215–16nn; images of, in restored Germany, 224–33; left's failure to deal with, 217; and medical profession in West Germany, 219–24; and Nazism as aberration, 211; quarrel among historians about Hitler and Nazism, 217–18, 218nn, 230; reconstructing history, 216–17; and scapegoating of Hitler and Nazis, 212–14

Pastoralization of Germany, 58–59

Patton, George S., Jr., 68, 182

PDS. *See* Party of Democratic Socialism (PDS)

Peace movement. *See* Protest movement

Peenemünde commemoration, 374, 374–75n33

Perot, H. Ross, 362n11

Persian Gulf war, 372–73, 374

Peterson, Edward N., 66

Physicians. *See* Medical profession

Pléven, René, 368

Poland, 24, 31, 35, 36, 36n, 61, 66, 116, 121, 141, 142n26, 374, 408n

Political parties: and 5 percent clause, 391, 391–92n; German public opinion on, 327–30, 329n; left-wing parties, 115–20, 406; multiparty political system favored, 102–3; neo-Nazi parties, 102–15, 398–99; and newspapers, 308–9; in postwar Germany, 102–20; and right-wing extremism, 102–15, 398–99; and U.S. occupation of Germany, 264–66. *See also* specific parties

Politics, participation in, 327–30, 328n12

Pollock, James K., 391

Potsdam Conference, 63–68, 181, 182, 241, 352, 352n

Prager, Emily, 233n36

Prisoners of war: German prisoners of war, 194, 198, 216, 243n6, 286; German treatment of, 149, 180, 180n

Propaganda, 28n9, 72–73

Protest movement, 118–19, 203–4, 217, 361, 372, 375, 406, 407–8. *See also* APO

Public opinion: British research on, 74; of East Germans, 78, 81; Germans trained in polling techniques, 82–83; historical development of measurement of, 71–74; and intelligence agencies, 72; and propaganda, 72–73; structured questionnaires and interviewing techniques in, 73; of West Germans, 77–83; on World War II, 121–22. *See also* American public opinion; German public opinion

Public Safety Manual, 179, 181

Publicists, Anglo-American, 26–34

Quebec Conference, 57–59

"Racial hygiene," 223, 223n23, 258n. *See also* Eugenics

Racism, 132–40, 133nn, 135n, 379–81, 381n. *See also* Anti-Semitism

Radio: Adenauer proposal for national radio, 401; Allied policy on, 297–300, 298nn, 300n19, 355; American Forces Network (AFN), 291; Communist party members speaking on, 310, 361; decentralized programming for, 300; evaluation of, 305–6, 305nn, 312–13; free versus controlled radio, 309, 309n32, 310; listenership of, 301–3; in Nazi Germany, 294, 294nn; num-